# History and Progress

# History and Progress

IN SEARCH OF THE EUROPEAN
AND AMERICAN MIND

**Margarita Mathiopoulos**

FOREWORD BY GORDON A. CRAIG

PRAEGER

New York
Westport, Connecticut
London

**Library of Congress Cataloging-in-Publication Data**

Mathiopoulos, Margarita, 1956–
  History and Progress.

  Translated from German.
  Bibliography: p.
  Includes index.
  1. Progress.   2. Historiography—United States.
3. United States—Historiography.   4. Europe—Intel-
lectual life.   5. Political science—United States—
History.   6. United States—Politics and government.
7. Europe—Politics and government—20th century.
I. Title.
CB151.M26   1989      907',2073      89-8841
ISBN 0–275–92792–X (alk. paper)

Library of Congress Catalog Card Number: 89–8841
ISBN: 0–275–92792–X

First published in 1989

Praeger Publishers, One Madison Avenue, New York, NY 10010
A division of Greenwood Press, Inc.

Printed in the United States of America

The paper used in this book complies with the Permanent
Paper Standard issued by the National Information Standards
Organization (Z39.48–1984).

10   9   8   7   6   5   4   3   2   1

Material contained herein is taken from the author's German publication, *Amerika—Das Experiment
des Fortschritts: Ein Vergleich des politischen Denkens in den USA und Europa* (Paderborn: Ferdinand Schöningh, 1987). Translation from German into English by Jessie Lenagh.

For my parents
Elsie and Vassos

"What Athens was in miniature, America will be in magnitude. The one was the wonder of the ancient world; the other is becoming the admiration, the model of the present."

Thomas Paine, *The Rights of Man*, Part II, Chapter 3, 1792

# Contents

# Foreword

In his life of Samuel Johnson, James Boswell tells of an encounter between his subject and a Mr. Edwards, who had been with him at Pembroke College, Oxford, forty-nine years earlier, although they had not seen each other since then. In the course of a rather strained conversation, Mr. Edwards said, "You are a philosopher, Dr. Johnson. I have tried too in my time to be a philosopher; but, I don't know how, cheerfulness was always breaking in."

It is surely not too far-fetched to suggest that this charming story of temperamental incompatibility can serve as a kind of parable to illuminate the recent dissonances in the relationship between the United States and its European allies. As their mutual confidence has eroded under the impact of sharp differences about such things as fiscal and economic policy on the one hand and defensive nuclear strategies on the other, there has been a growing fear among our European, and especially our German, friends that cheerfulness is becoming a national disease on this side of the Atlantic and that American optimism, always excessive, is now being carried to the point of fecklessness, failure to recognize limitations, and unwillingness to face up to facts that challenge presuppositions. Simultaneously, a feeling, not always clearly articulated, has become perceptible in American official circles that there has been too much ratiocination, too much idle speculation, too much philosophical doubt in recent European attitudes and that this has all too frequently lamed the will and prevented or crippled expedient action.

It would not be difficult to parade facts from the political record of the past decade to support either of these cases, but it would be a partisan and idle exercise. It is more important to note that, underlying the disputes that the Atlantic partners have engaged in with respect to specific contemporary issues, there is a more fundamental difference of attitude about direction and purpose in history and about the possibility and meaning of progress.

The idea of progress has intrigued human minds for thousands of years; it has been a subject requiring definition and explication in all major religious and philosophical systems; it has animated and inspired thought and action in revolutionary periods and times of affluence and growth. But perhaps in no part of the world has it exercised a greater and more continuous dominance, from earliest times to the present, than in the United States of America.

In other countries its incidence and strength have generally been at the mercy of external events, of invasion, war, and pestilence. Who in the German states could take much stock in progress in the wake of the Thirty Years War? And was it not true that such catastrophes created persistent reservations in the mind, so that the idea of progress that was inherent in the Enlightenment was internalized in Germany and limited to a belief in the possibility of individual intellectual betterment (*Verbesserung*), which was, however, combined with a tacit acceptance of the uncontrollability of the external world? But Americans were subject to no such doubts and hesitations. From colonial times onward, they were sure that they were building a *novum ordinem saeculorum* in which there would be no limits to human growth, institutional improvement, and national expansion. Not even the greatest tragedy in their history, the Civil War, diminished the ebullient faith in the national mission or cast doubts upon Whitman's evocation of the peculiarly American self-confidence:

> Have the elder nations halted?
> Do they droop and end their lesson, wearied over there beyond the seas?
> We take up the task eternal, and the burden and the lesson . . .
> Fresh and strong the world we seize, world of labor and the march,
> 　　　Pioneers! O pioneers!

Nor did either of the great wars of our century—whose horrors, to be sure, were never visited upon its shores—cause more than a wavering of faith in the inevitability of new advances and achievements. If there were any American intellectuals who felt, like Paul Valéry after the First World War, that the fundamentals of life had been changed by these conflicts and "the Mind [so] cruelly wounded [that] it passes a mournful judgement upon itself; it doubts itself profoundly," they had no power to dam the prevailing tide of optimism, nor did European philosophers like Georges Sorel and Oswald Spengler, who declared that progress was an illusion and proclaimed the decline of the West. These last writings were little read in the United States, where respect for philosophers (except for those who, like Emerson, confirmed native assumptions) was never high, although there is no doubt that they made a powerful contribution to the totalitarianization of the idea of progress in Europe, so that in the 1930s and 1940s even the country whose *philosophes* had helped to inspire the work of the American founding fathers lost faith in the principles of the Enlightenment that they had been the first to propagate.

There have been earlier studies of the idea of progress in the United States, but none that have placed it adequately within the context of European intellectual history, showing the common roots and historical interdependence of European and American thinking about progress, explaining the divergence that took place after the force of the Enlightenment was spent, and analyzing the varieties and depth of faith in progress in American historiography, in American literature and culture, and in the American consciousness. In this remarkably comprehensive volume, which shows a thorough knowledge of classic and contemporary texts and a shrewd appreciation of American perceptions and prejudices, Dr. Mathiopoulos has made an important contribution to scholarship. She may also prove in the long run to have done something to ease the strains in the alliance. For this is a book that can give Europeans a clearer understanding of the historical reasons for the American preoccupation with progress, its reflection in American romanticism and nationalism, the way in which it influences all aspects of American political theory and practice, including its historical attitudes with respect to foreign affairs, and the positive, as well as the negative, aspects of this influence. Perhaps, too, by helping Americans appreciate the intellectual heritage that they share with Europe, it may even induce administration spokesmen to diminish the emphasis upon American exceptionalism that is often so exasperating to our friends and allies.

Gordon A. Craig

# Acknowledgments

Many people have supported the work on this book, and I wish to express my thanks to all of them. I am indebted to my instructor and mentor, Professor Karl Dietrich Bracher, former head of the Department of Contemporary History and Political Science, University of Bonn. For his continuous support of my scholarly work and valuable suggestions, I will remain deeply grateful.

I also want to express my gratitude to Professors Gordon A. Craig (Department of History, Stanford University) and Gerhard Wirth (Department of Ancient History, University of Bonn), both of whom always had time to discuss my research with me. Many thanks go to Professor Richard E. Neustadt, former adviser to President Truman and now professor in the John F. Kennedy School of Government at Harvard University. His support and critical judgment were central to the completion of this work, especially the chapter on the American presidents. He, too, frequently gave generously of his time in thorough discussions with me. During my studies and research at Harvard University from 1980 through 1982, I had the chance to conduct interviews with Professors Don K. Price (former dean of the Kennedy School of Government), Samuel P. Huntington (director of the Center for International Affairs), and Stanley Hoffmann (director of the Center for European Studies), all of whom offered valuable advice on my work. I am grateful to them all. At the same time I would like to thank the following people for their interest and support: Dr. R. Gordon Hoxie (president of the Center for the Study of the Presidency, New York), Professor Costas Proussis, and Dr. Nancy Reinhardt (director of the Special Student Office at Harvard).

For their generosity in granting so much of their time, I thank those individuals who patiently endured my interviews: Clark Clifford (former Secretary of Defense), Lawrence Eagleburger (Deputy Secretary of State), Senator William Fulbright, Norman Podhoretz (editor of *Commentary*), Walt W. Rostow (former National Security Adviser), Dean Rusk (former Secretary of State), Cyrus Vance (former Secretary of State), and the late Governor Sherman Adams (also former chief of staff under President Eisenhower).

Further appreciation goes to the Friedrich-Neumann Foundation, which supported my research from 1981 through 1983.

I am most grateful to Nick Mitropoulos, close adviser to Governor Michael Dukakis and consultant at the Kennedy School of Government, Harvard University. He directed me to many helpful American scholars and politicians. I will not forget the many insightful conversations with the late Mrs. Elisabeth (''Johnny'') Fainsod.

Friedbert Pflüger, my husband and colleague, deserves special merit for his patience and his critical and constructive comments, which I deeply appreciated.

Berlin
April 1989                                              Margarita Mathiopoulos

The original German manuscript was completed in the summer of 1986. For the most part, subsequent events and publications have not been considered.

# History and
# Progress

# Introduction: The Idea of Progress in the American Political Tradition and Present

America and Europe have difficulty understanding one another. Mutual misunderstandings, prejudices, and distortions exist on both sides of the Atlantic. But while the European's image of America since the birth of the United States has been ambiguous and subject to fluctuation, criticism of American policy in Western Europe has taken on almost grotesque characteristics in the recent past, especially in the Federal Republic of Germany.[1] Indeed, the debates over America in recent years have centered on such emotionally loaded terms as Pershings, cruise missiles, pacifism, nuclear war, and Star Wars.

Scholarly discussion in Europe is concerned primarily with American foreign and security policies, which are generally severely criticised, although few of the critics have bothered to take American history into account. This discrepancy has long escaped notice, especially in the Federal Republic of Germany. Only recently has a greater effort been made to gain a better understanding; exchange programs for students, scholars, journalists, and politicians have been created. Although German Historical Research Institutes have existed for many years in Paris, London, and Rome, it was not until 1987 that one was finally opened in the United States (Washington, D.C.).

This book will attempt to promote a better understanding of America in Europe, particularly in Germany. Crucial to understanding American politics and history is the idea of progress. The fact that the idea of progress—an idea that galvanized humankind for centuries—has existed in the United States without interruption for more than two hundred years immediately piques intellectual curiosity. America was a product of the cultural legacy of the European Enlightenment and the desire to realize reason, freedom (including religious freedom), equality, democracy, and human rights in the New World:

The foundations of our image of man, of his dignity, his rights and responsibilities, his coexistence with others, are all part of the common inheritance of European culture. That which we call Western is not American but European. And that which makes Americans "Western," is European. The American idea of freedom is rooted in the thought of Europe. In this respect we are irrevocably bound to one another, or, more exactly, Americans are bound to us. (Richard von Weizsäcker, Speech at the Katholikentag in Aachen, 1986)

The progressive idealism of the European Enlightenment brought the "American Dream" to life, which even today remains deeply rooted in the consciousness of the American population and continues to shape the country's foreign and domestic policy. The object of this study is to portray and analyze the idea of progress in the political tradition and daily reality of America.

In the process, the influence of the various manifestations of the key term "progress" in the European history of ideas since classical antiquity cannot be neglected.[2] For this reason Part I is devoted to the origins and transformations of the idea of progress in European intellectual history. The development of the idea of progress will be traced over the course of the epochs from the flowering of the Enlightenment to ideological decline, liberal consensus to historical crisis, and individual self-realization to collectivist dictate.

Part II emphasizes the historical interdependence of European–American thought, portraying the European influence on the idea of progress in American historical interpretation. The following transatlantic comparison attempts to illustrate the individual convergences and divergences in the European–American understanding of history and progress. This understanding continues today to bind both continents together even as it drives them apart.

Part III deals with the political and philosophical bases of the American idea of progress. National identity and the American creed,[3] revolutionary constitutionalism and presidential democracy,[4] and their realization in political theory and praxis are analyzed and discussed.

Part IV examines the domestic political manifestations of the American idea of progress. Explored first are the motivation and problems of an internal continental sense of mission, which transposed the concept of progressivism into the ideas of the "frontier" and manifest destiny. This discussion is followed by an analysis of the popularization of the idea of progress in Jacksonian democracy, the romantic and nationalist origins of the idea, and its first crisis at the outbreak of the Civil War. Finally, the appearance in populist thought of criticism of civilization and its channeling and integration into the Progressive movement are discussed.

Part V attempts to explain the role of the idea of progress in foreign policy. Here the international impact of the American Revolution and its exemplary function for the rest of the world are examined. Its effects reach from the French Revolution all the way to the recent past, encompassing even the decolonization processes and the independence movements of the Third World. This issue is extended into a broad analysis of the idea of progress in light of foreign policy dualism between an expansionist sense of ideological mission and continental isolationism from the Washington Doctrine to the Reagan Doctrine.[5]

# Part I

## ORIGINS AND METAMORPHOSES OF THE IDEA OF PROGRESS IN THE EUROPEAN HISTORY OF IDEAS

*The attempt to arrive at a conclusive definition of progress would be as presumptuous as trying to prove or disprove the existence of supernatural powers. The modern effort to incarnate the concept of progress is comparable to the course of two parallel lines, which, at least within finite space, never touch. Mathematicians have indeed conjectured that two parallel lines will ultimately converge in infinity, but in earthly life the desires of people run parallel to their hopes without ever reaching the convergence point of perfection.*

*Nonetheless, doctrinaire ideologues unwearyingly stress the alleged determinism of history, which after several "necessary" dialectical, even violent, intervening stages finally reaches its ultimate conclusion, the seamless harmony of the ideal society. The dogmatic prophets of various religions, in turn, locate the bliss of humankind in an alleged netherworld. Here, oddly, mathematics and Christian eschatology seem to meet. While the one places the point of convergence of the transformed parallelism (or futility) of straight lines in outer space, the other shifts this point to the spiritual perfection achieved at the moment physical existence ceases. "Happily we are left with the conviction that many things can and must exist together which would otherwise repress each other: the spirit of the world is more tolerant than we often think" (Johann Wolfgang von Goethe, 1826).*

*In this context, European awareness of the existence of history is one of the first prerequisites for meaningful human life. The study of history as an immutable fact enables us to understand our present existence, thus fulfilling a second meaningful prerequisite. On the basis of knowledge of the past and reconciliation to it, the self-aware contemporary can subject historical events to analysis and criticism and perhaps even avoid them in the future. This results simultaneously in the creation of the third and fourth prerequisites.*

*Certainly, interpretations of specific historical phenomena in each epoch, as well as the conclusion to be drawn from them for the future, will remain contentious. Of special importance for the historian is the continuous consciousness of the basic premise of the open-endedness of history. Those who desire to prove the inescapable causal historical principles responsible for shaping the past are, for this reason, working in vain. Nothing happened because it had to happen. History knows no laws. Of course, the lessons that can be extracted from the study of history—that is, if they are recognized as such—can give people the power to shape their future, perhaps even for the better. This is the mark of change from one epoch to another. The criteria for measuring progress have always been more demanding. For this reason, homogeneity of argument cannot be the ultimate aim of a multidimensional attempt to define the idea of progress. The most important task here is to identify, respect, and fully exploit the possibilities of a pluralist spectrum of opinion in democracies, which codify freedom.*

*Upon closer observation, the four prerequisites of meaningful existence described above combine to form a basic principle of Western culture—to live with history and exploit its open-endedness. This principle stands in fundamental opposition to Eastern doctrine, which takes the causal determination of history as given and entertains hope for a promised and all-inclusive utopia, one that often demands brutal sacrifices. It should also be noted that since the end of the Second World War the West, and specifically Europe (however paradoxical this might at first seem), not America, is being threatened by an ahistoricism that could mean the end of a belief in the future as well as progress as a whole.[6] In fact, all of these general considerations about the idea of progress have their beginnings in classical antiquity.*

# 1

## From Classical Antiquity to Modern Times

### THE CLASSICAL IDEA OF PROGRESS AND DECLINE

Beginning with classical antiquity, the history of political thought can be interpreted as the product of tension between progress and decline, democracy and dictatorship. Almost all the historical images and modes of inquiry of political theory were developed by the ancient thinkers. The first and most influential intellectual equivalents of the idea of progress, whether defined as the recurring key to the political history of ideas (Karl Dietrich Bracher),[7] as the experience of freedom enabling people to overcome the sorrows of the past and the frustrations of history (Henry Kissinger),[8] or as the idea that has marked Western civilization for over three thousand years (Robert Nisbet),[9] can be found in Greek and Roman antiquity. At the same time the question that arises is, to what degree does the multidimensional polymorphy of the idea of progress[10] intervene in the process of Greek and Roman political themes such as democracy and dictatorship, freedom and equality, or natural and human rights? Concurrently, it is interesting to identify the appearance of a specific characteristic of the progressivist idea in the thought of this historical epoch, which is evidenced in the cyclical model of classical antiquity and which determined the ambivalence of progress in relation to ethical decline.

However dominant the static element may have been in the Greek conception of history, the absence of a straightforward and encompassing conception of progress should not be construed as indicating an absence or negation of the idea. New studies of Greece and Rome clearly show the prevalence of a sense of improvement (*auxesis, progressus*) and increasing abilities, as well as pride in the achievements of civilization, technology, culture, and politics at levels hitherto unknown.[11] These older equivalents of a progressivist idea are evidence of the movement of classical thought. One need only recall the philosophy of Heraclitus, *panta rei,* although the category of progress was not granted the same politicohistorical position of social function as in later epochs.[12]

For the classical thinkers, the ambivalence of human thinking and creativity was a self-evident historical experience: from the patronal polis democracy to Hellenist universalism, from the idealized *res publica,* to the time of the emperors. Peace without war was just as unthinkable as technological, scientific, and cultural achievements without moral decline; art without tragedy; creativity without leisure; competition (*agon*) without pleasure; self-confidence without the myth of barbarism; freedom without self-awareness and self-control—all would have been completely inconceivable, and gods without human faces and weaknesses totally implausible.

Thucydides repeatedly posed the critical question of whether the increase of knowledge, power, and size was automatically accompanied by the ethical improvement of society. Even Polybius, an admirer of Rome, could not repress thoughts of the potential decadence of a monarchic-aristocratic constitution mixed with democratic elements. The Romans Seneca and Lucretius perceived this dilemma similarly: where the development of external culture failed to coincide with the power of the individual, progress lost its value, was only *sagacitas* (cunning) and not *sapientia* (wisdom).[13] Thucydides, in turn, valued human experience, the inquisitiveness of human nature, and the understanding of political imperatives (especially in war), as well as the human striving for power as important steps forward.[14] The reconstruction and understanding of past events, prerequisites for realizing the power of future knowledge, formed the core of his philosophy, which lent Thucydides' historical works a timeless validity (*ktema es aei*). Certainly, this was not to imply that the exploration of anthropomorphy would simultaneously resolve human faults. Rather, it was precisely human limitations that checked the high expectations of progress. Thus, Thucydides knew that certain historical events (war) would continue to occur, for he was convinced of the permanence of irrational and irredeemable elements in human nature.[15]

The idea of the cycle, of becoming and dissolution, thus remained bound to concepts of change, increase, improvement, and progress in the classical awareness of history.

As little as the antique cosmos experienced the need for a dynamic historical interpretation of the idea of progress, so much more strongly did Greek philosophy place ethical speculations above intellectual or technical achievements, with its stress on education (*paideia*) to moral action, persuasive oratory and proper leadership,[16] the determination of the goals of natural processes, as well as the best possible forms of state and constitution.

The tersely rational, yet so revolutionarily enlightening, axiom of Socrates—"Know thyself"—can be regarded not only as a preconditional maxim of Greek philosophical reflection but also as characteristic of human potential for progress. It may be seen not as an end in itself, but rather as an instrument for the prevention of individual hybris and limitless political ambition, and thus beneficial for society as a whole.

The idea of progress is manifested in different forms of Aristotle's constitutional theory and Plato's ideal state. According to Aristotle, only in the democracy of the Greek polis, with its ideal of a free and individualistic citizen, that is, only in the city-state, can a person attain the status assigned by nature, that of citizen, and only within this context is the good life possible.[17] Plato believed in the social theory of a gradual social metamorphosis into a statist utopia: "My law will be made with a general view to the best interests of society at large . . . as I rightly hold the single person and his affairs of minor importance."[18] The transformation of democracy into dictatorship, the mutation of an open social system into a closed one, can also be traced back to classical theories of government. From "the magic of Plato," through various Christian and church chiliasms and eschatologies up to the "false prophets" Hegel, Marx, and their epigones (Karl Popper),[19] modern utopias and versions of racist or communist totalitarian solutions have possessed "suggestive seductive power over all mixed pluralist forms of social and state order" (Karl Dietrich Bracher).[20] The danger has existed of a "reduction of diversity to uniformity" (Fritz Stern),[21] of a belief in an absolute and unitary principle of progress which abuses humankind's hope for a better world.

The turn to Hellenism—initiated in Chaironeia (338 B.C.) and firmly established with the founding of the world empire of Alexander the Great[22]—confirmed the inevitable extinction of the Athenian polis. It also marked the privatization and universalization of Greek thought, both in antipolitical Epicurean provincialism ("free yourself from the prison of the arts and political life"[23]) and in Stoic egalitarian cosmopolitanism. Whereas Plato and Aristotle still believed in the institution of slavery and the distinction between Greeks and barbarians,[24] the idea of progress propounded by Stoic natural philosophy lay, first, in the emphasis on the general public and the equality of the human race, in the unity (harmonia, concordia) of all people, slave and masters, barbarians and Greeks, in the concept of international community, the reign of reason, world civilization, and a consensus gentium (Cicero, Grotius). Second, it ascribed to the postulate of life led in accordance with nature. The criterion of immutable law was no longer sought in the state itself, but in a world reason transcending ordinary state boundaries. It must be acknowledged that the Epicurean negation of political duties and the Stoic maxim of a general claim to human rights without conformity to a state contained the seed of an ancient, apolitical cult of alternativism as well as the relativization of concrete political bonds. In extreme cases, it resulted in the questioning of all forms of political order or even anarchistic dissolution of all common political entities based on structures of power or domination, as was also true of the ideal of the Cynics.[25] The ambivalent explosiveness of the Stoic philosophy of humankind did not, however, come to fruition in ancient times, even if the cosmopolite Diogenes did set the tone for later alternative thought with his retreat from politics into the self-contained microcosm of his barrel.[26] Its power would remain for the anarcho-revolutionary movements of later epochs.

Rome ultimately profited as well from the positive aspects of this progress of civilization toward universal history and an order transcending state boundaries and constituted by natural laws. The rise of the Roman Empire was legitimized by protecting the world from the African and Germanic barbarians and ensuring general prosperity. The basic Hellenist theories of natural and human rights were fused in the supranational claim and moral-philosophical sanctioning of an eternal, universal, and self-proselytizing ideal of Rome as *progressus* into a Roman imperial synthesis.[27]

Various crisis theories had evolved even before Rome's power began to wane. While the Hellenist historiographers and philosophers Polybius, Poseidonios, Sallust, and Vellius Paterculus pointed to the danger of Roman decline, identifying the source of the crisis and fall of Rome in the improvisation of foreign policy (the destruction of Carthage, 146 B.C.), Cicero saw the Republic's system of decadence manifested exclusively in personal ineptitude and in failure of domestic political factors crucial to the existence of the state: in the decline of morality (*mores*), religion, free order and justice (*auctoritas, libertas*), and the *consensus omnium bonorum.*[28]

After domestic political improvisation (the assassination of Caesar in 44 B.C.), Marcus Tullius Cicero strove to prevent the collapse of the *res publica* on the eve of the Augustinian principate dictatorship. Through his fourteen orations (Phillipics), he tried to convince the divided and powerless Roman Senate to restore the Republic owed to Rome and its people. It was then that the greatness and tragedy of this Roman statesman became clear; his uncompromising and embittered struggle with Antony, who personified the crisis for him, opened the way for Octavius to establish the Augustine dictatorship.[29]

The possibilities for the ideologization of Plato's ideal state, as well as the paralysis of historical and cultural thought in the "metahistorical dogmatization of the idea of Rome into a worldwide mission," are manifested in prototypal form in the later phase of the development of Rome.[30]

If we attempt to define the ancient version of progressivist thought, we will note that it can also lay claim to a timeless historical and political quality, for the origin of the idea of freedom also contains the engine of later human and inhumane progress. The historical cyclical model of antiquity was naturally unable to foresee the ambivalent politicorevolutionary consequences of a modern progressivist idea of freedom, for its historical consciousness was cyclical and static, not dynamic and progressive. The themes of Greek and human antiquity were not utopian evolution in the future, but rather concrete existence in the present, the idea of culture, of art, of scholarship, the idea of the intellectual enlightenment of the individual, translated into a humanist philosophy for reasoning, free, self-aware citizens called to the formation of a free polis democracy (*res publica*) and polis culture. However, ancient thought always placed the individual attainment of political and intellectual freedom against awareness of the limits of human ability. The ancients also experienced the ambivalence of freedom, which can reveal itself in the abuse of power (when unbridled by self-criticism and not limited by legal rulings).

First set in motion in the classical period, the process of historical questioning, of the formulation of philosophical principles, and the assertion of moderate political ideals—and finally their ideological overemphasis as well—incited, provoked, and influenced succeeding currents of regressive or progressive historical thought in the European, and later, American history of ideas.

## PROGRESS AS DOGMATIC CHRISTIAN ESCHATOLOGY

The idea of human progress underwent a change with the evolution of Christianity, which itself later profoundly affected the concept of history in the Middle Ages. The "wretched cycles" of heathen antiquity were abandoned in favor of a chiliastic belief in the hereafter. Progress was henceforth related to the eschatological expectation of a "new heaven and new earth" as the result of a divine plan of salvation, presented by Augustine in his *Civitas Dei* as the maxim for the salvation of human fate. The humanistic and enlightened concepts of classical antiquity, which had communicated to the individual a sense of, and an aptitude for, philosophical and political thought, fell victim to a misanthropic philosophy of the individual's subordination to absolute obedience and humility to Christianity and the church.[31] If the individual failed to fulfill his or her moral and religious duties, the Church of Rome reserved the ultimate right to discipline the sinner through the Inquisition.

The lasting theocratic dualism between the spiritual (pope) and worldly (emperor) administrators of the medieval politicohistorical synthesis of eschatological yearnings for the hereafter and static conceptions of the here and now of *renovation mundi* produced passionate religious conflicts. Initially, at least, these conflicts could be channeled into the ideology of progressive salvation during the Crusades. Increasing doubt as to the extent of papal infallibility resulted, however, in the emergence of a reform movement within the church, and nation-states began to make their claims to sovereignty heard. In 1324 Marsilius of Padua demanded the separation of church and state in his work, *Defensor Pacis*. Such claims would be confirmed by the later development of absolutism and by the principle of national sovereignty.[32]

The ambiguous role of the idea of progress in the historical milieu of the Middle Ages is exemplified by the recent debates on the meaning of Christianity for the formation of a modern attitude to nature and for the development of a technology based on the natural sciences.

While, in ancient times, nature stood in constant balance with Becoming, the American historian Lynn White, in his controversial essay "The Historical Roots of Our Ecological Crisis," attributes some of the responsibility for the unscrupulous exploitation and destruction of nature to the Christian concept of history.[33] Both Holy Scripture and nature have been regarded as sources of the knowledge of God, but while the Eastern Church interpreted nature as a type of symbolic language of God, in the Western Church the idea of exploring nature as a means of coming to know God and nature gained prominence. Today's "ecological crisis," claims White, is the product of scientific and technological power unleashed by the subjugation of nature, which had been made possible in the Middle Ages by the Christian world-view.[34]

St. Francis of Assisi may well have been the first proponent of an alternative line of thought in the Middle Ages by criticizing the then reigning school of thought concerning the relationship between the human being and nature and realizing the thesis of Christ's renunciation of worldly possessions, a thesis declared heretical by John XXII in 1323. A hundred years earlier Joachim von Fiore had already broached this subject with his alternative utopian theory of the Trinity. According to this theory, history proceeds through three stages: first, in a pre-Christian era, then in the contemporary crisis between "the flesh and the spirit," and finally in an era of contemplation in which heaven is to be realized on earth.

Although this revolutionary chiliastic interpretation of history (condemned in 1215 by the Lateran Council and, later, by Thomas Aquinas) posed no danger to the established order of the Middle Ages, the sectarian and fanaticizing aspects of the apocalyptic prophecies of Joachanism served as the inspirational ideology for later utopian expectations of progress.[35]

The variety of the sociopolitical and especially the religious currents of the Middle Ages lent this epoch a (seemingly?) mystical, almost indecipherable character, which for decades has appeared especially well suited for provoking historical analyses—whether for a "history of mentalities" (Marc Bloch), an "archeology of knowledge" (Michel Foucault), or even a "structural anthropology" (Claude Levi-Strauss).[36]

In addition to these exclusive interpretations, mention should also be made of those historical approaches that are connected to White's view of history and that define the twelfth and thirteenth centuries as the "origin of modern times" by attempting to locate the beginning of the Industrial Revolution and technological dynamism in the Middle Ages.[37] Of course, even these scientifically oriented theories cannot evade the fact that the medieval sense of progress was limited to the internalization of religious dogma that made earthly humility a precondition for the eschatological postponement of life to a paradise in the hereafter.

## BETWEEN WESTERN ENLIGHTENMENT AND MODERN UTOPIA

The transition from the Middle Ages to modern times was characterized by a demystification and secularization of the salvational expectations of progress.

The discoveries and inventions in all fields, the development of Protestantism, the rediscovery of ancient Republicanism in the humanist cultural and political thought of the Renaissance, the conclusive establishment of the natural sciences (Kepler, Galileo, Newton) as an area of thought separate from theology and morality, the rationalist philosophy of Descartes (*de omnium dubitandum est*), the empiricism of Spinoza and Leibniz as well as that of Bacon, with its stress on the power inherent in knowledge and learning—all resulted in the individual's liberation from "self-willed mental immaturity" (Kant), giving way to the seemingly inevitable process of progress. The idea of a total mastery of nature by the human being and science as one of the modern principles of secularized change of the world in the sense of a forward-moving linear improvement was first propounded by Francis Bacon in his utopian essay "Nova Atlantis" (1627) and remained influential well into the second half of the twentieth century.

Following the revolutionary successes of scientific progress, physics replaced theology, and the function of prophecy was replaced by a concept of foreseeable progress, thus making possible the definition of a modern progressivist doctrine that considered the ambivalence of progress resolved. The classical awareness of the limits of human freedoms and abilities now seemed to have been refuted scientifically, and the medieval trauma over the theory of salvation preached by the church was written off as superstition. Precisely this development, which, simultaneously with the establishment of the natural sciences, brought about the establishment of a limitless sense of progress, contained complex consequences for the idea of progress itself. Disavowing the ambivalence of progress, which now seemed to be under the scientific control of humans, did not totally negate it, but rather made it manageable. The result was that progress and power became identical.

From this point on, both categories became mutually dependent and subject to the constant threat of negative ideologization as instruments of manipulation by systems with progressivist utopian claims (Morus, Campanella). Armed with these new qualities of power, humankind found itself confronted by the temptation of the path of total progress—which is no different from the path of its own eradication.[38]

It would be a misunderstanding of the modern concept of progress to consider its influence only on the multidimensional, by no means strictly negative, development of science and technology without simultaneously stressing its enlightening quality for the political thought processes of the modern period.

The modern concept of the state can undoubtedly be traced back to Machiavelli's rational, pragmatic, and equally blunt definition of state rationale, which he considered to be dependent on successful leadership (*Il Principe*, 1513), as well as on a fortunate coincidence of personal and pragmatic political determinants. His view of history, influenced by the cyclical thought of Livius and Polybius and the conviction of the immutability of human nature, remained, understandably enough, pessimistic.[39] Bodin's (*De la Republique*, 1513) and Hobbes's (*Leviathan*, 1651) absolutist contractual theories emerged later from a historical skepticism shared by David Hume in his examination of the limits of human understanding.[40]

The liberal, pluralist concept of society and state as well as that of a rational, optimistic desire for freedom and a sense of progress made their breakthrough—as the basic philosophies behind modern liberal democracy—in the constitutional theories of Locke and Montesquieu. They succeeded in expanding the catalogue of basic historical subjects in constitutional law, subjects such as human and civil rights, national sovereignty, and the principle of the majority, the ideas of freedom and equality, minority rights, and the separation of power, while limiting their roles in the politics of power. The influence that Locke's theories had on the English Revolution and the rise of English parliamentarianism as well as, later, on the American Revolution is unmistakable. In 1776, the economic revolution occasioned by Adam Smith's epochal book, *The Wealth of Nations,* supplied the liberal idea of progress with a new dynamic and capitalist quality, one closely bound to special interests and competition and still prominent today.[41]

The Enlightenment's idea of progress reached its philosophical climax in the writings of Voltaire and Immanuel Kant. Kant's political ethos of the dignity, freedom, and autonomy of the individual, his maxims of the individual's responsibility for reasoned pursuit of knowledge and of the voluntary obligation to self-restraint, as well as his postulate of teaching humanistic values, cosmopolitanism, and "eternal peace," tied into the ideals of classical antiquity, developed them further, and repeatedly served liberal conceptions as a source of inspiration for the human dignity of existence and progress.[42]

Of course, these advances were not greatly respected by those messianic perfectionists who saw the greatest value in the maximal deployment of power, rather than in freedom, equilibrium, and restraint for the creation of a utopian order. An outstanding cultural theoretician of his time, transformer of nature, and harbinger of pessimistic utopianism—part of the same sequence of alternative thought from Diogenes to Joachim—was Jean-Jacques Rousseau, who through his overemphasis on the egalitarian components of democracy (*Contrat Social,* 1762) and his partial prognostications prepared the way for the exaggeration of political equality by absolute social conformity and the populist ideologization of progress (*Volonte General*) even beyond Robespierre's regime of terror.[43]

The high point of modern optimism toward progress was manifested in the American and French revolutions. One must take care, however, to differentiate between the situation in France, where absolute legal and moral claims on the state and society gave way, after initial euphoria, to disillusionment, polarization, and the ideologization of progressivist thought, and the American version of a constitutionally attested policy of checks and balances between change and preservation, freedom and consensus, which after 1787 made a conscious effort to end the political Europeanization of America and strive toward the practical realization of the idea of progress.

## PHILOSOPHICAL DECADENCE AND POLITICAL
## IDEOLOGIZATION

The nineteenth-century sky was still bright with the guiding stars of freedom, equality, fraternity, justice, reason, and truth, but the brightness of their light blinded the French (Saint-Simon, Comte) and to an even greater degree the German (Hegel, Marx) thinkers. These self-appointed inheritors of the revolutionary events of 1789 were convinced that they could eliminate the causes of failure by declaring progress to be an "immanent law" of history that was, in fact, "scientifically verifiable." The humanistic progressive thought of the Enlightenment, which had appealed to reason and the self-responsibility of the individual, was replaced by an "objective" and materialist principle of progress: the supremacy of the world spirit, the dialectic of capitalistic means of production, or natural law with its attendant forces of biological (Darwin, Spencer) or racial (Joseph Arthur de Gobineau, Houston Stewart Chamberlain) selection.[44] Of course, the assumption that history is subject to laws alterable by human intervention was the source of fateful historical fallacies. These continued to express themselves in certain social systems in the ambivalence of the Hegelian, linear model of progress of the Marxist totalitarian concept of progress well into the twentieth century.[45]

The nineteenth century can be characterized as a time of great political discontinuities and ideological transformations. At the same time, drawing on the crises arising from these changes, there emerged a decadence and paramorphosis of the idea of progress whose effects lasted well into the twentieth century.

The ambiguous quality of the French Revolution in the eighteenth century was by no means resolved. Its exaggerated ideals were vented all the more vehemently on the nineteenth century as a conglomerate of distorted revolutionary ideas of conflicting or cooperating negative ideologies: as intolerant political nationalism and rapacious imperialism, as the destructive confrontation between culture and technology, or as a pessimistic, anarchistic, or apocalyptic romanticism.[46] Irrational political chaos was brought about by the parallel emergence of a restorative conservatism (propounded in its moderate version by Edmund Burke, and in more reactionary form by René Chateaubriand, Karl Ludwig von Haller, and de Maistre),[47] of a bourgeois emancipatory market liberalism (Jeremy Bentham, John Stuart Mill),[48] and of an anticapitalistic socialism (Marx, Engels).[49] This initiated the polarizing collision of these competing "isms" to the point of their dogmatic exaggeration: on the one hand, in the Romantic transfiguration of the medieval feudal monarchic state willed by God and the scholastic persistence of its restoration, and on the other, in the Marxist ideology of a communist seizure of power and utopian establishment of a proletarian mass dictatorship. The exception here, of course, was liberalism, whose nineteenth-century influence remained fatally limited to the Anglo-Saxon countries, and the self-understanding of which obviated any form of indoctrination.

The political ideologization and irrational hardening of fronts were followed, thanks to the economic successes of capitalism and the Industrial Revolution, by unstoppable changes that exploded traditional economic ties, created deep uncertainty, and increased susceptibility to easily digestible ideologies, with the ultimate result that the individual was consigned to a social vacuum.[50]

Earlier progressivist optimism changed into a nihilistic cultural pessimism; the scientifically controllable ambivalence of progress no longer seemed so easy for the human psyche to bear, sociopolitically or spiritually. An unstable and passive sense of crisis set in, drawing its political and philosophical legitimation from various theoretical directions. The French thinker Tocqueville was one of the first to foresee the hidden dangers of the approaching mass society in the tyranny of the majority over the minority.[51] Arthur Schopenhauer, Jacob Burckhardt, and Søren Kierkegaard had already taken flight into romantic-conservative and religious existential criticism of civilization, just as their alternativist predecessors before them, and had satisfied themselves with the role of pessimist interpretors of a hopeless present. Nietzsche surpassed all previous patterns for the cultivation of apocalyptic nostalgia with his own brand of nihilistic philosophy. On the basis of its linguistically brilliant, irrationally seductive articulation, Nietzsche's thought had an impact that extended far beyond fin de siècle Europe.[52]

All of them had in common an antimodernist skepticism and a moral critique of the arising mass systems, the emerging mass social culture, the loss of individuality ensuing from the individual's absorption into the mass, the headlong development of scientific and industrial progress, and the materialist biological evolutional theory of Darwin, which was understood in a destructive sense. The "valuelessness of earlier values" (Nietzsche) was postulated. Beguiled by the anarchistic apocalypse of their own historical analyses, they allowed their theories to flow like molten lava, without presenting their confused contemporaries any constructive means to grope their way out of this seemingly desperate existence and continuing decline.[53]

In the emerging sciences of sociology (Herbert Spencer, Max Weber) and psychology (Le Bon, Wundt, Freud), the attempt was made to compensate for this failure. But the discerning explanatory approaches of even those disciplines were unable to break completely free from the prevailing lines of thought and escape the vortex of those dispirited times.[54]

If nineteenth-century European political thought about progress reflects a historical change that is characteristic of the twentieth century, then the changes in thought within relevant historical categories can be shown as follows. In antiquity and the Middle Ages, the ambivalence of progress was interpreted as historical experience, but it also served as an appropriate scale for human self-control and political self-restraint and as a God-given boundary beyond which the individual could not pass. In the sixteenth and seventeenth centuries, modern scientific knowledge seemed to dissolve the historical and transcendental boundaries that had been imposed on the ambivalence of progress. All obstacles facing the individual's power over nature and the cosmos were swept away.

Yet, by no means did eighteenth-century thought witness an absolute dessication of the sources of reflection on rational scientific progress toward the ethical and political enlightenment of the individual and achievement of an appropriate liberal democratic social order. Even the ancient maxim of the limitation of everything political, as well as a secularized form of the limit imposed by the Middle Ages, continued to exist as a result of enlightened redefinition, until a few French revolutionaries temporarily declared them no longer valid.

But the partial political reforms proferred in the eighteenth century led only to the theoretical capitulation of the nineteenth. The dissolution of all previous limits and Nietzsche's proclamation of nihilism ("God is dead" or "the will to power") heralded the reversal of progress and its misunderstood ambivalence. Such a decadent philosophy of resignation naturally provided additional impetus for the destructive unleashing of rigid political ideologies: conservatism and nationalism versus Marxism and anarchism (Proudhon, Bakunin, Sorel). These ideologies were embraced throughout Europe, from socialism to anarchism in the doctrinaire application and monopolization of progressivist thought (from Marx to Lenin), and in the reaction of nationalist conservative policies of restoration (from Napoleon to Kaiser Wilhelm II).[55]

The coincidence of political polarization and ideological fanaticism, antimodernism, and romanticism, and increasing scientific, technological, and economic dynamics, sowed confusion, complicating and indeed hindering the analysis, classification, or understanding of the conflicting strains of thought. In addition, it slowly but surely prepared the way for the most extreme example of political irrationality thus far: the clash between fascism, socialism, and communism. The theoretical arrogance of European thought in the nineteenth century ultimately facilitated the virtual capitulation and moral catastrophe of the twentieth century.

# 2

## The Crisis of Europe in the Twentieth Century

The twentieth century saw the unleashing of the insatiable, destructive force of a crude ideological potential. With almost every rational political current paralyzed by the overriding cultural pessimism fomented by European intellectuals well into the 1920s and 1930s, the "progressivist" claims and uncompromising objectives of both Left and Right no longer seemed resolvable by peaceful means and were conquered by the barbarous use of military force. The events of the First and, especially, Second World Wars accelerated unscrupulous theories of decline and simultaneously triggered a lasting crisis in the European concept of progress as the consequences of perfectly organized and ideologically abused technical progress became clear.

One is faced with the question of whether the free Europeans, in the wake of the historical trauma of fascist, national socialist, and communist orchestration, perversion and totalitarianization of a progressivist idea pursued ad absurdum, could actually find the political ethos and moral power to recapture their belief in enlightened, humanist progress.

The beginning of the twentieth century was replete with analyses revealing progress as an illusion (Georges Sorel), with prophecies of the "Twilight of the West" (Oswald Spengler) or the decline of capitalism and democracy (Carl Schmitt, Joseph Schumpeter, Ludwig Marcuse), and prognoses of the end of European history (Alfred Weber, Arnold Toynbee). The philosophical articulation of the spirit of the times was the intellectual continuation of long existent sentiments. Indeed, the pending apocalypse and tragic extermination of the human race, culture, and a vision of the future was eventually realized in practice as a result of the dominant politico-ideological mentalities, together with the aid of new military technology.[56]

The question must remain unresolved whether the philosophical vacuum was indeed partly responsible for the political vacuum that manifested itself within Europe in the parochial, somewhat racially oriented competition among the states and that outwardly was motivated by colonial and imperialistic ambitions. Those historical epochs in which a harmonious rapprochement of philosophy and politics, theory and practice, between the individual, state, and rationality was still possible remain a challenging ideal today. The actual realization of the ideal is difficult because philosophy is no longer generally accepted as the mediator between politics and organized knowledge.

This change was completed in the nineteenth century, when the discrepancy between scientific achievements and philosophical knowledge expanded, ensconced itself in a nihilistic atmosphere, and thus allowed the classical dialogue between philosophy and politics to degenerate into culturally pessimistic, ideologically totalitarian, or romantic utopian monologic processes. The cleft between the natural sciences and the humanities, detailed for the first time by Giambattista Vico (see Isiah Berlin),[57] has not been bridged by philosophy since the nineteenth century. If the eighteenth century can be termed the century of progress, then a sure and ominous characteristic of the nineteenth century was the decline of progress, in which German thinkers figured prominently—Hegel and Marx on the one hand, Nietzsche and Schopenhauer on the other. The "philosophical penetration of the natural sciences" (Carl Friedrich von Weizsäcker),[58] which since classical antiquity had been one of the main tasks of philosophy, gave way to the socialist determinism of a continuing movement toward freedom, allegedly verifiable scientifically, and to the decadent brooding over a self-induced pathology of progress. Certainly history is an open-ended process, and thoughts are free. But where philosophy fails, the miscarriage of politics is not far behind. The path to the century of violence, to the totalitarianism of Left and Right (were not fascism and national socialism legitimized in advance by racism and nihilism, and communism in its turn by Marxist-Leninism?), and finally to the "crisis of Europe" (K. D. Bracher) had already been clearly delineated, although this did not presuppose that it must be traveled.[59]

## THE TOTALITARIANIZATION OF PROGRESS IN NATIONAL SOCIALISM AND COMMUNISM

Germany's political development in the first five decades of this century played a devastating and central role for the peoples of Europe. It contained a totalitarian rejection of liberal, humanist assumptions about civilization, replacing them instead with racist discrimination; the negation of the idea of humanity; the destruction of the legacy of Western culture, which the Germans had themselves helped to create; and a European vision that was beginning to take form (Briand,

Stresemann). This development ultimately dealt the idea of progress one of the heaviest blows it had ever suffered.[60]

To interpret Hitler as a strictly German phenomenon, however, could be a completely distorted evaluation of the historical and political relationships and ideological ambiguities of the interwar years. Hitler was a German phenomenon, he was a European phenomenon, and he is a global phenomenon of our century. By analyzing the development of world history, one can perhaps understand how Europe made Hitler a possibility; and by analyzing modern European history, how Germany produced him.[61]

Hitler's domestic political path to power was characterized by Germany's defeat in the First World War, the failure of the Weimar Republic and its intellectuals, and the particular status of what, by Western European standards at least, was a "late nation" (Helmuth Plessner). His success was facilitated also by an outmoded Wilhelminian social structure that combined characteristics of a reactionary belief in authority with an alternative, avant-gardist cultural and artistic romanticism while regarding economic and technological progressivism with an antimodernist, anti-industrial skepticism.[62] Hitler simultaneously personified the phenomenon of perfidious ideological insanity and economic success and was able to exacerbate unresolved ideological problems with his blood-and-soil ideology.[63] He firmly established in a teutonic myth of community and a totalitarian leadership cult the dilemmas of cultural lag and modern technological complexity, which had led to the social isolation of the individual and a paralyzing apprehensiveness, individual egoism, and "the malaise of civilization" (Freud). In addition, Hitler used the competitive ethos of capitalism to form a socio-biological Darwinist theory of the struggle for existence and to legitimize the territorial claims of a racially superior Germanic people in his domestic and foreign policy. Finally, he fought mass unemployment by promoting highway construction and a technologically ultramodern armaments program.[64]

Hitler astutely used the "legend of betrayal," the Versailles treaty and its consequences, which were so traumatic for the German people, to propagate a "Third Reich": the alternative ideology of "German National Socialism," an anticommunist, anti-American, anti-Western, and antidemocratic "Third way." His accessible, populist phraseology and mass-oriented slogans, technologically aided by the use of the new media of radio and film, were supposed to instill in the people a new sense of self-confidence, unity, and security, and ultimately motivate and mobilize them for Hitler's own purposes.[65]

In less than a decade, Hitler came to power legally, liquidated Germany's constitution and democracy, converted skepticism and discontent into an absolutely destructive, programmatically expedient mass ideology and mass psychosis, and incited Germans to turn against their European neighbors and Jewish citizens. The result was Europe's catastrophe, the final solution of Auschwitz, and the moral annihilation of the Germans.[66]

But Hitler was also a European phenomenon. The establishment of a free and democratic Europe after 1918 in cooperation with the United States had not been successful.[67] Ideologists chose to philosophize on the twilight of Western civilization, thereby strengthening predilections toward political self-fragmentation and ideological self-estrangement. The "golden" twenties evolved into a decade of crisis for the democracies, especially in Eastern and Southern Europe, with the rise of fascism under Mussolini in Italy and of communism under Lenin in Russia as the most extreme examples.[68] However immune the Western democracies may have remained to fascism and communism, they failed to appreciate the extent to which the young and endangered German democracy required support in order to flourish domestically and to redeem itself abroad. France and England's behavior toward Germany after the First World War is understandable psychologically, especially since the war had been the prelude to the collapse of the colonial empires of all three nations. But the obduracy of French politics, which denied the democratically elected German governments those successes Hitler would later be accorded without resistance, proved afterward to have been at the least foolish, certainly devastating, and probably opportunistic.[69]

Unlike the French, and unlike the German conservatives, the English showed themselves—admittedly with massive American aid—to be much less corruptible as democrats in time of need.[70] Even so, Hitler's barbarism brought Europe the greatest cultural and political humiliation in its history thus far—a humiliation that, although based on other intentions, had already been experienced by the peoples of Africa and Asia as the result of Europe's colonial and missionary policies.

At the same time, Hitler was and remains a global phenomenon of this century. Initially, it was the worldwide economic crisis and the increasing misery of mass unemployment that combined to propel him to power. With interwar Europe suffering from conditions akin to civil war and from a power vacuum, Hitler seemed to be the only European leader at the time capable of offering potentially successful political and economic answers to the crises. Weimar Germany, rife with antiparliamentary feuding between political parties, was a model of the "ungovernability" of democracy that created a power vacuum and strengthened the appeal of dictatorship, making Hitler appear as the logical alternative to the other German parties and their self-destructive infighting.[71] In the wake of the First World War, America succeeded Great Britain as leader of the development of a modern, worldwide capitalist system. So it was that the United States under Franklin D. Roosevelt's New Deal gave the only effective democratic response to the economic crisis. The solution, however, had negligible meaning for Europe because of American isolationist sentiment (after Wilson's European "overengagement"). This does not mean that the world economic crisis inevitably enabled Hitler to come to power. The partly European, particularly German historical responsibility for the horrors and consequences of the Second World War cannot be even partly—much less wholly—denied by citing American isolationism. The fate of Europe lay in the hands of the Europeans. Any political action would be meaningless if one were not always ready to believe in the existence of alternatives.

Hitler's seizure of power has in many ways remained a global phenomenon characteristic of the twentieth century.[72] At first his momentous role in world history was not primarily that of subjecting lesser races to Nordic domination and creating a world empire. Actually, the motif of world domination at the hands of "great men" can be traced back far into Western as well as Oriental history, from Darius, Alexander, Caesar, and Genghis Khan to Napoleon, although the specific political and economic conditions of each epoch must be evaluated differently. First, Hitler was a European trying to realize this goal in a Europe and a world where the sense of equality was very advanced, even successfully institutionalized in some countries. Second, he attempted to realize this goal through the use of totalitarian, ideological means of extermination, causing potentially irreparable damage both to the idea of humankind and the humanist tradition of Western civilization. On the other hand, the phenomenon of Hitler refuted Hegel and his epigones by proving, regardless of the high level of cultural and political development of a particular epoch, that its people and democratic institutions remain vulnerable to the seductions of totalitarianism.

History is by no means necessarily the progress of freedom. By showing that technological progress can ultimately lead to historical regress, Hitler also demonstrated the degree to which the increasing technological progress of the twentieth century contributed to a more systematic exploitation of subtle and terrorist violence for ideological ends. Hitler refuted Nietzsche as well. In a time when intellectual play on the brink of the abyss of civilization was in fashion, when radical criticism from the Left and Right did not coincide with an awareness of responsibility or consistency, the "will to power" was able to produce the nihilistic explosion of a presumptuous and irrational cultural and political pessimism, the consequences of which Nietzsche had failed to consider.[73] These factors culminated in "superman" Hitler as a pathological racist design for rightist totalitarian power and apotheosis.

After thorough theoretical preparation in the nineteenth century, the principle of leftist totalitarianism, in the form of the Russian Revolution and the theory of Marxist-Leninist dictatorship and world domination, came into practical realization in the twentieth. Initially, however, the political transformation from czarist despotism to the communist myth of the proletariat remained a purely Russian affair. The new dictatorial regime did not apparently worsen conditions for the Russian people, who had been living under oppression for hundreds of years.[74]

Hitler's aggressive military plans against Russia produced a fundamental reevaluation of communist ideology. His declaration of war had the unintended effect of handing trumps to Stalin and the leftist totalitarian camp, a consequence that still has historical and political significance. As a result, Stalin was able to justify his pact with Hitler as a prescient, carefully thought out tactical move for the preparation of his own armed forces. He was also able to stabilize his own rule of terror domestically, to legitimize it morally, and finally to rally the Russian people to the idea of communism and world revolution[75] as part of the struggle against national socialist and fascist enemies. In addition, Stalin was able to present his alliance with Churchill and Roosevelt, both to his suspicious comrades and to world opinion, as the great common cause of democracy against tyranny. After the victory over Hitler, Stalin freely exploited this situation for his own totalitarian purposes.

Hitler, the "greatest promoter of Bolshevism in Europe" (Walter Hofer),[76] with his rightist totalitarian seizure of power and megalomaniac military strategy, was responsible for the Soviet Union's imposition of leftist totalitarian rule on the peoples of Eastern Europe. This process began after the collapse of the Third Reich and continues into the present. It includes the division of Europe, the continuing leftist totalitarian rule over the German Democratic Republic at the hands of the victorious Soviet Union, the division of Germany, and the continuing forced division of the city of Berlin into East and West. Hitler's strategy made possible the ascendancy of the United States and the Soviet Union as competing superpowers, replete with worldwide confrontation between liberalism and collectivism from the First to the Fourth World, and ensured the decline of Europe's influence on international politics, relegating the Old World to the periphery of the superpowers.

The principle of rightist and leftist totalitarianism as the attempt, in the twentieth century, to realize a totalitarian concept of progress by means of force has consigned the idea of progress to an abyss and has deeply shaken the historical consciousness of the Europeans, in particular.

The confrontation between liberal, pluralist democracies and totalitarian and authoritarian systems has prevailed since 1945. The totalitarian regimes range from the leftist totalitarianism of a geographically enlarged and ideologically strengthened Soviet Union and the spread of communist ideas in the countries that emerged from the destruction of the colonial empires after the Second World War to form the Third World to a wide variety of rightist totalitarian regimes. The rightist military dictatorships of Spain, Portugal, Greece, and Turkey in postwar Europe, which resulted from the legacy of rightist totalitarian dictatorships, have, with the exception of Turkey, all been superseded by democratic regimes. In many of the lesser developed nations in Africa, Asia, and Central and South America, the rightist ideology has been exhibited in nationalist or authoritarian dictatorships. Racist authoritarianism is the driving force behind the South African regime, whereas Iran is dominated by an Islamic fundamentalism bordering on a theocratic totalitarian reign of terror. The conflict between these systems and liberal pluralism cannot be seen merely as the global historical consequence of national socialism. Rather, it has to be understood precisely in respect to the relative totalitarian threat of the Soviet Union as a basic historical experience and as an ideological challenge to free political thought in the twentieth century.[77]

## THE POLITICOHISTORICAL DIALECTIC OF THE IDEA OF PROGRESS AFTER 1945

Forty years have passed since the end of the war, and the "crisis of Europe" seems to be just as pertinent today as in 1917–18, 1933, or 1945. The paradigms of political discussion might have changed in recent decades, but the contemporary revisions and renewed proclamations of crisis in progressivist thought, or the sobering analyses of its end as an ideology, suggest that attempts to cope with politicohistorical events or the persistent, even widening, philosophical gap between the natural sciences and the humanities have either faltered or utterly failed. In this view, society's consciousness is marked by uncertainty, an attitude that recalls the previous cultural pessimism at the beginning of this century.

Have the theoretical erosions—communism, fascism, Nazism—in the Western idea of progress or the practical consequences of these mass ideologies in the First and Second World Wars ever been mastered or subdued? Has the ideological division of Europe also resulted in a sociocultural separation among the Europeans themselves? Is the contemporary intellectual articulation of crisis symptoms at many levels indeed a sign of a "search for lost times," for a repressed past, for a historical identity, or fear of an unrecognizable future? On what politicohistorical basis could the renaissance of the liberal democracies of Western Europe hope to flourish after the war? Which philosophical and social value structures should the democratic societies have attempted to link themselves to, if they were able?[78]

At first, a historical paradox confronted free Europe and ultimately provided the key to understanding the initial Western political position after the war. On the one hand, the task consisted of restoring an awareness of history and historical responsibility as the most important prerequisites for human identity and social progress. On the other hand, it was necessary to bring about a break with the past through the repulsion and containment of totalitarian ideologies and their implications.[79]

Germany was especially affected by this historical discontinuity. The young Federal Republic found itself faced with the traumatic task of creating a political form of organization and a legal framework that would simultaneously include the limitation and the status of a provisional or "transitional" state (Theodor Heuss) as an intermediate stage on the way to a reunified Germany. The conscious maintenance of this tentative status, however, precluded the development of any strong sense of history or state. It was also crucial that a basic political consensus be achieved despite the fact that the German question remained unresolved. This meant the repression of both the past and the contemporary historical circumstances and the postponement of the search for German identity to some indefinite day of national unity.[80]

This abnormal German process of alternating between the repression and mastery of history, between lachrymose self-denial and constructive democratic reidentification, was relatively painless at first, owing to conscious acceptance of Western integration and generous American economic aid. The latent socio-political strains of coming to terms with the past were balanced out by means of a cross-partisan economic consensus, which lasted until the youth and student rebellions of the mid-1960s.

The continuing political controversy over Germany's attempts to cope with the German question and the past has great contemporary relevance thanks to political debate within the framework of a new policy of rapprochement between the two German states, a new search for identity, and self-determination, and the recent emergence of anti-American, antimodernist Green national neutralism and pacificism. When reviewing the actual sociopolitical development of the Federal Republic, however, one sees that it also has analytical resonance.[81]

A similar, extensive public discussion about the German past and the European/ Atlantic present and future would have had to occur when the Federal Republic was established as a constitutional state in order to regain political freedom, historical responsibility, and a sense of German identity and Europeanness, and to neutralize the natural fragmentation of society into an embittered, vulnerable older generation and a younger, questioning, critical generation. It is quite possible that this failure to analyze the past, and the unwillingness or refusal of the older generation to engage in open dialogue with the younger, was one of the most important causes for the emergence of the German protest movement at the end of the 1960s. The youth movement in Germany, because of its extreme potential for aggression and frustration and because of its escalation into violence and terrorism, differed from the youth revolts in the United States and France.[82] It may be just as possible that the movement represents a further consequence of unresolved German history and a lack of social harmony. The specific contemporary problem posed by the Greens contains parallels to the Weimar Republic's vulnerability to irrational cultural pessimism about progress. The Alternatives openly disavow reality. With their own antiparliamentarian stance, they are attempting to undermine parliamentarianism by turning it back on itself.

These anachronistic tendencies in the contemporary history of the Federal Republic of Germany should be neither dramatized nor trivialized.[83] If one were to take stock, West Germany would be shown to have a high degree of democratic stability, even though it was made possible only through an inflexible consensus at the cost of the homogeneity of social transformation. This was accomplished despite the extreme hardship of its initial political position and the ambiguity of this position historically: "as far as our sense of history was concerned, we Germans initially fell into a deep slumber" (Richard von Weizsäcker).[84] It may be that the unresolved German question permitted an immediate public effort to cope with the past, to transmit a new awareness of German history and identity, but it is equally possible that the German people had been too devastated to complete this effort. Regardless, it was necessary that an attempt be made, for one's own sake and above all for the sake of postwar youth. The reconciliation of the generations did not take place—to the misfortune of the German social mentality.[85]

The unresolved German question and the open course of German history remain inextricably linked to open European history.[86] The division of Germany and the division of Europe were not and are not a reason for neglecting the unification of the free European countries and the institutionalization of the United States of Europe. It remains the historical task of the West to promote the fusion of West German and West European responsibility for the realization of the European idea, the United States of Europe, in order to ensure the political, cultural, and economic survival of the old continent.[87]

The Federal Republic of Germany was not the only country to find itself confronted by a political vacuum after the war; a similar situation faced the other countries of East and West. In Eastern Europe the imposition of totalitarian leftist regimes brought with it the categorically defined communist ideologization of the past, present, and future. The Western European states were presented with the task of salvaging Western civilization from the ruins of the Second World War, since only the open avowal of this tradition would allow them the possibility of regaining historical perspective and awareness, and give them the power to rediscover the idealistic and humanist qualities of the past.

Yet, even if the Europeans recognized the necessity of restoring a historical awareness for the preservation of the Western tradition of ideas as well as for the democratic, responsible, and realistic management of future challenges, and even if historical awareness was interpreted by all parties as a fundamental historical and political realization, as a necessary condition of the idea of progress, as a prerequisite for future thought, the motivation behind the search for a common historical identity and the vision of a unified European future was made vastly more difficult as a result of six factors brought about by the Second World War.

*First,* the oppressive fact that the pervasive phenomenon of totalitarianism had become a historical constant in the twentieth century must be acknowledged. This realization, in turn, occasioned disillusionment in Western Europe's recent political past, for totalitarianism of the Right as well as the Left could ultimately be traced back to the domination and perversion of the European idea of progress. This disillusionment, in turn, made the act of remembrance a burden. Thus, the repression of history seemed to be the only solution. But the repression of history remains pointless, for history remains *us,* which, in this case, means that we are only repressing or denying ourselves. Hence, we never have a choice other than to accept, analyze, and answer for history in its negative as well as in its positive aspects. Otherwise we stand for nothing.

*Second,* in their efforts to come to terms with the past, the Europeans focused primarily on the war in order to relieve themselves of as much guilt as possible.

To cope with the historical baggage of the Second World War, they simply relegated it to the Germans. Undeniably, it was Hitler who plunged Europe into chaos and committed irreparable crimes against the Jewish people. German responsibility for the Second World War cannot be quibbled out of existence.

Nonetheless, the Europeans had sufficient occasion to begin a basic revision and analysis of their own political roles in the First World War, in the interwar years, and during the Second World War. Italy had the chance to reflect on Mussolini; England, on Chamberlain; France, on Marshall Pétain; and Norway, on Quisling. Political conditions in the Southern European countries of Spain, Portugal, and Greece would not permit reflection on Franco, Salazar, and Metaxas and the devastating Greek civil war, respectively, until thirty years after the Second World War had ended. Certainly, no epoch has ever lacked historical material for reflection. Generally, all that has been lacking are political and democratic maturity, a consistent sense of responsibility, and voluntary self-criticism.

However understandable postwar European resentment of the Germans may have been, for many years it obstructed European unification, a European future, and coordinated political, economic, and social progress.

*Third,* both wars had emasculated the centuries-old international power structure of the Old World, divided Europe geographically and ideologically, and thus condemned it to the quasi-provincialization of its political and economic goals. The rise of the United States and the USSR to the role of superpowers, attended by the bipolarity of an ideological confrontation, left the Western Europeans with only one realistic possibility: to preserve their open and democratic social systems by accepting the path of political humility and entering into an alliance with the Americans as a guarantee of freedom, economic prosperity, and antitotalitarian involvement. Eastern Europeans were given no such choice by the Soviet Union. They were politically subjugated by the totalitarian means of a closed system.

Europe's new status and its reduced political and economic capacities in the world, the loss of the past, and the diminution of future possibilities all changed and inevitably narrowed the horizon of its historical and political thought. The Europeans were no longer the hub of the universe (Ortega y Gassett); the wars had robbed them of their *élan vital* (Stanley Hoffmann)—perhaps forever.[88]

The Western humanist roots of Europe, the rare historical combination of intellectual inspiration and scientific progress, religious power and economic courage, historical awareness and political optimism had been transplanted to the New World with the first migrations of Europeans to America at the beginning of the seventeenth century—before they ultimately fell victim to Europe's own ideologies. This was a revolutionary process, which, however, had little impact on the politicohistorical thought and action of the Europeans until the Second World War sharpened their powers of perception and allowed cooperation with the United States to become a strategy that was both politically expedient and vital to Europe's economic survival.[89]

*Fourth,* the American Marshall Plan for the economic revitalization and prosperity of Western Europe provided for political stability and forged consensus for the restoration of the European democracies. But the Europeans were not able to exploit this new economic impulse by joining together immediately and cooperating without reservation in a European-wide community to guarantee themselves a relevant political future by recreating and ensuring their economic dynamism.[90]

There was no shortage of good intentions, realistic concepts (especially from Jean Monnet, Robert Schuman, and Paul-Henri Spaak), British superiority complexes (Winston Churchill's remark in January 1952 that ''I love France and Belgium, but we cannot let ourselves be reduced to that level''),[91] and successful French obstruction (one need only recall the failure of the European Defence Community [EDC] and the ten-year stonewalling of English negotiations for entry into the European Economic Community [EEC], both brought about by use of the French veto).[92] What the Western Europeans lacked was a common historical orientation toward the future, the discerning vision to redefine European identity, and the ability to translate economic dynamism into common European projects, large or small.

In retrospect, it might be quite embarrassing for the Europeans to recognize that, at that time, the Americans were thinking more like Europeans than many Europeans themselves.[93] Postwar Europe demonstrated, perhaps paradigmatically, that periods of economic growth, social comfort, and political stability could be attended by periods of historical sluggishness, and that the two categories of history, dynamism and inertia, need not be mutually exclusive. Progress in one sector can mean decline in another.[94]

It is not difficult to point to the political and economic, though not military, successes of Western Europe—disregarding for the moment the Western European Union (WEU) with its workable defense plan: the Council of Europe, the European Parliament (EP), the EEC, and the program of European Political Cooperation (EPC) on the intergovernmental level of the twelve European Community member states.[95] Today, however, the overwhelming economic and bureaucratic differences between the various countries, their internationally weakened political and economic position, as well as the irrational and the concrete disharmonies in relationships between Western Europe and the United States, can partially be traced to the understandable, but disastrous, problems of the postwar period.[96] They missed the opportunity to exploit American economic aid for the establishment of a common European commitment, and they neglected to understand the importance of work on a common political vision as a historical task of the West and as the future of Europe.

But who trusted the Germans enough after the war? The French did not even trust the Americans.[97] The Gaullist trauma of the Americanization of Europe, which was the driving force behind French politics until the end of the Pompidou period, not only turned out to be unsuitable for the idea of Europe but also helped to promote those tendencies that Charles de Gaulle had most wanted to avoid.[98] If Roosevelt had had the chance to form a different image of the French general ("the bride"),[99] perhaps de Gaulle might have been spared his American trauma; Europe, Gaullism; and the United States, the political and military capriciousness of the French.

*Fifth*, the various historical interpretations found in Western European textbooks of the 1940s, 1950s, and 1960s on the causes of the Second World War probably did not help promote a common historical identity, a future European desire for unification, and supranational education toward European citizenship. All of these were important prerequisites for the creation of a sense of solidarity with the Germans, which, at that time, was a very difficult proposition indeed.[100]

In the Federal Republic, meanwhile, lessons on European and German history stopped with the end of the First World War. Until the end of the 1960s, reference to events that occurred after World War I was taboo, both in textbooks and in the thinking of older history teachers. The difficulties involved in the development of a historical, European, and German consciousness were undoubtedly much greater for students in the Federal Republic of Germany (and probably for those in the German Democratic Republic as well) than in other Western European countries.[101] An additional factor was provided by a program of school reform in the Federal Republic of Germany at the beginning of the 1970s, which ultimately accelerated the decay of a thinly sown sense of history. The new guidelines of "modern emancipatory pedagogy" did not provide for the long overdue analysis of the causes of the two world wars, of the failure of Weimar and the rise of Hitler, of the division of Germany and the phenomenon of totalitarianism. Rather, they presented the sociocritical illumination of conditions in the Third World and of the "capitalistic methods of exploitation" of the West.

Progressive education aiming to ensure emancipation would also have to consider the formation of historical awareness as one of its most important tasks before any serious thought is given to the Third World. For this reason it is ironic that precisely this "emancipatory pedagogical practice," camouflaged as "modern educational reform," completely dismissed the study of history and thus unwittingly brought about the same result ultimately intended by the all-powerful and omnipresent state depicted in Orwell's utopia.[102]

With the entry of this "progressive" generation of teachers into German schools, the direction of the rather anachronistic history that had been taught up to that point took an exotic turn. Fidel Castro's Cuba, the Vietnam War, the Shah of Iran, Biafra, or Allende's Chile were the themes that stimulated these teachers (who were already deficient in history) and increased the ignorance of their students. The entire undertaking was not without its sensationalist aspects. The Americans' war in Vietnam was condemned in the classroom by teachers whose knowledge of American history was restricted to the *Mayflower*, the Pilgrim fathers, and the Boston Tea Party; whose knowledge of German history could be reduced to the simplistic phrase "we have nothing to do with the fascist Nazi past"; and whose knowledge of real communism had been fed by the utopian writings of the nineteenth century. The freedom and economic well-being of those teachers had been made possible by the Americans after the war and continues to be guaranteed by them today. It may be, however, that their elder colleagues and their parents may have defrauded these teachers of knowledge and understanding of their ability to evaluate freedom and economic well-being, democracy and tolerance, historical identity, and European consciousness.[103]

By the end of the 1970s, the wave of interest in the Third World had petered out, and, as has been shown by recent studies, the concept of the "European dimension" moved increasingly to the fore of history classes in Germany as well as the other Western European countries. Such an early awakening and cultivation of a European consciousness among young people, and the perspective this lends, promised to inculcate an unprejudiced approval as well as a denationalized approach to the formation of a free and united Europe.[104] The success of any attempt to release fresh energies for a "model of the future" for Europe will ultimately depend on the meaning that the new European teaching curricula ascribe to the history of Europe.

The greater our chronological distance from the Second World War, the greater chance that a sober and honest communication of historical material will grow. Greater possibilities for the formation of a sense of history as well as for the refinement of a European identity will occur, and new hopes for a benevolent future will be discovered.[105]

The beginning of the television era has posed new challenges for the open and pluralistic social systems of the Western world. The multiplication of macrotechnological elements and microelectronic instruments has not only altered the polymedial presentation of history and current events, but has also affected the self-awareness of those who until now had fulfilled the role of the mediators of history, of the intellectuals, for instance. Their longing for socialist, conservative, and liberal philosophies has indeed remained unchanged, but in the wake of the growing society of information and mass communication, their methods of communicating history must now begin to conform to the demands of the consumers of history or fall into oblivion altogether. Television is therefore the new "opium of the intellectuals" (Raymond Aron). Its new role in the mass processing of history, science, and politics might define intellectuals henceforth as mass communicators.

The degree to which television has contributed to a populist "democratization" and dissipation of the understanding of history in the Western democracies since the Second World War has not yet been sufficiently verified empirically. It has yet to be explored whether or not, and to what degree, television through its manipulation of European historical material in documentary films, continues to promote historical antagonism and cynicism among viewers.[106]

The problematic themes of history and television and their accompanying controversies about the meaning and possibilities of political (mis)education will lend a new dimension to the New Media, whose technical qualities guarantee an incredible growth of political power.[107] The rapid technological transformation of public as well as private media within the framework of general public education offers opportunities for cultivating political awareness and sophistication, but it also harbors the risk of the totalitarianizing and barbarization of human consciousness. Risks that the New Media, as all-around vehicles of communication, might penetrate the liberal ethical and sociopolitical sphere of individuals do exist. By perfecting visual hypnosis and subliminal suggestion, one can overcome the average television consumer's resistance to the "magic box." Television itself can bring about an "industrialization of consciousness, a new, deep degree of estrangement" (Richard von Weizsäcker). With the explosion of information, essential political facts become indistinguishable from unessential ones, and television systems function as simplifiers of history and popularizers of culture (Dieter Stolte). On the one hand, all this leads to the "end of enlightenment through a flattening-out of theoretical consciousness" (Günter Gaus) and the elimination of critical reflection. On the other, the effect is to reduce human fantasy and individual dimensions of experience through manipulated visual effects and textual statements.[108]

Although television technology can be misused for purposes ranging from political propagandizing to the creation of ideological conformity (as communist regimes have already demonstrated), it is not in itself dangerous. Rather, the threat lies in the possible infiltration of an "imperialism of instrumental reason that will divide the *ratio technica* from the *ratio ethica*," if Western societies entrust the media with the diversity of the democratic spectrum of opinion.[109]

The primary task of all political and scientific supporters of a pluralist democracy who regard its freedom and openness to history as crucial to survival is to develop and formulate principles for a new consciousness of responsibility and ethics in the age of technological and electronic expansion.[110] In this context, the New Media offer the West not only Orwellian visions but also challenging opportunities. They can be used to communicate and promote a European consciousness and a common politicohistorical and cultural identity, or to eliminate those persistently cultivated clichés that occur to some reporters when they have nothing else to say, in particular during reports on foreign countries. The many new private television broadcasters can be seen and used here as a guarantor of the diversity of opinion: the prejudices of one media journalist can then be compensated by the fairness of a different media historian in a private television production.

Modern media systems offer additional opportunities for the universalization of image, language, and communication. Over the long term, they can promote broader understanding among Europeans as well as between Europeans and other peoples of the world. They can foster political pluralism and can widen cultural cosmopolitanism, both of which are conducive to peace.

*Sixth*, with the invention and use of the atomic bomb, technological progress made it possible to realize a hitherto utopian category of thought: the end of history. This new dichotomy of progress would henceforth reveal itself as nuclear schizophrenia—indeed, as one of the greatest philosophical, psychological, and political challenges to human reasoning. Could history, under these circumstances, still be managed and endured? "Europe's secret is that it no longer loves life," was Camus's interpretation of the historical vacuum that followed the war.

What chance was there for historical optimism to redevelop in view of the newly acquired power of progress, which gave humans the capacity to destroy the entire material and ideological cosmos and placed in human hands the "godlike" freedom of decision over all earthly life? Inevitably, the existence of the atomic bomb transformed the European sense of freedom, responsibility, and history: historical fatalism and cynicism moved into the foreground to brace against psychic strains. The degree to which the consequences of the nuclear revolution have since become an integral part of the scientific, humanistic, and political fate of Western Europe can be understood through a discussion of the last four decades.

Even if the articulation of a common historical identity and the vision of a unified Western European future was made more difficult by the six political factors described above, the question remains how the idea of progress has been understood and realized despite the historical burdens in philosophical thought, social conditions, and political decisions of Western Europe after the Second World War.

# 3

## Progress and Ideology: On the Future of European History

### THE CRISIS BETWEEN PHILOSOPHY AND SCIENCE

"Living with the bomb" (Carl Friedrich von Weizsäcker)[111]—that was the initial situation and the post-1945 leitmotif of a future and permanent uncertainty that would henceforth plague humankind. The old apparatus of philosophy, knowledge, truth, and ethics seemed helpless in the face of the new technical and scientific challenges.

The last great physicists of this century (Einstein, Bohr, Planck, Hahn, Heisenberg, Oppenheimer)—great because they were humanists at the same time—still strove to draw spiritual identity from Western philosophy and history as the vital condition for their scientific investigations. They sought to analyze their knowledge in a historical, political, and social context, and to make this knowledge fruitful for humankind. They assumed responsibility for their knowledge; some, like Oppenheimer, were ruined spiritually by the weight of their discoveries. A later generation of physicists would not share this attitude.[112]

Indeed, the production of the atom bomb demonstrated the ambivalence of progress more clearly than ever before: the "divine" omnipotence of the individual was assured, while human powerlessness to resist human abilities seemed more fixed than ever. Once the war was over, the philosophical conflict with the idea of progress thus fell prey to the pessimistic prognoses of the future deeply rooted in a predominantly nihilistic pathos. Once more philosophy's role as mediator between the sciences and humanities was sacrificed to the current feeling of resignation and was focused on more or less fatalistic and groundless speculations.

The competing polymorphy of the critique of reason proved characteristic of various philosophical currents in the postwar era, whether because rationality had failed so colossally in the First and Second World Wars or because of its enslavement in the twentieth century by science and technology. This critique can be broken down into three main directions: a school of cultural pessimism centered on Karl Jaspers, Aldous Huxley, and others; the meta-Marxists of the Frankfurt school; and the irrational mysticism of sects, Greens, and Alternatives. Three less spectacular but more original philosophical schools that developed parallel to these directions can be seen as their antithesis: the rationalist and pragmatic, basically pessimistic existentialism of Jean-Paul Sartre; the anti-Enlightenment structuralism of Claude Levi-Strauss and Michel Foucault, with its challenge to knowledge of historical structures; and the rationalist and pragmatic, basically optimistic critical rationalism of Karl Popper.[113]

Drawing on Spengler's and Toynbee's criticism of civilization, Jaspers set out in the 1940s and 1950s to seek ways to restore transcendentalism to guide the individual's return to a limit called "God" in order to overcome the crisis of thought caused by the increasingly dubious achievements of science and technology. The existentialism of Sartre, by contrast, was linked to Nietzsche's thesis "God is dead" and left the individual adrift in the "meaninglessness" of existence, which was bereft of hope for life after death or life in a chiliastic and progress-oriented future. The individual had to find and recognize the meaning and purpose of his or her actions alone in each phase of life in the "here and now." As Sartre saw it, the individual was also condemned to "torturous" freedom.[114] In fact, the philosophy of existentialism explains the postwar historical vacuum with the greatest conciseness: in the apparent absence of future and past in the life of the individual thrown into the "hopelessness" of the present.

The renaissance of critical theory at the hands of the Frankfurt meta-Marxists proved to be a disturbing social philosophy and progressivist terminology, with significant effects on the American, German, and French student generation of the late 1960s and early 1970s.[115] The main critique in the writings of Adorno, Habermas, Horkheimer, and Marcuse was directed at the scientific and technical concept of progress and reason in the twentieth century, whose reversal had been revealed by the "dialectic of the Enlightenment" to be a "return to the barbarism of civilization." Progress, wrote Horkheimer, now threatened to eliminate the goal that it was once supposed to realize—the ideal of human existence. To Adorno, progress thus occurred where it ended, whereas Marcuse attacked the "repression by the capitalist society of wealth and class domination," and the "system-immanent compulsions," such as "terrorized consumption," "meritocracy," the "cultural hypocrisy of the Establishment," and the "technocratic self-estrangement of the individual," which led to the individual's "unidimensionality." Marcuse ultimately came to the conclusion that this social situation could only be overcome by "the negation of everything existing." This theory gave rise to a destructive dynamic in both Italy and the Federal Republic of Germany. Only in this way, according to Marcuse, could progress toward a maximum development of human existence be assured.[116]

As youthful optimism and the euphoria over the transformation of society gave way to violence and terrorism,[117] the discouraged critical theorists disassociated themselves from the "arsonists." Positive elements of inquiry can be found today in the thinking of the Frankfurt school, which continues to develop primarily under the leadership of Habermas. This school is concerned primarily with problems of the roles and interaction of reason, science, and philosophy in developed industrial societies, as well as with the tasks and possibilities of philosophical rationale in the face of the technological and scientific triumphs of individual applied disciplines.[118] "The task of philosophy is to criticize science" (Habermas); this was the reason for the establishment of the Max Planck Institute in Starnberg, West Germany, under the aegis of Carl Friedrich von Weizsäcker, for the study of living conditions in the technological world.[119] The closing of the Institute in 1980 thwarted an attempt to pursue meaningful interdisciplinary research in the age of technological perfectionism and nuclear threat. At the same time, perhaps, it was an unconscious step toward the decline of philosophy.[120]

In the 1970s, the vision of "progressive" social change was replaced by one of hysterical announcements of apocalypse. Where critical theory had attempted to replace an allegedly negative scientific and technological theory of progress with a philosophy of social utopia, now the idea of progress fell victim to a global and categorical negation of progressivism, stimulated in particular by the apologists of the Club of Rome.

In view of the serious consequences for the Western nations of the economic and energy crises of the 1970s, and given the heightened awareness of increasing world population and world hunger, dramatic prognoses about increasing water, air, and soil pollution, and, of course, a number of accidents within the nuclear energy industry, the belief became widespread that the political "forcing" of economic, scientific, and technological progress was responsible for the "crisis" of Western industrial society. The apocalyptic analyses of the Club of Rome and the Global 2000 report not only supplied the corresponding theses and data about pollution, population, and scarcity in the world, but simultaneously demanded that humankind rigorously change its belief in progress. The new philosophy was called "doing without."[121] To avoid consuming the future today, so the theory went, the quantitative-multidimensional concept of growth behind the previous idea of progress had to be abandoned once and for all. The limits of economic and technological change seemed to have been discovered, and they ushered in the idea of an alternative economy that has since been described as an ideology of zero growth, zero progress.[122]

Attacks on the idea of progress did not cease in the 1980s. On the contrary, there was a tremendous revival of fear of the nuclear threat. The nuclear di-

mension of progress has become, as in the 1940s and 1950s, the new subject
of contemporary discussion and catastrophe literature. Whereas in the 1970s
Western Europe was preoccupied with the economic and ecological aspects of
progress (triggered by the world economic and environmental crisis), the focus
in the 1980s has shifted to the military possibilities of technological progress
(triggered by Soviet armament and Western rearmament) and a philosophy of
pacifism.

The potential for protest already extant in the different European environmental
groups was now joined by the civil disobedience of an antinuclear "peace movement" fixated specifically on the deterrence doctrine of Western nuclear theology. The problems of progress were stylized by the "peace" and alternative
movements as well as by the Greens of the Federal Republic of Germany into
an all-encompassing phobia syndrome.[123]

The formation of the German movements can be traced to the tradition of
alternative philosophy from Diogenes to Rousseau (although the whining mel-
odrama of the Green melancholics is dominated by an adolescent obstinance
rather than the spirited nonconformism of the Greek or the French thinker) and
is characterized by a backward, ahistorical desire for a medieval-like, mystical
internalization of Joachimist utopias, microstructural units, and idyllic social
harmony—all as a counterreaction to the macrotechnical achievements of modernity. One also discerns astounding analogies to the romantic and irrational
criticism of the late nineteenth and early twentieth centuries, a revolt against the
Enlightenment with its guiding concepts of critical reason and spiritual emancipation, and the strange fusion of antiprogressivist nihilism and neo-Marxist
revivalism.[124]

Another contemporary world phenomenon of the aggressive and apocalyptic
mythology of doom and the abhorrence of reason is the spread of parareligious
sects and movements whose leaders understand how to transform the philosophical void of the present into morbid visions of salvation. Bhagwan Shree
Rajneesh claims to be the personal manifestation of "God," and the Bhagwanis
believe it. They understand how to convert their disciples, despite the dogmatic
and physical harassment connected with life in the semidictatorial, Orwellian
camps of these sects, into slavish subjects lacking all self-will. The most tragic
example of this phenomenon is the "ecstasy without return," the horrible mass-
suicide of Jonestown.[125]

If these lines of Western thought reflect a philosophical uncertainty, a more
or less agnostic pessimism concerning the increasing technological, economic,
and nuclear ambiguity of progressivist thought in the twentieth century, then the
biological revolution already underway presents philosophical thought with a
new technological challenge. In addition, it could well mean the end of philosophy itself, indeed, the end of a two-thousand-year-old tradition of culture and
humanism. For does not Western culture in particular, with its concentration on
the ideal of human dignity and freedom, become superfluous at the very moment
when the human creature can be genetically manipulated, meaning that the human
being is possibly damned to cloning or even immortality? If this development

takes place (and recent advances in biogenetic research make it plausible), then the entire course of history until now will lose all meaning. If, with the help of genetic mutation, human beings can be duplicated, individuality will be flattened out by mass copies.[126]

The idea of breeding humans is an ancient utopian ideal that has surfaced repeatedly in various destructive theoretical guises. Particularly crass were the decay of the Darwinian theory of evolution into Social Darwinism, the "superman-ideology" of Nietzsche, and the hysteria over racial purity in the Third Reich. Beginning in the 1930s, the first technologically feasible solutions were proposed for the biological adaptation of those individuals who could no longer cope with the demands of modern civilization. The genetic self-domestication of the human being became a feature of the second biological revolution, promoted by the followers of Pavlov, the behaviorists, and by the followers of Darwin, the genetic engineers.[127] For Joan Broadus Watson, one of the first "theologians of behavior," the task of behaviorist psychology consisted of exploring human behavior through experimental methods to predict and monitor behavior.[128]

Well into the 1970s, the behaviorist Skinner was still claiming that "A scientific view of man offers exciting possibilities. We have not yet seen what man can make of man."[129] The 1980s, however, have witnessed the testing of genetic surgical procedures for transplanting foreign genetic material as well as synthetic anthropomorphic genetic substances.[130] It is possible that, within the near future, nothing more will stand in the way of the genesis of a "new man" without soul or depression, freed from the weight of a sense of history and progress.

One must emphasize here the invaluable medical knowledge to be gained through genetic research.[131] Yet, the "forbidden" visions remain: "perfection" of human material is possible as well as a retardation, weakening, and degradation of the individual.

The atomic bomb gave human beings the power to destroy external structures and vitality of the material cosmos; the biological revolution has now added the power for them to destroy their inner essence as well. The possibility of "progress" may henceforth be manifested in the creation of passionless, positively adapted, and future-oriented beings with computer-like brains, through the deactivation of the human soul and the capacity for historical memory. Yet humankind's path to a regression of culture and civilization is also an open-ended one, since a genetic reversion and paramorphosis of the human creature could bring about a reversal of Darwin's theories of evolution. For the time being, however, the variety of scientific trends for the coming decades is not ripe for political consensus, undefined legally, and has certainly not been subjected to sufficient philosophical analysis.[132] Richard von Weizsäcker's hopeful statement that "the nature of man is stronger than technology"[133] may be premature, but the ambiguity of progress for the twenty-first century—superman versus primate—remains a fictive vision of horror.

The idea of progress confronts the second half of the twentieth century with the same series of questions that philosophy faced following the Cartesian separation of physics from ethics and the concomitant growth of the gap between the natural sciences and the humanities. Although the development of postwar philosophy was marked by acquiescence to a fin de siècle pessimism and a return to nihilistic views of the idea of progress, there was also evidence of a renaissance of critical rationalist philosophy that struck out passionately against any sign of irrational cultural pessimism or dogmatic theories of salvation.[134]

It is perhaps characteristic that even an exotic figure such as Michel Foucault should, at the end of his life, give up the structural view of a historical psychology and direct his philosophical speculations to ancient thought, ethics, and the rationality of the individual (of voluntary moral asceticism as well as balanced responsible self-realization and social freedom[135]). Even after the theoretical ideologization of the theory of progressivism in the nineteenth century and its utter totalitarianization and perversion in the twentieth century, rational aspects and enlightened tendencies in contemporary thought once again became recognizable. These aspects and trends were basically attempts to overcome the crisis in philosophy, the crisis in the sense of history and progress, the crisis of Europe. It is perhaps a sign of hope that, despite all the ideologizing and mysticizing instabilities of reason in its present form, the philosophical maxims of ancient times have not completely disappeared. Precisely the redefinition of the ethical dimension of the idea of progress, which presupposes the preservation of the individual as well as a sense of responsibility to the liberal reform of democracy, is also a main concern of critical rationalism.[136]

Only the struggle for ethical maturity can save the individual from scientific irresponsibility and the ambivalence of progress: In the face of the dialectic of the Enlightenment, enlightenment has become a conservative task, as the sociologist Ernst Topitsch put it.

If contemporary thought succeeds in reinterpreting the historical and ethical quality of ancient thought—the recognition of the limits on human freedom and ability, of the need to balance human curiosity and capriciousness, of the double-edged sword represented by progress as the dialectic of human nature—and if it also succeeds in reacquiring the reasoned options of the Enlightenment, then it will be possible to restore the philosophical link between science and ethics. This is the only way progress can be humanized in the twentieth century.

Interesting new approaches toward reconciling science and philosophy are offered by the College Internationale de Philosophie founded in 1984 under the direction of Jacques Derrida. He and his colleagues view their task as that of awakening a need for philosophy in all areas of the sciences. Thus, the famed astrophysicist Jean-Claude Pecker, working in close association with the newly established French think-tank, describes his own discipline's numerous links to philosophy as follows: "In my opinion philosophy can only make progress by maintaining a close relationship to the sciences as a whole. Equally obvious is the fact that astronomy contains a large number of problems which have philosophical significance."[137]

Why would it not also be possible in the future to found a *European* Academy that would promote the influence of rational philosophy in our present "eminently unreasonable era,"[138] precisely in the context of interdisciplinary scientific research? Human fear of the nuclear threat and the danger of biogenetic devastation of the Western mind and individual freedom must be mastered. There must be recognition of the inseparability of the common efforts of philosophical and scientific responsibility for the ethical resolution of the ambivalence of progress. Only the philosophical rediscovery of a historical and transcendental limit, one seemingly dissolved ever since the scientific discoveries of the sixteenth century, can imbue the individual with moral respect for the dichotomy of progress and inspire acceptance of the cosmopolitan responsibility implied by a two-thousand-year-old tradition.

This is not to advocate an antiscientific anachronism. The power to reflect on rational scientific progress toward the ethical and political enlightenment of the individual should be cultivated anew in order to free us from progressivist megalomania, ideological obfuscation, and technological excess.

A crisis in the idea of progress also means a crisis of philosophy, which is the failure to communicate to humankind an open, free, historical, and personal optimism. In this sense, formulating a rational philosophical critique of the contemporary Western idea of progressivism is the best way to introduce the age of a Second Enlightenment and to restore belief in the humanist qualities of Western civilization.

## UNIVERSAL TECHNOLOGICAL PROGRESS VERSUS HUMAN SELF-LIBERATION?

Just as philosophical thinking was deeply affected after 1945 by the historical and political turbulence of the Second World War and the accompanying multidimensional consequences for social progress, so was Western Europe's social development and psychological condition. After the totalitarian dissolution of the Western value system, the reappearance of culturally pessimistic moods of decline as expressions of European impotence was hardly surprising. Indeed, the return of European societies to the philosophical, ethical, and political value structures of the Enlightenment was hampered by the diversity of causes behind the change of progress.

The dynamic forces of capitalism and the Industrial Revolution were greeted by pessimistic cultural critics as the senseless pursuit of progress, a deep confusion of the social and moral consciousness of the individual, and the fall of civilization, and were finally taken to an extreme in Nietzsche's nihilistic lament about the "valuelessness of all previous values." In fact, since the age of scientific progress, the human psyche has been exposed to those modern psychic strains usually accompanying technical progress and rapid social change.[139]

The degree of homogeneity or difference with which social changes took place always depended on social political analyses and interpretations, which vary from Schopenhauer to the Greens, from Freud to Fromm.

The two world wars threw the Europeans into what was undoubtably the deepest depression they had hitherto experienced. This depression led to a (temporary?) devitalization of culture and society. Similarly, the creation of the atomic bomb brought with it a new fear of war and social uncertainty, which was reflected in sociopolitical radicalness and anomic resignation.[140]

If one tries to characterize the transformation of Western values in correlation to the idea of progress in postwar Europe, then the social development can be roughly divided into two phases: an economically oriented era and a postmaterialistic era.[141]

The economic era coincided with Europe's reconstruction, which lasted until the end of the 1960s. In this period, the supporting behavioral norms and institutions of the technologically advanced industrial societies were based largely on economic values, with values concerning social ideals playing a secondary role.

While the German sociologist Helmut Schelsky spoke of the necessity of overcoming the ''inherent imperatives'' of technological progress with technologically oriented values, Erich Fromm and Bertrand de Jouvenel proposed that the industrial societies shed the purely economic and technological values of prosperity and achievement. They believed that the individual was in danger of personal and social isolation and ultimate degeneration into indifferent neuroticism and estranged ignorance.[142]

In light of these two opposing positions, the dilemma of sociology and psychology also becomes clear: to overcome, on the basis of the individual's adjustment to the conditions of a highly industrialized society, the social discrepancy between technological progressivism and psychological well-being in a way that neither neglects the argument for technological progress nor relinquishes the idea of individual freedom.

The aforementioned decreasing historical awareness and the universal advance of technology undoubtedly predestined the initial postwar situation of the Western European democracies for the psychological estrangement of the ''lonely crowd'' (David Riesman).[143] As Robert MacIver's definition explains, anomie means the spiritual condition of someone torn away from his or her moral roots, someone who no longer has any norms, only discordant impulses, who is no longer able to develop any sense of continuity, established groups, or obligation. The anomic individual is spiritually sterile, completely self-oriented, isolated, and frustrated, has no values, and feels responsibility to no one. He or she has lost the crucial sense of commitment to social coherence—the main source of social security—and now lives on the narrow emotive line between a past that is lacking because it has been repressed and a future that is lacking because it appears to be hopeless.[144] Precisely at this point, at the end of the 1960s, the Frankfurt school took up its generalized Marxist critique of society, a perspective that widely influenced Western youth and the student generation of the day, transforming its mood into one of anticapitalist, anti-industrial, and antitechnological revolt. Particularly influential was Marcuse's philosophy of anarchistic ''ideology of refusal'' as opposed to ''an aggressive society of surplus'' ''obsessed with technocratic progressivism" that had brought about a "total estrangement" of the individual from the self, the environment, and nature.[145]

The effects of these so-called antiauthoritarian protest movements were varied. On the one hand, they brought about a lethargic hippy-and-hashish generation, roaming peacefully and aimlessly around the world; on the other, in Italy and the Federal Republic of Germany, they developed into historically and chronologically specific variants of violent terrorism, which was expressed as a total negation of modern Western culture, society, and values.[146]

Parallelling the extremes of the student revolt since the late 1960s was a transformation of Western political culture, one determined by two closely related factors. First, a change of generations occurred, highlighting the significant differences in the value systems of the young and old. Second, this change brought about the transition from the era of economic growth to that of postmodern society. The values of the "affluent society" (John Kenneth Galbraith) of the 1950s and 1960s, which had been shaped by the experience of the war, were primarily materialistic. They focused on maximizing work and individual achievement for the socioeconomic reconstruction of democratic institutions. By contrast, the values of the "postindustrial society" (Daniel Bell) changed drastically in the 1970s and 1980s. The postulate of the achievement-oriented work ethic was replaced by the slogan "the quality of life," which was understood as the maximization of leisure time with as many state-provided social benefits as possible and elevated to the level of an individual desideratum.

This postmaterialist change of values was initially the product of loud revolt and ultimately gave way to a "silent revolution" (Ronald Inglehart). It was marked by a blatant paradox: as tempting as the hedonistic elements of an improved quality of life might have been for everyone, they were, and remain, inconceivable without the assiduous development and preservation of the Western democracies. These systems are based on a political and economic, as well as technological and scientific, progressivist optimization of modern industrial society.[147] For this reason, the most recent polemical attacks directed against Western industry, science, and technology by the ecological, alternative, and Green descendants of the 1960s movements should not be interpreted solely as a recurrence of the intellectual themes of nineteenth-century critique of progress and civilization. They should also be regarded as a reflection of the contradictory dialectic of the welfare state, a dialectic created through the institutionalization and bureaucratization of social benefits.[148]

The "renunciation of technocratic industrial society," the society that the Alternatives regard with complete antipathy and which they consider to present "no future," is clearly not completely thought out. Their postmaterialist values do not prevent them from taking further advantage of the material benefits of the welfare state.[149] On the contrary, it is even regarded as "clever" to enjoy an "alternative existence" for as long as possible at the cost of the state welfare system without producing anything at all in return—an attitude that only attests to the convenience of this seemingly unconventional lifestyle.

Criticism of the highly developed industrial, technological, and communications society is justified by the plea to eliminate the negative consequences of the technological, ecological, and nuclear development, and by the maxims of rational and human formation of an open society. The problem of the classic tensions between real and ideal values, between reconciliation with the past and visions of the future, between individual and communal realization of goals cannot, however, be solved by means of the dogmatic alternative choice between "elimination of technological progress or renunciation of the present systems of society." It can only be overcome through the liberal struggle for a compromise involving both sides of the problem. The further development of modern industrial and democratic society, with all of the advantages and disadvantages of the contemporary ambivalence of progress, must be accepted. Concurrently, an attempt must be made to utilize fully the possibilities of liberal democracy for the improvement of individual and social potential.[150]

Because of the consistency of human needs and weaknesses, the homogeneity of social change as well as the option of a political consensus of values has been reached in the past only when the individual has been able to summon energy for the voluntary recognition of a necessary balance between freedom and justice, human rights and civic duties. In the age of hypermodern social change, a policy of balance becomes a virtual priority because of the new multidimensional challenges to progressivist ideals. It now appears that only the political assurance of a balanced coexistence between economics and ecology, between technological progress and individual well-being, can guarantee a positive social attitude and a democratic consensus toward new technological achievements in the future.[151]

The social stability and moral values of the individual depend not only on liberal political aspirations toward the broadest possible social gratification of material claims and ideological goals for self-realization, but also on the autonomous cultivation and maintenance of his or her spiritual equilibrium. That the twentieth century is the century not only of ideological extremes, but also of addiction to excess, is shown by the alarming statistics on crime and drug abuse of recent decades as well as the growth of certain morbid social phenomena caused by individual neuroses and psychoses. All this points to the temporary loss or destruction of inner spiritual equilibrium. Among these phenomena is anomie, a pathological narcissism derived from feelings of boredom and emptiness. These feelings are manifested in an egocentric mania for self-realization and self-interest marked by a brutish urge for gratification. The result has been a perfidious, misanthropic wave of pornography that attempts to dismantle sexual taboos and maximize the addiction to pleasure that can only be sated by a deadening sensory bombardment. One feels compelled to ask whether the free market should cease at the point where it begins to violate human dignity. These phenomena have led to the appearance of the alleged salvational dogmas of various esoteric therapeutic groups or occult sects, which represent only the degeneration of human capability for communication and dialogue.[152]

Do these contemporary phenomena signal the kind of decadence of European

culture that Pier Paolo Pasolini, with calculatedly horrifying effects, attempted
to portray in his film *One Hundred Days of Sodom* (1975) with scenes of co-
prophagy, or a decline of values and customs in ancient Rome and recurrent
visions of approaching doom such as that Federico Fellini vividly parodied in
his cheerfully cynical films *Satyricon* (1969) and *Ship of Dreams* (1984)? In the
age of splendid isolation, modern individuals do indeed seem to be unable to
cope with the technological and scientific dimensions and the attendant social
implications of progress. They therefore seek to numb their strained minds with
deadening and intoxicating agents.

Sociologists and psychologists have also been attempting to deal with the
transformation of the problems of progress for over a century. At the same time
their messages have only become more dramatic: more or less pessimistic cultural
diagnoses, dire analyses of the social situation, and prophecies of the end of the
responsible individual after the Second World War, of a revived nuclear threat,
of worldwide increase in technology, rigid bureaucratization, computerization
of the environment and the private sphere, and the pending scientific ambivalence
of accelerating progressivism.[153] Yet, somewhat more optimistic prognoses of
the possibilities for rational and homogeneous management of the modern dialectic of society have also emerged from the assortment of pessimistic, antimodernist, or radical arguments.

The fact that the present condition of Western societies can be characterized
from the viewpoint of the individual as anomie and from that of civilization as
a crisis of culture is explained by the sociologists Raymond Aron and Richard
Löwenthal as part of the emergence of long-term social changes. These changes
often take place so rapidly and so turbulently that they exceed the limit of human
capacity for experience and adaptation (cultural lag). In the process, a redefinition
of values and the adaptation of behavioral norms have been unable to keep pace.
As a result, the applicability of norms, the authority of institutions, and the
credibility and binding social power of values have been challenged. Aron and
Löwenthal argue for a creative reinterpretation of basic values and a readaptation
of the behavioral norms and institutions based on traditional Western values in
line with the new conditions of high-tech industrial society.[154]

At the same time, the "survival of humankind" depends, as the psychologist
Alexander Mitscherlich emphasizes, on that task of the "reinforcement of the
self" that humanist psychology has set itself. Neither a radical behaviorism
desiring to manipulate and control human behavior nor a neo-Marxist critique
of society hoping for a revolutionary transformation of pluralist democracy,
neither depressing summaries of past and present sociopolitical mistakes nor the
summoning of future catastrophes can help the individual to understand and
overcome the "ever-changing environment" and the enormous powers of technological and scientific development. Instead, Mitscherlich pins his hope for the
future on a humanistic psychology, in which "the reinforcement of the self" is
understood as an aid to self-help and as a precondition for the creation of a
humane society.[155]

The starting point for this line of thought is based in the liberal and individualist human ideal of classical Greece, which saw in the philosophical reflection toward self-awareness the possibility of human self-realization. It was not, however, to be abused as an end unto itself, but rather as a way to avoid individual hubris, excessive political ambitions, and social immorality. It is important that the modern individual attempt to free Western values and ideals from the ideological rubble of history. The historical identity of Europeans is rooted in these values, which can still illuminate the way to their cultural and political socialization and self-liberation.

The philosophical and political ethos of classical antiquity and the Enlightenment was documented in the conviction that the individual could achieve harmony with self and nature through moderation and self-control. If the contemporary individual succeeds in internalizing these maxims, then he or she may also be able to regain inner equilibrium and be able to cope with a highly technologized environment. Knowledge and the capacity for human progress are also the preconditions for the sociopolitical acceptance of rapid social change and further technological and scientific progress—in the service of humanity.

## THE RENAISSANCE OF LIBERTY—BETWEEN IDEOLOGICAL CHALLENGE AND THE TRIAL OF DEMOCRACY

Unlike the philosophical pessimism of the postwar era and the modern critique of civilization, the ideas of popular sovereignty, freedom, and equality were revived in the political thinking of Western Europe after the catastrophes of the two world wars in the forms of republicanism, liberalism, and democracy. It was both astounding and encouraging that the political ideals of liberalism, conservatism, and socialism (social democracy) did not become victims of the pessimistic cultural propaganda of the 1940s and 1950s. These attitudes were expressed in the nihilistic thinking in the face of a cultural "Americanization" of Europe, the acceleration of technological progress, and the increasingly threatening character of its ambivalence.[156] After 1945, many began to wonder what solutions the classical political theories would propose for the new multidimensional challenges of progressivist thought in the wake of Europe's socioeconomic, ideological, and scientific transformation. At the same time, the political decisions of the West were profoundly influenced by the continuous existence of totalitarianism and communism. The leftist totalitarianism of the Soviet Union and its satellite states had not only become a depressing historical constant in the second half of the twentieth century, but also posed an ideological threat for the political and economic development of the Western European democracies. Even while the postwar fragmentation of communism into Maoism, Titoism, and Eurocommunism signalled a crisis within the Marxist camp, variations of communist ideology continued and still have considerable impact on most liberal and pluralist social systems of the Western European countries and, particularly, on the former colonial states of the Third World.[157]

The decisive characteristic of postwar Western history was documented in the free world's clear political commitment to building and maintaining "Europe as a continent of democracy" (K. D. Bracher).[158] With the help of the United States, the Europeans have succeeded in creating a model of progressive Western European democracy representing "the freest, most just, most humane, and best—because of its capacity for improvement—experiment" (Karl R. Popper) in its history to date.[159] The renaissance of European freedom was, however, overshadowed by the division of the Old World into East and West and by the accompanying bipolar confrontation of the two superpowers. Within the Western democracies themselves, the situation repeatedly promoted political and ideological challenges to antitotalitarian policies.

The history of the political conflict over a definition of the idea of progress in Western European thought after the Second World War can be divided into four phases. In the first phase, from the mid-1940s to the 1960s, theories of progress and political decisions were influenced by the definition of the Western community of values, the consolidation of liberal democracy, and economic reconstruction. In the second phase, from the mid-1960s to the early 1970s, the political and economical consensus of the democratic parties was increasingly brought into question by the reideologization of neo-Marxist progressivist utopias. In the third phase, which extended from the early 1970s to the mid-1980s, romantic progressivist euphoria was transformed into an antiprogressivist cultural pessimism. Doomsayers made the established parties responsible for politically forcing technological and economic progress, which would, they claimed, lead to "the ecological exploitation and military destruction of the planet Earth." This critique of progress simultaneously caused an apparent reversal of progressive and regressive political fronts. In the fourth phase, which has been in progress since the mid-1980s, the crisis within progressivist thought is showing signs of drawing to a close. Among these signs are increasing theoretical discussion and inquiry, increased efforts on the part of conservatives, social democrats, and liberals to find new and practical solutions to the ultramodern dilemmas of progress within the context of a unified Europe.

The cornerstone for the rebirth of European democracy was laid in the first twenty years after the end of the war: "After Everything" (Roland N. Stromberg)[160]—after the totalitarianization and perversion of the idea of progress under national socialism and communism, the ideological experiences of the brutal regimes of Hitler and Stalin, and the mass extermination of the Jews. The European need for an "End of Ideology" (Daniel Bell)[161] and dogmatic salvational utopias (Judith N. Shklar),[162] and for the establishment of unified opinion on the value of liberal democracy and common requirements became the focus of thought. Accordingly, a Western European definition of political progress emerged (quite unambiguously) during the reconstruction of Europe. Its goals were to create the premises for an "open society" and to protect it from "its enemies" (K. R. Popper); to transform the new nuclear dimension of political responsibility into effective measures for insuring peace, which has since been achieved with the help of the doctrine of the "balance of terror"; and to re-establish the order and stability of a liberal and pluralistic system of democracy, as in the Federal Republic of Germany, or to reconfirm it, as in Great Britain. They aimed to produce the conditions for economic convalescence and social stability and to develop and exploit the possibilities of scientific and technological progress.

Differences in the realization of these ideals could definitely be identified among the conservative, socialist, and liberal arguments over the means and strategies to be employed. One should note that the German Social Democrats first declared themselves in favor of these guidelines in their Godesberg Program of 1959.[163] The decisive historical and political moment, however, lay precisely in the conviction of the necessity of a transparty consensus. This alone could ensure the existence and progress of Europe after 1945 in the face of the monolith of Soviet dogmatism and serve as the guiding spirit for coming world politi-cohistorical decisions. This consensus, which manifested itself in the fusion of European and transatlantic political, economic, and military alliances (such as the EEC and NATO), lasted into the beginning of the 1980s despite recurrent turbulence.[164]

European readiness for consensus on the pragmatic modification of the idea of progress and its reduction to values of economic, social, and military security allowed conservative technocrats, social democratic reformists, and liberal the-orists of freedom to appear as a democratic unit, immune to dogmatic authori-tarian ideologies of Left and Right and to meta-Marxist variants of theorists such as Korsch, Lukács, Bloch, Gramsci, and Thorez, whose tenets were embodied primarily in Italian and French eurocommunism.[165] There was, however, another side to this deemphasis of ideology. Coming to terms with the past and the establishing future European identity were less important than determining the most crucial issues of the present and soberly calculating practical objectives. In short, pragmatic political considerations superseded efforts to establish a philosophical and moral basis of liberal democracy in political thought.[166] The long-term inadequacy of this "restorative spirit" of the first postwar period ultimately came to light two decades later, as radical world outlooks once more came to the fore.

Since the mid-1960s, Western European political discussion on the definition of progressivist thought has been exposed to constant ideological fluctuation. Initially, the lack of an idealistic political vision after the phase of reconstruction, together with the change of generations and a corresponding shift in values, kindled the anger of a prosperous and well-educated youth and student generation over the pragmatic party consensus of the first postwar generation. The liberal understanding of the legitimacy of the democratic state's protection of individual, politica!, and economic freedom paled against the newly unleashed critique of democracy, which pronounced itself unsatisfied with the "mere" guarantee of basic values and demanded instead that the state provide an absolute realization of democracy, equality, and justice. Ahistorical comparisons were drawn between Western ideals and political reality, above all in the Third and Fourth Worlds (only 30 of the 160 member states of the United Nations have democratic constitutions), between capitalist prosperity and worldwide famine. Camus made the following observation about the history of ideas in the twentieth century: "The revolution of the twentieth century arbitrarily separated, for the sake of extreme goals of conquest, two inseparable concepts. Absolute freedom makes a mockery of justice. Absolute justice denies freedom. Both concepts must limit each other in order to become fruitful."[167] This observation was confirmed by the emergence of radical social theories and neo-Marxist progressivist utopias from the beginning of the 1960s to the beginning of the 1970s.

The quasirevolutionary progressivist visions of the rebelling youth and student movements in Europe and the United States were similar in some respects— abhorrence of the establishment's rational conservative belief in reconstruction and its materialist, bourgeois values, elimination of "authoritarian" structures, and establishment of an "antifascist" rather than antitotalitarian order. Supporters of these movements also believed in the absolute democratization of state and society for the purpose of overcoming the "crisis of legitimacy" of the Western system of government. They advocated the socialization of the capitalist "economy of exploitation," the complete equality and participation of citizens in a collectively organized democratic society "free of oppression," the achievement of neglected social reforms and of progressive educational curricula and university reform, and the breakdown of taboos in sexual relationships as a first step toward "emancipation."[168] The causes of the return to ideology, the sources of conflict and protest differed, however, according to national and historical boundaries. In the United States, the civil rights movement and the controversial military involvement in Vietnam stood in the foreground. Italy and France experienced sociopolitical antagonism promoted by powerful eurocommunist parties. In the Federal Republic of Germany, the problems were centered primarily on the national socialist past and the failure to come to terms with it, as well as the conceptions of totalitarianism and democracy specific to a country divided into East and West. Great Britain, as the oldest modern European democracy, was spared revolutionary leftism.

The theoretical ideological constructs of progressivist romantic utopias supplied by the humanist Marxist Frankfurt thinkers Horkheimer, Adorno, and Marcuse, who had returned from America, particularly fascinated the student avant-garde of the "extraparliamentary opposition." It suddenly seemed possible to set a "progressive cultural revolution" in motion with the help of social Marxism without having to identify oneself with Soviet or East German communism or French or Italian communism. However, this leftist progressive euphoria soon proved to be "leftist fascism": "violence against things" escalated to "violence against people" and ultimately gave way, in Italy and the Federal Republic of Germany, to irrational terrorism.[169] The fragmented remnants of the protest movements experimented with the "march through institutions" and subsequently more or less merged with parties of the Left or disappeared into a "subversive" underground in order to readapt themselves to an alternative ideological spirit of the times with fresh decadence a few years later.

The third phase of progressivist discussion, which lasted from the beginning of the 1970s into the 1980s, took place against the background of a new wave of ideologization. The old leftist revolutionary euphoria over the change and improvement of society had, however, given way to an antiprogressivist cultural pessimism. This was occasioned by the worldwide economic and energy crises (1973), which hit the European industrial nations especially hard. There were calls for new political responses to the technological and economic ambiguities of progress, which the apodictic school of the Club of Rome ideologists discussed under such headings as "limits of growth," "scarcity of resources," "destruction of the environment," and "the decline of man." The continuing globalization of the Western idea of progressivism together with its technological and scientific dimensions was no longer considered a liberating force, but rather one enslaving human beings and nature. The effect of this change was to provide hysterical prophets with horrifying ideological visions and speculations about humankind's doomed future.[170]

This fatalistic, antimodern shift to outmoded variants of Rousseauian civilizational criticism reflected a certain frustration with the emotional progressivist romanticism of the movements of 1968. However, it also served to clarify the crisis in the materialist and growth-oriented concept of progress in which the conservatives, social democrats, and liberals had placed their faith with much hope and initial success, though with different conceptual ambitions after 1945.[171] For the first time, the boundaries between the three largest Western schools of thought on the idea of progress seemed to soften. The increasingly ecological emphasis of debate on progress began to dominate political thought and reversed previous Right-Left divisions and ideological fronts in an astonishing, though rather superficial, way.

The concurrent development of leftist, neoconservative, and alternative skepticism was a response to the mounting "regressive" side effects of "progressive" achievements, side effects that were emerging more and more clearly because of the scientific, technological, and idealistic political ambivalence inherent in progress.[172] A number of theoretical attempts to respond to "structural conservatism," "technocratic liberalism," or "progressive socialism" by vaguely labeling the "shift of trends" since the mid-1970s as a "value conservativism" proved not only problematic but also wrong. A gradual shift in the perception of progress began to make itself felt within the parties, which increasingly made the preservation of the natural environment important planks in their platforms. However, because of the variety of political means and paths to this goal, this progressive realization of the vital necessity of conserving nature did not legitimize the general validity of the term "value conservatism." In addition, the neoconservative shift signalled a broad critical change of consciousness in both the American and European attitudes, notably with respect to the practical consequences of Left progressivist political models.[173]

With the formation of ecological and "peace" movements such as the Green party in Europe (the German Greens being an especially exotic form),[174] the critique of the industrial societies' ideas of technological progress took up where the revolts of the 1960s had left off, driven by another presupposition. Previously, the chiliastic utopias of the Left had arisen from the optimistic belief that "capitalist pseudo-democracy" could be progressively transformed and overcome. Now, visions of cultural doomsday emerged from an apolitical fatalism that proposed, after the failure of attempts at a "progressive change of society," to combat the alleged expansion of "techno-fascism" (Robert Jungk) with the help of an "ecological dictatorship" (Wolfgang Harich), a total refusal of progress, and a restrictive dogma of renunciation. It does seem rather inconsistent that Green technology-haters of antiparliamentarian, anti-Western, and antitechnological provenance swear by the ideals of a "value conservatism" while professing their faith in an alternative political and economic culture of Europe without a liberal and pluralistic understanding of democracy. They wish to construct a Europe without economic growth and without nuclear deterrence, pleading for a return to a technological and industrial Middle Ages and "gentle structures of non-Enlightenment," for pacifist demilitarization and a "bow-and-arrow doctrine."[175]

Social democratic lip service to the ecological and postindustrial challenges of the 1970s proved to be much more complex. While the Left more or less disassociated itself from the alternative ideologies of a Green social paramorphosis, avowals such as those of the German Social Democrat Erhard Eppler on the "value conservatism" illustrate democratic socialism's progressivist dilemmas, which came to light at roughly the same time as the neoconservative shift. The European idea of progress, monopolized by the Left since the French Revolution, now became the chief theme of an increasingly liberalized Right. They recognized that the main issue was no longer one of regressive preservation, but of preserving continuity in the state, environment, and society. It was precisely the unilaterally acknowledged necessity of preserving humankind from the ambivalence of scientific progress that gave rise to progressivist perplexity in Western socialism. The changes in the historical conditions governing the progress of the political and ecological economy seemed to have bankrupted the classical repertoire of social democratic economic and social policies materially as well as idealistically.

The financial resources of the social democratic parties that formed the governments of the 1970s (the Labour party in Great Britain, the SPD/FDP coalition in the Federal Republic of Germany, and the social democratic models of Scandinavia) for achieving more democracy, more equality, more government, more reforms, or more quality of life were soon exhausted. Moreover, the political consequences of these progressivist meliorist concepts had been discredited. In the first place, the gigantic bureaucracies that had been erected to carry out boundless reform projects in welfare, social security, education, and government employment programs now stood in the way of the individual's maturity and private initiative. Second, the expansion of the welfare system and the intervention of the state in the free-market economy resulted in an increasing concentration of power and centralization of political, social, and economic structures, complicating the democratic functioning, efficiency, and innovation of these institutions. Third, the average citizen ended up associating the ambiguous concept of the "quality of life" with benefits and claims presumably guaranteed by the state. This hindered individual independence, creativity, and willingness to take risks, and falsely attributed to the state the role of an all-encompassing welfare institution. In the fourth place, the "equalizing" reforms within the educational systems led not only to an unjust decline in the quality of education, but also to a catastrophic rise in the number of unemployed university graduates. Finally, the democratic socialists began to doubt their own belief in economic growth as a result of ecological and technological ambivalence.[176]

Accordingly, the neoconservatives responded by questioning whether the modern state was "governable" under such conditions or was indeed already suffering from ideological and socioeconomic "overloading." The theoretical vacuum that ensued from the multidimensional contradictions of socialist progressivism and the alternative Green antiprogressivist negative utopia directly provoked a conservative backlash whose understood purpose was to redefine the idea of progress. Since then, "progressive and liberal conservatism" (G. K. Kaltenbrunner, Christian Graf von Krockow) has striven to dismantle social, state, and economic progress. The conservatives' primary goals have been to debureaucratize and decentralize complex modern industrial societies, to desocialize the economy, and to disencumber the state socioeconomically. In addition, they have attempted to deideologize and pragmatize the ecological, peace, and disarmament debate and prove that the tensions between liberty, equality, and majority rule cannot be harmonized in liberal pluralist democracies. In short, they want to ensure the preservation and improvement of human progress.[177]

Liberalism turned out to be both a winner and a loser in the 1970s. Conservatives, socialists, and social democrats not only absorbed the ideas (especially the antidogmatic political philosophy of Critical Rationalism), but also coopted its terminology—for example, "social-liberal" and "liberal conservative."[178] While the conservatives used the crisis in the idea of progress for purposes of political reidentification, the socialists and social democrats and liberals have yet to face this challenge, which has existed since the beginning of the 1980s.

The controversy over the idea and the crisis of progressivist ideology has been in its fourth phase since the beginning of the 1980s. Whereas in the first three postwar periods the European discussion of progress was occupied with the themes of consolidation, ideologization, reideologization, and deideologization, a "cease-fire of ideas" in Western thought seems to be developing as the twentieth century draws to a close. In an age dominated by an oversimplifying cult of feasibility, that is, "everything is feasible," and a pessimistic cult of fatalism, that is, "everything can be made obsolete," one is forced to ask whether the idea of progress is not in danger of degenerating into a historical code bereft of substance. The contemporary sense of reality, which is supported by the technological mastery of nature and obtains its reserves from the cult of feasibility, is influenced by a concept of time as an empty continuum evolving into infinity, a continuum that appears to be mercilessly enmeshing all things. Even a planet in a nuclear explosion would not remain exempt from the endless frozen death of evolution. Such a sense of time may purge substantial expectations and hopes and spawn that secret anxiety that gnaws at the soul of the postmodern individual. This concept of life, based on the timelessness of time, may shatter the great visions of Western civilization and trivialize or even eliminate the great utopian concepts. This process is often found just beneath the surface of current political life.

Secret fear of the timelessness or banality of time also nourishes the phenomenon that in recent times has been called the cynicism of postmodernism. It is the cult of apathy, the desire to slip away from the danger zones of political and historical responsibility, the urge to conform socially and avoid making waves, to prefer concealment in apolitical and asocial niches, living and thinking for the short term. Thus, it is a mentality that transforms the individual into a voyeur of his or her own decline.[179] These tendencies seem to point to alarming symptoms of serious historical exhaustion in Europe.

The last four decades saw the multidimensional ambivalence and postmodern dichotomy of the idea of progress debated and problematically propounded by conservatives, liberals, and socialists (social democrats) after the recurring postulate of "the end of the ideological age" (Daniel Bell, 1960; Peter Bender, 1981) had been proved a myth and the West returned to an "age of ideologies" (Karl Dietrich Bracher, 1982).[180] As a result, one is compelled to ask whether Western progressivist ideocratic thought has not reached its zenith, and whether Europe is now setting course for an ideological age in which history and progress are absent. Does the idea of progress, the idea of democracy, and human, political, and economic liberty still have a future in Europe? For liberal, pluralistically oriented governments, the commitment to democratic responsibility and rational mastery of the tasks approaching with the end of the twentieth century requires an extraordinarily differentiated, multifaceted, open, and humane capacity for reflection. In view of the increasingly ambiguous qualities of postmodern progress, intellectual and sober analyses will remain necessary to ward off the danger of alternative flirtation with forms of dictatorship and to protect democracy's institutions from impotence. This thesis was recently demonstrated by Jean-François Revel in *How Democracies Perish* (1984): "Communism may be a 'spent force,' as Milovan Djilas has repeatedly said. Some might even call it a corpse. But it is a corpse that can drag us with it into the grave!"[181]

The major themes and challenges of the 1980s and 1990s that will determine the future of Western Europe have been recognized by observers of almost all political orientations. *First,* the technological, nuclear, and biological revolution and its attendant social and economic consequences must be brought under control ideologically as well as practically. The new technologies, particularly those in microelectronics (microprocessors/chips), the military sector (space weapons), communications and information (New Media), and genetic technology (gene therapy, genetic engineering), have the potential to push, along with the United States and Japan, the Western European countries into a phase of "super industrialism" with unimaginably high economic growth rates.

Solutions to the risks accompanying this development have still not been found and applied. The labor market has registered high unemployment and job rationalization, trends that necessitate a broad redefinition of work and leisure and a reconsideration of the role and function of unions, which are increasingly anachronistic. In the military sphere, the value of the American Strategic Defense Initiative (SDI) for defense, research, and the guarantee of peace remains unclear for Europeans and Americans alike. The introduction of the New Media may mean that the informational "hookup" of different planes of interpersonal communication could be accompanied by cultural devastation, social and individual estrangement, perhaps even psychological depression, and the decline of the human being's critical faculties. One must also take into account ethical reservations about the manipulation of human genetic material along with the medical and ecological successes of genetic technology. If a biogenetically "new man" is actually created, as suggested earlier, all previous values and conceptions will be revolutionized.[182]

*Second,* the pollution of water, air, and soil requires that ecology and economic activity be reconciled in an undogmatic way that does not threaten economic growth. Approaches for an innovative ecological policy that does not ideologize environmental protection, but instead recognizes it as an economic opportunity, have already been formulated and even pursued. Of course, genuine success will be achieved only when all Europeans have reached a consensus on environmental policy. It remains to be seen whether the Chernobyl nuclear accident will prove the catalyst necessary for such a consensus.[183]

*Third,* humanitarian reasons, political ideology, and economic and financial policy seem to make it imperative to find a more intense and productive approach to the problems of the Third and Fourth World—hunger, poverty, economic and financial insolvency, and overpopulation. Instead of bewailing the expansion of communist influence in less developed or nonindustrialized countries, it would be more sensible for Europeans and Americans to cooperate in pursuing a North-South dialogue alongside the East-West dialogue. No country with an even moderately successful economy and a just government has ever selected a communist or rightist authoritarian government of its own free will.[184]

*Fourth,* in Europe as in the United States, despite the legally protected equality of all people, an awareness of the need for equal rights between men and women has arisen and can no longer be suppressed. This awareness has emerged as a result of the frequent lack of real—rather than just statutory—sociopolitical recognition of women's individual and professional rights to self-determination.

Although the statistics may indicate a decrease in discrimination against women in the private and public spheres as well as in professional life, percentage rates in the West vary from country to country. The United States has the best record, whereas the Federal Republic of Germany's is quite poor. The goal of all Western countries can only be to move away from an exhausting conflictual relationship between men and women to equality between the sexes. Constructive directives for the establishment of equal rights, or even for the targeted assistance of professional women, were issued by the European Community at the beginning of the 1960s. In addition, the EC Commission's report, "New Program for the Equal Rights of Women 1982–85," recommended that business and social institutions in all European member states take the initiative toward positive measures. There remains, of course, a long way before anything approaching parity between men and women in top positions will be reached. Immature feminist rigorism cannot accelerate the social revolution, nor can immature male demonstrations of power delay it. The idea that increased female presence in public and governmental positions and in private business and industry contains the long-term chance to make society more peaceful is the controversial thesis of Margarete Mitscherlich's work on the peaceful woman (1985).[185]

*Fifth,* it is questionable whether the ambiguities of scientific freedom can or should be controlled by pluralistic democratic processes. Before the discovery of the atomic bomb, the maxim still held that the freedom and curiosity of scientists should not be limited in any way. Faced with the immense but mortally dangerous achievements of technological progress, political experts cannot alone manage consequences of scientific discoveries for politics and society. The role of the scientist in society, as well as the role of the politician in scientific decision-making processes, will have to be redefined. Scientific freedom unbridled by social and political responsibility could mean a future paramorphism of Western ideals and the decline of the hard-won enlightenment of humankind.

The problems in which we have entangled ourselves with the help of science and technology will not be obviated by ideologized technological skepticism or dogmatic opposition to modernization, but rather through science and technology themselves. Science and technology must, however, be guided by perceptive ideals that serve human existence and correspond to the natural contexts of life. These would chiefly emphasize *knowledge for preservation* rather than *knowledge for destruction,* the classical awareness that, even after two thousand years, the ambivalence of progress ultimately signals nothing other than the *limits* of being mortal. Democracy has always required voluntary self-limits and freedom of self-limitation. Which knowledge is worth knowing, and thus worth its freedom, hardly lends itself to scientific proof but can probably be considered philosophically and decided politically.[186]

*Sixth,* there are alarming symptoms of a creeping historical exhaustion among Europeans.[187] Nothing could have a more devastating effect on the future of Europe than the spread of historical pessimism. This phenomenon, which the Americans call Euro-sclerosis, seems to have deep roots. Although the historical vacuum that ensued after the Second World War has prevented the flourishing coalescence of a European identity to this day, the Western Europeans, with the help of the Marshall Plan and American moral support, did succeed in bringing about the economic and political reconstruction of democratic societies. Admittedly, these projects also served to divert attention from the painful search for a common historical identity and the idea of realizing political union in Europe. It is clear that all Europeans, East and West, had to pay the heavy price of forced Soviet division of Europe and the ensuing conflicts of the Cold War in return for the German national socialist past. The mere fact that a spirit of political community continued to evolve and was confirmed in such a postwar climate was at least an encouraging sign for the future of Europe. Although not entirely sufficient, it was, perhaps, all that could be expected. The fact that Western Europeans have for forty years nonetheless cultivated, defended, and maintained a homogeneous political, economic, and military consensus of values is a historical achievement.[188]

It is also clear that Europe finds itself today in a new historical identity crisis, or, more optimistically, in a process of political transformation. The ideals of the postwar period and a commitment purely to antitotalitarianism no longer suffice now that the work of the economic and military reconstruction and the democratic consolidation of Western Europe have been completed. Those ideals no longer seem convincing in the face of the new technological and military challenges of scientific progress, or even in the view of past and redefined currents, ideologies, and anxieties—of a sovietization, neutralization, Europeanization, or Americanization of Europe.[189]

Western Europe must summon up a vigor and a will that extends beyond any ideology to realize a new utopia, a new vision, a rekindling of progress—in sum, the United States of Europe. Only in this way can it maintain a significant political, economic, and military stature and avoid stagnation in historical insignificance.[190] This obviously requires more than "The Solemn Declaration on European Union" (Stuttgart, 1983), which impose no binding commitment on European governments, and the constant formation of new intergovernmental committees, which basically exist only in order to revise European political initiatives that already exist (such as the Draft Treaty of the European Parliament, EP/1984).[191] Without the renunciation of the European *sacro egoismo,* without the merciless debureaucratization of the European idea and the honest coming to terms with entrenched prejudices and cliches, without sincere efforts to produce a European sense of history, to preserve Western culture and to manage forthcoming challenges democratically and responsibly, the future of European history may be endangered. It is necessary to redefine European identity, cultural unity, and politicohistorical vitality to form an innovative European community of research and technology (EURECA), to convert economic dynamism into a single European market, supposedly to be born in 1992, to encourage common defense initiatives, and to maintain close multilateral ties and cooperation with the United States.[192]

*Finally,* one must ask whether the answers and solutions of the conservative, liberal, and social democratic parties of Europe to the problems and consequences of scientific, economic, political, and ethical progress can also be of help in overcoming the European crisis of progressivist thought. Although thus far all democratic parties have been concerned with guaranteeing the functional competence of pluralistic democracy and its parliamentary goals and with realizing humanist values, and although modernization and efficiency have been more or less recognized as the prerequisites of economic and socioeconomic progress, the various ways and means for preserving and improving human conditions in a just political and social order have differed vastly.[193]

Interestingly, since the beginning of the 1980s the discrepancy of methods has been limited. At the "end of the socialist epoch" (Ralf Dahrendorf), we are experiencing the phenomenon of a split within the leftist democratic camp into an ecological socialism and a metasocialism. Although the concept of metasocialism can be defined as an ideological migration toward liberalism and conservatism, the vocabulary of ecological socialism is clearly a rejection of neoliberal and neoconservative theories of progress. It is the Left's own growing doubts about the efficiency of the welfare state, of state expansion of a multilateral social network, of regimented economic policies and state employment programs, that characterize the slow expiration of the historical repertoire of socialist ideas,[194] reflected paradigmatically in the policies of the leading metasocialist politicians François Mitterrand, Bettino Craxi, Felipe González, and Mario Soares. Their first commandment is a positive attitude toward progress and innovativeness; their absolute priority is the social market economy. All of them share the conviction that the key to the solution of the crisis in economics and employment, the real crisis of progress, lies in a progressive program of economic and technological modernization.[195] An "anachronistic" exception to this rule was presented by the Greek socialist Andreas Papandreou during his first term, when he was pressing for an anticapitalistic socialism as well as fusion of his party (PASOK) to the state. One wonders whether or not the rigid socialist leadership style of Papandreou did not appear curiously paradoxical to a people who live and think as individualistically as the Greeks.[196]

German Social Democrats (SPD) now occupy the other end of the democratic-Left spectrum, and are currently expressing increasing doubts about traditional leftist progressivist thinking. The new catchwords of the SPD are ecological modernization and ecological socialism, as Oscar Lafontaine's plea for a "different kind of progress" (1985) signals new approaches to a technological and economic concept of progress, thus continuing and reinforcing the concept promoted by Erhard Eppler in *Ende oder Wende* (1975) ten years earlier.[197] Ever since the departure of Helmut Schmidt and the ascendance of the Christian-Liberal coalition (1982–83), the Social Democrats have been seeking a new profile. As unavoidable and even understandable as that search may be, the SPD is nonetheless in danger of moving into an alternative "Green cul-de-sac" if it opposes economic growth and technological modernization and if it fails to keep up with the development of a high-tech and computerized society. It would be just as disastrous to continue supporting the socialist mentality of security and benefits regardless of its negative effects on economic risk-taking, innovative thought, career motivation, and the work ethic, to say nothing of its inability to reduce unemployment.[198] In 1985 Bruno Kreisky astutely pointed out that "socialism needs a new identity" in order to prevent the "historical end of socialism," and the future ideological and practical usurpation of the idea of progress by the conservative and liberal camps.[199]

Whether we are facing the dawn of a liberal epoch is equally uncertain. Although the United States since the Nixon administration, Great Britain under Margaret Thatcher, the Federal Republic of Germany under Helmut Kohl, and even some Southern European administrations have witnessed a neoconservative progressive idealism characterized by support of laissez-faire economic policies, and although neoconservatism tries to present itself as this decade's only democratic ideology capable of guaranteeing successful adaptation to technological progress, every progressive-conservative policy requires a strategy that can cope with the moral consequences of scientific progress and thereby preserve society's liberal-pluralist structure.[200]

Although the problems of the postmodern progressivist ideal have at least been identified, no line of political thought has yet been able to provide satisfactory answers to the ethical, social, economic, and security dilemmas of the nuclear, biological, and technological revolution. Yet, it may be precisely in this age of progressivist crisis that liberalism will recognize the ideological challenge and the attendant chance to reorient itself. In their role as progressive thinkers, European liberals are challenged to seek new possibilities for the humane use of the New Technologies in order to do justice to their own maxims of the humanistic and democratic formation of society and steady human progress toward greater freedom. These maxims can be guaranteed only by alert institutional monitoring and greater clarity of increasingly complex and ambiguous power relationships.[201] Reasonable solutions for human problems have always existed, and will continue to exist, as Isaiah Berlin once put it with a few simple words: "Man is, in principle at least, everywhere and in every condition able, if he wills it, to discover and apply rational solutions to his problems."[202] But one wonders whether national solutions alone will suffice to overcome the postmodern historical and progressivist fatigue of Western civilization, or whether the technological and nuclear revolution, as well as the belated pretensions to cultural unity, do not make the unification of Europe imperative.[203]

More than forty years have passed since the end of the Second World War, and the wounds, if not completely healed, have at least been stitched. Perhaps the time has come for Europeans, aided by their intellectual curiosity and enlightened skepticism, to consider their tradition and mutual heritage with an open historical élan, thereby creating a new political vitality for the future. This tradition embraces elements of Greek philosophy, Christian religion, and rational enlightenment that created the image of a modern, autonomous, and self-determining individual; the religious coloring of politics by the Reformation and Counter-Reformation; the secularization of politics by the revolution in the natural sciences; the bureaucratization and rationalization of policies, which led to a balanced relationship between state and society; the universal ideals of humanity and general human rights, as proclaimed in the French Revolution; the subsequent ideologization of politics; the process of industrialization and its social implications; the crisis of the liberal system and the emergence of communism, fascism, and national socialism; and finally, the rebirth of democracy on a broad Western European basis. The time may well have arrived for Europeans to make the effort to achieve a renaissance of historical optimism, a new vision of political freedom, a new intercultural harmony. Perhaps, too, the time has come for Europeans to recognize the crisis of Europe as their own failure to convert, after the war, their historical heritage into a common public philosophy and common European identity.[204]

Hitler, the division of Europe, and Soviet totalitarianism almost destroyed Western civilization. Western Europeans themselves have the task of refusing to allow these barbaric shocks to undermine their ideals. The Europe of Twelve can serve as a beginning in reactivating the continent's spiritual energy, in mobilizing an incipient Southern European dynamism, and in homogenizing European policies, the Common Market, the European university system, and European technological research. The Europe of Twelve can prove to be the catalyst for renouncing national provincialism in favor of cosmopolitan humanism, for institutionalizing the United States of Europe as an expression of European sovereignty, European political and economic cultural identity, and equal partnership and friendship with the United States of America.[205]

The establishment of the European Union can also contribute to a lasting peace within and beyond Europe, with the Federal Republic of Germany fulfilling a key function. The recognition of a European identity would help the Germans to come to terms with their past and their divided present, to give them the strength, finally, after forty years, "to look the truth in the eyes as honestly as we can" (Richard von Weizsäcker),[206] to avoid repeating "gestures of reconciliation à la Bitburg" (1985) or debates like "the war of the German historians" (1986–87), which made the unfruitful attempt to downplay Hitler's genocide through historical comparison to Stalin's purges.[207] It would also avoid discussions of reunification and the unresolved German question until the day when all of Eastern Europe is freed from the Soviet yoke, making the division of Europe a thing of the past.[208]

The Federal Republic of Germany needs Europe, but Europe needs the Federal Republic of Germany just as much.[209] It is time for the Europeans to clear up their mutual misunderstandings and to begin to know and appreciate one another. The future of European history depends on their historical sense of responsibility and their future sense of political duty.

# Notes to Introduction and Part I

## INTRODUCTION

1. See Gordon A. Craig, *The Germans* (New York, 1982).

2. For a basic discussion of European progressivist thought, see Karl D. Bracher, *The Age of Ideologies: A History of Political Thought in the Twentieth Century,* trans. Ewald Osers (New York, 1984).

3. For a basic discussion of this topic, see Samuel P. Huntington, *American Politics: The Promise of Disharmony* (Cambridge, Mass., 1981).

4. For a basic discussion of the American presidency, see Richard E. Neustadt, *Presidential Power: The Politics of Leadership from FDR to Carter* (New York, 1980).

5. For basic opposing perspectives on American foreign policy, see Henry A. Kissinger, *American Foreign Policy,* 3d ed. (New York, 1977); Stanley Hoffmann, *Primacy or World Order? American Foreign Policy since the Cold War* (New York, 1980).

## PART I

6. See Stanley Hoffmann, Fragments Floating in the Here and Now: Is There a Europe, Was There a Past, and Will There Be a Future? or, The Lament of a Transplanted European, in *Culture and Society in Contemporary Europe,* ed. Stanley Hoffmann and Paschalis Kitromilides (Winchester, Mass., 1981), 213–31. See further the controversial book by Allan Bloom, *The Closing of the American Mind* (New York, 1987), who also argues that the American sense of history is declining.

## CHAPTER 1

7. See Karl Dietrich Bracher, Fortschritt-Krise einer Ideologie, in *Geschichte und Gewalt* (Berlin, 1981); K. D. and Dorothee Bracher, *Schlüsselwörter in der Geschichte*

(Düsseldorf, 1978). K. D. Bracher, Verfall und Fortschritt im Denken der frühen Römischen Kaiserzeit, Studien zum Zeitgefühl und Geschichtsbewußtsein des Jahrhunderts nach Augustus, Ph.D. thesis, Tübingen, 1948.

8. See Henry Kissinger, The Meaning of History, Reflections on Spengler, Toynbee and Kant, unpublished Honors Thesis, Harvard University, 1951.

9. Robert Nisbet, *History of the Idea of Progress* (New York, 1980).

10. On the problematic of the idea of progress, see Carl Becker, *Progress and Power* (New York, 1936). Frederick J. Teggart, *Theory and Processes of History* (abridged edition with a preface by Kenneth Bock) (Berkeley, 1941) (The Idea of Progress and the Foundations of the Comparative Method, 82–98). John Baillie, *The Belief in Progress* (New York, 1950). John U. Nef, *War and Human Progress, An Essay on the Rise of Industrial Civilization* (Cambridge, Mass., 1950). J. B. Bury, *The Idea of Progress: An Inquiry into Its Growth and Origin* (New York, 1955). R. G. Collingwood, *The Idea of History* (New York, 1956). Fritz Stern, ed., *The Varieties of History, From Voltaire to the Present* (Cleveland, 1956). Raymond Aron, *Introduction to the Philosophy of History* (Boston, 1962). Ernst Bloch, *Differenzierungen im Begriff Fortschritt, Tübinger Einleitung in die Philosophie I* (Frankfurt, 1963). Sidney Pollard, *The Idea of Progress, History and Society* (New York, 1968). Reinhart Koselleck, *Vergangene Zukunft* (Frankfurt, 1979), 130 ff., 339 ff. David Brion Davis, Slavery and the Idea of Progress, in *Oceans Apart? Comparing Germany and the United States,* ed. Erich Angermann and Marie Luise Frings (Stuttgart, 1981).

11. See K. D. and D. Bracher, *Schlüsselwörter in der Geschichte,* 39. See also Christian Meier, Der Wandel der politisch-sozialen Begriffswelt im 5. Jh. v. Chr., *Archiv für Begriffsgeschichte* 21 (1977): 7 ff. See Chr. Meier, Ein antikes Äquivalent des Fortschrittsgedankens, *Historische Zeitschrift* 226 (1978).

12. For a discussion of the controversy over the existence or nonexistence of a classical conception of progress, see J. B. Bury, *The Idea of Progress;* Collingwood, *The Idea of History.* Radoslav A. Tsanoff, Ancient Classical Alternatives and Approaches to the Idea of Progress, *Greek and Byzantine Studies* 1, no. 2 (1958): 90 ff. A. G. Drachmann, *The Mechanical Technology of Greek and Roman Antiquity* (Copenhagen, 1963). Ludwig Edelstein, *The Idea of Progress in Classical Antiquity* (Baltimore, 1967). W. K. C. Guthrie, *A History of Greek Philosophy,* 3 (Cambridge, Mass., 1969). Kurt von Fritz, *Grundprobleme der Geschichte der antiken Wissenschaft* (Berlin, 1971). E. R. Dodds, *Der Fortschrittsgedanke in der Antike* (Munich, 1977).

13. See also K. D. Bracher, Verfall und Fortschritt im Denken der frühen Römischen Kaiserzeit, 36. On Polybius, see K. E. Paetzold, Kyklos und Telos im Geschichtsdenken des Polybius, *Saeculum* 28 (1977): 253 ff.

14. See Jacqueline de Romilly, Der Optimismus des Thukydides u. das Urteil des Historikers über Perikles (Thuk. II 65), in *Perikles u. seine Zeit,* ed. G. Wirth (Darmstadt, 1979), 290–311. J. de Romilly, Thucidide et l'Idée de Progrès, *Annali della Scuola Normale Superiore di Pisa,* Ser. 2 (1966): 177.

15. On this question today, see also Daniel Bell, *The Cultural Contradictions of Capitalism* (London, 1976), 12, 13: "Does human nature change over historical time, in response to changes in modes of production or some other historicist turn, or is human nature invariant? If human nature remains the same, how can we speak of a growth of 'consciousness'? But if human nature changes, how do we understand the past?" See also D. Bell, Technology, Nature, and Society, in *The Frontiers of Knowledge,* The Frank Nelson Doubleday Lectures, 1st series (Garden City, N.Y., 1975).

16. See Gerhard Wirth, Der Weg an die Grenze. Blüte und Schicksal der antiken Bildungstradition, in *Schulgeschichte im Zusammenhang der Kulturentwicklung,* ed. L. Kriss-Rettenbeck and M. Liedtke (Bad Heilbrunn, 1983). George Kennedy, *The Art of Persuasion in Greece* (Princeton, N.J., 1963). G. Kennedy, *The Art of Rhetoric in the Roman World* (Princeton, N.J., 1972).

17. See C. Meier, *Die Entstehung des Politischen bei den Griechen* (Frankfurt am Main, 1980).

18. Plato, *Laws,* 923 b (Princeton, N.J., 1982). On classical theories of the state, see Michael Rostock, *Die antike Theorie der Organisation staatlicher Macht* (Meisenheim, 1975). W. Robert Connor, *The New Politicians of Fifth-Century Athens* (Princeton, N.J. 1971). See also Jochen Bleicken, *Die athenische Demokratie* (Paderborn, 1984).

19. See Karl Popper, *The Open Society and Its Enemies* (London, 1957); see also Kurt von Fritz, *The Relevance of Ancient Social and Political Philosophy for Our Times* (New York, 1974).

20. K. D. and D. Bracher, Schlüsselwörter in der Geschichte, 25. K. D. Bracher: "Totalitarianism," in *Dictionary of the History of Ideas* 4 (New York, 1973), 406 ff.

21. See Fritz Stern, *The Politics of Cultural Despair, A Study in the Rise of the Germanic Ideology* (Berkeley, Calif., 1961).

22. See G. Wirth, *Alexander der Große* (Reinbek, 1979).

23. On the philosophy of Epicurus, see *Philosophie der Freude* (Stuttgart, 1973), 25.

24. See also Joseph Vogt, Die Sklaverei im antiken Griechenland; und Die Sklaverei im antiken Rom, *Antike Welt* 9, no. 2 (1978): 49 ff; and no. 3: 37 ff.

25. On the origins of human and natural rights, see K. D. Bracher, Menschenrechte und politische Verfassung, in *Geschichte und Gewalt,* 28 ff. Olaf Gigon, *Der Begriff der Freiheit in der Antike* (Munich, 1977).

26. See D. R. Dudley, *A History of Cynicism from Diogenes to the Sixth Century AD* (London, 1937).

27. See also Chr. Meier, *Res publica Amissa, Eine Studie zu Verfassung und Geschichte der späten römischen Republik* (Frankfurt, 1980). H. C. Baldry, *The Unity of Mankind in Greek Thought* (Cambridge, 1965). Arnaldo Momigliano, *Alien Wisdom: The Limits of Hellenization* (Cambridge, 1975).

28. See also E. Badian, *Roman Imperialism in the Late Roman Republic* (Oxford, 1968). E. Badian, Crisis Theories and the Beginning of the Principate, in *Romanitas-Christianitas, Untersuchungen zur Geschichte und Literatur der römischen Kaiserzeit* (Festschrift for Johannes Straub), ed. G. Wirth (Berlin, 1982), 18–41. Martin L. Clarke, *The Roman Mind. Studies in the History of Thought from Cicero to Marcus Aurelius* (London, 1956). Edward Gibbon, *The Decline and Fall of the Roman Empire* (New York, 1932).

29. See also Ronald Syme, *The Roman Revolution* (London, 1952). E. S. Gruen, *The Last Generation of the Roman Republic* (Berkeley, Calif., 1974). Chr. Meier, Cicero, Das erfolgreiche Scheitern des Neulings in der alten Republik, in *Die Ohnmacht des allmächtigen Diktators Ceasar, Drei biographische Skizzen* (Frankfurt, 1980).

30. See also K. D. Bracher, Fortschritt-Krise einer Ideologie, 215.

31. On Christianity's destruction of the classical educational tradition, see also G. Wirth, Der Weg an die Grenze, Blüte und Schicksal der antiken Bildungstradition, 95 ff.

32. See K. D. Bracher, Fortschritt-Krise einer Ideologie, 220 f.

33. See Lynn White, The Historical Roots of Our Ecological Crisis, in *Dynamo and Virgin Reconsidered, Essays in the Dynamism of Western Culture* (Cambridge, Mass., 1968, 1976), 75–94.

34. See ibid., 88 ff. On the same theme, see also Iring Fetscher, *Überlebensbedingungen der Menschheit—Zur Dialektik des Fortschritts* (Munich, 1980). Carl Amery, *Das Ende der Vorsehung—Die gnadenlosen Folgen des Christentums* (Hamburg, 1974). John Passmore, *Man's Responsibility for Nature: Ecological Problems and Western Traditions* (London, 1974).

35. See R. Nisbet, Medieval Currents, in *History of the Idea of Progress,* 94 ff. K. D. Bracher, Fortschritt-Krise einer Ideologie, 222. L. White, The Context of Science, in *Dynamo and Virgin Reconsidered,* 95 f. Norman Cohn, *The Pursuit of the Millenium, Revolutionary Messianism in Medieval and Reformation Europe and Its Bearing on Modern Totalitarian Movements* (New York, 1961).

36. A book written by Marc Bloch and first published forty years ago, has been issued in German as *Die Feudalgesellschaft* (Frankfurt, 1982). Bloch summarizes medieval history as a complex network of traditions and myths, geography and economic structures, of social strata and their transformations and shifts as the result of migrations and invasions. This historiography recognizes no first cause, but rather the interconnectedness of all its components, all of which condition each other. The element that holds the structure of feudal society together and makes its unity possible is the *atmosphère mentale,* that is, the spiritual climate of the time, the type of social feeling, collective ideas of reality, pictures of the world in which the legal forms and social customs of the European Middle Ages are created. Bloch does not describe the ideas and ideologies of the period, but rather the largely preconscious attitudes of social groups, the unquestioned axioms and norms, the basic postures that make up the human community. There are parallels here to the radical structural philosophy of Foucault, who attempted to isolate the unsayable from the unsaid, the unthinkable from the unthought.

Bloch further investigates the relations of human beings, during the period of transition from late antiquity to the Middle Ages, to nature, time, and space, and comes to the conclusion that the common denominator is uncertainty. In this world of migrations, invasions, and catastrophes, only the clan, and then serfdom and the feudal system, offer security. This form of the history of the attitudes of medieval and early modern folk culture has since been rediscovered; see especially Robert Muchembled, *Kultur des Volkes—Kultur der Eliten. Die Geschichte einer erfolgreichen Verdrängung* (Stuttgart, 1982), and Peter Burke, *Helden, Schurken und Narren. Europäische Volkskultur in der frühen Neuzeit,* ed. with a preface by R. Schenda (Stuttgart, 1982). A history of social attitudes during the French Revolution is now available in German as well: Michel Vovelle, *Die Französische Revolution—Soziale Bewegung und Umbruch der Mentalitäten (Ancien Régime, Aufklärung und Revolution,* vol. 7) (Munich, 1982). See also Michel Foucault, *Die Archäologie des Wissens* (Frankfurt am Main, 1973). Claude Lévi-Strauss, *Structural Anthropology* (London, 1968).

37. See Marie-Dominique Chénu, *L'éveil de la conscience dans la civilisation médiévale* (Paris, 1969). R. Nisbet, *Medieval Currents.* William H. McNeill, *The Pursuit of Power, Technology, Armed Force and Society since A.D. 1000* (Chicago, 1983).

38. See also G. Negley and J. M. Patrick, *The Quest for Utopia: An Anthology of Imaginary Societies* (New York, 1952). Paul Hazard, *La crise de la conscience européenne 1680–1715* (Paris, 1961). William Leiss, *The Domination of Nature* (New York, 1972).

Alexander Koyré, *From the Closed World to the Infinite Universe* (New York, 1958). P. Mathias, ed., *Science and Society: 1600–1900* (Cambridge, 1972).

39. Of the almost three thousand works on Machiavelli, the following are a few examples: P. H. Harris, Progress in Machiavelli Studies, *Italica* 18, no. 1 (March 1941). Leo Strauss, *Thoughts on Machiavelli* (Glencoe, Ill., 1958). De Lamar Jensen, ed., *Machiavelli: Cynic, Patriot, or Political Scientist?* (Boston, 1960). J. G. A. Pocock, *The Machiavellian Moment. Florentine Political Thought and the Atlantic Republican Tradition* (Princeton, N.J., 1975). Isaiah Berlin, *Against the Current* (chapter: The Originality of Machiavelli, 25–79), ed. Henry Hardy, with an introduction by Roger Hausheer (New York, 1980). Herfried Münkler, *Machiavelli: Die Begründung des politischen Denkens der Neuzeit aus der Krise der Republik* (Florence, 1982). For background on the Renaissance see John U. Nef, *Western Civilization since the Renaissance. Peace, War, Industry, and the Arts* (New York, 1963).

40. See Julian H. Franklin, *Jean Bodin and the Rise of Absolutist Theory* (Cambridge, 1973). Quentin Skinner, *The Foundation of Modern Political Thought,* 1 (Cambridge, 1978).

41. On Montesquieu and Locke, see John Dunn, *The Political Thought of John Locke* (Cambridge, 1969). J. H. Franklin: *John Locke and the Theory of Sovereignty* (Cambridge, 1978). Isaiah Berlin, *Against the Current* (chapter: Montesquieu, 130–61). On Adam Smith, see Robert Heilbroner, *The Worldly Philosophers* (see chapter: The Wonderful World of Adam Smith), (New York, 1953).

42. On Voltaire and Kant, see J. S. Spink, *French Free Thought from Gassendi to Voltaire* (London, 1960). Karl Jaspers, *Die großen Philosophen* (chapter: Kant), (Munich, 1961). Karl R. Popper, *The Open Society and Its Enemies,* 1 (chapter on Kant).

On the Enlightenment, see Charles Frankel, *The Faith of Reason: The Idea of Progress in the French Enlightenment* (New York, 1948). Franco Venturi, *Utopia and Reform in the Enlightenment* (Cambridge, 1971).

43. On the ideologization of the French Revolution, see Albert Camus, *The Rebel* (New York, 1956). On the origins of the populist (progressive) ideologization of the political will as the source of the totalitarian principle and the basis of every modern dictatorship, see K. D. Bracher, *Geschichte und Gewalt* (Berlin, 1981), 38 ff; K. D. Bracher, *The Age of Ideologies: A History of Political Thought in the Twentieth Century* (New York, 1984). Jacob L. Talmon, *The Origins of Totalitarian Democracy* (New York, 1960).

44. See also R. Nisbet, Progress As Power, in *History of the Idea of Progress,* 237 ff., 286 ff. Geoffrey G. Field, *Evangelist of Race, The Germanic Vision of Houston Stewart Chamberlain* (New York, 1981).

45. See also K. R. Popper, *The Open Society and Its Enemies,* 2 (chapter on Hegel). Charles Taylor, *Hegel* (Cambridge, 1975). Peter Hans Reill, *The German Enlightenment and the Rise of Historicism* (Berkeley, Calif., 1975). Robert C. Tucker, *The Marxian Revolutionary Idea* (London, 1970). Hal Draper, *Karl Marx's Theory of Revolution,* 1, 2 (New York, 1977).

46. See James H. Billington, *Fire in the Minds of Men, Origins of the Revolutionary Faith* (New York, 1980). Donald R. Kelly, *The Beginning of Ideology, Consciousness and Society in the French Reformation* (Cambridge, 1981). For a characterization of the fundamental ideological developments of the nineteenth century and their consequences for the twentieth century, see K. D. Bracher, *The Age of Ideologies.* On the characterization of the nineteenth century as the century of counter-Enlightenment, see the essay

by I. Berlin, *Against the Current*, 1–24. See also Jacob L. Talmon, *Political Messianism* (London, 1960).

47. On European conservatism, see Jacques Droz, *Le Romantisme politique en Allemagne* (Paris, 1963). Jack Lively, ed., *The Works of Joseph de Maistre* (New York, 1965). G. K. Kaltenbrunner, ed., *Konservatismus in Europa* (Freiburg, 1972). G. K. Kaltenbrunner, *Konservatismus International* (Stuttgart, 1973). Fritz Valjavec, *Die Entstehung des europäischen Konservatismus*, ed., H. G. Schumann (Cologne, 1974). Especially on Germany, see Klaus Epstein, *The Genesis of German Conservatism* (Princeton, N.J., 1975).

48. See George H. Sabine, *A History of Political Theory* (London, 1966). Alan Ryan, *The Philosophy of John Stuart Mill* (London, 1970). Gertrude Himmelfarb, *On Liberty and Liberalism: The Case of John Stuart Mill* (New York, 1974).

49. On Marxism, see Richard N. Hunt, *The Political Ideas of Marx and Engels,* vol. 1, *Marxism and Totalitarian Democracy 1818–1850* (London, 1975). Ernst Nolte, *Marxismus und Industrielle Revolution* (Stuttgart, 1983).

50. See also David Landes, *The Unbound Prometheus: Technological Change and Industrial Development in Western Europe from 1750 to the Present* (Cambridge, 1969). Raymond Williams, *Culture and Society 1780–1950* (New York, 1958).

51. See Michael Hereth, *Alexis de Tocqueville, Die Gefährdung der Freiheit in der Demokratie* (Stuttgart, 1979).

52. See also Karl Jaspers, *Nietzsche* (Berlin, 1950). Karl Löwith, *From Hegel to Nietzsche, The Revolution in Nineteenth Century Thought* (London, 1964). Arthur C. Danto, *Nietzsche as Philosopher* (New York, 1965).

53. See also F. Stern, *The Politics of Cultural Despair.*

54. See also Paul-Laurent Assaun, *Freud et Nietzsche* (Paris, 1980). Raymond Aron, *Main Currents in Sociological Thought: Durkheim, Pareto, Weber,* vol. 2 (New York, 1976). David Beetham, *Max Weber and the Theory of Modern Politics* (London, 1974).

55. On the paradoxes of Marxist ideology, see also G. Lichtheim, *Marxism: A Historical and Critical Study* (London, 1961). Leszek Kolakowski and Stuart Hampshire, eds., *The Socialist Idea: A Re-appraisal* (London, 1974). On the origins of nationalism, see Eugene Kamenka, ed., *Nationalism, the Nature and Evolution of an Idea* (London, 1976). On the significance and influence of nationalism on the thought of Marx, Disraeli, and Sorel, see the essays of I. Berlin, Benjamin Disraeli, Karl Marx and the Search for Identity; Georges Sorel; and Nationalism: Past Neglect and Present Power in *Against the Current,* 252–86, 296–332, 332–55. For more background on the political thought of the nineteenth century, see Robert Pearson and Geraint Williams, *Political Thought and Public Policy in the Nineteenth Century, An Introduction* (New York, 1984).

## CHAPTER 2

56. On this topic see Georges Sorel, *Les Illusions du progrès* (Paris, 1908). Jack J. Roth, *The Cult of Violence: Sorel and the Sorelians* (Berkeley, Calif., 1980). Oswald Spengler, *The Decline of the West* (New York, 1932). H. Stuart Hughes, *Oswald Spengler—A Critical Estimate* (London, 1962). P. Ch. Lutz, ed., *Spengler heute* (Munich, 1980). Gerhard Masur, *Prophets of Yesterday, Studies in European Culture 1890–1914* (New York, 1965). Carl Schmitt, *Die Diktatur* (Munich, 1921). Joseph A. Schumpeter, *Capitalism, Socialism and Democracy* (New York, 1942). Walter Struve, *Elites against Democracy, Leadership Ideals in Bourgeois Political Thought in Germany, 1890–*

*1933* (Princeton, N.J., 1973). Ludwig Marcuse, *Das Märchen von der Sicherheit*, ed. and introduction by H. von Hofe (Zürich, 1981). (These are essays, portraits, and polemics written by Marcuse in French exile in the 1940s; for Marcuse the great words of the past 150 years—God, Christ, reason, freedom, and democracy—all met their downfall in the century of Hitler's Germany and Stalin's Russia.) Alfred Weber, *Farewell to European History* (New Haven, Conn., 1949). Arnold J. Toynbee, *A Study of History*, 2 vols. (New York, 1947). Henry A. Kissinger, The Meaning of History, Reflections on Spengler, Toynbee and Kant; James Joll, *Europe since 1870* (New York, 1973). S. Pollard and C. Holmes, *The End of the Old Europe, 1914–1939* (New York, 1973). Felix Gilbert, *The End of the European Era, 1890 to the Present* (New York, 1970). H. Graml, *Europa zwischen den Kriegen* (Munich, 1969). Oron Hale, *The Great Illusion 1900–1914* (New York, 1971). Raymond J. Sontag, *A Broken World 1919–1939* (New York, 1971). H. Stuart Hughes, *Consciousness and Society: The Reorientation of European Social Thought 1890–1930* (New York, 1958). Michael Biddiss, *The Age of the Masses. Ideas and Society in Europe since 1870* (New York, 1978).

57. See I. Berlin, The Divorce between the Sciences and the Humanities in *Against the Current*, 80–110. On the "two cultures" theory, see C. P. Snow, *The Two Cultures and the Scientific Revolution* (Cambridge, 1959). F. R. Leavis, *Two Cultures? The Significance of C. P. Snow* (London, 1963).

58. See Carl Friedrich von Weizsäcker, *Der bedrohte Friede, Politische Aufsätze 1945–1981* (Munich, 1981). See also Henri Lefèbvre, *Einführung in die Modernität, Zwölf Präludien* (Frankfurt am Main, 1978).

59. See N. Stone, *Europe Transformed 1878–1919* (Glasgow, 1983). George C. Mosse, *Rassismus, Ein Krankheitssymptom in der europäischen Geschichte des 19. und 20. Jahrhunderts* (Königstein, 1978). Ernst Nolte, *Der Faschismus in seiner Epoche* (Munich, 1979). D. E. Ingersoll, *Communism, Fascism and Democracy, The Origins and Development of Three Ideologies* (Columbus, Ohio, 1971). Hannah Arendt, *The Origins of Totalitarianism* (New York, 1951). Leonhard Schapiro, *Totalitarianism* (London, 1972). K. D. Bracher, *Die Krise Europas, 1971–1975* (*Propyläen Geschichte Europas*, vol. 6) (Frankfurt am Main, 1976), Jean-François Revel, *The Totalitarian Temptation* (New York, 1977). For a discussion of the concept of totalitarianism, see C. J. Friedrich and Z. K. Brzezinski, *Totalitarian Dictatorship and Autocracy* (Cambridge, Mass., 1956). K. D. Bracher, Totalitarianism, in *Dictionary of the History of Ideas*. K. D. Bracher, *Zeitgeschichtliche Kontroversen—Um Faschismus, Totalitarismus, Demokratie* (Munich, 1984).

60. See also Fritz Stern, *The Politics of Cultural Despair, A Study in the Rise of the German Ideology*. F. Stern, *The Failure of Illiberalism, Essays on the Political Culture of Modern Germany* (New York, 1972). Gordon A. Craig, *Germany, 1866–1945* (New York, 1978). Rudolf von Thadden, ed., *Die Krise des Liberalismus zwischen den Weltkriegen* (Göttingen, 1978). On the first political efforts toward realization of the European idea, see the essays on Briand and Stresemann by Klaus Schumann and Werner Weidenfeld, in *Persönlichkeiten der Europäischen Integration*, ed. T. Jansen and D. Mahnke (Bonn, 1981).

61. On this topic, see also C. F. von Weizsäcker, Speech on July 20, 1974, in *Der bedrohte Frieden*, 439 ff. K. D. Bracher, *Die deutsche Diktatur, Entstehung, Struktur, Folgen des Nationalsozialismus* (Cologne, 1979). Martin Broszat et al., ed., *Deutschlands Weg in die Diktatur* (Berlin, 1983). See likewise the colloquium on this topic organized by the Institut für Zeitgeschichte on November 26, 1981: Deutscher Sonderweg-Mythos

oder Realität? with contributions by H. Möller, Th. Nipperdey, K. Sontheimer, E. Nolte, M. Stürmer, K. D. Bracher (Munich, 1982).

62. See Helmuth Plessner, *Die verspätete Nation, Über die Verführbarkeit des bürgerlichen Geistes* (Stuttgart, 1959). Fritz Fischer, *Griff nach der Weltmacht. Die Kriegszielpolitik des kaiserlischen Deutschland 1914/18* (Düsseldorf, 1961). Kurt Sontheimer, *Antidemokratisches Denken in der Weimarer Republik* (Munich, 1962). Peter Gay, *Weimar Culture, The Outsider as Insider* (New York, 1968), with an introduction by K. D. Bracher. Walter Z. Laqueur, *Weimar: A Cultural History* (New York, 1975). David Calleo, *The German Problem Reconsidered, Germany and the World Order 1870 to the Present* (Cambridge, Mass., 1978). K. D. Bracher, *Die Auflösung der Weimarer Republik, Eine Studie zum Problem des Machtverfalls in der Demokratie* (Villingen, 1978). R. J. Evans, ed., *Society and Politics in Wilhelmine Germany* (New York, 1978). K. D. Erdmann, *Die Weimarer Republik* (Munich, 1980). Peter Graf Kielmansegg, *Deutschland und der Erste Weltkrieg* (Stuttgart, 1980). Alexander Schwan, *Weimar, Selbstpreisgabe einer Demokratie* (Düsseldorf, 1980). From the six-volume series: Die Deutschen und ihre Nation, see H. Schulze, *Weimar, Deutschland 1917–1933,* 4 (Berlin, 1982). Michael Stürmer, *Das ruhelose Reich, Deutschland 1866–1918,* 2 (Berlin, 1983). Ulrich Heinemann, *Die verdrängte Niederlage—Politische Öffentlichkeit und Kriegsschuldfrage in der Weimarer Republik* (Göttingen, 1983). Jeffrey Herf, *Reactionary Modernism in Weimar Germany* (Cambridge, 1986).

63. On Adolf Hitler, see the classic works by A. Bullock, *Hitler: A Study in Tyranny* (New York, 1962). J. C. Fest, *Hitler, Eine Biographie* (Berlin, 1973). Eberhard Jäckel, *Hitlers Weltanschauung, Entwurf einer Herrschaft* (Stuttgart, 1981).

64. On the concept of cultural lag, see William F. Ogburn, *Social Change* (New York, 1922). On the crisis of the individual, see the above-mentioned Freud study, *Civilization and Its Discontents* (London, 1951). As early as 1887, the sociologist Ferdinand Tönnies contributed to the typology of the concept of community and society. On this topic, see E. G. Jacoby, *Die moderne Gesellschaft im sozialwissenschaftlichen Denken von Ferdinand Tönnies* (Stuttgart, 1971). On the theme of the ideological vulnerability of intellectuals, see Karl Corino, ed., *Intellektuelle im Bann des Nationalsozialismus* (Hamburg, 1980). James Joll, *Intellectuals in Politics* (London, 1960). On Nazism and the Führer cult, see George L. Mosse, *Nazi Culture: Intellectual, Cultural, and Social Life of the Third Reich* (New York, 1966). Saul Friedländer, *Kitsch und Tod— Der Widerschein des Nazismus* (Munich, 1984). Friedländer analyzes *kitsch* as a way of finding personal identity. In the case of Hitler and Nazism, political kitsch served as a medium for the Führer cult, for the identification of the "little man" with the "great cause."

65. On the theme of a German "third way" and on the source of the success of Hitler's alternative ideology, see K. D. Bracher, *The Age of Ideologies.* H. L. Müller, Der "dritte Weg" als deutsche Gesellschaftsidee, *Aus Politik und Zeitgeschichte,* B 27/ 84, (July 7, 1984). James M. Rhodes, *The Hitler Movement, A Modern Millenarian Revolution* (Stanford, Calif., 1980). Jacob L. Talmon, *The Myth of the Nation and the Vision of Revolution, The Origins of Ideological Polarization in the Twentieth Century* (London, 1981).

66. See Martin Broszat, *Der Staat Hitlers, Grundlegung und Entwicklung seiner inneren Verfassung* (Munich, 1969). M. Broszat, *Der Nationalsozialismus, Weltanschauung, Programm und Wirklichkeit* (Stuttgart, 1960). Hans-Adolf Jacobsen, *National-*

*sozialistische Außenpolitik 1933–1938* (Frankfurt am Main, 1968). Gerhard L. Weinberg, *The Foreign Policy of Hitler's Germany, Diplomatic Revolution in Europe 1933–1936* (Chicago, 1970). G. L. Weinberg, *The Foreign Policy of Hitler's Germany, Starting World War II, 1937–1939* (Chicago, 1980). V. R. Berghahn and M. Kitchen, eds., *Germany in the Age of Total War* (Festschrift for F. L. Carsten), (London, 1981).

67. See Werner Link, *Die amerikanische Stabilisierungspolitik in Deutschland 1921– 1932* (Düsseldorf, 1970). Klaus Schwabe, *Deutsche Revolution und Wilson-Friede, Die amerikanische und deutsche Friedensstrategie zwischen Ideologie und Machtpolitik 1918/ 19* (Düsseldorf, 1974); K. J. Newman, *Zerstörung und Selbstzerstörung der Demokratie, Europa 1918–1938* (Cologne, 1972). G. A. Craig and A. L. George, *Force and State-craft: Diplomatic Problems of Our Time* (New York, 1983).

68. On fascism and communism, see Denis Mack Smith, *Mussolini, A Biography* (London, 1981). A. J. Gregor, *Young Mussolini and the Intellectual Origins of Fascism* (Berkeley, Calif., 1979). R. Collier, *Duce: A Biography* (New York, 1971). J. D. Forman, *Communism: From Marx's Manifesto to 20th-Century Reality* (New York, 1972). D. E. Ingersoll, *Communism, Fascism and Democracy.*

69. On France's posture, see V. Wieland, *Zur Problematik der französischen Militärpolitik und Militärdoktrin in der Zeit zwischen den Weltkriegen* (Boppard, 1973). L. E. Ambrosius, Wilson, the Republicans, and French Security after World War I, *Journal of American History* 59 (1972–73).

70. On England, see M. Cowling, *The Impact of Hitler, British Politics and British Policy 1933–1940* (Cambridge, 1975); Winston S. Churchill, *The Second World War* (Boston, 1948–53).

71. See David Abraham, *The Collapse of the Weimar Republic, Political Economy and Crisis* (Princeton, N.J., 1983). John M. Keynes, *The Economic Consequences of the Peace* (London, 1950). Theodor Eschenburg: *Die Republik von Weimar. Beiträge zur Geschichte einer improvisierten Demokratie* (Munich, 1984).

72. See the speeches held in the Berlin Reichstag on January 30, 1983, the fiftieth anniversary of Hitler's seizure of power, printed in *Geschichte mahnt,* January 30, 1933– January 30, 1983, ed. by the Presse- und Informationsamt der Bundesregierung, esp. the speeches of Richard von Weizsäcker, Willy Brandt, K. D. Bracher. Wolfgang Michalka, ed., *Die nationalsozialistische Machtergreifung* (Paderborn, 1984). Eberhard Jäckel, *Hitler in History* (Hanover, N.H., 1985).

73. See K. D. Bracher, *The Age of Ideologies.*

74. On this topic, see M. Hellmann, ed., *Die Russische Revolution von 1917, Von der Abdankung des Zaren bis zum Staatsstreich der Bolschewiki* (Munich, 1964).

75. On the controversial question of "world revolution or socialism in one country," see the new theses of Piero Melograni, cited by K. D. Bracher in *The Age of Ideologies;* Adam B. Ulam, *Stalin, the Man and His Era* (New York, 1973).

76. Quoted according to K. D. Bracher's speech on the fiftieth anniversary of Hitler's seizure of power, in *Geschichte mahnt, 30. Januar 1933–30. Januar 1983,* ed. Presse- und Informationsamt der Bundesregierung (Bonn, 1983).

77. This discussion of the concept of totalitarianism is not intended to question the terroristic and ideological mechanism of the mass subordination of society (*Gleichschaltung*) characterized as leftist and rightist totalitarianism. Rather, this characterization is used to distinguish between the leftist totalitarian principles of communism and the rightist totalitarian principles of national socialism, since both have different ideological origins and pursue different approaches and goals, albeit with identical means. Although

the principle of leftist totalitarianism continues to be practiced as communism (most flagrantly in the Soviet Union, but also, for example, in the People's Republic of China, Vietnam, and Cuba), the extinction of the principle of rightist totalitarianism as national socialism disappeared with its collapse. However, it does continue to live only in the sense of a warning against the recurrence of political perversion.

Today's rightist military dictatorships and nationalist authoritarian dictatorial variations—mostly in the Third World—cannot be understood from the perspective of rightist totalitarianism. First, the principle of total subordination of society (*Massengleichschaltung*), the forced involvement of all citizens in the fulfillment of dominant ideological projects is not used. Second, no concept of world domination is involved and there is no claim to the dissemination of a specific doctrine. Third, authoritarian military dictatorships can revert to democracy, while thus far there has been no precedent for such a development among totalitarian systems (with the possible exception of the Federal Republic of Germany, under the condition of the two Germanies). Lastly, the principles of the free-market economy are not infringed upon. These four observations are not intended to obscure the dictatorial character of the various countries, one marked by oppression of the freedom of opinion, the persecution and torture of political opponents, violations of general human rights, and social injustice. On the topics of totalitarianism, communism, and fascism, see note 59. On the theme of communism and authoritarianism and its emergence, see Samuel P. Huntington and Clement H. Moore, eds., *Authoritarian Politics in Modern Society* (New York, 1970). David Collier, ed., *The New Authoritarianism in Latin America* (Princeton, N.J., 1979). M. M. J. Fischer, *Iran from Religious Dispute to Revolution* (Cambridge, Mass., 1980).

78. See Arnold J. Toynbee, *Civilization on Trial* (New York, 1958). H. Stuart Hughes, *Contemporary Europe: A History* (Englewood Cliffs, N.J., 1966). Walter Laqueur and George L. Mosse, eds., *Literature and Politics in the Twentieth Century* (New York, 1967). Maurice Crouzet, *The European Renaissance since 1945* (New York, 1971). George Lichtheim, *Europe in the Twentieth Century* (New York, 1972). Roland N. Stromberg, *An Intellectual History of Europe* (Englewood Cliffs, N.J., 1975). Robert O. Paxton, *Europe in the Twentieth Century* (New York, 1975). K. Jaspers, *Die geistige Situation der Zeit* (Berlin, 1979).

79. See Stanley Hoffmann, Europe's Identity Crisis: Between the Past and America, *Daedalus* 93 (Fall 1964): 1249, 1252 f. R. Nisbet, Progress at Bay, in *History of the Idea of Progress*, p. 323 f.: " . . . the past is sacred ground for any genuine, creative and free civilization. . . . Without the past as represented by ritual, tradition, and memory, there can be no roots; and without roots, human beings are condemned to a form of isolation in time that easily becomes self-destructive. The past, as I stressed several times, is vital to the idea of progress. Fundamental in all periods in which faith in progress has prospered has been the remembered past. The ancient Greeks, even at the highest point of their exploration of the present, were nevertheless profoundly interested in their past, in finding or recreating its great events, in revering it in all, in giving it permanent representation in such structures as the Parthenon.''

80. See the preliminary remarks of the editors (K. D. Bracher, Theodor Eschenburg, Joachim C. Fest, and Eberhard Jäckel) in *Geschichte der Bundesrepublik Deutschland* (5 vols.), Deutsche Verlagsanstalt—Stuttgart, F. A. Brockhaus-Wiesbaden. See also D. Blackbourn and G. Eley, *Mythen deutscher Geschichtsschreibung* (Berlin, 1980); Gordon A. Craig, *The Germans*. K. D. Bracher, *Theodor Heuss und die Wiederbegründung der Demokratie in Deutschland* (Munich, 1971).

81. See Eberhard Schulz, *Die deutsche Nation in Europa, Internationale und historische Dimensionen* (Bonn, 1982). Werner Weidenfeld, ed., *Die Identität der Deutschen* (Munich, 1983). Robert Gerald Livingstone, Once Again, the German Question, *German Studies Newsletter*, no. 2 (April 1984): 11–15. Charles E. McClelland and Steven P. Scher, eds., *Postwar German Culture: An Anthology* (New York, 1974).

On the German alternative "scene" and a newly awakened patriotism on the Left, see Wolfgang Pohrdt, *Endstation* (Berlin, 1982). The contribution of P. Brandt and H. Ammon, Patriotismus von links, in *Die deutsche Einheit kommt bestimmt*, ed., W. Venohr (Bergisch-Gladbach, 1982), proves that the Green movement is not only an alternative, environmentalist, and peace movement, but also a specific expression of an unsatisfied German special awareness (*Sonderbewußtsein*), with the themes of pacifism and nuclear technology functioning as welcome discussions for a reunification of the two Germanies.

82. See also Helmut Schelsky, *Die skeptische Generation, Eine Soziologie der deutschen Jugend* (Düsseldorf, 1957). On the French student revolution, see Raymond Aron, *The Elusive Revolution* (London, 1968). On the American youth movement, see Theodor Roszak, *The Making of a Counterculture: Reflections on the Technocratic Society and Its Youthful Opposition* (London, 1969). J. Rothschild and S. B. Wolf, *The Children of the Counterculture* (New York, 1976). From the vast amount of literature on terrorism, see the standard work, Y. Alexander, ed., *International Terrorism, National, Regional and Global Perspectives* (New York, 1976). On the causes of Italian terrorism, see Giorgia Bocca, *Il terrorismo italiano, 1970–1978* (Milan, 1978). Generally, on the theme of violence, see S. Bialer and S. Sluzar, eds., *Radicalism in the Contemporary Age*, 3 (Boulder, Colo., 1977).

83. See also Kendall L. Baker, Russell J. Dalton, and Kai Hildebrandt, *Germany Transformed: Political Culture and the New Politics* (Cambridge, Mass., 1981). Kurt Sontheimer, *Zeitenwende?. Die Bundesrepublik Deutschland zwischen alter und alternativer Politik* (Hamburg, 1983). P. Reichel, *Politische Kultur in der Bundesrepublik* (Opladen, 1981). Wilfried Röhrich, *Die verspätete Demokratie. Zur politischen Kultur der Bundesrepublik Deutschland* (Cologne, 1983). B. Faulenbach, *Deutscher Sonderweg, Zur Geschichte und Problematik einer zentralen Kategorie des deutschen Weges* (Munich, 1980).

84. Richard von Weizsäcker, *Die deutsche Geschichte geht weiter* (Berlin, 1983), 299.

85. See Kurt Biedenkopf, *Demokratische Gesellschaft, Konsensus und Konflikt*, (Munich, 1975). K. D. Bracher, *The German Dilemma: The Throes of Political Emancipation* (London, 1974). Frederick D. Weil, Post-Fascist Liberalism: The Development of Political Tolerance in West Germany Since World War II, Harvard University, Department of Sociology, Ph.D. diss., 1981. G. K. Romoser and P. Wallach, eds., *West German Politics in the Mid-Eighties—Crisis and Continuity* (New York, 1985).

86. See U. Albrecht et al., eds., *Deutsche Fragen—Europäische Antworten* (Berlin, 1983). Günter Gaus, *Wo Deutschland liegt, Eine Ortsbestimmung* (Hamburg, 1983).

Also the question arises here as to whether European culture has ever been Europeanized, whether it has been destroyed by the division of Europe, or whether it has, as a real factor, ever ceased to function as a binding force between an open and a closed society. On this topic, see François Bondy, Europa ohne Grenzen, *Aus Politik und Zeitgeschichte*, B 23-24/84 (June 9, 1984): 21–30.

87. On the idea of Europe in the postwar years, see Carlo Schmid, *Europa und die Macht des Geistes* (Bern, 1973). Arnold Bergstraesser, *Europa als Idee und Wirklichkeit*

(Freiburg, 1955). Walter Lipgens, *Sources for the History of European Integration, 1945–1955* (Stuttgart, 1980). H. Brugmans, *L'idée européenne 1920 à 1970* (Brügge, 1970). E. B. Haas, *Uniting of Europe, Political, Social and Economic Forces 1950–1957* (Stanford, Calif., 1968). Pierre Gerbet, *La Construction de l'Europe* (Paris, 1982).

88. In his book *The Revolt of the Masses* (Notre Dame, Ind., 1985), Jose Ortega y Gasset described the new, diminished European consciousness as follows (p. 135): "For the first time, the European, stymied in his plans—whether economic, political, or intellectual—by the limitations of his nation, feels that his vital possibilities, his life-style, are incommensurable with the collective body in which he is enclosed. He has discovered that to be English, French, or German is to be provincial. He finds himself, then, to be "less" than before, because previously the Englishman, the Frenchman, or the German thought himself to be, each one, a universe."

Stanley Hoffmann has also noted that Europe is suffering from its increasing historical disinterest, that the shrinkage of its former world political role has diminished its spiritual élan.

It takes a combination of faith in, ideas about, and will to build one's future to keep an interest in the past from becoming mere scholarship or leisure. . . . First, can one live for ever in the economic present, confronting oneself with comparative statistics and half-cozy, half-worried enjoyment of goods, freedom, and rights? Secondly, to what extent are the poverty of inspiration and imagination, the concentration on the here and now, related to the European nation's fall from international eminence? Are images of the past and visions of the future tied either to struggles for national identity or to the possibility of strutting on the world's stage, to fighting or speaking out for a great cause, national or not? . . . Only a uniting Europe that could look at the whole of its fragmented past would be able to will a future. See *Fragments Floating in the Here and Now,* 230.

89. One of the few European thinkers to foresee Europe's coming dependence on the great powers of Russia and America was Alexis de Tocqueville, *Democracy in America*, 2 vols. (New York, 1945). On the topic of the European repression of America *and the Amerika-Bild* in Germany, see Manfred Henningsen, *Der Fall Amerika, Zur Sozial- und Bewußtseinsgeschichte einer Verdrängung, Das Amerika der Europäer* (Munich, 1974), and Ernst Fraenkel, *Amerika im Spiegel des deutschen politischen Denkens* (Cologne, 1959).

90. See also W. W. Rostow, *The United States in the World Arena: An Essay in Recent History* (New York, 1960), 195 ff., 209 ff. Raymond Aron, *The Imperial Republic* (Englewood Cliffs, N.J., 1974).

91. On the idea of Europe, see Jean Monnet, *Memoirs* (Garden City, N.Y., 1978). P. -H. Spaak: *Combats inachevés, 1969,* 1, 2. On judgments from the British point of view, see Anthony Eden, *Memoiren. 1945–1957* (Cologne, 1960). On German points of view, see Konrad Adenauer, *Erinnerungen,* 1–4 (Stuttgart, 1965–68). The Churchill quotation is printed in Alfred Grosser, *Das Bündnis. Die westeuropäischen Länder und die USA seit dem Krieg* (Munich, 1978), 175.

92. On the topic of the EDC, see Arnulf Baring, *Außenpolitik in Adenauers Kanzlerdemokratie, Bonns Beitrag zur Europäischen Verteidigungsgemeinschaft* (Munich, 1969). Paul Noack, *Das Scheitern der Europäischen Verteidigungsgemeinschaft* (Düsseldorf, 1977). On the Anglo-French disputes and on the special British self-awareness in respect to the rest of Europe, see K. D. Bracher, *Die Krise Europas* (chapter: Westeuropa und England, 286 ff.). From a general point of view, see the evaluation by André Fontaine, The Real Divisions of Europe, *Foreign Affairs,* no. 2 (January 1971): 302–14.

93. One need only recall, for example, Monnet's excellent relationship to Dean

Acheson or George W. Ball, who, just like the American Congress and the American press, supported the realization of the idea of Europe. D. Acheson, *Present at the Creation. My Years in the State Department* (New York, 1969). G. W. Ball, *The Past Has Another Pattern, Memoirs* (New York, 1982) (chapter: Jean Monnet and the Parturition of Europe, 69 ff., 84 ff.). See also the American source material in the Library of Congress, European Affairs Division, *The United States and Postwar Europe, a Bibliographical Examination of Thought Expressed in American Publications during 1948–52.* Further see Max Beloff, *The United States and the Unity of Europe* (Washington, 1963). C. L. Sulzberger, *Seven Continents and Forty Years, A Concentration of Memoirs* (New York, 1977). For a critical view of the American commitment in Europe, see Pierre Melandri, *La politique extérieure des Etats-Unis de 1945 à nos jours* (Paris, 1982).

94. See Robert L. Heilbroner, *The Future As History, The Historic Currents of Our Time and the Direction in Which They Are Taking America* (New York, 1960). Heilbroner works out some of the differences in American and European historical thought (chapter: The Inertia of History, 193 ff.). See also K. Jaspers, *Vom Ursprung und Ziel der Geschichte* (Frankfurt am Main, 1955). A. J. Toynbee, *Die Zukunft des Westens* (Munich, 1964).

95. See Walter Lipgens, Der Zusammenschluß Westeuropas, in *Geschichte in Wissenschaft und Unterricht, 1983/84,* 345–72. Hans Jürgen Küsters, *Die Gründung der Europäischen Wirtschaftsgemeinschaft* (Baden-Baden, 1982). R. Rummel and W. Wessels, eds., *Die Europäische Politische Zusammenarbeit* (Bonn, 1978). Emmanuel Richter, *Die erste Direktwahl des Europäischen Parlaments, Motive, Wahlkampf, Resultate und Perspektiven* (Bonn, 1981). R. Hrbek: 30 Jahre Römische Verträge, Eine Bilanz der EG-Integration, *Aus Politik und Zeitgeschichte,* B 18/87 (May 2, 1987).

96. At the beginning of the 1960s, Stephen G. Graubard, in his book *A New Europe?* (Boston, 1964), regarded the Europeans' federation plans with some skepticism. At the beginning of the 1970s, sixteen Europeans were still able to view the future with some optimism. See R. Mayne, ed., *Europe Tomorrow, 16 Europeans Look Ahead* (London, 1972). At the beginning of the 1980s, the European Community seemed to be in a crisis. For example, see K. Kaiser, C. Merlini, Th. de Montbrial, W. Wallace, and E. Wellenstein, *Die EG vor der Entscheidung, Fortschritt oder Verfall* (Bonn, 1983). Paul Taylor, *The Limits of European Integration* (New York, 1983). U. Everling, *Sind die Mitgliedstaaten der Europäischen Gemeinschaft noch Damen der Verträge?* (Festschrift for H. Mosler), (Berlin, 1983). Marcello Dell'Omodarme, *Europa. Mito e Realtà del Processo d'Integrazione* (Milan, 1981).

97. For an analysis of de Gaulle's policies as viewed by an American Atlanticist, see Harold van B. Cleveland, *The Atlantic Idea and Its European Rivals* (New York, 1966).

98. On the trauma of de Gaulle, see H. von d. Groeben, *Aufbaujahre der Europäischen Gemeinschaft.* Milder judgments of de Gaulle's political methods can be found in Pierre Gerbet, *La Construction de l'Europe.* On de Gaulle's phobia about the economic and cultural Americanization of Europe, see Edward A. McCreary, *The Americanization of Europe. Americans and American Companies in the Uncommon Market* (New York, 1964). Michel Crozier, France's Cultural Anxieties under Gaullism: The Cultural Revolution Revisited, in *Culture and Society in Contemporary Europe,* 105–116. On the Anglo-Saxon attitude toward de Gaulle, see the critical book by John Newhouse, *De Gaulle and the Anglo-Saxons* (London, 1970).

99. The degree to which political decision-making processes are influenced by good

or bad relations between public figures is demonstrated paradigmatically by the poor relationship between Franklin D. Roosevelt and de Gaulle. See here the correspondence of FDR and Churchill during the Second World War, especially the letters of May 8, 1943, and June 17, 1943 (FDR to Churchill), printed in F. L. Loewenheim, H. D. Langley, and M. Jones, eds., *Roosevelt and Churchill. Their Secret Wartime Correspondence* (New York, 1975). In his interview with *Der Spiegel* on November 25, 1968, 162–66, the American ambassador at large Averell Harriman confirmed and simultaneously regretted the "misunderstandings between the two great men." Jean Monnet describes in his memoirs that de Gaulle, who had a "memory which knows no forgetting," was buffeted by political "phantasmata," and believed that his honor had been besmirched by the Americans once and for all (p. 282). On the uneven de Gaulle–Roosevelt relationship, see likewise Maurice Ferro, *De Gaulle et l'Amérique* (Paris, 1973). Milton Viorst, *Hostile Allies, F.D.R. and Charles de Gaulle* (New York, 1965). See also Stanley Hoffmann, *Decline or Renewal? France since the 1930s* (New York, 1977). On French policy since the 1930s, see as well Grosser's new book, *Affairs Extérieures, La politique de la France 1944/84* (Paris, 1984).

100. See also the case studies on the United Kingdom (W. H. Cavill and T. W. Randle, *Cooperation in Europe since 1945 as Presented in Resources for the Teaching of History, Geography and Civics in Secondary Schools* [Strasbourg, 1979], Doc. DECS/EGT/79/ 61); on Sweden (B. Thelin, *Cooperation . . .*, [Strasbourg, 1979], Doc. DECS/EGT/79/ 60); and on France (Y. Pasquier, *La coopération . . .*, [Strasbourg, 1979], Doc. DECS/ EGT/79/56), which was prepared for the Committee of Cultural Cooperation of the European Council.

101. See David P. Conradt, Changing German Political Culture, in *The Civic Culture Revisited,* ed. Gabriel A. Almond and Sidney Verba (Boston, 1980), 234. Manfred Hättich, Geschichtsbild und Demokratieverständnis, in *Die zweite Republik, 25 Jahre Bundesrepublik Deutschland—eine Bilanz,* ed. R. Löwenthal and H. -P. Schwarz (Stuttgart, 1974/1979), 905–26; Agnes Blänsdorf: Zur Konfrontation mit der NS-Vergangenheit in der Bundesrepublik, der DDR und Österreich, *Aus Politik und Zeitgeschichte,* B 16/ 87 (April 18, 1987): 3.

102. For more background on German educational policy in general, see also Willy Strzelewicz and Ferdinand Wiebecke, Bildungspolitik, in *Die zweite Republik,* 865–904.

103. On the German educational system, see S. Verba, Germany: The Remaking of Political Culture, in *Political Culture and Political Development,* ed. Lucian W. Pye and S. Verba (Princeton, N.J., 1966), 169. David C. McClelland, *The Roots of Consciousness* (Princeton, N.J., 1964). Edward C. Devereux, Urie Bronfenbrenner, and George J. Suci, Patterns of Parent Behavior in the USA and the Federal Republic of Germany: A Cross National Comparison, *International Social Science Bulletin,* no. 14 (Fall 1962): 488– 506.

An analysis of the differences between the U.S. and the Western, Southern, and Eastern European educational systems, as well as an excursus on the structure of Japanese society are presented in Samuel P. Huntington: *American Politics, The Promise of Disharmony* (Cambridge, Mass., 1981) (chapters: The Gap: The American Creed Versus Political Authority, 31 ff., and European Societies, 42 ff.).

104. The theme of "Europe" in the political education of five EC member states (FRG, Denmark, UK, France, and the Netherlands) was examined in the period from Spring 1983 to Spring 1987 in a study commissioned by the Committee of Cultural Cooperation of the European Council. See also Wolfgang W. Mickel, Der Begriff der

"europäischen Dimension" im Unterricht, *Aus Politik und Zeitgeschichte*, B 41/84 (October 13, 1984). M. Grosjean and G. Renner, *Die europäische Integration in den Rahmenplänen für Unterricht der Länder der Bundesrepublik Deutschland* (Berlin, 1981). I. Goodson, European Cooperation in Education: Historical Background and Contemporary Experience, *European Journal of Teacher Education*, no. 5 (1982). Lionel Elvin, ed., *The Education Systems in the European Community. A Guide* (Windsor, 1981). F. Karasek, *Zusammenarbeit in Europa und Erziehung in Europa* (Vienna, 1981). K. Winter, *Das europäische Bildungswesen im Prozeß seiner Internationalisierung* (Weinheim, 1980). W. Weidenfeld, ed., *Die Vermittlung der europäischen Einigung in Schule und Massenmedien* (Bonn, 1981).

105. On the topic of history as a human orientational factor, see Hermann Lübbe, *Geschichtsbegriff und Geschichtsinteresse—Analytik und Pragmatik der Historie* (Basel, 1977). Jörn Rüsen, Geschichtsbewußtsein und menschliche Identität, *Aus Politik und Zeitgeschichte*, B 41/84 (October 13, 1984). On the difficulties of Germany's effort to cope with its history, see Christian Graf von Krockow, Tradition und Geschichtsbewußtsein im sozialen Wandel, *Aus Politik und Zeitgeschichte*, B 17/81 (April 25, 1981): 7 ff. Andreas Hillgruber, *Die Last der Nation. Fünf Beiträge über Deutschland und die Deutschen* (Düsseldorf, 1984). For an opposing view see Alfred Heuß, *Versagen und Verhängnis. Vom Ruin deutscher Geschichte und ihres Verständnisses* (Berlin, 1984).

106. On the problems of "history and medium," see K. D. Bracher, Geschichte und Medium im Fernseh-Zeitalter, in *Geschichte und Gewalt*, 253–67. Siegfried Quandt, ed., *Geschichtswissenschaft und Massenmedien* (Gießen, 1981), 5 ff. Wolfgang Bergsdorf, *Die Vierte Gewalt, Einführung in die politische Kommunikation* (Mainz, 1980), 133 ff. See also Otto Ulrich, Computer, Wertewandel und Demokratie, *Aus Politik und Zeitgeschichte*, B 25/84 (June 23, 1984): 14–25.

107. See also Hermann Boventer, Neue Medien und politische Bildung, *Aus Politik und Zeitgeschichte*, B 41/84 (October 13, 1984). W. Wunden, *Medienpädagogik, Führerschein fürs Fernsehen?* (Stuttgart, 1984).

108. See Ithiel de Sola Pool, *Technologies of Freedom* (Cambridge, Mass., 1983), 24 f. K. W. Deutsch, Soziale und politische Aspekte der Informationsgesellschaft, in *Die Zukunft der Informationsgesellschaft*, ed. P. Sonntag (Frankfurt am Main, 1983), 68–88. National Institute of Mental Health, *Television and Behavior. Ten Years of Scientific Progress and Implications for the Eighties* (Washington, D.C., 1982). H. Oberreuter, *Übermacht der Medien. Erstickt die demokratische Kommunikation?* (Zürich, 1982).

109. Quote by H. Boventer, *Neue Medien und politische Bildung*, 15.

110. See M. Schöneberger, Kultur und Kabel. Die Neuen Medien als Auftrag für die Politik, *Die politische Meinung* (March/April 1984). Simone Weil, *Die Einwurzelung. Ein Vermächtnis. Einführung in die Pflichten dem menschlichen Wesen gegenüber* (Munich, 1956).

## CHAPTER 3

111. See C. F. von Weizsäcker's essay of the same title from 1958: *Der bedrohte Friede*, 43–87.

112. See R. Nisbet, Disowning the Past, in *History of the Idea of Progress*, 329. Joseph Ben-David, *The Scientist's Role in Society* (Englewood Cliffs, N.J., 1971).

113. See also Claus Grossner, *Der Verfall der Philosophie* (Hamburg, 1971).

114. On Jaspers's philosophy, see K. Jaspers, *Die geistige Situation der Zeit*, 72–76;

K. Jaspers, *Über Bedingungen und Möglichkeiten eines neuen Humanismus* (Munich, 1951), 51 f. On the cultural pessimism of this period, see Ludwig Marcuse, Kultur-Pessimismus, in *Club Voltaire I*, ed. G. Szczesny, (Munich, 1964), 246. Aldous Huxley, *Brave New World* (New York, 1932). On Sartre's philosophy, see Arthur C. Danto, *Jean Paul Sartre* (New York, 1975).

115. On the German student revolt, see G. Langguth, *Protestbewegung. Entwicklung, Niedergang, Renaissance, Die neue Linke 1968* (Cologne, 1983). On the French and American student revolt, see William R. Schonfeld, *Obedience and Revolt: French Behavior toward Authority* (Beverly Hills, Calif., 1976). Stanley Hoffmann, Paradoxes of the French Political Community, in S. Hoffmann et al., *In Search of France* (Cambridge, Mass., 1963). Raymond Aron, *The Elusive Revolution* (London, 1968). George Kennan, *Democracy and the Student Left* (Boston, 1968).

116. See Max Horkheimer and Theodor W. Adorno, *Dialektik der Aufklärung* (Frankfurt am Main, 1969); Th. W. Adorno, *Negative Dialektik* (Frankfurt am Main, 1967); Herbert Marcuse, *One-Dimensional Man* (Boston, 1964). On the criticism of the Frankfurt School, see Kurt Sontheimer, *Das Elend unserer Intellektuellen* (Hamburg, 1976) and H. Lenk and R. Simon-Schaefer, Vernunft-Wissenschaft-Praxis, Zur Kritik der "kritischen Theorie," *Aus Politik und Zeitgeschichte*, B 50/81 (December 12, 1981): 42 ff. Another view of these issues was presented by Ernst Topitsch at the beginning of the 1960s: *Sozialphilosophie zwischen Ideologie und Wissenschaft* (Neuwied, 1961–71).

117. On terrorism, see note 82 above.

118. From the vast literature on the interrelation of science, reason, and philosophy, see Edgar Zilsel, The Genesis of the Concept of Scientific Progress, *The Journal of the History of Ideas* 6 (1945): 325–49. Jürgen Habermas, *Erkenntnis and Interesse* (Frankfurt am Main, 1968). J. Habermas, *Technik und Wissenschaft als Ideologie* (Frankfurt am Main, 1968). Thomas S. Kuhn, *The Structure of Scientific Revolutions* (Chicago, 1970). Imre Lakatos and Alan Musgrave, eds., *Criticism and the Growth of Knowledge* (Cambridge, 1970). Karl R. Popper, *Objective Knowledge* (Oxford, 1972). Robert F. Almeder, Science and Idealism, *Philosophy of Science* 40 (1973): 242–54. R. Harré, ed., *Problems of Scientific Revolution* (Oxford, 1975). Gerard Radnitzky and Gunnar Anderson, eds., *Progress and Rationality in Science* (Dordrecht, 1978). Kurt Hübner, *Kritik der wissenschaftlichen Vernunft* (Freiburg, 1978). Paul K. Feyerabend, *Ausgewählte Schriften* (vol. 1: *Der wissenschaftliche Realismus und die Autorität der Wissenschaften;* vol. 2: *Irrwege der Vernunft*), (Wiesbaden, 1979). Nicholas Rescher, *Wissenschaftlicher Fortschritt, Eine Studie über die Ökonomie der Forschung,* ed. Roland Posner, (Berlin, 1982).

119. See C. F. von Weizsäcker, Aufzeichnungen zur Begründung eines Max-Planck-Instituts zur Erforschung der Lebensbedingungen der wissenschaftlich-technischen Welt, in C. Grossner, *Verfall der Philosophie,* 239–42.

120. See Jost Herbig, Mittelmaß aller Dinge. Über die Schließung des Max-Planck-Instituts zur Erforschung der Lebensbedingungen, *Der Spiegel,* no. 19 (May 5, 1980).

121. On the Club of Rome philosophy, see D. and D. Meadows, E. Zahn, and P. Milling, *The Limits of Growth* (New York, 1972). The Global 2000 Report to the President (Washington, D.C., 1980); *Global Future: Time to Act* (Washington, D.C., 1981). See also the discussions of G. Brunner, J. S. Nye, N. Belknap, and E. Teller, in *Probleme der Kernenergie, Chancen, Risiken und Perspektiven in einer sich wandelnden Energiewirtschaft* (Bonn, 1977), as well as the growth-oriented study by Ralf-Dieter Brunowsky and Lutz Wicke, "Der Öko-Plan"—Durch Umweltschutz zum neuen Wirtschaftswunder,

(Munich, 1984), which understands environmental protection not only as an ethical principle, but also as an economic opportunity for an innovation-oriented ecological policy.

122. The most important no-growth primer was written by the American Lester Thurow, *The Zero-Sum Society, Distribution and the Possibilities for Economic Change* (New York, 1980). The book had almost no influence in the United States, while meeting with great interest in the Federal Republic of Germany, particularly among the Greens.

123. From the extensive literature on doomsday issues, see a few characteristic examples: Jonathan Schell, *The Fate of the Earth* (New York, 1982). Günther Anders, *Die atomare Drohung, Radikale Überlegungen* (Munich, 1983). An opposing view is found in Andre Glucksmann, *Philosophie der Abschreckung* (Stuttgart, 1984). On the evangelical church and the peace movement, see G. Baadte, A. Boyens, and O. Buchbender, eds., *Frieden stiften, Die Christen zur Abrüstung. Eine Dokumentation* (Munich, 1984). On the fear and denial of progress among Greens and Alternatives, see Walter Jens, ed., *In letzter Stunde* (Munich, 1982). Rolf Peter Sieferle, *Fortschrittsfeinde? Opposition gegen Technik und Industrie von der Romantik bis zur Gegenwart* (Munich, 1984). See also note 83 above. On the Green concept of civil disobedience, see the interview in *Die Zeit* with the former speaker of the Greens, Rainer Trampert: "Hoffen auf einen gewaltfreien Bürgerkrieg," by H. Bieber, D. Buhl, and G. Spörl, *Die Zeit*, no. 9 (February 25, 1983), 3 and 4.

124. On the alternative philosophy of jadedness toward progress and moroseness toward reason, which has been influencing the political culture of the Federal Republic of Germany for more than a decade, see Ralf Dahrendorf, Die Denunziation der Aufklärung, *Die Zeit*, no. 14 (March 28, 1975). Nina Grunenberg, Aufklärung heute: Gegenaufklärung?, *Die Zeit*, no. 5 (January 25, 1980). Fritjof Capra, *The Turning Point* (New York, 1982). Peter Sloterdijk, *Kritik der zynischen Vernunft*, 2 vols. (Frankfurt am Main, 1983). K. H. Bohrer, ed., *Mythos und Moderne* (Frankfurt am Main, 1983). Fritz J. Raddatz, Die Aufklärung entläßt ihre Kinder. Vernunft, Geschichte, Fortschritt werden verabschiedet: Mythos ist der neue Wert (Part I), *Die Zeit*, no. 27 (June 29, 1984), (Part II): Unser Verhängnis als unsere Verantwortung, *Die Zeit*, no. 28 (July 6, 1984). On the theme of "reason today," see also the large poll on philosophy organized by *Le Monde* in the summer of 1984. The participants included Jean François Lyotard, Michel Tournier, Alain Touraine, Lucien Sere, and Jürgen Habermas. On the return of nihilism today, see E. Severini, *Vom Wesen des Nihilismus* (Stuttgart, 1983). W. Kraus, *Nihilismus heute oder die Geduld der Weltgeschichte* (Vienna, 1983). An interesting analysis of Green and alternative ideology and its affinity for medieval structures is presented by Christian Graf von Krockow in a series of articles in three parts: Groß oder Klein?/ Haben oder Sein?/Gemeinschaft oder Gesellschaft?, *Die Zeit*, no. 39 (September 24, 1984), no. 40 (October 1, 1984), and no. 41 (October 8, 1984).

125. See Gunther Duda, *Im Bann religiösen Wahns, Die Jugendsekten* (Tutzinger papers), (Stuttgart, 1982); Albrecht Schöll, ed., *Handbuch Jugendreligionen, Informationen-Analysen-Alternativen* (Gießen/Basel, 1981).

126. See Christian Flämig, Die genetische Manipulation des Menschen, *Aus Politik und Zeitgeschichte*, B 3/85 (January 19, 1985), 3–17. Ruppert Riedl, *Die Strategie der Genesis* (Munich, 1984). K. Lorenz, *Der Abbau des Menschlichen* (Munich, 1983). B. Nussbaum, *Das Ende unserer Zukunft* (Munich, 1983). D. Rorvik, *In This Image: The Cloning of a Man* (New York, 1978).

127. On the idea of breeding human beings, see H. Conrad-Martius, *Utopie der*

*Menschzüchtung. Der Sozialdarwinismus und seine Folgen* (Munich, 1955). Günther Altner, ed., *Der Darwinismus. Die Geschichte einer Theorie* (Darmstadt, 1981). Aldous Huxley, *Brave New World;* Pierre Teilhard de Chardin, *The Phenomenon of Man* (New York, 1959). E. Klee, "Euthanasie" im NS-Staat (Frankfurt am Main, 1983); (Klee's book illuminates the progression from Social Darwinism to national socialism.) On biogenetic research into the breeding of human beings since the 1930s, see Hermann J. Müller, *Out of Night. A Biologist's View of the Future* (New York, 1935). Joan Broadus Watson, *Behaviourismus* (Stuttgart, 1930). Should We Strengthen or Weaken our Genetic Heritage?, *Daedalus* (Summer 1961): 432–76.

128. See J. B. Watson, *Behaviourismus,* 113 f.

129. B. F. Skinner, *Beyond Freedom and Dignity* (New York, 1971), 215.

130. See Ch. Flämig, *Die genetische Manipulation des Menschen,* 15.

131. Ibid., 9 ff.

132. At the initiative of the SPD and the Greens, the German Bundestag approved the establishment of an investigative commission on the "Chances and Risks of Genetic Engineering." See also Ernst Benda, Erprobung der Menschenwürde am Beispiel der Humangenetik, *Aus Politik und Zeitgeschichte,* B 3/85 (January 19, 1985): 18–36.

133. Quoted according to an interview with President Richard von Weizsäcker in SWF 3 (German Radio Station), September 18, 1984 (9:00 to 11:00 P.M.).

134. See also Hermann Lübbe, *Zeit-Verhältnisse. Zur Kulturphilosophie des Fortschritts* (Graz, 1983). W. Lienemann and I. Tödt, eds., *Fortschrittsglaube und Wirklichkeit* (Munich, 1983). Rudolf Wendorf, *Zeit und Kultur* (Opladen, 1980). Karl Popper, Selbstbefreiung durch das Wissen, in *Der Sinn der Geschichte* ed. L. Reinisch (Munich, 1961). K. Popper, *The Open Society and Its Enemies,* 2.

135. See Jürg Altwegg, Empörung gegen die vorschreibende Vernunft, Michel Foucault's Auseinandersetzung mit den Erben der Aufklärung, "Frankfurter Allgemeine Zeitung," no. 249 (November 3, 1984).

136. See Karl R. Popper, *Auf der Suche nach einer besseren Welt. Vorträge und Aufsätze aus dreißig Jahren* (Munich, 1984). P. A. Schlipp, ed., *The Philosophy of Karl Popper* 2 vols. (La Salle, 1967).

137. The quotation is taken from Walter von Rossum's article, Mobile Denkfabrik, Das neu gegründete, "Collège international de Philosophie" in Paris, *Die Zeit,* no. 43 (October 19, 1984), 64.

138. C. F. von Weizsäcker, *Wahrnehmung der Neuzeit* (Munich, 1983) (articles from 1945 to 1983).

139. See also S. N. Eisenstadt, *Tradition, Wandel und Modernität* (Frankfurt, 1979); Leslie Sklair, *Die Soziologie des Fortschritts* (Munich, 1972).

140. On the topic of war and social change, see the comparative study of A. Marwick, *War and Social Change in the Twentieth Century, A Comparative Study of Britain, France, Germany, Russia and the United States* (London, 1974). See also Lewis Mumford, *Values for Survival* (New York, 1946).

141. The Harvard sociologist Daniel Bell coined the concept of postindustrial society and postmaterial values in 1959. On this matter, see K. D. Bracher, *The Age of Ideologies.* See also E. J. Trueblood, *The Dawn of the Post-Modern Era* (New York, 1954).

142. For a critical view of the economic values of industrial society, see Erich Fromm, *To Have or to Be?* (New York, 1976); David Riesman, *Abundance for What?* (New York, 1964). For an opposing view, see Helmut Schelsky, *Auf der Suche nach Wirklichkeit*

(Düsseldorf, 1965), 439 ff. Raymond Aron, *In Defense of Decadent Europe* (Washington, D.C., 1979).

143. See D. Riesman, *The Lonely Crowd, A Study of the Changing American Character* (New Haven, Conn., 1950).

144. Robert MacIver's definition of anomie is printed in Ralf Dahrendorf, *Die Chancen der Krise, Über die Zukunft des Liberalismus* (Stuttgart, 1983), 125. See also Roderick Seidenberg, *Post-historic Man: An Inquiry* (Boston, 1957).

145. See Herbert Marcuse, Die Idee des Fortschritts im Lichte der Psychoanalyse, *Frankfurter Beiträge zur Soziologie* 6 (1957): 432 f. and 89 n. 116.

146. On the protest movement and terrorism, see note 82 above.

147. On change in the values of Western industrial nations, see Alain Touraine, *Die postindustrielle Gesellschaft* (Frankfurt am Main, 1982). E. Noelle-Neumann, *Werden wir alle Proletarier?* (Zürich, 1978); Ronald Inglehart, *The Silent Revolution: Changing Values and Political Styles among Western Publics* (Princeton, N.J., 1977); D. Bell, *The Coming of Postindustrial Society* (New York, 1973). John Kenneth Galbraith, *The Affluent Society* (Boston, 1958). On the continuity and change of the political culture of Western Europe, see the study of Peter Reichel, *Politische Kultur in Westeuropa. Bürger und Staaten in der Europäischen Gemeinschaft* (Frankfurt am Main, 1984). On change in the work ethic of the Federal Republic of Germany, see E. Noelle-Neumann and B. Strümpel, *Macht Arbeit krank, macht Arbeit glücklich* (Munich, 1984). Werner Kaltefleiter, Changes in Social Values in Industrial Societies—The Example of the Federal Republic of Germany, in *Structural Change: The Challenge to Industrial Societies,* Eighth German-Japanese Economics and Social Sciences Seminar, Cologne, September 24–27, 1984, ed. H. Hax, W. Kraus, and T. Kiyoshi (New York, 1985).

148. See Ph. Herder-Dornreich, H. Klages, and H. -G. Schlotter, eds., *Überwindung der Sozialstaatskrise* (Baden-Baden, 1984). H. Klages, *Überlasteter Staat—verdrossene Bürger? Zu den Dissonanzen der Wohlfahrtsgesellschaft* (Frankfurt am Main/New York, 1981). H. Schelsky, *Der selbständige und der betreute Mensch* (Stuttgart, 1976).

149. See K. W. Brand, D. Brüsser, and D. Rucht, *Aufbruch in eine andere Gesellschaft, Neue soziale Bewegungen in der Bundesrepublik* (Frankfurt am Main/New York, 1983). W. Kaltefleiter, *Changes in Social Values in Industrial Societies* (chapter: The Dropouts).

150. See also K. D. Bracher, *The Age of Ideologies.*

151. See Hasso von Recum, Dimensionen des Wertewandels, and Otto Ulrich: Computer, Wertewandel und Demokratie, *Aus Politik und Zeitgeschichte,* B 25/84 (June 23, 1984): 3–13, 14–25; R. -D. Brunowsky and L. Wicke, "Der Öko-Plan"—Durch Umweltschutz zum neuen Wirtschaftswunder.

152. See the interesting research of the American sociologist Richard Sennett, *The Fall of Public Man* (New York, 1983). See also Helge Pross and Eugen Buß, *Soziologie der Masse* (Heidelberg, 1984); Christopher Lasch, *The Culture of Narcissism: American Life in an Age of Diminishing Expectations* (New York, 1978); D. A. Hughes, ed., *Perspectives on Pornography* (New York, 1970).

153. See notes 140, 142, and 145 above; R. P. Sieferle, *Fortschrittsfeinde? Opposition gegen Technik und Industrie von der Romantik bis zur Gegenwart.* K. W. Deutsch, *Soziale und politische Aspekte der Informationsgesellschaft,* 68–88. Henry Jacoby, *Die Bürokratisierung der Welt* (Frankfurt am Main, 1984).

154. See R. Löwenthal, Gesellschaftswandel und Kulturkrise, Zukunftsprobleme der

westlichen Demokratien (Frankfurt am Main, 1979), 21–36. R. Aron, *Progress and Disillusion, The Dialectics of Modern Society* (London, 1968).

155. See Alexander Mitscherlich, *Versuch, die Welt besser zu bestehen* (Frankfurt am Main, 1970), 169 f.

156. On political thought in the postwar period, see Maurice Grouzet, *The European Renaissance—since 1945* (New York, 1971). Frederick M. Watkins, *The Political Tradition of the West: A Study in the Development of Modern Liberalism* (Cambridge, 1948). On the cultural pessimism of the postwar years, see Karl Jaspers, *Die geistige Situation der Zeit.*

157. See Wolfgang Leonhard, *The Three Faces of Marxism: The Political Concepts of Soviet Ideology, Maoism, and Humanist Marxism* (New York, 1970). Alexander Sinowjew, *Kommunismus als Realität* (Zürich, 1981). Milovan Djilas, *The Unperfect Society* (London, 1968).

158. K. D. Bracher, Europa zwischen National- und Weltpolitik: Historische Wandlungen und politische Entscheidungen, *Integration* (March 1980): 103.

159. K. R. Popper, *Auf der Suche nach einer besseren Welt, Vorträge und Aufsätze aus dreißig Jahren* (Munich, 1984), 128.

160. R. N. Stromberg, *After Everything: Western Intellectual History since 1945* (New York, 1975).

161. D. Bell, *The End of Ideology, On the Exhaustion of Political Ideas in the Fifties* (Glencoe, Ill., 1960).

162. J. N. Shklar, *After Utopia: The Decline of Political Faith* (Princeton, N.J., 1957).

163. On the program of the SPD during its postwar opposition period, see Kurt Klotzbach, *Der Weg zur Staatspartei, Programmatik, praktische Politik und Organisation der deutschen Sozialdemokratie 1945 bis 1965* (Berlin, 1982). Gordon D. Drummond, *The German Social Democrats in Opposition, 1949–1960: The Case Against Rearmament* (Norman, Okla., 1982).

164. On the Western transparty consensus in the postwar years, see K. D. Bracher, *The Age of Ideologies.*

165. On Italian and French eurocommunism, see William E. Griffith, ed., *The European Left, Italy, France and Spain* (Lexington, Mass., 1979). D. L. M. Blackmer and Annie Kriegel, *The International Role of the Communist Parties of Italy and France* (Cambridge, Mass., 1975).

166. See K. D. Bracher, *The Age of Ideologies.*

167. Albert Camus, *The Rebel.*

168. On this topic, see R. Aron, *The Elusive Revolution* (London, 1968). George Kennan, *Democracy and the Student Left* (Boston, 1968). Richard Löwenthal, *Der romantische Rückfall* (Stuttgart, 1970). Gabriel Almond and Sidney Verba, *The Civic Culture, Political Attitudes and Democracy in Five Nations* (Princeton, N.J., 1963). Helmut Schelsky, *Systemüberwindung, Demokratisierung, Gewaltenteilung* (Munich, 1973). S. H. Barnes, M. Kaase, et al., *Political Action, Mass Participation in Five Western Democracies* (London, 1979). Ralf Dahrendorf, *Über den Ursprung der Ungleichheit unter den Menschen* (Tübingen, 1966). Alexander S. Neill, *Summerhill: A Radical Approach to Child Rearing* (New York, 1960). Wilhelm Hennis, *Die deutsche Unruhe, Studien zur Hochschulpolitik* (Hamburg, 1969). Sidney Hook, *Academic Freedom and Academic Anarchy* (Boston, 1971).

169. The legitimation for acts of violence was supplied to some extent by John Gal-

tung's thesis of "structural violence" of the bourgeois system and its institutions, cited in his book *Strukturelle Gewalt* (Reinbek b. Hamburg, 1977).

170. On Club of Rome literature, see note 121 above. See also Iring Fetscher, *Überlebensbedingungen der Menschheit, Ist der Fortschritt noch zu retten?* (Munich, 1985). H. Lübbe, *Fortschritt als Orientierungsproblem* (Freiburg, 1975).

171. See Raymond Aron, *Progress and Disillusion, The Dialectics of Modern Society* (London, 1968). Zbigniew Brzezinski, *Between Two Ages, America's Role in the Technetronic Era* (New York, 1970). Maurice Duverger, *Demokratie im technischen Zeitalter* (Munich, 1973). Jürgen Habermas, ed., *Stichworte zur geistigen Situation der Zeit*, 1, 2 (Frankfurt am Main, 1980). R. Inglehart, *The Silent Revolution: Changing Values and Political Styles among Western Publics*. F. Capra, *The Turning Point*.

172. One of the protagonists of leftist skepticism is Erhard Eppler. See his *Ende oder Wende, Von der Machbarkeit des Notwendigen* (Stuttgart, 1975); Sind die Grünen Kulturpessimisten?, *Der Spiegel*, no. 4 (January 22, 1979): 56, 57. G. K. Kaltenbrunner analyzed the topic of ecology from a conservative perspective; see his article Schöpferischer Konservatismus und konservative Aktion heute, in *Konservatismus International*, ed. G. K. Kaltenbrunner (Stuttgart, 1983), 223, 257, 258. The book by the alternative Marxist Rudolf Bahro, an emigré from the German Democratic Republic, has had substantial influence on the Green and alternative "scene": *Die Alternative* (Cologne, 1977). On change within the German parties, see Warnfried Dettling, ed., *Deutsche Parteien im Wandel* (Munich, 1983).

173. On neoconservative tendencies in the Federal Republic of Germany, see the collection edited by Clemens Graf Podewils, *Tendenzwende, Zur geistigen Situation der Bundesrepublik* (Stuttgart, 1975). The controversial term *Wertkonservativismus* (value conservatism) was coined by E. Eppler in *Ende oder Wende*, 28 ff. On American neoconservatism, see Peter Steinfels, *The Neoconservatives, The Men Who Are Changing America's Politics* (New York, 1980). On the German debate, see Christian Graf von Krockow, Der fehlende Konservatismus, in *Konservatismus—Eine deutsche Bilanz* (Munich, 1971), 99, 101 ff., 116. G. K. Kaltenbrunner, ed., *Rekonstruktion des Konservatismus* (Freiburg, 1972). M. Greiffenhagen, *Das Dilemma des Konservatismus* (Munich, 1977).

174. The unique characteristic of the German Greens and Alternatives is their interest not only in topics of "peace" and "ecology," but also in totally new ways of living in a "gentle and peaceful idyll" and in the total transformation of the political, institutional, and economic system of the Federal Republic of Germany. They are an expression of the recurrent German phenomenon of unsatisfied romantic yearnings, of skepticism toward progress and civilization. At the same time, they are an expression of the apparent inability to cope with the past, of the search for a German identity and national unity. In contrast to their predecessors of the 1968 movement, who either withdrew resignedly or chose the path of terrorism, the Greens are attempting to achieve a "total democratization" of the West German system through legal parliamentary means and with the help of their popular commitment to the environment. See the eloquent testimony of two Greens, Joschka Fischer, *Von Grüner Kraft und Herrlichkeit* (Reinbek b. Hamburg, 1984), and Antje Vollmer: " . . . und wehrt Euch täglich! Bonn—ein Grünes Tagebuch" (Gütersloh, 1984). See also Brigitte Sauzay, *Le Vertige Allemand* (Paris, 1985), who sees a parallel between Nazi ideology and the ecopacifist ideology of the Greens, its world without technology, capitalism, and Pershings, without harmful scientific and technological prog-

ress, but with grass-roots democracy, small, comprehensible production units, a happy and liberated Third World, and a history from which the German legacy of guilt has been extinguished and in which a Green national and neutral future can flourish. In this world the state is despised instead of glorified, and there is no racial hatred.

To the irritation of the Greens, Rudolf Bahro drew parallels between the Greens and the Nazi party at the Green party convention in Hamburg in December 1984: "From a formal and structural point of view, movement, state, and society confront each other today just as they did in the Republic of Weimar, and the Greens are rising along quite similar lines as the Nazi party did. In order to come out all right this time, that is, so that the popular uprising remains a peaceful one, the Greens cannot be allowed to fail" (quoted according to Gerhard Spörl, Ein Prophet ohne Jünger, Die Zeit, no. 51, December 14, 1984: 5). See also Richard Löwenthal, Reflections on the "Greens": Roots, Character, and Prospects, in German Studies Newsletter, no. 4 (February 1985): 11–18. Jean-Paul Picaper, Vers le IV^E Reich, Ecologistes et Gauchistes contre la démocratie en Allemagne Fédérale (Paris, 1983), 153 passim.

175. See Wolfgang Harich, Kommunismus ohne Wachstum? Babeuf und der "Club of Rome" (Reinbek b. Hamburg, 1975). On communist conceptions on the theme of "technology, economy, and ecology," see: Soetozar Stojanovic, Kritik und Zukunft des Sozialismus (Munich, 1970). Christoph Huhle, Vom Nahziel Kommunismus zu den Grenzen des Wachstums? Sowjetische Kommunismus-Konzeptionen seit 1961 (Frankfurt am Main, 1980). Igor Bestuschew-Lada, Die Welt im Jahr 2000. Eine sowjetische Prognose für unsere Zukunft (Freiburg, 1984). On Green standpoints and political objectives, see Die Grünen, Das Bundesprogramm (n.d.), 6 ff, 18–21 (deprivatization of economic structures, German and European neutrality); Die Grünen, Sinnvoll arbeiten—solidarisch leben (final program from the federal delegate conference of January 15–16, 1983, in Stuttgart-Sindelfingen), 6 ff. (grass-roots democratic control of the economy); Die Grünen, Programm für Bonn (n.d.), 3. "The self-management of businesses is impossible without change in the conditions of ownership." A closer reading of Green programs reveals a number of Marxist components (especially in economic issues) which have thus far been given little scholarly attention. On Green ideology, see also Günther Rüther and Klaus Weigelt, eds., Die Grünen und der Parlamentarismus (Melle, 1985). Franz Alt, Frieden ist möglich (Munich, 1983). On the emergence of the Green party and its electoral potential, see Kim Holmes, The Origins, Development, and Composition of the Green Movement, in The Greens of West Germany, ed. Robert L. Pfaltzgraff et al. (Cambridge, Mass., and Washington, D.C., 1983), 15–46 (Institute for Foreign Policy Analysis). Elim Papadakis, The Green Movement in West Germany (New York, 1984). G. Langguth, Der grüne Faktor, Von der Bewegung zur Partei (Zürich, 1984). Despite national and international interest in the German phenomenon of the "Greens," one should not underestimate the possibility of the movement's rapid obsolescence, which is already becoming noticeable among the younger, more technologically oriented generation as an anti-Alternative posture. See M. Horx, Das Ende der Alternativen oder Die verlorene Unschuld der Radikalität (Munich, 1985).

176. On the basic principles of democratic socialism in the 1970s, see Horst Ehmke, Demokratischer Sozialismus und demokratischer Staat (Bonn-Bad Godesberg, 1973). Willy Brandt, Bruno Kreisky, and Olof Palme, Briefe und Gespräche 1972–1975, eds. G. Grass, E. Jäckel, and D. Lattmann (Frankfurt am Main, 1975); E. Eppler, Ende oder Wende. R. Löwenthal, ed., Demokratischer Sozialismus in den 80er Jahren (Cologne, 1979). O. Palme, Demokratischer Sozialismus und der Kampf der Vollbeschäftigung, in Demokratischer Sozialismus in den 80er Jahren, 103–16. Erik Lundberg, Aufstieg und

Fall des schwedischen Modells, in *Trendwende, Europas Wirtschaft in der Krise,* ed. R. Dahrendorf (with a foreword by Gaston Thorn), (Zurich, 1981), 247–66. Thomas Meyer, ed., *Demokratischer Sozialismus, Geistige Grundlagen und Wege in die Zukunft* (Munich, 1980). For opposing views, see M. D. Hancok and G. Sjoberg, *Politics in the Post-Welfare State,* (New York, 1972). Walter Leisner, *Der Gleichheitsstaat, Macht durch Nivellierung* (Berlin, 1980). Gerhard Szczesny, *Vom Unheil der totalen Demokratie, Erfahrungen mit dem Fortschritt* (Munich, 1983).

177. On the topic of ungovernability, see Wilhelm Hennis, *Politik und praktische Philosophie* (Stuttgart, 1977), 240–42. On the emergence of a neoconservative theory, see Kurt Sontheimer, Der Konservativismus auf der Suche nach einer Theorie, *Merkur,* 7 (1974). G. K. Kaltenbrunner, Gibt es eine konservative Theorie?, *Aus Politik und Zeitgeschichte,* B 42 (1974). Rudolf Schottlaender, Geschichtsphilosophische Aspekte konservativer Fortschrittsbejahung, in *Konservatismus International.* For a critical view of neoconservative theory, see M. Greiffenhagen, *Der neue Konservatismus der 70er Jahre* (Hamburg, 1974). Hans Kremendahl, *Pluralismustheorie in Deutschland* (Leverkusen, 1977), 428 f.

178. Both Helmut Kohl and Helmut Schmidt, as adherents of Kant, have identified themselves with the political philosophy of critical rationalism, which can be traced back to the liberal thinker Karl R. Popper. See H. Kohl, *Zwischen Ideologie und Pragmatismus, Aspekte und Ansichten zu Grundfragen der Politik* (Stuttgart, 1973), 11 f. Georg Lührs et al., eds., *Kritischer Rationalismus und Sozialdemokratie* (Berlin, 1975) (with a preface by Helmut Schmidt). On critical rationalism, see K. R. Popper, Philosophische Selbstinterpretation und Polemik gegen die Dialektiker, in C. Grossner, *Verfall der Philosophie* (Reinbek b. Hamburg, 1971). On liberalism, see M. Salvadori, ed., *European Liberalism* (New York, 1972). Ralf Dahrendorf, *Die neue Freiheit, Überleben und Gerechtigkeit in einer veränderten Welt* (Munich, 1975).

179. On the meaning of utopia, see Ernst Bloch, *Geist der Utopie* (Frankfurt am Main, 1964). Frank E. Manuel, *Utopias and Utopian Thought* (Boston, 1966). Georg Picht, *Mut zur Utopie* (Munich, 1969). Ulrich Hommes, Brauchen wir die Utopie, *Aus Politik und Zeitgeschichte,* B 20 (1977): 3–17. Hommes offers an interesting definition of utopia: "It is a part of freedom to discover something which might be called possibility without actually having to demonstrate its realizability, to discover something which creates space and makes possible an idea of a direction which can be taken, if one decides in favor of it. This utopia is a discovery, determined by the interest of freedom and guided by the historical experience of freedom, of the possibilities of the real." On the meaning of religion for humankind, see J. Bauer, ed., *Entwürfe der Theologie* (Graz, 1985).

180. D. Bell, *The End of Ideology.* Peter Bender, *Das Ende des ideologischen Zeitalters, Die Europäisierung Europas* (Berlin, 1981).

181. J. F. Revel, *How Democracies Perish* (New York, 1984), 20. That Soviet totalitarianism has not been extinguished is the thesis of the volume by Guy Hermet, Pierre Hassner, and Jacques Rupnik, *Totalitarismes* (Paris, 1984).

182. On the new technologies, see Dieter Bullinger, Die Neuen Technologien, *Aus Politik und Zeitgeschichte,* B 4/85 (January 26, 1985): 47–60. H. Kahn, *The Coming Boom: Economic, Political, and Social* (New York, 1982). A. Toffler, *The Third Wave* (New York, 1980). On the varied, as yet unsolved, risks connected with application of the New Technologies, see Detlef Eckert, *Risikostrukturen industrieller Forschung und Entwicklung. Theoretische und empirische Ansatzpunkte einer Risikoanalyse technologischer Innovationen* (Berlin, 1985). Walter Sauer, ed., *Der dressierte Arbeiter, Ge-*

*schichte und Gegenwart der industriellen Arbeitswelt* (Munich, 1984). Oskar Negt, *Lebendige Arbeit, enteignete Zeit. Politische und kulturelle Dimensionen des Kampfes um die Arbeitszeit,* (Frankfurt am Main, 1984). Wolfgang Lecher, Überleben in einer veränderten Welt, Ein Konzept für die zukünftige Arbeit der Gewerkschaften, *Die Zeit* (April 26, 1985): 44–45. (Lecher argues that the German unions in particular have to rethink their position. According to Lecher, shrinking membership, high unemployment rates, stagnating growth, and technological change will make it more difficult for them to defend their position in society). Hartmut v. Hentig, *Das allmähliche Verschwinden der Wirklichkeit. Ein Pädagoge ermutigt zum Nachdenken über die Neuen Medien* (Munich, 1984). E. Feigenbaum and P. McCorduck, *Die Fünfte Computer-Generation— Künstliche Intelligenz und die Herausforderung Japans* (Basel, 1984). M. Ferguson, *Die sanfte Verschwörung—Persönliche und gesellschaftliche Transformation im Zeichen des Wassermannes* (Munich, 1984). (Ferguson is considered a cult figure of the "New Age Movement," which sees a spiritual transformation of society with new qualities in the technological transformation of society).

183. See Andreas Troge, *Technik und Umwelt* (Cologne, 1985). Europäisches Parlament, ed., *Plan für den wirtschaftlichen Wiederaufschwung in Europa* (resolution of March 27, 1984), (Luxembourg, 1984), 16, 51. Peter Cornelius Mayer-Tasch, Die internationale Umweltpolitik als Herausforderung für die Nationalstaatlichkeit, *Aus Politik und Zeitgeschichte,* B 20/85 (May 18, 1985): 3–13.

184. On the issue of the Third World, see the recent report of the Brandt Commission, *Common Crisis, North-South: Cooperation for World Recovery* (London, 1983), with a preface by Willy Brandt. Robert Boardman, Timothy M. Shaw, and Panayotis Soldatos, eds., *Europe, Africa and Lomé III* (Washington, D.C., 1985).

185. On the issue of equal rights for men and women, see Berndt Warnat, Gleichberechtigung von Männern und Frauen—Ist der Staat am Zuge?, and Helge Pross, Von der Rechtsgleichheit zur Gleichberechtigung, *Aus Politik und Zeitgeschichte,* B 45/81 (November 7, 1981): 3–13, 14–25. EG-Kommission, ed., *Gleiche Chancen für die Frauen, Stichwort Europa,* 4/84 (February 1984). On the theme of women in business and society, see Elisabeth Noelle-Neumann, *Frauen in Beruf und Politik, Allensbacher Report,* quoted from Eva Witte, Gleichberechtigt in 245 Jahren?, Auch gutgemeinte Programme erhöhen die Chancengleichheit der Frau nicht, *Die Zeit* (May 17, 1985): 22. (This study analyzes the professional situation of German women. Only 3 percent of German women manage to rise to top posts as compared to a European average—France, Great Britain—of 6 to 8 percent. In the United States, every fifth management position is already held by a woman.) Europäisches Parlament, ed., *Stellung der Frau in Europa* (Entschließung zur Situation der Frau in Europa vom 17. January 1984), (Luxembourg, 1984). On women in politics, see Liselotte Funcke, ed., *Die Liberalen, Frei sein, um andere frei zu machen* (Stuttgart, 1984), with a foreword by Walter Scheel. Antje Huber, ed., *Die Sozialdemokratinnen, Verdient die Nachtigall Lob, wenn sie singt?* (Stuttgart, 1984), with a foreword by Herbert Wehner. Renate Hellwig, ed., *Die Christdemokratinnen, Unterwegs zur Partnerschaft* (Stuttgart, 1984), with a foreword by Helmut Kohl. If one compares the party programs of the CDU, SPD, FDP, and the Greens on equal rights for men and women in politics and society, the Greens and the FDP emerge better owing to the relatively high representation of female Green and FDP politicians in parliament as well as in party politics. Only after the CDU discovered increasing defections of female voters did it elevate the issue of "new partnership between man and woman" to a guiding slogan of its party convention in Essen in March 1985. See also Margarete

Mitscherlich, *Die friedfertige Frau* (Frankfurt am Main, 1985); Birgit Meyer, Frauen an die Macht!? Politische Strategien zur Durchsetzung der Gleichberechtigung von Mann und Frau, *Aus Politik und Zeitgeschichte,* B 9–10/87, (February 28, 1987): 15–27.

186. On the scientist's role in society, see Don K. Price, *The Scientific Estate* (Cambridge, Mass., 1965). Joseph Ben-David, *The Scientist's Role in Society* (Englewood Cliffs, N.J., 1971). Klaus Michael Meyer-Abich, *Wege zum Frieden mit der Natur, Praktische Naturphilosophie für die Umweltpolitik* (Munich, 1984). Richard von Weizsäcker, Mehr Fragen als Antworten, Gentechnologie, Verantwortung der Wissenschaft, Neue Medien, Kunst, *Die Zeit* (January 18, 1985).

187. See also Stanley Hoffmann, *Fragments Floating in the Here and Now, Is There a Europe, Was There a Past, and Will There Be a Future?, or The Lament of a Transplanted European,* 213–31. S. Hoffmann, Europe's Identity Crisis: Between the Past and America, *Daedalus* 93 (Fall 1964): 1249, 1252–53.

188. On the idea of Europe, see Sebastian Haffner, *Im Schatten der Geschichte, Historisch-politische Variationen* (Stuttgart, 1985). Michel Richonnier, *Les Métamorphoses de l'Europe de 1769 à 2001* (Paris, 1985).

189. See O. Franz, Am Wendepunkt der europäischen Geschichte (Göttingen, 1981). D. Hasselblatt, ed., *1984—Orwells Jahr* (Berlin, 1984). P. Bender, *Das Ende des ideologischen Zeitalters, Die Europäisierung Europas.* Fernand Spaak, The U.S. and Europe: Partners at Last? (The First Annual Paul-Henri-Spaak Lecture, April 8, 1981, sponsored by the Frank Boas Foundation and the Center for International Affairs, Harvard University, with a preface by Robert D. Putman, CFIA, Harvard University, 1981, October). François Bondy, *Der Nachkrieg muß kein Vorkrieg sein, Europäische Orientierungen* (Zürich, 1985).

190. See Raymond Aron, *In Defense of Decadent Europe* (Washington, D.C., 1979). Dolf Sternberger, Komponenten der geisten Gestalt Europas, *Merkur* 34 (1980): 228–38. A. Danzin, *Wissenschaft und Wiedergeburt Europas,* (Frankfurt am Main, 1980). Franz König and Karl Rahner, eds., *Europa, Horizonte der Hoffnung* (Cologne, 1983). "Die Zukunft Europas—Kann die Technik eine Antwort geben" (On the seventy-fifth birthday of Gräfin Dönhoff, the Aspen-Institute in Berlin held a conference on this topic with Gräfin Dönhoff, Henry Kissinger, Reimar Lüst, Helmut Schmidt, Theo Sommer, Herwig Schopper, Fritz Stern, Shepard Stone et al.), printed in *Die Zeit,* Mit Grips, Geld und Gremien, Was können die Technik und die dritte industrielle Revolution zur Einigung Europas beitragen?, January 4, 1985, 9–11.

191. See *Integration* (January 1984) (special issue on the draft treaty of the European Parliament). Jürgen Schwarze and Roland Bieber, eds., *Eine Verfassung für Europa. Von der Europäischen Gemeinschaft zur Europäischen Union* (Baden-Baden, 1984). Rudolf Hrbek, Welches Europa? Zum Zwischenbericht des Ad-Hoc-Ausschusses für institutionelle Fragen ("Dooge-Committee"), *Integration* (January 1985): 3–10.

192. On European nationalism, provincialism, and egoism, see K. D. Bracher, *Europa zwischen National- und Weltpolitik.* Europe 1984, Colloque A l'Assemblée Nationale Avec Simone Veil, Jacques Chirac et Michael Albert, Jacques Baumel, Jean-Marie Domenach, Kai-Uwe von Hassel, Alain Juppé, Alain Pohrer, Pierre-Bernard Reymond, Paris, 1984 (Les Cahiers de la Fondation du Futur, April 1984). Harald Hotze, *Skandal Europa. Die Europäische Gemeinschaft oder: Wie sich eine Idee zu Tode subventioniert* (Frankfurt am Main, 1985). *Europäische Defizite, europäische Perspektiven–eine Bestandaufnahme für morgen,* ed. Werner Weidenfeld (Gütersloh, 1988). On mutual European prejudices and on lack of information in public opinion on the European idea,

see Michael Wolffsohn, Das Bild der Deutschen im Ausland, "Süddeutsche Zeitung," no. 223 (September 26, 1984), 11.

In October 1977, the following question was asked in Italy, the United States, Great Britain, Sweden, Greece, the Netherlands, Denmark, and France: "Do you have reservations about Western Germany or its inhabitants? If reservations exist, what do they consist of?" The most frequent answer was, "the country still cannot be trusted completely because of the Nazi period." France was clearly at the top with 41 percent, followed by Great Britain with 38 percent and the United States with 31 percent, in Sweden it was 29 percent, while in the other countries the numbers were below 20 percent. The reservations in Greece were the lowest, with only 9 percent. Despite all claims to the contrary, Germans today know little about the French mentality, and vice versa; see B. Sauzay, *Le Vertige allemand.*

The question also arises as to whether the Germans have an idea of the mentality or contemporary political culture of the British, Belgians, Greeks, Portuguese, or Dutch, or whether the Danes and the Italians have ever thought about the French, German, and British mentalities. The Europeans seem to have a lot of catching up to do in this area. Similarly, the European institutional concepts of "Brussels, Luxembourg, and Strasbourg" still summon up an image of disease among Europeans. In the Federal Republic of Germany, for example, a politician's assignment to the European Parliament or the European Commission is usually regarded as a political defeat and personal failure. On this topic, see also E. Noelle-Neumann and G. Herdegen, Die Europäische Gemeinschaft in der öffentlichen Meinung: Informationsdefizite und enttäuschte Erwartungen, *Integration* (March 1983): 95–195; see also note 104, above. On the problems of European identity and culture, see O. Marquard and K. Stierle, eds., *Identität,* (Munich, 1979); Hans Mayer, Widersprüche einer europäischen Literatur, *Die Zeit,* no. 42 (October 14, 1983): 57. Paul Harro Piazolo, Europäische Kulturgemeinschaft—notwendige Schritte auf ein großes Ziel, *Integration* (March 1983): 79–90; François Bondy, *Europa ohne Grenzen,* 21–30. Thomas Nipperdey, *Im Zwielicht der Geschichte. Vom Nutzen und Nachteil der Geschichte für das Leben* (Munster, 1985), 37–75.

The philosophy of strengthening a technological community consists of supporting Europe's high technologies in those areas where they are presently behind those of the United States and Japan and adapting them to a new internal European infrastructure. This would be the case in the areas of biotechnology and telecommunications, especially in the sector of data base networks, where the United States currently controls 90 percent of the data market and thus possesses a strategically important information monopoly.

The philosophy behind EURECA consists of the supplementation of American SDI projects by means of a European civilian enterprise that would also have some military uses. The French initiative proposes cooperation in high-speed microelectronics, optical electronics, new materials, high performance lasers, large computers, and artificial intelligence. See "Neue Züricher Zeitung": Europäische Antwort auf die SDI-Initiative? (April 24, 1985).

On the discussion of a mutual European defense initiative, see also Jean Klein, Zur französischen Debatte über die europäische Verteidigung, *Integration* (February 1985): 68–79. Hans-Gert Pöttering, ed., *Sicherheit in Freiheit für Europa, Plädoyer für eine europäische Sicherheitspolitik* (Bonn, 1988). William G. Hyland, Lawrence D. Freedman, Paul C. Warnke, and Karsten D. Voigt, *Nuclear Weapons in Europe,* ed. Andrew J. Pierre (New York, 1984). For the strengthening and expansion of mutual European large-scale projects, new initiatives and proposals can be expected from the European Atomic

Research Center (CERN), from the European Space Agency (ESA), and the European strategic program of the EC for information technology (ESPRIT). See Kommission der Europäischen Gemeinschaften ed., *Eine Industriestrategie für Europa* (June/July 1984).

193. See John Dunn, *Western Political Theory in the Face of the Future* (Cambridge, 1980).

194. See Gesine Schwan, *Sozialismus in der Demokratie?* (Stuttgart, 1982). Klaus Haefner, *Mensch und Computer im Jahre 2000. Ökonomie und Politik für eine human computerisierte Gesellschaft* (Basel, 1984). Henner Kleinewefers, *Reformen für Wirtschaft und Gesellschaft, Utopien, Konzepte, Realitäten* (Frankfurt am Main, 1985).

195. On France's economic and technological policies, see Henrik Uterwedde, Mitterrands Wirtschaftspolitik—Was bleibt vom Sozialismus?, *Aus Politik und Zeitgeschichte*, B 19/85 (May 11, 1985): 3–13. Jacques Attali, *La figure de Fraser* (Paris, 1984). Jean-Louis Servan-Schreiber, *Die 90-Minuten-Stunde* (Düsseldorf, 1984). Catherine Nay, *Le Noir et le Rouge ou l'histoire d'une ambition* (Paris, 1984). (Nay's biography of Mitterrand offers support for the thesis of the moderate leftist Mitterrand, who has thus far always managed to establish ties to the French Right.) On Italy, see Istituto Nazionale per lo Studio della Congiuntura, ed., *L'Evoluzione Congiunturale dell'Economia Italiana* (Rome, 1985) (Rapporto Semestrale February 1985). On Spain and Portugal, see Peter Frey, Spanien and Portugal, in *Jahrbuch der Europäischen Integration*, ed. W. Weidenfeld and W. Wessels (Bonn, 1984), 390–400.

196. On Greece, see Heinz Jürgen Axt, *Die PASOK in Griechenland. Aufstieg und Wandel eines verspäteten Sozialismus* (Bonn, 1985). Roy C. Macridis, *Greek Politics at a Crossroads, What Kind of Socialism?* (Stanford, Calif., 1984), 56 ff.

197. See O. Lafontaine, *Der andere Fortschritt, Verantwortung statt Verweigerung* (Hamburg, 1985). Johano Strasser and Klaus Traube, *Die Zukunft des Fortschritts, Der Sozialismus und die Krise des Industrialismus* (Bonn, 1985).

198. On the discussion of a new social democratic profile, see Willy Brandt, *Zeit* Interview conducted by Fritz J. Raddatz: Unsere Welt ist von Waffen vergiftet (December 31, 1982): 29. "In the old SPD there is . . . , along with unbelievable devotion to progressive ideology, a horrifying amount of petty bourgeois attitudes." Peter Glotz, *Die Arbeit der Zuspitzung, Über die Organisation einer regierungsfähigen Linken* (Berlin, 1984); Claus Offe: "Arbeitsgesellschaft," Strukturprobleme und Zukunftsperspektiven (Frankfurt am Main, 1984). Jochem Langkau and Claus Köhler, eds., *Wirtschaftspolitik und wirtschaftliche Entwicklung* (Festschrift for Walter Hesselbach) (Bonn, 1985). On the discussion of a German work ethic, desire for security, and high expectations of welfare state benefits, as well as an (increasing?) hostility toward progress, see E. Noelle-Neumann and B. Struempel, *Macht Arbeit krank, macht Arbeit glücklich?* (Cologne, 1984). Werner Kaltefleiter, *Changes in Social Values in Industrial Societies—The Example of the Federal Republic of Germany.* Hans Jakob Ginsburg, Computer, nein danke. Mit dem Vormarsch der neuen Technik wächst die Angst um den Job, *Die Zeit* (May 31, 1985): 27, 28. (In comparison to Japan, the United States, Great Britain, and France, this poll depicts the Germans as veritable sticks-in-the-mud in respect to computers and technology.)

199. First indications of a social democratic search for a new leftist identity, now being understood by the SPD for the first time in a European context, is presented by Peter Glotz's book, *Manifest für eine neue europäische Linke* (Berlin, 1985), which has been widely discussed in Germany.

200. On American neoconservatism, see Peter Steinfels, *The Neo-Conservatives, The Men Who Are Changing America's Politics* (New York, 1980). Hans Rühle, Hans-Joachim Veen, and Walter F. Hahn, eds., *Der Neo-Konservativismus in den Vereinigten Staaten und seine Auswirkungen für die Atlantische Allianz* (Melle, 1982). On American and British economic policy, see Jürgen Kromphardt, Die neue Wirtschaftspolitik in Großbritannien und in den USA, *Aus Politik und Zeitgeschichte*, B 12/84 (March 24, 1984): 21–32. For criticism of Margaret Thatcher's conservatism, see the book of the former conservative MP Julian Critchley, *Westminster Blues: Minor Chords* (London, 1985). On British technological politics and research, see Reiner Luyken, Utopia in Schottland, Livingston—europäischer Stützpunkt für Amerikaner und Japaner, *Die Zeit* (March 1, 1985): 43. Robert Dunn, Microcomputers in Britain's Schools, *Survey of Current Affairs* (April 1984). This article, by the Parliamentary Under-Secretary of State for Education and Science, R. Dunn, explains the success of the British "Microelectronic Education" program, initiated in March 1980 and extended in March 1983, to equip all secondary schools and 70 percent of the primary schools in Britain with microcomputers; today Great Britain is the leader in computer use.

COI reference No. 216/83, British Technology Group, (London, 1983), together with the National Research Development Corporation (NRDC) and the National Enterprise Board (NEB), the British Technology Group (BTG)—since 1981, there has been a mutual board of directors—promotes the intensification of research possibilities in universities and government institutions, as well as possibilities for innovation and New Technologies in British industry. On German economic policy, see Schritte der Erneuerung, soziale Marktwirtschaft für die achtziger Jahre, ed. Presse-und Informationsamt der Bundesregierung (Bonn, 1985).

On German technological policies, see Thierry Gaudin, *Die Innovationsbremse—Der lange Weg des technischen Fortschritts durch Bürokratien und Unternehmen* (Frankfurt am Main, 1981). A. Probst, Schlüsseltechnologien und politische Rahmenbedingungen in der Bundesrepublik Deutschland, in Institut der Deutschen Wirtschaft, ed., *Technik kennt keinen Rückschritt—Veränderte Rahmenbedingungen für den betrieblichen Bildungsprozeß* (Cologne, 1984). Dieter Stolze, *Die Zukunft wartet nicht—Aufbruch in die neunziger Jahre* (Munich, 1984). *Die Bundesrepublik Deutschland 1985/1990/2000— Die Entwicklung von Wirtschaft und Gesellschaft in der Bundesrepublik und den Bundesländern bis 2000*, by Peter Hofer, Stefan Rommerskirchen, Detlef Franzen, Heinfrid Wolf (Stuttgart, 1983) (Prognos AG—Report/Basel).

201. See W. Becker, *Die Freiheit, die wir meinen. Entscheidung für die liberale Demokratie* (Munich, 1982). Ralf Dahrendorf, *Die Chancen der Krise, Über die Zukunft des Liberalismus* (Stuttgart, 1983).

202. I. Berlin, *Four Essays on Liberty* (New York, 1970) (Chapter: Political Ideas in the Twentieth Century), 8.

203. See also Peter Reichel, ed., *Politische Kultur in Westeuropa. Bürger und Staaten in der Europäischen Gemeinschaft* (Frankfurt am Main, 1984). Jürgen Hartmann, *Politische Profile der westeuropäischen Industriegesellschaft—Ein vergleichendes Handbuch* (Frankfurt am Main, 1984).

204. Stanley Hoffmann defines the problem of the Europeans as follows: "There never was a single common faith in Western Europe," in Fragments Floating in the Here and Now, 217.

205. The entry of Spain and Portugal into the EC (in January 1986) may well give

Europe new dynamic impulses. Although the Southern Europeans still lag behind their Western and Northern European counterparts in the business, industrial, and technological sectors, with their still unexhausted potential of energy, imagination, and creativity they can contribute to their own economic situation and thus to that of the EC. They can also promote and enrich intellectual harmony in Europe with their own polymorphic political culture. Note that in the last fifty years Nobel Prizes have been awarded to five Southern Europeans: Salvadore Quasimodo, George Seferis, Eugenio Montale, Vincente Alexandre, and Odysseus Elytis. In the framework of a cosmopolitan humanism, perhaps the Europeans will succeed in overcoming the cultural barriers of national isolationism. See Stanley Hoffmann and Paschalis Kitromilides, eds., *Culture and Society in Contemporary Europe,* 13–29 and passim. See also Hans Magnus Enzensberger's interesting efforts to get closer to a different culture: Italienische Ausschweifungen, Eine ideologische Reportage, *Die Zeit* (March 16, 1984): 41 ff.; Norwegische Anarchronismen I und II, *Die Zeit* (November 2, 1984): 39 ff., (November 9, 1984): 65 ff.; Ungarische Wirrungen, *Die Zeit,* (May 3, 1985): 57 ff.

On the homogenization of the European college and university system, see P. H. Piazolo, *Europäische Kulturgemeinschaft—notwendige Schritte auf ein großes Ziel.* On the revitalization of the Action Committee for the United States of Europe led by Jean Monnet during the committee's existence into the mid-1970s, see Helmut Kohl's luncheon speech held for the Aktionskomitee für Europa, June 7, 1985, Presse-Mitteilung, No. 249/85 of the Presse- und Informationsamtes der Bundesregierung.

206. Richard von Weizsäcker, 8th of May speech, Mitteilung für die Presse, Bundespräsidialamt, May 8, 1985 (Bonn, 1985).

207. See Rudolf Walter Leonhardt, Bergen-Belsen und Bitburg, Was immer die Toten uns zu sagen haben, es darf nicht gegen die Lebenden gehen, *Die Zeit* (April 26, 1985): 3. James M. Markham, Bitburg Visit: Is "Reconciliation" Needed?, *New York Times* (May 1, 1985): 16. On the war of the German historians, see Gordon A. Craig, The War of the German Historians, *The New York Review* (January 15, 1987): 16–19; Christoph Bertram: Disputes Among Historians Indicate Changing Cultural Moods, *International Herald Tribune* (March 31, 1987): 9.

208. On the discussion of Deutschlandpolitik from the perspective of the Greens and the peace movement, see W. Pohrdt, *Endstation* (Berlin, 1982); Wilfried von Bredow, Friedensbewegung und Deutschlandpolitik, *Aus Politik und Zeitgeschichte,* B 46/83 (November 19, 1983): 34–46. Antje Vollmer, Interview with *Die Zeit* (April 5, 1985); Neutralismus ist kein Schimpfwort, 50. For a critical view of this, see R. G. Livingston, Once Again, the German Question, *German Studies Newsletter,* no. 2 (April 1984): 11–15. On the debate over Deutschlandpolitik, which was given new life by Hans Apel's remark in August 1984 that "the German question is no longer open," see Gerd Bucerius, Die deutsche Einheit ist unaufhaltsam, *Die Zeit* (August 24, 1984): 4. William Stivers, The March to German Consensus, *International Herald Tribune* (October 15, 1984): 4. Egon Bahr, ed., *Mut zur Einheit.* Philipp von Bismarck, Joseph Rovan, Werner Weidenfeld, and Heinrich Windelen, *Die Teilung Deutschlands und Europas* (Bonn, 1984), with a preface by Walter Scheel.

209. See E. Schulz, *Die deutsche Nation in Europa, Internationale und historische Dimensionen* (Bonn, 1982); E. Schulz, Die europäische Integration und die deutsche Frage, in *EG-Mitgliedschaft: Ein vitales Interesse der Bundesrepublik Deutschland?,* ed. R. Hrbek and W. Wessels, (Bonn, 1984): 443–68. W. Weidenfeld, *Ratlose Normalität— Die Deutschen auf der Suche nach sich selbst* (Zürich, 1984). Gabriele Weber, Die

europapolitische Rolle der Bundesrepublik Deutschland aus der Sicht ihrer EG-Partner. Deutscher Sonderweg oder europäische Musterrolle? (Bonn, 1984). Eberhard Schulz and Peter Danylow, *Bewegung in der Deutschen Frage?/Die ausländischen Besorgnisse über die Entwicklung in den beiden deutschen Staaten,* (Bonn, 1985).

# Part II

## THE HISTORICAL INTERDEPENDENCE OF THE EUROPEAN AND AMERICAN IDEA OF PROGRESS

*The American idea of progress can be explained only in the context of the philosophical debate that has surrounded the idea of progress in Europe for centuries. The political as well as the economic development of America evidenced the longings, desires, and hopes of many Europeans for the creation of a New World that would allow a greater chance for realizing the ideals of the Old World (freedom, democracy, equality, and human self-determination). Although the story behind the founding of North America was deeply influenced by European progressivist ideas and elements, one should also note the development of a distinctively American historiography and historical interpretation, which gave the idea of progress an American profile.*

*The following analysis of the idea of progress in American historical imagery illustrates the influence and relevance of European trends of progress and decline. In the process, the historical interdependence of European-American thought as well as the distance and emancipation of America from European political culture are demonstrated. The unique historical chance to formulate and practice the best possible form of state and society from the inherited European history of ideas was recognized and utilized by the Founding Fathers of the United States, who had carefully analyzed Greek and Roman historical interpretation and theories of state. Thomas Jefferson, Alexander Hamilton, James Madison, Benjamin Franklin, and John Adams, all understood how to avoid the Europeanization of America and how to adopt and apply only the progressive elements and guiding images of European history, philosophy, and politics. This understanding has been proved by the two-hundred-year history of American democracy.*

*A transatlantic comparison may also illustrate the individual convergences and divergences within the European-American understanding of history and progress that links and at the same time separates the two continents. It is, after all, the tension between history and the awareness of the multifaceted concept of progress that continues to determine the acceptance or discrepancy of consensus and conflict, democracy and dictatorship, in the political history of Europe and the United States. Europe was repeatedly shaken by the recurring negative ideologization of history and progress, which expressed itself in various forms of utopianism, dogmatism, and totalitarianism. This manner of dealing with history and progress established the ambivalence of progress as an empirical verity in European history and as a unique precondition to the Old World's historical thought. By contrast, America succeeded in developing a positive ideologization of history and progress. The idealized acts of progress in 1776 and 1787 offered historical precedents that had only to be preserved in order to guarantee future progress. In this way American progressivist idealism can be understood as its own ultimate historical necessity. America not only had it better, as Goethe once remarked, but apparently also chose better routes than Europe.*

*Of course, it remains to be examined to what degree various European-American interpretations of the politicohistorical phenomenon "revolution," as well as the years of European (and especially German) ignorance and repression of the phenomenon of "America," not only determined the mutual images held, but reflected the different concepts of history and progress as well.*

# 4

## The Idea of Progress in the American Interpretation of History

When analyzing American historiography, one notes the overwhelming preoccupation of Americans with their own rather than world history. Nevertheless, numerous works by American historians on European history testify to the New World's interest in the Old.[1] This fact is important in that the American interpretation of certain European periods also sheds some light on American interpretations of history. To a certain degree, American historians rediscovered elements of the European idea of progress, which they reminded their readers were preconditions for the founding of America, and which they presented as models for the formulation of an American idea of progress. Although the main topic of this chapter is the idea of progress in the American interpretation of history from Puritan fragments to recent research concepts of contemporary history, a brief portrayal of the development and state of research of the historical interpretation of Europe in the United States may well help illuminate American progressivist thought.

Within American historiography on Europe, one can distinguish between two schools that seek to connect the history of the Old World with the historical experiences of the New. The first employs a chronological conception: European history is seen primarily as a prehistory of America, as a kind of introductory phase to later ideas, traditions, and political occurrences that formed the New World. The second builds on a sense of historical community, in which America and Europe are equal partners and poles of the same Western history and civilization. It is understandable that representatives of the first school focused on the earlier epochs of European history and devoted themselves in particular to political institutions, culture, and religion, while representatives of the second school directed their gaze to contemporary events and explored problems in economic and diplomatic history as well as international relations. Historians of the first line of thought emphasized the commonness and unity of the cultural inheritance, whereas the historians of the second school placed the history of Western civilization in an Atlantic context, which they defined as a common destiny. Until the end of the nineteenth century, the interest of American Euro-historiographers was centered on bringing out the unity of the historical heritage of Western civilization. At the turn of the century, particularly after the United States' entry into the First World War and its elevation toward superpower status, American historical research shifted increasingly to the elaboration of the idea of common destiny.[2] One began to speak of a turning point in American historiography, marked by an increasing professionalism and scholarliness in research methods. In the words of the historian Leonard Krieger, American historiography before the twentieth century was "amateur in authorship, romantic in tone, literary in style, nationalist in mission, and multivolumed in scope."[3]

American historians did not begin to address European themes until the nineteenth century. Practically no works on the history of Europe appeared in the seventeenth and eighteenth centuries, although the Puritan era did produce several isolated works on motives of Divine Providence, which included the traditional Christian concept of the four holy empires, the inner spiritual conflict of each Christian between the power of the good and the power of Satan, the dramatic events of the Reformation, the persecution of many religious dissenters, and the flight to New England. Worthy of mention here are Cotton Mather's *Magnalia Christi Americana* (1702) and Thomas Prince's *Chronological History of New England* (1736).

The historians of the revolutionary phase, in turn, considered all events from a secularized point of view and saw their main task in explaining the American Revolution as a part of human history to the rest of the world and for posterity. From the need to create a unified basis of experience for the young nation grew a cult of hero- and patriot-worship, to which historians such as David Ramsay (*History of the American Revolution,* 1789) or Mason Locke Weems (*Life of George Washington,* 1800) paid homage in their writings.[4] At the same time, in the first decades after the Revolution and the founding of the nation the desire emerged for emancipation from the Old World. The attempt was made to divorce oneself mentally as well as physically from the motherland, whose dominion had been cast off, while at the same time to contrast the moral decline of the Europeans (especially of the British government) with "the rising glory" of the new empire of virtues and freedom.[5] In any case, it remains characteristic of the colonial and revolutionary historiography of the United States that no historical work concerned itself with European themes.

The "national" or "romantic" period of the first half of the nineteenth century is of decisive importance in the development of American historiography concerning Europe. Historians such as Washington Irving (*Columbus,* 1828), William Hickling Prescott (*History of the Reign of Ferdinand and Isabella, the*

*Catholic*, 1838), or John Lothrop Motley (*The Rise of the Dutch Republic*, 1856 and on, 6 vols.), all of whom pass under the milieu of New England Unitarianism, were poets and literary figures until they later discovered their Puritan passion for historical writing.[6] As familiar with the works of Scott and Cooper, Wordsworth, Coleridge, and Byron as with Schiller, Goethe, and Herder, they represented to some extent the American counterpart to Romantic historiography. Their goal was to use their historical studies as a means of depicting the European past as "prenatal" American history. They were not interested in the historical and philosophical analysis of past epochs, but rather in the search for usable empirical values. This rejuvenation of European empirical values was regarded by Romantic historiography as a moral guide for American history, as pointed out by Richard Hofstadter:

What they found most generally and consistently was progress toward liberty—progress which they interpreted with a distinct Protestant bias, as though all the world had been preparing for nineteenth-century Unitarianism. The medieval inheritance, Latinity, Catholicism, stood as the foe against which the impulse toward progress had to assert itself.[7]

Prescott viewed Spanish history and culture as a motor for the progress of Western civilization and praised the development of liberal Teutonic traditions and institutions for the cultivation of national vitality, which had ultimately contributed to the release of the West's energies for the founding of the New World as the great achievement of Ferdinand and Isabella. He only mentioned, however, the impact of clerical bigotry and the rise of monarchic authoritarianism, both of which finally led to the destruction of individual freedoms and the fall of the Spanish Empire.[8] Motley, in turn, wanted to alert his contemporaries to the "dangers [in Europe] which come from superstition and despotism and the blessings which flow from the maintenance of religious and political freedom."[9] Ultimately, he perceived this problem to be the key to a universal law, which ruled "all bodies political as inexorably as Kepler's law controls the motion of planets. The law is Progress; the result Democracy."[10]

Together with George Bancroft, the first famous historian of American historiography, Prescott and Motley were convinced that the idea of freedom, which reached its zenith in the establishment of the United States of America, was continuing to spread throughout the world. They claimed to have found its roots in the Renaissance of Teutonic virtues and institutions, which had remained buried for centuries beneath the burden of European feudalism. Motley took his Romantic belief in progress and naive admiration for the alleged continuity of Germanic tradition and ideology in the Old as well as the New World so far that he was able to overlook the serious differences in German and Anglo-American culture and enlightenment and openly declare that

Ever since the great rising for freedom against the German Empire, down to this hour, Germany has been the main source of European and American culture. The common

mother of nations and empires—*alma mater felix prole*—she still rules the thought of
her vast brood of children; Franks, Goths, Saxons, Lombards, Normans, Netherlanders,
Americans—Germans all.[11]

That Bancroft, Prescott, and Motley, with their narrow historical perspectives
and religious prejudices, were able to regard Germany as an outpost of progress
may, as Gordon A. Craig puts it, be understandable from their point of view,
but no impartial observer of international events of the time could have come
to such a conclusion.[12] It seems indisputable that Romantic historiography was
concerned primarily with emphasizing the legacy of ideals common to Europe
and America and at the same time with stressing America's uniqueness, where
moral progress was able to unfold as freedom and democracy under the leadership
of God—in contrast to Europe, where political restoration was increasingly
attended by stagnation of progressivist ideas.

In the second half of the nineteenth century, and especially after the end of
the Civil War, the school of scientific history emerged, having been influenced
by German historicism and the Darwinian theory of evolution. Although historicism was never completely integrated into American thought, American interest in the German method of historiography and in German history itself grew.
This was ascribable to the emigration of German historians—mainly students of
Leopold von Ranke or Friedrich Meinecke—to the United States toward the end
of the nineteenth century.[13] Despite the increasing scholarliness of research
methods and academic conferences, however, the study of European history in
America remained confined to the display of intercultural legacy and the summary
and presentation of European history, which was treated and interpreted simply
as the period prior to the colonial period of North America. Under the leadership
of Herbert Baxter Adams, Johns Hopkins University evolved as the most important center of the scientific school, next to Harvard and Columbia (where
Henry Adams and John Burgess taught). By now, defined as a scientific theory
of historical continuity, Teutonism had reached full bloom.

Additionally, religious motifs, as links between the Old and New World,
provided material for new research projects. John William Draper's *History of
the Intellectual Development of Europe* (1863) and *History of the Conflict between
Religion and Science* (1874), as well as Andrew Dickson White's *History of the
Warfare of Science with Technology in Christendom* (1896), are documents of
the intellectual conflict at the end of the nineteenth century over the struggle
between science and religion, which was projected by both rather anachronistic
historians back into the classical period and the Middle Ages of the Old World.
Draper, a somewhat belated eighteenth-century encyclopedist and adherent to
the theory of evolution and Comtian positivism, attempted to use the methods
and tools of the scientific school to portray the contrast between the "dark age
of faith," which lasted until the end of the fifteenth century, and the "enlightened
age of reason," which began in the Renaissance and reached its climax in modern

America.[14] White, historian, diplomat, and first president of Cornell University, saw his task in confronting his readers with the European past in order to help them "to understand our own time and its problems in the light of history."[15] Both historians attempted rather clumsily—and Draper much more uncritically than White—to underline the necessity of cultural progress.

Critical historiography and the attempt to preserve traditional ideals were first combined in the works of Henry Charles Lea. Much as his colleagues in the scientific school, Lea studied the history of the institutions of Western civilization, specializing in the history of the European churches. His most important works, which brought him international fame and the presidency of the American Historical Association (1903), included the *History of the Inquisition in the Middle Ages* (1888) and *History of the Inquisition in Spain* (1906–1907). In contrast to many of his contemporaries, however, he understood his task as a historian to be the critical presentation of facts, which, as he believed, spoke for themselves, and not the celebration of American and European cultural unity. Lea was especially interested in the destructive spiritual powers of certain medieval lines of religious thought that had ultimately taken control of the church and, in the process, had become obstacles to human progress. For the medievalist Lea, "human progress" meant "the liberty of conscience, tolerance, and democracy." He saw the honorable task of the American nation as anchored in the preservation of these ideals, in order to thwart the recurrence of European misfortunes in the United States.[16] Although other historians among Lea's contemporaries were concerned with issues of European church history, in particular various consequences of the Reformation, the diaspora of Protestant movements, or spiritual prosopographies (such as Henry M. Baird's *History of the Rise of the Huguenots of France* [1879], Samuel M. Jackson's *Huldreich Zwingli* [1900], and Williston Walker's *John Calvin, the Organizer of Reformed Protestantism, 1509–1564* [1906][17]), none of them approached the scholarly level of Lea's works.

Around the turn of the century, American historiography of Europe began to move in a new direction, one that established itself in the "Imperial School" and that was first reflected in the famous trilogy of Admiral Alfred R. Mahan on *The Influence of Sea Power upon History, 1660–1783*.[18] The change in theme was particularly notable: for the first time in the course of the nineteenth century an American author dedicated himself to a hitherto unexplored area of the European past, thus abandoning the traditional areas of scholarly interest within European history, such as the history of institutions, the church, or devotional literature. His main thesis was power as the moving force of history, power that Mahan saw as equally embodied in America and Europe. Both continents had fused into an ideological and political unit, as equal partners in a transatlantic common destiny, and had simultaneously developed as globally dominant powers capable of transforming history. It is probably no accident that the rise of historical interest in the so-called Anglo-American imperial tradition coincided with the imperial expansion of the United States, and that this interest found its expression in the writings of the "colonial historians"—Charles M. Andrews, Herbert Lewis Osgood, and George Louis Beer.

Around the beginning of the twentieth century, almost paralleling the Imperial School, a circle of young scholars formed around the Columbia historian James Harvey Robinson (*The New History,* 1912), which at various times included Charles A. Beard, Carl Lotus Becker, James T. Shotwell, Carlton Hayes, and Lynn Thorndike. This historical movement was also interested in reaching a new understanding of the history of the Old World, one that transcended the hitherto depicted humanistic tradition of mutual cultural heritage.[19] In fact, the premises of "New History" initiated a new period in the American interpretation of history:

History is a continuous process; its chief goal is to learn from the past in order to contribute not only to the understanding but to the improvement of the present. The historian must encompass all the varied interests and activities of man; he must try to understand conditions and institutions, and not simply reproduce the facts.[20]

American experts on Europe would henceforth develop a sense of the "common contemporary connexions and destinies" that had already been demonstrated by the experiences of the First World War. More books on Atlantic foreign policy and diplomacy appeared between 1917 and 1930 than at any time before, a fact that offered proof of the increasing global role of the United States in world history.[21] The controversy between the revisionist and antirevisionist interpretations of the origins of the First World War and American intervention in it cannot go unmentioned in this context. The most prominent representative of the revisionists, Harry Elmer Barnes, met with considerable approval, especially among the Germans.[22]

Along with the great expansion of research in American historical writing on Europe in the fields of diplomatic, economic, and social history, and in the discussion of problems of nationalism and imperialism, the interest in the study of medieval history not only remained constant during the 1920s, but, with works such as Henry Osborn Taylor's *Medieval Mind* (1911), Charles Homer Haskins's *Renaissance of the Twelfth Century* (1927), or Henry Adams's *Mont-Saint Michel and Chartres* (1913), actually reached its apex.[23] The contributions of the Americans George Sarton and Lynn Thorndike were particularly important for the research of the Middle Ages in their attack on Burckhardt's conception of the Renaissance. As true adherents of the idea of linear scientific progress, they saw in the Renaissance not the reawakening of the intellectual powers of humankind, but rather a pause between the Middle Ages and the Enlightenment, indeed, a moment of regression.[24] That these theses produced a revolt within the historical guilds of both the Old and New World is self-evident, since the majority of American medievalists continued to cite the ideas of European and American "cultural unity" and repeatedly spoke with pride of the common intellectual heritage of Western civilization, which, as Charles Homer Haskins put it in 1923, did not belong to the Europeans alone: "Whether we look at Europe genetically as the source of our civilization, or pragmatically as a large part of the world in which we live, we cannot ignore the vital connections between Europe and America, their histories are ultimately but one."[25]

In the interwar years, especially during the time of Hitler, American historiography received new impetus from the emigration of primarily Jewish European scholars to the United States.[26] In particular, experiences with national socialism and the Second World War reinforced the Atlantic perception of the Americans, who no longer experienced the common Western destiny as a gradually developed historical configuration, but as a recently concluded cohesion of the Free World against the phenomenon of totalitarianism. The degree to which the emigré scholars actually influenced the development of American scholarly work on Europe is, of course, hard to determine exactly. Certainly, however, the numerous articles and books of the American representatives of "Atlantic history" (Carl Becker, Louis Gottschalk, and Crane Brinton) as well as their European representatives (Fritz Stern, Gordon A. Craig, Hajo Holborn, and Henry Kissinger) helped to bring the transatlantic political and intellectual cosmos closer together. In fact, the European "sister continent" remained the main focus of American research until the end of the 1960s, when the factor of wartime and postwar emigration still played an important role in American society. Of course, the new constellations of political power and the historical changes after the Second World War also broadened the perspectives and horizons of American historians to include Asia and Africa. It is still too early to appreciate fully what effects the repeated political and economic strains that have plagued U.S.-European relations since the 1970s may have on American historiography.[27]

## HISTORY AS PROVIDENCE: "A CITY ON A HILL"

The beginning of American history was dominated by a Christian world outlook: specifically, Calvinism, which penetrated all expressions of life. With no serious contemporary historiography in the first half of American history, that is, from the colonial period until independence in 1776, Americans have been unable to develop a sense of history during this period and have relied on an episodic mythology.[28] The Puritan fragments of the Pilgrim Fathers, which were based primarily on religious and moral messages, must be understood as a substitute for a historical conception and summary of this period. The roots of American history and the American idea of progress cannot, however, be understood without studying the Puritan fragments.

Calvinism, which in its American form is called Puritanism, constitutes the starting point of the development of American history, culture, and government as an experiment in the practical and political realization of religious faith. It ultimately became the vehicle of a religious conviction of the providential progressivist mission of the New World of America. The first Puritan settlers were drawn to New England by the spiritual and moral goal of religious freedom and the belief that they had been elected by God to carry out this historical mission. To realize this pious goal in the practical world, they created the authoritarian theocracy of Massachusetts.[29]

John Winthrop, the later governor of the Massachusetts Bay Colony, had already formulated the Puritan ideology of a religiopolitical community during the crossing to the Promised Land in 1620: "The work we have in hand, it is by a mutuall consent through a special overruleing providence . . . to seeke out a place of Cohabitation and Consorteshipp under a due forme of Government both civill and ecclesiasticall."[30] Indeed, the political goal was subordinated to the religious one at least initially: "To improve our lives to do more service to the Lord . . . that ourselves and posterity may be the better preserved from the common corruptions of this evil world to serve the Lord and work out our Salvation under the power and purity of his holy ordinances."[31]

After all, these ardent Calvinists had fled from England, turning their backs on the Old World and its feudal monarchical social structure. In America they sought the New Jerusalem of humankind, the realization of a Christian community (covenant) supported by God's plan of salvation in an Old Testament sense, aided by God's leadership and providence for a Chosen People. The Englishness of their origins was, in newly established New England, unmistakable. Their self-confidence corresponded to the Protestant English missionary zeal exemplified by the great poet John Milton: "Let not England forget her precedence of teaching nations how to live."[32] It was above all this practical and moral tone that distinguished the Anglo-Saxon national consciousness from other national manifestations of missionary zeal. As a result, it was confronted with the ideas of democratic, parliamentary, and constitutional political and social theories much earlier than continental Europe was.[33] Only against this background can the Calvinistic ethos be understood correctly. It must be noted, however, that the first demonstration of American identity did not testify to democracy and political freedom, but rather to hard living conditions and divinely willed missionary tasks, as Harriet Beecher Stowe portrayed in her work *Oldtown Folks* (1869): "The underlying foundation of life . . . in New England, was one of profound, unutterable, and therefore unuttered melancholy, which regarded human existence itself as a ghastly risk, and, in the case of the vast majority of human beings, an inconceivable misfortune."[34] Jonathan Edwards's description of the new situation of fate in New England also attested to the Puritan belief in human impotence:

Natural men are held in the hand of God, over the pit of hell. . . . The devil is waiting for them, hell is gaping for them, the flames gather and flash about them, and would fain lay hold on them, and swallow them up; the fire pent up in their own hearts is struggling to break out. . . . You have nothing to stand upon, nor any thing to take hold of; there is nothing between you and hell but the air.[35]

Initially, however, only the Congregational Church of New England was democratically structured. This occurred not because the Puritans valued the forms of democracy but because their leaders, John Cotton and Thomas Hooker, had insisted on modeling the first churches of Boston and Hartford after the first churches of Corinth and Philippi. Cotton and Hooker knew little about these churches, owing to the sparseness of apostolic and evangelical descriptions. The religious factor stood indisputably in the foreground during the establishment of the New England colonies and placed the Puritans in the larger context of God's plan of salvation, the renewal of the church, and ultimately that of humankind as well.[36] The consciousness of membership in the elect (as Increase Mather said, "without doubt, the Lord Jesus hath a peculiar respect unto this place, and for this people"[37]), the belief of a mission, indeed, of the duty to provide an example for other people and nations, corresponded to the conviction that one had been set above others by God—"For wee must Consider that wee shall be as a Citty upon a Hill, the eies of all people are upon us."[38]

From the beginning, American Puritanism had to confront two great tasks. First, it was crucial to realize a Christian community according to the Protestant, Calvinist self-understanding of the rigorous unity of belief and politics (for this was the ultimate motive for their emigration from Europe). In addition, it had to be proven that their religious undertaking would be accorded a unique place in God's providence analogous to that of Judeo-biblical history and would ultimately serve as a paragon and ephocal phenomenon for all humankind. As Jonathan Edwards wrote, "The most glorious renovation of the world shall originate from the new continent. . . . The latter day glory, is probably to begin in America."[39] It is in this sense that Puritan writings are to be understood as the single source of historiography of that time, which pursued the goal of tracing *The History of New England,* or *Wonder-Working Providence of Sions Saviour* (Edward Johnson, 1654) in the wilderness of the New World and ensuring its promulgation among their contemporaries as well as for posterity.[40] Thus, Johnson wrote: "Know this is the place where the Lord will create a new Heaven, and a new Earth in new Churches, and a new Commonwealth together."[41]

The work by the Boston theologian Cotton Mather entitled *Magnalia Christi Americana* (1702) described the miracles of Christ in America with conscious reference to the history of Christian civilization and its effects on the American present (which was lauded as far more advanced than the rest of the world in the fulfillment of the Godly plan of salvation). The work must also be understood as a review of contemporary history.[42] Remarkably, Mather's ideas contain many reflections on the classical period, which contributed to his belief that he was the Virgil of the New World and to the expectation, shared by many of his contemporaries, of a New Golden Age in New England—"The God of Heaven had carried a nation into a wilderness upon the designs of a glorious reformation." He supported his theses with quotations from the Roman poet and compared the crossing of the *Mayflower* to the founding of Rome and the flight of Aeneas from Troy. Much as Virgil began his *Aeneid* with "arma virumque cano,"

Mather's own book begins with sentences such as, "In short, the First Age was the Golden Age: To return unto That, will make a Man a Protestant, and I may add, a Puritan."[43] This long-term development of Puritan messianic ideology of progressivism was reflected several years later in Jonathan Edwards's important writing *Thoughts Concerning the Present Revival of Religion in New England,* in which American contemporary history was interpreted as the fulfillment of the biblical promises of the prophets. Edwards was convinced that America had taken on the sacred legacy of Israel, the Orient, and finally Europe, that it was America's task to develop this legacy anew and transmit it for Europe and the rest of the world, that the course of events in the spiritual as well as the worldly realm had turned away from the Old to the New World, that God's providence would once again turn the earth back into Paradise in a development evolving from the wilderness of America, that the sun of the new heaven and the new earth would thus rise in the West.[44]

The Christian idea of "providential history," which had penetrated the Greek and Roman philosophy of cyclical progress and the decline of empires with Augustine's chiliastic world outlook of the *Civitas Dei,* now appeared to the Puritans to be hastening toward its completion in America. The imperial, cultural, and spiritual mandate as well as the messianic beliefs of Western civilization appeared to have been propelled from the Orient to Rome, the Middle Ages to modern times, and ultimately to the New World. As Winthrop believed, God had reserved America for those faithful believers who had been elected and called "to save out of this generall callamitie," as he had once rescued Noah by providing the ark.[45] "New England," as Arthur Schlesinger wrote in 1977 on the occasion of the American bicentennial, was "certainly a part, perhaps the climax of redemptive history; America was divine prophecy fulfilled."[46] Reverend Timothy Dwight, Jonathan Edwards' grandson, called the Americans "this chosen race."[47] Finally, the idea of an elect nation (Sacvan Bercovitch) or redeemer nation (Ernest Lee Tuveson) had simultaneously given birth to an American national destiny (Schlesinger), which did not conceive of itself in the Puritan missionary zeal but rather in its later, secularized form as the liberal-democratic guiding image for the progress of humankind.[48] Not only has this motif of a sense of mission permeated American history from the landing of the *Mayflower* in New England (1620) to the landing of the Marines in Grenada (1983), but it may also be viewed as an intrinsic element of the American idea of progress.

As inevitable as such associations as intolerant messianism, martial readiness for sacrifice, doctrinaire bigotry, or clerical oligarchy might seem upon first exposure to the rigorous religious culture of the New England Puritans, associations that reveal the ambivalence or indeed the apparent contradictions of *Puritanism and Democracy* (Ralph Barton Perry, 1944), Puritan receptiveness toward democratic ideas, which made possible the secularization of the Puritan missionary zeal into a transnational democratic missionary idea, cannot be overlooked despite the orthodox theocracy of New England.[49] The transition from the American *saeculum theologicum* to the *saeculum politicum* (Vernon Louis Parrington), from the biblical justification of the religious salvational task in the seventeenth century to the rational, optimistic, and natural justification of democracy and its secular task in the eighteenth century, took place most clearly in the work *Vindication of the Government of New England Churches* (1717), by the preacher and Harvard graduate John Wise. It was based on a theory of natural law and natural freedom, the democratic form of government, and the natural equality of human beings. "The End of all good Government is to Cultivate Humanity, and Promote the happiness of all, and the good of every Man in all his Rights, his Life, Liberty, Estate, Honor, etc., without injury or abuse done to any."[50] Wise's phrase anticipated the famous Jeffersonian version of the American slogan of independence and democracy "life, liberty, and the pursuit of happiness." This secularized use of the Puritan idea of the state reflected the electness of American "exceptionalism," preserving its meaning without basing it on divine providence, but rather on the unique effects of reason:

For if we should make a new Survey of the Constitution before named under the brightest light of Nature, there is no greater Example of natural Wisdom in any settlement on Earth; for the present and future security of Humane Beings in all that is most Valuable and Grand, than in this.[51]

Puritan and democratic thought had already been combined in a similar way by the Connecticut preacher Thomas Hooker, one of the drafters of the "Fundamental Orders of Connecticut" (1639). This document turned away from the Massachusetts theocracy and approved a quasidemocratic order of self-administration that would no longer form the community according to the model of the church, but rather would make participation in political life independent of certain religious commitments. Despite its various dogmatic regulations, Hooker's political thought proved that Puritanism contained not only the roots of American ideas of mission and providence, but also elements of liberal democratic thought, indeed, "the combination of political emancipation and membership to a religious elect" (Karl Dietrich Bracher). Hooker's speech before the legislative convention in Hartford on May 31, 1638, which ended with the famous phrase "because the foundation of authority is laid firstly, in the free consent of the people," was characterized by the English historian G. P. Gooch as the first written constitution of modern democracy. It interpreted the idea of the covenant with God as a contract between free individuals, referring to the theory of popular sovereignty and the limitation and checks on political authority and power.[52]

Roger Williams, the famous liberal Calvinist, political preacher, and critic of theocratic authoritarianism continued this process of the secularization of the Puritan missionary zeal. He was expelled from Massachusetts because of his democratic, tolerant, and antiauthoritarian beliefs and fled to Rhode Island, where he founded "Providence." There he established a liberal Christian "think-tank," a "laboratory for a democratic future" (Clinton Rossiter), in which principles such as tolerance and democracy, equality and freedom, individualism and pragmatism were fused into an early American self-awareness and concept of progress.[53] The largely democratically self-administered colony of Rhode Island became the first American community to achieve the principle of the separation of church and state ("no bishop, no king"), and with it the unlimited freedom of belief. Moreover, Williams's philosophy of the sober experience and daily practice of community life asserted itself against the traditional Puritan theocracy. Nonetheless, his 1644 pamphlet entitled *The Bloody Tenents* did not challenge the idea of electness, or providence, and belief in a mission, the conviction of an inseparable connection of political and religious thought, or the idea of popular sovereignty and of a system of government based on free consent as the will, command, and order of God.[54]

For the Americans, with their love of experimentation, the liberal and Puritan city of Providence in Rhode Island, to which John Locke also paid tribute, was the embodiment par excellence of their optimistic belief in the future. It simultaneously prepared the ground for the secularization of the New England missionary zeal and the triumph of humanistic, progressivist deism, and rationalism in the eighteenth century.[55] But the development of democratic thought in America would remain closely bound to the idea of religious mission: "religion is an important, perhaps an indispensable clue to what America is like" (William Lee Miller). It was this bond that lent to the American concept of democracy its universal progressivist and missionary quality, which was so clearly divergent from the European concepts of democracy.[56]

All the elements of enlightened rationalism in the first decades of the eighteenth century provoked theological as well ideological tensions within the American churches. As a result, orthodox reaction and a new mood of authoritarian religious momentum set in. Out of these reactionary elements emerged in the 1740s and 1750s the so-called Great Awakening, a revivalist and charismatic movement triggered by the enthusiastic traveling priest George Whitefield. It temporarily swept the colonies, but the process of secularization and the ideas of the Enlightenment could no longer be stalled.[57]

Unlike Europe, North America and its history emerged from a voluntary act on the part of religious fanatics and Calvinists hungry for freedom. The Puritan sense of history had always been a religious conviction that American history was "providential and redemptive." American history as divine providence, redemption, and example ("a Citty upon a Hill"), the promising salvation of humankind, these were the catchwords of the New England Puritans. America became the symbol of a "geopolitical specification of the millennium," of an "identification of the New Jerusalem with a particular place and people" (Arthur Schlesinger).[58] As Bercovitch wrote, "What in England, Holland, Germany, and Geneva was an a priori antithesis [between the saints and the state] became in America the twin pillars of a unique federal eschatology."[59]

Even the basic American values of today—the idea of democracy and freedom, of equality and individual human dignity, of the sense of universal mission, and of the moral responsibility of the individual, all of which combined to form the American ideology of progress—were anticipated by Puritan thought and work. The American success ethos, which later inspired Max Weber to write his study *The Protestant Ethic and the Spirit of Capitalism*, was also born under the aegis of the Puritans. This ethos not only accepted the concept of the accumulation of wealth and material happiness, but even regarded it as a duty to the commonweal, according to the Calvinist motto "God helps those who help themselves."[60] Institutions of higher education also owed their emergence and continued existence to the initiatives of the churches, particularly to the Puritans of Massachusetts, who founded Harvard College in Cambridge as early as 1636. This was followed by the founding of William and Mary College in Williamsburg in 1693, Yale College in New Haven in 1701, and, around the middle of the eighteenth century, Princeton, Brown, Rutgers, and Dartmouth, all of which ultimately helped to break the ground for the secularization of Puritan ideology and the evolution of an American Enlightenment.[61] The Puritan Age had long since enabled history and progress, science and freedom to fuse into the *Providentia Americana* (Karl Dietrich Bracher).

## HISTORY AS EXPERIMENT: "LIFE, LIBERTY, AND THE PURSUIT OF HAPPINESS"

Whereas the writings of the Puritans were the first historical fragments of American thought, it was the Declaration of Independence of 1776 that first created the political and constitutional preconditions for the formation of the American Republic and the actual development of American history. Unlike any of the other great modern revolutions, the American Revolution marked the birth of a nation. A new period in the history of the American people commenced with the Revolution; indeed, it marked the real beginning of the Americans' national identity. Thus, it inevitably became an existential point of reference, a progressive ideology for the historical self-understanding of the United States of America.[62]

The earlier Puritan missionary zeal was now transformed into a secularized idealism that understood itself to be enlightened rational progress for humankind. The Founding Fathers of the North American republic participated in an essential way in this revolutionary process of enlightenment, not only as political theoreticians, but indeed as *uomini universali*. As scholars and intellectuals, as politicians and theorists of constitutional law, their influence on the American historical consciousness was profound. Their historical view of the world and their pragmatic national interpretation of progress were determined by the belief that the future of freedom and worldwide democracy depended on America's unique experience ("that we are acting for all mankind").[63] Their enlightened vision was centered primarily around the social option of an "experimental humanism" (Adrienne Koch), as well as the political claim of a state "workshop of liberty" (James Madison): America would henceforth reveal itself to be the protagonist of Western historical progress.[64]

The origin of this way of thought lay in the Founding Fathers' candid examination of the classical heritage of Greek and Roman historiography as well as in the intellectual achievements of the European Enlightenment, the secularized concept of history as a progressive, linear process. Their knowledge of the classic period was enormous; the American elite of the end of the eighteenth century possessed a fluent command of Greek and Latin. As was noted by the Reverend John Witherspoon, the president of Princeton (1768–94) and the only religious figure to sign the Declaration of Independence, Greek and Latin were not only useful for literary or rhetorical reasons, but were also indispensable "to fit young men for serving their country in public stations."[65] The correspondence of the two American presidents John Adams and Thomas Jefferson contains discourses on Greek metrics, Ciceronian vocabulary, interpretations of Cleanthes, Theocritus, and Theogenes as well as critical remarks on Dionysius, Isocrates, and Hesiod. Jefferson even sent copies of Polybius from Paris to the delegates of the Constitutional Convention (1787) to serve as inspiration.[66]

For Benjamin Franklin (according to Jefferson "the father of American philosophy"), who embodied the cosmopolitan and scholarly spirit of the American Enlightenment, Socrates was the ideal philosopher with whom he identified. The natural wisdom of the Greek scholar symbolized for Franklin the virtue of human happiness. Indeed, wisdom seemed to him a virtual precondition for a happy life. Thus, he converted the stoic and epicurean element of socratic wisdom ("tranquility, modesty, temperance, order, social intercourse, sleep, eating and drinking, and a host of other activities and qualities") into a personal philosophical wisdom with the slogan, "to be happy even in Paradise requires a happy disposition."[67] On the other hand, the following humorous remark has also been attributed to Franklin, who was a connoisseur of the Romans as well: "It is better to bring back from Italian travel a receipt for Parmesan cheese than copies of ancient historical inscriptions."[68]

Even Thomas Paine, the radical Anglo-American representative of rationalist enlightenment, compared America to Greece: "What Athens was in miniature, America will be in magnitude. The one was the wonder of the ancient world; the other is becoming the admiration, the model of the present" (*The Rights of Man*, Part II, Chapter 3, 1792). The Founding Fathers were beguiled by classical thought. Their great aim to create a new republic that would serve as a source of hope for humankind led them inevitably back to the ideals of Athens and Rome, to the first and noblest forms of expression of free people desirous of self-government. "The Roman republic," wrote Alexander Hamilton in *The*

*Federalist Papers,* who not only admired Caesar as the most brilliant statesman of the Roman world but also considered himself a Caesarian, "attained to the pinnacle of human greatness."[69] The degree to which the first generation of the American republic had internalized this conviction was also demonstrated by their neoclassical buildings and toga-clad statues, the designation of the legislature as the "Senate," and Hamilton's signature of his pamphlets with "Publius." "One is hagridden," complained Edmund Trowbridge Dana in 1805, "with nothing but the classicks, the classicks the classicks!"[70] (As a result of this heretical statement, Dana failed his Harvard exams, and only after eighty years had passed was he finally awarded his AB degree.)

In all their admiration of the ancient cosmos, and despite Hamilton and Adams's differences with Jefferson and Madison over Greek and Roman political ideology, the first American statesmen were in agreement about the fragility of individual and collective aspirations, the ambivalence of human nature. On the trail of classical historiography, of the historical awareness of a Thucydides, Polybius, Plutarch or Cicero, Sallust or Tacitus, they searched for ways to escape the fate of the Greek polis and the decline of the Roman Empire.[71] As pragmatic realists, they understood how to interpret the historical lessons of ancient thought; namely, that it was not "the inevitability of progress," but rather "the perishability of republics, the subversion of virtue by power and luxury, the transience of glory, the mutability of human affairs" that shaped the basic historical and political patterns of human societies. In contrast to conventional conceptions, J.G.A. Pocock observed that this line of American thought was not only indebted to John Locke, but had also been strongly influenced by the "Machiavellian moment," the *Discorsi* from Harrington to Montesquieu and Hobbes. During the period of the political and constitutional establishment of America, the "Machiavellian moment," writes Pocock, meant nothing other than the realization that a republic "is seen as confronting its own temporal finitude, as attempting to remain morally and politically stable in a stream of irrational events conceived as essentially destructive of all systems of secular stability." The concept of the "mortality of states," "the unceasing contest between corruption and virtue," proved to be a vital element for the "sensibility of Philadelphia in 1787."[72]

Alexander Hamilton had the fewest illusions about the process of American history:

Have we not already seen enough of the fallacy and extravagance of those idle theories which have amused us with promises of an exemption from the imperfections, the weaknesses, and the evils incident to society in every shape? Is it not time to awake from the deceitful dream of a golden age and to adopt as a practical maxim for the direction of our political conduct that we, as well as the other inhabitants of the globe, are yet remote from the happy empire of perfect wisdom and perfect virtue?[73]

The Founding Fathers obtained their familiarity with the political examples of Athens and Rome and their conviction of the immutability of human nature

("there is a human nature and that . . . human nature is the same in all men"—
Thomas Jefferson) primarily from the works of Tacitus and Polybius.[74] Jefferson,
whom John Dewey considered "the first modern to state in human terms the
principles of democracy," viewed Tacitus as "the first writer of the world without
a single exception. His book is a compound of history and morality of which
we have no other example." "To live without having a Cicero and a Tacitus at
hand," said John Quincy Adams two decades later, "seems to me as if it was
a privation of one of my limbs." Adams's cousin, William Smith Shaw, later
summarized Tacitus's work as follows: "The writings of Tacitus display the
weakness of a falling empire and the morals of a degenerate age. . . . They form
the subject of deep meditation for all statesmen who wish to raise their country
to glory; to continue it in power, or preserve it from ruin."[75]

The writings of Polybius also had significance for the creation of America—
"for delineating the cycle of birth, growth, and decay that constituted the destiny
of states; and for sketching the mixed constitution with balanced powers that the
founding fathers seized as a glimpse at remedy."[76] Drawing on these classical
historical principles, the fathers of the Constitution attempted to define their own
historical standpoint: "History was valued in a special way as the laboratory
where human relations had been tried and had partially failed or partially succeeded . . . "[77] They sought to imbue American history with an optimistic outlook
propounding the principles of "life, liberty, and the pursuit of happiness." Of
course, from the beginning they were conscious of "the improbability of their
undertaking" to create as liberal and free a form of a presidential republic as
possible, even though the geographic and demographic advantages of their country made it much more promising than the more humble experiments of earlier
times. Benjamin Franklin ascribed the historical unavoidability of America's
independence from England to such material factors as the increase of population
and unclaimed lands, and not to divine intervention or providence. Yet these
advantages could not, as Franklin suspected, "be counted on to prevail against
history and human nature."[78]

In the ratifying convention of New York, Hamilton added: "The tendency of
things will be to depart from the republican standard. This is the real disposition
of human nature." In 1802, when the American Constitution was fifteen years
old, Hamilton called it "a frail and worthless fabric." "Every republic at all
times," he wrote, "has its Catilines and its Caesars. . . . If we have an embryo-
Caesar in the United States, 'tis Burr."[79] (Aaron Burr, vice-president under
Jefferson, was Hamilton's arch enemy.) Jefferson and John Adams were convinced that Hamilton himself was the Caesarian. Abigail Adams, indignant over
Hamilton's attempts to have himself appointed commander-in-chief of the army
in 1798, wrote, "That man would in my mind become a second Buonaparty if
he was possessed of equal power."[80] But even Hamilton's less pessimistic rivals
did not always possess great optimism about the future of the American republic.
"They looked upon the new federal organization," Woodrow Wilson remarked
later, "as an experiment, and thought it likely it might not last."[81] "Commerce,

luxury, and avarice have destroyed every republican government,'' John Adams wrote Benjamin Rush in 1808. ''We mortals cannot work miracles; we struggle in vain against the constitution and course of nature.''[82] ''I tremble for my country when I reflect that God is just,''[83] was Jefferson's reaction in the 1780s and 1790s to the problems of slavery and ''monarchist'' tendencies, which were reflected in 1798 in the Alien and Sedition Acts before disappearing again shortly thereafter. (These acts were passed by the Federalist President John Adams for the arrest and imprisonment of oppositional government critics and the expulsion of undesired foreigners without trial. When Jefferson was elected president in 1800, he released all the prisoners.)

Yet, despite all of the rational pessimism and critical sense of history among the first American politicians—''these are the times that try men's souls'' (Thomas Paine, *The American Crisis,* 1776)[84]—by no means did they allow the study of classical historiography on political progress and ideological decline of the Athenian and Roman republics, the premises of the constancy of human nature, or the pragmatic political teachings of the first modern political theorist, Machiavelli, to deteriorate into thoughts of decadence and crisis *à l'europeéne*. On the contrary, strengthened by the historical perception and knowledge of human, societal, and political existence, Franklin and Washington, Jefferson and Madison all entertained an enlightened belief in the American potential to achieve freedom and democracy, equality and self-determination, human rights and self-fulfillment more freely and unprejudiced in the New World than in Europe. With the pragmatic estimation of human limits and possibilities, there developed in the Founding Fathers' thought a historical optimism that was manifested as a bold liberal experiment and model of an ideal democracy for universal, sociopolitical, ethical, economic, and scientific human progress.

George Washington, in his first inaugural speech, delineated the forthcoming tasks: ''The preservation of the sacred fire of liberty and the destiny of the republican model of government are justly considered, perhaps as *deeply,* as *finally,* staked on the experiment intrusted to the hands of the American people.''[85] Toward the end of his life, James Madison described America's role in world history as a free system of government so congenial with reason, with common sense, and with a universal feeling that it must produce approbation and a desire of imitation, as avenues may be found for truth to the knowledge of nations. The country, if it did justice to itself, would be the workshop of liberty to the civilized world and would do more than any other for the uncivilized.[86]

If one compares Madison's cosmopolitan conception of a ''workshop of liberty'' with Jeffersonian philosophical idealism of the ''pursuit of happiness'' based on Locke's *Essay Concerning Human Understanding,* then both approaches can be seen as complementary elements of an American humanist framework. First, the pursuit of happiness encompasses the hard work and discipline of free individuals; and second, the instruments of freedom make possible the pursuit of happiness in a society. These are the proper preconditions of happiness, which is considered a virtue. In the controversy surrounding the correct definition of the pursuit of happiness, Adrienne Koch notes that Jefferson did not understand it to be the accumulation of material goods, but interpreted it in a purely Aristotelian sense, "implying the happiness appropriate to the human condition, substantial happiness that is achieved by the mature development of man's fullest potentialities."[87] Thus, the universally applicable core of the Declaration of Independence written by Jefferson, "life, liberty, and the pursuit of happiness," can be interpreted as the enlightened American articulation of the idea of progress, " . . . [the] expressed faith in progress—agreed that progress ultimately meant the approximation of human happiness," and as the optimistic American historical motif, as "a rationalist prescription for history."[88] As David W. Marcell wrote: "Happiness . . . was given a rationalistic definition; it was not simply physical pleasure or psychic euphoria. Happiness was the rational perception of the fitness of the human condition within the order of nature."[89] Happiness was, in the American history of ideas of the eighteenth century in general and the historical thought of the Founding Fathers in particular, the main precondition of progress.

The combination of happiness and progress was simultaneously influenced by the new historical components of science and technology. The scientific achievements and modern knowledge ("the new science"), in particular the works of Descartes, Bacon, and Newton, inspired the intellectual thought of the American philosophers, politicians, scholars, and journalists of the rationalist phase (1750–1815), whose ranks included Benjamin Franklin, Thomas Jefferson, James Madison, John Adams, George Washington, Thomas Paine, Joel Barlow, Timothy Dwight, Joseph Priestly, Philip Freneau, Benjamin Rush, James Wilson, Benjamin Barton, and Charles Willson Peale.[90] The European Enlightenment's definition of history as a progressive linear process, which through the new scientific and technological discoveries had made possible the control of nature and the improvement of social, political, and economic conditions, exerted a lasting influence on America.[91] This is corroborated by the historian R. E. Delmage (*The American Idea of Progress,* 1947)—"the dominant note in American thought between 1750 and 1800 was that of progress"[92]—or by his predecessor Joel Barlow in a book entitled *The Columbiad* (1807), which summarized the American credo from Columbus's discovery of America up to the beginning of the nineteenth century as "history's progressive march toward perfection." Madison's formula for progress of a "workshop of liberty" was indebted to the new ideology of science and technology. The "workshop" was understood as a symbol of technology, and technology was devised to lighten humankind's innumerable burdens. In the long run, technology would flourish most in a society based on free inquiry, a society that would zealously guard the intellectual freedom of its thinkers and scientists.[93]

In the same way, Franklin, Jefferson, and Madison expressed their interest, as politicians and as scientists, in the promotion of scientific and technological research. They were interested "not merely for its intellectual aspects, nor even for its material benefits," according to Don Price, "but also for the liberating effects it would have on the politics of all nations.''[94] Only ''through the control of machines'' would ''liberty'' as well as a ''bettering of man's estate'' (Adrienne Koch) be provided. They wanted to create the preconditions for a new society, *Novus Ordo Saeculorum,* consisting of ''reasonable men,'' ''reasonable actions,'' and ''reasonable compromises.'' In this sense, the Founding Fathers understood the American experiment as a scientific experiment as well, ''suffused through and through with the spirit of controlled experimentation.''[95]

Religious belief in the New World was by no means repressed by scientific progress as it was in the Old. On the contrary, there emerged an American symbiosis of rationalism and Christianity, technological progress and moral challenge, that remains uncontested to today. This uniquely American progressivist synthesis has been referred to repeatedly, as is demonstrated by William Paley's *View of the Evidences of Christianity* (1794) or Benjamin Rush's lectures of 1799 with the confusing title ''Three Lectures upon Animal Life.'' In these lectures Rush observed, ''There is an indissoluble union between moral, political, and physical happiness.''[96] This thesis also appeared in later writings:

Franklin, Jefferson, Rush, and Priestly all espoused a rationalistic conception of progress, but, unlike Paine, they found that science and reason did not require them to reject completely their Christian heritage. Rather, Christianity supplied them with a comfortable ethical system whose telic projections could be made entirely harmonious with the methods and conclusions of science.[97]

It was precisely the combination of traditional Christian ethics and modern science that, as Daniel J. Boorstin wrote, enabled the American rationalists of the eighteenth century ''to read in the peculiar conditions of America the Creator's designation of a special role. . . . Had such a vast and fertile continent not been destined for prosperity and for a special example for mankind, there would have been an unthinkable poverty in the Creator.''[98]

Of course—despite all the self-sufficiency and emancipation of American thought and the American progressivist idea of European conditions, feudalism, colonialism, and dogmatism—

People could come to and live in the New World legitimately seeking to break with the Old because it was the New World, because it was America. They could come and break restraints, as they saw them, on ideas or on creed, on religion or politics. They could come and perfect institutions they saw as corrupt or decayed or imperfect. . . . And many would come to the New World only to improve themselves in the eyes of the Old. Thus, in reality, Columbus discovered a New World of the mind.[99]

Despite the moral and political conviction of a national and transnational missionary consciousness—paradigmatically expressed in the correspondence of Thomas Jefferson and John Adams—

We are destined to be a barrier against the returns of ignorance and barbarism. Old Europe will have to lean on our shoulders, and to hobble along by our side, under the monkish trammels of priests and kings, as she can. What a colossus shall we be, when the southern continent comes up to our mark! What a stand will it secure as a ralliance for the reason and freedom of the globe![100]

Even with all of these qualifications, it remains a historical fact that the intellectual, political, and economic independence of the American continent, the progressive frame of mind of the American "Emile," and the American gamble at a historical experiment of universal progressive quality—all would have been unthinkable without the intellectual influence of Europe. Without the mixture of classical philosophical wisdom, the advance of human self-knowledge, political ethos, and historical decline, without the scientific and technological revolution of modernity, the encyclopedic knowledge and cosmopolitan thought of the rationalists, pessimists, and enlighteners Niccolò Machiavelli, Thomas Hobbes, David Hume, Edmund Burke, Jean-Jacques Rousseau, John Locke, Adam Smith, Voltaire, Condorcet, and Denis Diderot, and finally without the historical experience of Western tragedy and the achievements of humanist high culture, the American experiment would have been unrealizable.[101]

On the other hand, the singularity of the American experiment and American progressivism lay in its refusal to become a second Europe. Adrienne Koch characterized the "America" experiment by stressing that there is no single idea that correctly portrays the American development; that there is no inevitable "march" to the American history. "We are not part of a wave of the future," she says, "nor are we assured that our 'destiny' will delight us." "What we are and will become is not independent of our united conduct; our history has been and still is the outcome of our own individual efforts." Koch further argues that American history and tradition do present ideas and ideals that may serve as operating models in helping us to realize a great idea—that human beings can make their history so that they will be free to realize their best nature. In this sense, one may select aspects of the American tradition that emphasize the more enduring and the better qualities of American endeavor and that can serve as guidance in the future.[102] The historical experiment of the New World would prove to be the moving force and national identity and consensus of the young republic, for the political ideology of the future and the progress of America.

## HISTORY AS HEROISM: "THE RISING GLORY"

The first historiographers of the American Revolution and national independence distinguished themselves in a crucial way from the political actors and intellectual contemporaries of the early phase of the United States of America. In contrast to the Founding Fathers, whose sense of history had been formed by the study of classical sources, by the credo of rational enlightenment and pragmatic optimism, the historical interpretations of the Revolutionary historians remained regionally confined to the perspectives of a national local patriotism. These writers were interested in the Revolution primarily as a regional, and not a national, phenomenon: its origins, its resonance, its heroes, and its effects, especially in South Carolina, New York, and Massachusetts. They produced such works as David Ramsay's *History of the Revolution of South Carolina* (1785), Jeremy Belknap's *History of New Hampshire* (1784–92, in 3 vols.), or John Sanderson's *Biography of the Signers of the Declaration of Independence* (1820–27, in 9 vols.). Their main concern was documented in a historical conception characterized by the English historian Herbert Butterfield as the *Whig Interpretation of History*, "in which the idea of progress is a central tenet" and the presumed needs and tasks of the present are addressed and complex historical and political events reduced to simple, easily dramatizable moral positions.[103]

As the American historian Richard Hofstadter has attempted to demonstrate, the dominant political loyalties of the various states formed the basis for this regional but rather cosmetic approach. In addition, the growth of critical historical scholarship was inhibited by technical difficulties, the strains of travel, and the inaccessibility of well-equipped libraries or archives. The historians of the time between the Peace of Paris (1783) and the ratification of the Constitution (1787), when documentation and source collections were especially rare, thus had no alternatives but plagiarism, compilation, or naive hagiography. Not even John Marshall and David Ramsay were able to resist the temptation to use large sections of Edmund Burke's reports in Dodsley's "British Annual Register," since all the important materials for the study of American history were located primarily on the other side of the Atlantic in English archives.[104] "The first colonial historians had been . . . [promotional], celebratory, and then perhaps nostalgic or defensive," wrote Hofstadter, "and after 1776 the state historians built upon this legacy a literature touting the revolutionary merits of their own states, commemorating local heroes, and dwelling poignantly on the particular grievances each one had against British policies."[105]

At the beginning of the nineteenth century, in fact, there existed no general history of the United States; there was merely a two-volume chronological summary of events presented in 1805 by Abiel Holmes, the father of Oliver Wendell Holmes. In 1810 Benjamin Trumbull published a general history of America, but it did not go beyond the year 1761. As late as 1839, the first professor of American history at Harvard, Jared Sparks, was forced to recommend the work of the Italian Carlo Botta as a textbook for his lecture on the American Revolution from 1763 to 1783, "all the other historians of the same period being out of print."[106]

At the same time, hagiographic biographies of the outstanding figures of the Revolution appeared, books that not only appealed to patriotic feelings but that also falsified facts or colored the deeds of the heroes in order to convey "the rising glory" of America in all its lustre.[107] George Washington, through his republican virtues and statesman-like qualities (both genuine and self-stylized), offered a particularly ideal heroic type.[108] The Supreme Court Justice John Marshall used the biographical framework of his Washington myth as a pretext for a parallel history of his own time and country from the standpoint of the Federalists—a five-volume compendium of "blunt and garrulous scholastic-ship" (1804–1807).[109] It was Parson Weems, traveling preacher and book sales-man, however, who advanced the Washington myth to the heart of American political folklore. In his biography of Washington, published in 1808, he com-bined true material with fictional anecdotes into a larger-than-life monument of exemplary virtue and morality in the service of the nation.[110] Neither the twelve-volume edition of Sparks's *The Writings of George Washington* (1834–37), nor Ramsay's biography of Washington was entirely free of well-meaning falsifi-cations that served to maintain the glorious image of the American national hero as long and as unscathed as possible.[111]

In general, one can say that certain common tendencies and inclinations emerged among the early nationalist Whig historians toward the harmonization of possible sources of conflict, mythologization of the deeds of historical actors, and moralizing about social conditions. All these concerns were reflected in speeches for Independence Day on the Fourth of July or Washington's birthday on the twenty-second of February.[112] On the other hand, in the 1820s, 1830s, and 1840s historians began to compose the first truly scholarly works about the Revolutionary period. In 1822 Hezekiah Niles published *Principles and Acts of the Revolution in America,* in 1836 Jonathan Elliot published the four-volume *Debates in the Several State Conventions on the Adoption of the Federal Con-stitution,* and in 1837 Peter Force began his nine-volume compendium, *American Archives.* Sparks managed, in turn, to bring out a comprehensive edition on the diplomatic correspondence of the Revolutionary period for research into Amer-ican history.[113] After 1830 there were already two dozen historical organizations, and the individual states began to compile their own document collections, although at this time the most important material on the colonial period was still housed in English archives. That the profession of the historian was to remain a very expensive and exclusive affair for at least another century in America had already been noted by Henry Adams: "History has always been the most aristocratic of all literary pursuits, because it obliges the historian to be rich as well as educated."[114]

American research has only recently begun to deal with the works and views of the early national historians in greater detail.[115] As Erich Angermann has summarized, this early historiography is characterized by four interrelated ele-ments. First, it was not the first-rank political actors who described the pre- and post-Revolution events (Thomas Jefferson and John Adams preferred to confine their historical observations to journals and letters), but participants of a third or fourth remove, such as Jeremy Belknap, William Gordon, David Ramsay, Mercy Otis Warren, as well as Noah Webster and Jedidiah Morse. As indirect participants in political decision-making, these historians were almost completely dependent on the "British Annual Register," since they had no access to primary sources. Second, the Revolution did not play as great a role in the shaping of historical awareness as the corrosive process of confederation, which began soon after independence. As a result, they consciously placed their historiography in the service of national unity, consolidation, and (as Richard Hofstadter pointed out) local patriotic affairs. This is also the background of the Whig interpretation of the American Revolution with its moral evaluation of the British government, and the ideology of America's virtuous uniqueness. Indeed, the young nation's sense of mission, which saw the New World as the avant-garde of freedom in the entire world and which later developed into the idea of manifest destiny stemmed from this notion. Third, this mode of historical portrayal resulted not least from the fear that the American experiment could fail. Appeals to patriotism and the unifying, identity-building impulse of the American Revolution were intended to compensate for all doubts and to produce a historical consensus. The democratic achievements and moral and political values were essentially uncontested. Almost all party conflict centered on discerning the best ways to preserve, expand, and strengthen "the rising glory." These concerns gave rise to the fourth characteristic: the use of biographies to transmit the American ideology via the popularization of heroic deeds. The numerous biographies of Washington serve as the clearest examples of patriotic historiography, which would soon be supplanted in its turn by romantic historiography.[116]

## ROMANTIC HISTORIOGRAPHY: "THE NECESSITY, THE REALITY, AND THE PROMISE OF THE PROGRESS OF THE HUMAN RACE"

Romantic historiography, represented foremost by George Bancroft,[117] developed as a reaction and revolt against rationalism and the Enlightenment. Yet it distinguished itself from patriotic historiography insofar as its plea for the strengthening of an American nationalism, individualism, and humanism was much more articulate, demanding, and scholastically more credible. Although William Hickling Prescott, John Lothrop Motley, Francis Parkman, and Richard Hildreth can all be characterized as historians of America's Romantic phase, the most influential and important Romantic historiographer of the democratic ideals and their realization in the United States (God's chosen providence) was indisputably George Bancroft.[118] His monumental ten-volume work, *The History of the United States of America from the Discovery of the Continent*, which he began in 1834 and which because of his political and diplomatic career he did not finish until 1874, revealed his view of history as an "organic process culminating in a rebirth of human opportunity in America."[119] Using his knowledge of sources, he composed with democratic passion, theological insight into God's plan of salvation, and enthusiastic nationalism an image of American history up to the ratification of the Constitution. In accordance with Whig tradition, this image emphasized the progress of freedom under the leadership of God and allowed no doubt as to the moral superiority of the Americans.[120]

Bancroft believed the task of the historian was similar to that of the philosopher, namely, the vivid dramatization of the past, a treatment that would enable people to better understand their destiny. "The unifying principle was progress ordained and planned by God," wrote Hofstadter of Bancroft's sense of history, which was filled by the belief that

the advance of liberty, justice, and humanity, all of which were particularly exemplified in American history, where providential guidance had brought together a singularly fit people and fit institutions. The genius of the American people was particularly adapted to liberty, their political order to its advance. American history could be seen as a kind of consummation of all history; Bancroft was supremely confident of the superiority of the United States to other countries, and in particular of the unvarying rightness of the American side in all the issues of the Revolution.[121]

It was Bancroft's spirit, shaped by the Old Testament, German idealism, and contemporary political events, specifically the personage of Andrew Jackson, that made him such an enigmatic historian. It was no accident that numerous later writings addressed themselves to Bancroft's political and intellectual life, his political role during Jackson's presidency, his study at Harvard and Göttingen, or his diplomatic missions in London and Bismarck's Germany.[122] This rich mixture of scholarship, politics, and diplomacy sharpened his historical and political powers of judgment and, along with the experience of the Civil War, led the not uncritical admirer of Andrew Jackson—" . . . he would endorse Jackson and cry out for democracy and egalitarianism, but was quickly disgusted with the coarseness of Jackson's levees where he saw 'all the refuse that Washington could turn forth from its workshops and stables' "[123]—from a belief in Jeffersonian democracy to a more conservative assessment of the protective and stabilizing power of American life. His opalescent character, "a tough Yankee man, of many worthy qualities more tough than musical," as Carlyle once described him to Emerson, enabled Bancroft to feel just as comfortable among English diplomats in London, the Junkers of Berlin, or at his summer house in Newport, to which only the most privileged American intellectuals had access. "I like to watch the shouts of the multitude," he wrote in his younger years, "but had rather not to scream with it."[124] "He wrote of American institutions like a visionary," described Hofstadter, "but played the game of the party spoilsmen like a professional. He attacked slavery with eloquence and unquestionable sincerity, but had no difficulty in adjusting himself to the Democratic party of the planters or in supporting the war with Mexico."[125]

Bancroft's biographer, Russell B. Nye, thus came to the conclusion that "beneath his theory lay a substratum of innate conservatism that colored his practice."[126] Bancroft's ideas were quite easy to define: "history taught a lesson, the inevitable movement of human affairs toward the goal of liberty under providential guidance," and was given its form by nineteenth-century Romantic nationalism and a manifest sense of mission.[127] His Romantic nationalist ideology came to the fore most clearly in his essay *The Necessity, the Reality, and the Promise of Progress of the Human Race* (1854):

The course of civilization flows on like a mighty river through a boundless valley, calling to the streams from every side to swell its current, which is always growing wider, and deeper, and clearer, as it rolls along. . . . Since the progress of the race appears to be the great purpose of Providence, it becomes us all to venerate the future. We must be ready to sacrifice ourselves for our successors, as they in turn must live for their posterity.[128]

The metaphor of the river, flowing on "through a boundless valley" and "always growing wider, and deeper, and clearer," reflects paradigmatically the Romantic historical interpretation of progress, which saw the source of democratic energy and republican virtues in the American landscape and nature. The myth of the Garden of Eden, as a symbol of nature and a motif of perfect progress, had also inspired Bancroft in his *History:*

The earth glows with the colors of civilization. . . . The yeoman, living like a good neighbor near the fields he cultivates, glories in the fruitfulness of the valleys, and counts with honest exultation in the flocks and herds that browse in safety on the hills, the thorn has given way to the rosebush; the cultivated vine clambers over the rocks where the brood of serpents used to nestle; while industry smiles at the changes she has wrought, and inhales the bland air which now has health on its wings.[129]

Like the other Romantics of his time, influenced by the German idealists Kant, Fichte, Herder, Lessing, Goethe, and Schiller, the Englishmen Coleridge, Carlyle, Wordsworth, and Shelley, and the French thinkers Lamartine, Cousin, Rousseau, Jouffroy, and Chateaubriand, Bancroft saw in nature an inexhaustible potential for the moral instruction and true knowledge of humankind. American civilization's unique interweaving with nature enabled the Romantics to regard American history as simultaneously progressive and heroic.[130] Scientific research "was widely assumed merely to confirm that progress through organic growth was God's law and plan," as the leading Yale geologist James Dwight Dana attempted to emphasize in 1865: "Science should not be feared. Her progress is upward as well as onward, to clearer and clearer visions of infinite beneficence."[131]

On the other hand, Romantic historiography was not so blind to the economic and scientific vision of the boundless possibilities of humans as not to also emphasize the necessity of building a tolerant and social community as prerequisites for individual self-fulfillment. The ongoing urbanization and industrialization of America since the middle of the nineteenth century had brought about a transformation of sociopolitical relations, so that it had now become very important to preserve a high standard of humanity in order to avoid endangering democracy and progress. This development was not lost on the Romantic reformer Bancroft, as is demonstrated in his prophetic speech given at Williams College in 1835:

The public happiness is the true object of legislation, and can be secured only by the masses of mankind themselves awakening to the knowledge and the care of their own interests. Our free institutions have reversed the false and ignoble distinctions of men, and refusing to gratify the pride of caste, have acknowledged the common mind to be the true material for a commonwealth. The exact measure of the progress of a civilization is the degree in which the intelligence of the common mind has prevailed over wealth and brute force; in other words, the measure of the progress of a civilization is the progress of the people.[132]

George Bancroft had an affinity for social reforms and democratic ideals, with the apotheosis of the Founding Fathers manifesting itself in his works again and again. Moreover, he more than any contemporary personified the American nineteenth-century sense of history. Nonetheless, because of his Romantic conservative ideology of nationalism and progressivism he remained the American "archetype of historical mystification" (Charles A. Beard).[133]

Bancroft's contemporaries evaluated and interpreted the problems of America's industrialization much more skeptically. Francis Parkman, who symbolized the transition from Romantic historiography to the conservative nationalism of the Gilded Age around the end of the century, lamented in 1878:

Now . . . the village has grown into a populous city, with its factories and workshops, its acres of tenement-houses, and thousands and thousands of restless workmen, foreigners for the most part to whom liberty means license and politics means plunder, to whom the public good is nothing and their own most trivial interests everything, who love the country for what they can get out of it, and whose ears are opened to the promptings of every rascally agitator.[134]

Unlike Bancroft and Parkman, and although outwardly indebted to the New England Federalist tradition, Richard Hildreth was a radical and romantic reformer. He was a supporter of temperance, an abolitionist, an opponent of the Whig-supported National Bank, and an anticlericalist, although he was by no means an advocate of the nativists. Hildreth tried vainly to present himself as an intellectual counterfoil and alternative historian to Bancroft by writing a six-volume history of America up to 1821. His unattractive, clumsy style, lacking in eloquence and elegance, combined with a sociocritical slant that viewed social processes primarily from the perspective of economic determinism and the competition of material interests, was not what the American public wanted to read.[135] "Of centennial sermons and Fourth-of-July orations, whether professedly such or in the guise of history, there are more than enough," Hildreth informed his readers in the beginning of his *History*. He continued: "It is due to our fathers and ourselves, it is due to truth and philosophy, to present for once on the historic stage, the founders of our American nation unbedaubed with patriotic rouge, wrapped up in no finespun cloaks of excuses and apology."[136]

Beyond this combative and abusive language, Hildreth also subjected his readers to sharp criticism of Jefferson's alleged opportunism, and portrayed Alexander Hamilton as the hero and advocate of a strong national government in the face of regional or state particularism. But other ideological inconsistencies in his works complicated a more or less one-dimensional politicohistorical portrayal. On the one hand, the powerful influence of nineteenth-century Romanticism and nationalism, and his opposition to slavery, shaped the tone of his books. On the other, his writings contained elements of a utilitarian and materialist philosophy, motifs of proletarian struggle, indeed, of a "Marxist" conception of historical progressivist development. In 1853 he wrote provocatively in his *Theory of Politics:* "The clergy, the nobles, the kings, the burghers have all had their turn. Is there never to be an 'Age of the people'—of the working classes? Is the suggestion too extravagant that . . . the middle of this current century is destined to be that age?"[137] For a Federalist historian of nationalist provenance, this question was rather unusual. The response of his American contemporaries to this dogmatic historical and progressivist ideology was accordingly negative: Hildreth's work remained unread.

## EVOLUTIONARY AND EXPANSIONIST THINKING IN SOCIAL DARWINISM: "SURVIVAL OF THE FITTEST"

In the wake of the frenzied building and continuing development of modern American industrial society after the Civil War, new ideas of nationalism and imperialism came to the fore, inevitably affecting historians of the time. The works of the German-American Hermann von Holst and the influential Columbia law professor John Burgess represent two examples of the intimate relationship between doctrinaire nationalism, moralist abolitionism, expansionist ideologies of racial superiority, and superficial scientific beliefs.[138] Holst, a rigid adherent of Treitschke and Bismarck, was aggravated by the particularism of the Confederation. He promoted the thesis that the Union, though older than the individual states, was now exposed to steady decline owing to the weakness of the central government. His German erudition and severity, which often extended to a tactless officiousness, often antagonized his American readers. At the same time, however, his nationalism and conspicuous social conservatism allowed him to blend well into the intellectual landscape of the United States of the late nineteenth century.[139]

The German intellectual influence was especially noticeable with John W. Burgess and, later, his student Archibald Dunning. Burgess, a Tennesseean, studied at Amherst College and later in Germany, whence he returned a convinced "Teuton" and nationalist. He supplemented his pro-Southern writings on Reconstruction with books on the "benefits of imperialism and the exceptional political genius of the Teutonic peoples."[140] Influenced by Darwin's theory of evolution, Hegel's national idealism, and Gobineau's racist ideology, Burgess came to the conclusion that only the "Aryan" nations had sufficient abilities of political organization and that these qualities were unevenly distributed throughout the world. He believed that the national state represented an achievement of the Teutonic spirit and the most perfect solution to problems of political organization, and therefore the leadership role in the establishment and administration of their own and foreign states would fall to the Teutonic nations.[141] Since "history as the revelation of Providence, . . . intends national states as the prime organs of human development" and "the highest duty of the state" was "to preserve and strengthen . . . its own national character," and since he was convinced of the superiority of the Teutonic nations in this regard, it was natural to Burgess that, as a "conclusion for practical politics," these Teutonic nations "[be] intrusted, in the general economy of history, with the mission of conducting the political civilization of the modern world."[142]

[From the] manifest mission of the Teutonic nations . . . it follows that interference in the affairs of populations not wholly barbaric . . . but with manifest incapacity to solve the problem of political organization with any degree of completeness, . . . is a justifiable policy. . . . It is in the interest of the world's civilization that law and order and the true liberty . . . shall reign everywhere. . . . A permanent inability on the part of any state or semi-state to secure this status is a threat to civilization everywhere. Both for the sake of the half-barbarous state and in the interest of the rest of the world, a state or states, endowed with the capacity for political organization, may righteously assume sovereignty over, and undertake to create state order for, such politically incompetent population. . . . The civilized states themselves are the best organs . . . in history for determining the proper time and occasion for intervening in the affairs of unorganized or not sufficiently organized populations, for the execution of their great world duty.[143]

Darwin himself encouraged many of these opinions and their application to America:

There is apparently much truth in the belief that the wonderful progress of the United States, as well as the character of the people, are the results of natural selection; the more energetic, restless, and courageous men from all parts of Europe having emigrated . . . to that great country, and having there succeeded best.[144]

For Darwin, it was a scientific fact that the Americans were "the heir of all the ages, in the foremost files of time."[145] This sense of history, which combined Social Darwinist evolutionism and expansionism, manifest destiny, and Anglo-Saxon, Puritan myths of superiority, was shared by other American contemporaries such as James Schouler, John Bach McMaster, James Ford Rhodes, Andrew C. McLaughlin, and William A. Dunning. They were all united by their nationalism and conservatism, an aversion to radical democratic forms, and the idea of a common American mission ("jingoism").[146] One need only think of von Holst's observation that the Declaration of Independence was descended from the "crude theories" of Rousseau; McMaster's defamatory remarks that Jefferson was "saturated with democracy in its rankest form" and had been "to the last day of his life a servile worshipper of the people"; Schouler's condemnation of the "unlettered and boozy foreigners, the scum of European society"; Rhodes's pedantic analysis attributing the social strife and industrial poverty of the Reconstruction period to the "constantly deteriorating character of the European immigration,'' or his characterization of foreigners and striking workers as ''mobs'' who spent their free time ''mainly in whisky-drinking''; or, finally, Dunning's racist claim that ''the negro had no pride of race and no aspirations or ideals save to be like the whites.''[147]

The foundation for these ideas came in part from a strengthened sense of power and nostalgic unease over the phenomena accompanying modern, urban, and industrial society, including the unprecedented rate of economic growth with its increasing difficulties, the crass, irresponsible accumulation of wealth by the robber barons, the massive influx of immigrants, the misery and neglect, corruption, criminality and violence, the disintegration of old social formations, and the decline of traditional norms of behavior. It was the reaction of a traditional America of white Anglo-Saxon Protestants (WASPs), who felt themselves to be the established, the rightful, the true Americans, to the materialist, free-living, amoral modernity brought about during the Gilded Age.[148] That the Social Darwinist ideologies of race and history reached their peak at this time, in domestic and foreign policy, is by no means a coincidence.[149]

The main adherents of expansionist Anglo-Saxonism included the historical scholars of the Imperial School, Herbert Levi Osgood, George Louis Beer, and Alfred Thayer Mahan. Although Osgood and Beer strove to emphasize Anglo-American relations and the interdependence of their foreign-political interests, the influential naval historian Mahan, who strongly influenced Theodore Roosevelt, invoked the United States' protagonistic role as a guardian of Western civilization and the divine will of history. He demanded the build-up of American sea power, and warned that religions which maintained no missions were doomed to extinction—''may it not be so with nations?'' But, more openly than many of his colleagues, Mahan's analysis contained unconcealed considerations of national interest: economic motives, prestige, and influence.[150] And yet Richard Hofstadter, in his monograph *Social Darwinism in American Thought*, came to the conclusion that ''although concrete economic and strategic interests, such as Chinese trade and the vital necessity of sea power, were the prominent issues in the imperial debate, the movement took its rationale from more general ideological conceptions.''[151]

John Fiske, the American *locum tenens* of Darwin and Spencer, may be considered the most important popularizer of late nineteenth-century ''ideological conceptions,'' particularly the mixture of historical nationalism (*The Critical Period of American History, 1783–1789*), the myth of electness, and pseudoscientific Social Darwinism.[152] As a convinced Darwinist, he was deeply imbued with the notion of the moral and cultural superiority of the ''Anglo-Saxon Teutonic and Germanic race,'' and certain of its providential mission. Thus, referring to the ''doctrine of evolution'' in his essay ''Manifest Destiny,'' he wrote with great self-confidence of the ''English race,'' since ''the spirit of English liberty is alike indomitable in every land where men of English race have set their feet as masters.''[153] America, he stated, had now assumed the role of England. American achievements were the greatest contribution to the development of humankind. For Fiske, this progressive undertaking was "destined to go on until every land of the earth's surface that is not already the seat of an old civilization shall become English in its language, in its political habits and traditions, and to a predominant extent in the blood of its people."[154]

"English" in this case referred to the language of America. Fiske understood and formulated the theory of evolution as a progressive historical process of the "survival of the fittest," in line with Spencer's assertion that

all excesses and deficiency must disappear; that is, all unfitness and all deficiency must disappear; that is, all unperfections must disappear. Thus the ultimate development of the ideal man is logically certain—as certain as any conclusion in which we place the most explicit faith; for instance, that all men will die.... Progress, therefore, is not an accident, but a necessity.... The modifications mankind have undergone, are still undergoing, result from a law underlying the whole of organic creation; and provided the human race continues, and the constitution of things remain the same, those modifications must end in completeness.[155]

Of course, Fiske left no doubt that this theory of evolution was a "godly theory," a "created order in the hands of God"; or, as the president of Princeton, James McCosh, put it in 1871, a "progressive progression" that was the will of God.[156] In his most important works, *Outlines of Cosmic Philosophy* (1874), *Darwinism and Other Essays* (1879), *The Destiny of Man Viewed in the Light of His Origin* (1884), *The Idea of God as Affected by Modern Knowledge* (1885), and *Through Nature to God* (1899), Fiske did not tire of repeatedly emphasizing that "natural selection" was the *vera causa* of the evolutionary process of progress, that "the law of progress" was "the law of history":

When the kindly earth shall slumber, lapt in a universal law, and when the desires of each individual shall be in proximate equilibrium with the ... desires of all surrounding individuals. Such a state implies at once the highest possible ... integration among the units of the community; and it is the ideal goal of intellectual and moral progress.[157]

This social historian owed his enormous success (he was the most read historian of his age) to his populist narrative style. He succeeded in presenting Americans with the Darwinian and Spencerian theories of evolution as the metaphysical, historical, and scientific notion of progress, since his works gave "the traditional faith of nineteenth-century Americans in God, progress, and the moral law its most optimistic, eloquent, and unified post-Darwinian expression."[158]

Other intellectually more demanding contemporaries of Fiske, such as Chauncey Wright, considered one of the most important members of the Charles S. Pierce Metaphysical Club, remained accessible only to a small circle because of his philosophically empirical, even critical approach to the theory of evolution: "Wright insisted that science and metaphysics were fundamentally separate concerns ... that the teleological interpretation of the cosmos was merely wishful thinking, if not a subtle kind of intellectual dishonesty."[159] Wright's skepticism of the Darwinian conclusions about the progressive evolution of history and humankind caused him to set the significance of scientific knowledge strictly apart from positive dynamism and moral progress in the course of history:

Progress is a grand idea,—Universal Progress is a still grander idea. It strikes the keynote of modern civilization. . . . What the ideas God, the One and the All, the Infinite First Cause, were to an earlier generation, such are Progress and Universal Progress to the modern world,—a reflex of moral ideas and feelings. . . . Theories of society and the character and origin of social progress . . . are all liable to the taint of teleological and cosmological conceptions,—to spring from the order which the mind imposes upon what it imperfectly observes. . . . Evidence of progress in life through any ever so considerable portion of the earth's stratified materials would not, in our opinion, warrant us in drawing universal cosmical conclusions therefrom. Alternations of progress and regress relatively to any standard of ends or excellence which we might apply, is to us the most probable hypothesis that the general analogy of natural operation warrants.[160]

That the theory of evolution held a certain fascination for the American contemporary spirit in the late nineteenth century was due to concepts of change, growth, development, natural selection, and manifest destiny, all of which lay at the heart of this age's ambience. If Americans were to remain true to their ideals, however, logic did not allow them to accept the determinism of a Spencer for long. They believed in progress. Their own history was the most convincing proof of the soundness of this belief. Sustained belief in an evolutionary notion of progress over which they had no influence and to which they had nothing to contribute would surely have been both logically and psychologically impossible.[161] The temporary advantage that Spencer's social philosophy gave to the sense of history of individual interest groups in America was obvious. Any further dissemination of and continued adherence to Social Darwinistic progressivist ideology, however, had to be judged an aberration, not least because it violated the principle of equality.

## PROGRESSIVE HISTORIOGRAPHY: BETWEEN FRONTIER ROMANTICISM AND ECONOMIC CONFLICT ANALYSIS

No great new historical laws were discovered at the turn of the century, and early twentieth-century history could not boast of a Newton or a Darwin. Although no prominent historians stood out, three scholars had an enduring influence on American historical writing, just as Lester Frank Ward had indelibly stamped his personality on sociology, and just as Thorstein Veblen had influenced economics and Oliver Wendell Holmes jurisprudence. The politicoeconomic thought of the historians Frederick Jackson Turner, Vernon Louis Parrington, and Charles A. Beard found support in the broadest American circles, as well as from other progressivist historians such as the representatives of the New History.[162]

The unique value of the American historical experience, the pioneer virtues of unlimited individualism and frontier spirit (Turner), were uppermost in their minds, at a time, of course, when the frontier had long since become a thing of the past. On the other hand, a muckraking spirit prevailed in the age of populism and the intellectual climate of the Progressive movement, an almost compulsory drive to expose conspiratorial intrigues and thereby, directly or indirectly, affect reform in public life. These impulses and experiences had two aspects in common: (1) the orientation toward conflict as a pattern of enlightenment for sociohistorical processes (Parrington); and (2) the preoccupation with economic interests (Beard). This new point of view was understandable in light of the earlier historical writing of the nineteenth century, with its excessive tendency toward mythologization and idealization. But as historical interpretation, this angle offered only a new distortion of perspectives, setting one type of one-sidedness against another.[163]

Viewed superficially, Turner, Parrington, and Beard seemed diametrically opposed in terms of character and interests. Turner, who came from Wisconsin, was straightforward, learned, and cautious, wrote passionately about the frontier and particularism, and trained an army of pupils to apply the frontier formula to the whole of American history. Parrington taught at the University of Oklahoma and was prosperous, fastidious, and aristocratic, a moralist who saw history as a struggle between the powers of darkness and those of light. During his entire life he wrote just one work, the monumental *Main Currents in American Thought* (1927). Beard, a professor at Columbia University, was sharp-witted, inquisitive, critical, and intellectually cultivated in almost all areas of history. His boundless energy took him beyond the boundaries of the humanities to a broad cross section of public life, until he finally rejected his original concept of a historical science and took refuge in a type of neotranscendentalism. Common to all three historians, however, were their Midwestern origins and their sympathy for the reform movements, liberalism, and agrarian radicalism of the 1890s.[164]

Turner first brought his influence to bear—and ultimately it was he who remained the most influential—by emphasizing the peculiar conditions of the New World that had shaped the historical development and especially the Americans' sense of history. They included the experience of the frontier settlement and the dynamic expansion of civilization into the open West. "The west looks to the future, the east toward the past," wrote Turner in 1887.[165] The belief that human civilization was following a westward course was already deeply rooted in mythology and had been revived by the Renaissance: "Arcadia, Atlantis, and the Fortunate Isles all were located vaguely in the West. By the eighteenth century, numerous heralds of this mythic tradition were proclaiming America its fulfillment."[166] Similarly, as early as 1726 Bishop George Berkeley had written that "westward the course of empire takes its way."[167] The heyday of the pioneer was already past in Turner's time, but the wealth of frontier literature that had grown out of it, influencing the European image of the New World, had become in itself an ideological political factor of the first order. Turner's

work expressed the dualist concept of Rousseauen Enlightenment with pronounced ambivalence: on the one hand in the form of a consummate civilization
guided by reason in the service of human progress, and on the other as a romantic-
agrarian idea of the return to pure, unspoiled nature as the deepest source of
progressive vitality.[168] Turner's fame and his influence on an entire generation
of historians are based largely on his startling lecture "The Significance of the
Frontier in American History" (1893).[169] These same historians first converted
his thesis into a concrete statement of the frontier movement. Turner's main
hypothesis was expressed in his historical ideology that a westward advance of
the frontier represented progress and the Americanization of American history:

The West believed in the rule of the majority . . . the East feared an unchecked democracy,
which might overturn minority rights, destroy established institutions, and attack vested
interests. . . . The frontier is the line of most rapid and effective Americanization. . . . In
place of old frontiers of wilderness, there are new frontiers of unwon fields of science,
fruitful for the needs of the race; there are frontiers of better social domains yet unexplored.[170]

At the same time, Turner interpreted the advance of the frontier as a progressive
renunciation of European influence, as a steady growth of independence on
American terms. Naturally, critics often noted that his frontier thesis was characterized by inner ambiguity and inconsistency: centralist and federalist, idealist
and economic views, progressivist conviction and civilizational critique were
juxtaposed with scarcely any philosophical support whatsoever.[171] Turner's terminology also gave rise to criticism owing to his combination of terms such as
progress, development, evolution, process, expansion, advance, movement, rise,
mobility, fluidity, waves, adaptation, adjustment, transformation, consolidation,
stages, and civilization, despite the fact that they were, strictly speaking, not at
all synonymous. Turner simply equated development with progress, identified
the law of continuity and development as the specific progressive experience
from frontier to frontier, and blindly defined the American process of progress
as a continuation of world progress:[172]

This ever retreating frontier of free land is the key to American development. . . . The
existence of an area of free land, its continuous recession, and the advance of American
settlement westward, explain American development. The true point of view in the history
of this nation is not the Atlantic Coast, it is the Great West. And to study this advance,
the men who grew up under these conditions, and the political, economic, and social
results of it, is to study the really American part of our history. The problem of the West
is nothing less than the problem of American development. The Mississippi Valley has
been the especial home of democracy. The forest clearings have been the seed plots of
American character. . . . This forest philosophy is the philosophy of American democracy.
This at least is clear: American democracy is fundamentally the outcome of the experiences
of the American people in dealing with the West. This new democracy that captured the
country and destroyed the ideals of statesmanship came from no theorist's dream of the

German forest. It came stark and strong and full of life, from the American forest. American democracy was born of no theorist's dream; it was not carried in the *Sarah (Susan) Constant* to Virginia, nor in the *Mayflower* to Plymouth. It came out of the American forest, and it gained new strength each time it touched a new frontier. Not the constitution, but free land and an abundance of natural resources open to a fit people, made the democratic type of society in America for three centuries while it occupied its empire. . . . It is in the Middle West that society has formed on lines least like those of Europe. It is here, if anywhere, that American democracy will make its stand against the tendency to adjust to a European type.[173]

Turner recognized European influence only in early American history. He saw the individual nature of American progress as rooted in the peculiar character of the American frontier. There was a clearly nationalistic bias to the Turnerian frontier ideology, based on the feeling of the pioneer life, achieved more than inherited, and thus a renunciation of the Old World as well as the Eastern states, which were more closely allied with it. For Turner, American progress originated from the depths of the West and signified a progression of the Americanization of politics, economics, and society while simultaneously harboring some consciously anti-European traits. On the other hand, frontier idealism was also a democratic ideological formula: frontier ideology enabled all Americans to participate equally in the progress of their country, offered each new generation an equal opportunity, made every American into a collaborator, and turned this sense of cooperation into a permanent mentality. The frontier permitted economic restlessness to function as a safety valve and served simultaneously as social laboratory, democratizing factor, and impulse for individual, social, psycho-spiritual self-development. The frontier was the bearer and the object of American progressive ideology extending from Jefferson to Jackson, and from the Puritan missionary zeal to manifest destiny.

In any evaluation of the Turnerian interpretation of history, it must be emphasized that the classical frontier era was irrevocably over. In 1890, three years before Turner's famous lecture, the official census report had declared that the country had possessed land open for colonization through 1880. At the time of the census, the unsettled area had been penetrated to such an extent by individual pockets of settlement that it was no longer possible to speak of a frontier. The work of Turner and his pupils basically recapitulated a completed phase of inner-American expansion and would henceforth face grave transitional crises and a future that would demand new interpretations of the principle of progress and continuity.[174]

Turner's new interpretation of the American idea of progress was adapted, with a strongly anticapitalist and agrarian accent, by the influential literary historian Vernon Louis Parrington. Like Turner, Parrington was convinced of the strength of American ideals and was at constant pains to redefine them: "To enter once more into the spirit of those fine old idealisms, and to learn that the promise of the future has lain always in the keeping of liberal minds that were never discouraged from their dreams, is scarcely a profitless undertaking."[175]

However, he was not in the least convinced that these ideals had sprung from
the American environs and historical experience. He was equally unconvinced
of their powers to resist the influence of the Old World. Coming from the Midwest
and devoted to the spirit of Populist rebellion, Parrington concentrated a large
part of his work on combatting the intellectual supremacy of Harvard University:
"The past five years I have spent in study and writing, up to my ears in the
economic interpretation of American history and literature, getting the last lin-
gering Harvard prejudices out of my system."[176]

For all his apparent provincialism and his fidelity to the Midwest, Parrington
was a cultivated scholar in every respect. Familiar with the literary and philosophical thinking not only of America, but also of England and the European
continent, he did not fall victim to the error of interpreting the intellectual
development of America as an isolated individual phenomenon. As a historian,
he knew that ideas have a genesis reaching far into the past. However original
the American frontier may have been in its practices and organization, however
much the frontier was able to resist political or economic pressures, ideas could
ultimately not be stopped.[177] Thus, in 1917 Parrington wrote: "To love ideas is
excellent, but to understand how ideas themselves are conditioned by social
forces is better still."[178] Although Parrington, as a professor of literature, analyzed mainly the literary currents in American thinking in his three-volume work,
*Main Currents in American Thought,* his analysis still included theological,
economic, legal, political, historical, journalistic, and belletristic questionings.
More alert than many other important historians to the interaction of European
and American thought, he devoted himself both to the Americanization of imported ideas and to the effect of those ideas on the American spirit. In his view,
it was crucial to understand the principle of natural selection and the consequence
of transplanting ideas. European ideas, once transplanted to American soil, would
take root in various places and stimulate Americans' thought, supplying ideas
for new utopian ventures and intellectual advances for new political experiments.
"Eminently liberalizing" in effect, these ideas seemed to Parrington to lend
impetus and form to native idealism and to contribute to the deepening of social
experience. He viewed America as the child of two continents, possessed of a
specific nature and character impossible to attribute exclusively to either one of
its parents.[179]

Parrington was one of the few American historians to develop a historical
philosophy, to reject Ranke's view that the historian's task was confined to the
collection of facts and that this edifying function could be fulfilled in a completely
impartial manner. Accordingly, Parrington's historiography was enormously
biased. He interpreted the American history of ideas as a struggle between the
forces of freedom and the defenders of privileges, and he resolutely took sides
in this conflict: "The economic interpretation of things is in the air. . . . It is fast
becoming for us both the law and the prophet."[180] All the decisive battles of
American history were refought in his books: the ideological progressivist dispute

between theocracy and independence, federalism and republicanism, slavery and emancipation, frontier and coast, populists and capitalists, labor and industry.

From the outset Parrington had declared the tradition of liberalism, progressivism, and rebellion to be the philosophical political tradition of American thought.[181] In the first two volumes of his work[182] Parrington introduced his heroes. He particularly admired Roger Williams, whom he saw as a predecessor of Locke, Paine, the French Romantics, Channing, and Emerson, as a great thinker and bold restorer, as a bulwark of liberalism in the age of Puritanism.[183] These were followed by Jefferson—whom he considered a perpetual inspiration to all those professing allegiance to the democratic ideal—Jackson, Lincoln, Wendell Phillips, Henry George, and Edward Bellamy, among others.[184] Richard Hofstadter expressed his opinion of the style and message of this opus: "It is avowedly partisan, it takes the side of dissenters and protestants against establishment, of democrats against aristocrats, of revolutionaries against old regimes; it seems to be telling a story of steady progress, pointing toward a certain satisfaction with the enlightened ideas of the present."[185] The third volume of his *Main Currents* proved to be quite different.[186] It reflected his populist disillusionment with the development of industry after the Civil War and a melancholy and pessimistic attitude toward the acceleration and consequences of economic and technological progress. In fact, Parrington was much closer to Turner on this point. Both historians shared the ultimate fear that "the disappearance of the frontier and free land, the . . . fear that American democracy, once separated from its agrarian and particularist base, might be doomed to go down before the machine and the city."[187] While Parrington and Turner admittedly appreciated the inevitability of the approaching industrial and technological culture, they were in no position to accept the modern progressivist development as a new glimmer of hope on the American horizon. Although Parrington was often described as "a diluted Marxist" because of his economically colored interpretation of American history, his "affection for the ideals of humanitarianism and progress" intellectually allied him with eighteenth-century thought. "For him the American Enlightenment remained the high point in national thought" (Hofstadter).[188]

The controversial historical theories of Charles A. Beard were considerably more economically radical and socially critical than those of Turner, Parrington, and other progressive historians. While the Whig historians and Romantics had interpreted the American Constitution as the most prominent symbol of national consolidation and political identity, and as a bulwark against radical democratic and antiproprietary infringements, representatives of the "New History" such as Carl L. Becker and Edwin R.A. Seligman, but above all Charles Beard, now attempted to portray the Constitution as an obstacle to progress both politically and economically.[189] The stimulus came in part from Europe and could be traced back to historical materialism. It was also part American in origin, marked by a philosophical antiformalism (William James), Progressive instrumentalism (John Dewey), and an extreme Populism (Henry George).[190]

The appearance in 1913 of Beard's book *An Economic Interpretation of the Constitution of the United States* strengthened the trend toward a one-sided economic approach oriented toward class conflict and congenial to the Progressive movement much more forcibly than any of the Progressive historians had done.[191] The essence of Beard's thesis was that the members of the Constitutional Convention of 1787—almost without exception members of the landed classes and administrators of government bonds—had, motivated by class, ratified a constitution that favored property ownership, was remote from democratic liberal aspirations, tended toward social conservatism, and favored a small property-owning elite at the expense of the mass of the agrarian population. By projecting the class and proprietary ideas of the radical progressivists and populists of the nineteenth and early twentieth century back into the Revolutionary period, Beard failed to note the almost self-evident acceptance of the right to liberty and property at the time the nation was founded. From this distorted historical and political perspective, it was possible for him to see in the Constitution of 1787 only a kind of counterrevolutionary instrument for the suppression of democratic aspirations, instead of the fulfillment and consolidation of the national legal order securing liberty and property won in the Revolution.[192]

Beard's later research used sound arguments to refute assumptions, basic sources, and patterns of interpretation. Beard had in fact succeeded in introducing a tendentious picture into American historical science with his economically determined research methods that lasted for decades, even if he later fundamentally revised his position and always repudiated the accusation that his historiography had embraced the cause of the radical reformists.[193] His ambiguous fame was closely identified with this adherence to the populist-progressive bases of political and economic interpretation of history. He believed that the main political questions were economic in nature, that the essence of politics was acquisition and exploitation, and that party conventions, electoral addresses, and congressional debates could only be accounted for from the viewpoint of classes and pressure groups. This materialistic historical interpretation also originated from realistic disenchantment and the realization that progress tends to sharpen the conflict between the ideal and the possible. This notion was expressed by Beard himself:

The essence of the crisis [lies] in the tragic sense of the conflict between the *ideal* and the *real*, between the noblest visions of man and his performances. The essence of the crisis itself is dissatisfaction with the present disarray of things. Were there no dissatisfaction there would be no crisis. Now dissatisfaction springs from the belief that the present state of things is not wholly good, does not meet the requirement of some ideal existing in the mind. . . . The ideal, however dim, is at the bottom of the difficulty. No ideal, no intellectual discontent. No intellectual discontent, no crisis in economy or thought.[194]

This discrepancy between ideal and reality, which Beard defined as a crisis, reflected for him the fact that political and social philosophy had lagged behind technological change. Science and technology had not, in Beard's eyes, furnished any acceptable political solutions. "Technology has not made a single important contribution to the philosophy of government," he declared irrefutably in *The American Leviathan* (1930),[195] and continued:

To make a swift summation, the crisis in Western thought may be said to spring from the disconcerting recognition of the fact that science cannot of itself provide the certainty, understanding, and unequivocal direction to policy and practice profoundly expected after theological supremacy and assurance were disrupted in a conflict extending through several centuries.[196]

Not even Beard could dispute the fact that laissez-faire individualism and its principles had brought American society demonstrable advances, but he considered this philosophy no longer applicable in the age of rapid scientific and technological change:

The cold truth is that the individualist creed of everybody for himself and the devil take the hindmost is principally responsible for the distress in which Western civilization finds itself. . . . Whatever merits the creed may have had in the days of primitive agriculture and industry, it is not applicable in an age of technology, science, and rationalized economy. Once useful, it has become a danger to society.[197]

In Beard's opinion, what American society now needed was the reassessment of state intervention, the admittance of state measures "to a new role in the process of civilization."[198]

Beard's career had been extraordinarily eventful and varied. Not only was the extent of his writing on history and politics, culture and society, economics, administration, English and European agriculture, and foreign policy impressive,[199] but he also created a stir as adviser to the governments of Japan and Yugoslavia, and to a number of foreign and native leftist movements, and as spiritual leader of the isolationists.[200] At the end of his career, Beard repudiated his pseudohistorical theories of the necessity of state economic determinism, only to fall into the embrace of a no less ahistorical historicism. This was perhaps ultimately due to the psychic constitution of a resigned cosmopolitan who, having become a cultural pessimist, had abnegated the search for ideals.[201]

Perhaps Beard's obtrusive demonstration of an alleged subjectivity of all historical writing, and his metaphysical definition of history as a mere "act of faith,"[202] were ultimately indebted to the influence of the German historians Meinecke, Mannheim, Riezler, Heussi, and Vaihinger, or the historical conception of Machiavelli or Croce, all of whom Beard had examined in great detail.[203] Nonetheless, with the fourth volume of their joint work, *The Rise of American Civilization,*—entitled *The American Spirit: A Study of the Idea of Civilization in the United States* (1942)—he and his wife, Mary Beard, had arrived at the conclusion that "the intellectual qualities which made American history unique in origins, substance, and development" amounted to objective, undeniable progress in human civilization.[204] A new interpretation of history and progress, one that did away with resignation and cultural pessimism, developed only after the end of the Second World War and the ensuing new power constellations.

## PESSIMISM AND THE CRISIS OF IDEALISTIC FAITH IN PROGRESS

At first glance, it seems paradoxical that a historical school of pessimists and critics of civilization should have arisen in the middle of the Populist and Progressive era in America. In his collection of essays entitled *Winds of Doctrine* (1913), which attacked both the theory of evolution and pragmatism, both determinism and irrationalism, emigrant philosopher George Santayana wrote that his contemporaries had enslaved their intelligence and rather than liberating it, they were attempting to avoid it. Santayana also contended that their lack of moral independence made them incapable of achieving a dispassionate view of worldly things, of life itself, and of the ambivalence of technological change and scientific progress. In the end, he wrote, it was feelings and instincts, and not the intellect, that dominated their thinking.[205] Not entirely free of critical reservations about Americanism ("that striving, sweating, progressive utilitarianism"), Santayana enjoyed referring to the aristocratic society of the Greeks. He particularly admired their ideal of *kalokagathia* (kind-heartedness) and intellectual independence, and their definition of classical happiness, one linked to their understanding of calamity. He attacked the American version of nihilism and decadent thinking represented by writers and historians such as Ernest Hemingway, Gertrude Stein, Ezra Pound, Brooks and Henry Adams, Carl Becker, and Lewis Mumford.[206]

Toward the end of the nineteenth century, indeed, a fin de siécle atmosphere did seem to gain ground in both Europe and the United States, an uncertainty with regard to progressivism seemed to crystallize, and a bleak premonition of the historical pattern of the progress and decline of cultures (the tragic truth in Europe) appeared to take hold. However, in contrast to political, philosophical, and historical irrationalist and decadent thought in Europe, America at the beginning of the twentieth century displayed several differing intellectual tendencies simultaneously. On the one hand, there emerged the theoretical foundation of Progressive reform and a new definition of Jefferson's liberalism, above all by Herbert Croly (*The Promise of American Life*, 1909, and *Progressive Democracy*, 1914), Walter Lippmann (*Preface to Politics*, 1913), and Walter Weyl, publisher of *The New Republic*, and their political conversion owing to the Progressive presidents Theodore Roosevelt and Woodrow Wilson. There also existed an optimistic outlook of a progressive American history (Frederick Jackson Turner, Vernon Louis Parrington, Charles Beard, James Harvey Robinson), philosophy (William James, John Dewey), economics (Thorstein Veblen, Richard T. Ely), and law (Oliver Wendell Holmes, Jr., Louis Brandeis). They recognized the problems of the advancing modern age but were convinced of the progressive democratization and reform of American society: "There can be no question that the progress of science and the application of science to industry will go on in a geometric ratio, and that eventually every country will benefit by this advance."[207]

In addition, there was the school of the doubters, who interpreted the apparent acceleration of historical progress and the factual popularization of democracy as a consequence of technological and mechanistic transformation, industrialization and urbanization as the dissolution of the uniform, cultural, and political ethos of Americans and their values. "By 1900," wrote David W. Marcell, "the number of serious and reflective doubters was growing. In sum, a vast and pervasive ambivalence toward the idea of progress marked American thought at the turn of the century."[208] Two historians, the prominent brothers Brooks and Henry Adams (of the presidential family), were American supporters of Nietzschean nihilism and the will to power and Spengler's apocalyptic historical philosophy of the decline of cultures.[209] Brooks Adams was the less important historian of the two, but as friend and adviser to Theodore Roosevelt, he had a certain degree of influence on the president's policies.[210] His historical and political orthodoxy is extremely difficult to classify because of its contradictions. He was characterized simultaneously as a "rebel with a passion for social justice," "absolute authoritarian," "pseudo-progressive," "constructive conservative," "prophet and reformer," "strategist of *Realpolitik*," "Jeffersonian-Jacksonian-Bryanian Democrat," "neo-Hamiltonian aristocrat," "Left-wing New Dealer," or "proto-fascist."[211] Basically, all the paradoxical, unfermented American currents of thought seeking new certainty and unity in an age of the upheaval of the idealistic notion of progress were reflected in these descriptions of Brooks Adams's personality.[212]

Clinton Rossiter and Daniel Aaron made a plausible attempt to place one paradox next to the other and eradicate the contradictions.[213] On the one hand, Brooks Adams was the author of the pessimistic philosophy of history entitled *The Law of Civilization and Decay* (1895). This work compared American civilization with the late Roman Empire and the conditions prevailing in Greece under the successors of Alexander. This tome, which included a preface by Theodore Roosevelt, attempted to portray the decline of American culture as an inevitability owing to a popularization of democracy, the rise of a mass society, the dominance of science and technology, and the deification of the Stock Exchange and capitalist machinations.[214] On the other hand, Adams involved himself with élan in the daily business of politics. As a "conservative at heart who advocated a radical program of reform," he supported, and even idolized, Roosevelt's Progressive politics ("on his success depends the success or failure of

American civilization''[215]). He repeatedly advocated the national greatness and unity and international supremacy of the United States. As Charles Hirschfeld noted, it was necessary

to create a national community pursuing the national interest by means of efficient and continuous administration, with all that it implied of planning and welfare measures. This organic community . . . was made necessary, and could only be achieved, by the strategic and economic growth of the United States to a position of supremacy in the world; the one was not possible without the other.[216]

At any rate, in his article "The New Industrial Revolution" (1901) Brooks was optimistic enough to imagine the integration of internal and external American policies as an opportunity to overcome the multidimensional phenomena of crisis:

In proportion as the United States consolidate within, in order to evolve the largest administrative mass, so must they be expected to expand without; and as they expand, they must simplify and cheapen the administrative machinery, until in this direction, also, the limit of economy by mass has been attained.[217]

The fact that Adams viewed the "state socialism" model as the least expensive and most important instrument of "national power" in a world full of conflicts remains without doubt one of his most blatant contradictions.[218]

His brother Henry, a professor of history at Harvard, also submitted to the apocalyptic discontent prevalent at the turn of the century. His intellectual struggle with the idea and the crisis of progress, the essence of nature, and the course of history was an ambitious and substantial one. He did not believe in the order and progress of history and set out to disprove the existence of order.[219] For him such notions were illusory:

Chaos [is] the law of nature; Order [is] the dream of man. . . . Every day Nature violently revolt[s], causing so-called accidents with enormous destruction of property and life, while plainly laughing at man. . . . An immense volume of force [has] detached itself from the unknown universe of energy, while still vaster reservoirs, supposed to be infinite, steadily [reveal] themselves.[220]

As did his brother, Brooks, and later Oswald Spengler, Henry Adams also distinguished between culture and civilization. Culture embodied for him the constructive, creative, devout phase of history, which was succeeded by the destructive countercurrent of civilization, the senseless, raw unleashing of material energies, the desolation, waste, deformation, and desecration of life. Upon returning to America after a ten-year stay in London, he was confronted with a different world that strengthened his belief in the imminent collapse (which he forecast for 1921) of American culture as the result of some natural catastrophe.[221] Thus, he wrote gloomily that his homeland in 1900 was fundamentally different from what it had been in 1860. He saw himself as a complete stranger in a world where the concentration and incessant development of powerful mechanical energies (coal, iron, steam power), rather than development of the mind, appeared unstoppable and had decisively superseded the old standards of industry, that is, agriculture, the crafts, and education.

Adams struggled in vain to find a new frame of reference; he had lost sight of his own path and had become an old-fashioned dreamer and preoccupied academic.[222] "At the rate of increase of speed and momentum, as calculated on the last fifty years," wrote Henry to Brooks in 1901, "the present society must break its damn neck in a definite, but remote, time, not exceeding fifty years more."[223] Arthur Schlesinger was later to describe him as a "reverse millennialist, convinced that science and technology were rushing the planet toward an apocalypse unredeemed by a Day of Judgment."[224] Henry, like Brooks, drew historical parallels between antiquity and his own age. In his despair, he agonized over "this secret belief that one stands on the brink of the world's greatest catastrophe; for it means the fall of Western Europe, as it fell in the fourth century."[225] He identified with Augustine: "I aspire to be bound up with St. Augustine. . . . My idea of what it should be proved beyond my powers. Only St. Augustine ever realized it."[226] Augustine, however, had the advantage of his chiliastic belief in the "City of God," whereas *The Rule of Phase Applied to History* (1909) left Adams room only for a modern belief in the "City of Chaos." "A law of acceleration," wrote Adams in 1909, "definite and constant as any law of mechanics, cannot be supposed to relax its energy to suit the convenience of man."[227] As the most progress-oriented country in the world, the United States was especially affected. "The United States, like everything else, was finished." A few weeks before the outbreak of the First World War, he once more resignedly remarked: "No one anywhere . . . expects a future. The life is that of the fourth century, without St. Augustine."[228]

Adams's fame rests above all on two extraordinary works, *Mont-Saint Michel and Chartres* (1904), and *The Education of Henry Adams, A Study in Twentieth Century Complexity* (1907). Taken together, these works form a polar unity, which might be termed his philosophy of history. (He himself would term it "tourist philosophy.") *The Education,* an enigmatically appealing self-contemplation in the third person, can be compared with Goethe's *Fact and Fiction.* But whereas the merit of Goethe's life is displayed in all its depth and breadth, in Adams's book the reader encounters ironic self-deprecation and an erratic style. Adams treated himself in the same way as a chemist who observes an element for its reactions in a variety of combinations. His target was the essential question—why does the modern human live? He sought an answer in each phase of his life, and every attempt ended in defeat, in nonanswer. The text reads like a satire of calculating reason, artfully used by an inscrutable narrator for purposes of personal revelation. Here the reader witnesses the reverse of Hegel. The ironic fate of knowledge in the modern, confused twentieth century lay in the disintegration of the tangible intellectual unity of Western civilization, in a progressive acceleration of chaos.[229] "History," wrote Adams in his *Education,* "was a hundred years behind the experimental sciences."[230]

Adams indefatigably devoted his energy to the illumination of the history of his country and the character of its people. In the midst of the advances and discoveries of science, he sought a historical formula that would rationalize history in a scientific way. In his opinion the future of thought, and therefore of history, now lay in the hands of the physicists, and the historian had to gain his education from the world of mathematical physics.[231] In the omnibus volume *The Degradation of the Democratic Dogma* (1919), which was edited by his brother and which contained the famous essays "The Tendency of History," "A Letter to American Teachers of History," and "The Rule of Phase Applied to History," this dynamically physical theory of history darkened to a naturalistic pessimism. History was seen here as part of a cosmic process, operating on the basis of thermodynamic law. In this way, Adams linked his dynamic theory of history with the physical theory that history tended to dissipate the extant forces of progress and nature, or even accelerated their dissipation:

nature shows no known machinery for restoring the energy that she dissipates. . . . From the beginnings of philosophy and religion, the thinker was thought by the mere act of thinking, to take for granted that his mind was the highest energy of nature. . . . As a force [reason] must obey the laws of force; as an energy it must content itself with such freedom as the laws of energy allow; and in any case it must submit to the final and fundamental necessity of Degradation. The same law by still stronger reasoning, applies to the Will itself.[232]

For Adams, the reduction of material force and energy, the human consumption of natural resources, the destruction of the environment by the age of industry and machines proved that "From the physicist's point of view, Man as a conscious and constant, single, natural force, seems to have no function except that of dissipating or degrading energy."[233] David W. Marcell wrote that "industrialization, technology, science"—all the advances of contemporary civilization—

became evidence of the charging, impending doom toward which all human energies were directed. Adams's theory of degradation inverted the mainstream of contemporary historical opinion and turned progress against itself: silence and death were to be the ultimate rewards of human effort. The "Letter" was Adams's impious rebuttal to the cheerful orthodoxy of evolutionary progressivism.[234]

Adams's tirades were, of course, directed mainly against Darwin's and Spencer's progressivist theory of evolution and selection. On the basis of his portrayal of thermodynamic law, Adams regarded the twentieth-century idea of progress as nothing more than a hypothesis that historians had deliberately manipulated and that he denounced as a fallacy. Compared with the eighteenth century, vividly embodied for him by the intellectual enthusiasm and statesmanlike ideals of his grandfather John Adams, scientific progress and modern democracy could only appear to him as a "degradation" of humankind.[235] The *Education* had been a study of the polymorphy and dividedness of modernity, an attempt to trace the penetration of scientific ideas through the course of modern American history. It depicted the shift of political emphasis from New England to the West, from farming to industry and then to finance, from the individual to the masses, the transformation in the structure of political power from intelligence to instinct, from reason to strength (reminiscent of Nietzsche's apotheosis of the "will to power"), the transition from evolutionary optimism to naturalistic pessimism, and from the conception of theological universe to a mechanistic one, the replacement of philosophy by the natural sciences, of people by machines, and of the Virgin by the dynamo. Now, in *Mont-Saint-Michel*, Adams recapitulated and showed a lively interest in the unity of medieval thinking and culture. The old creeds—the puritanical Calvinism of the seventeenth century, the enlightened deism of the eighteenth century, and the romantic transcendentalism of the nineteenth century—had disappeared; the determinism of Spencer and Fiske, which condemned the present in favor of an uncertain future, was unacceptable. Polymorphy, chaos, and stagnation were the characteristics of the age of the dynamo, which for Henry Adams had begun with the closing of the frontier in 1890 and had taken over from the age of the Virgin:[236] "Among the thousand symbols of ultimate energy, the dynamo . . . [is] the most expressive. . . . The new American like the new European, [is] the servant of the powerhouse, as the European of the twelfth century was the servant of the church."[237]

Adams's revolt against the chaos of modern science led him back to the unity of the church. In *Mont-Saint-Michel* he reconstructed the synthesis that had also occupied the mind of his grandfather; but the difference was that Adams built up this theory from the consciousness of his age, as a "tourist." In 1895, together with Senator Henry Cabot Lodge, he visited Normandy and its surroundings—Amiens, Bayeux, Coutances, Mont-Saint-Michel, Vitré, Le Mans, and Chartres. Enchanted by the divine architecture, which he interpreted as a symbol of veneration for the Virgin Mary, Mother of God, he returned to America and wrote his brilliant work. Happy to have at last found a "mistress" who was not interested in her lover's age, he devoted himself to an unusually human and rather avant-garde worship of the Virgin. In contrast to medieval Catholicism, Adams saw "the greatest and most mysterious of all energies" as embodied in the Virgin.[238] Whether a symbol or a source of power, "the Virgin had acted as the greatest force the Western world had ever felt, and had drawn man's activities to herself more strongly than any other power, natural or supernatural, had ever done."[239]

Disappointed by the decline of this source of power (could he have meant source of progress?), Adams wrote the following:

The Woman had once been supreme; in France she still seemed potent, not merely as a sentiment, but as a force. Why was she unknown in America? . . . American art, like

American language and education, was as far as possible sexless. Society regarded this victory over sex as its greatest triumph.[240]

For him, Mary integrated the collective rebellion of humankind against fate; the entire protest against divine law; general contempt for human law ensuing from the respect for its divine counterpart; and all the unspeakable madness of human nature, which charges against the prison walls and suddenly gathers hope that, in the Virgin, the individual has found a door to freedom. She was above the law and obtained female satisfaction in making hell into a pleasure palace. She spurned social differences in this life and the next. She knew that, in terms of any moral theory, the universe remained just as incomprehensible to her as it did to her worshippers, and just like them, she doubted whether its creator understood it any better.[241] Adams was probably not aware that his veneration of the Virgin in *Mont-Saint-Michel* and *Chartres* read like a heretical, socialist, feminist, even despairingly Progressive manifesto. Uprooted and demoralized, tortured by a helplessness that found no repose in thought and saw no objective in action, convinced of the bankruptcy of the future and the vanity of all knowledge, disappointed in its belief in progress and evolution, resigned to the reduction of energy, the exhaustion of society, and the fall of humankind, and lost in a universe he viewed as incomprehensibly mechanistic and chaotic, Adams found consolation only in that single symbol of unity personified by the Virgin. A stranger in spirit to the modern Catholic Church, one of the greatest American historians indulged in what he considered to have been the significance of the Virgin for an uncomplicated age. Her compassion, he knew, was infinite.

## PROGRESS AND CONSERVATION AS NATIONAL HISTORICAL CONSENSUS

In the years between the two world wars, an atmosphere of nihilism and pessimism continued to be present in American thought. This mood, reflected above all in American literature, forced the idealistic notion of progress onto the defensive. American irrationality was largely modern and almost exclusively European in origin. It is indicative that the greatest obscurity, immaturity, and decadence were displayed by those American literary works with the greatest affinity to European literature. These works were often indebted to the French, particularly the Symbolist poets Mallarmé, Verlaine, Rimbaud, Valéry, Laforgue, and Paul Fort, critics such as Remy de Gourmont and philosophers such as Henri Bergson, with his glorification of the *élan vital,* and other authors such as André Gide and, especially, Marcel Proust. The debt was even greater, however, to Freud in Vienna, Jung in Zürich, and Pavlov in Russia, who did not merely contribute to a sense of the essence of the subconscious, but ultimately even became overconscious of it. However, doubtless owing to the common language, the greatest influence was exercised by the philosophers, poets, and authors of the British Isles: pioneers of sexual science such as Edward Carpenter and the dogmatic Havelock Ellis; novelists such as Dorothy Richardson, Aldous Huxley, D. H. Lawrence, and Virginia Woolf; the Irish experimentalists William Butler Yeats, George Moore, Oscar Wilde, and, above all, James Joyce.

The attack on reason, on any historical meaning, on clarity, normality, grammar, and morality, were characteristic features of this new American literary school, which included naturalists such as London, Crane, Norris, and Dreiser. Dreiser was among the last naturalists whose determinism was still directly descended from Darwin and Haeckel, and who consciously acknowledged Nietzsche's influence on his work. The new school also included primitivists and irrationalists such as Anderson, Hemingway, Faulkner, Sinclair, Caldwell, Pound, Stein, Jeffers, Fitzgerald, Dos Passos, and Steinbeck; traditionalists such as Wharton, Glasgow, Field, Young, Robinson, Santayana, Frost, and Benét; conservatives such as W. C. Brownwell; humanists such as Irving Babbitt; and classicists such as Paul Elmer More. In philosophical terms, all of them represented the reflection of that attitude of doubt following Victorian progressivist optimism and the invasion of determinism, naturalism, pragmatism, and realism.[242] At the same time, these philosophical and literary currents reflected the disillusionment that set in after Wilson's idealistic Messianism and the return to normality, demonstrated in the flight from reason triggered by the collapse of Newtonian physics, the triumph of Freud's psychology, and the political disintegration of the Old World. In addition, the atmosphere of general pessimism was strongly influenced by the economic depression that played such an important role in American history from the early 1890s into the 1930s.[243]

In summary (as indicated by H. S. Commager), these negative trends of the interwar era were inspired by seven political and irrational motives and apocalyptic elements, and shaped by the modern ambivalence of progress that was also making itself felt in the United States. First, a pseudoscientific rejection of reason, sense, normality, historical continuity, and context, indeed, the rejection of American civilization itself as eccentric and decadent, all took place. Second, a passionate interest in the subconscious and unconscious, an enthusiasm for emotion, instinct, and anarchy, as opposed to thought, rationality, and discipline, had developed. Third, the number of intellectual "fellow travelers" grew in the 1930s, consisting above all of the staff members on the Marxist periodical *The Partisan Review*, founded in 1934, whose romantic utopian yearnings and political and ideological illusions compelled them to convert to communism. Fourth, an affinity arose for sexuality, especially in its abnormal manifestations, regarded as the most powerful and ubiquitous instinct, and the explanation for all human behavior. Fifth, a weakness for primitivism crystallized in the selection of literary themes, for "primitive" cultures such as those of the Africans and Indians, for myths, for peasant and native folklore, for primitive emotions and activities such as eating, drinking, sleeping, fighting, and loving—and, closely connected, a predeliction for violence, anarchy, and revolt, wherever and however they arose. Sixth, all orthodox moral conceptions, all conformity and convention were negated, while people abandoned themselves to a perverse amorality in which submission to the instincts counted as the highest virtue. Seventh, and finally, a new language and grammar were formed to permit a better expression of the capricious impulses springing from the subconscious.[244]

But these pessimistic intellectual currents prevalent in the 1920s and 1930s did not influence historical writing and politics in America as they did so disastrously in Europe. Historical realism dominated as a reaction to the traditional progressivist and religious belief in the American mission. This vein of thought found its ardent spokesman in Reinhold Niebuhr:[245] "we had a religious version of our national destiny which interpreted the meaning of our nationhood as God's effort to make a new beginning in the history of mankind."[246] Niebuhr categorically defined Messianism as "a corrupt expression of man's search for the ultimate within the vicissitudes and hazards of time," and warned at the same time of "the deep layer of Messianic consciousness in the mind of America." He considered the myth of American innocence to be fatal. "Nations, as individuals, who are completely innocent in their own esteem, are insufferable in their human contacts." According to Niebuhr, self-righteous nations should be aware of the divine judgment on human arrogance and never forget "the depth of evil to which individuals and communities may sink, particularly when they try to play the role of God in history."[247] Thus, "in an ultimate irony of American history," wrote Arthur Schlesinger, "Niebuhr used religion to refute the religious version of the national destiny."[248]

The confrontation with the phenomenon of twentieth-century totalitarianism in the Second World War, and subsequently in the Cold War, was the initial cause of the development from progressive history, through pessimism and realism, to "consensus history." There arose a conservational attitude towards historiography that emphasized the common, bonding nature of the American historical experience. The political collapse of Europe, the horror of the war, and the concentration camps brought in a shift in postwar historical thought, a renunciation of the ideologization and antagonization of European society and politics, and a reawakening of the pioneer spirit and Americanism, the conviction that the United States was different and superior. Along with this came a transformation in the viewpoints of American historiography, with the methods and statements of conflict history relinquished in favor of consensus history.[249] Richard Hofstadter, one of the most important American consensus historians, succinctly interpreted this new intellectual current:

The cold war brought a certain closing of the ranks, a disposition to stress common objectives, a revulsion from Marxism and its tendency to think of social conflict as carried à outrance. The apocalyptic end of capitalism so widely expected during the 1930's had not been brought by the war—nor had the precipitate end of American democracy the isolationists had so confidently predicted. Instead of the expected catastrophic depression, an unprecedented economic boom followed the war, and the star of Keynes rose as that of Marx waned. Even the bomb, the most disquieting reality of the era, set in motion a current of conservativism, insofar as it made men think of political change with a new wariness and cling to what they had. . . . The populism of the right inspired a new skepticism about the older populism of the left. While Daniel Bell was writing about the end of ideology in the West, historians were returning to the idea that in the United States it had hardly ever begun.[250]

This transformation of historical consciousness can also be interpreted symbolically, using the example of a speech held in 1950 before the American Historical Association by its president, Samuel Eliot Morison. Morison pleaded for a historical approach that, though still dedicated to the critical search for truth, would not neglect the positive sides of history and would preserve traditions by debunking them: "We need a United States history written from a sanely conservative point of view."[251] As early as 1942, the third edition of Samuel Eliot Morison's and Henry Steele Commager's consensus history *The Growth of the American Republic,* a highly influential historical monument to the self-perception of a nation dedicated to freedom, democracy, and progress, had met with a warm reception.[252] A further work of "consensus" history that contributed substantially to the mood and historiography of the 1950s and that has remained very influential was Richard Hofstadter's *The American Political Tradition and the Men Who Made It* (1948). His analysis of ten representative American politicians, the Founding Fathers of the Revolution and the "spoilsmen" after the Civil War, came to the conclusion that a "reinterpretation of our political traditions" was necessary, one that "emphasizes the common climate of American opinion. The existence of such a climate has been much obscured by the tendency to place political conflict in the foreground of history."[253]

Hofstadter attempted to prove that all influential American presidents and politicians had agreed on a consensus-building ideological framework binding for all, composed of the ideal achievements of the nation—freedom, democracy, equality, property, economic individualism, and competition—and which guaranteed them basic agreement even in the event of superficial differences of opinion. "In these pages I have tried," wrote the pluralist historian in the book's introduction, "without neglecting significant conflicts, to keep sight of the central faith and to trace its adaptation to varying times and various interests."[254] This historical approach figured conspicuously not only in his elaboration of the political tradition of America, but also again and again in his treatment of certain other epochs and phenomena. He never whitewashed the conflicts in American history; his books on the anti-intellectualism, violence, and paranoia in American history are eloquent evidence of this.[255] Even in his later years, however, Hofstadter continued to regard consensus history as an important corrective of the progressivist historical writing which was cast in terms of simple contrasts. He also emphasized the sociopolitical complexity of American history:

If there is a single way of characterizing what has happened in our historical writing since the 1950's, it must be, I believe, the rediscovery of complexity in American history: an engaging and moving simplicity, accessible to the casual reader of history, has given way to a new awareness of the multiplicity of forces. To those who find things most interesting when they are simple, American history must have come to seem less interesting in our time; but to those who relish complexity, it has taken on a new fascination. When we look at the diffuseness of what has taken their place, we may appreciate once again the allure of the progressive schematizations, but we can hardly continue to believe in them.[256]

For Hofstadter, the study of history had been synonymous from the outset with the creation of a sense of social responsibility and progress. This is not to say that he did not allow for the inevitability (so familiar to the historian) of frustration and failure. Whereas Bancroft and Beard regarded historiography as an instrument of struggle or of romantic and dialectical instruction, Hofstadter rejected that view as a tragic historical fallacy. He hoped that historical science would remain the most humane of the arts: "In an age when so much of our literature is infused with nihilism, and other social disciplines are driven toward narrow positivistic inquiry, history may remain the most humanizing of the arts."[257] This long-term development of a new sense of history should, however, be seen primarily as closely linked to the creators of the consensus thesis characterizing the whole of American history. This consensus had spared Americans from a "real" revolution and its attendant ideological conflicts. Daniel J. Boorstin and Louis Hartz were the prime "homogenizers" of American history. Both Boorstin's influential book *The Genius of American Politics* (1953) and Hartz's classic *The Liberal Tradition in America* (1955) evolved from the search "for a usable past," as a critical Hofstadter cynically observed.[258]

Boorstin attributed the uniqueness of American political and democratic development and of American socioeconomic progress to the particularly fortunate circumstances and especially nurturing environmental conditions of the United States; to the historical continuity of the country's idealistic traditions; to the strength of American institutions and modes of behavior, a strength ensuing from their flexibility. In short, he ascribed it to the pragmatism and conservativism of the American way of life. He candidly noted that the genius of the New World "comes not from any special virtue of the American people but from the unprecedented opportunities of this continent and from a peculiar and unrepeatable combination of circumstances."[259] In this respect, his work is reminiscent of Turner's; not of Turner's internal struggle between the men of the frontier and the capitalists, but of his search for the primary source of American uniqueness (*e pluribus unum*). Hofstadter pointed out that "in Boorstin the frontier becomes a source not of agrarian conflict but of American conservatism."[260] For Boorstin, American values were so deeply rooted in the American character that he viewed them as not merely transcendent of all borders but as indestructible. Thus, he defined the American values as products of everyday practical experience, and not as philosophical perceptions:

We do not need American philosophers because we already have an American philosophy, implicit in the American Way of Life. . . . We must find a way of defending our institutions without insisting on propagating them. . . . We must refuse to become crusaders for conservatism in order to conserve the institutions which have made America great.[261]

In conjunction with a distinct "belief in the *continuity* or homogeneity of our history," this very givenness of particular historically and environmentally conditioned factors had apparently never aroused among Americans the need, so apparent in Europeans, for an explicit political theory beyond the extent of those basic values defined by the Founding Fathers. Boorstin did not even regard the American "Revolution" as such. For him, therefore, the Revolution could function neither as the instrument of a political theory nor as the initiator of ideological confrontation.[262] Hofstadter vehemently contradicted this opinion and countered Boorstin's view with the truly revolutionary aspects of the American Revolution:

Certainly the pattern of the American Revolution was different from that of the Puritan, French and Russian revolutions. But will it do to conclude that since Americans were in this sense born free, they had no revolution at all? . . . If we conclude that the American Revolution lacked a true revolutionary character because of the traditionalism of its *ideas,* we may miss a vital point. This Revolution represented the inheritance of the most radical ideas in Western civilization . . . it took the demand for popular government out of the realm of slogans and rallying cries and showed that it was actually susceptible to being translated into living institutions and being made to work. If our test for a revolution is the formation of a radically new ideological system, or regicide, or a widespread lethal terror, the American revolution will not qualify. But if our criterion is the accelerated redistribution of power among social classes or among various social types, a pragmatic disrespect for vested interests, the rapid introduction of profoundly important constitutional changes, we must reconsider it.[263]

The Yale historian Edmund S. Morgan (*The Birth of the Republic, 1763–89,* 1956), and especially the neo-Whig historian Bernard Bailyn from Harvard University, also argued along these lines. In his award-winning book *The Ideological Origins of the American Revolution* (1967), Bailyn used pamphlets to bring attention to the origins of the ideological and sociopsychological impulses of the American Revolution, which were still unexplored (except in pamphlets) at that point.[264] Ultimately indicative of Bailyn's perception of the American Revolution was his address to the 1975 International Congress of Historical Sciences in San Francisco:

It developed into a revolution shaped to the broader ideals of the enlightenment and of Anglo-American libertarianism, its ultimate aim nothing less than to perfect the condition of mankind by those lights at least in this one land, so highly endowed with natural wealth and so naturally free from the burdens of ancient institutions. . . . So idealism has mingled with realism, brutality with the loftiest aspirations; and while there has always been cynicism, there has always been hope.[265]

In Boorstin's opinion—which was classified by Richard Hofstadter as anti-intellectual and therefore specifically American—the Americans' practical political genius made a system of political theory superfluous. But it was precisely this same phenomenon that the brilliant intellectual historian Louis Hartz regarded as a defect. Like Tocqueville, Hartz attributed the Americans' political consensus to the lack of a feudal system and, after the eradication of the Loyalists, to the lack of a conservative opposition as an intellectual antagonist. Hofstadter criticized Hartz's premise that

lacking a feudal past, America was "born free," and needed no democratic revolution to become democratic. The American Revolution itself was a colonial revolution only, marked by an astonishing traditionalism and legalism in its leading ideas. The basically liberal-bourgeois ideas of Europe had been transported to America and here were given an exceptionally open environment in which to develop virtually unopposed. In the absence of feudal reactionary traditions and feudal patterns of dominance and submission, the principles of bourgeois liberalism, as embodied in the intellectual heritage of Locke, enjoyed here an almost exclusive control of the spectrum of political belief. Absorbed in constitutionalism, America developed, in place of a class of political thinkers, a class of argumentative lawyers. . . . The working class, so little affected by the dreams of socialism, became preoccupied with individualistic opportunity and advancement, not with class solidarity and class struggle.[266]

To Hofstadter this thesis was confined to a purely political history of ideas and detached from the actual development of history. It was this point that he thought constituted the inherent weakness of Hartz's interpretation:

It is a highly rationalist and intellectual approach to the ways of a nonintellectual people. . . . With his [Hartz's] easy and knowing allusions to European political thinkers of the second and third rank whom most of us have never read and have not, in some cases, even heard of, [he] seems like some splendid exotic bird, cruelly forced to live on the coarse and indigestible flora of America.[267]

With all due respect to the possible justness of the critique of consensus historiography, voiced in particular by John Higham in his attack in 1959 against the "cult of the 'American Consensus' " as "pure homogenizing" of the American past,[268] Hartz's progressive account of the predominantly liberal traditions of the United States on the foundation of historical and current political experience, has proved itself sound, remaining valid even today. The key to the idealist American sense of progress and its conversion into practice lies precisely in this abiding, nonpartisan national consensus on the values first formulated by the Founding Fathers. In fact, the political motivation for the preservation of progressivist historical values has characterized the thoroughly liberal element of American conservativism so fundamentally different from its European counterpart. In this light it seems that a liberal-pluralistic historiography such as consensus history does the most justice to the American historical and political tradition.

## REVISIONIST HISTORIOGRAPHY: PROGRESS AS PSEUDO-IDEOLOGY

In the 1960s, and to a lesser degree in the 1970s, American historiography increasingly directed attention to the role of economic and social conflicts of interest. The approach was considerably more radical, however, than that of previous progressivist historians. Obeying the motto of a protagonist of the historiography of the New Left, Edward Hallet Carr ("Before you study history, study the historian . . . before you study the historian, study his historical and social environment"),[269] a group of younger historians began to experiment with a new revisionism. They were influenced by the sharp ideological contrasts of the 1960s, and they consciously continued the conflict-oriented model of progressive history.[270]

These historians devoted themselves primarily to the political, social, and racial tensions in American society, issues that became the distinctive focal point of their analyses. The contemporary civil rights movements, race and minority issues, poverty, social disintegration in the slums, the vested privileges of the "Establishment," alleged repression under the slogan of "law and order," the disillusionment ensuing from the assassinations of John F. Kennedy, Robert Kennedy, and Martin Luther King, Jr., and the Vietnam War were among the key problems and areas of conflict. Many of the New Left historians became spokespersons for these causes and helped to promote their goals with historical research and analysis. To this end, they propagated their selectively biased and instrumental (in the sense of helping to encourage social change in contemporary history) radical democratic ideas.[271] Worthy of mention here are Staughton Lynd and Howard Zinn, who referred to a somewhat undiscerning interpretation of New History and a Marxism based mainly on early writings.

They did not hesitate to profess their support for a "radical history" as an impetus for social action, and they worked to orient historical questions to current political interests.[272] Most of the New Left historians—largely from the so-called Wisconsin School associated with names such as Fred Harvey Harrington and William Appleman Williams—devoted themselves exclusively to the "imperialistic" foreign policy of the United States.[273] Others, however, wrote on the history of minorities, particularly blacks and Indians, Abolition, the history of the industrial labor movement, or the reform movements of the twentieth century.[274] In 1968 Jesse Lemisch staged a frontal attack on the entire course of American historiography up to that point with his demands for a "history from the bottom up," a history of the "little people," the workers, craftsmen, small farmers, sailors, and slaves, who had always been "trampled on," in place of history of the elite and the victors in decisive historical processes. Lemisch polemicized against the tendency of traditional historiography to consider history from the perspective of the ruling classes. He pointed out that the lower class's radicalizing function, which he considered a positive one, had affected the "true" progress of history. Inspired by Herbert Marcuse, he demanded greater sympathy for the powerless, a sympathy that, he contended, could only be guaranteed by "historic objectivity":

In practice, it [this sympathy] leads the historian to describe past societies as they appeared from the bottom rather than from the top, more from the point of view of the inarticulate than of the articulate. . . . A small part of the necessary work has been done, and a radically new view is just now becoming visible: it is hoped that some of the readers of this essay will do more.[275]

Lemisch does not seem to have considered that such an endeavor is in fact hardly feasible methodologically. In any event, the New Left historians were not granted lasting fame. Initially, they suffered from the delusion that the academic historical Establishment would simply block their research work.[276] It is more likely, however, that their failure can be attributed to the New Left's loss of unity and impetus after 1969, especially after the end of the Vietnam War. Moreover, a new sobriety arose among American historians, an attitude that emphasized meticulous elaboration of research findings rather than ideologically motivated studies.[277] Thus, William Appleman Williams's book *America Confronts a Revolutionary World, 1776–1976* (1976) proved to be not only a left-wing anachronism, but also a grotesque example of historical philosophy. In his analysis, Williams declared the Constitution of 1787 a regression, the end of any potential for structural change in the new state. "It established the foundation of a superstate, a political giant that had the power to override any single state (or culture). It did so by making population the bedrock of power: a majority could impose its will upon *any* minority."[278] The principle of self-determination set down in the Declaration of Independence had been abandoned, he stated, and the preservation of the status quo had become the overriding aim. At the same time, the Founding Fathers' "Establishment" had embarked on a course of constant expansion, in order to divert the internal tensions of the new antiprogressivist system to international political actions. Thus, contrary to the ideals it had formulated at the outset, America had risen to a counterrevolutionary power that attempted to impose its own ideology on its neighbors, indeed on the entire world. Of course, if one is even vaguely familiar with the political and legal structure of power in the Union up to the Civil War, such allegations can only be characterized as "phantasmagoria."[279]

The ideological combination of political moralizing and dogmatic accusation characteristic of New Left history continues to find resonance even now in some of the most recent projects on contemporary historical research. To some degree, however, current American historiography also reflects a trend toward both pessimism and consensus history.

## AMERICAN CONTEMPORARY THINKING: BETWEEN NEW REALISM AND NEW IDEALISM

The creative revision of history is one aspect of a larger recent trend in contemporary history and literature whose goal is the reconstruction of the American past. In the 1960s, revisionist historians began to question the traditional view of American history, which focused on consensus, assimilation, and progress. These historians undeniably opened up extremely interesting, new, and previously overlooked areas of the history of the so-called silent groups, such as blacks, women, and workers. But this new historiography was based largely on quantitative research and microhistorical studies that tended to fragment insight into American history and to reduce its accessibility to the wider public. Many of these studies tended to apply modern expectations to historical events, to make rough generalizations of isolated and peripheral events, and to indulge in New Left moralizations.[280] Without doubt, works on the race question and on the history of slavery occupy a prominent place in the latest historical research. Noteworthy here are Winthrop D. Jordan's far-reaching history *White Over Black,* which examines white supremacy in America from the sixteenth to the early nineteenth century, and David Brion Davis's *Slavery and the Idea of Progress,* which discusses the problem of slavery in the Revolutionary age and the arguments for and against its abolition.[281] Mention should also be made of the increased research on the history of women. Although earlier works had demonstrated an interest in women of the Revolutionary period, the "Founding Mothers," they concentrated almost exclusively on such famous personalities as Abigail Adams, Mercy Warren, or Martha Washington, all of whom belonged to the upper echelons of society.[282] Under the influence of the "Women's Lib" movement, there has been an upsurge of women's studies in the United States since the 1960s.[283]

Interpretation of the American Revolution as a source of historical self-understanding continues to be an essential characteristic of contemporary American historiography. Studies regularly appear on the American Revolution, its intellectual and social basis, and its effect on the existence and identity of the American people. This identity can still be paraphrased with the words of Oscar Wilde: "The youth of America is their oldest tradition."[284] Numerous political studies of the American Revolution appeared for the Bicentennial in 1976 and in the period following it. Good examples are the articles published in *American Historical Review* in 1977[285] and Morton White's book *The Philosophy of the American Revolution,* works that trace the philosophical foundations of the concepts behind the American Revolution back through Western civilization. White concludes that, although the Founding Fathers did not develop any new, original thoughts about human social existence, they did transform much of the philosophical wisdom of their age into actual political practice. White offers convincing evidence for his thesis, substantiating it with the use of some of the Revolution's central concepts—"self-evident truth," "nature," "progress," and the "essence of man." These concepts remain valid because of their traditions, contemporary meaning, and timeless relevance.[286]

The study by the English historian J. R. Pole entitled *The Pursuit of Equality in American History* is also worth mentioning. Pole analyzes the idea of equality and the importance of the role it has played in American political thought since the Revolution. He establishes a convincing connection between intellectual history and general historiography by defining the impact of the principle of equality, always noting its interaction with the complementary idea of freedom, in all areas of human existence, up to and including current sociocultural relationships and political practices.

Finally, Michael Kammen created a sensation with his work *A Season of Youth, the American Revolution and the Historical Imagination*. Working from the perspective of cultural anthropology, Kammen concludes that the Revolution proved to be the formative event for the American sense of self and value. In his examination of the polymorphic imagination of Americans and their scientific, literary, and artistic interaction with history, Kammen perceives the Revolution as a basic historical element in the political and cultural thought of his countrymen. Despite all change and progress, it triumphs as a self-contained conservative myth.[287]

At the same time, around the end of the 1970s and the beginning of the 1980s, a new avant-garde trend was developing in American literary and historical circles. In the words of Herbert G. Gutman, a new synthesis is necessary, one that incorporates the New History and goes beyond it. Semiologists and historians are beginning to question the traditional distinction between historiography and literary fiction.[288] By pointing out the similarities between the linguistic structures and rhetorical strategies of historical and fictional texts, Roland Barthes and Hayden White had already attacked the special status of history as a representation of reality. For them there was apparently no privileged perspective for the past and no "objective" history. Facts were not unambiguous; rather, they were selected and organized according to the specific narrative vision that historians brought to their subjects.[289]

Many writers noted the dissolution of the traditional barriers between history and literature. In the 1960s, authors like John Barth (*The Sot-Weed Factor*), Thomas Berger (*Little Big Man*), and William Styron (*Confessions of Nat Turner*) had already begun to reshape American history in their novels. Closer to the present, the newly awakened interest in history repeatedly directed itself toward political themes, as seen in E. L. Doctorow's *Ragtime*, Gore Vidal's *Burr*, or John A. Williams's *Captain Blackman*.[290] In 1978 Doctorow explained in an interview why American novelists were turning to history as a theme in their work:

Well, first of all, history as written by historians is clearly insufficient. And the historians are the first to express skepticism over this "objectivity" of the discipline. A lot of people discovered after World War II and in the fifties that much of what was taken by the younger generations as history was highly interpreted history. And just as through the guidance and wisdom of magazines like *Time*, we were able to laugh at the Russians' manipulation of their own history—in which they claimed credit for technological advances that had clearly originated in other countries, and in which leaders who had fallen out of favor were suddenly absent from their texts—just around that time, we began to wonder about our own history texts and our own school books. And it turned out that there were not only individuals but whole peoples whom we had simply written out of our history—black people, Chinese people, Indians. At the same time, there is so little a country this size has in the way of cohesive, identifying marks that we can all refer to and recognize each other from. It turns out that history, as insufficient and poorly accommodated it may be, is one of the few things we have in common here. . . . For all of us to read about what happened to us fifty or a hundred years ago suddenly becomes an act of community. And the person who represented what happened fifty or a hundred years ago has a chance to begin to say things about us now. I think that has something to do with the discovery of writers that this is possible.[291]

Partly as a reaction to the excessive subjectivity in the literature of the 1950s and partly as a reaction to the political and cultural events of the 1960s, this renewed interest in history was shown in the writings of numerous authors. Their ranks extended from orthodox modernists like William Styron and Gore Vidal to unorthodox postmodern novelists like Thomas Pynchon and Ishmael Reed. In their novels, fact and fiction, as well as conventional and experimental form, are united in order to question the concept of historical objectivity and to destroy the assumption that a demonstrable order lies at the base of history. In Reed's *Mumbo Jumbo* and Doctorow's *Ragtime,* for instance, the traditional interpretation of modern American history is turned on its head and rewritten from the "bottom up." In these books, blacks, women, immigrants, and workers—the people who do not appear in history books—assert themselves as personalities in modern American culture.[292]

It would probably be going too far to claim that history has become the paradigm of recent American literature, as Marxism was in the 1930s and existentialism in the 1950s. Many American authors are trying to achieve the new synthesis that Herbert Gutman found lacking in contemporary historiography, but in fact, several of today's writers are now concerning themselves with the end of history. In the 1980s, American literature began to strike an apocalyptic note, as in Jonathan Schell's much-discussed apology of decline *The Fate of the Earth,* in Norman Mailer's description of the fall of a great empire in *Ancient Evenings,* or in Jayne Anne Phillips's settling of accounts with the "American Dream" in her most recent book, *Machine Dreams.*[293] Bernard Malamud's *God's Grace* depicts a world of catastrophe and heralds the end of the world. On the first page of his novel, for example, God speaks to the only survivor of a nuclear holocaust in the language of a seventeenth-century Puritan sermon:

They have destroyed my handiwork, the conditions of their survival: the sweet air I gave them to breathe; the fresh water I blessed them with, to drink and bathe in; the fertile green earth. They tore apart my ozone, carbonized my oxygen, acidified my refreshing rain. Now they affront my cosmos. How much shall the Lord endure?[294]

These religiously motivated American indictments of progress seem very different from certain alternative and radicalized, European (and especially German), antiprogressivist, and antitechnological ways of thinking. The ambivalence of progress is making waves in literature and contemporary historiography on both sides of the Atlantic. The overlapping impressions are still too fresh to distinguish who is influencing whom. Turning to the picture of contemporary American society in recent literature, one is inevitably confronted by the same apocalyptic feeling. "History," observes the protagonist in John Updike's *Rabbit Is Rich,* "the more of it you have, the more you have to live it. After a little while there gets to be too much of it to memorize and maybe that's when empires start to decline."[295]

The theme of decline also plays a central role in Saul Bellow's book, *The Dean's December,* which is about contemporary life in Chicago and Bucharest. Bellow's novel is a portrait of two societies plagued by different symptoms of decline. The liberal society of the West is constructed on the pleasure principle, but suffers from loss of authority and is threatened by an oppressed, anarchic lower class. The authoritarian society of the East is based on the principle of suffering, but is undermined by apathy and governed by a cynical new class. For Bellow, the "soft" nihilism of the West, where permissiveness undermines the community, contradicts the "hard" nihilism of the East, where terror seizes legal authority.[296] *The Dean's December* describes what the last days of civilization may be like in terms similar to those in Christopher Lasch's controversial study, *The Culture of Narcissism: American Life in an Age of Diminishing Experience.*[297]

In these last days we have a right and even a duty to purge our understanding. In the general weakening of authority, the authority of the ruling forms of thought also is reduced, those forms which have done much to bring us into despair and into the abyss. I don't need to mind them anymore. For science there can be no good or evil. But I personally think about virtue, about vice. . . . In the American moral crisis the first requirement was to experience what was happening and to see what must be seen.[298]

For Bellow, the writing of literature is an act of regaining reality, as well as a process of revealing its meaning. This reclaiming of social reality requires more than a simple admission that the environment is deteriorating. It calls for a confrontation with "the slums we carry around inside us. Every man's *inner* city."[299] Bellow thus feels that the problem of progress is not just a poisoned atmosphere, but also poisoned thoughts and a poisoned theory. For this reason a new realism is necessary, one that would help us to recover the world we have lost contact with, or, in Bellow's words: "To recover the world that is buried under the debris of false description or non-experience."[300]

The political writer Renée Winegarten also argues from this perspective:

We remain content to speak of sick ages and cultures, rather than a misguided or perverted individual. We attribute too much to the fatality of decline. Perhaps, after all, it is not decadence itself, so much as the ready acceptance of the idea of an all-pervasive decadence, which is insidiously demoralizing, especially in vulnerable democracies. For, as has been well said, it is often not the real losses in battle which prove disastrous, but the imaginary loss and the discouragement which drain away the strength that fate had left untouched.[301]

This new realism in contemporary American history and literature appears to be a reaction to the contemporary intellectual atmosphere vis-à-vis an idea of progress in need of redefinition, as well as a critical reexamination of the utopian revisionism of the 1960s. American literature and contemporary history have become, in fact, more political—proof of this is given in Allan Bloom's thesis of the "closing of the American mind"—and in the process have consciously gone beyond the "truths" defined by the prevailing ideology of the recent past. For Bellow, these new directions of thought mean the restoration and rehabilitation of humanism in a world dominated by scientific materialism. For Doctorow, it means resuming the search for justice in a world of complexity and bipolarity. According to Doctorow, a feeling of total spiritual exhaustion developed in the face of the political alternatives of progress in the twentieth century, a state of exhaustion (one could add) ultimately making itself noticeable physiologically as well, namely, in the newest social disease, AIDS. For Doctorow, no system, whether religious or nonreligious, capitalist or planned by the state, is immune from the hate, greed, and insanity of humankind. The literary historian Paul Levine feels that the best recent American literature and contemporary historiography is characterized by this new realism, a realism not without hope, but also not without wisdom.[302]

A neoconservative political and historical ethos, already in existence prior to Ronald Reagan's presidency but undoubtedly reinforced by it, can be detected in American political culture today. For the moment, however, it is too early to say whether this neoconservative consciousness has made inroads into American contemporary history. Certainly, an effort to return to the true basic values of American history, to human rights, freedom, equality, and justice, has become manifest, with the study of the nation's birth in its complex context of revolution and conservation continuing to play an important role. Undoubtedly, the experiences of many Americans since the Second World War have led to the conclusion that elements of preservation and stability are as important to the existence of society as factors of activity for its progress. A renaissance of consensus history seems to be in the offing in American historiography, although conclusive evidence for it is not yet available.[303]

# 5

---

# History and Progress: Convergence and Divergence in Transatlantic Comparison

An understanding of the historical character of the Old and New World requires comparison, as attempted in the preceding chapter, of the European and American ideas of progress. The convergence of European and American thought is defined through the values and motifs of Western ideas. While Europe evolved over the centuries from various power constellations and their displacement, America was born of concrete principles. American history can be regarded as the realization of liberal and democratic ideas of progress, as "applied Enlightenment."[304] The uniqueness of the American nation stems precisely from its creation as a conscious act on the part of the Founding Fathers, who based their ideas on universally applicable ethical and political maxims. In Ralf Dahrendorf's words, American history is nothing more than the development of a single principle: the process of rationalization, democratization, mobilization, and communalization, that is, the perfection of elements contained in the beginnings of every society.[305]

The divergence of the political ideas of America and Europe actually begins with the French and American revolutions, with their different aims, courses, and consequences. The phenomena of the American Revolution and independence resulted in a national historical consensus and pragmatic political progressivist idealism that still exist today. Thus, a positive ideologization, so to speak, of American history was created that spared Americans from political extremism. At the same time, the absolute progressive ideals set up by French Revolution continuously antagonized and polarized European sociopolitical models. Thus was created a negative ideologization that expressed itself in utopian, dogmatic, and totalitarian theories and political forms. The phenomena of "America" and its revolution were, simultaneously, ignored and suppressed for over a century by many Europeans, who basically did not understand, or accept, the historical independence of the United States from Europe until the Second World War.

The interdependence of European and American progressivism did not remain unaffected by the historical and political denial of America. Mutual perceptions have fluctuated since the French and American revolutions. From Benjamin Franklin to Henry Kissinger, the American image of Europe, from the observation post of isolationism as well as from an activist position of strength, has always been more or less sympathetic and balanced. In contrast, the European view, from Abbé Raynal, Alexis de Tocqueville, and Hegel, all the way up to the Greens, has always been more arrogant. Ultimately, all anti-American trends in European behavior have always revealed only the Old World's own fears, uncertainties, and weaknesses. The Americans' claim to the universality of their moral progressivism, along with the increasing Americanization of Europe, and indeed of the entire Western world, is a thorn in the sides of many Europeans. On one hand, they cannot bear to see the superior culmination and perpetuation of the classical Western values of freedom, democracy, human rights, and equality in the New World rather than in the Old. They are jealous and at odds with themselves. On the other hand, they are afraid (perhaps because they no longer believe in themselves) not to regain the European identity lost with Hitler and Stalin. At this point it becomes apparent that history and progress represent one indivisible, progressive phenomenon for America. For Europe, history often stands in the way of progress. Whether or not the Second World War has destroyed Europe's idea of progress may perhaps be revealed in the twenty-first century.

## THE AMERICAN REVOLUTION VERSUS THE FRENCH REVOLUTION

The American Revolution has a timeless significance because it was the first modern revolution and because it marked the beginning of the modern political world in certain decisive respects. The Revolution proclaimed popular sovereignty, the right to political participation through elections, the structuring of political life according to written constitutions, the recognition of basic human rights, liberty, and the pursuit of happiness. All of these achievements symbolized the Revolution's modernity. Although many of these ideas had been articulated during the English Revolution in the middle of the seventeenth century, they were not the "official" revolutionary doctrine, but the thoughts of a minority that was unable to implement them. In the American Revolution the "rights of Englishmen" became human rights; the Americans' common-law claim to the right of equality with English citizens across the Atlantic led to the idea of human equality, at first, admittedly, in rather vague form but nonetheless with a high degree of universality.

The revolutionary characteristics of the founding of the United States have not always been defined as such in the way Americans see themselves historically.

In the period directly after the Revolution, the military aspect and heroics initially gained prominence, and the accent and the interest of the historians shifted to the "War of Independence." Soon a flood of hagiographic biographies of George Washington appeared. The historians David Ramsey (*History of the American Revolution*, 1789) and Mason L. Weems (*Life of George Washington*, 1800) presented and celebrated heroic, even superhuman, images of Washington. But soon, with the domestic political controversies between the Federalists around Alexander Hamilton and John Adams and the Republicans around Thomas Jefferson, this issue developed into a dispute about the interpretation and preservation of the legacy of the Revolution and the founding ideals of the Union. These arguments provided the real content of Mercy Otis Warren's multivolume work entitled *History of the Rise, Progress, and Termination of the American Revolution* (1805).

The conflict over the correct interpretation of the American Revolution greatly affected American contemporary history in the decades leading up to the Civil War. It was essentially left to the most important historian of Romanticism, George Bancroft (who dedicated the last two volumes of his lengthy *History of the United States* [1834–82] to the ratification of the Constitution in 1787), to put an end to the controversy by pointing out the altered domestic situation and to draw attention to the promising progressivist future. The entire history of America since the Colonies, in which the American Revolution was harmoniously embedded, was for Bancroft the irrepressible expression of democracy's triumphal march through the world. Although it may seem to be only a small interpretative step from Bancroft's Romantic view of the Revolution to the liberalism thesis of the consensus historian Louis Hartz, historiography about the Revolution did not draw a straight line between them. During the rapid industrialization of America around the end of the nineteenth century, economic, political, social, and regional conflicts entered the picture. Under these conditions the American Revolution was interpreted as an expression of the internal opposition between the urbane East and the backward agricultural West. *The Critical Period of American History, 1783–1789* (1888), by the popular historian John Fiske, reflected this attitude.

During the following decades, from the reform movements of the Populist and Progressive eras and into the 1920s, these conflict-oriented interpretations of the American Revolution became even stronger. The works of such historians as Carl L. Becker, Charles A. Beard, and J. Franklin Jameson are particularly characteristic. In *The History of Political Parties in the Province of New York, 1760–1776*, Becker concluded that the American Revolution was not just a matter of "home rule," but of the question "who would rule at home." This position remains controversial to the present day. Along with the issue of independence from England, according to Becker, a domestic political power struggle was being fought around the question of political participation. Charles Beard's provocative work, *An Economic Interpretation of the Constitution of the United States* (1913) in turn discredited the Founding Fathers of the republic as the

"Funding Fathers," who, as Beard contended, had identical economic interests and obtained economic advantages from the Constitution they created.

J. Franklin Jameson's lectures, collected in his book *The American Revolution Considered as Social Movement* (1926), examined the interrelationships of the social classes, the institution of slavery, the system of landownership, and the forms and substance of intellectual and religious life. Although Jameson avoided the term "social revolution," his conflict analysis of the American Revolution met with vehement criticism from conservatives and moderate liberals, as had also been the fate of the interpretations of Becker and the "Marxist" Beard. Louis Hartz later stated in testimony before the Senate Committee on Foreign Affairs in 1968 that the liberal political culture of the country had its foundation in the Puritan immigration of the seventeenth century and not in a social revolution. This, contended Hartz, was the reason why Americans had such problems in understanding social revolutionary movements in other parts of the world. Of course, Hartz's conception of the almost natural character of America's political liberalism was, from the outset, an expression of the thinking of the 1950s and 1960s vis-à-vis totalitarianism in the Soviet Union. During the Cold War, it was necessary to demonstrate the superiority of Western ideals and to emphasize unity, freedom, democracy, and constitutional government. Thus, the objective of consensus history's debate about the phenomenon of the American Revolution was not the reinterpretation of the Revolution itself, but rather the refutation of the Progressive historians.

The most important works of this period included Richard Hofstadter's *The American Political Tradition* (1948), Frederick B. Tolle's *The American Revolution Considered as a Social Movement: A Re-Evaluation* (1954–55), and Louis Hartz's *The Liberal Tradition in America* (1956). All of these authors attempted to portray the Revolution as a unique phenomenon of liberal principles in politics and society—principles established in a consensus-based Constitution approved by the people—and as a means of securing individual rights and protecting the people from every form of despotism. This neo-Whiggist interpretation of the American Revolution, based on the ideology of consensus, came to fruition especially in Bernard Bailyn's *The Ideological Origins of the American Revolution* (1967). In this work, he analyzed the Revolution from the perspective of its ideological roots and interpreted it exclusively as a constitutional dispute about the correct form of government. Bailyn defined the outbreak of the Revolution not as the result of social dissatisfaction, economic unrest, or growing poverty, but as a rebellion that took place in the context of a prosperous economy and a society with relatively small class differences in order to achieve independence from England. For Bailyn, as for other consensus historians, social conflicts had no significant influence on the essence of the American Revolution.

The deep-seated unrest and conflicts within American society from the mid-1960s into the 1970s then posed anew the question of the phenomenon of the "American Revolution," raising new doubts about consensus history. For example, conflicts in the Revolutionary era once again became the focus in new books, including Michael Kammen's *A Season of Youth, the American Revolution and the Historical Imagination* (1978), Richard A. Ryerson's *The Revolution Is Now Begun: The Radical Committees of Philadelphia, 1765–1776* (1978), Gary B. Nash's *The Urban Crucible: Social Change, Political Consciousness, and the Origins of the American Revolution* (1979), Edward Countryman's *A People in Revolution: The American Revolution and Political Society in New York, 1760–1790* (1981), and Rhys Isaac's *The Transformation of Virginia, 1740–1790* (1982). Even if these studies bear similarities to the research approaches of the Progressive historians, by no means did they represent a complete return to the academic positions of the early twentieth century. The authors use new methods in their attempt to direct the reader's attention to the middle and lower classes—"the people"—in order to offer a different interpretation of the American Revolution.

These contrasting interpretations reflect the polymorphism of the phenomenon of "revolution" not only in American historiography, but in the national self-understanding as well.[306] The image of the American Revolution as the breakthrough of the optimist belief in enlightenment and progress can still be seen in the American spirit of the times: both as an actual historical process that led to the founding of the United States two hundred years ago and as the myth revealed by James Oliver Robertson in *American Myth, American Reality* (1980). This myth was formed at the end of the eighteenth century and is preserved today as the conserving, progressivist strain in America's political culture and national consciousness. It is reaffirmed in ritualized form every year on the Fourth of July.

Apart from the American historical self-image with regard to the phenomenon of "revolution," the revolutionary qualities of the events in America should be investigated, especially in terms of their political ideas, their ramifications for the development of constitutional law, and the progressivist meaning of the American Revolution as compared to the French. About 130 years ago, Leopold von Ranke made the following observation about America to King Maximilian II of Bavaria:

This was a larger revolution than any other in the world before it, a complete reversal of principle. Before it was the king, by the grace of God, who organized everything around him; and then the idea appeared that that power should rise up from below.... These two principles face each other as two worlds, and the modern world is but trapped between the two.[307]

Ranke's attempt to characterize the American Revolution was only partly successful. Although the most important domestic impacts of the Revolution had been the "democratization," "modernization," and "advancement" of American society and its political system, the residents of Rhode Island or Connecticut would probably not have understood Ranke's argument. After all, even though many of them had participated in the American Revolution, few of them saw any reason to change the constitutional bases of their own states and to give themselves new constitutions as the other eleven states had done. For the Americans, nothing fundamental changed in the legitimization and practice of governing.

The leaders of the American Revolution were by no means united in their opinion of the meaning and importance of the Revolution. According to John Adams, the Revolution took place in the hearts of the people, from 1760 to 1775, beginning fifteen years before the first drop of blood was shed in Lexington.[308] A great change took place in the minds of America's Revolutionary elite during these years. Their loyalty turned away from the monarchical mother country to create an independent republic. In 1788 Madison took it to be self-evident that the general form and organization of the American government had to be strictly republican, although he was aware that this contradicted prevailing theories of the state, according to which—as Montesquieu emphasized—the republic was, as a form of government, fitting only for small territories, for larger states would inevitably become victims of corruption.[309] Thus, from a domestic standpoint, the establishment of a republic in America seemed a logical conclusion. Viewed from the outside, however, it was a novelty, an expression of will, something of revolutionary freshness. At the same time, this reflected the feelings Americans had of the deep caesura caused by the Revolution and of a new beginning in world history. Even if opinions differed as to when the Revolution began and when it ended, it is safe to say that the rebellious Americans were conscious of a new start. A feeling of "the pathos of a new beginning" reigned in the United States, a feeling that, as expressed by Hannah Arendt, legitimized talk of revolution.[310]

For Madison and the other Founding Fathers, these innovative processes could mean lasting success only if they were linked to a representative republican government under elite leadership. Here one of the most important differences between the French and American republicanism becomes clear. The revolutionary character of France was, from August 10, 1792, and onward, much more closely tied to the concept of equality and direct popular government, and much less to the concepts of freedom and representative democracy that so strongly influenced America.[311] This fundamental quality of the American Revolution made possible the creation of a constitution derived directly from the people; it "ushered in a new era in the history of mankind." It was precisely in modern constitutionalism, with its constitutional anchoring of human rights, its principles of checks and balances, and the establishment of the Constitution as the highest level of legal authority, that the progressivist quality of the American Revolution found its fullest expression. The global importance of the American Revolution lies in the fact that it was a democratic, *constitutional revolution* and, at the same time, the birth of a state that until then had not existed in any form, comprised of thirteen neighboring colonies without any common history and homogeneous population. The American Revolution symbolized a *radical redefinition of the concept of government*, without basic changes in the structures of ownership or society, without a rigorous replacement of the ruling class, and without even the abandonment of already existing constitutional elements.

For the first time in modern history the sovereignty of the people was made the foundation of the state order. The American Revolution adopted the idea that public power must be exercised by and for those who are subject to it. The revolutionary element lay not just in the proclamation and rationale of this idea, but, as Robert Palmer has emphasized, in the practical realization of the idea of popular sovereignty.[312] The state was constituted as a democracy based on the principle of checks and balances, and the Constitution was interpreted as the establishment of a principle of law of higher order and power because it was derived directly from the people. The creation of the Constitution was synonymous with the exercise of popular power and, because it stemmed from the people, it was of higher rank. Government by constitution replaced government by will. All of this was, to use Klaus Stern's phrase, "not pure *popular sovereignty*, but *constitutionalized popular sovereignty, that is, limited by fundamental rights.*"[313] The Revolution led to a clear separation of law and constitution, of legislative and constitutional assembly. The Bill of Rights effected the idea of inalienable rights, which were protected even from legislative intervention. The Constitution and the Bill of Rights became the normative limits of the power of the state.[314]

In contrast to its French counterpart, therefore, the Constitution of the United States was interpreted as a document for the control of relationships between the individual and the state, rather than between the state and society. The concepts of the French declaration of the rights of the individual, such as *société, corps social, distinctions sociales, nation,* and *la loi* (the law of collective, social reason) are absent from the American Bill of Rights, which became part of the Constitution as the first ten amendments in 1787. Its themes were those of the personal security of the individual, protection from the arbitrary power of the state and legal system, the right to personal freedom from injury, and the right to lead one's own life. That is, it was concerned with the borders of power between the state and the individual, and not with those separating the state from society. Unlike the case in France, in the United States this individualism thus became a basis of the Constitution.[315]

With its views that constitutions were feasible and revisable in the light of experience or change, the American Revolution documented the modernity of its understanding of the world and the state. At the same time it directly opposed the English constitutional conception, where the idea of an unalterable constitution had vehement support from, of all quarters, the radicals. Eventualities of change and progress were, to an extent, even calculated into the revision clauses of most articles in the American Constitution. This strategy could be traced back (in the cases of Jefferson and Paine) to the wise insight that each generation should have the right to make its own decisions without being unnecessarily burdened by the problems of its predecessors.[316]

The American Revolution was primarily a *constitutional* revolution; definable not only negatively through the mistakes of deep socioeconomic conflicts and change, but also positively in the same way. For one thing, the conflict with the mother country was a constitutional conflict, where a colonial constitutional order had been cast off violently; for another, the break with the traditional order and the innovative establishment of republicanism lay in a creative process of "constitution-making." For the American revolutionaries themselves, the understanding of the new historical beginning and of their role in world history had its basis in the single act of creating the Constitution.[317] The Americans were, as John Jay said, the first people to have been favored by heaven with the opportunity to choose and discuss the form of government under which they wanted to live; all other constitutions owed their existence to power or fate.[318] James Wilson celebrated the American Constitution by noting that forms of government are generally the result of violence, deception, or fate. During the more than six thousand years since the creation of humankind, the United States presented the first example of a nation where the people had decided, without being attacked by an external enemy and without being shaken by domestic revolts, on a new system of government under which they and their descendants could live peacefully.[319]

The question of whether the Revolution was revolutionary must thus be answered in the affirmative, for Americans were highly convinced that their actions were setting a good example. During the Revolution Americans took up the old Puritan missionary zeal again, the idea of being "a Citty upon a Hill," emphasizing the uniqueness of the American anticolonial revolts.[320] It offered the possibility of a link to religious chiliasm and its reinterpretation in political terms.[321] The Puritan ideology of America as the center of salvation and the elected instrument of God repeatedly appeared in secularized form during the Revolution and lent a universal dimension to the event.

A further progressive quality of the American Revolution manifested itself in the creation of the "new people" of the first new nation, "the Americans," who no longer regarded themselves primarily as New Yorkers or Virginians, but developed a new feeling of belonging that extended beyond provincial boundaries, transcending not just the old political and geographic borders that had existed until that time, but, increasingly, ethnic and religious barriers as well, on the way to a new "American" identity and a new society of the homogeneous "melting pot."[322]

In addition, it produced a certain social dynamic in many areas, an *élan vital* in the material expansion and acquisition of property. Before the deaths of Thomas Jefferson and John Adams in 1826, the last living signatories to the Declaration of Independence, the original thirteen states had grown to twenty-three members of the Union. This sociopolitical dynamic was in part a result of the gradual success of a bourgeois capitalist form of production, which strove to overcome the mercantile production and trade limits that had been imposed on the colonies earlier by London's imperial policies. It was Alexander Hamilton who, in his role as secretary of the Treasury during the Washington administration, favored introducing industrialization and capitalism to the American economy and ushered in important changes and strategies for the country's subsequent economic boom.[323] The American Revolution not only facilitated steady growth toward the West, bringing about rapid change in rural America, but also helped lend economic success a new, socially progressive status that was decisive for the the country's future political culture. This revolutionary combination of capitalist economy and libertarian politics gave the American social organization its new fundamental structures, whose dynamism became more manifest in the course of the nineteenth century. In essence, these structures have survived to the present day.

Despite the predominantly positive course of the American Revolution, it is still necessary to point out the failures of its development, including the unsolved problem of slavery and the unchanged question of the Indians. The Indian territory west of the settlement boundary of 1763 was increasingly encroached upon and to some extent destroyed by white Americans.[324] The American Revolution's ideological effect on the problem of slavery was ambiguous. On the one hand, equality and freedom called for the elimination of slavery; on the other hand, slavery was protected by the strong emphasis on "property rights."[325] Nonetheless, the changes and impulses of the 1770s and 1780s speak for the revolutionary quality of these events in America. By 1804 all of the Northern states had passed emancipation laws, and even in the South, despite the continued existence of slavery, the ideas of the Revolution brought about a certain change in the white population's attitudes toward the slavery question, which was, of course, resolved only by the Civil War. The emancipation of the slaves, very difficult in the eighteenth century, was made gradually easier by a series of legal decisions. It can definitely be seen that the number of free blacks between 1790 and 1810 increased more rapidly than the number of slaves as a result of the American Revolution.[326] Both the Declaration of Independence and the Bill of Rights enabled American blacks to perceive of freedom as a right belonging to them as a people, not one that could be sought only on an individual basis.

In conclusion, a comparison between the American and French Revolutions with regard to the divergent future development of American and European ideas of progress could well be illuminating. The unique qualities of the American Revolution lay precisely in its untypical, exceptional course: no missed aim or deformation, no strong swing of the pendulum in one direction or another, no reign of terror, no sudden dictatorial takeover, no restoration. In this sense it differed greatly from the other major revolutions of modern history, the English, French, and Russian. Clearly, freedom is at the center of the American Revolution, just as the creation of the Constitution was regarded as the act giving this freedom a form.[327] This liberal orientation was possible because the United States had a healthy economy, the promises of the Revolution were more modest, and the socioeconomic impulses toward Revolution much weaker than in other revolutions.

At the same time, the American Revolution did not manifest the dualism of a political and a social rebellion so evident in other revolutions in the history of humankind. For this reason, it can be viewed as an almost purely political revolution. None of the divisive rifts seen in other countries appeared in the revolutionary camp, nor did the powers-that-be form an opposing coalition. Unity was the order of the day. By contrast, the French Revolution has been classified as a revolution of the nobility, a revolution of the bourgeoisie, a revolution of the peasantry, and a popular revolution waged mostly by the sansculottes. In a word, its social representatives were as varied as its demands. While the bourgeoisie concentrated on the emancipation of property and the liberalization of the economy, the Parisian people's movement was opposed to laissez-faire economic policies and wanted to increase traditional economic regulations in the area of food production and distribution. All these ways of thinking were alien to the American Revolution; certain basic elements of American revolutionary ideology, such as mistrust of power, fear of dictatorship and corruption, and rejection of a standing army, helped to prevent its degeneration into a military dictatorship of the type experienced by the English, then the French, and finally the Russians. It was precisely this eminently antiauthoritarian "spirit of apprehension" that, in the end, prevented the political deformation of the American Revolution.[328]

America's Revolutionaries seem to have made a maxim of John Dickinson's remark of 1768, a paraphrase of Machiavelli: Happy are the people, and happy is the country, that become wise through the misfortune of others. Because of their sober historical thinking and awareness, the American Revolutionaries were definitely influenced by the Enlightenment's temperate belief in reason, not by the utopian belief of the unlimited human potential for perfection.[329] Patrick Henry, the revolutionary leader from Virginia, noted in 1775: "I have but one lamp by which my feet are guided, and that is the lamp of experience. I know no way of judging of the future but by the past."[330] The French Revolution, on the other hand, was dominated by a grand belief in reason, as exemplified by the works of Abbé Sieyes: "Never before was it a more urgent task to bestow reason with all its power and to wrest the facts away from might, which, to the misfortune of man, took them for itself."[331] For the Americans, however, it was more important to take into account the recognizably negative facts of history and to take rational precautions to prevent them from recurring.[332] The American Revolution was favored by the long-extant structures of self-rule, the country's de facto republicanism, its fluid social order, and the fact that there was no absolutist autocracy under the old regime, as was the case in France or Russia. Unlike the sansculottes, even the vast majority of the radical Americans accepted the principle of representation. The American Revolution lacked, perhaps uniquely in history, violent purges or the dissolution of existing parliaments.

Unlike France, America never clung to the utopian fiction that the people

should directly govern themselves.[333] The historian François Furet described the
year 1793 in France:

The right to vote is suspended because the people rule; the right of defense, because the
people judge; freedom of the press, because the people write; and freedom of opinion,
because the people speak: an enlightening lesson; to which the proclamations and terroristic
laws are nothing more than a long commentary.[334]

As expressed by Robespierre in the trial against Louis XVI, the people possessed
absolute power (*toute-puissance*). The conception of the people as a collective
body with a united will never asserted itself in the United States. A distance
between the governed and those governing was taken for granted in America,
and the idea of popular sovereignty was never, as in France, (mis)understood
as mobocracy. Even the radicals in America understood ''the sovereignty of
the people'' to mean the autonomy of the individual and his inviolable sphere
of rights, which were protected by the concept of ''limited government'' and
the Bill of Rights. For the Americans the Bill of Rights concretely assured
freedom for the individual, whereas the French declaration of human and civil
rights had the character of a ''national catechism,'' as Barnave called it. Despite
the declarations of civil and human rights, the principle of unbounded and
dogmatic government power again made itself felt in France, not least because
of the Revolution's failure to justify itself both domestically and internationally.[335] These differences were definitely recognized on both sides of the Atlantic
even at the time. According to Condorcet the French Revolution differed from
the American in that:

It was more comprehensive than the American Revolution, and its internal course was
thus more violent, for the Americans were satisfied with the civil and penal laws that
came to them from England. They had neither an inadequate tax system to reform, nor
a feudal tyranny and inherited class differences, nor rich and privileged institutions, nor
a system of religious intolerance to overcome. They were thus able to limit themselves
to introducing new powers, with which they replaced the people who had governed them
until that point as the agents of the British. The details of these reforms did not affect
the mass of the people in any way; relationships between individuals hardly changed.
For the opposite reasons, the revolution in France had to encompass the entire structure
of society, to alter all social relationships, and to penetrate all political contexts, including
individuals who lived peacefully from their possessions or trade, and who normally took
no part in public movements either through their views and activities, or through their
desires for fortune, honor, or glory.[336]

Madame d'Houdetot had already argued in a similar vein in a letter to Jefferson
in 1790:

The characteristic difference between your revolution and ours is that you didn't need to
hurt anything, because you had nothing to destroy, and because you worked for a small,

unspoiled population spread out over a large area, you were able to avoid all of the unpleasantnesses of a situation opposite to yours in every respect.[337]

According to the American poet, revolutionary, and speculator Joel Barlow, the moderate American "exceptional revolution," and its function as a conserver of spiritual and moral continuity, were possible because the previous reign in America had deformed human nature far less than previous reigns had in other countries.[338]

Despite idealism and optimism, the existing philosophical fund of political experience (self-government) and knowledge of democratic structures and their limits actually led to a fundamental mistrust of government power (regardless of the system involved). At the same time it prevented the kind of utopian, extremely moralizing, excessive demand on politics and on the discourse of égalité in the "sociétés de pensées" that as a consequence of the old regime in France, had led to Robespierre's reign of terror.[339] In addition, America did not have the human will to punish ("volonté punitive") resulting from years of maltreatment, a feature that the historian Georges Lefèbvre singled out as a distinguishing characteristic of the French Revolution. Nor did it have an egalitarianism so loaded with resentment that it overshadowed the desire for freedom. The United States also had no comparable social reservoir of revenge, created in conditions of dependency and humiliation, as represented by the employees of the nobility, the coachmen, cooks, maids, and butlers.[340] This phenomenon and motive of unsparing revenge has not died out; it lives on today in countless bloody revolutions in the Third World. The more cruelly people are treated, the less mercy they show when given the opportunity for revenge.

From the outset, there was no glorification of violence in the American Revolution and no concept of social extermination, no "delirium of collective violence" like the September murders, and no vision of the "orgy of the primitive justice of the people, of butchery, of revenge and plundering," as Babeuf admitted of the first phase of the populist coup in France. Nor was there any "holy rebellion" like that propagated by the sansculottes, who spoke enthusiastically of the guillotine as the "sickle of equality." There was no Marat among the radicals in America, no one who shared his conviction that "the solution of most problems begins with the massacre of as many personal enemies as possible."[341] Hannah Arendt has fittingly observed that this vindictive egalitarianism had no place in the United States. In the American Revolution, the "right to freedom" was uppermost, owing to the lack of a privileged upper class; in the French Revolution, the "right to a livelihood" or "right to bread" was central.[342] It is testimony to the extremism and doctrinaire ideological excesses of the French Revolution that a man like Thomas Paine, who was regarded in America as a man of the far left wing, who was rejected by the American Whigs because of his democratic radicalism, and who had even praised the French Revolution in his *Rights of Man* (1791) as being less bloody than the American, himself almost became a victim of the *terreur* when he renounced the death penalty.[343]

Finally, several other important political factors distinguish the French and American revolutions from one another. First, the United States, unlike France, had an administrative, or almost ideological, continuity. Almost two-thirds of the Senate and half of the House of Representatives in the first Congress convened under the Constitution had also been delegates at the Continental Congress. The American Revolution did not "devour its own children."[344] Second, the revolutionary regime in America was never as isolated and discredited from the outside as was later the case with the revolutionary regimes of France or Russia. Rather, it was England that found herself isolated militarily and politically, while the United States received military aid from Spain and France from the beginning. French support played an especially important role in America and helped to prevent a military crisis like the one that facilitated the French Revolution's drastic transformation into a terroristic regime.[345] Third, the war with England had a cohesive effect on the revolutionary situation in America. Benjamin Franklin's saying, "We must all hang together, or assuredly we shall all hang separately" makes this point clear in a humorous way. Even if they were shocked by many manifestations of the Revolution, the moderate revolutionaries were unable to return to the mother country once ties had been cut. In contrast, French officers left the country after the king's failed attempt to flee in 1791. Treason, counterrevolutionary intrigue, and extreme radicalism, all features of the French Revolution, were almost totally absent from the American Revolution.[346]

Fourth, and last, the unique character of the American Revolution is revealed in one very important point: its assessment of human nature. Although the Americans also saw virtue as an important prerequisite for a republican state, this recognition never turned into a rigorous enforcement of virtue. In France, the obsession with virtue led the French to enforce *virtus* with violence.[347] In the United States, the requirement of virtue was pragmatic and realistic, reduced to an elite minority designated to guard public well-being. But disappointment at the lack of "virtue" was given a productive outlet in the theoretical innovations of the Constitution. Instead of striving for moral perfection or the perfection of its citizens, the United States strove for institutional perfection. These institutional safeguards are most obvious in the system of "checks and balances" built into the "frame of government" by John Adams in Massachusetts, as well as in constitutionally proscribed limits to the direct rule of the majority in the individual states and the balancing of various special interest groups.

The design of new constitutional mechanisms and the achievement of a new federal constitution as rational measures against egoism and self-righteousness testify to the unique connection established by American political theory of the revolutionary phase and the periods following: namely, the linkage of a classical, pessimistic assessment of human nature and an optimistic belief in traditional institutions. The trust in rationally constructed political mechanisms satisfied the knowledge that virtue is nonexistent and that human beings are irrational and directed it into constructive and progressive channels.[348] The two-hundred-year existence of the American republic and its Constitution is the best proof of the functional and democratic capabilities of the American political system. The next chapter will attempt to show that the polymorphic divergence in both the French and American revolutions, as described above, deeply influenced the historical and progressivist ethos of the Americans as well as of the Europeans and that the roots of modern totalitarian ideologies are to be found in the French Revolution.

## PROGRESS AS IDEAL VERSUS PROGRESS AS LAW

As the preceding investigation has tried to show, the modern origin of the divergent conceptions of progressivist thought in America and Europe was manifested very clearly in both the American and French revolutions. The way revolutionaries perceived themselves, as well as the course of events, differed in both cases. The consequences for the understanding of history and progress, democracy and utopia, the individual and society, have proved weighty indeed. Summarizing the divergences of the two revolutions into a coherent thesis, one comes to the conclusion that a historical convergence existed between the Old and New Worlds in respect to Western tradition but that the values and progressive ideology that came out of the American Revolution created a political consensus, whereas those of the French Revolution produced political dissent.

Assuming that the term "ideology" means a system of ideas that spreads political and social values and that is recognized by a significant social group, then this statement applies to the revolutionary eras in both the United States and France. However, an important qualification must be added, namely, that American revolutionary ideology led to a positive ideologization, whereas French revolutionary ideology led to a negative ideologization of progress. Comparing the sociopolitical situations of France and America before their respective revolutions, one recognizes that the British colonization of the New World was quite bearable in comparison to the feudalist systems and absolutist monarchies of Europe. This explains Hannah Arendt's astute observation that the more lawless the preceding reign, the more absolutist the revolution.[349] This was the case in France. But one cannot speak of such a period of terror in any phase of the American Revolution. Thus, in the course of the French Revolution, the progressivist ideas of liberty, equality, and brotherhood were exaggerated, dogmatized, and absolutized, Robespierre's reign of terror totalitarianized, and, ultimately, converted into a restorative dictatorial regime, the opposite of the liberal democratic social order originally aspired to in their name. With its claim to absolute equality, the French model not only decisively reduced the freedom of the individual, but also produced the distorted idea of an "elite," which was later totally perverted and finally destroyed in Marxist-Leninism, fascism, and national socialism. The French Revolution also revived the idea of the mutability of human nature, the possibility of perfecting the human creature. This illusory combination ultimately promoted a utopian understanding of history in Europe that, in its extreme form, regarded history as manipulable, displaced progress into the future, and strove toward a collectivist ideal as the ultimate egalitarian condition.

This constant exaggeration of progressivist ideas, of this "all-or-nothing" mentality, made the negative ideologization of progressivism in Europe possible. It expressed itself in various pessimistic and nihilistic circles that led to fascism and national socialism. It also gave way to the chiliastic utopia of Marxist-Leninism, which in turn led to communism. The last stage of an absolute progressivism was reached in the totalitarian phenomena of the twentieth century.

The pragmatic, progressive idealism of the Founding Fathers, centered primarily on the creation of a constitutional and liberal democratic system, was the crucial factor in the development of the American Revolution. Tellingly, the dates 1776 and 1787 are the symbolic pillars of American history and ideology, providing Americans with an unblemished historical connection to a lasting identity not found in France. This is especially true because the birth of the United States through revolution, its independence, and its constitutionality has been accepted and institutionalized in all quarters. In the United States, unlike in Europe, this self-perception promoted the growth of a conservative sense of history regarding the ideals of the revolution—freedom, democracy, human rights, and equality—as a generally valid progressivist tradition that was worth preserving. For Americans, history and progress were therefore identical categories from the outset. American history required no manipulation, since progress was not understood as a vision of the future, but rather as a daily experience.

The European utopia of liberty was achieved in the United States because the positive ideologization of progress promoted individualism as the supreme manifestation of freedom and accepted the approximation of political and human ideals as the only realistic possibility. Unlike the case of the French Revolution, Thomas Jefferson, in the Declaration of Independence in 1776, had not only assured his countrymen of the "inalienable right" to life and liberty, but also posited the "pursuit of happiness" as a constitutional right. Yet, Jefferson's philosophical formulation did not imply the pursuit of political and human perfection, but rather the striving for self-knowledge and self-control in the Socratic sense. The Founding Fathers had as little belief in the mutability of human nature as did the historians and philosophers of classical antiquity. Thus, in 1786 George Washington wrote to John Jay: "We must accept human nature as it is. Perfection is not granted to mortals."[350] However, they did believe that they could use rational political means and compromises to create the constitutional preconditions for a free, democratic, and stable social order. They called on all Americans to participate in this process. In the United States, equality meant "equal opportunity" from the very beginning, and never the denial of the individual for the good of the community. The open, unperverted, and historically unencumbered American elitist ethos made it possible to promote the "best" and the "brightest." In the end, the pragmatic assumptions of their progressivist thought spared the Americans the European experience of extremism and eschatological ideology. The gulf between theory and practice, progress and utopia, aspiration and reality, a gulf that has challenged Europe for centuries, remains unknown in America.

## AMERICAN VERSUS EUROPEAN HISTORY:
## THE DENIAL OF AMERICA

Any discussion or analysis of the differing European and American understanding of history and progress should include an outline of the European view of Americans and the American perception of Europeans. Interestingly, closer examination of the European image of America reveals a process of repression of the phenomenon of "America," a process native to German thought in particular.

The American view of Europe since the founding of the United States has been quite positive, despite a certain skepticism toward the political structures of the Old World. Anti-Europeanism essentially did not exist. Franklin, Paine, Madison, Washington, and Jefferson were well known as European experts not only because of their studies, but because of the time they had spent in Europe—mostly in Paris and London—acquainting themselves with European politics and society. In 1822, Alexander Hill Everett, a diplomat from Boston and editor of the *North American Review,* the leading political and literary publication of its time, published an unusually well-informed book about Europe. Indeed it was incomparable with anything that Americans had written about the Old World up to that time.[351] His work, which appeared anonymously, was a systematic, knowledgeable overview, country by country, of European politics, with predictions of each nation's prospects for the future. It was based on his extensive reading and his diplomatic experience, for he had served as personal secretary to John Quincy Adams during his service as an American diplomat in Russia, as an embassy secretary in the Hague, and as an ambassador to Spain, to name but a few. The book was so well researched, with Everett quoting the newest European books, magazines, and newspapers, that English reviewers refused to believe that the book, whose author was named merely as a "citizen of the United States," had been written by an American.[352]

In the subsequent volume of 1827, entitled *America,* Everett concerned himself with future options of a European and American alliance against Russia. He emphasized the uniqueness of America's "internal development" and the settlement of the continent, praising a "progress of improvement unheard of, unthought of, in any former age or region." He compared this to the peculiarity of the despotic Russian system: " . . . a picture in every respect precisely the reverse of this."[353] Everett's contemporary, John Bristed, was born in England and settled in New York in 1806 to become a lawyer and publisher. He was thus equally at home on both sides of the Atlantic. In his book *The Resources of the United States* (1818), which he wrote as a response to the "grievous misrepresentations" by European writers of America, he viewed European-American relations at the time quite skeptically: "The great question now at issue between America and Europe, is, which of the two shall change its form of government? Whether Europe shall become more democratic, or the United States more aristocratic?"[354] In any case, the Americans ultimately preferred to continue their isolationist policies for almost an entire century, thus ensuring their independence from European quarrels.

The view of Europe held by American Romantics, influenced in particular by the historians Bancroft, Motley, and Prescott, all of whom had developed a particular liking for Germany, was overwhelmingly positive.[355] German influence on American philosophy also reached its high point in the second half of the nineteenth century. Kant, Fichte, Schelling, and especially Hegel, all had a receptive swarm of apostles, such as Henry Philipp Tappan (1805–81), the first president of the newly founded University of Michigan. He ultimately yielded to reproaches of a "Prussification" of American scholarship and spent the last years of his life in Germany and Switzerland. George Sylvester Morris (1840–89) who also taught at the University of Michigan, brought out a series of books entitled *German Philosophical Classics,* published in Chicago. Frederick A. Rauch studied under Hegel before coming to America in 1831, where he became the first Hegelian in the United States and president of Marshall College in Pennsylvania. Francis Lieber (1800–72), who, with his works about an idealistic, democratic liberalism, belonged to the radical group "Junges Deutschland," became a professor of social sciences and politics at the University of South Carolina in 1835.[356]

Regard for Germany reached its zenith in the United States in the second half of the nineteenth century. Many of the most respected Americans studied in Germany. German immigration went into the hundreds of thousands. The capital (and Hegelian metropolis) of this German period in America was St. Louis. The period's most outstanding figures included Henry Conrad Brokmeyer (1826–1906), a Hegel admirer who at seventeen fled from the "autocratic demon of the Old World" to find his fortune in the "free, democratic self-government of the New World." He ultimately managed to become governor of Missouri, founded a philosophical society, and provided the impetus for the founding of a philosophical journal in English, the *Journal of Speculative Philosophy* (1867–93), the most significant and representative work of the St. Louis School. Other members of the school included W. T. Harris, who taught at the Concord School of Philosophy, and Denton Snider, who wrote *The History of the St. Louis Movement,* both loyal adherents of Brokmeyer. Less closely associated with the school were Carl Schurz, a great political mind and liberal philanthropist; Adolf Kroeger, a Fichtean and translator of Fichte; Susan Blow, at the center of the kindergarten movement and assistant to Harris; Joseph Pulitzer, the great journalist and later press magnate; George H. Howison, professor of philosophy in California and teacher of Josiah Royce; the historian James Hosmer; the pedagogue Frank Soldan; and the legal scholar and writer Johann Gabriel Woerner, whose novel *The Rebel's Daughter* recalled the St. Louis School in fictional form.[357]

This German-American philosophical school also had an influence on the romantic, idealistic poetry of Walt Whitman in *Democratic Vistas* (1871), in which he related Hegel's philosophy of history to his own vision of the United States' mission to become the new "world people," a people destined to fuse all of the one-sided national traditions of Europe. Its influence was also strong on John Dewey's philosophy of instrumentalism, the American expression of Hegelian economic and historical materialism.[358] The most important critics of Hegel in America included Charles Sanders Pierce (1839–1914), whose views fluctuated between great admiration and complete rejection, and William James (1842–1910), who had also studied in Germany. With his pragmatism he led the attack against Hegel's ideology of "block universalism" and "absolute determinism," which attempted to save existential uncertainty and individual decision-making responsibility from a general metaphysical logic.[359] Even though Cornell University has remained the bastion of American Hegelianism, it must be stressed that this German philosophical tradition has, in the final analysis, represented only a marginal phenomenon in American thought.

In the first half of the twentieth century, Americans' perceptions of Europe were strongly affected by the two world wars, which revived the image of the Europeans as brilliant thinkers and philosophers who were, at the same time, obsessed with their own self-destruction. Admittedly, the totalitarian catastrophe of World War II did not leave the American progressivist consciousness entirely unaffected. A crisis mentality of European origin infiltrated the booming economic prosperity of the 1950s. One of its manifestations was the historical interest in the theme of the progress and decline of Western ideology, exemplified by Walter Lippmann's famous work *The Public Philosophy, On the Decline and Revival of the Western Society* (1955), Max Lerner's comparison of America to Rome in *America as a Civilization* (1957), or Daniel Bell's *The End of Ideology* (1960). Another characteristic theme was the increasing loneliness and alienation of the individual in advanced industrial societies, as depicted, for example, in *The Lonely Crowd* (1950), a major work by the Harvard sociologist David Riesman.[360] None of this, of course, meant that American progressivist thought was undergoing "Europeanization"; it was simply that certain European trends of thought with profound effects on the Western spirit of the times could not be ignored by America in its role as Europe's savior from dictatorship.[361] That the European political Left, which has always been very critical of the historical and political phenomenon of "America," underwent an Americanization of its ideology from about 1960 to the mid-1970s can only be viewed as the ironic fate of leftist ideology. European student revolts were almost entirely inspired by the United States.[362]

The further development of American perceptions of Europe up to the present day cannot be treated here in detail.[363] Ostensible tendencies toward increasing interest in Asia at the costs of the Old World cannot yet be taken seriously on the basis of constantly changing political prognoses. Nonetheless, the pithy, sarcastic advertising slogan of an American travel agency—"Travel to Europe while it's still there"—gives cause for reflection on both sides of the Atlantic.

While the ad was related "merely" to the possibility of Europe's destruction in a nuclear holocaust, in fact the issue is a larger one: that of the future of Europe's economy, defense, technology, and vitality. America has been largely free of resentment against Europe since the founding of the United States. Thus, the image of Europe in America has been determined mostly by the Europeans themselves. Ever since the Revolution, the Americans have not considered the Europeans as particularly progressive.

The Europeans' perception of America has been ambivalent from the very beginning. From the founding of the American republic to the present, various images of America have prevailed in the European mind, images ranging from a recurrent, ideologically motivated anti-Americanism to an insistence that America is a spiritual province of Europe. Despite the flood of information about the New World that has swamped Europe since the eighteenth century, the perception of the phenomenon "America" as *terra incognita* in Europe's mental map of the world has not been overcome. Europe's relation to America until the Second World War was constricted by the social and attitudinal repression of American history.[364]

The origin of this denial goes back to the French Revolution, which was seen in European politics and history as a great turning-point and advance of world history, thus diverting attention from the New World. The political, intellectual, economic, and social development of America according to its own successful laws contradicted the popular thesis of America as a simple country of immigrants. Every year the millions of European emigrants leaving the misery of the Old World behind them proved that, for them, America represented a model of the future that was *the* alternative to the rhetorical promises of the French Revolution.[365] As Europe's antagonistic structures hardened and, owing to leftist and rightist ideologies in the first half of the twentieth century, finally collapsed in a bloody European civil war, the progressivist revolution of American society went peacefully on. The Europeans failed to recognize the polymorphic meaning of the internal American progressivist process or the European emigration that confirmed the revolutionary character of this process. The exodus of millions seemed to justify the denial, for the fact that the New World granted asylum to the "rabble" of Europe underlined, for European arrogance, the unrefined nature of American society.

The United States' entry into the First World War forced the Europeans to reconsider America's role. This process reached a new stage with the expulsion of intellectual elites from continental Europe beginning in 1933. The reversal of the European denial of America was the direct result of internecine European wars. The image held of America suddenly changed, and, the new immigrants in the United States, representatives of European philosophy, literature, art, music, humanities, and social and natural sciences, were forced to come to terms with the American phenomenon, even to adjust to America as their new home. In the European intellectuals' encounter with the New World, the centuries-old denial of America broke through. It demonstrated the lack of German literature's viability in the United States, for that literature was committed to the notion that European culture was superior. At the same time, genuine attempts were made to legitimize the real America in the eyes of Europe's revolutionary and philosophical intelligentsia. Europe's problems, which were connected with the years of denial, were revealed by the Frankfurt school's attempt to understand American reality through critical theory, an experiment that ended in melancholy. They were evident, too, in the attempt in political philosophy to see America as the heir of Western culture, an endeavor that ended in silence. America's historical independence had not been understood. It was the French Revolution, Hegelianism, and Marxism that formed the matrix of political ideologies in Europe—and anti-Americanism was one of the byproducts of these ideologies. The true discovery of America through European political philosophy, and the realization that the Europeanization of America had in fact never taken place, had in essence been delayed by two hundred years.

A short historical overview, from Richard Price to Godfrey Hodgson, from Abbé Raynal through Alexis de Tocqueville to Michel Crozier, from Hegel to the Greens, is necessary for a more exact understanding of the long development of European perceptions of America.

Before and after the American Revolution, England's relationship to the United States was to a large extent determined by the hostilities of the wars.[366] With the exception of Richard Price's *Observations* (1784),[367] the English view of America at that time was so unobjective that one of the first British travelers to set foot on American soil after the War of Independence complained about the inadequacy of the reports he had been given to read before the journey.[368] The so-called second Anglo-American war of independence (1812–14) brought with it the intensification of the English criticism of America. The forces of change that made themselves felt at the beginning of the nineteenth century, and that finally, in the form of political, social, and economic revolution, transformed aristocratic England into a bourgeois democracy, ultimately drew attention to America as a model of those new principles that appeared to be triumphing with the progress of republicanism and democracy. For the Tories, the simple fact that the United States existed was a threat to traditional British institutions. By contrast, the Liberal party in England owed its strength and inspiration almost exclusively to America.

The English argument repeatedly opened with condescending references to the youth of America and the subordinate rank to which America was assigned owing to its short history and undeveloped national identity. At this level, the English observer displayed a conscious air of superiority, based on an awareness of a longer tradition and a culture of taste and intellect.[369] Thus, an 1821 issue of the London *New Monthly Magazine and Literary Journal* contained the following preachy sentences: "America is yet in her infancy, and must not, like a forward child, born to a great estate and the dupe of domestic adulators, im-

maturely assume the tone and pretensions of a riper period; she must be docile
and industrious, and patient of rebuke that conveys instruction."[370] The famous
and arrogant description of Americans, from the pen of the renowned Reverend
Sidney Smith, is written in a similar vein:

They have hitherto given no indications of genius, and made no approaches to the heroic,
either in their morality, or character. . . . They have yet done marvellously little to assert
the honour of such a descent (from the English) or to show that their English blood has
been exalted or refined by their Republican training and institutions.[371]

These examples reflect the British attitude toward America in the nineteenth
century, which explains the acute sensitivity of Americans to English judgments.[372] This "special" love-hate relationship was expressed in a number of
more objective works from the early and mid-nineteenth century, such as John
Bristed's Resources of the United States of America (1818), Basil Hall's Travels
in North America in the Year 1827 and 1828 (1829), Francis Trollope's Domestic
Manners of the Americans (1832), Harriet Martineau's Society in America
(1837), Charles Dickens's American Notes (1842), or Philip Schaff's America:
A Sketch of Its Political, Social, and Religious Character.[373]
After the British Empire came to terms with the United States' increasing
position as a world power in the twentieth century, the English began to engage
in a more serious effort to understand the phenomenon of America from a political
and scholarly perspective. Worthy of mention is James Bryce's classic work The
American Commonwealth (1907), as well as Harold Laski's The American Democracy (1948).[374] The current British view of America, now purged of historical
and political rivalries, has once again become more critical. Godfrey Hodgson,
a long-time correspondent in America, represents this new point of view.[375]
However, there has been no virulent British anti-Americanism for the last one
hundred and fifty years.

The relationship between France and America took a positive turn with the War
of Independence. After the war, the influence of French culture spread in American education and society, in literature as well as in politics,[376] while in France
revolutionary groups around Lafayette and Brissot de Warville tried to undertake
reform with the help of American principles and ideals.[377] Before the end of the
century, the multifaceted relationships between the two countries had given rise
to a series of books, the most important of which included Hector St. John de Crèvecoeur's Letters from an American Farmer.[378] Four more names, Raynal, Mably,
Chastellux, and Brissot, continued to influence the French idea of America.
Abbé Raynal's understanding of America was superficial, haughty, and full
of shortcomings. Whereas in the middle of the eighteenth century Georges Buffon
had made pseudoscientific claims of the biological inferiority of American animals, Raynal went a step further and declared the Americans themselves to be
inferior, greedy, and corrupt.[379] Raynal, in his book Philosophical and Political

*History of the Settlements and of the Commerce of Europeans in the Two Indies*
(1770), saw European innocence threatened by American depravity. He claimed
to have found the basis for the degeneration of the Europeans in the climatic
and geological conditions of America. He commented without hesitation that:

The men have less strength and less courage . . . and are but little susceptible of the lively
and powerful sentiment of love. . . . Let me stop here, and consider ourselves as existing
at the time when America and India were unknown. Let me suppose that I address myself
to the most cruel of Europeans in the following terms. There exist regions which will
furnish thee with rich metals, agreeable clothing, and delicious food. But read this history,
and behold at what price the discovery is promised to thee. Does thou wish or not that
it should be made? Is it to be imagined that there exists a being infernal enough to answer
this question in the affirmative! Let it be remembered, that there will not be a single
instant in futurity, when my question will not have the same force.[380]

After the Declaration of Independence, Raynal added injury to his insults. As
a gesture of gratitude for being named a member of the Academy of Lyon,
Raynal established a prize of 1,200 francs for the best essay on the theme "Was
the discovery of America a blessing or a curse to mankind? If it was a blessing,
by what means are we to conserve and enhance its benefits? If it was a curse,
by what means are we to repair the damage?"[381] The Founding Fathers were
understandably indignant over the claim that America might have been a miscarriage; Franklin, Jefferson, Adams, and Paine all rejected these supercilious
reproaches. Hamilton responded in *The Federalist,* saying:

Africa, Asia, and America have successively felt her [Europe's] domination. The superiority she has long maintained has tempted her to plume herself as the mistress of the
world, and to consider the rest of mankind as created for her benefit. Men admired as
profound philosophers have in direct terms attributed to her inhabitants a physical superiority and have gravely asserted that all animals, and with them the human species,
degenerate in America—that even dogs cease to bark after having breathed awhile in our
atmosphere. Facts have too long supported these arrogant pretensions of the European.
It belongs to us to vindicate the honor of the human race, and to teach that assuming
brother moderation. . . . Let Americans disdain to be the instruments of European greatness! Let the thirteen States, bound together in a strict and indissoluble Union, concur
in erecting one great American system superior to the control of all transatlantic force or
influence and able to dictate the terms of the connection between the old and the new
world![382]

Gabriel Bonnot de Mably was by no means as scathing as Raynal, yet he
remained pessimistic about the long-term survival of the proclaimed ideals of
America: freedom and equality. This was expressed with particular clarity in his
book *Observations sur le Gouvernement et les Lois des Etats-Unis d'Amérique,*
in which he overdramatized the weaknesses of the future republic.

If you take proper measures to prevent commerce from multiplying your wants; if you
oppose the progress of luxury, if your laws are prudently diffident of women, by whom

corruption has been introduced into every republic, if you set bounds to the ambition of the rich, who are naturally inclined to think that every thing is their due, because possessed of that wealth, to which every thing submits; in a word, if you endeavor to establish among all your citizens . . . such an equilibrium, as leaves reason to conclude that you have exerted every possible effort to fix liberty firmly on the basis of laws, you need not fear that the evils, with which America may at any time be afflicted, will be imputed to you. . . . But however . . . it is beyond a doubt, that as soon as your republics are enriched by an extensive commerce, their citizens will assume the genius and character peculiar to traders. . . . This prospect of prodigious wealth makes me tremble for the lot that awaits you. . . . Every bale of merchandize, imported or exported, will certainly become, like Pandora's box, a source of evils to the republic.[383]

In contrast to Raynal and Mably, François Jean Marquis de Chastellux and Jean Pierre Brissot de Marville were much more optimistic about the future of America. In 1788, the enthusiastic republican Brissot even founded a Société des amis des noirs, after having previously studied the question of the blacks in America.[384] For the radical philosopher and progressivist European Brissot, the founding of the United States of America was something to be admired. To characterize it as a "miscarriage" was, for him, to serve the reactionary forces in Europe. In his main works *Nouveau voyage dans les Etats-Unis de l'Amerique Septentrionale, fait en 1788* (1791) and *Recherches Philosophiques sur le droit de propriété et sur le vol, considérés dans la nature et dans la société* (1782), he came to the following conclusions:

Splendid Europeans, you hardly deign to notice these mortals who have too few wants to be able to reach your rank. But how much are they above you! You degrade nature, but they preserve her in all her simplicity. . . . I see Happiness and Industry, smiling side by side, Beauty adorning the daughter of Nature, Liberty and Morals rendering almost useless the coercion of Government and Laws, and gentle Tolerance taking [the] place of the ferocious Inquisition. I see Mexicans, Peruvians, men of the United States, Frenchmen, and Canadians, embracing each other, cursing tyrants, and blessing the reign of Liberty, which leads to Universal Harmony.[385]

Marquis de Chastellux also believed in America's progress toward a perfect society. In his main work *De la Félicité Publique, ou Considérations sur le sort des hommes dans les différentes époques de l'histoire* (1772), he confirmed his progressivist thesis:

I will not say that all is well, but all is better. There is progress; there is ground for hope. . . . Hence the public evils spring much less from present than from past errors, and it is unjust to mistrust human reason, the progress of which would have a more rapid effect if it had not to combat prejudices and customs, all of which arose and were formed in the times of ignorance.[386]

At the same time he compared classical antiquity with the enlightening effect of America:

If we pass to North America we can defy the Solons and Lycurgus in opposing to them the Lockes and William Penns. Read the laws of Pennsylvania and Carolina and compare them to those of Sparta, and you will find the same difference as between the rule of St. Benedict and the domestic administration of a farm. Who would not experience an agreeable sensation in realizing that a territory of more than a hundred thousand square miles is now being populated under the auspices of liberty and reason, making equality the principle of its morals and agriculture that of its politics?[387]

Chastellux wrote these sentences before ever having set foot on American soil. He made his first journey to America with Rochambeau's troops during the War of Independence, and it was there that he began work on his second book *Voyages dans l'Amérique septentrionale dans les années 1780, 1781 et 1782* (1782), which became renowned for its portrayal of events around 1776.[388]

The affinity of Americans for everything French emerged clearly against this background; they did not intentionally lead the French astray, nor did they show only a certain side of themselves. In short, America presented itself to the French observer naturally, and with no inhibitions, so that Alexis de Tocqueville, the most influential nineteenth-century observer in France, if not in all of Europe, was able to report, shortly after his arrival in America with his friend Gustave de Beaumont in 1830, that "All the Americans of all the classes seem to rival each other as to who will be the most useful and agreeable to us."[389] An event at the time contributed to these tendencies. In 1824 Lafayette came to America, and his triumphal procession through the Union reminded the young republic of the tradition of its military alliance with France, and concomitantly of the richness of the relationship between the two countries. Thus, Tocqueville arrived in the United States at a particularly favorable moment, especially as the Americans still felt that the English did not yet properly appreciate the United States. However strongly Tocqueville's journey across the Atlantic had been motivated by the young aristocrat's own ambition and his worries about France, the Americans expected the Frenchman to paint a just, comprehensive, and possibly even sympathetic picture of the young, aspiring republic and its principles and ideals.

These hopes were expressed by, among others, the American historian Jared Sparks, who anticipated that Tocqueville's *Democracy in America* would prove "a more accurate and judicious account of the United States than has yet appeared from the pen of any European traveller."[390] The Americans had had a high opinion of French visitors from the beginning, as was documented by William Hickling Prescott's evaluation of French reporting:

There is a mixture of frivolity and philosophy in their composition, which is admirably suited to the exigencies of their situation. They mingle readily with all classes and races, discarding for the time their own nationality,—at least their national antipathies. The Frenchman can even accomodate himself to habits alien to his own, that he can tolerate those of the savages themselves, and enter into a sort of fellowship with them, without either party altogether discarding his national tastes. . . . The most comprehensive and truly philosophic work on the genius and institutions of this country, the best exposition of its social phenomena, its present condition, and probable future, are to be found in the pages of a Frenchman.[391]

Tocqueville actually succeeded in casting off his French prejudices, and he strove to be as impartial to the enthusiasm of the liberals as he was to the hatred of the conservatives, in his desire to describe reality as fairly as possible. Where European awareness, rather than ignorance, of the processes and developments in the United States existed, there was also the awareness—and this applied in particular to Tocqueville—that if democracy were to triumph in Europe it would bring with it not only a redefinition of political life and thought, but a transformation in all other areas of life as well, the consequences of which were unpredictable. This was the source of the antidemocratic tendencies of British travel literature as well as the strong political and ideological controversies in France and England.

Interestingly, during their stay in the area of the Great Lakes, Tocqueville and Beaumont were accompanied for a time by an Englishman, Godfrey T. Vignes. Differing from his countrymen in his relative lack of bias, Vignes was able to close his report of *Six Months in America* (1832) with the remarkable words,

I advise you to go to America: at this period there is no country equally interesting, nor one so likely to remain so, till it falls to pieces . . . by its own weight. If you are an ultratory you will, perhaps, receive a lesson, that may reduce you to reason; if you are a radical, and in your senses, as an Englishman and a gentleman, you are certain of changing your opinions before you return. . . . You will be gratified by visiting a land, that . . . must ever remain a land of liberty, which the Saxon blood alone is capable of enjoying. . . . You will be gratified by seeing so much of what may be termed the aristocracy of nature . . . and still more so by having visited a land where man is supposed to be more his own master than in any other civilized part of the world, and where his energy meets with co-operation in the natural resources of the country, and commands success at the hands of his fellow men. You will then be able to form an opinion whether the state of society be more or less enviable than that to which you have been accustomed; whether the fine arts are more likely to flourish; whether men in their public and private characters as husbands, as fathers, as brothers, as gentlemen, are better, more honest, or more amiable than among yourselves; or whether the government under which they live is more calculated for the encouragement of true religion, the shelter of virtue, the enjoyment of life and liberty; or, if fair allowance be made for the advantages incidental to a new country, whether it is better adapted for the advancement of national prosperity, than the institutions of your native land.—Go to America, canvass the pretensions of the Americans, and then judge for yourself.[392]

Vignes's remarks on the effects of political institutions on religion and morality, family life, and the prosperity of a country demonstrate the honesty with which he attempted to reach a comprehensive understanding of the United States from a political, rather than an ideological, perspective.

In the light of such evidence, contemporary efforts toward a comprehensive interpretation of the United States culminated in Tocqueville's *Democracy in America*. His work is characterized, above all, by three observations or prognoses about the progressive development of America. With a relevance unprecedented in the modern age, these simultaneously determined the global perspectives for Europe's historical self-understanding: first, the realization that the idea of progress was the key concept of the American ideology of success; second, that the emergence of American mass democracy would become the dominant force in future world affairs; and third, that a world political polarization between the principles of freedom (America) and subjugation (Russia) could ensue, with Europe placed in a corresponding position of dependence. Already in his first investigation of the American national character, Tocqueville had pointed to the idea of progress as the dominant sociopolitical and democratic component of the American system. For him this included the concept of *perfectibilité humaine* as well as that of material progress. "L'ambition est le sentiment universel" was Tocqueville's formulation of the essence of American democratic society, in which the "empire moral de la majorité" manifested itself. These first solid principles of progress gave rise to the *mouvement démocratique, the grande mobilité de la plupart des actions humaines,* in which Tocqueville saw the release of the American individual from the rigid fabric of a hierarchical social structure, such as that which existed in Europe.[393] It was in this context that Tocqueville felt the actual progress of the Americans lay in their exploitation of favorable conditions to produce responsible, self-confident, and freedom-loving citizens who regarded and practiced this republican system as their own, and whose civic spirit—nurtured by a democratic constitution, liberal institutions, and constantly changing values—kept liberty and progress alive in a continuous self-education of society.[394]

In the two volumes of his *Democracy in America,* Tocqueville concentrated almost entirely on the domestic affairs of the United States, measuring them against his general theme of democracy. In the foreword to the first printing (1835), he admitted that he saw more in America than just America itself. He sought there the image of democracy itself. In the foreword to the twelfth printing (1848), he spoke more precisely of his thesis of the inevitable rise of mass democracy as the dominant factor in history. The Americans were intending, he commented, to reap the fruits of democratic revolution without having to experience it themselves. With his description of the transatlantic miracle, the young aristocrat wanted to reach not only America, but his home country of France as well. He intended his work to fulfill a pedagogical and ideological function and to gather evidence for the superiority of democratic societies in order to provide France (and Europe) with the courage for overdue and inevitable reforms. The demand of equality, which had nourished the energies of the American soul from the very beginning, had, according to Tocqueville, been persistently ignored in the Europe of the Restoration.[395]

Tocqueville's liberal-conservative belief in democracy and equality offered a constructive alternative to the reactionary and authoritarian nationalism of the nineteenth century. The author was convinced that he had discovered the secret behind the Americans' successful combination of freedom and equality: religion. No one before and few after him were able to show with such clarity the insoluble link between American progressivism and American religiosity. The liberal Frenchman presented his contemporaries with a picture of American life that is no more understandable now for the Europeans than it was over one and a half centuries ago: the degree to which the religious impulse penetrates almost every aspect of public life in America. The careful reader of Tocqueville's book can hardly be surprised by the deeply religious Harry Truman—"Truman firmly believed that America was God's own chosen country"[396]—or the evangelical preacher Jimmy Carter, who tried to reconcile his actions with the precepts of Christianity in every facet of his life, and who asked for God's "guidance" in important decisions.[397] Both presidents came from deep within the tradition described so precisely by Tocqueville. What today still appears to Europeans as an absurd hypocrisy, namely, the alliance between politics and religious belief, had always been the essence, according to Tocqueville's analysis, of the American spirit. Enlightenment and the belief in progress, religion and rationalism, freedom and equality, revolution and reformation did not meet in a deadly opposition in the New World, but rather joined together in a frequently tense, ultimately productive symbiosis.

Still another of Tocqueville's messages continues to have relevance today. The Count's fame was based to a large degree on a misunderstanding, namely, the reduction of critical interest to the visionary passage at the end of the first volume of his study of the United States:

There are at the present time two great nations in the world, which started from different points, but seem to tend towards the same end. I allude to the Russians and the Americans. Both of them have grown up unnoticed; and while the attention of mankind was directed elsewhere, they have suddenly placed themselves in the front rank among the nations, and the world learned their existence and their greatness at almost the same time.

All other nations seem to have nearly reached their natural limits, and they have only to maintain their power; but these are still in the act of growth. All the others have stopped, or continue to advance with extreme difficulty; these alone are proceeding with ease and celerity along a path to which no limit can be perceived. The American struggles against the obstacles that nature opposes to him; the adversaries of the Russian are men. The former combats the wilderness and savage life; the latter, civilization with all its arms. The conquests of the American are therefore gained by the plowshare; those of the Russian by the sword. The Anglo-American relies upon personal interest to accomplish his ends and gives free scope to the unguided strength and common sense of the people; the Russian centers all the authority of society in a single arm. The principal instrument of the former is freedom; of the latter, servitude. Their starting-point is different and their courses are not the same; yet each of them seems marked out by the will of Heaven to sway the destinies of half the globe.[398]

This prognosis of the future confrontation between freedom and subjugation, and of the future polarization of Europe and its relegation to a position of dependence on America and Russia, was not entirely new. The forecast of a universal Russian influence goes as far back as Leibniz in the late seventeenth century.[399] As far as the American side was concerned, Alexander Hamilton, in the famous last sentence of *The Federalist* (1787), had advised the newly independent states to move the American system toward a position of superiority: "Let the thirteen States, bound together in a strict and indissoluble Union, concur in erecting one great American system superior to the control of all transatlantic force or influence and able to dictate the terms of the connection between the old and the new world!"[400]

John Bristed (*The Resources of the United States of America*, 1818), Dominique-Georges-Frédéric Dufour de Pradt (*L'Europe et l'Amérique en 1822 et 1823*, 1824), Conrad von Schmidt-Phiseldeck (*Europa und Amerika, oder die künftigen Verhältnisse der zivilisierten Welt*, 1820), or Alexander Hill Everett (*America; or a General Survey of the Political Situation of the Several Powers of the Western Continent with Conjectures on Their Future Prospects*, 1827) were all predecessors of Tocqueville and early prophets of the destinies of America, Russia, or Europe.[401] Of course, even later prophets of the Cold War such as Theodore Poesche and Charles Goepp (*The New Rome: or the United States of the World*, 1853) did not succeed in making their predictions of the future positions of America and Europe with the same force and foresight as Count Tocqueville.[402] Yet, Tocqueville's presentiments were hardly noticed by his European contemporaries, who were more interested in eliminating the phenomenon of America—and American progress—from their historical awareness. Tocqueville's work had to wait until the twentieth century to find proper appreciation in Europe.

The French view of America remained positive well into the twentieth century. In the 1950s Simone de Beauvoir gave an excellent report of her trip to America, giving her impressions from East to West, North to South in her book *L'Amérique au jour le jour* (1950).[403] Like the Swede Gunnar Mydral (*An American Dilemma, The Negro Problem and American Democracy*, 1944),[404] Beauvoir also described the weaknesses of American society. Nonetheless, she was overwhelmed by the extent of equal rights for women in the United States, by the Americans' kindness, hospitality, openness, ability to learn, tolerance, and their freedom. Her companion Jean-Paul Sartre was more restrained in his judgment of America. Unlike Beauvoir, he was unable to open himself up to the "American phenomenon" without preconceptions.[405] Despite their critical aspects, other, later books—such as Jean-Jacques Servan-Schreiber's *The American Challenge* (1968), Raymond Aron's *The Imperial Republic: The United States of America and the Rest of the World since 1945* (1973), or Michel Crozier's *Le mal américain* (1981)—also are testimony to the historical indestructibility and warmth of French-American relations.[406] The extent to which Tocqueville remains a living presence in the United States is shown by the American journalist Richard Reeves's successful attempt (*American Journey: Travelling with Tocqueville in*

*Search of America,* 1982) to compare the Frenchman's travel experiences with his own today.[407]

Germany's relationship to America began with German emigration to the New World, with the thirteen families from Krefeld who first touched American soil in Philadelphia on October 6, 1683.[408] They were followed by seven million of their countrymen, who sought to build on the other side of the Atlantic a freer, more tolerant existence, superior economically and socially as well, since the realization of their hopes and aims seemed impossible either in their home country or the rest of Europe. Although the immigrants from Germany contributed vastly to the creation of the United States, as farmers and merchants, soldiers and teachers, politicians, scientists, and artists, it was also clear that they had become and wanted to remain Americans.[409] The German immigration, like the European immigration of which it was a part, was motivated primarily by the prospect of building a new existence. It was much more a flight from politically or socially intolerable conditions in Europe rather than an attempt to cultivate transatlantic relations. Quite a few Europeans turned their backs on the Old World in order to rid themselves, in America, of their old identities and replace them with new ones. The emigrants left Europe willingly and assimilated themselves with equal willingness into the political, economic, and social culture of America. It was precisely the voluntary and individual contributions of the Teutonic, Latinate, Slavic, Asiatic, and African (here, however, initially unwilling) potential, that continues to this day to make up the seemingly inexhaustible *élan vital* of American society. President Reagan expressed this unique cultural and political experiment in 1984 as follows:

The United States is a nation of great size and many resources, but our richest resource is our people. They are fiercely independent and . . . they cherish their liberty above all else. It is a place where the cultures of many nations have blended to produce one culture—that which we call "American."[410]

If one can speak today of fifty million Americans of German or at least partly German descent, then it must be emphasized that these people consider themselves 100 percent American and possess far more knowledge of and commitment to the American political and democratic tradition than to a German culture and history that they have never experienced. The yearly Steuben parades, the German Wursthäuser found across the entire country, or the diverse clubs and organizations for the preservation of German tradition testify more to the maintenance of German folklore, than to the influence of a German lobby on the political course of Washington. Americans of German descent, from General von Steuben to Henry Kissinger, have actively contributed to the political culture of the United States, but they have always clearly acted in the name of American rather than German interests.[411] By no means does this represent a devaluation

of the three-hundred-year history of German-American ties. It is more a question
of providing a more sober view of the exaggerated expectations that continue to
be connected to German-American relations in order to explain and hopefully
avoid misunderstandings on both sides.

The German immigrants in the United States had little will or reason to
influence the German view of America. This attitude is reflected in the lack of
understanding and enlightenment concerning the American political system and
its actors, indeed, the repression of the "American phenomenon," on the part
of the scholars, writers, and politicians who remained in Germany.

If one takes into account the fact that the American Revolution coincided with
a climax of German cultural and intellectual life, that Franklin, Washington,
Hamilton, and Jefferson were the contemporaries of Kant, Goethe, Schiller,
Herder, and Lessing, then it comes as a surprise that the American idea of
freedom met with no significant response in Germany, despite efforts by such
teutonophile American historians as Prescott, Motley, or Bancroft to communicate it.[412] The reason for this was the fundamental difference between the
national development of Germany and that of the United States. The great
intellectual movement of the eighteenth century, the Enlightenment, was interpreted and absorbed differently in the two countries.

In America, the momentum of the Enlightenment was pragmatic and political,
and resulted in the establishment of a constitutional system based on the principle
of popular sovereignty. By contrast, in Germany its momentum rested on moral
and metaphysical postulates, and brought with it a strengthening of existing
authoritarian structures. The generation that had carried out the revolution in
America in 1776 had not only studied the ideas and ideals of the Enlightenment,
rationalism, and John Locke's teachings about natural rights and the social
contract, but had actually internalized and carried them forth. The intellectual
and political leaders of America were also rational people who wanted to create
a new commonwealth; they regarded ideas as tools for the realization of their
aims of freedom and democracy. Locke's theories were accordingly translated
into institutional forms, his conception of atomistic social freedom was transformed into a theory of revolution, with constitutional power vested in the people.
By contrast, the enlightening philosophies of Kant, Lessing, and Lichtenberg
had little effect in their home country, since Germany, whose village and urban
communities remained closely bound by custom and tradition, was not particularly open to external intellectual influences. In addition, the ideas of the social
contract and popular sovereignty, which were so characteristic for the Enlightenment in the West, proved to be relatively powerless in Germany, and the
impetus of the movement was diverted to questions of morality and self-perfection. The fleeting phenomenon of the Enlightenment in Germany and the subsequent domination of a cultural nationalism, indebted to the philosophy of
Herder, and a pessimistic Romanticism, favored an image of the individual that
was diametrically opposed to that ascendant in America. This image tended to
regard individuality not in terms of pragmatic, political, and egalitarian rela-

tionships, but rather metaphysically and mystically as "a particular physical manifestation, in which the divine spirit reveals itself from time to time, whether it be in the guise of individuals or in those communal institutions larger than the individual."[413] Under these circumstances it seems almost understandable that a large segment of German intellectual life remained closed to the ideas of the New World.

The exclusion or repudiation of the United States as the expression of historical repression (on a social as well as a mental level) of Americanism appeared as early as Hegel's "Lectures on the Philosophy of History" in the winter semester of 1822: "Now that we have dispensed with the New World and the dreams connected with it, we can move to the Old World, that is, to the center of world history."[414]

Hegel's contemporary, Friedrich Schlegel, in a series of lectures in Vienna entitled "The Philosophy of History," reproachfully transferred responsibility for the French Revolution to the Americans: "the revolutionary educational institution for France and the rest of Europe was North America." Heinrich Heine called the Americans "egalitarian bumpkins," while at the same time (1840) cursing the "horrifying prison of freedom, where . . . the most disgusting of all tyrants, the mob, conducts its uncouth rule." The complacent superiority and ignorant juxtaposition of German "culture" and American "barbarian civilization" seemed to know no limits. Instead of criticizing themselves, intellectuals chose to criticize others.

European malaise manifested itself in anti-American moods that found expression in such books as Ferdinand Kürnberger's *Weary of America* (1855). This type of displacement can be traced like the thread of Ariadne through the German disposition. Almost all learned quarters and political camps of the nineteenth century agreed that the "barbarians" on the other side of the Atlantic were only interested in hunting the dollar to the tunes of Negro music, leaving corpses behind and not troubling themselves an iota about intellect and culture. Although remaining the uncontested center of the world, Europe and Germany nonetheless bore an animosity that wavered between envy, uncertainty, and fear. Thus, Nikolaus Lenau (despite his being an emigrant) denounced the American spirit as "petty." For Hebbel the Americans had "no sense of poetry," for Schopenhauer they were "inferior utilitarians," for Jacob Burckhardt "nothing but business," for Thomas Mann, who had his own experience of America, "speculators and businessmen," and for the returned emigré Karl Zuckmayer "without tradition or culture."

Although Robert von Mohl's monograph on the constitutional structure of the United States (1824), Werner Sombart's discussion of the lack of socialism in the United States (1906), Hugo Münsterberg's study of the Americans (1912), Georg Jellinek's examinations of American human and civil rights (1927), and Max Weber's treatise on Protestant ethics and the spirit of capitalism (1922) all represented serious attempts to come to terms with the political, social, and economic system of the United States, they were all exceptions. In the cases of

Brecht and Tucholsky, C. G. Jung, and Ferdinand Tönnies, it was an arrogant posture of general disapproval rather than a detailed criticism of American faults that formed the basis for aversion toward "the unknown continent." Oswald Spengler summarized his anti-Americanism in *The Years of Decision* (1933) with the observation: "The 'new society' of Western Europe after 1918, a mixture of snob and mob, fantasizes about a young, strong, superior, and model Americanness, but it confuses records and dollars with the spiritual power and depth of national tradition, and . . . business cleverness with spirituality."[415] For most German philosophers and writers, America was and remains the "automobile-radio-jazz-band-five-and-ten-cent-store civilization" (Adolf Halfeld), which they looked down on and considered to be capable of anything.[416]

The political anti-Americanism of the German conservatives had already become clear in 1848–49, with the German Democrats' first tentative experiments with American constitutional practice.[417] But Marx's and Engels's image of America was also full of prejudices.[418] At the beginning of the twentieth century, political anti-Americanism in Germany continued. The educated German middle-class juxtaposed German culture and Western civilization, German spirit and Anglo-Saxon commercial instinct. The reactionary rightists of the Kaiserreich and the revolutionary rightists and leftists of the Weimar Republic perpetuated the antipathy by condemning a presumed cultural and economic mass Americanism and equating the United States with capitalism, and imperialism. Finally, the intellectual propagandists of national socialism adopted the entire spectrum of anti-American ideas and integrated political, cultural, and economic points of view that had previously been only vaguely connected with each other; a self-contained and negative monumental picture of "the extreme and decadent continent" was the result.[419]

Despite an inadequate knowledge of the American system of government, Carl Schmitt reinforced this image with his destructive critique of the modern constitutional democracy. The more the Germans became fascinated with the functioning of America's economic and technological system and the more they rejected this system at the same time, the less prepared they were to recognize the continued existence of deeply rooted traditions beneath the surface of an allegedly hypermodern apparatus. The more the Germans discredited the American process of the maintenance and expansion of a pluralist state and social order as "uniformization," the less they were able to understand that the creation of a "total state" in Germany would inevitably stand in opposition to the United States of America. Because public opinion in the Weimar Republic misgauged the United States, failing to recognize in America the model for a means to escape from its own domestic crises, the U.S. reaction to the Third Reich came to the Germans as a surprise.[420]

Adolf Hitler hated Franklin D. Roosevelt more fanatically than any other politician because Roosevelt had succeeded, more convincingly than any other national leader of the times, in disproving Hitler's thesis that economic chaos could be overcome only by means of political dictatorship.[421] Goebbels's propaganda did its best to portray the United States as the prototype of an outmoded, liberal, highly capitalized mass society, in which the individual was completely at the mercy of "anonymous" forces and the development of a "national" community had been rendered impossible by the tyranny of a mechanical "head-count democracy." With the increasing radicalization of the national socialist movement, the inclination to regard the United States as the antithesis of the Nazi regime increased. Yet American public opinion and large sections of Congress responded to the dramatic events in Germany with apathy for almost an entire decade. Attempts such as those of the Dickstein Committee to convince America of the necessity of abandoning its policy of isolationism remained fruitless for a long time. The American administration changed the course of its foreign policy for the first time in President Roosevelt's famous "quarantine" speech in 1937.

The source of postwar Germany's exaggerated attention to the partial failure of the New Deal, rather than to its lasting effects, probably lay in the fact that the merits of the reform-minded President Roosevelt remained hidden from the Germans because for a long time they were convinced of the failure of the wartime President Roosevelt. German revisionism from the Right as well as the Left had also contributed significantly to this conviction. Indeed, as long as the names Wilson and Roosevelt summon the emotional reactions "Versailles" and "Yalta," a historical shadow will continue to fall on German-American relations.[422]

Many representatives of the intellectual elite in the Weimar Republic who had emigrated to the United States in an involuntary mass exodus after the Nazi seizure of power confronted the American phenomenon defensively, having been thoroughly indoctrinated by anti-American clichés. One need only recall Thomas Mann, Heinrich or Klaus Mann, Alfred Döblin, René Schickele, Stefan Zweig, Carl Zuckmayer, Franz Werfel, or Bertolt Brecht. Their personal and literary work in the years of the emigration testifies to the "inability of German literature to survive in America." The experience of the German scientists, who found an academic milieu waiting for them in the United States, was quite different. They were able to continue their research at universities and research institutions which, in the America of the 1930s, still stood under the aegis of German scholarship. German emigration enriched America with Einstein, the theory of relativity and the atomic bomb, gestalt psychology and psychoanalysis, epic theater and some of the more esoteric variants of Marxism—the Frankfurt school succeeded in advancing to an "import-export philosophy" on the German-American market for fifty years.[423] European and German scholars who opened themselves to America and its society without prejudice were able to discover new horizons. Hannah Arendt, Hans Morgenthau, Karl Mannheim, Carl Joachim Friedrich, Eric Voegelin, Ernst Fraenkel, Arnold Bergstraesser, Golo Mann, and Karl Dietrich Bracher were among those who sought to examine the historical and cultural connection of the European and American models of civilization.[424]

After the Second World War, the division of Germany introduced a new phase of German-American relations and perceptions. The Federal Republic of Germany became America's number one European partner, with all of the attendant consequences for domestic and foreign policy.

From the 1950s until the end of the 1970s, the German view of America was largely a positive one. During the Adenauer era a broad wave of idealization of American political culture and ideology asserted itself. This new feeling was based, however, less on well-founded factual knowledge of the democratic political structures of American society than on a mood of deep gratitude toward a country that had rescued Germany from its ruins and offered it generous assistance in the construction of political economic democracy.

This unquestioning pro-Americanism, which helped to repress their own past as well as the actual role of the United States during the war, would be reversed three decades later by the renaissance of a German idealism in the cultural pessimism of the Greens. But the first cracks and emotional polarizations in the German view of America had already appeared in the intervening decades of the 1960s and 1970s, through the Vietnam War and Watergate, although they were overwhelmingly restricted to the leftist student and intellectual community and left the broader population untouched. In fact, German-American relations were undamaged by the riots of the radical Left, which were, of course, not restricted to Germany.[425]

Germany's relationship to America began to become genuinely explosive at the beginning of the 1980s, when national security issues became a mass political theme, and the "peace movement" and the Greens began to demonstrate anew the connection between anti-Americanism and German national (reunification) romanticism.[426] Their disconcertingly naive longing for an ideal, pure, anti-modern, anti-Western, and "homey" world seems to be the reexpression of an old and arrogant idealism, nihilistic cultural pessimism, and ignorant nationalism—all of which have contributed to the recurrent denial of the phenomenon "America" in German history. Today it is especially clear that the emergence of the Green and Alternative movements, which have set off the search of a German identity, a definition of *Heimat* (homeland) and patriotism, is the consequence of repressed German history and a lack of self-assuredness.

The new anti-American and anti-Western course of these movements can also be explained as the "alienation of certain European intellectuals from the values and institutions of their own democratic society." This remark by the late American ambassador to Bonn, Arthur F. Burns, is indeed appropriate, since identification with Western values is by no means self-evident for a large section of the German population. In German schools up until the late 1960s Western values were prescribed from above more than they were voluntarily learned and internalized. If one considers that the recent German past, specifically national socialism and the resulting division of the country, was until very recently taboo in West German history classes, then it is understandable that identification with an "enigmatic Germany" was just as problematic as identification with an "unexplained America.'' It may be that the spontaneous pro-Americanism of the 1950s is being expressed in the 1980s as a spontaneous "pro-Germanism.''

This anti-Western view of the world can be understood as a relic of the unresolved problems of the past and inhibited self-awareness, and possibly even as the "resentment of a defeated people" (Klaus Harpprecht) toward the victorious United States, indeed, as the Germans' search for their identity Helmut Kohl's controversial gesture of reconciliation with Ronald Reagan at the Bitburg Cemetery in 1985, which marked the fortieth anniversary of the surrender of the Nazi regime and the liberation of Western Europe, amounted to a significant declaration of unreflected feelings of new German patriotism—a declaration that led to strong criticism on both sides of the Atlantic. Richard von Weizsäcker's historic speech on May 8 presented a counterpoint to it:

We Germans observe the day among ourselves, and that is necessary. We must find our own standards of measurement. The protection of our feelings on our part or by others no longer helps. We need, and we have the strength, to look the truth in the eye as well as we are able, without extenuation and without bias. The 8th of May is for us above all a day of remembering what people had to suffer. . . . The more honestly we observe it, the freer we are to face the responsibilities of its consequences.[427]

As a prime example of reflection on German history, this speech eased the irritations that had arisen in German-American, as well as German-European, relations. The wounds of German history are still open. Anti-Americanism in Germany will disappear only when the Germans have found themselves.

If one compares the view of Europe held by many Americans with the Europeans' image of America, then it becomes apparent that America has generally confronted European history with admiration mixed with skepticism and curiosity, whereas Europe has generally interpreted American history as an unsuccessful offshoot of Europe, repressed it because of superiority complexes, or simply ignored it as an unfathomable phenomenon. This process reflects a transatlantic divergence vis-à-vis history and progress. From its very beginning, American orthodoxy had defined itself according to the idea of liberalism, which authoritatively shaped the American idea of progress. By contrast, European orthodoxy defined itself after the French Revolution according to Hegelianism and Marxism. It ultimately formed the matrix for the political (progressivist) ideologies of Europe and their catastrophically antagonistic exaggerations—with anti-Americanism as a by-product of these ideologies.

Today, after the strenuous reconstruction of democratic structures and economic prosperity, Europe seems to have reached a point where the consequences of the Second World War are reemerging in the form of plaguing questions: What is Europe today? Can its division ever be overcome? Does Europe still play any kind of political or historical role between the two blocs? Does Europe still have an identity beyond 1992 worth preserving and asserting? Or is Europe's future, and its belief in progress, being continued in America? Has the "European dream" perhaps been fulfilled by the "American dream"? Is Europe historically dead?

Today the intellectual self-awareness of the West, once developed in the context of European history, can in principle only be explained in relation to the achievements of American political thought, if Western ideology does not want to succumb to provincial atrophy. Neither a nostalgic picture of Europe on the part of the Americans nor anti-American assertions on the part of the Europeans can halt the continuing Americanization of Europe. Even Mikhail Gorbachev's grand design of a Common European House will have to include the opening up of Eastern Europe to Western influence if it does not want to fail. The antagonistic ideological history that once distinguished Europe from America belongs to the past. In the process, European anti-Americanism has revealed itself to be the product of Europe's fears and doubts about its own present and future. Whereas America always staked its future on fulfilling the dreams of progress envisioned already in 1776, and whereas the country's political and social renewal has always sprung from belief in tradition, Europe was and remains dependent on activating its historical dynamism and political vitality by shaping new visions of progress and the future.

History and progress in Europe did not, as in America, run parallel; Europe was blessed by a far greater share of failures and crises. And yet the great philosophies of Western civilization—those of classical antiquity and the Enlightenment—have forfeited none of their power. An enormous reservoir of ideas and policies is waiting to be revived. All efforts to play American against European history, or European against American history, can only be viewed as ahistorical. Europe's historical hope for the future lies in its *Europeanization*, in the classical, not the Marxist sense of the word.

# Notes to Part II

## CHAPTER 4

1. See Leonard Krieger, European History in America, in J. Higham, L. Krieger, and F. Gilbert, *History, Humanistic Scholarship in America,* (Englewood Cliffs, N.J., 1965).

2. See Hans R. Guggisberg, The Uses of the European Past in American Historiography, in A.N.J. Den Hollander, ed., *Diverging Parallels, A Comparison of American and European Thought and Action,* (Leiden, 1971), 59.

3. Krieger, *European History,* 238.

4. See Sydney G. Fischer, The Legendary and Myth-making Process in Histories of the American Revolution, *Proceedings of the American Philosophical Society* 51 (1912): 53–75. Dixon Wecter, *The Hero in America. A Chronicle of Hero-Worship* (New York, 1941).

5. See Erich Angermann, To steer clear of permanent alliances. Neutralität, Parteipolitik und nationale Konsolidation in der Frühgeschichte der Vereinigten Staaten von Amerika, in *Vom Staat des Ancien Régime zum modernen Parteienstaat* (Festschrift for Theodor Schieder), ed. H. von Berding, K. Düwell, L. Gall, W. J. Mommsen, and H.-U. Wehler (Munich, 1978), 133–144.

6. See David Levin, *History as Romantic Art: Bancroft, Prescott, Motley, and Parkman* (Stanford, Calif., 1959), 3–23.

7. Richard Hofstadter, *The Progressive Historians. Turner, Beard, Parrington* (New York, 1970) (Chapter 1: Historical Writing Before Turner), 14.

8. See H. R. Guggisberg, William Hickling Prescott und das Geschichtsbewußtsein der amerikanischen Romantik, *Jahrbuch für Amerikastudien* 11 (1966): 176–193.

9. John L. Motley, *History of the United Netherlands from the Death of William the Silent to the Twelve Years' Truce* (London, 1901), 1, iv.

10. John L. Motley, *Democracy, the Climax of Political Progress and the Destiny of Advanced Races: An Historical Essay* (London, 1869), 6.

11. J. L. Motley, Historic Progress and American Democracy, in *Representative Selections, with Introduction, Bibliography, and Notes,* ed. Chester P. Higby and B. T. Schantz (New York, 1939), 105. See also H. R. Guggisberg, *Das europäische Mittelalter im amerikanischen Geschichtsdenken des 19. und 20. Jahrhunderts* (Basel, 1964), 33.

12. See Gordon A. Craig, Germany and the US: Some Historical Parallels and Differences and Their Reflection in Attitudes Toward Foreign Policy, in *The Federal Republic of Germany and the United States,* ed. J. A. Cooney, G. A. Craig, H.-P. Schwarz, and F. Stern, (Boulder, Colo., 1984).

13. See Jürgen Herbst, *The German Historical School in American Scholarship* (Ithaca, N.Y., 1965), 99–128. See also George G. Iggers, The Image of Ranke in American and German Historical Thought, *History and Theory* 2 (1962): 17–40.

14. H. R. Guggisberg, The Uses of the European Past in American Historiography, 65 f.

15. *Autobiography of Andrew Dickson White* (New York, 1905), 1, 83.

16. See H. R. Guggisberg, Uses of the European Past, 67.

17. On the topic of the Reformation, the American journals *Church History, The Mennonite Quarterly Review,* and the German-American *Archiv für Reformationsgeschichte* present the most up-to-date research developments.

18. A. T. Mahan, *The Influence of Sea Power upon History, 1660–1783* (1890); *The Influence of Sea Power upon the French Revolution and Empire, 1793–1812* (1893); *Sea Power in Its Relation to the War of 1812* (1905).

19. See Charles Homer Haskins, European History and American Scholarship, *American Historical Review* 28 (January 1923): 215 ff. Chester P. Higby, The Present Status of Modern European History in the United States, *Journal of Modern History* 1 (March 1929): 3–8. Daniel Boorstin, *America and the Image of Europe* (New York, 1960).

20. L. Krieger, European History in America, 260 f.

21. See ibid., 263, 269 ff.

22. See Günther Moltmann, *Revisionist Historiography in the United States and Its Importance for German-American Relations in the Weimar Period, Deutschland und die USA 1918–1933* (Braunschweig, 1968); Warren J. Cohen, *The American Revisionists: The Lessons of Intervention in World War I* (Chicago, 1967).

23. An example of this development is the founding of the Medieval Academy of America (1925), which has been publishing the journal *Speculum* since 1926. In 1929, there appeared the first issue of the *Journal of Modern History,* specializing in modern European history.

24. See G. Sarton, *Introduction to the History of Science,* (Baltimore, 1927–48), 3 vols., 5 parts. G. Sarton, Science in the Renaissance, in *The Civilization of the Renaissance,* eds. J. W. Thompson, G. Rowley, F. Schevill, and G. Sarton (Chicago, 1929), 79. L. Thorndike, *A History of Magic and Experimental Science* (New York, 1923–58), 8 vols. See Wallace K. Ferguson, *The Renaissance in Historical Thought: Five Centuries of Interpretation* (Boston, 1948). H. R. Guggisberg, Jacob Burckhardt und Amerika, *Jahrbuch für Amerikastudien* 13 (1968): 53–68.

25. C. H. Haskins, European History and American Scholarship, 215.

26. See Rudolph J. Vecoli, European Americans: From Immigrants to Ethnics, in *The Reinterpretation of American History and Culture,* ed. William H. Cartwright and Richard L. Watson (Washington, D.C., 1973), 81–112. Donald Fleming and Bernard

Bailyn, eds., *The Intellectual Migration, Europe and America, 1930–1960* (Cambridge, Mass., 1969). Gerald Stourzh, Die deutschsprachige Emigration in den Vereinigten Staaten: Geschichtswissenschaft und politische Wissenschaft, *Jahrbuch für Amerikastudien* 10 (1965): 59–77, 232–66 and 11 (1965): 260–317. Franz L. Neumann, The Social Sciences, in F. L. Neumann et al., *The Cultural Migration: The European Scholar in America* (Philadelphia, 1953), 4–26.

27. For background, see L. Krieger, European History in America, 288 ff. See also the Festschrift in honor of Hajo Holborn, the German-born Yale Professor of German history, who was elected president of the American Historical Association in December 1966. L. Krieger and F. Stern, "Editors' Introduction," *The Responsibility of Power, Historical Essays in Honor of Hajo Holborn* (Garden City, N.Y., 1967). See also Henry Kissinger, The Meaning of History, Reflections on Spengler, Toynbee and Kant, unpublished Honors Thesis, Harvard University, 1951. H. Kissinger, *A World Restored. Castlereagh, Metternich and the Restoration of Peace, 1812–1822* (Boston, 1957). F. Stern, *The Politics of Cultural Despair. A Study in the Rise of the Germanic Ideology* (Berkeley, Calif., 1961); F. Stern: *The Failure of Illiberalism, Essays on the Political Culture of Modern Germany* (New York, 1972). G. A. Craig, Germany, 1866–1945 (New York, 1978). Jeffrey Herf, *Reactionary Modernism: Technology, Culture, and Politics in Weimar and the Third Reich* (Cambridge, Mass., 1984). The newest research on the United States' economic decline is Paul Kennedy's book, *The Rise and Fall of the Great Powers: Economic Change and Military Conflict from 1500 to 2000* (New York, 1988).

28. On these theses, see Richard Hofstadter, *The Progressive Historians* (Chapter: Historical Writing Before Turner), 5. James Oliver Robertson, *American Myth, American Reality* (New York, 1981), 3–22. Francis Jennings, *The Invasion of America: Indians, Colonialism, and the Cant of Conquest* (Chapel Hill, N.C., 1975). Michael Kammen, *People of Paradox: An Inquiry Concerning the Origins of American Civilization* (New York, 1972). Thomas A. Bailey, The Mythmakers of American History, *Journal of American History* 55 (June 1968): 5–21. One of the most important portrayals of the colonial period is presented in Samuel Eliot Morison, *The Oxford History of the American People, Prehistory to 1789*, vol. 1 (New York, 1965).

29. See Alan Heimert and Andrew Delbanco, eds., *The Puritans in America* (Cambridge, Mass., 1985). K. D. Bracher, *Geschichte und Gewalt* (Berlin, 1981), 221. Knud Krakau, *Missionsbewußtsein und Völkerrechtsdoktrin in den Vereinigten Staaten von Amerika* (Frankfurt am Main, 1967), 30. Perry Miller and Thomas H. Johnson, eds., *The Puritans* (New York, 1938). Edmund S. Morgan, *The Puritan Family* (New York, 1966).

30. "A Modell of Christian Charity," quoted according to Perry Miller, *Errand into the Wilderness* (Cambridge, Mass., 1956), 5.

31. John Winthrop, quoted by Oscar Handlin, ed., *American Principles and Issues, The National Purpose* (New York, 1961), 33.

32. See K. D. Bracher, Demokratie als Sendung: das amerikanische Beispiel, in *Deutschland zwischen Demokratie und Diktatur* (Bern, 1964), 318. (Milton's quote is also on p. 318.) See Ralph Barton Perry, *Amerikanische Ideale*, vol. 1 (Nürnberg, 1947), 87 ff. Charles L. Sanford: *The Quest for Paradise. Europe and the American Moral Imagination* (Urbana, Ill., 1961).

33. See also Ralph Henry Gabriel, *The Course of American Democratic Thought* (New York, 1940), 30 ff.

34. H. B. Stowe, *Oldtown Folks* (Boston, 1869), 368.

35. "Sinners in the Hands of an Angry God," quoted by Arthur Schlesinger, in America: Experiment or Destiny? *The American Historical Review*, 82, no. 3 (1977): 506.

36. See S. E. Morison, *The Oxford History of the American People*, 102. Herbert Wallace Schneider, *The Puritan Mind*, (Ann Arbor, Mich., 1958), 33 ff.

37. Quoted in Sacvan Bercovitch, *The Puritan Origins of the American Self* (New Haven, Conn., 1975), 54 f.

38. J. Winthrop, *A Modell of Christian Charity*, quoted by P. Miller, *Errand into the Wilderness*, 11. See E. S. Morgan, *The Puritan Dilemma: The Story of John Winthrop* (Boston, 1958).

39. See K. D. Bracher, Demokratie als Sendung: das amerikanische Beispiel, 319–21 (the quote of Edwards, 321). P. Miller and Th. H. Johnson, eds., *The Puritans*, 243 ff.; P. Miller, *Jonathan Edwards* (New York, 1949).

40. See K. D. Bracher, Demokratie als Sendung, 319 f.; Knud Krakau, Missionsbewußtsein und Völkerrechtsdoktrin in den Vereinigten Staaten von Amerika, 32.

41. Quote in H. W. Schneider, *The Puritan Mind*, 8.

42. See Knud Krakau, Missionsbewußtsein, 34. Max Lerner, *America as a Civilization* (New York, 1957), 705. Erich Voegelin, *Über die Form des amerikanischen Geistes* (Tübingen, 1928).

43. See K. D. Bracher, Demokratie als Sendung, 320. P. Miller and Th. H. Johnson, eds., *The Puritans*, 163–79; H. W. Schneider, *The Puritan Mind*, 31.

44. See K. D. Bracher, Demokratie als Sendung, 321. See also Brian Klunk, The American Mission, in Kenneth W. Thompson, ed., *Political Traditions and Contemporary Problems* (American Values Projected Abroad Series, Vol. II), (New York, 1982). Edward McNall Burns, *The American Idea of Mission* (New Brunswick, N.J., 1957). Clinton Rossiter, The American Mission, *The American Scholar*, 20 (1950–51): 19–28.

45. See S. Bercovitch, *The Puritan Origins of the American Self*, 89 f.

46. A. Schlesinger, *America: Experiment or Destiny?*, 515.

47. Quote in A. K. Weinberg, *Manifest Destiny* (New York, 1963), 40.

48. See E. L. Tuveson, *Redeemer Nation: The Idea of America's Millenial Role* (Chicago, 1968), and S. Bercovitch, The Typology of America's Mission, *American Quarterly* 25 (1978): 135–55.

49. See R. B. Perry, *Amerikanische Ideale*, 39 ff., 84 ff., 226 ff. Clinton Rossiter, *Seedtime of the Republic, The Origin of the American Tradition of Political Liberty* (New York, 1953).

50. Quote in P. Miller and Th. A. Johnson, eds., *The Puritans*, 268, 269. See also K. Krakau, Missionsbewußtsein, 37.

51. Wise quote in P. Miller and Th. A. Johnson, *The Puritans*, 257.

52. See R. B. Perry, *Amerikanische Ideale*, 231; K. D. Bracher, Demokratie als Sendung, 325–28. A. Heimert and A. Delbanco, *The Puritans in America* (Chapter: John Wise).

53. See C. Rossiter, *Seedtime of the Republic*, 185; P. Miller, *Roger Williams, His Contribution to the American Tradition* (Indianapolis, Ind., 1953).

54. This discussion of the American principle of the separation of church and state was inspired by conversations with Professor Don K. Price on May 16, 1984, at the

Kennedy School of Harvard University. See also K. Krakau, Missionsbewußtsein, 36 and 37.

55. For a discussion of Locke's influence on Williams (who has sometimes been called Locke's predecessor), see James Ernst, *Roger Williams* (New York, 1932), 205 ff. R. B. Perry, *Amerikanische Ideale*, 233.

56. See K. D. Bracher, *Demokratie als Sendung*, 326; E. L. Tuveson, *Redeemer Nation*, A. Schlesinger, *America: Experiment or Destiny?*

57. See Alan Heimert, *Religion and the American Mind: From the Great Awakening to the Revolution* (Cambridge, Mass., 1966).

58. See A. Schlesinger, *America: Experiment or Destiny?*, 515.

59. S. Bercovitch, *The Puritan Origins of the American Self*, 89–90.

60. See K. Krakau, *Missionsbewußtsein*, 54 ff. R. B. Perry, *Amerikanische Ideale*, 113, 349 ff. Ernst Troeltsch, *Protestantism and Progress, A Historical Study of the Relation of Protestantism to the Modern World* (Boston, 1958).

61. See S. M. Morison, *Three Centuries of Harvard, 1636–1936* (Cambridge, Mass., 1936). New England's First Fruits: Description of Harvard College (1643), in *The Puritans*, ed. P. Miller and Th. H. Johnson, 701 ff.

62. On the significance of the American Revolution for the historical self-perception of the Americans, see Daniel J. Boorstin, *The Genius of American Politics* (Chicago, 1953), 10–22. Richard B. Morris, *The American Revolution Reconsidered* (New York, 1967). Bernard Bailyn, The Central Themes of the American Revolution. An Interpretation, in *Essays on the American Revolution*, ed. Stephen G. Kurtz and James H. Hutson (New York, 1973), 3–31. Edmund S. Morgan, *The Birth of the Republic, 1763–89* (Chicago, 1977). Michael Kammen, *A Season of Youth. The American Revolution and the Historical Imagination* (New York, 1978). Erich Angermann, *Die Amerikanische Revolution im Spiegel der Geschichte*, ed. E. Angermann, (Munich, 1979), 13. Seymour Martin Lipset, *The First New Nation, The United States in Historical and Comparative Perspective* (chapter: Revolution as the Source of National Identity), (New York, 1979), 74 ff. Hans-Christoph Schröder, *Die amerikanische Revolution* (Munich, 1982), 147 ff. Horst Dippel, *Die Amerikanische Revolution 1763–1787* (Frankfurt am Main, 1985), 112 ff.

63. See A. Schlesinger, *America: Experiment or Destiny?*, 507–509, 511–13. Robert Nisbet, *History of the Idea of Progress* (chapter: The Founding Fathers), (New York, 1980), 193–206.

64. See A. Koch, *Power, Morals, and the Founding Fathers. Essays in the Interpretation of the American Enlightenment*, (Ithaca, N.Y., 1966), (chapter: Madison and the Workshop of Liberty, 103–106), 5, 145 f.

65. Quote in Richard M. Gummere, *The American Colonial Mind and the Classical Traditions—Essays in Comparative Culture* (Cambridge, Mass., 1963).

66. Ibid., 173 f. Meyer Reinhold, ed., *The Classick Pages: Classical Reading of Eighteenth-Century Americans* (University Park, Pa., 1975), 121.

67. Quote in A. Koch, *Power, Morals, and the Founding Fathers* (chapter: Franklin and Pragmatic Wisdom), 18, 19. See also Benjamin Franklin, *Collected Works* (The Library of America Series), (New York, 1985). Ronald W. Clark, *Benjamin Franklin: A Biography* (New York, 1983). Catherine Drinker Bowen, *The Most Dangerous Man in America: Scenes from the Life of Benjamin Franklin* (Boston, 1974). Leonard W. Labaree et al., eds., *The Autobiography of Benjamin Franklin* (New Haven, Conn., 1964).

68. Quote in R. M. Gummere, *The American Colonial Mind*.

69. Alexander Hamilton, No. 34, in *The Federalist Papers, Alexander Hamilton, James Madison, John Jay* (Introduction: Clinton Rossiter), (New York, 1961), p. 206. Arthur Schlesinger points out that "some of the Founders' allusions are to Rome as a Republic, some to Rome as an empire. It is not clear that they drew too sharp a distinction between these phases in Roman history" (*America: Experiment or Destiny?*, 508 n. 14). For an example of this thesis, see Fisher Ames: "Rome was a republic from its very birth. It is true, for two hundred and forty-four years it was subject to its kings; but the spirit of liberty was never more lofty at any period of its long troubled life than when Rome was governed by kings. They were, in war, generals; in peace, only magistrates. For seven hundred years Rome remained a republic" (Seth Ames, ed., *The Works of Fisher Ames* (Boston, 1854), 332–33. On Hamilton's admiration for Caesar, see A. Koch, *Power, Morals, and the Founding Fathers* (chapter: Hamilton and the Pursuit of Power, 67, 75). Gerald Stourzh, *Alexander Hamilton and the Idea of Republican Government* (Stanford, Calif., 1970).

70. T. Dana, The Winter of Criticism, *Monthly Anthology and Boston Review* 12 (October 1805). Lewis P. Simpson ed., *The Federalist Literary Mind* (Baton Rouge, La., 1962), 209, 230.

71. See A. Koch, *Power, Morals, and the Founding Fathers*, 26 f., 31 f., 104. A. Schlesinger, *America: Experiment or Destiny?*, 507.

72. Quote in J. G. A. Pocock, *The Machiavellian Moment: Florentine Political Thought and the Atlantic Republican Tradition* (Princeton, N.J., 1975), viii. See Gordon S. Wood, *The Creation of the American Republic, 1776–1787* (Chapel Hill, N.C., 1969). David E. Ingersoll, Machiavelli and Madison: Perspectives on Political Stability, *The Political Science Quarterly* 85, no. 2 (June 1970): 259–80. Richard Hofstadter, *The American Political Tradition and the Men Who Made It* (New York, 1948), with a preface by Christopher Lasch (chapter: The Founding Fathers: An Age of Realism, 3–21).

73. Alexander Hamilton, No. 6, in *The Federalist Papers*, 59.

74. Quote in A. Koch, *Power, Morals, and the Founding Fathers*, 26.

75. Quote in W. O. Clough, ed., *Intellectual Origins of American National Thought*, (New York, 1961), 71.

76. Quote in Meyer Reinhold, ed., *The Classick Papers*, 121. Meyer Reinhold points out that Polybius was widely read during the revolutionary phase, specifically Book IV of his history "partly as mediated through Machiavelli's 'Discourses' and Montesquieu's 'Laws'."

77. A. Koch, *Power, Morals, and the Founding Fathers* (chapter: The Idea of America), 130.

78. Quotations in Joseph Ellis, Habits of Mind and an American Enlightenment, *American Quarterly* 28 (1976): 161. A. Schlesinger, *America: Experiment or Destiny?*, 509.

79. Hamilton in G. Stourzh, *Alexander Hamilton*, 71, 98. See *Jonathan Daniels: Ordeal of Ambition: Jefferson, Hamilton, Burr* (Garden City, N.Y., 1970). John C. Miller, *Alexander Hamilton: Portrait in Paradox* (New York, 1969).

80. Abigail Adams, in A. Koch, *Power, Morals, and the Founding Fathers*, 75.

81. W. Wilson, *Constitutional Government in the United States* (1908; reprint New York, 1961), 44–45.

82. Adams to Rush, September 27, 1808, in Adrienne Koch and William Peden,

eds., *The Selected Writings of John and John Quincy Adams* (New York, 1946), 149–50. See also Robert A. East, *John Adams* (Boston, 1979).

83. Thomas Jefferson, *Notes on the State of Virginia* (1785), Query XVIII.

84. Paine, in K. D. Bracher, Politische Institutionen in Krisenzeiten, *Vierteljahreshefte für Zeitgeschichte* 1 (1985): 4.

85. George Washington, First Inaugural Address in the City of New York, April 30, 1789, in *Inaugural Addresses of the Presidents of the United States, from George Washington 1789 to Richard Milhous Nixon 1973* (Washington, D.C., 1974), 3. See also the most recent Washington biography, *John R. Alden: George Washington*, (Baton Rouge, La., 1984).

86. Madison in A. Koch, *Power, Morals, and the Founding Fathers*, 105.

87. A. Koch, *Power, Morals, and the Founding Fathers* (chapter: Jefferson and the Pursuit of Happiness, 23–49, and chapter: Madison and the Workshop of Liberty, 103–21), 28 f., 105, 130 f. A. Koch, *Jefferson and Madison: The Great Collaboration* (New York, 1950). See also David W. Marcell: *Progress and Pragmatism. James, Dewey, Beard, and the American Idea of Progress* (chapter: The Heritage of Progress), (Westport, Conn., 1974), 52–69. Howard Mumford Jones, *The Pursuit of Happiness* (Cambridge, Mass., 1953), 1–28.

88. Quotations in Rutherford E. Delmage, The American Idea of Progress, 1750–1800, *Proceedings of the American Philosophical Society* 91 (1947): 313, and D. W. Marcell, *Progress and Pragmatism*, 56. See also Carl L. Becker, *The Declaration of Independence: A Study in the History of Political Ideas* (New York, 1956), 25–26.

89. D. W. Marcell, *Progress and Pragmatism*, 56.

90. For a discussion of the influence of the scientific revolution on American thought, see J. Bernard Cohen, *Revolution in Science* (Cambridge, Mass., 1985), 208, 232, 325, 513–14. Gary Wills, *Cincinnatus: George Washington and the Enlightenment* (Garden City, N.Y., 1984). Zoltan Haraszti, John Adams and the Prophets of Progress, *Mississippi Valley Historical Review* 38 (December 1951): 387–402; R. E. Delmage, The American Idea of Progress, 307–14; V. E. Gibbens, Tom Paine and the Idea of Progress, *Pennsylvania Magazine of History and Biography* 66 (April 1942): 191–204. E. T. Martin, Thomas Jefferson and the Idea of Progress, Ph.D. diss., University of Wisconsin, 1941. Macklin Thomas, The Idea of Progress in the Writings of Franklin, Freneau, Barlow, and Rush, Ph.D. diss., University of Wisconsin, 1938.

91. See Merle Curti, *Human Nature in American Historical Thought* (Columbia, Mo., 1969), passim. R. G. Collingwood, *The Idea of History* (Oxford, 1964). Howard M. Jones, *O Strange New World* (New York, 1964).

92. R. E. Delmage, The American Idea of Progress, 313.

93. Madison in A. Koch, *Power, Morals, and the Founding Fathers*, 129.

94. See Don K. Price, *The Scientific Estate* (Cambridge, Mass., 1965), vii.

95. See A. Koch, *Power, Morals, and the Founding Fathers*, 129 f. See also Sidney J. French, The Spirit of American Science, in *The American Idea* (New York, 1976).

96. B. Rush, *Three Lectures upon Animal Life* (Philadelphia, 1799), 62.

97. D. W. Marcell, *Progress and Pragmatism*, 61.

98. D. Boorstin, *The Lost World of Thomas Jefferson* (Boston, 1948).

99. James Oliver Robertson, *American Myth, American Reality* (New York, 1981), 42.

100. Quoted in Arthur A. Ekirch, *The Idea of Progress in America, 1815–1860* (New

York, 1944), 32. See Henry Steele Commager, *Jefferson, Nationalism and the Enlightenment* (New York, 1975).

101. See also J. B. Bury, *The Idea of Progress* (New York, 1920), 98–176. Sidney Pollard, *The Idea of Progress: History and Society* (New York, 1968), 18–96.

102. See A. Koch, *Power, Morals, and the Founding Fathers,* 123.

103. See Herbert Butterfield, *The Whig Interpretation of History* (London, 1931). R. Hofstadter, *The Progressive Historians* (chapter: Historical Writing Before Turner), 7. E. Angermann, *Die Amerikanische Revolution im Spiegel der Geschichte,* 16 f.

104. See R. Hofstadter, *The Progressive Historians,* 9. Orin Grant Libby, Some Pseudohistorians of the American Revolution, *Proceedings of the Wisconsin Academy of Sciences and Arts* 13 (1900): 419–25. O. G. Libby, Ramsay as Plagiarist, *American Historical Review* 7 (1902): 697–703. Sydney G. Fisher, The Legendary and Myth-Making Process in Histories of the American Revolution, *Proceedings of the American Philosophical Society* 51 (1912): 53–75. Thomas A. Bailey, The Mythmakers of American History, *Journal of American History* 55 (June 1968): 5–21. T. A. Bailey, *Probing America's Past: A Critical Examination of Major Myths and Misconceptions* (Lexington, Mass., 1973).

105. R. Hofstadter, *The Progressive Historians,* 9.

106. Herbert Baxter Adams, *Life and Writings of Jared Sparks* (Boston, 1893), 2, 375.

107. See Dixon Wecter, *The Hero in America. A Chronicle of Hero-Worship* (Ann Arbor, Mich., 1963). Clinton Rossiter, *The American Quest, 1790–1860. An Emerging Nation in Search of Identity, Unity, and Modernity* (New York, 1971).

108. On the Washington myth, see Marcus Cunliffe, *George Washington, Man and Monument* (Boston, 1958). Bernard Mayo, *Myths and Men: Patrick Henry, George Washington, Thomas Jefferson* (Athens, Ga., 1959). James T. Flexner, *Washington, The Indispensable Man* (Boston, 1974). Lawrence J. Friedman, *Inventors of the Promised Land* (New York, 1975) (chapter: The Flawless American. The Invention of George Washington).

109. See John Marshall, *The Life of George Washington* (Philadelphia, 1804–1807), 5 vols. Critical on this topic is E. Angermann, *Die Amerikanische Revolution im Spiegel der Geschichte,* 22.

110. See Mason Locke Weems, *The Life of George Washington. With curious anecdotes, equally honourable to himself and exemplary to his young countrymen* (Philadelphia, 1808; new edition: Cambridge, Mass., 1962).

111. See Jared Sparks, *Writing of George Washington. Being his Correspondence, Addresses, Messages, and Other Papers, Official and Private* (Boston, 1834–37), 12 vols. David Ramsay, *The Life of George Washington* (Baltimore, 1807).

112. See Paul C. Nagel, *This Sacred Trust. American Nationality, 1789–1898* (New York, 1971). P. C. Nagel, *One Nation Indivisible. The Union in American Thought, 1776–1861* (New York, 1964); Merle Curti, *The Roots of American Loyalty* (New York, 1946).

113. See H. Niles, ed., *Principles and Acts of the Revolution in America* (Baltimore, 1822). J. Elliot, ed., *Debates in the Several State Conventions on the Adoption of the Federal Constitution* (Washington, D.C., 1836), 4 vols. P. Force, ed., *American Archives—Consisting of a collection of authentic records, state papers, debates, and letters . . . forming a documentary history of the origin and progress of the North American*

*Colonies* . . . (Washington, D.C., 1837–53), 9 vols. J. Sparks, ed., *Diplomatic Correspondence of the American Revolution* (Boston, 1829–30), 12 vols.

114. H. Adams, in *History*, ed. J. Higham, L. Krieger, and F. Gilbert, 70.

115. See Lester H. Cohen, *The Revolutionary Histories: Contemporary Narratives of the American Revolution* (Ithaca, N.Y., 1980). Arthur H. Shaffer, *The Politics of History, Writing the History of the American Revolution, 1783–1815* (Chicago, 1975). Bert James Loewenberg, *American History in American Thought. Christopher Columbus to Henry Adams* (New York, 1972). David D. Van Tassel, *Recording America's Past. An Interpretation of the Development of Historical Studies in America, 1607–1884* (Chicago, 1960).

116. See E. Angermann, *Die Amerikanische Revolution im Spiegel der Geschichte*, 17–23. See also Richard Buel, *Securing the Revolution. Ideology in American Politics, 1789–1815* (Ithaca, N.Y., 1972).

117. The most recent biography of Bancroft was written in 1984: Lilian Handlin, *George Bancroft: The Intellectual as Democrat* (New York, 1984).

118. See David Levin, *History as Romantic Art: Bancroft, Prescott, Motley, and Parkman* (Stanford, Calif., 1959), passim.

119. D. W. Marcell, *Progress and Pragmatism*, 75; G. Bancroft, *The History of the United States of America from the Discovery of the Continent* (Boston, 1934–74), 10 vols. See Russel B. Nye, *George Bancroft, Brahmin Rebel* (New York, 1945).

120. See E. Angermann, *Die Amerikanische Revolution im Spiegel der Geschichte* (chapter: Romantik und Realismus), 23 f.

121. R. Hofstadter, *The Progressive Historians* (chapter: Historical Writing before Turner), 16.

122. See R. B. Nye, *George Bancroft, Brahmin Rebel*. R. B. Nye, *George Bancroft* (New York, 1964). A. M. Schlesinger, *The Age of Jackson* (Boston, 1945). R. Canary, *Brief Life* (New York, 1974). L. Handlin, *George Bancroft: The Intellectual as Democrat*.

123. Quote in R. Hofstadter, *The Progressive Historians*, 19.

124. Ibid., 17–19. See William R. Taylor, *Cavalier and Yankee: The Old South and American National Character* (New York, 1961), 95–141.

125. R. Hofstadter, *The Progressive Historians*, 19. See also R. B. Nye, *George Bancroft* (New York, 1964), 74, 76, 81, 83–84.

126. R. B. Nye, *George Bancroft, Brahmin Rebel*, 87, 92, 127, 139, 167, 188, 204, 306.

127. Quote in R. Hofstadter, *The Progressive Historians*, 15. See L. Handlin, *George Bancroft* (Chapter 7).

128. G. Bancroft, *Literary and Historical Miscellanies* (New York, 1855), 516.

129. G. Bancroft, *History of the United States* . . . (Boston, 1856), 2, 267, 269. On the discussion of Bancroft's conception of progress, see Merrill Lewis, Organic Metaphor and Edenic Myth in George Bancroft's "History of the United States," *Journal of the History of Ideas* 26 (October–December 1965), 587–92.

130. On European influence, see Howard Mumford Jones, The Influence of European Ideas in Nineteenth-century America, *American Literature* 7 (March 1935–January 1936): 241–73, and especially René Wellek, *Confrontations: Studies in the Intellectual and Literary Relations Between Germany, England and the United States during the Nineteenth Century* (Princeton, N.J., 1965), passim.

131. J. D. Dana, Science and the Scientific Schools, *American Journal of Education* 2 (September 1856): 364.

132. G. Bancroft, *Literary and Historical Miscellanies*, 418–19.

133. See R. Hofstadter, *The Progressive Historians*, 18–20. See also A. A. Ekirch, *The Idea of Progress in America, 1815–1860*, 267. Rush Welter, The Idea of Progress in America, *Journal of the History of Ideas* 16 (June 1955): 401–15. John L. Thomas, Romantic Reform in America, 1815–1865, *American Quarterly* 17 (Winter 1965): 656–81. Yehoshua Arieli, *Individualism and Nationalism in American Ideology* (Cambridge, Mass., 1964), 246–76.

134. F. Parkman, The Failure of Universal Suffrage, *North American Review* 127 (1878): 7. On Parkman see also Howard Doughty, *Francis Parkman* (New York, 1962).

135. See Donald E. Emerson, *Richard Hildreth* (Baltimore, 1946), 133, 140, 162. E. Angermann, *Die Amerikanische Revolution im Spiegel der Geschichte*, 24 ff.

136. R. Hildreth, *The History of the United States of America* (New York, 1849–52), 6 vols., here vol. 1, iii.

137. R. Hildreth, in R. Hofstadter, *The Progressive Historians*, 22.

138. See H. von Holst, *Verfassung und Demokratie der Vereinigten Staaten von Amerika*, vol. 1 (Düsseldorf, 1873), vols. 2–5 (Berlin, 1878–92) [*The Constitutional and Political Theory of the United States*, 8 vols.: Chicago, 1889–92]. J. W. Burgess, *Political Science and Comparative Constitutional Law*, vol. 1 (*Sovereignty and Liberty*), (Boston, 1896).

139. See Eric F. Goldman, Hermann E. von Holst, Plumed Knight of American Historiography, *Mississippi Valley Historical Review* 23 (1936–37): 511–32. R. Hofstadter, *The Progressive Historians* (chapter: Historical Writing Before Turner), 24–30. E. Angermann, *Die Amerikanische Revolution im Spiegel der Geschichte* (chapter: Nationalismus nach dem Bürgerkrieg), 28 ff. Jürgen Herbst, *The German Historical School in American Scholarship. A Study in the Transfer of Culture* (Ithaca, N.Y., 1965).

140. See R. Hofstadter, *The Progressive Historians*.

141. See K. Krakau, *Missionsbewußtsein und Völkerrechtsdoktrin in den Vereinigten Staaten von Amerika*, 136 f.

142. See J. W. Burgess, *Political Science and Comparative Constitutional Law*, 44.

143. Ibid., 46–48.

144. Charles Darwin, *The Descent of Man, and Selection in Relation to Sex* (New York, 1871), 179. On Darwin's influence in the United States, see *Darwinism Comes to America*, ed. George Daniels (Waltham, Mass., 1968).

145. C. Darwin, *The Descent of Man*.

146. See John Dewey, *The Influence of Darwin on Philosophy* (New York, 1910). Stow Persons, ed., *Evolutionary Thought in America* (New Haven, Conn., 1950). R. Hofstadter, *Social Darwinism in American Thought* (Boston, 1955). Loren Eiseley, *Darwin's Century* (New York, 1961). R. J. Wilson, ed., *Darwinism and the American Intellectual* (Homewood, Ill., 1967). Gertrude Himmelfarb, *Darwin and the Darwinian Revolution* (New York, 1968). Paul F. Boller, *American Thought in Transition: The Impact of Evolutionary Naturalism, 1865–1900* (Chicago, 1969).

147. Quotations in R. Hofstadter, *The Progressive Historians*, 28. On this topic, see Edward Saveth, *American Historians and European Immigrants, 1875–1925* (New York, 1948), 36, 49, 172, 232 f. John Higham, *Strangers in the Land. Patterns of American Nativism, 1860–1925* (New York, 1963).

148. See James C. Malin, *Confounded Rot about Napoleon. Reflections upon Science and Technology, Nationalism, World Depression of the Eighteen-Nineties, and Afterwards* (Lawrence, Kan., 1961). H. Wayne Morgan, ed., *The Gilded Age* (Syracuse, N.Y.,

1970). Paul C. Nagel, *This Sacred Trust, American Nationality 1798–1898* (New York, 1971). Morton Keller, *Affairs of State. Public Life in Late Nineteenth Century America* (Cambridge, Mass., 1977). E. Angermann, *Die Amerikanische Revolution im Spiegel der Geschichte*, 30 f.

149. See R. Hofstadter, *Social Darwinism in American Thought*, 170–200. Hanns-Joachim W. Koch, *Der Sozialdarwinismus. Seine Genese und sein Einfluß auf das imperialistische Denken* (Munich, 1973), 87 ff., 113 ff.

150. See H. L. Osgood, *The American Colonies in the Eighteenth Century* (New York, 1924), 4 vols. G. L. Beer, *The English-speaking People* (New York, 1918). A. T. Mahan, *The Interest of America in Sea Power, Present and Future* (London, 1898). In general on "Imperial School": Lawrence H. Gipson, The Imperial Approach to Early American History, in Ray Allen Billington, ed., *The Reinterpretation of Early American History* (San Marino, Calif., 1966), 185–99.

151. R. Hofstadter, *The Progressive Historians*, 179.

152. See J. Fiske, *The Critical Period of American History, 1783–1789* (Boston, 1888). On Fiske, see Milton Berman, *John Fiske: The Evolution of a Popularizer* (Cambridge, Mass., 1961).

153. J. Fiske, Manifest Destiny, in *American Political Ideas Viewed from the Standpoint of Universal History* (New York, 1885), 121.

154. Ibid., 143.

155. Herbert Spencer, *Social Statics* (New York, 1865), 74, 76, 79–80.

156. See J. Fiske, *Outlines of Cosmic Philosophy* (Boston, 1875), 1, 184. James McCosh, *Christianity and Positivism* (New York, 1871), 51. See Herbert W. Schneider, The Influence of Darwin and Spencer on American Philosophical Theology, *Journal of the History of Ideas* 6 (January 1945): 3–18.

157. J. Fiske, *Outlines of Cosmic Philosophy*, 2, 228.

158. See J. Fiske, A Century's Progress in Science, *Atlantic Monthly* 78 (July 1896). Quote from D. W. Marcell, *Progress and Pragmatism* (chapter: The Evolutionary Dialogue), 114.

159. Quote from D. W. Marcell, *Progress and Pragmatism*, 122, 124 f. For a description of Wright's life work, see Edward H. Madden, *Chauncey Wright and the Foundations of Pragmatism* (Seattle, Wash., 1963), 3–30.

160. C. Wright, in *Philosophical Discussion by Chauncey Wright*, ed. Charles Eliot Norton (New York, 1898), 69, 73, 16.

161. See also H. S. Commager, *The American Mind: An Interpretation of American Thought and Character since the 1880's* (New Haven, Conn., 1950) (chapter on Fiske). D. Hull, *Darwin and His Critics* (Cambridge, Mass., 1973). J. White, The Americans on Herbert Spencer: Some Reaction to His Social and Evolutionary Thought, 1860–1940, Ph.D. diss., Hull University 1975. On American atheism, see, in addition, James Turner, *Without God, Without Creed. Origins of Unbelief in America* (Baltimore, 1985).

162. See H. S. Commager, *The American Mind* (chapter on Turner, Parrington, and Beard). Peter M. Rutkoff, and William B. Scott, *New School, A History of the New School for Social Research* (New York, 1986).

163. See E. Angermann, *Die Amerikanische Revolution im Spiegel der Geschichte* (chapter: "New History," Progressive Historians), 38 ff. H. R. Guggisberg, Sozialpolitisches Engagement in der amerikanischen Historiographie des 20. Jahrhunderts, in H. R. Guggisberg, *Alte und Neue Welt in historischer Perspektive, Sieben Studien zum amerikanischen Geschichts- und Selbstverständnis* (Bern, 1973), 120–50. Lee Benson,

*Turner and Beard, American Historical Writing Reconsidered* (Glencoe, Ill., 1960). James Harvey Robinson, *The New History, Essays Illustrating the Modern Historical Outlook* (New York, 1912).

164. See R. Hofstadter, *The Progressive Historians,* 41–43. H. S. Commager, *The American Mind.*

165. F. J. Turner, in Ray A. Billington, Young Fred Turner, *Wisconsin Magazine of History* 46 (1962): 45.

166. D. W. Marcell, *Progress and Pragmatism,* 65.

167. George Berkeley, *Works,* ed. A. C. Fraser, (Oxford, 1871), 3, 232.

168. See K. D. Bracher, Der "Frontier-Gedanke": Motiv des amerikanischen Fortschrittsbewußtseins, Ein ideologienkritischer Versuch, *Zeitschrift für Politik* 2 (1955): 230.

169. This lecture is printed in F. J. Turner, *The Frontier in American History* (New York, 1920).

170. F. J. Turner, *The Frontier in American History,* 302–303, 299–300.

171. See K. D. Bracher, Der "Frontier-Gedanke," 231, 233, 235. See Warren I. Susman, The Useless Past: American Intellectuals and the Frontier Thesis: 1910–1930, *Bucknell Review* 11, (1963): 1–20.

172. See R. Hofstadter, *The Progressive Historians* (chapter: Frontier and Section and the Usable Past; and The Frontier as an Explanation), 84–164; K. D. Bracher, Der "Frontier-Gedanke," 231.

173. F. J. Turner, in *Frontier and Section* ed. R. A. Billington (New York, 1961), 29. F. J. Turner, *The Frontier in American History,* 1, 3, 4, 205, 206–207, 266, 216, 293.

174. See H. S. Commager, *The American Mind;* K. D. Bracher, Der "Frontier-Gedanke," 234–36.

175. Parrington, in R. Hofstadter, *The Progressive Historians* (chapter: Criticism and Political Thought), 396.

176. Parrington, in R. Hofstadter, *The Progressive Historians* (chapter: Economics and Criticism), 364. On Parrington's academic career, see William T. Utter, Vernon Louis Parrington, in *The Marcus W. Jernegan Essays in American Historiography,* ed. W. T. Hutchinson (Chicago, 1937).

177. See H. S. Commager, *The American Mind.*

178. Parrington, in R. Hofstadter, *The Progressive Historians,* 396.

179. See Robert A. Skotheim and Kermit Vanderbilt, Vernon Louis Parrington: The Mind and Art of a Historian of Ideas, *Pacific Northwest Quarterly,* 53 (1962): 102 ff. H. S. Commager, *The American Mind.*

180. Parrington, in R. Hofstadter, *The Progressive Historians* 389. See also Parrington's 1917 essay Economics and Criticism, published for the first time many years later by his son, Vernon Parrington, Jr., in *Pacific Northwest Quarterly* 44 (1953): 91–105.

181. See A. A. Ekirch, Parrington and the Decline of American Liberalism, *American Quarterly* 3 (1951): 295–308.

182. V. L. Parrington, *Main Currents in American Thought,* vol. 1: *The Colonial Mind, 1620–1800;* vol. 2: *The Romantic Revolution in America, 1800–1860* (New York, 1927).

183. Ibid., 1, 74–75.

184. See V. L. Parrington, *Main Currents in American Thought,* 2, 415–416. In

addition, see R. Hofstadter, Parrington and the Jeffersonian Tradition, *Journal of the History of Ideas* 2 (1941): 391–400.

185. R. Hofstadter, *The Progressive Historians*, 428.

186. V. L. Parrington, *Main Currents in American Thought*, vol. 3: *The Beginnings of Critical Realism in America, 1860–1920* (New York, 1930).

187. R. Hofstadter, *The Progressive Historians*, 429.

188. Quotations in ibid., 429, 434. On problems of progress in America around the turn of the century, see David W. Noble, *The Paradox of Progressive Thought* (Minneapolis, 1958).

189. See E. R. A. Seligman, *The Economic Interpretation of History* (New York, 1902). James Harvey Robinson, *The New History. Essays Illustrating the Modern Historical Outlook* (New York, 1912). Cushing Strout, *The Pragmatic Revolt in American History: Carl Becker and Charles Beard* (New Haven, Conn., 1958), 13–29. Charles Crowe, The Emergence of Progressive History, *Journal of the History of Ideas* 27 (1966): 107–24.

190. See D. W. Marcell, *Progress and Pragmatism*, 146–334. John L. Thomas, *Alternative America. Henry George, Edward Bellamy, Henry Demarest Lloyd and the Adversary Tradition* (Cambridge, Mass., 1983).

191. Charles A. Beard, *An Economic Interpretation of the Constitution of the United States* (New York, 1913) (New edition: 1935, with an introduction revising his own standpoint). For a critical response, see R. Hofstadter, *The Progressive Historians*, 207 ff. Robert E. Brown, *Charles Beard and the Constitution. A Critical Analysis of "An Economic Interpretation of the Constitution"* (Princeton, N.J., 1956).

192. See also E. Angermann, *Die Amerikanische Revolution im Spiegel der Geschichte* (chapter: "New History," Progressive Historians), 43 f. Howard K. Beale, ed., *Charles A. Beard: An Appraisal* (Lexington, Ky., 1954).

193. For a critical view of Beard and his sphere of influence, see Edmund S. Morgan, ed., *The American Revolution: Two Centuries of Interpretation* (Englewood Cliffs, N.J., 1965), 172 ff. R. Hofstadter, The Progressive Historians, 285 ff., 344–46. H. S. Commager, *The American Mind*.

194. Charles Beard and G. H. E. Smith, *The Open Door at Home* (New York, 1934), 135–136. Charles Beard, The Task Before Us, *Social Studies* 25 (May 1934): 215.

195. Charles Beard and William Beard, *The American Leviathan* (New York, 1930), 9.

196. Charles Beard, Limitations to the Application of Social Science Implied in Recent Social Trends, *Social Forces* 2 (May 1933): 506.

197. Charles Beard, *The Myth of Rugged American Individualism* (New York, 1932), 26–27.

198. Charles Beard and W. Beard, *The American Leviathan*, 3.

199. On Beard's life and work, see Ellen Nore, *Charles A. Beard: An Intellectual Biography* (Carbondale, Ill., 1983). Bernard C. Borning, *The Political and Social Thought of Charles A. Beard* (Seattle, Wash., 1962). Mary R. Beard, *The Making of Charles A. Beard* (New York, 1955). Charles Beard, Self-Education, *Young Oxford* 1 (October 1899): 17 ff.

200. See Charles Beard, Rebuilding in Japan, *Review of Reviews* 68 (October 1923): 382 f. Charles Beard, Municipal Research Abroad and at Home, *Journal of Social Forces* 3 (March 1925): 495 f. H. S. Commager, *The American Mind*.

201. See Charles Beard, *The Discussion of Human Affairs* (New York, 1936), 79 f.

Charles Beard, Grounds for a Reconsideration of Historiography, in *Theory and Practice in Historical Study: A Report of the Committee on Historiography* (New York, 1946), 6 ff.

202. Charles Beard, Written History as an Act of Faith, *American Historical Review* 39 (January 1934): 219, 229.

203. Charles Beard and Mary Beard, *The American Spirit: A Study of the Idea of Civilization in the United States* (New York, 1942), 7, 581. See also the theses of Robert Skotheim, *American Intellectual Histories and Historians* (Princeton, N.J., 1966), 105–106, who interprets *The American Spirit* as Beard's answer to the challenges of totalitarianism.

204. On the German influence on Beard, see Charles Beard and Alfred Vagts, Currents of Thought in Historiography, *American Historical Review* 42 (April 1937): 481 f. Lloyd R. Sorenson, Charles A. Beard and German Historical Thought, *Mississippi Valley Historical Review* 42 (September 1955): 274–87. Gerald D. Nash, Self-Education in Historiography: The Case of Charles A. Beard, *Pacific Northwest Quarterly* 52 (July 1961): 108–15. On Croce's influence on Beard, see G. D. Nash, Self-Education in Historiography, 112–14. Beard obtained his ideas of Machiavelli's image of history from F. Meinecke's book *Die Idee der Staatsräson* (Munich, 1924). On this topic, see Charles Beard, *The Nature of the Social Sciences* (New York, 1934): 191.

205. See George Santayana, *Winds of Doctrine* (New York, 1913), passim.

206. For additional background on decadent thought at the turn of the century, see Carl Becker, *Progress and Power* (New York, 1936). Lewis Mumford, *The Human Prospect*, ed. H. T. Moore and K. W. Deutsch (Boston, 1955). Lewis Mumford, *The Transformation of Man* (New York, 1962). Timothy Paul Donovan, *Henry Adams and Brooks Adams: The Education of Two American Historians* (Norman, Okla., 1961). H. S. Commager, *The American Mind* (chapter: The Cult of Irrationality).

207. Quote from the journal *Living Age* from February 26, 1901.

208. D. W. Marcel, *Progress and Pragmatism* (chapter: Formalism, Degradation, and Pragmatism), 31. See also D. Noble, The Religion of Progress in America, 1890–1914, *Social Forces* 22 (Winter 1955): 417–40. D. Noble, *The Paradox of Progressive Thought* (Minneapolis, 1958), passim. Henry F. May, *The End of American Innocence: A Study of the First Years of Our Own Time, 1912–1917* (Chicago, 1959), 20–29 ff. Frederick Cople Jaher, *Doubters and Dissenters: Cataclysmic Thought in America, 1885–1918* (New York, 1964), passim.

209. See R. P. Blackmur, Henry and Brooks Adams: Parallels to Two Generations, *Southern Review* 5, no. 2 (1939): 309 f. William F. Dowling, The Political Thought of a Generation of Adamses, Ph.D. diss., Harvard University, 1950, passim. T. P. Donovan, *Henry Adams and Brooks Adams*.

210. On this topic, see Thornton Anderson, *Brooks Adams, Constructive Conservative* (Ithaca, N.Y., 1951), 106–17. Arthur F. Beringause, *Brooks Adams: A Biography* (New York, 1955), 247–50, 257–59, 266 f., 274–79, 283–94. Charles Hirschfeld, Brooks Adams and American Nationalism, *American Historical Review* 69, no. 2 (January 1964): 380.

211. Daniel Aaron, *Men of Good Hope* (New York, 1951), 245, 252, 255; T. Anderson, *Brooks Adams*, 2f, 207; Samuel P. Huntington, *The Soldier and the State* (Cambridge, Mass., 1957), 270–72. A. F. Beringause, *Brooks Adams*, 371. William A. Williams, Brooks Adams and American Expansionism, *New England Quarterly* 25 (June 1952): 225–28.

212. "Paradox had become the only orthodoxy . . ." was Henry Adams's commentary on the intellectual trends of his time, in Louis Hartz, The Coming of Age of America, *American Political Science Review* 51 (June 1957): 483.

213. For a more detailed discussion, see Clinton Rossiter, *Conservatism in America* (New York, 1955), 166. D. Aaron, *Men of Good Hope,* 252.

214. See Brooks Adams, *The Law of Civilization and Decay* (London, 1895; New York, 1955, with an essay as preface by Theodore Roosevelt).

215. Quotations in D. Aaron, *Men of Good Hope,* 252, 273–74. See also Brooks Adams, The American Democratic Ideal, *Yale Review* 5 (January 1916): 225–27, 231–33. Brooks Adams, The Incoherence of American Democracy, in *Proceedings Bunker Hill Monument Association 1916* (Boston, 1916), especially 30–48.

216. C. Hirschfeld, Brooks Adams and American Nationalism, 391.

217. Brooks Adams, The New Industrial Revolution, *Atlantic Monthly* 87 (February 1901): 165.

218. See C. Hirschfeld, *Brooks Adams and American Nationalism,* 372, 375, 377 f., 383, 386 f., 392.

219. See also the interesting and critical correspondence that Henry Adams conducted with the Harvard philosopher and colleague William James, printed in Henry James, ed., *The Letters of William James* (Boston, 1920), 2 vols. Harold Dean Cater, ed., *Henry Adams and His Friends: A Collection of His Unpublished Letters* (Boston, 1947). Worthington Chauncey Ford, ed., *The Letters of Henry Adams, 1892–1918* (Boston, 1938), 2 vols. Ernest Samuels, *Henry Adams: The Middle Years* (Cambridge, Mass., 1958).

220. Henry Adams, *The Education of Henry Adams* (Boston, 1918), 451, 495.

221. See Henry Adams, *The Tendency of History* (chapter: The Rule of Phase Applied to History), (New York, 1919), 172. See also Howard M. Munford, Henry Adams and the Tendency of History, *New England Quarterly* 32 (March 1959): 88.

222. See W. C. Ford, ed., *The Letters of Henry Adams,* 279.

223. Henry to Brooks Adams, November 23, 1900, and May 7, 1901, in H. D. Cater, ed., *Henry Adams and His Friends,* 502.

224. Arthur Schlesinger, *America: Experiment or Destiny?,* 519.

225. Henry to Brooks Adams, November 23, 1900, to May 7, 1901, in H. D. Cater, ed., *Henry Adams and His Friends,* 508.

226. Henry Adams, quoted in A. Schlesinger, *America: Experiment or Destiny?,* 519–20.

227. Henry Adams to H. O. Taylor, November 22, 1909, in W. C. Ford ed., *The Letters of Henry Adams,* 526.

228. Henry Adams to C. M. Gaskell, June 1, 1914, and to Ferris Greenslet after December 22, 1915, in W. C. Ford, ed., *The Letters of Henry Adams,* 625, 635.

229. See G. E. Müller, *Amerikanische Philosophie* (chapter: Henry Adams), 274 ff.

230. Henry Adams, *The Education of Henry Adams,* 301.

231. See William H. Jordy, *Henry Adams: Scientific Historian* (New Haven, Conn., 1952).

232. Henry Adams, *The Degradation of the Democratic Dogma* (New York, 1919), compiled by Brooks Adams, 212, 207–208.

233. Henry Adams, *The Degradation of the Democratic Dogma,* 218.

234. D. W. Marcell, *Progress and Pragmatism,* 15.

235. See H. S. Commager, *The American Mind.* G. E. Müller, *Amerikanische Philosophie,* 278.

236. Adams discovered the "dynamo" in 1900 at the Trocadero exhibit in Paris. See also Lynn White, *Dynamo and Virgin Reconsidered, Essays in the Dynamism of Western Culture* (Cambridge, Mass., 1968), 57–73.

237. Henry Adams, in L. White, *Dynamo and Virgin Reconsidered*, 59.

238. Ibid., 57 f. Melvin Lyon, *Symbol and Idea in Henry Adams* (Lincoln, Nebr., 1970).

239. Henry Adams, in L. White, *Dynamo and Virgin Reconsidered*, 58.

240. Ibid.

241. See Henry Adams, *Mont-Saint-Michel and Chartres* (1904), (Boston, n.d.), 213.

242. See H. S. Commager, *The American Mind* (chapter: The Cult of Irrationality).

243. See David A. Shannon, ed., *Progressivism and Postwar Disillusionment 1898–1928* (New York, 1965). K. D. Bracher, Turn of the Century and Totalitarian Ideology, in *Totalitarian Democracy and After* (Jerusalem, 1984), 72–74.

244. See H. S. Commager, *The American Mind*.

245. See Reinhold Niebuhr, *Faith and History* (New York, 1949), passim. R. Niebuhr, An Adequate Faith for the World Crisis, in *Representative American Speeches*, ed. A. C. Baird, 20, no. 4 (New York, 1948).

246. Reinhold Niebuhr, *The Irony of American History* (New York, 1952), 4.

247. Ibid., 42, 69–70.

248. A. Schlesinger, *America: Experiment or Destiny?*, 520.

249. See R. Hofstadter, *The Progressive Historians* (chapter: Conflict and Consensus in American History), 438 f.; Robert A. Skotheim, *American Intellectual Histories and Historians* (Princeton, N.J., 1966).

250. R. Hofstadter, *The Progressive Historians*, 439. See also Raymond Aron, Nations and Ideologies, *Encounter* 4 (1955): 24–33. Daniel Bell, The End of Ideology in the West, in *The End of Ideology: On the Exhaustion of Political Ideas in the Fifties* (Glencoe, Ill., 1960).

251. S. E. Morison, Faith of a Historian, *American Historical Review* 56 (1950–51): 273. See also E. Angermann, *Die Amerikanische Revolution im Spiegel der Geschichte* (chapter: Consensus History), 51 f.

252. See S. E. Morison and H. S. Commager, *The Growth of the American Republic* (New York, 1942), 2 vols.

253. R. Hofstadter, *The American Political Tradition and the Men Who Made It* (New York, 1948), xxxvi.

254. R. Hofstadter, *The Progressive Historians*, xxxviii.

255. See Stanley Elkins and Eric McKitrick, Richard Hofstadter. A Progress, in *The Hofstadter Aegis. A Memorial*, ed. S. Elkins and E. McKitrick (New York, 1974), 300–67. Arthur M. Schlesinger, Richard Hofstadter, in *Pastmasters. Some Essays on American Historians*, ed. Marcus Cunliffe and Robin W. Winks (New York, 1969), 278–315.

256. R. Hofstadter, *The Progressive Historians*, 442.

257. Ibid., 466.

258. Daniel J. Boorstin, *The Genius of American Politics* (Chicago, 1953). D. J. Boorstin, *The Americans*, vol. 1: *The Colonial Experience*, vol. 2: *The National Experience* (New York, 1958, 1965). Louis Hartz, *The Liberal Tradition in America. An Interpretation of American Political Thought since the Revolution* (New York, 1955). See R. Hofstadter, *The Progressive Historians*, 445; Critical here is John Higham, Beyond Consensus: The Historian as Moral Critic, *American Historical Review* 67 (1962): 609–625. E. H. Carr, *What Is History?* (New York, 1962). Warren Susman, History and the

American Intellectual: Uses of a Usable Past, *American Quarterly* 16 (Summer 1964): 243, 263. J. R. Pole, The American Past: Is It Still Usable?, *Journal of American Studies* 1 (1967): 63–78. Bernard Sternsher, *Consensus, Conflict, and American Historians* (Bloomington, Ind., 1975).

259. D. Boorstin, *The Genius of American Politics,* 162. See also E. Angermann, *Die Amerikanische Revolution im Spiegel der Geschichte,* 56.

260. See R. Hofstadter, *The Progressive Historians,* 449.

261. D. Boorstin, *The Genius of American Politics,* 163, 189.

262. See E. Angermann, *Die Amerikanische Revolution im Spiegel der Geschichte,* 56 f. J. R. Pole, Daniel J. Boorstin, in *Pastmasters,* ed. M. Cunliffe and R. W. Winks, 210–38.

263. R. Hofstadter, *The Progressive Historians,* 459–60.

264. E. S. Morgan, *The Birth of the Republic, 1763–89* (Chicago, 1956). E. S. Morgan, ed., *The American Revolution. Two Centuries of Interpretation* (Englewood Cliffs, N.J., 1965). Bernard Bailyn, *The Ideological Origins of the American Revolution* (Cambridge, Mass., 1967). B. Bailyn, The Central Themes of the American Revolution. An Interpretation, in *Essays on the American Revolution,* ed. Stephen G. Kurtz and James H. Hutson (Chapel Hill, N.C., 1973), 3–31.

265. B. Bailyn, Lines of Force in Recent Writings on the American Revolution, Paper, 14, International Congress of Historical Sciences, San Francisco, August 22–29, 1975, hectographed manuscript. On this topic see E. Angermann, *Die Amerikanische Revoluton im Spiegel der Geschichte,* 70 f.

266. R. Hofstadter summarizes Hartz's theses in *The Progressive Historians* (chapter: Conflict and Consensus in American History), 446.

267. R. Hofstadter, *The Progressive Historians,* 448 f.

268. See J. Higham, The Cult of the "American Consensus," Homogenizing Our History, *Commentary* 27 (1959): 93–100.

269. E. H. Carr, *What Is History?* (New York, 1962), 54. Critical on this topic is G. R. Elton, *The Practice of History* (London, 1969). J. H. Hexter, *Doing History* (London, 1971). Peter Gay, *Style in History* (New York, 1974).

270. See Irwin Unger, The "New Left" and American History. Some Recent Trends in United States Historiography, *American Historical Review* 72 (1966–67): 1237–63. H. R. Guggisberg, Sozialpolitisches Engagement in der amerikanischen Historiographie des 20. Jahrhunderts, 136 ff. For background on the "New Left," see I. Unger, *The Movement. A History of the American New Left, 1959–1972* (New York, 1974) and Lawrence Lader, *Power on the Left, American Radical Movements since 1946* (New York, 1979).

271. See E. Angermann, *Die Amerikanische Revolution im Spiegel der Geschichte* (chapter: "New Left"), 76 ff.

272. See S. Lynd, *Intellectual Origins of American Radicalism* (New York, 1968). H. Zinn, *Politics of History* (chapter: What Is Radical History"?), (Boston, 1970), 35–55. H. Zinn, *A People's History of the United States* (New York, 1980). Lynd and Zinn were also very active in the civil rights movement, the Vietnam War protest, and the creation of alternative professional institutions. See also E. Angermann, *Die Amerikanische Revolution im Spiegel der Geschichte,* 77.

273. See Lloyd C. Gardner, Walter La Feber, and Thomas J. McCormick, *Creation of the American Empire. U.S. Diplomatic History* (Chicago, 1976). W. A. Williams, *The Tragedy of American Diplomacy* (New York, 1962).

274. See Barton J. Bernstein, ed., *Towards a New Past. Dissenting Essays in American History* (New York, 1968). Alfred F. Young, ed., *Dissent—Explorations in the History of American Radicalism* (De Kalb, Ill., 1968).

275. J. Lemisch, The American Revolution Seen from the Bottom Up, in *Towards a New Past*, ed. B. J. Bernstein, 6. See also E. Angermann, *Die Amerikanische Revolution im Spiegel der Geschichte*, 79.

276. See here in particular Jesse Lemisch's self-pitying study, *On Active Service in War and Peace. Politics and Ideology in the American Historical Profession* (Toronto, 1975).

277. See E. Angermann, *Die Amerikanische Revolution im Spiegel der Geschichte*, 79 f.

278. W. A. Williams, *America Confronts a Revolutionary World, 1776–1976* (New York, 1976), 17.

279. See E. Angermann, *Die Amerikanische Revolution im Spiegel der Geschichte*, 80.

280. See Paul Levine, Der neue Realismus in der zeitgenössischen nordamerikanischen Literatur, *Aus Politik und Zeitgeschichte*, B 39–40/1984, (September 29, 1984): 21. E. Angermann, *Die Amerikanische Revolution im Spiegel der Geschichte* (chapter: Neue Interessengebiete), 82.

281. See W. D. Jordan, *White over Black. American Attitudes toward the Negro, 1550–1812* (Chapel Hill, N.C., 1968). D. B. Davis: *The Problem of Slavery in the Age of Revolution, 1770–1823* (Ithaca, N.Y., 1975). D. B. Davis, Slavery and the Idea of Progress, in *Oceans Apart? Comparing Germany and the United States*, ed. E. Angermann and M.-L. Frings (Stuttgart, 1981), 13–28.

282. See Elizabeth F. Ellett, *The Woman of the American Revolution* (New York, 1853–54), 3 vols. Linda Grant De Pauw, *Founding Mothers. Woman in America in the Revolutionary Era* (Boston, 1975). L. Grant De Pauw, Conover Hunt, and Miriam Schneir, *Remember the Ladies. Woman in America, 1750–1815* (New York, 1976). Paul Engle, *Woman in the American Revolution* (Chicago, 1976). E. Angermann, *Die Amerikanische Revolution im Spiegel der Geschichte*.

283. See Betty Friedan, *The Feminine Mystique*. New York, 1963. Jean E. Friedman and William G. Shade, *Our American Sisters, Woman in American Life and Thought* (Boston, 1976). Carol Berkin, ed., *Woman of America* (Boston, 1979). Sheila Ruth, *Issues in Feminism: A First Course in Woman's Studies* (Boston, 1980). The problem of women was also given increasingly broad treatment in American literature. On this topic, see Marge Piercy, *Small Changes* (Garden City, N.Y., 1973). M. Piercy, *Vida* (London, 1980). Gail Godwin, *The Odd Woman* (New York, 1974). Alice Walker, *Meridian* (New York, 1976).

284. Two interesting works on this subject are Lester H. Cohen: *The Revolutionary Histories: Contemporary Narratives of the American Revolution* (Ithaca, N.Y., 1980); and James Oliver Robertson, *American Myth, American Reality* (New York, 1980).

285. See Richard B. Morris, "We the People of the United States": The Bicentennial of a People's Revolution, *The American Historical Review* (AHR), 82, no. 1 (February 1977): 1–19. C. Vann Woodward, The Aging of America, *AHR* 82, no. 3 (June 1977): 583–94. Robert Kelley, Ideology and Political Culture from Jefferson to Nixon, *AHR* 82, no. 3 (June 1977): 531–62. Arthur Schlesinger, America: Experiment or Destiny?, *AHR* 82, no. 3 (June 1977): 505–22. A. Schlesinger, *The Birth of a Nation: A Portrait of the American People on the Eve of Independence* (Boston, 1982).

286. See Morton White, *The Philosophy of the American Revolution,* (New York, 1978). E. Angermann, *Die Amerikanische Revolution im Spiegel der Geschichte,* 86.

287. See J. R. Pole, *The Pursuit of Equality in American History* (Berkeley, Calif., 1978). M. Kammen, *A Season of Youth, The American Revolution and the Historical Imagination* (New York, 1978). E. Angermann, *Die Amerikanische Revolution im Spiegel der Geschichte,* 86.

288. See H. G. Gutman, Whatever Happened to History?, *The Nation* (November 21, 1981): 554. See also John Higham and Paul K. Conkin, *New Directions in American Intellectual History* (Baltimore, 1980).

289. See P. Levine, Der neue Realismus, 21. Michael Kammen, ed., *The Past Before US: Contemporary Historical Writing in the United States* (Foreword by John Hope Franklin), (Ithaca, N.Y., 1980).

290. See P. Levine, Der neue Realismus, 21.

291. P. Levine, The Writer as Independent Witness: An Interview with E. L. Doctorow, in *E. L. Doctorow: Essays and Conversations,* ed. R. Trenner (Princeton, N.J., 1983), 58–59. See also Dominick LaCapra, *History and Criticism* (Ithaca, N.Y., 1985).

292. See E. L. Doctorow, *Ragtime* (New York, 1975). Ishmael Reed, *Mumbo Jumbo* (New York, 1972).

293. See J. Schell, *The Fate of the Earth* (New York, 1982). Norman Mailer, *Ancient Evenings* (New York, 1983). J. A. Phillips, *Machine Dreams* (New York, 1984).

294. B. Malamud, *God's Grace* (London, 1982), 5.

295. J. Updike, *Rabbit Is Rich* (London, 1982), 229.

296. See S. Bellow, *The Dean's December* (London, 1982).

297. C. Lasch, *The Culture of Narcissism, American Life in an Age of Diminishing Expectations* (New York, 1979).

298. S. Bellow, *The Dean's December,* 278, 123.

299. Ibid., 207.

300. Ibid., 243.

301. R. Winegarten, The Idea of Decadence, *Commentary* 58, no. 3 (September 1974): 69.

302. See P. Levine, *Der neue Realismus,* 23.

303. Representative of this trend is the most recent politicohistorical work by Samuel P. Huntington, *American Politics, The Promise of Disharmony* (Cambridge, Mass., 1981).

## CHAPTER 5

304. See Ralf Dahrendorf, *Die angewandte Aufklärung* (Frankfurt am Main, 1968).

305. Ibid., 100.

306. For an interpretation of the American Revolution from the German point of view, see Horst Dippel, *Die Amerikanische Revolution 1763–1787* (Frankfurt am Main, 1985). Hans-Christoph Schröder, *Die Amerikanische Revolution* (Munich, 1982). Erich Angermann et al., eds., *New Wine in Old Skins. A Comparative View of Socio-Political Structures and Values Affecting the American Revolution* (Stuttgart, 1976). E. Angermann, *Die Amerikanische Revolution im Spiegel der Geschichte.* Hans-Ulrich Wehler, *200 Jahre amerikanische Revolution und moderne Revolutionsforschung* (Göttingen, 1976).

307. Leopold von Ranke, *Über die Epochen der Neueren Geschichte* (1854), quoted in H.-C. Schröder, 199–200.

308. John Adams und Thomas Jefferson, August 24, 1815, in L. J. Cappon, ed., *The Adams-Jefferson Letters. The Complete Correspondence Between T. Jefferson and A. and J. Adams* (Chapel Hill, N.C., 1959), 2, 455.

309. Madison, No. 39, in *The Federalist Papers*. Hamilton, Madison, Jay (with an introduction by Clinton Rossiter) (New York, 1982), 240–46.

310. See Hannah Arendt, *Über die Revolution* (Frankfurt am Main, 1968), 41.

311. See also H. Dippel, *Die Amerikanische Revolution 1763–1787*, 113. Otto Vossler, *Die amerikanischen Revolutionsideale in ihrem Verhältnis zu den europäischen* (Munich, 1929).

312. See H.-C. Schröder, 198–200. H. Dippel, *Die Amerikanische Revolution, 1763–1787*, 115 f. *Fundamental Testaments of the American Revolution*, Library of Congress Symposia on the American Revolution (Washington, D.C., 1973). R. R. Palmer, *The Age of Democratic Revolution* (Princeton, N.J., 1959), 1, 185. Pauline Maier, The Beginnings of American Republicanism, in *The Development of a Revolutionary Mentality*, Library of Congress Symposia on the American Revolution (Washington, D.C., 1972).

313. See Klaus Stern, *Grundideen europäisch-amerikanischer Verfassungsstaatlichkeit* (Berlin, 1984), 13 f. Karl Carstens, *Grundgedanken der amerikanischen Verfassung und ihre Verwirklichung* (Berlin, 1954).

314. The quarrel between George Jellinek and Emile Boutmy is a famous one in constitutional history. The basis for the argument was the question of which country should receive credit for producing the document that originally established basic rights as an integral part of constitutions: The Virginia Bill of Rights of June 12, 1776, or the Déclaration des droits de l'homme et du citoyen of August 26, 1789. See G. Jellinek, *Die Erklärung der Menschen- und Bürgerrechte* (1895), and E. Boutmy, *Die Erklärung der Menschen- und Bürgerrechte und Georg Jellinek* (1902), in *Zur Geschichte der Erklärung der Menschenrechte*, ed. R. Schnur (Darmstadt, 1964). However great the initial influence of the French "Déclaration" in Europe, the American Constitution ultimately played the more decisive role, particularly in its relevance for the judiciary. In Klaus Stern's words, the American constitutional documents institutionalized a "basic rights constitutionalism" in contrast to a French "basic rights abstraction." For a more detailed discussion, see K. Stern, especially 17. See also, H.-C. Schröder, Die Grundrechtsproblematik in der englischen und amerikanischen Revolution, Zur "Libertät" des angelsächsischen Radikalismus, in Günter Birtsch, ed., *Grund- und Freiheitsrechte im Wandel von Gesellschaft und Geschichte* (Göttingen, 1981), 75–95.

315. See H. Dippel, *Die Amerikanische Revolution, 1763–1787*, 118 f.; K. Stern, *Grundideen europäisch-amerikanischer Verfassungsstaatlichkeit*, 14 ff. On the universality of basic and human rights, see Kenneth W. Thompson, ed., *The Moral Imperatives of Human Rights* (Washington, D.C., 1980).

316. See H.-C. Schröder, *Die Amerikanische Revolution*, 200–201. H.-C. Schröder, Die amerikanische und die englische Revolution in vergleichender Perspektive, in *200 Jahre amerikanische Revolution und moderne Revolutionsforschung*, ed. H.-U. Wehler, 9–37.

317. On this thesis, see especially Bernard Bailyn, *The Ideological Origins of the American Revolution*, passim. See also Edward Handler, *America and Europe in the Political Thought of John Adams* (Cambridge, Mass., 1964).

318. John Jay, in H. S. Commager, *The Empire of Reason, How Europe Imagined and America Realized the Enlightenment* (London, 1978), 182.

319. James Wilson, in H. S. Commager, ibid., 189.

320. See Nathan O. Hatch, *The Sacred Cause of Liberty, Republican Thought and the Millenium in Revolutionary New England* (New Haven, Conn., 1977), 44 f.

321. H.-C. Schröder, *Die Amerikanische Revolution*, 195.

322. The *locus classicus* for the description of Americans as the "new people" is *Letters from an American Farmer* published in 1782 by Hector St. John de Crèvecoeur. See H. St. John de Crèvecoeur, What Is an American?, reprinted from *Letters from an American Farmer*, in *The Character of Americans*, ed. Michael McGiffert (Homewood, Ill., 1964). See Denis W. Brogan, *The American Character* (New York, 1944). R. W. B. Lewis, *The American Adam* (Chicago, 1959). Seymour Martin Lipset, *The First New Nation* (New York, 1963).

323. See Herbert McClosky and John Zaller, *The American Ethos, Public Attitudes toward Capitalism and Democracy* (chapter: The Foundations of the American Ethos: Capitalism and Democracy, 1–17), (Cambridge, Mass., 1984). Gerald Stourzh, *Alexander Hamilton and the Idea of Republican Government*.

324. See Roy H. Pearce, *The Savages of America: A Study of the Indian and the Idea of Civilization* (Baltimore, 1965). Angie Debo, *A History of the Indians of the United States* (Norman, Okla., 1970). Dee Brown, *Bury My Heart at Wounded Knee: An Indian History of the American West* (New York, 1971). Wilcomb E. Washburn, *The Indian in America* (New York, 1975).

325. See D. B. Davis, *The Problem of Slavery in the Age of Revolution, 1770–1823* (Ithaca, N.Y., 1975), 161 f.; R. B. Morris, *The American Revolution Reconsidered* (New York, 1968), 72. J. R. Pole, *The Pursuit of Equality in American History* (Berkeley, Calif., 1978).

326. See Benjamin Quarles, *The Negro in the American Revolution* (Chapel Hill, N.C., 1961), 107 f., 199. Gerald W. Mullin, *Flight and Rebellion, Slave Resistance in Eighteenth-Century Virginia* (New York, 1972), 24 f., 128 f., 136 f. D. B. Davis, *The Problem of Slavery*, 60.

327. See H. Arendt, *On Revolution* (New York, 1963).

328. See H.-C. Schröder, *Die Amerikanische Revolution*, 196 f. A comparative study of the French and American revolutions was published as early as 1800 by a conservative German publicist: Friedrich von Gentz, *The American and French Revolutions Compared* (Chicago, 1955), originally published as *Der Ursprung und die Grundsätze der Amerikanischen Revolution, verglichen mit dem Ursprunge und den Grundsätzen der Französischen*, Berlin, 1800.

329. See Paul Leicester Ford, ed., *The Writings of John Dickinson* (Philadelphia, 1895), 1, 375. Franco Venturi, *Utopia and Reform in the Enlightenment* (Cambridge, 1971).

330. Quoted in H. Trevor Colbourn, *The Lamp of Experience, Whig History and the Intellectual Origins of the American Revolution* (Chapel Hill, N.C., 1965).

331. Emmanuel Joseph Sieyes, *Politische Schriften 1788–1790* (Darmstadt, 1975), 35.

332. See H.-C. Schröder, *Die Amerikanische Revolution*, 172. Douglass Adair, *Fame and the Founding Fathers* (New York, 1974).

333. See also H. S. Commager, *The American Mind;* Hannah Arendt, *On Revolution*. Alexis de Tocqueville had already referred to these differing ideological situations in his work, *The Old Regime and the French Revolution*, (New York, 1955).

334. F. Furet, *1789—Vom Ereignis zum Gegenstand der Geschichtswissenschaft* (Frankfurt am Main, 1980), 215.

335. See K. Stern, *Grundideen europäisch-amerikanischer Verfassungsstaatlichkeit*, 20–23. H.-C. Schröder, Die Grundrechtsproblematik in der englischen und amerikanischen Revolution, Zur "Libertät" des angelsächsischen Radikalismus, in Grund- und Freiheitsrechte im Wandel von Gesellschaft und Geschichte, ed. Günter Birtsch (Göttingen, 1981), 89 ff.

336. Condorcet, *Entwurf einer historischen Darstellung der Fortschritte des menschlichen Geistes,* ed. Wilhelm Alff, (Frankfurt am Main, 1976), 167.

337. Quoted in Joyce Appleby, America as a Model for the Radical French Reformers of 1789, *William and Mary Quarterly,* Ser. 3, vol. 28 (1971): 286.

338. See Henry F. May, *The Enlightenment in America* (Oxford, 1978), 240.

339. See also Franco Venturi, *Utopia and Reform in the Enlightenment.* Morton White, *The Philosophy of the American Revolution* (New York, 1978).

340. See Georges Lefèbvre, *Etudes Sur la Révolution Française* (Paris, 1963), 129.

341. See Albert Soboul, *Französische Revolution und Volksbewegung: die Sansculotten* (Frankfurt am Main, 1978), 131, 281. F. Furet and Denis Richet, *Die Französische Revolution* (Frankfurt am Main, 1968), 224, 276, 323. R. B. Rose, *Gracchus Babeuf, The First Revolutionary Communist* (Stanford, Calif., 1978), 242.

342. See H. Arendt, *On Revolution.*

343. On Tom Paine's role in the French Revolution, see David Freeman Hawke, *Paine* (New York, 1974).

344. See J. James Henderson, *Party Politics in the Continental Congress* (New York, 1974), 434.

345. See H.-C. Schröder, *Die Amerikanische Revolution,* 184.

346. See Jacques Godechot, *The Counter-Revolution* (London, 1972), 143. M. Kammen, *A Season of Youth, The American Revolution and the Historical Imagination* (New York, 1978), 133 ff.

347. See Richard Cobb, *Reactions to the French Revolution* (London, 1972), 216.

348. See Gordon S. Wood, *The Creation of the American Republic* (Chapel Hill, N.C., 1969), 428 f. Peter Gay, *The Enlightenment,* vol. 2: *The Science of Freedom* (New York, 1969), 563.

349. H. Arendt, *On Revolution.*

350. Quoted in H.-C. Schröder, *Die Amerikanische Revolution,* 137.

351. See *"Europe," or, a General Survey of the Present Situation of the Principal Powers, with Conjectures on Their Future Prospects: By a Citizen of the United States* (London, 1822). On the author's identification, see Joseph Sabin, *Bibliotheca Americana . . . ,* (New York, 1873), 278 f.

352. On the author Everett, see Allan Johnson, ed., *Dictionary of American Biography* (London, 1931), 220 f. Hans Kohn, *American Nationalism* (New York, 1957). Heinz Gollwitzer, *Geschichte des weltpolitischen Denkens* (Göttingen, 1972).

353. See *"America"; or a General Survey of the Political Situation of the Several Powers of the Western Continent, with Conjectures on Their Future Prospects: By a Citizen of the United States* (Philadelphia, 1827), 21 f.

354. John Bristed, *The Resources of the United States of America* (New York, 1818), 237.

355. See D. Levin, *History as Romantic Art: Bancroft, Prescott, Motley, and Parkman* (Stanford, Calif., 1959). H. R. Guggisberg, William Hickling Prescott und das Ge-

schichtsbewußtsein der amerikanischen Romantik, *Jahrbuch für Amerikastudien* 11 (1966): 176–93. See Jürgen Herbst, *The German Historical School in American Scholarship* (Ithaca, N.Y., 1965), 99–128.

356. See G. S. Morris, *Hegel's Philosophy of the State and of History* (Chicago, 1887). F. A. Rauch, *Psychology, or, a View of the Human Soul, Including Anthropology* (New York, 1841). F. Lieber, *Civil Liberty and Self-government* (Philadelphia, 1853). Charles M. Perry, *Henry Philipp Tappan* (Ann Arbor, Mich., 1933).

357. See H. C. Brokmeyer, *A Mechanic's Diary* (privately printed by H. C. Brokmeyer), (Washington, D.C., 1910). W. T. Harris, *Hegel's Logic: A Book on the Genesis of the Categories of the Mind: A Critical Exposition* (Chicago, 1890–95). C. M. Perry, *The St. Louis Movement in Philosophy, Some Source Material,* (Norman, Okla., 1930).

358. See John Dewey, *Reconstruction in Philosophy* (New York, 1955). G. E. Müller, *Amerikanische Philosophie* (Stuttgart, 1950), pp 122, 134.

359. See C. Pierce, *Principles of Philosophy* (Cambridge, Mass., 1931). William James, *Pragmatism and the Meaning of Truth* (Introduction by A. J. Ayer), (Cambridge, Mass., 1978).

360. See Walter Lippmann, *The Public Philosophy, On the Decline and Revival of the Western Society* (Boston, 1955). M. Lerner, *America as a Civilization* (New York, 1957). (Parallels to classical antiquity, usually along the lines of Greece/Europe versus America/Rome, were a favorite theme of European historians in the postwar years, one that was, however, made obsolete by the actual constellation of the East-West politics.) See K. D. Bracher, *The Age of Ideologies;* D. Bell, *The End of Ideology* (Glencoe, Ill., 1960). D. Riesman, *The Lonely Crowd, A Study of the Changing American Character* (New Haven, Conn., 1950).

361. See Vera M. Dean, *Europe and the United States* (New York, 1950). *America and the Mind of Europe* (Collection, introduction by Lewis Galantiere), (London, 1951), especially the essays of R. Aron, S. Spender, and M. Lasky.

362. See A. N. J. Den Hollander, On "Dissent" and "Influence" as Agents of Change. An Introduction, in *Contagious Conflict, The Impact of American Dissent on European Life,* ed. A. N. J. Den Hollander (Leiden, 1973). Kurt L. Shell, The American Impact on the German New Left, in *Contagious Conflict.* Marianne Debouzy, Influence of American Political Dissent on the French New Left, in *Contagious Conflict.* J.-F. Revel, *Without Marx or Jesus* (New York, 1971).

363. On the image of Europe in America during the 1970s, see Robert J. Schaetzel, Das Europabild der Amerikaner, in *Amerika und Westeuropa,* ed. K. Kaiser and H.-P. Schwarz (Stuttgart, 1977), 29–40. On the image of Germany presented by American history textbooks, see also Robert Multhoff, Das Bild der Deutschen Geschichte im Spiegel amerikanischer Geschichtslehrbücher (The Alumni Funnel: U.S. Educational Commission in the Federal Republic of Germany, vol. 2), 1960, no. 1, 5–36. See in particular G. A. Craig's study, *The Germans* (New York, 1982).

364. See also Manfred Henningsen, *Der Fall Amerika, Zur Sozial- und Bewußtseinsgeschichte einer Verdrängung. Das Amerika der Europäer* (Munich, 1974), 9 ff.

365. See Oscar Handlin, *The Uprooted. The Epic Story of the Great Migration That Made the American People* (Boston, 1951).

366. An overview of this period through British eyes is provided by Allan Nevins, *America through British Eyes* (New York, 1948).

367. See R. Price, *Observations on the Importance of the American Revolution and the Means of Rendering It a Benefit to the World* (London, 1784).

368. See H. Wansey, *An Excursion to the United States of America, in the Summer 1794* (Salisbury, 1798).

369. See Bernhard Fabian, *Alexis de Tocquevilles Amerikabild* (chapter: England, Frankreich und die Vereinigten Staaten: Das englische und das französische Amerikabild um 1830 und ihre geschichtlichen Voraussetzungen), (Heidelberg, 1957).

370. *The New Monthly Magazine and Literary Journal* 1 (1821): 155 (anonymous).

371. Quoted from *The Works of the Reverend Sydney Smith* (London, 1839), 2, 15–17.

372. See Jane Louise Mesick, *The English Traveler in America, 1785–1835* (New York, 1922).

373. See J. Bristed, *The Resources of the United States of America; or, a View of the Agricultural, Commercial, Manufacturing, Financial, Political, Literary, Moral, and Religious Capacity and Character of the American People* (New York, 1818). B. Hall, *Travels in North America in the Years 1827 and 1828* (Edinburgh, 1829), 3 vols. F. M. Trollope, *Domestic Manners of the Americans* (New York, 1949). H. Martineau, *Society in America* (New York, 1837), vols. 1 and 2. Charles Dickens, *American Notes (1842)* (London, 1893). P. Schaffs, *America: A Sketch of Its Political, Social, and Religious Character* (Cambridge, Mass., 1961 reprint). See Max Berger, *The British Traveller in America, 1836–1860* (New York, 1943).

374. See J. Bryce, *The American Commonwealth* (New York, 1907), vols. 1 and 2. H. Laski, *The American Democracy* (New York, 1948). On British-American relations, see also H. C. Allen, *Great Britain and the United States: A History of Anglo-American Relations* (London, 1954). Arnold Wolfers and Lawrence Martin, eds., *The Anglo-American Tradition in Foreign Affairs* (New Haven, Conn., 1956).

375. See G. Hodgson, *America in Our Time: From World War II to Nixon; What Happened and Why* (New York, 1976).

376. See Bernard Fay, *The Revolutionary Spirit in France and America: A Study of Moral and Intellectual Relations between France and the United States at the End of the Eighteenth Century* (New York, 1929; Paris 1925); Howard Mumford Jones, *America and French Culture, 1750–1848* (Chapel Hill, N.C., 1927). Gilbert M. Fess, *The American Revolution in Creative French Literature (1775–1932)* (Columbia, Mo., 1941). Durrand Echeverria, *Mirage in the West: A History of the French Image of American Society to 1815* (Princeton, N.J., 1968). René Rémond, *Les Etats-Unis devant l'opinion française 1815–1852* (Paris, 1962).

377. See Olivier Bernier, *Lafayette: Hero of Two Worlds* (New York, 1983). Louis Gottschalk, *Lafayette between the American and the French Revolutions, 1783–1789* (Chicago, 1950). W. Stark, *America: Ideal and Reality, The United States of 1776 in Contemporary European Philosophy*, ed. Karl Mannheim (London, 1947) (chapter: Brissot the Admirer, 80–100).

378. See J. Hector Saint John de Crèvecoeur, What Is an American?, reprinted from *Letters from an American Farmer* (1782), in *The Character of Americans*, ed. Michael McGiffert (Homewood, Ill., 1964).

379. See Antonelli Gerbi, *The Dispute of the New World: The History of a Polemic, 1750–1900* (Pittsburgh, 1973). W. Stark, *America* (chapter: Raynal the Fatalist, 16–35).

380. Quoted in Henry Steele Commager and Elmo Giodanetti, eds., *Was America a Mistake? The Eighteenth-Century Controversy* (New York, 1967), 126, 129, 138.

381. See ibid., 16.

382. Hamilton, No. 11, in *The Federalist Papers*, 90–91. In a footnote Hamilton

quoted in this context Cornelius de Pauw, *Recherches philosophiques sur les Américains ou mémoires intéressantes pour servir à l'histoire de l'Espèce humaine* (Berlin, 1768–69).

383. G. B. de Mably, Observations on the Government and Laws of the United States of America (London, 1784), 98, 84. See also W. Stark, *America* (chapter: Mably the Pessimist, 36–57).

384. See B. Fabian, *Alexis de Tocquevilles Amerikabild*, 18.

385. J. P. Brissot, *New Travels in the United States of America performed in 1788* (London, 1792), 288, 482. See also W. Stark, *America* (chapter: Brissot the Admirer, 80, 86, 100).

386. F. J. Marquis de Chastellux, *Essays on Public Happiness*, quoted in W. Stark, *America* (chapter: Chastellux the Critic, 58).

387. Ibid., 69.

388. See Chastellux, *Travels in North America in the Years 1780–1781, and 1782* (London, 1787).

389. Quoted from G. W. Pierson, *Tocqueville and Beaumont in America* (New York, 1938), 67.

390. H. B. Adams, Jared Sparks and Alexis de Tocqueville, *Johns Hopkins University Studies in Historical and Political Science* 16, no. 12 (1898), quoted from B. Fabian, *Alexis de Tocquevilles Amerikabild*, 20 ff.

391. William Hickling Prescott, in *The North American Review*, 56 (1843): 145 and 146.

392. Godfrey T. Vignes, *Six Months in America* (London, 1832), 2, 273–76. See also the comprehensive study by Oscar Handlin, *This Was America: True Accounts of People and Places, Manners and Customs, as Recorded by European Travelers to the Western Shore in the Eighteenth, Nineteenth, and Twentieth Centuries* (Cambridge, Mass., 1949).

393. See Alexis de Tocqueville, *Democracy in America* ed. P. Bradley (New York, 1945). Here quoted from B. Fabian, *Alexis de Tocquevilles Amerikabild*.

394. See also Michael Hereth, *Alexis de Tocqueville. Die Gefährdung der Freiheit in der Demokratie* (Stuttgart, 1979), 44.

395. See also Klaus Harpprecht, *Der fremde Freund. Amerika-eine innere Geschichte* (chapter: Die fromme Utopie oder: Wiedersehen mit Tocqueville, 460–72), (Stuttgart, 1982).

396. Author's conversation with Professor Richard E. Neustadt, Harvard University, John F. Kennedy School of Government, Cambridge, Mass. (May 5, 1981). Richard E. Neustadt was a staff member in the Truman presidency—Bureau of the Budget from 1946 to 1950, Special Assistant in the White House Office during 1950–53, and consultant to Presidents Kennedy and Johnson in 1961–66.

397. See D. Kucharsky, *The Mind and Spirit of Jimmy Carter* (New York, 1977), 13.

398. Alexis de Tocqueville, *Democracy in America*, 2:452.

399. See B. Fabian, *Alexis de Tocquevilles Amerikabild*, 82–85.

400. Alexander Hamilton, No. 11, *The Federalist Papers*, 91.

401. See J. Bristed, *The Resources of the United States of America*. D.-G.-F. Dufour de Pradt, *Des colonies et de la révolution actuelle de l'Amérique* (Paris, 1817). Pradt, *L'Europe et l'Amérique en 1821* (Paris, 1822) (2 parts). Pradt, *L'Europe et l'Amérique en 1822 et 1823* (Paris, 1824) (2 parts). C. von Schmidt-Phiseldeck, *Europa und America, oder die künftigen Verhältnisse der zivilisierten Welt* (Copenhagen, 1820).

402. See also Theodore Draper, Die Idee des "Kalten Krieges" und ihre Propheten, Über Tocqueville und andere, *Der Monat,* no. 290 (February 1984): 180–98.

403. See Simone de Beauvoir, *L'Amérique au jour le jour* (Paris, 1950).

404. See Gunnar Myrdal, *An American Dilemma, The Negro Problem and American Democracy* (New York, 1944), vols. 1 and 2.

405. See Jean-Paul Sartre's essays: New York, ville coloniale (1946); Villes d'Amérique (1945); Individualisme et conformisme (1945), in *Situations* (Paris, 1949), vol. 3.

406. See Jean-Jacques Servan-Schreiber, *The American Challenge* (New York, 1968). Raymond Aron, *The Imperial Republic* (Englewood Cliffs, N.J., 1974). Michel Crozier, *Le mal américain* (Paris, 1981).

407. See Richard Reeves, *American Journey: Travelling with Tocqueville in Search of America* (New York, 1982).

408. See Klaus Wust and Heinz Moos, eds., *300 Jahre deutsche Einwanderer in Nordamerika,* (Munich, 1983). Günter Moltmann, ed., *Germans to America. 300 Years of Immigration, 1683–1983* (Stuttgart, 1982). Frank Trommler, ed., *Amerika und die Deutschen, Bestandsaufnahme einer 300 jährigen Geschichte,* (Opladen, 1986).

409. See Thomas Piltz, ed., *Die Deutschen und die Amerikaner* (Munich, 1977), 69 ff. Hartmut Wasser, Deutsche und Amerikaner—Verwandte speziellen Grades? Ein historisch-politischer Exkurs über das Verhältnis beider Staaten, *Der Monat,* no. 290 (February 1984): 108–20. In addition, see the letters of German emigrants to America during the period 1820–1920, ed. Wolfgang Helbich: "Amerika ist ein freies Land . . . ", *Auswanderer schreiben nach Deutschland* (Darmstadt, 1985).

410. Ronald Reagan, America Is "Inextricably" Linked to Europe, Interview with *France Soir Magazin* (November 3, 1984).

411. See also Manfred Jonas, *The United States and Germany, A Diplomatic History* (Ithaca, N.Y., 1985). G. M. Eisenstadt and D. Oberndörfer, eds., *200 Jahre deutsch-amerikanische Beziehungen* (Bonn, 1976). T. Hübener, *The Germans in America* (Philadelphia, 1962).

412. On the impact of the American Revolution on Germany, see Horst Dippel, *Germany and the American Revolution, 1770–1880. A Sociohistorical Investigation of late Eighteenth-Century Political Thinking* (Chapel Hill, N.C., 1977). See also Ernst Fraenkel, *Amerika im Spiegel des deutschen politischen Denkens* (Cologne, 1959), 11–48.

413. The quotation and some elements of this discussion were taken from Gordon A. Craig's lecture: Deutschland und die Vereinigten Staaten: Historische Gleichartigkeiten und ihr Niederschlag in der Einstellung zur Außenpolitik, reprinted in J. A. Cooney, G. A. Craig, H.-P. Schwarz, and F. Stern, eds., *The Federal Republic of Germany and the United States* (Boulder, Colo., 1984). On German national consciousness, see Peter Alter, Nationalbewußtsein und Nationalstaat der Deutschen, *Aus Politik und Zeitgeschichte,* B 1/86 (January 4, 1986): 17–30.

414. See E. Fraenkel, *Amerika im Spiegel des deutschen politischen Denkens.* H. Wasser, *Die USA—der unbekannte Partner* (chapter: Die Deutschen und Amerika—Umrisse einer Beziehung), (Paderborn, 1983), 15 ff. Alexander Ritter, ed., *Deutschlands literarisches Amerikabild* (Hildesheim, 1977).

415. Quote from E. Fraenkel, *Amerika im Spiegel des deutschen politischen Denkens,* 298.

416. On the German perception of America, see also W. P. Adams and K. Krakau, eds., *Deutschland und Amerika: Perzeption und historische Realität* (Berlin, 1985).

417. See E. G. Franz, *Das Amerikabild der deutschen Revolution von 1848/49* (Heidelberg, 1958). Erich Angermann, Der deutsche Frühkonstitutionalismus und das amerikanische Vorbild, *Historische Zeitschrift* 219 (1974): 1 ff.

418. See Manfred Henningsen, Das Amerika von Hegel, Marx und Engels, *Zeitschrift für Politik*, no. 3 (1973): 224 ff.

419. See Günther C. Behrmann, Geschichte und aktuelle Struktur des Antiamerikanismus, *Aus Politik und Zeitgeschichte*, B 29–30 (1984): 11; G. Moltmann, Deutscher Anti-Amerikanismus heute und früher, in *Vom Sinn der Geschichte*, ed. F. Otmar (Stuttgart, 1976), 85–105. G. Wirsing, *Der maßlose Kontinent* (Jena, 1942).

420. See E. Fraenkel, *Amerika im Spiegel des deutschen politischen*, 45. P. Berg, *Deutschland und Amerika 1918–1929, Über das deutsche Amerikabild der zwanziger Jahre* (Hamburg, 1963).

421. The Hitler quotations cited here repeatedly on this issue come from Rauschning's *Conversations with Hitler*, which can no longer be regarded as an absolutely reliable source in view of Wolfgang Hanel's forthcoming exposé of Rauschning's apparently spurious conversations with Hitler. See Karl-Heinz Janßen, Kümmerliche Notizen, Rauschnings "Gespräche mit Hitler"—wie ein Schweizer Lehrer nach 45 Jahren einen Schwindel auffliegen ließ, *Die Zeit* (July 19, 1985): 16. On the relationship between Hitler and Roosevelt, see Gordon A. Craig, Roosevelt and Hitler: The Problem of Perception, in *Deutsche Frage und europäisches Gleichgewicht* (Festschrift for Andreas Hillgruber), ed. K. Hildebrand and R. Pommerin (Cologne, 1985), 169–94.

422. See E. Fraenkel, *Amerika im Spiegel des deutschen politischen Denkens*, 45 ff. On German rightist revisionism, see B. E. Schönborn, *Los von Amerika. Eine nationaldemokratische Analyse* (Kalbach, 1974). C. B. Dall, *Amerikas Kriegspolitik, Roosevelt und seine Hintermänner* (Tübingen, 1975). B. Colby, *Roosevelts scheinheiliger Krieg* (Berg, 1977). H. Fish, *Der zerbrochene Mythos. F. D. Roosevelts Kriegspolitik 1933–1945* (Berg, 1982). J. Bruhn and D. Bavendamm, *Roosevelts Weg zum Krieg* (Munich, 1983). On German leftist revisionism, see A. Charisius et al., Weltgendarm USA (Berlin, 1983). G. Kade, *Die Amerikaner und wir* (Cologne, 1983). B. Grüner and K. Steinhaus, *Auf dem Weg zum 3. Weltkrieg? Amerikanische Kriegspläne gegen die USSR, Eine Dokumentation* (Cologne, 1980).

423. See H. Wasser, *Die USA*, 31 f. Robert Boyers, ed., *The Legacy of the German Refugee Intellectuals* (New York, 1972). J. Radkau, *Die deutsche Emigration in den USA. Ihr Einfluß auf die amerikanische Europapolitik 1933–1945* (Düsseldorf, 1971). Helge Pross, *Die deutsche akademische Emigration nach den Vereinigten Staaten 1933–1941* (Berlin, 1955). Gertrude Himmelfarb, American Democracy and European Critics, *The Twentieth Century* 151 (1952): 320–27.

424. See the following examples: Golo Mann, Der Fortschrittsglaube Amerikas, *Universitas*, no. 10 (1950): 1153–61. G. Mann, *Vom Geist Amerikas, Eine Einführung in amerikanisches Denken und Handeln im zwanzigsten Jahrhundert* (Stuttgart, 1954). E. Fraenkel, *Das amerikanische Regierungssystem* (Cologne, 1962). K. D. Bracher, Demokratie als Sendung: das amerikanische Beispiel, in *Deutschland zwischen Demokratie und Diktatur* (Bern, 1964).

425. See M. Mathiopoulos, The American President Seen Through German Eyes: Continuity and Change from the Adenauer to the Kohl Era, *Presidential Studies Quarterly* (Fall 1985); Herbert von Borch, *Amerika—Die unfertige Gesellschaft* (Munich, 1960). H. von Borch, *Amerika—Dekadenz und Größe* (Munich, 1981). Walter Leisler Kiep, *Good Bye Amerika—was dann?* (Stuttgart, 1972).

426. See two representative books from the Greens: Joschka Fischer, *Von Grüner Kraft und Herrlichkeit* (Reinbek b. Hamburg, 1984), and Antje Vollmer: " . . . und wehrt Euch täglich!" (Bonn—ein Grünes Tagebuch, Gütersloh, 1984). See Kim F. Holmes, *The West German Peace Movement and the National Question* (Cambridge, Mass., 1984). Andrei S. Markovits, On Anti-Americanism in West Germany, *New German Critique,* no. 34 (Summer 1985).

427. R. von Weizsäcker, The 8th of May 1945—Forty Years After, in *A Voice from Germany* (London, 1986), 43.

# Part III

## THE POLITICAL AND PHILOSOPHICAL FOUNDATIONS OF THE AMERICAN IDEA OF PROGRESS

*American history and American political ideology are, as Samuel Huntington argues, based on four Great Awakening periods and four Creedal Passion periods.[1] All of these periods, as sources of national identity, simultaneously reflect the American idea of progress. The values and progressivist ideals of the American creed were tested for their ability to survive in the four periods of religious revival. The First Awakening swept the colonies between 1730 and 1740, the Second Awakening began in the first years of the nineteenth century and lasted until 1830, the Third Awakening began around 1890 and continued until the first decade of the twentieth century, and the Fourth Awakening originated in the 1950s. These values and ideals were tested as well in four confrontations in political belief: during the revolutionary phase between 1760 and 1770, the Jacksonian revolution of 1820 to 1830, the age of populism and progressivism from 1890 to 1910, and the years of protest and reform from 1960 to 1970.*

*That most of these periods coincided chronologically was not accidental. "The promise of American politics" (Samuel Huntington), or as one could add, "the promise of American progress" to realize their ideals motivated Americans, from the very beginning of their history, to seek paths of religious and moral-political renewal. The gap between ideal and institution, of course, compelled (and still compels) Americans to live with a certain form of cognitive dissonance. In times when this dissonance remained latent, it developed into a central struggle and gave way to the periods of Great Awakening and Creedal Passion. Although the characteristics of these periods varied from epoch to epoch, they were all marked by rapid economic and social change resulting in moral and political ideologization. Although rapid change in Europe historically meant a sharpening of class conflicts, the Americans tended to see themselves as committed instead to revival of traditional values—"the American mission for the future was to realize the values of the American past."[2]*

*The following discussion presents the Americans' basic ethical and political values and progressivist ideals, namely liberty, freedom, equality, individualism, and democracy. All of these ideals are rooted in the Protestantism of the seventeenth century and the Lockean liberalism of the eighteenth. As Alexis de Tocqueville remarked, in no other country in the world did the Christian religion have as great an influence on the souls of people as in America. The American form of Protestantism as "democratic and republican religion" and as an element of individual conscience contributed substantially to the establishment of a republic and democracy in American public life.[3] Nowhere else in the world was the institutional separation of church and state carried out as thoroughly ("no bishop, no king"), and nowhere else were religious and political ideals and symbols interwoven in national thinking as inextricably as in America. Precisely because American national identity is defined as a combination of religious and political ideals, both the American creed and political reality contain religious aspects.[4] G. K. Chesterton appropriately characterized the United States as "a nation with the soul of a church."[5]*

*At the same time, in contrast to those of other societies, the values of the American creed were and remain liberal, atomistic, democratic, egalitarian, and thus antigovernmental and antiauthoritarian by their very nature. While other ideologies legitimized established authority and institutions, the American creed served to create a revolutionary constitutional order legally excluding all hierarchical, compulsory, or authoritarian structures. The core of the American Constitution was the limitation of "governmental power through fundamental law."[6] The core of American liberalism was, as Bernard Bailyn summarized the progressivist argument of the American revolution, "freedom from governmental control, the vindication of liberty against power." The core of American individualism was the right of each person to act in accordance with his or her conscience and to guide his or her own fate free from external compulsion, without infringing on the rights of others. The core of the American idea of equality was the rejection of the idea of one citizen exerting power over another. The core of American democracy was "popular control over government, directly or through representatives, and the responsiveness of governmental officials to public opinion."[7] The revolutionary aspect of the American idea of progress seemed to be manifested in the constitutional basis of the American idea of progress as well: "The American constitution is unlike any other: it represents the lifeblood of the American nation, its supreme symbol and manifestation. It is so intimately welded with the national existence itself that the two have become inseparable."[8] From this point on it was up to the American president, and not, as in Europe, to individual parties, to balance the scope of his constitutional authority between power and freedom. According to Richard E. Neustadt's key definition of "presidential power," that is, the president's power to convince or convert, the transformation of American progressivist ideals into practical political concepts has always required a president who was able to act in a convincing manner in addition to knowing how to utilize his power to the fullest. To fulfill credibly this role between political power and social freedom has been the maxim (though not always recognized as such) of American presidents since Washington.[9] Adlai Stevenson once said that American history is largely the history of the American presidency; that it is a history of people rising to the demands of their time in an office that afforded them the power to govern; and that great presidents made government an engine of progress toward their objectives.*

*Finally, the ambivalence of the American idea of progress will be examined on the basis of American political theory and practice, which differs from its European counterpart. Unlike Europeans, Americans have never seen a contradiction in pursuing moral ideals by means of pragmatic realism. In contrast to Europe, in America liberalism has* *always been the dominant ideology, thus effecting different consequences for American conservatism and progressivism than for Europe. The frustrations encountered by Burkean conservatives in America have been described in great detail by Louis Hartz (*The Liberal Tradition in America, *1955). Because the United States was never faced with the historical burdens of feudalism, monarchy, and an entrenched aristocracy, because it knew no established national church and was spared from deep-seated class conflict, the only traditions and institutions that exist for preservation by American conservatives are liberal ones. The frustrations of progressivist reformers, on the other hand, are rooted in the idea of liberal consensus in American political theory and American society. Although the conservative may object to the fact that American political institutions are formed according to liberal ideas, these same institutions do not necessarily correspond to the progressivist ideal of the reformer. It is, however, precisely this liberal ambivalence in the idea of progress that has ultimately made America immune to trends in socialist, communist, and fascist thought.*

# 6

## National Identity and American Creed

The emergence and definition of the American idea of progress cannot be understood without first analyzing Americans' unshakeable belief in certain key values and ideals. The ideas of providence, freedom, and equality, as well as the fusion of different races, formed the bases of American ethics from the very beginning. The following discussion will show how the consistent linkage of deep religiosity, liberal rationalism, unbridled capitalism, and individual willingness to experiment ultimately coalesced into the ideology of Americanism and the foundation of the national identity. That American values have remained almost completely unchanged is one of the most essential characteristics of the American idea of progress.[10]

### PROTESTANTISM AND CAPITALISM

No other concept of values has been rooted so deeply in the ethos of the New World, in its political, economic, and social culture, as the idea of freedom. As Clinton Rossiter observed:

We have always been a nation obsessed with liberty. Liberty over authority, freedom over responsibility, rights over duties—these are our historic preferences. From the days of Williams and Wise to those of Eisenhower and Kennedy, Americans have talked about practically nothing else but liberty. Not the good man, but the free man has been the measure of all things in this "sweet land of liberty"; not national glory but individual liberty has been the object of political authority and the test of its worth.[11]

These ideas originated in the American version of Protestantism, the Calvinist Puritanism of the seventeenth century, which interpreted the idea of freedom and democracy as a mission. It is in the interweaving of religion and politics—"religion is an important, perhaps an indispensable clue to what America is like"[12]—that American political thought found many of the moral and political impulses that continue to shape the political philosophy and terminology of the American president even today.[13] The vision of America as a new promise for humankind, America as a new Israel, was fed by the Puritan belief in electedness and mission: "to create a city upon the hill, the last best hope of earth, and to bring about a new heaven and a new earth through its errand in the wilderness of the world."[14] It was this belief that, in its secularized form, helped to determine the liberal democratic credo of the eighteenth century and valorized the connection of politics and religious morality, of democratic ethical universalism and the historical experience of the turn away from a corrupt, unfree Old World and the beginning of a New.

The exceptional significance of Puritanism lay in the role it played for the American creed and the beginning of American civilization and state. Puritanism's orientation—common to Protestantism as a whole—toward the individual, the individual's direct relationship to God, self-responsibility, and freedom of decision, formed the actual moral element in Puritan orthodoxy.[15] At the same time, after its failure in England, it was the first experiment in the practical and thus political realization of Puritan belief. Alexis de Tocqueville had already pointed out that Puritanism was almost as much a political theory as a religious dogma.[16] His contemporary, the German theologian Philip Schaff, likewise noted in 1853 that "everything in America had a Protestant beginning."[17]

The religious factor, specifically, the intolerant theocracy of Massachussetts—surely was a prominent one. The Puritans saw themselves as the "soldiers of Christ," as God's chosen who would take advantage of their fresh start in the New World to work in covenant with God to realize His plan of salvation on earth. They understood this sense of selectness to refer not merely to the few, but to all humanity. This way of thinking thus contained the roots for the moral optimism and claim to universality underlying the American missionary idea.[18] The transition from a biblical basis of the religious salvation—"this new world is probably now discovered, that the new and most glorious state of God's church might commence there" (Jonathan Edwards)—to the rationalist founding of democracy, and its task for humankind, is manifested equally clearly in John Wise's monograph *Vindication of the Government of New England Churches* (1717).[19] Wise's work is based on the idea of natural law, natural freedom, and the equality of men—"the first formulation of secular republicanism." "The end of all good government is to Cultivate Humanity, and Promote the happiness of all, and the good of every Man in all his Rights, his Life, Liberty, Estate, Honor, etc., without injury or abuse done to any."[20]

At such points, Wise's Puritan democratic ethos anticipates Jefferson's enlightened liberal ethos of "life, liberty, and the pursuit of happiness." Despite the gradual softening of these originally religious values as a result of the secularization of Puritan thought, the deep conviction of the special and elect position of America—serving as a beacon and an example for the rest of the world—and of the exceptional mission of America as "the form of the American spirit" (Eric Voegelin)[21] continued to exist. This conviction determined the new secular values and their objectives: democracy, equality, happiness, and freedom. These values initially strengthened the democratic and republican tendencies in the political thought of the eighteenth century. They ultimately formed the ethical substance and progressive basis for the American liberal sense of mission and American political and social ideology.

Another aspect of Puritanism proved essential for the development of national identity and the American creed: the ethos of success, that is, economic virtue. It is clearly connected with the American sense of missionary purpose. The works of Max Weber and Ernst Troeltsch were responsible for directing attention to the links between the Protestant Reformation—especially in its Calvinistic manifestations—and the spirit of modern capitalism.[22] Luther tended to regard the idea of a profession with the resigned acceptance of the human lot; one must accept even so insignificant a position in God's grand scheme of things. In Calvin's case, however, individuals were constantly called on to prove their unwaning zeal by constantly striving to improve their position. In contrast to Lutheran Quietism, Calvinism had much to offer to aspiring people, whose ambitions knew no limits. For this reason, as Max Weber emphasized, the Puritan believer would never be able to find rest at any particular level of achievement.

According to Cotton Mather, the relations of the creatures were organized according to God's plan so that self-interest and general well-being were in complete harmony with each other. The Puritan ideology of success was that if God showed one a path that could lead to more success than another, without doing another soul any harm in the process, and if the one then rejected this path and chose one less profitable, then this would mean renunciation of the goals of one's profession and the end of one's role as God's servant, as well as the refusal to use one's God-given talents to God's advantage. The individual was allowed to work in order to become rich for God, but not for the flesh or sin. In this way wealth becomes evidence of piety, and riches the total result of constant piety and virtuousness. The aspiration toward success, wealth, and earthly happiness was more or less sanctioned theologically, for the success with which one pursued one's earthly affairs was the visible proof of God's mercy, of one's place among the Elect.[23] In the reflexive effect of this ethic of success lay another root of the American missionary awareness, namely, "the idea that wealth implied both the favor of God and a duty to be the instrument of divine beneficence."[24] The oldest Puritan tradition of the "Citty upon a Hill" is reflected here. Ultimately, Puritan theology accustomed its adherents to the idea that they comprised a privileged group of individuals, one enjoying a monopoly on divine forgiveness.

The equivalent of this notion in democratic American ideology was the establishment of the human "pursuit of happiness," which clearly included economic success. Jefferson can be regarded as a particular exponent of the political and democratic ethic of success. Whereas the Puritans saw virtue and grace as the basis for success, Jefferson believed that success of the individual personality was measured according to personal happiness, political freedom, and respect for the equality of people. He did not, as his critics claim, consider only economic prosperity and economic success as the prerequisites for civic virtue and duty.

The success of the American experiment in the New World for the American progressivist creed—with its origin in Puritan thought—seems to be based on the assumption that the conviction of electness and the special American mission, which was there from the beginning, were justified. Many foreign and American observers, from the Frenchman Alexis de Tocqueville, the Englishman Geoffrey Gorer, and Reinhold Niebuhr, who called this phenomenon of activism and dynamism "Yankeeism," to James Oliver Robertson's *American Myth, American Reality* (1980),[25] have agreed that the ethos of success plays an important role in the daily life of Americans: from Benjamin Franklin's instrumental philosophy of success, which secularized the moral discipline of New England, that is, of Puritanism, all the way to the widely admired achievements of Andrew Carnegie, the cult of the self-made person, and Horatio Alger's mythologization of "success stories."

The fundamental idea of modern American capitalism can also be traced back to the Puritan ethos. The rights of individuals do not lie merely in possessing and enjoying the fruits of their labor, but rather in using these rights to further the general good. That the values of capitalism and democracy have remained the foundation of the American ethos until the present day is proven conclusively in the newest study by Herbert McClosky and John Zaller, entitled *The American Ethos: Public Attitudes toward Capitalism and Democracy* (1984):

Two major traditions of belief, capitalism, and democracy, have dominated the life of the American nation from its inception. Whether these beliefs are described as the *American creed,* the *Lockean settlement,* the *American consensus,* or as we prefer, the *American ethos,* it is clear that capitalist and democratic values have strongly influenced the course and character of American development, and that they continue to serve as the authoritative values of the nation's political culture.[26]

In conclusion, it can be said that the root of the American creed, national identity, and belief in progress are all to be found in the Puritan belief in mission, in its basic ideas of covenant and social contract, individualism, freedom, and moral responsibility of individuals as well as in the ethical duty for the common realization of economic success. The periodic return of Great Awakenings ultimately constitutes a crucial reminder and contemporary redefinition of Americans' original ideals.

## AMERICANISM AND INDIVIDUALISM

Leon Samson gave the concept of "Americanism" an appropriate definition: "Americanism is to the American not a tradition or a territory, not what France is to a Frenchman or England to an Englishman, but a doctrine—what socialism is to a socialist."[27] Dava Sobel, in turn, defined the concept of individualism: "The desire to be unique—a universal goal."[28] The first definition shows the influence of the specifically American version of the idea of progress, which initially contained the Puritan idea of a divine plan and was subsequently replaced, in the period of Reason, by democratic energy and scientific inventiveness. Since then, Americans have remained firmly convinced that they enjoy the best version of the good life, thanks to their political, social, and economic system. Never before in human history has a people known so exactly what it wanted, while at the same time finding such a surplus of sources of help and space for the accomplishment of its ideal goals. Almost all dreams could be realized in this rich, new country. The idea that progress belonged to the "American way of life" was nourished by the immigrants' new freedom to keep moving on, to find and to form their own place to live. The immigrants had, after all, freely elected to become Americans. Unlike the French, the Germans, or the English, they were not confronted with the problem of conforming to a social system. They were not faced with the alternative of becoming either Marxists or reactionaries. They had emigrated to America of their own free will, they helped to build this new system, and it seemed good to them. It was a system they believed in, and they worked with all their power to realize its basic premises, which they regarded with approval. In spite of their willingness to criticize details, they never questioned the basic presuppositions on which the American system is based. After all, these presuppositions had motivated them to emigrate from Europe. In this way the belief in progress of all Americans— whether of Irish or Italian, German or French, Greek or Slavic origin—began to play an important role in the thought of the New World.[29]

In addition, an absolute belief in the validity of their own idea of progress predestined a desire to share this progress with the rest of the world. Here progressivist thought and missionary conviction correlated. America had indeed turned away from the Old World, but in so doing it had offered a new beginning for the rest of humankind. In the political and moral foundations of their progressivist experiment, Americans saw the bases of human existence itself. These principles were not limited to the New World. Thus, in 1821 John Quincy Adams described the Declaration of Independence and its principles as the "only *legitimate* foundation of civil government"; it was the "cornerstone of a new fabric, destined to cover the surface of the globe."[30] The same remained valid for President Herbert Hoover, the supreme example of one who advocated the teaching of American individualism for whom the American system was "the only safe avenue of human progress."[31] Here Puritan tradition and democratic universalism, liberalism and moralism in its American variants, which lay at the base of the break with the Old World, make themselves felt as a new quality of progress, namely, that of "Americanism."[32] Richard Hofstadter characterized this development with the words: "It has been our fate as a nation not to have ideologies, but to be one."[33] Unlike any other society, in the United States the ideology of Americanism appears to form not just the political theory, but rather the national identity of the New World. A weakening of Americanism would mean the end of the American nation.

Both the frontier experience and the passionate sense of individualism belong to this context. Americanism, the frontier experience, the pioneer spirit, and individualism cannot be isolated from one another, for they have constituted a unity from the very beginning. As James Oliver Robertson points out, frontiers and lines were powerful symbols for Americans. The moving frontier was never only a geographical line, but a palpable barrier that separated the wilderness from civilization. "It distinguished Americans," says Robertson, "with their beliefs and their ideals, from savages and strangers, those 'others' who could not be predicted or trusted." Indeed, these symbols set the American nation apart from other nations and marked its independence. "What was at stake," continues Robertson, "in the drawing of lines and the establishment of frontiers was identity, personal, communal and national." What seemed to separate Americans from other people was the metaphorical image of the frontier. Behind that frontier, inside the community, all Americans appeared to be one, ideally. "The ideal of national homogeneity, the ideal of the 'melting pot,' was one of America's revolutionary, radically democratic ideals," says Robertson. "Anyone who volunteered was promised assimilation into a democratic, egalitarian, libertarian nation the like of which the world had never seen." He concludes his analysis by stressing that background, birth, wealth, inheritance, social position, and class did not count. In fact, the immigrant was required to give up national and class identity and culture and language, and that this was the dare, the challenge of crossing the frontier: to become an American![34]

Carl J. Friedrich once expressed it similarly: "To be an American is an ideal; while to be a Frenchman is a fact."[35] Frederick Jackson Turner, in particular, demonstrated the multifarious influence of the frontier motif in his famous collection of essays and lectures entitled *The Frontier in American History* (1920). On the one hand, it strengthened and deepened Puritan as well as liberal democratic convictions and experiences—idealism, individualism, the feeling of American uniqueness and electedness—and, as influenced by these qualities, permanently shaped the "unchanging American character."[36] On the other hand, it represented an independent politicohistorical factor of ideology. As a secular counterpart to the religious origin of the progressivist and missionary ideas, the frontier hypothesis influenced the American understanding of history and world outlook.[37] The pioneer existence of the American frontierspeople in their constant struggle against nature, their reliance on themselves, their own abilities, and the help of a few neighbors, nourished traits that continue to be regarded today as "typically American": self-confidence, the active desire for independence, distrust of authority, work and constant activity, optimism, a strong sense of individualism and belief in uniqueness, respect of equal opportunity and success.[38]

The frontier was the real "melting pot" of America. Under its influence immigrants of all origins became "Americans." The frontier mentality and the belief in progress ultimately fused into the "national identity" of every American. The self-made person remains today the incarnation of the success myth, nurtured by the individualist virtues of the pioneers. Everyone can be unique in America; everyone can make the climb upward from dishwasher to millionaire. "Anything is possible in America, if you work for it," said the democratic vice-presidential candidate Geraldine Ferraro in 1984. "American history," she went on, "is about doors being opened, doors of opportunity for everyone no matter who you are—as long as you are willing to earn it. . . . There is always an electricity in the air, an excitement, a sense of new possibilities, a pride."[39] The frontier phenomenon as individual, social, and scholarly challenge has returned again and again in American history and politics: from a pioneer existence in the wilderness to the modern struggle of the individual against the urban jungle or the mass tendencies of political and social culture; from John F. Kennedy's "new frontier" ideology, which has become a generally recognized symbol of dynamism, progress, optimism, activity, and initiative, to Ronald Reagan's scientific vision of the "new frontier" of SDI. To be an American means to find again and again the courage to face the new frontiers of tomorrow.

## SCIENTISM AND EXPERIMENTALISM

Science and progress are two inseparable historical categories in American thought. The outstanding significance of scientific and technological progress in the American ideology and politics found its first form of expression—if one considers the transatlantic crossing of the Puritan pilgrims to America as a religious progressivist experiment—in the philosophy of the Founding Fathers of the United States: "Ever since Benjamin Franklin and Thomas Jefferson, Americans have been inclined to put their faith in a combination of democracy and science as a sure formula for human progress."[40] The central dream of the Founding Fathers during the Enlightenment was to give "experimental humanism" a philosophical basis and to realize it politically. Indeed, as Adrienne Koch points out, the American Enlightenment was characterized by its profound attachment to experimental empiricism and its equally profound attachment to the humanistic ideal of the whole person, whose knowledge is neither fragmented nor fragmentary, but moral or ethical in its concern for others and the world.[41] In the "Age of Experiments" (Benjamin Franklin), in a society that rediscovered "the pursuit of happiness" (Thomas Jefferson) of classical civilization, the American Enlightenment as the "workshop of liberty" (James Madison) was to serve as a symbol of democratic, economic, scientific, and technological progress of humankind.[42] Convinced of the progress of the republic and with pragmatic hope for the future, George Washington wrote the following letter to the governors of the thirteen states in 1783:

The foundation of our Empire was not laid in the gloomy age of ignorance and superstition, but at an Epoch when the nights of mankind were better understood and more clearly defined, than at any former period; the researches of the human mind after social happiness, have been carried to a great extent, the treasures of knowledge, acquired by the labours of Philosophers, Sages and Legislators, through a long succession of years, are laid open for our use, and their collected wisdom may be happily applied in the establishment of our forms of Government. . . . At this auspicious period, the United States came into existence as a Nation, and if their Citizens should not be completely free and happy, the fault will be entirely their own.[43]

This affinity to the revolutionary scientific discoveries of modernity—especially Descartes' establishment of rationalism and Newton's *Principia Mathematica*—and to the possibilities of political and scientific knowledge on which the ideas of democracy and the perfectibility of the individual through reason ultimately rest was reflected in particular in Franklin, the founder of the American Philosophical Society (1743).[44] Thus he wrote these characteristic sentences to his friend Joseph Priestly:

The rapid progress true science now makes occasions my regretting sometimes that I was born too soon. It is impossible to imagine the height to which may be carried, in a thousand years, the power of man over matter. . . . O that mortal science were in as fair a way of improvement, that men would cease to be wolves to one another, and that human beings would at length learn what they now improperly call humanity.[45]

The Founding Fathers also believed in the progress of education and culture, made possible by the liberating effect of the sciences. John Adams's statement can be considered representative:

The science of government is my duty to study more than all other sciences. . . . I must study politics and war, that my sons may have liberty to study mathematics and philosophy, geography, natural history and naval architecture, navigation, commerce, and agriculture, in order to give their children a right to study painting, poetry, music, architecture, statuary, tapestry, and porcelain.[46]

The nineteenth-century mixture of scientific optimism, moral and political belief in progress, and technological daring continued in American thought until the Second World War, though fits of cultural pessimism and warnings of decline were not unheard of.[47] Lewis Mumford and the brothers Henry and Brooks Adams are especially cogent examples.[48] In contrast to Europe, however, in America these elements of civilizational critique remained without significant influence on politics or society. Americans first became aware of the ambiguity of scientific technological progress with the invention of the atomic bomb and the destruction of Hiroshima. The skepticism of scientists at the end of World War II toward an increasing technical complexity between the acquisition of scientific knowledge and political decision-making processes did not, however, drive them to despair. Rather, they were spurred to renewed efforts to ensure the progress of science, and with it that of American society. The path-breaking scientific report "Science—The Endless Frontier" (1945), commissioned by President Franklin Delano Roosevelt and written under the auspices of Vannevar Bush, the director of the Office of Scientific Research and Development, turned the previous research policies of the United States upside down. The report succeeded in convincing American universities and private research institutions to request financial support from the government, and in convincing the government to reverse its practice and strongly support not only applied research but also neglected basic research. The appeal was based on the motto that "basic research is the pacemaker of technological progress" since otherwise the "health, prosperity, and security" of the nation would be endangered.[49] Since then the principles of research policy have remained changed only little.

After the dropping of the atomic bomb, scientists did criticize the program (a criticism principally articulated in the *Bulletin of the Atomic Scientists* over several decades), and a sense of despair over the new power role of technological expansion sporadically found expression in political and sociological literature. However, damage to the belief in progress was not nearly as profound in America as it was in Europe.[50] President Dwight D. Eisenhower's warning against the fusion of science and the military-industrial complex, in his farewell address in 1961, provided the next shock to American scientists.[51] Shortly thereafter appeared a book that would ultimately become a classic work in the field: *The Scientific Estate* (1965), by Don K. Price, later president of the American Association for the Advancement of Science (1967). Price dealt directly with crucial questions of whether the ambiguous qualities of scientific freedom could, should, or must be controlled by pluralistic democratic processes, and of the extent to which science should serve military purposes.[52] In addition, he addressed the classic themes of scientific power and political truth:

Fundamental is the way men think about the desirability of organizing truth in the service of power, and using power to determine truth. Whether truth is conceived in the old terms of religion, or the new terms of science, the greatest source of tyranny is the conviction that there is a single way of determining truth and that it should be interpreted by a single disciplined organization.[53]

Whether future science would lead to tyranny or freedom, Price argued, would depend not on a state's technological progress, but rather on its ideology. Referring to closed political systems, Price concluded:

In view of the way in which science seems to condemn us to live in a world of rapid social change, we may have to get used to a constitutional system that does not operate according to absolute rules or fixed procedures, but one that adjusts itself to meet new conditions in a world that we do not expect to become perfect in the predictable future. Perhaps indeed a nation can be free only if it is in not too great a hurry to become perfect. It can then defend its freedom by keeping the institutions established for the discovery of truth and those for the exercise of political power independent of each other.[54]

Since 1945 American critics have spoken out time and again against the apparently uncontrollable development of technological progress. Their reasons vary. While some regard the ethical implications as no longer socially acceptable and perceive a crisis in the idea of progress in a postmodern culture,[55] others are simply no longer willing to believe or hope that politically independent and humane strategies still exist for the solution of problems stemming from the growing multidimensional power of progress, problems manifested in a highly technological, biological, and nuclear revolution.[56] On the other hand, it should be stressed that Americans' traditional trust in science as the ally of political, economic, and social progress, their conviction of America's role as the pro- tagonist of experimentation, a conviction that has repeatedly given them the courage to move out to new frontiers, and their optimistic philosophy of "never giving up" on the "American way of life," all continue to be shared by the majority.[57]

Doomsayers of imminent environmental catastrophes, of the limitations of economic growth, of computerization, or the dangerous ascendance of the media, have always had more of an audience in Europe than in the United States.[58] If President Jimmy Carter's term is remembered in the history books as having been less than successful, it will have a considerable amount to do with the fact that Carter was the first U.S. president to demand material moderation and economic restrictions from his fellow citizens and to regard as necessary the slowing of technological progress in the land of unlimited opportunities.

We have learned that *more* is not necessarily *better,* that even our great nation has its recognized limits, and that we can neither answer all questions nor solve all problems. We cannot afford to do everything, nor can we afford to lack boldness as we meet the future. So together, in a spirit of individual sacrifice for the common good, we must simply do our best.[59]

Carter's successor Ronald Reagan may attribute his greater success in part to his revision of Carter's policies and his plan to help America to new political, economic, and technological heights. In the past few years almost all of the Nobel Prizes in the sciences have been awarded to Americans, which may also have something to do with the unique research climate in the United States.[60] At the same time, however, the Reagan administration's new strategy for the advancement of research may not be an entirely positive one for the nation's general scientific well-being. In 1986 *Scientific American* disclosed the research and development allotment of the proposed budget: 73 percent of the $63 billion went directly or indirectly to military research. There were cutbacks in all areas—

biology, medicine, energy and environmental research, and the geological and human sciences—except physics and data processing, the two most important components of the SDI program initiated in March 1983.[61] No matter how one may assess Ronald Reagan's new frontier project in space,[62] it may be that Donald K. Price's cogent phrase may also apply to the West: "Perhaps indeed a nation can be free only if it is in not too great a hurry to become perfect."[63]

# 7

## Revolutionary Constitutionalism and Presidential Democracy

The two hundredth anniversary of the American Constitution was celebrated in 1987. "The genius of the American Constitution," as has been stressed repeatedly, lies in its adaptability: "Institutional continuity has been the product of institutional adaptability."[64] Drafted during an agricultural era, it survived the Civil War, the demands of the Industrial Revolution, massive waves of immigration, two world wars, a devastating economic depression, the resignation of a president, and America's geopolitical expansion after 1945. Today, in the transitional phase from the industrial to the technological era, in a period of potential worldwide nuclear destruction, the American Constitution has lost none of its vitality. Apart from the Bill of Rights, only sixteen amendments to the Constitution have been passed in over two centuries. This stability is generally attributed to the Supreme Court, but in reality the impressive two-hundred-year continuity of American constitutional history, and its fundamental importance for presidential democracy and the country's political culture, were made possible by the specific characteristics of the American Constitution, in particular by the principle of checks and balances. The Constitution of 1787 was essentially the legal institutionalization of the Declaration of Independence of 1776 and its proclaimed ideals of "life, liberty, and the pursuit of happiness," a guarantee for the continuity of fundamental American values, and the main pillar of American stability. Here, more or less as the culmination of the American Revolution, American values were realized and their long-term preservation ensured.

This chapter portrays the revolutionary character of the American constitutional system and describes some of its underlying intellectual principles, that is, the influence of European political philosophy and Anglo-Saxon style of government on American constitutional development, as well as the unfolding of genuine American solutions. The United States is a common-law and not a civil-law country. This, and the combination of written and unwritten constitutional rights—the latter based on Supreme Court constitutional practices and jurisdiction—resulted (and results) in a unique mixture of traditional constraints and consensus, elasticity and change. This mixture makes it possible to satisfy the American people's passion for reform as well as their aversion to authority by means of "restraint of governmental power through fundamental law," without prejudicing their need for an unassailable symbol of national unity.[65] By virtue of the presidential office, the head of state of the United States is responsible for using legal authority to guarantee and promote societal ideals of freedom. The American Revolution's ideals of progress, as institutionalized in the Constitution, are thus supposed to be perpetuated and constantly redefined by the president. The problematic differences that have arisen between the modern presidential democracy and the classical model of the executive as conceived by the Founding Fathers will also be illustrated in the following discussion.

## TRADITION AND CONSENSUS

The ratification of the Federal Constitution of the United States represented the conclusion of a historical process begun on the Fourth of July 1776, with the Declaration of Independence of the thirteen colonies from the rule of the English monarchy. The victorious ending of the American Revolution (1775–83) led to the international recognition of the sovereign nation "The United States of America." The Constitution of the United States originated neither in the fever of enthusiasm surrounding the Declaration of Independence nor in the triumphal atmosphere following the end of the Revolution. In the eleven years between 1776 and 1787, the basic values of the American Revolution (liberty, democracy, equality, and human rights) had had time to ripen in the Founding Fathers' minds until they were institutionalized in a politically and ideologically "conservative" document.[66] The fact that the American Constitution is by no means a foregone conclusion for Americans even today is shown by the words of Chief Justice Warren E. Burger:

Our great and remarkable Constitution created for the American people a unique system of separated and divided powers to provide internal checks and produce the balance that has given us an ordered liberty unparalleled in history. We must constantly remind ourselves of the wonders of this constitution. We must not take it for granted. We hear and read daily of other people who seek freedom and opportunity, and we know that their struggles do not always achieve those goals. . . . The planning and execution of a revolution is no easy business, and the pages of history are replete with countless revolutions. But the business of putting together a government, a system of governing that will last, is even more difficult.[67]

In the New World, the creators of the constitutional state had no history of political ideas of their own to fall back on; they had to look to the Old World for ideas, knowledge, and achievements that had developed there. It was precisely this state-forming *élan vital* that gave the American constitutional state the power to offer a universal perspective for the future.[68] (As "philosopher-statesmen" [Adrienne Koch], the Founding Fathers had the vision of a political system for the American republic, as well as the ability to realize political leadership in a new environment with the option of resorting to European political traditions.) As James Madison wrote in *The Federalist Papers* (presented as a commentary on the Constitution and today considered a classic text of political theory), the constitutional state was to become "the greatest of all reflections on human nature":[69] "In any case it is without doubt that, since the emergence of the American constitutional state, the written legal constitution based on certain principles became 'an irresistible idea' (Immanuel Kant)."[70]

The Founding Fathers wanted to bind the authority of the state to norms and to establish constitutional legitimacy. An *imperium limitatum* was to replace the *imperium absolutum*. Although the birth of the constitutional state took place in America, the cradle of its intellectual predecessors was clearly to be found in Europe. The constitutional development of the United States can thus be traced back to the influence of Europe. In their attempt to design and realize a liberal democratic and republican system, the American revolutionaries and nation-builders had two stimuli: first, European political theory as developed since the beginning of the seventeenth century; and second, English governmental policy as practiced in the Colonies.[71] The Founding Fathers were familiar not only with the classical texts, but also with the modern political theories of John Locke and Charles de Montesquieu. The most significant section of the Declaration of Independence presented no revolutionary novelty:

That all men are created equal; that they are endowed by their Creator with certain inalienable rights; that among these are life, liberty, and the pursuit of happiness; that to secure these rights, governments are instituted among men, deriving their just powers from the consent of the governed; that whenever any form of government becomes destructive of those ends, it is the right of the people to alter or abolish it, and to institute new government, laying its foundation on such principles, and organizing its powers in such form, as to them shall seem most likely to effect their safety and happiness.[72]

The attempt to put these progressive axioms into practice, to construct a system of government that would dispense with all forms of traditional authority, was revolutionary, however.

The political values and goals conceived in the Declaration of Independence had been anticipated long before in John Locke's *Two Treatises of Government* (1689):

The Reason why Men enter into Society, is the preservation of their Property; and the end why they chuse and authorize a Legislative, is, that there may be Laws made, and

Rules set as Guards and Fences to the Properties of all the Members of the Society, to limit the Power, and moderate the Dominion of every Part and Member of the Society. For since it can never be supposed to be the Will of the Society, that the Legislative should have a Power to destroy that, which every one designs to secure, by entering into Society, and for which the People submitted themselves to the Legislators of their own making; whenever the *Legislators endeavour to take away, and destroy the Property of the People,* or to reduce them to Slavery under Arbitrary Power, they put themselves into a state of War with the People, who are thereupon absolved from any further Obedience, and are left to the common Refuge, which God hath provided for all Men, against Force and Violence. . . . The Power . . . devolves to the People, who have a Right to resume their original Liberty, and, by the Establishment of a new Legislative (such as they shall think fit) provide for their own Safety and Security, which is the end for which they are in society. What I have said here, concerning the Legislative, in general, holds true also concerning the *supreame Executor.*[73]

As Louis Hartz showed, Locke's ideas were similar to American thought because the material circumstances of the country corresponded to his political ideal of a social contract. The Americans were a people with natural rights that had been awarded to them neither by state nor society, rights to life, liberty, equality, work, property, and happiness; Americans were autonomous individuals who willingly committed themselves to a contractual state arrangement with other individuals for the long-term preservation of these rights. These were all assumptions coinciding with existential experiences that the "frontier" had given the pioneers.[74] Tocqueville once wrote fittingly that the Americans "arrived at a state of democracy without having to endure a democratic revolution, and . . . are born equal instead of becoming so."[75] James Bryce emphasized that "Americans had no theory of the state and felt no need for one. . . . The nation is nothing but so many individuals. The government is nothing but certain representatives and officials."[76]

American antipathy to concentration of power in the state has its source in this line of thought. "Indicative of the American antipathy to power and government is the virtual absence of the concept of the 'state' in American thought" (Samuel Huntington).[77] It was accepted that the government was "necessary," but only in the form of a "trust," of an entrusted task, of delegated authority, created in order to realize the social polity, which society as a whole defined as community purpose. A breach of trust on the part of the ruling class justified the right to resistance. The Lockean postulate that all power must come from the people—the democratic concept of popular sovereignty—was incorporated into the American Constitution in 1787.

That majority rule would not necessarily eradicate abuse of political power was understood by the Founding Fathers Madison and Hamilton as well as by the Englishman Locke. The "tyranny of the majority," a legislative absolutism in the name of the majority, should be eliminated as far as possible to protect individual and minority rights.[78]

The answer to the institutional compatibility of majority rule and the preservation of freedom was provided by the work of Charles de Montesquieu, who was aware of English constitutionalism and Lockean thought when he developed his political philosophy. Individual as well as group liberty were to be protected by preventing a concentration of political power. Montesquieu saw modernity's great chance for freedom in the principle of the separation of power, an idea he developed in Book XI of his work *De l'espirit des lois* (1748), which was often quoted by the Americans. Here he developed a system of checks and balances, a strict separation of the executive, legislative, and judicial branches of government, while attributing to this system unambiguous sociopolitical powers. Political change and social transformation would only be possible as a result of consensus among the classes, thus imbuing the system's various areas of authority with vitality. Although Montesquieu's political theory was based on European class structure, which was not only foreign but also inherently suspect to American thought, the Founding Fathers were fascinated by the idea that, by means of an institutional anchoring of a variety of checks and balances in the realm of political power, they could lessen the threat of tyranny of the majority that was so dangerous to the preservation of liberty.[79]

In addition to European political theory, the Founding Fathers were also able to draw on practical experiences and institutional patterns of self-government and administration from most of the colonies, from the vastly symbolic Mayflower Compact of 1620, from Massachusetts' open town meetings in 1635, the Fundamental Orders of Connecticut in 1639, and Pennsylvania's Charter of Privileges in 1701. The institutional legacy of the Cromwell Era and the Glorious Revolution provided further stimulus, such as the idea of codification of the Constitution, the documentation of inalienable human rights, the clear demarcation of executive and legislative authority, and the independence of the courts.[80] In 1891 James Bryce himself had already shown with great clarity how smoothly colonial tradition adapted itself to the drafted constitutional text.[81]

American statements of fundamental and human rights, as far as concrete protection of citizens from state encroachments was concerned, were clearly anticipated by the British tradition of the Magna Charta of 1215, the Petition of Rights in 1627, the Habeas Corpus Act in 1679, the Bill of Rights in 1689, and a variety of corresponding colonial documents. It should be emphasized here, however, that basic rights and the idea of human dignity can be explained with reference to a variety of religious, philosophical, anthropological, ethical, and political spheres of thought. Natural rights, Christianity, humanism, Enlightenment, individualism, and liberal and democratic constitutionalism played important roles. In retrospect, the famous historical dispute between George Jellinek and Emil Boutmy, as to whether the Virginia Bill of Rights of June 12, 1776, which emerged as the Bill of Rights in 1787 or the "Déclaration des droits de l'homme et du citoyen" of August 26, 1789, served as inspiration for the incorporation of fundamental rights in the Constitution, no longer has the relevance once accorded by their contemporaries.[82] Even if the French Déclaration enjoyed greater influence in Europe, history has shown American constitutional documents to be more important with respect to political and legal developments. They led to what Klaus Stern calls "basic-rights constitutionalism." The future would belong to this constitutional concept rather than to the French abstractions of basic rights.[83] The French were concerned primarily with the creation of political maxims of abstract purity, which, because of their absolute claim to truth, would ultimately be given concrete substance solely by the legislators. Most of the deputies of the National Assembly did not want to formulate a legal catalogue of rights because they believed that fundamental rights would evolve of their own accord once the philosophical theory of natural rights was recognized. They wanted to avoid legal norms that could have been applied by the courts or that might have provided bases for claims against those norms.[84]

The Founding Fathers, on the other hand, thought very differently: abstractions, theories, or philosophies of basic rights, natural rights or English birthrights, were replaced by constitutional rights that could be effortlessly understood, interpreted, and applied, and above all used as positive legal bases for countering state authority. A further step was required in order to make "basic rights constitutionalism" manifest. It was this step that was actually revolutionary in the constitutional sense, namely, that all rights of individuals in respect to the state had to be set down in a form that could neither be questioned nor misinterpreted. These had to be individual rights that were binding for state authority as a whole, rights that were "to be the foundation of the government." As the highest rights, the basic rights were to have their source in the authority vested by the Constitution and were at the same time incorporated into the Constitution itself.[85] In this way, the incorporation of basic rights into constitutional law transformed nonnormative constitutionalism into basic-rights constitutionalism, in the process creating a new material legitimacy for the American state. Since then the inclusion of basic rights,[86] the "heart of every constitution," as Chief Justice Earl Warren would later put it,[87] has been the leitmotif for all constitutions. The idea of the state in American constitutional government thus attained a liberal and legal maturity that, because it departed so widely from past models and has remained intact to this day, symbolizes the progress of human rights. The American missionary zeal can be understood primarily as a commitment to humankind based on the idea of human, citizen, and individual rights.

The fathers of the Constitution of the American republic were profoundly aware of the imperfection of human nature, of human suspiciousness, envy, egoism, of the individual's desire for power and the group's desire for domination:

But what is government itself but the greatest of all reflections on human nature? If men were angels, no government would be necessary. If angels were to govern men, neither external nor internal controls on government would be necessary. In framing a government which is to be administered by men over men, the great difficulty lies in this: you must first enable the government to control the governed; and in the next place oblige it to control itself.[88]

For this reason they tried to design a liberal, democratic system based as little as possible on European tradition and with the greatest potential for lasting consensus on the postulated ideals of the Revolution.

The creation of an empire of liberty required a constitution of liberty. Thus, in contrast to European revolutionaries, the pragmatic Federalists did not view the history of human rights as an irresistible ascent into the kingdom of absolute perfection. Rather, they knew that ideals could only be approached, and that refinement of political controls and improvement of social inadequacies were the most one could hope for. Madison noted soberly:

No government of human device and human administration can be perfect; . . . that which is the least imperfect is therefore the best government; that the abuses of all other governments have led to the preference of republican governments as the best of all governments, because the least imperfect.[89]

Clearly, the framers of the Constitution were aware that "liberty [was] not, as it was for Plato, a perfect archetype in the heavens but a hard-won compromise, a strategic ideal."[90] There was little revolutionary enthusiasm involved here; instead, there was a much greater portion of liberal skepticism, which took into account human weaknesses, the human inclination to abuse power, even as it recognized the individual's potential for reason. Thus, they set out to exploit the limitation of human existence in the creation of a liberal community, to make rationally interpreted interests politically and economically concrete, and to preserve and institutionalize these interests as the bases of a progressive constitutional order.

State power without social freedom would have been tyranny; social freedom without state power, utopia. Fortunately, however, the Founding Fathers possessed insights that precluded either of these extremes. Above all, they had a politicophilosophical, but at the same time pragmatic, vision and readiness to compromise, the desire to combine power and freedom and to limit political domination through institutional precautions according to the principle of checks and balances. In addition, they assumed a fully realized pluralism, that is, an appreciation of a social community organized among diverse particular interests, material property, and functions. Such a social entity ultimately prevented the formation of large majorities in the federal government or the individual states, and thus avoided the danger of the oppression of minorities. Through these qualities, the fathers of the Constitution were able to develop a representative and foresighted document, one that institutionalized and preserved the American progressivist ideology in a juridical and consensual manner:

American democratic "ideology" possesses an elaborately defined theory, a body of interrelated assumptions, axioms, and principles, and a set of ideals that serve as guides for action. Its tenets, postulates, sentiments, and values inspired the great revolutions of the . . . eighteenth century, and have been repeatedly and explicitly set forth in fundamental documents, such as the Constitution, the Declaration, and the Federalist Papers. They have been restated with remarkable unanimity in the messages of Presidents, in political speeches, in the pronouncements of judges and constitutional commentators, and in the writings of political theorists, historians, and publicists.[91]

At the same time, their achievement provided the constitutional thought of the Western world with lasting inspiration.[92]

## CONTINUITY AND CHANGE

If one contends that the American Revolution was a constitutional revolution that made possible the establishment of the United States of America as well as the institutionalization of national ideals (the American creed), then it is interesting to examine how little political and constitutional change affected the dominant quality of the American Constitution and judiciary. It would seem that the quality of the American Constitution crystallized precisely in this institutional continuity of the politicohistorical consensus on the American basic values and that socio-political change never succeeded in destroying the framework of constitutional consensus. One could dare pose the thesis that progressive sociopolitical change remains safe because of conservative constitutional continuity.

It has generally been recognized that the judiciary, especially the Supreme Court, has played a more important role in the political life of the United States than in comparable governmental systems. Observers of American constitutional culture have often correctly pointed out that the Supreme Court not only has the function of the highest court in the country, but also constitutes a political institution with the ability to influence national policy: ''To consider the Supreme Court of the United States as a legal institution is to underestimate its significance in the American political system. For it is also a political institution, an institution, that is to say, for arriving at decisions on controversial questions of national policy.''[93] In fact, the Supreme Court, whether in its role as a ''court of judicial activism'' or as a ''court of self-restraint,'' a ''court as guardian,'' or a ''court as oracle,'' has influenced the political, economic, and social interests of the American nation for two hundred years.[94]

The source of the Supreme Court's unusual authority is its power of judicial review, a power that has usually been interpreted in strongly activist terms. The Supreme Court's authority to examine legislation for its constitutionality was expressed only vaguely in Article III of the original text of the Constitution: ''The Judicial power of the United States shall be vested in one Supreme Court and in such inferior courts as the Congress may from time to time ordain and establish.''[95] Nor did Hamilton's argument (in *The Federalist Papers*, No. 78) that the Constitution was ''supreme,'' providing a framework and power for the government (''no legislative act therefore, contrary to the Constitution, can be valid''[96]), bring about a permanent decision. Judicial review was applied for the first time with the famous unanimous Supreme Court decision *Marbury vs. Madison* in February 1803, written by Chief Justice John Marshall. As Charles Grove Haines showed in *The American Doctrine of Judicial Supremacy* (1914),[97] the origin of the doctrine of judicial review rested on a decision made in 1610 by the English judge Sir Edward Coke.[98] On the basis of an incidental case, that of Dr. Bonham, Coke determined that common law actually controlled other laws and that those laws inconsistent with common law had to be declared invalid. Common law was regarded in England as the embodiment of law and reason, but not, however, as a constitution. Because English law did not accept a ranking of court and constitutional authority, because Parliament had the greatest power, Coke's decision did not prevail in England.[99] According to Haines, however, Coke's decision later enjoyed an enormous revival in America, for it contributed to the development of the American theory on the review of laws for their constitutionality:

It was the resistance to English authority [that] culminated in the American Revolution, that rendered the conception of a fundamental law and of individual natural rights popular and encouraged judges to regard it as their peculiar duty to guard and defend the superior laws. The doctrine that there were superior laws to which all legislation must conform was eloquently defined by James Otis.[100]

The acceptance of judicial review, Haines argued further, evolved over a period of about thirty years—from about 1774 to 1803:

It was in this period that the American doctrine of judicial review of legislation was formally announced and accepted as a feature of the public law of the states and of the nation. The gradual emergence of the principles that constitutions are fundamental laws with a peculiar sanctity, that legislatures are limited and receive the commission for their authority from the constitution, and that courts are to be considered the special guardians of the superior written laws may be observed in the evolution of political ideas which accompanied the separation from the British Empire and the establishment of an independent America.[101]

In the fundamental decision *Marbury vs. Madison,* Marshall made the claim, a vital one for the Supreme Court, of ultimate authority in decisions regarding the constitutionality of congressional legislation; the legislative branch had to yield to the judiciary. Only through the exercise of judicial power did the original Constitution become the ''supreme law of the land.'' In this way the Supreme Court became a constitutional court.[102]

In essence, Marshall argued that because the Constitution is the highest law, one based on the will of the people and limiting all state authority derived from it, it is the ruling derived from lower authority that must be overturned in the case of conflict. The ruling of lower origin is legally invalid, not a law, and cannot therefore be applied by the courts in their role as the authoritative interpreters and protectors of the law, and particularly of the Constitution.[103] In the Court decisions *Martin vs. Hunter's Lessee* (1816) and *Cohens vs. Virginia* (1821), the Supreme Court's normative jurisdiction was extended to the legislative process in the individual states. The constitutional foundation for a national state with unified federal legislation was laid quite early, with the unanimous declaration of the supremacy of federal law over the individual states and the authority of the federal government to regulate interstate commerce (*Gibbons vs. Ogden*, 1824).[104] This was not enough, however, to prevent the Southern states from seceding in 1861.

Of course, the Supreme Court's powerful role has not escaped political criticism, because the president appoints the nine members of the Supreme Court for life and because they usually belong to his party and share his ideological orientation.[105] As Franklin D. Roosevelt once argued, "nine old men" should not be in the position "to overrule representatives of the people."[106] Yet, even as critical a spirit as Charles A. Beard was able to write in 1938 that "Whatever controversies may arise in the future over the exercise of judicial power, it is not likely that the historic right of the Supreme Court to pass upon acts of Congress will again be seriously challenged."[107] The academic community took nearly an entire century after 1803 to begin paying serious attention to the subject of judicial review and the role of the courts as protectors of the Constitution.[108] The reason for this may well have been that more than fifty years passed until the Supreme Court once again made use of the right of judicial review to declare laws unconstitutional (*Dred Scott vs. Sandford*, 1857).[109]

After the strengthening of the central government and the limitation of the rights of individual states in the period between 1787 and 1865, the Supreme Court went on to exercise judicial self-restraint beginning with the appointment of Chief Justice Roger Taney (1836) by President Andrew Jackson. This period lasted through the Civil War, Reconstruction, and industrialization, and continued until the death of Chief Justice William Howard Taft (1930). The Court interpreted "judicial restraint" to mean strict maintenance of the laissez-faire economic system and the protection of corporate private ownership against the intervention of the federal government by invoking the "due process of law" and "equal protection of law" clauses in the Fourteenth Amendment (1868). In the area of economic policy, the "due process" clause was applied after 1868 initially for the protection of individual property rights from intervention by the states. Yet the trusts, which had already monopolized the most important sectors of trade and industry by the end of the nineteenth century, were also able to claim personal property rights as corporations, as "juristic persons."

As defenders of free enterprise, the judges certainly were in favor of laissez-faire capitalism, even though the two great judges Oliver Wendell Holmes and Louis A. Brandeis were to go down in American legal history as famed dissenters on this issue. Thus, in 1895 the Supreme Court declared a federal income tax unconstitutional, and the tax ultimately became law in 1913 by means of the Sixteenth Amendment. In addition, the Court limited enforcement of the first antitrust legislation (1895); prohibited the federal government from regulating child labor (1918), and prohibited the states from regulating working hours (1905). On the other hand, the Supreme Court permitted the states to control trade and industry that benefited the public interest (1877); supported state laws on mining safety regulations (1902); and allowed the states to regulate railroad companies operating in their territory (1886). The Supreme Court also supported the rights of the individual states in over 80 percent of the decisions regarding various aspects of economic life between 1887 and 1910.[110]

During the New Deal period, which began with President Herbert Hoover's appointment of Chief Justice Charles Hughes in 1930 and ended in 1946 under Chief Justice Harlan Stone, Franklin D. Roosevelt came into sharp conflict with the "third power" thanks to the role of governmental regulation in his economic policies. Much of Roosevelt's first New Deal legislation, such as the National Industrial Recovery Act (1933) for combatting the economic crisis, was declared unconstitutional by the Supreme Court in 1935. Between 1933 and 1937 twelve other federal laws, some of them of decisive importance for Roosevelt's social reform policies, were declared unconstitutional by the Supreme Court, mostly by votes of five to four.

After his reelection in 1936, Roosevelt used his "court-packing plan" of February 1937 in an unsuccessful attempt to force a change of course in the Supreme Court, which had thus far blocked his New Deal policies against the wishes of majorities in the House and Senate, as well as against public opinion and the president himself. Roosevelt presented Congress with a bill for reform of the federal judiciary system which would have given him power to add an additional justice to the Court for every justice over seventy years of age who was unwilling to resign voluntarily, until the Court had fifteen justices. It soon became clear, however, that Roosevelt's plan to shape the Supreme Court according to his own desires would divide not only the Congress, but also the Democratic party, indeed, the very country itself. A large part of the American people viewed the attempt as an attack on the protectors of the Constitution and the guarantee of the legal basis of the state, as a threat to the independence of the courts and the constitutional system. Nonetheless, by the end of 1937, as the result of deaths and resignations, the Supreme Court had a liberal majority; by 1941, seven of the nine justices were Roosevelt appointees. The example of FDR's dispute with the Supreme Court does demonstrate, however, how deeply rooted the historical liberal democratic consciousness of Americans in respect to their own constitutional culture and traditions was.[111]

After the Second World War, the main focus of the Supreme Court, under the leadership of Chief Justice Earl Warren (1953–1969), was on individual and civil rights:

The Warren Court period . . . was the most revolutionary in the modern Court's history. Operating according to the premises of judicial activism, the Court left hardly any area of the political system or society untouched. At times playing the role of oracle, . . . stressing its policy-making function as well as its role in identifying the meaning and direction of public morality, . . . and at times of guardian of due process of law, the Warren Court in fact became the spearhead for much-needed political and social reform.[112]

The era of a liberal, democratic, and politically activist Supreme Court began with President Eisenhower's appointment of Earl Warren to the post of chief justice, for Warren ultimately proved to be an advocate of the civil rights movement. In 1969 President Nixon appointed Warren Burger chief justice, and it was under Burger's leadership that the Supreme Court returned to judicial self-restraint. This period marked the completion of a conservative shift intended to close the gap, which had been increasing since the beginning of the 1970s, between the liberal decisions of the Warren Court and a public exhausted by issues of race, equality, and civil rights.[113] At any rate, the Supreme Court's role in the area of civil rights profoundly shaped the "political" significance of the "third branch" and its constitutional function as the sociopolitical conscience of the nation.[114]

The Supreme Court extended the principles of the supremacy of federal law and of normative control to the entire nation, that is, to legislation even in the individual states. For the first time since the Civil War (1865), the Court focused on civil rights, which have been of major importance to American politics since the renewed growth of the black civil rights movement of the late 1950s. The Bill of Rights, comprising the Constitution's first ten amendments, applied almost exclusively to federal decisions and not to those of the individual states, according to Chief Justice John Marshall's 1833 decision *Barron vs. Baltimore*.[115] It was the Fourteenth Amendment (1868) that first freed U.S. citizens from exclusive reliance on the civil rights guarantees and interpretations by the states in which they lived. The Fourteenth Amendment was in fact the most important of the three so-called Civil War amendments, enacted in order to complete the emancipation of slaves begun in 1863. The Thirteenth Amendment of 1865 gave constitutional status to the prohibition of slavery; the Fifteenth Amendment (1870) forbade the government as well as the individual states to prohibit or impede a citizen's right to vote.

The Fourteenth Amendment declared all "persons" born or naturalized in the United States "citizens" of their state and the United States. This paved the way for the revocation of the notorious 1857 court decision *Dred Scott vs. Sanford,* in which Chief Justice Taney had denied blacks the right to citizenship and declared their emancipation in the northern territories to be unconstitutional.[116] The actual text of the Fourteenth Amendment reads as follows:

All persons born or naturalized in the United States, and subject to the jurisdiction thereof, are citizens of the United States and of the State wherein they reside. No State shall make or enforce any law which shall abridge the privileges or immunities of citizens of the United States; nor shall any State deprive any person of life, liberty, or property, without due process of law; nor deny to any person within its jurisdiction the equal protection of the laws.[117]

The "due process of law" and "equal protection of the laws" clauses in the Fourteenth Amendment gave the federal government the role of protecting individual citizens from the governments of the individual states. This constitutional advance first became reality, however, under the new social and economic conditions and changes in attitude of the twentieth century. In the nineteenth century, Court decisions tended in the opposite direction, as in *Plessy vs. Ferguson* of 1896, where the state of Louisiana was brought to court for having made racial segregation in railroad cars into law. The Supreme Court decided that the equality of the races could be considered compatible with their legal separation. However, this so-called separate but equal doctrine led to the "legitimization of the social inferiority of blacks." Shortly after the decision, this doctrine was applied to schools and other public institutions.[118]

It was not until 1954, in *Brown vs. Board of Education of Topeka*, that the separate but equal doctrine was finally invalidated. Under the leadership of Chief Justice Warren, a liberal Supreme Court became the vanguard of the civil rights movement, which began at the end of 1955 with the famous boycott in Montgomery, Alabama.[119] The ground for the *Brown* decision had already been broken, however, when the Supreme Court decided in 1938 that blacks must be admitted to schools founded for whites only, if no other equal opportunity was available.[120] In 1950, the National Association for the Advancement of Colored People (NAACP), which had been founded in 1901, succeeded in confronting the Supreme Court with five cases illustrating the basic dilemma of racial integration in the public schools. (This effort was made under the leadership of the lawyer Thurgood Marshall, who in 1967 would become the first black to be appointed to the Supreme Court.) In the *Brown* decision, Earl Warren ruled that the separate but equal doctrine amounted to inequality in the public education system and that legal segregation of the races in the schools violated the equal protection of the law clause of the Fourteenth Amendment. The Court decision therefore required public schools to integrate students of different races under the supervision of the federal courts as quickly as possible.[121] In 1957 President Eisenhower was even forced to send in the National Guard to protect black students in Little Rock, Arkansas, after Governor Orval Faubus had deployed troops in an attempt to prevent integration of the schools.[122] President Kennedy sent paratroops to the University of Mississippi in 1962 on a similar occasion, and shortly afterward he sent the National Guard to the University of Alabama, where Governor George Wallace, later candidate of the Citizen party, tried to block the integration of black students.[123]

In 1964 only around 2 percent of the black students in the eleven Southern states were integrated; since the beginning of the 1970s more than 2,700 school districts of the South have been integrated. In 1971 the Supreme Court went a step further with the decision *Swann vs. Charlotte-Mecklenburg Board of Education,* in which it established that students could also be transported in school buses to different schools by court order to establish a uniform school system by means of "racial quotas."[124] This "mandatory busing system" has since become an extremely explosive political subject, one leading to friction particularly in the North. It has probably contributed more than any other problem to resistance to "big government" from Washington and Democratic reformist liberalism of the 1960s.[125] Busing has faced political opposition as well, with both presidents Nixon and Reagan calling for its elimination and a Democratic House of Representatives in the 1970s passing several laws restricting the policy. In March 1982 the Senate voted 57 to 37 to prohibit busing altogether; however, the House of Representatives did not consent.[126] The example of busing clearly shows the political limits of the Supreme Court's control over processes of social change that are not solidly supported by a majority of the citizens.

The Warren Court did succeed in anchoring civil rights in federal law through a series of basic legislative changes. From 1957 to 1970, six significant civil rights laws were passed, which, among other things, made infringement of individual voting rights or preregistration procedures for voters punishable by federal law. The Supreme Court appointed a commission to supervise elections, banned all types of discrimination in public institutions, and made discrimination in the hiring and dismissal of employees (Equal Employment Opportunity, 1964) as well as in the rental or sale of housing punishable by law. The Department of Health, Education, and Welfare even threatened all colleges and universities in the United States with federal funding cuts if they did not contribute to ending discrimination by demonstrating compliance with "affirmative action" plans for the acceptance of minority groups and women.[127] The introduction of these so-called racial quotas has since continued to spark its share of controversy. These quotas are sometimes interpreted as reverse discrimination, that is, discrimination against white men. The quotas have thus repeatedly become issues of political dispute, such as in the so-called *Bakke* case of 1978.[128] Without doubt, reverse discrimination is a highly ambiguous legal concept, and most of the suits have thus far been dismissed.

In the area of equal rights for women, the ratification of the Equal Rights Amendment (ERA), sponsored by the National Organization of Women, remains a desideratum. As far back as 1923 women's rights supporters designated the ERA as their most important objective. It received a green light from Congress in 1970, but since then the proposed amendment has failed to be ratified by the two-thirds majority of the state legislatures, as required for amendments to the Constitution.[129]

For the past twenty-five years, all the way from the liberal Warren Court, through John F. Kennedy's vision of a New Frontier, to Lyndon B. Johnson's attempts to realize the American Dream in his Great Society program, Europeans have followed the Americans' efforts to cope with the problems of a pluralistic society. The progress that the Americans have made in the area of equal, civil, and individual rights, rights that have shaped (and will continue to shape) American politics for decades, can only demand respect and admiration. It is impressive to note that America today has almost 6,000 elected black officeholders, from the local level to Congress, and that an increasing black middle class now comprises over a quarter of the black population. In addition, some of the country's largest cities are governed by blacks; Chicago, Philadelphia, Los Angeles, New Orleans, Washington, and Detroit all have black mayors.[130]

In 1984 and again in 1988, Jesse Jackson, a black, campaigned for the presidential nomination. Equality for other minority groups, such as women, has made enormous progress in American society. In 1981, President Ronald Reagan appointed Sandra Day O'Connor as the first woman associate justice of the Supreme Court. In 1984, Geraldine Ferraro became the first woman to campaign for the office of the vice-presidency. According to the economist Paul A. Samuelson, more than half of America's women now have jobs, 36 percent of them in middle and top positions. Between 1975 and 1984, the number of women employees rose from 37 million to 50 million. At the end of 1985, 54 percent of all female Americans over sixteen years of age were employed, as compared to 43 percent in 1970 and 38 percent in 1960. Interestingly, this last figure (38 percent) corresponds to the percentage of German women who pursued a career in 1984.[131]

When summarizing the achievements of the Supreme Court, one can make the following observation about the period following Earl Warren's tenure as chief justice:

The Court has declared Bible reading and all other religious exercises in public schools unconstitutional; it has ordered the reapportionment of the national House of Representatives, of both Houses of state legislatures, and of local government bodies on a one-man, one-vote basis; it has reformed numerous aspects of state and federal criminal procedure, significantly enhancing the rights of the accused, including juvenile offenders; it has laid down a whole set of new rules governing the admissibility of confessions in evidence, and in effect, the conduct of police throughout the country toward persons arrested on suspicion of crime; and it has held that wiretapping and eavesdropping are subject to the Fourth Amendment's prohibition against unreasonable searches and seizures. The Court has also enlarged its own jurisdiction to hear cases challenging federal expenditures. . . . [it] has limited the power of state and federal governments.[132]

In the words of the former Supreme Court Justice Arthur J. Goldberg, the achievements of the Warren Court were revolutionary:

To me the major accomplishments of the Supreme Court . . . in which Earl Warren was Chief Justice were the revolution in criminal justice both state and Federal; a translation of our society's proclaimed belief in equality into some measure of legal reality, and the beginning of the profound change in the mechanics of our political democracy.[133]

Neither democratic ideology nor the system of checks and balances provided room for a "judicialization" of politics or the creation of a "judiocracy," as critics have claimed.[134] On the other hand, the theory of American constitutional government and the doctrine of limited government had opened up possibilities for limiting power through law, thus giving the Supreme Court the rank of a respected and important "third force" in the creation of political will and in the utilization of power.[135] The function of the Supreme Court, defined by the Founding Fathers as the constitutional protector of American revolutionary values and ideals and as the moral and legal conscience of the nation, has over the course of the past two hundred years (with a few exceptions in the nineteenth century) proved itself a guarantor of institutional continuity and social change.

While the American experiment in the realization of freedom, equality, and human rights for all has been improved step by step, and while the black minority in the United States has been integrated for decades now, in South Africa (to cite the most extreme example) the rights of the black majority are daily being subjected to violent oppression at the hands of a white minority.

## POWER AND FREEDOM

For generations the American Constitution and presidency have enjoyed, as national and political symbols of integration, the unqualified respect and admiration of American society. In the course of the country's transformation from an agrarian state to a highly industrialized world power, the office of the American presidency has acquired numerous additional functions and meanings, and they have come to change its traditional definition and responsibilities. It is nonetheless amazing to consider that even today congressional investigative committees, official statements of the president, or scholarly investigations on the checks and balances of power continue to consult and quote the opinion of the Federalists, or the views of the oracle of Philadelphia, when deliberating on current political problems.[136]

The fathers of the Constitution selected the presidential system quite consciously as the form of government most appropriate for the New World. They had a vision of a strongly pluralistic, clearly federalist, representative republic, with the Federalists, above all Alexander Hamilton and John Adams, supporting a "strong central government," while the Republicans Thomas Jefferson and James Madison were convinced that "that government was best which governed least."[137]

In the modern presidential democracy of the twentieth century, these political fundamentals were to change places completely. Today it is the Democrats who favor a strong central government and the Republicans who aspire to the decentralization of power in Washington. The origins of present-day presidential democracy can be traced back to the beginning of modern American industrial capitalism, to the concepts of government articulated by presidents Theodore Roosevelt and Woodrow Wilson. Breaking with tradition, both men advocated an active, interventionist federal government led by the president as the sole governmental authority, able to act on the majority will of the nation's voters politically, economically, and ideologically. In keeping with the ideas and concepts of the framers of the Constitution, Congress was to serve as the dominant governmental organ, with the active involvement of numerous interest groups preventing the rule of simple majority governments on the federal level. By contrast, modern presidential democracy was chosen explicitly to preserve the dominance of majority interests on the national level against the powerful interest groups of the new capitalistic monopolies. Economic and social transformation brought about a fundamental shift of responsibilities in favor of the president within the power structure of constitutional policy. Today—expressed in rather simplified form—the media-oriented presidential democracy may be headed in the direction of a national, plebiscitary majority democracy.[138]

From the beginning it was the president's task to exercise constitutionally sanctioned presidential authority by balancing it against power and freedom. In order to convert ideals of progress into practical political concepts and strategies, every president since Washington has had to be persuasive and able to use his power to the fullest and yet limit it. The present chapter outlines this presidential role of exercising political power while preserving social liberty and explains the American presidential political philosophy of the "conjunction of power with liberty."

As Adlai Stevenson once observed, "American history is largely the history of the American presidency. It is a history of men rising to the demands of their time in an office which afforded them the power to govern. Great Presidents . . . made government an engine of progress towards their objectives."[139] Unlike the European parliamentary system, which depends on party ideologies, coalitions, and concessions in order to create a government capable of governing, the presidential system in the United States is based on the ideology of the president, who can advance policies without having to wait for entire governmental programs to be approved.[140] This is the basis for understanding the observation that great presidents were able to make "government an engine of progress towards their objectives."

The American presidential system presents itself as a guarantor of the tradition, consensus, and continuity of progress. Performing the key function of centralizing and nationalizing American policy, the president—and not, as in Europe, party platforms—initiates large-scale social and strategic programs. For this reason there is a drastic swing every four to eight years—as each new president proclaims a "revolutionary new beginning" and promises to do everything differently from and better than the preceding president. In a sense, it reflects the Americans' need to confirm and redefine their founding principles and progressivist ideology.[141] Each change in the presidency seems to initiate a new Creedal Passion period, in which the values of the past are revived by public philosophy and presidential style and the historical continuity of the American creed maintained despite political change. Richard Neustadt puts it this way: "Presidents have to wrap themselves in continuity, fundamentals, because their legitimacy is enhanced by it. And they have to move from party politics to be president of all the people and make the most they can of that imagery."[142]

Interestingly, the president, as philosopher-statesman (Adrienne Koch), uses terminology and rhetoric that often seem strangely lofty to European ears in order to achieve the strategic ideals of foreign and domestic policies, ideals that already had the ring of public philosophy in the inaugural address. John Mc-Diarmid even went so far as to speculate that "the verbal symbols in Presidential inaugural addresses . . . changed little during the first 150 years of American history."[143] Unlike Europe, presidential terminology and rhetorical slogans in America decisively shaped entire epochs.[144] Thomas Cronin wrote aptly:

A president who does not raise hopes is criticized as letting events shape his presidency, rather than making things happen. A president who eschewed inspiration of any kind would be rejected as un-American. For as a poet once wrote, "America is promises." For people everywhere cherishing the dream of individual liberty and self-fulfillment, America has been the land of promises, of dreams. No president can stand in the way of this truth, no matter how much the current dissatisfaction about the size of big government in Washington, and its incapacity to deliver the services it promises.[145]

To clarify the development of the American presidency and modern presidential democracy, several specific characteristics of the American presidency will now be analyzed in terms of the president's own understanding of the office.

The Constitution stipulated that "the executive power shall be vested in a President of the United States of America." The president of the United States is chief of state and head of the government in one, supreme administrator of the entire federal bureaucracy, commander-in-chief of the armed forces, and the country's highest diplomat. In keeping with the constitutional principle of checks and balances, the president also is the initiator and adversary of the legislative process as well as the leader of the party.[146] In Alexander Hamilton's words the following maxims were intended as the first commandment for the president: "Energy in the executive is a leading character in the definition of good government."[147] For Hamilton this also implied "the primacy of virtue and constitutionalism," by which he meant virtue in the Aristotelian sense of the word.[148]

The interesting and at the same time controversial thesis of Edward S. Corwin and Clinton Rossiter that "the modern theory of presidential power is the contribution primarily of Alexander Hamilton" will not be discussed further here.[149] It remains uncontested, however, that the "inventors of the presidency"—George Washington, Benjamin Franklin, James Madison, Alexander Hamilton, and Elbridge Gerry, among others—created a democratic system of government unique in history, one that would guarantee the progress of America for two hundred years.[150] "Their most remarkable, their most unique, creation was the American Presidency," according to R. Gordon Hoxie, the president of the Center for the Study of the Presidency.[151] Since then the president, presidential power, and presidential performance have stood at the center of the American political and scholarly discussion.[152] The questions connected with it were formulated by Richard Neustadt as follows: "When we inaugurate a president we give him the powers of our highest office. From the moment he is sworn the man confronts a personal problem: how to make those powers work for him."[153]

Furthermore, the public philosophy of a president is to be judged by how he acts on his progressivist policies: "What were his purposes and did these run with the grain of our history."[154] Emmet John Hughes described "the most difficult job in the world" in this way:

any President finds himself commanded to perform an almost interminable series of conjuring acts to control the ceaseless contradictions of Presidential life. He must proudly cherish and profess political principles—yet sometimes pursue his greater purposes unslowed by lesser scruples. He must summon his people to be with him—yet stand above, not squat beside them. He must question his own wisdom and judgment—but not too severely. . . . He must be aggressive without being contentious, decisive without being arrogant, and compassionate without being confused. . . . He must be pragmatic, calculating, and earthbound—and still know when to spurn the arithmetic of expediency for the act of brave imagination, the sublime gamble with no hope other than the boldness of vision.[155]

As indicated earlier, the two presidents especially responsible for the emergence of modern presidential democracy and the activist presidency were Theodore Roosevelt and Woodrow Wilson. In his "stewardship theory" Roosevelt explained his understanding of presidential power: "My belief was that it was not only his right but his duty to do anything that the needs of the nation demanded, unless such action was forbidden by the Constitution or by the laws."[156] Wilson saw his role as president similarly: "The President is at liberty, both in law and conscience, to be as big a man as he can."[157] This model of an activist presidential democracy would become the focal point of the political conceptions of government particularly of the Democratic party and its ideology of liberal democracy.

It was, of course, the most famous Democratic president in the twentieth century, Franklin D. Roosevelt—"The Presidency . . . is preeminently a place of moral leadership"—who made the governmental system of a strong presidential democracy into an example and symbol of modern (i.e., progressive, democratic, socially oriented) politics. This system should simultaneously realize the traditional American values and ideals of individual freedom and equality.[158] At least since Franklin D. Roosevelt, this image of presidential power and strategic performance has, as the ideal image for a "strong president," inspired and influenced presidential self-understanding and the political progressive concepts of the liberal Democratic presidents. For Hedley Donovan, Roosevelt was "the founder of the modern Presidency, the focus of authority and initiative in a greatly extended and centralized government."[159] As Neustadt observed in his classic work *Presidential Power* (1960), however, FDR did not develop a philosophical concept of the office of the presidency: "Roosevelt, almost alone among our Presidents, had no conception of the office to live up to; he was it. His image of the office was himself-in-office. The memories left by his associates agree on this if nothing else: he saw the job of being President as being F.D.R."[160]

With the presidency of Harry Truman, the era of the Cold War began. Vis-à-vis the all-encompassing Soviet dictatorship, the office of the American president had advanced under Roosevelt from a national to an international leitmotif. It was under Truman, however, that the new role of the president as the leader of the free world was conclusively established. This new global political constellation was reflected in Truman's inaugural address: "Events have brought our American democracy to new influence and new responsibilities. They will test our courage, our devotion to duty, and our concept of liberty."[161] In his speech on "Presidential Power" in 1954, he remarked:

a successful administration is one of strong presidential leadership. Weak leadership—or no leadership—produces failure and often disaster. . . . Today the tasks of leadership falling upon the President spring not only from our national problems but from those of the whole world. Today that leadership will determine whether our Government will function effectively, and upon its functioning depends the survival of each of us and also on that depends the survival of the free world.[162]

For Dwight D. Eisenhower, the president stood out in his capacity as a figure of moral leadership: "The President of the United States should stand, visible and uncompromising, for what is right and decent. . . . The highest national office should be sought and occupied less as an exercise of political power than as a test of personal virtue."[163] And John F. Kennedy saw the role of the president as the broadest exploitation of the possibilities of presidential power: "He must be prepared to exercise the fullest powers of his office—all that are specified and some that are not."[164]

Presidential democracy began to suffer an increasing loss of confidence and respect among the public under the leadership of Democratic President Lyndon Johnson during the Vietnam War. Johnson's commentary on the office of the presidency would prove almost prophetic for himself as well as for his successor Richard M. Nixon:

The office of the Presidency is the only office in this land of all the people. . . . At no time and in no way and for no reason can a President allow the integrity or the responsibility or the freedom of the office ever to be compromised or diluted or destroyed, because when you destroy it, you destroy yourselves.[165]

The dangers inherent in the modern presidential democracy, in view of its increasing power in economic, foreign policy, and military decision-making processes became visible in the discussion of the so-called imperial presidency. This designation, coined by Arthur M. Schlesinger (*The Imperial Presidency,* 1974), referred to the tendency to extricate the executive from its constitutional limits and constraints.[166] It was under President Richard M. Nixon that this development reached its pinnacle ("The days of a passive Presidency belong to a simpler past"[167]) during the Watergate affair. The phenomenon of the imperial presidency cannot, however, be attributed exclusively to Nixon's personal ambitions, and it was not extinguished following his resignation. Indications of the imperial presidency as latent danger are still present.[168] It was in this context that Gerald R. Ford formulated his philosophy of the presidency in a speech in Michigan in 1985. This conception was reflected during his brief term of office:

What we really want is balance, not the extreme here or the extreme there. We do not want an imperiled presidency, nor do we want an imperial presidency. We do not want an impotent one. We do have to find some reasonable balance where the President and the members of Congress can operate together in a responsible and in a cooperative way.[169]

Together with the neoconservative questioning of the liberal Democratic economic and social programs of the 1960s, and in the wake of the worldwide energy crisis in the mid-1970s and the weak leadership of Democratic President Jimmy Carter toward the end of that decade, American policy of the late 1970s led to a "crisis" in modern presidential democracy.[170] The image of the presidency under Carter lost authority. Carter himself remarked: "The erosion of our confidence in the future is threatening to destroy the social and the political fabric of America."[171] With his thesis of the "crisis of confidence" Carter conjured, and indeed, took on himself the burden of the crisis and his apparent lack of personal leadership qualities. In June 1984 he confessed quite frankly to a small group in the Woodrow Wilson Center in Washington: "One of the great things about President Reagan's personality is that he seems satisfied with the way the nation is doing. . . . Popularity has to do with the way you present yourself, and I must say I have great admiration for President Reagan because he does it so well."[172] With Ronald Reagan in the White House, the office of the president enjoyed a new glitter and glory. "So here came Reagan," writes Hedley Donovan, "not overworking himself but relishing the job and the power, using it with great gusto and skill to shrink the role of the Government and of the President."[173] Ronald Reagan assumed the office in 1981 with the goals of eliminating the economic crisis and loss of American foreign political prestige (especially because of Vietnam and Iran) and of reestablishing the confidence of Americans and the rest of the world in American institutions, the office of the president, and the American (progressivist) ideology. Significantly, Reagan succeeded in strengthening the role of the president and investing it with respectability without using the traditional strategy of the previously ascendant liberal presidential model, but precisely by means of decentralization, dismantling an active, interventionist federal government, and attempting to reduce big government. In his inaugural address in 1981, Reagan said: "In this present crisis, government is not the solution to our problem; government is the problem."[174]

Reagan's leadership qualities and persuasiveness, his populist rhetoric, and his ability to appear in the media as the Great Communicator all furthered the realization of his domestic as well as foreign policy concepts. It has also been pointed out, however, that the phenomenon of plebiscitary presidential democracy, based primarily on television, is occurring more dramatically in the Reagan era. This tendency became especially clear in the campaign year of 1984, when the Republican party concentrated exclusively on the personality and public effect of Ronald Reagan. The dangers of presidential democracy connected with this development, dangers resting in the most effective media presentation of presidential virtues and policies, is the subject of recent studies.[175]

If one were to read James Bryce's book *The American Commonwealth* (1891) today, one would notice that many of his satirical observations as to why great men are not elected president could be aptly applied to several American presidents of the past century.[176] The complexity of American twentieth-century presidential democracy, conditioned by an increasingly autonomous, egalitarian, and freer society, the global political antagonism between the pluralistic systems of liberal democratic pluralism and the ideologically dogmatic regimes of totalitarian or authoritarian character, that is, the defense of the free world by the United States in the face of communist expansion pursued by the Soviet Union, as well as the constantly growing nuclear threat faced by humankind, has required outstanding political personalities and presidents since the Second World War.

In accordance with Clinton Rossiter's definition of presidential functions, the president of United States has the following roles to assume:[177]

—*Chief of State* (The president is ceremonial head of government and represents the American nation.)
—*Chief Executive* (The president rules and runs the government.)
—*Commander-in-chief* (The nation's armed forces take their orders directly from the president.)
—*Chief Diplomat* (The president's position in foreign affairs is paramount.)
—*Chief Legislator* (The president plays a key role in determining legislative programs.)
—*Chief of Party* (The president has the absolute right and duty to be leader of the party, through which the president has reached the highest office.)
—*Voice of the People* (The president serves as spokesperson for the people, and is a formulator and expounder of public opinion.)
—*Protector of the Peace* (Americans expect the president to take the key role in times of crisis.)
—*Manager of Prosperity* (The president is expected to use the powers of the office to maintain stable economic conditions.)
—*World Leader* (The president's constituency is much broader than the United States— it stretches out to foreign shores; what America does or doesn't do has significant impact on world conditions and the environment in other countries.)

To follow Thomas E. Cronin, the Americans also expect a series of leadership qualities from their president:[178]

—Self-knowledge/self-confidence
—Vision, ability to infuse important, transcending values into an enterprise

—Intelligence, wisdom, judgment

—Learning/renewal

—Worldmindedness/a sense of history and breadth

—Coalition building/social architecture

—Morale-building/motivation

—Stamina, energy, tenacity, courage, enthusiasm

—Character, integrity/intellectual honesty

—Risk-taking/entrepreneurship

—An ability to communicate, persuade, and listen

—An understanding of the nature of power and authority

—An ability to concentrate on achieving goals and results

—A sense of humor, perspective, flexibility

If we were to evaluate presidential performance, public philosophy, presidential instruments, or the presidential character from Franklin D. Roosevelt to Ronald Reagan, and roughly weigh presidential progressive domestic and foreign policy strategies for a balance between power and freedom, then we would see that all were more or less successful in coping with the new geohistorical, geopolitical, and nuclear factors after 1945.[179] They all had in common a political awareness of commitment and responsibility to American values and American tradition, to the preservation of the progressivist ideology of the Founding Fathers and the concomitant guarantee of continuity and consensus in American history and politics.

Measured against Richard Neustadt's sentence, "what were his purposes and did these run with or against the grain of history," Franklin D. Roosevelt, four-time president-elect, will definitely go down in the annals of American history as *the* representative of the modern American presidency, *the* successful solver of the American economic depression in the 1930s, as *the* leader of the Democratic party, *the* savior of Europe ("we must be the great arsenal of democracy") from national socialist barbarism—though with Stalin's help—and *the* visionary of a democratic "world society": "we know it because democracy has constructed an unlimited civilization capable of infinite progress in the improvement of human life."[180] As Senator J. William Fulbright said in a conversation in 1982: "Roosevelt I considered a great politician, a great leader."[181]

Harry Truman set the course for American and, to a certain degree, European postwar foreign policy with the Truman Doctrine and the Marshall Plan. These policies were formed by the Cold War and the prominent dualism of liberal democracies in the West versus communist dictators in the East. In his inaugural address Truman emphasized:

Today marks the beginning not only of a new administration, but of a period that will be eventful, perhaps decisive, for us and for the world. . . . Communism is based on the belief that man is so weak and inadequate that he is unable to govern himself, and therefore requires the rule of strong masters. Democracy is based on the conviction that man has the moral intellectual capacity, as well as the inalienable right, to govern himself with reason and justice. Communism subjects the individual to arrest without lawful cause, punishment without trial, and forced labor as the chattel of the state. It decrees what information he shall receive, what art he shall produce, what leaders he shall follow, and what thoughts he shall think. Democracy maintains that government is established for the benefit of the individual, and is charged with the responsibility of protecting the rights of the individual and his freedom in the exercise of his abilities. Communism maintains that social wrongs can be corrected only by violence. Democracy has proved that social justice can be achieved through peaceful change. Communism holds that the world is so deeply divided into opposing classes that war is inevitable. Democracy holds that free nations can settle differences justly and maintain lasting peace. . . . I state these differences, not to draw issues of belief as such, but because the actions resulting from the Communist philosophy are a threat to the efforts of free nations to bring about world recovery and lasting peace. . . . The initiative is ours.[182]

To his close adviser Richard Neustadt, Truman not only was "the builder of American foreign policy," but also set "the standards for the postwar American Presidency."[183] Clark Clifford, speechwriter and closest adviser of the president, said once about Truman: "It is my belief that the United States during that period led by President Truman in reality really saved the free world."[184]

The more time that passes, the more positive the image of President Dwight D. Eisenhower becomes. During his two terms the country experienced its greatest economic upswing, one that carried over to other countries. Eisenhower himself interpreted this phenomenon with the following words:

The American experiment has for generations fired the passion and the courage of millions elsewhere seeking freedom, equality, and opportunity. And the American story of material progress has helped excite the longing of all needy peoples for some satisfaction of their human wants. These hopes that we have helped to inspire we can help to fulfill.[185]

In addition, Eisenhower kept the United States out of war and distanced the country from risk-laden conflicts with the Soviet Union. Senator Fulbright's evaluation of President Eisenhower is particularly illuminating from the perspective of contemporary history:

I think as I look back upon it, under the circumstances Eisenhower was a good leader. He did not involve us, he helped to avoid us from becoming entangled in insolvable problems. He had a sense of limitations and above all he had a sense of the military and the military shouldn't dominate the country.[186]

The cliché of Eisenhower leaving the most important domestic and foreign policy decisions to his advisers has also since been refuted.[187] Asked about this matter, his former chief of staff, Sherman Adams, responded as follows:

the harder the decision, the more difficult the confrontation, the more certain he was that he was right. He was a very positive person. When he came to a decision he stuck to it above everything else; it was his decision and not the decision of his staff or advisers.[188]

In his study of the Eisenhower era and Ike's seemingly modest political character, Eisenhower expert R. Gordon Hoxie wrote:

Eisenhower realized that following twenty years of social revolution and war, the nation both needed and yearned for a period of calm, consolidation, efficiency, and understanding. . . . For this admixture of seemingly calm persuasion rather than bombastic direction, for a recognition of the need for consolidation while moving ahead, for this mixture of affection and quiet strength, Eisenhower did not earn the sobriquet of the activist President. Yet an examination of his public papers and personal letters, his personal reminiscences, and the record of his two administrations reveal his mastery of command.[189]

John F. Kennedy's charisma bordered almost on Jefferson's or Lincoln's. Yet, if Lee Harvey Oswald's shots had missed him on the twenty-second of November 1963, it is doubtful that Kennedy would have gone down in the history of United States as the idol of progress for generations to come. Kennedy's presidency symbolized an era of turmoil and renewal, an era in which the time had come for equal rights for blacks and whites, an era of the "ascension to power of scientists and scholars" (Herbert von Borch)[190] by "the best and the brightest" (David Halberstam),[191] and an age of courage to move out to "new frontiers":

We stand today on the edge of a new frontier—the frontier of the nineteen-sixties, a frontier of unknown opportunities and paths, a frontier of unfulfilled hopes and threats. . . . The new frontier of which I speak is not a set of promises—it is a set of challenges. It sums up not what I intend to offer the American people, but what I intend to ask of them.[192]

At the same time, it was a presidency consisting of an indefinable mixture of intellectual hubris and compassion, the time when the first American advisers were sent into the Vietnam War. Not even his own advisers believe today that Kennedy would have prevented the escalation of the war.

Few presidents before Kennedy possessed an aura of inexorable progressivity and willingness to face risks and the ability to translate this aura into words and deeds (Alliance for Progress, civil rights). The following sentences have become legend, a classic version of the American Dream:

In the long history of the world, only a few generations have been granted the role of defending freedom in its hour of maximum danger. I do not shrink from this responsibility—I welcome it. I do not believe that any of us would exchange places with any other people or any other generation. The energy, the faith, the devotion which we bring to this endeavor will light our country and all who serve it—and the glow from that fire can truly light the world. And so, my fellow Americans: ask not what your country can do for you—ask what you can do for your country. My fellow citizens of the world: ask not what America will do for you, but what together we can do for the freedom of man.[193]

Kennedy himself felt a commitment to the values of the Founding Fathers, as attested to by his Secretary of State Dean Rusk: "Kennedy firmly believed, as Thomas Jefferson put it, that governments derive their just powers from the consent of the governed. . . . he believed, that this idea remained the most powerful and revolutionary political idea in the world today."[194]

Penetrating the sphinx-like character of Lyndon B. Johnson is one of the most difficult tasks confronting his biographers. No other president remains the subject of so many rumors and myths, as is demonstrated by the massive differences among historical and political evaluations of the Johnson presidency. On the one hand, he is cheered as the architect of the Great Society; remembered for his "compassion for the poor," as Walt Rostow, one of his closest advisers, put it;[195] and praised for his personal qualities as "a very human president" (Jack Valenti, 1975).[196] On the other hand, American history has forever consigned Johnson to be the president responsible for the debacle of the Vietnam War.[197]

Without doubt Johnson realized part of his vision of the Great Society with his civil rights programs and the "War on Poverty":

I do not believe that the Great Society is the ordered, changeless, and sterile battalion of the ants. It is the excitement of becoming—always becoming, trying, probing, falling, resting, and trying again—but always trying and always gaining. In each generation—with toil and tears we have had to earn our heritage again.[198]

Johnson owed his domestic political successes to two characteristics: first, the liaison between the White House and Congress during the Johnson era resembled a honeymoon; and second, Johnson understood how to formulate and shape his policies "with the grain of history" (Richard Neustadt). In 1982 Rostow wrote of LBJ:

Johnson judged that, in the cyclical rhythm of American history, he had come to responsibility at a rare, transient interval of opportunity for social progress. And so, on domestic issues, he used up his capital as he believed a President should achieve much, left Washington with a sense of how much he would have liked to do, but left also a nation determined to pause and rest and catch its breath rather than continue to plunge forward.[199]

At the same time Robert A. Caro, for whom Lyndon Johnson was "the goddamndest paradox in history," wrote a very critical biography of the thirty-sixth president of the United States. Caro's book *The Years of Lyndon Johnson: The Path to Power* (Vol. 1, 1982; two further volumes followed) has met with widely varying reactions among Johnson experts.[200] The last word on this enigmatic president clearly remains to be spoken.

While Johnson was unable to succeed in foreign policy, his successor failed miserably in the domestic political leadership of the country. However, Richard M. Nixon will go down in history with Franklin D. Roosevelt and Harry Truman as one of the most competent twentieth-century presidents in foreign policy. Although from the beginning the Europeans did not take Nixon's involvement in the Watergate scandal seriously (after all, scandals like the P-2 conspiracy in Italy, the Bokassa diamonds of Giscard D'Estaing, and the involvement of German politicians in the Flick affair have been routine occurrences in European politics since the Middle Ages), the morally puritanical Americans have only recently begun to rehabilitate Nixon and to recall his foreign policy triumphs. (*Newsweek* featured Nixon in May 1986 on its cover with the words: "He's back.")[201] However exaggerated Nixon's euphoric utterance about the SALT I agreement may appear today ("1972 will long be remembered as the year of the greatest progress since the end of World War II toward a lasting peace in the world"[202]), his foreign policy strategies, détente toward the USSR and China, ending the Vietnam War, and signing of the ABM and SALT treaties, not only influenced a decade of American politics, but also opened up the possibility of a change in postwar strategic thinking and behavior in the West as in the East:

After a period of confrontation, we are entering an era of negotiation. Let all nations know that during this Administration our lines of communication will be open. We seek an open world—open to ideas, open to the exchange of goods and people, a world in which no people, great or small, will live in angry isolation. We cannot expect to make everyone our friend but we can try to make no one our enemy.[203]

That the Soviet Union did not completely accept the American offer of rapprochement in various crisis areas, from Angola to Nicaragua, is not the fault of the Nixon administration.

Such Nixon sentences as "to a crisis of the spirit, we need an answer of the spirit," or "we see the hope of tomorrow in the youth of today," or "America's record in this century has been unparalleled in the world's history for its responsibility, for its generosity, for its creativity and for its progress"[204] will remain unforgotten. At the same time, they cannot mitigate the tragic paradoxes in Nixon's being and behavior. They were of his own making and ultimately led to the crass misuse of political power.[205]

Gerald Ford was destined to be president of the United States for only two years. His decision to pardon Nixon was a courageous one:

My concern is the immediate future of this great country. In this, I dare not depend upon my personal sympathy as a long-time friend of the former President, nor any professional judgement as a lawyer, and I do not. As President, my primary concern must always be the greatest good of all people in the United States whose servant I am. . . . My conscience tells me it is my duty, not merely to proclaim domestic tranquility but to use every means that I have to ensure it.[206]

Gerald Ford restored normality to American politics (which was characterized as *A Time to Heal* [1979]),[207] but he was unable to disassociate himself in the public eye from the negative Nixon-Watergate syndrome. Thus, Ford lost a close race to Jimmy Carter. The act of forgiveness could only be carried out credibly by "a man of substance," as Hedley Donovan praised Ford.

It is still too early to judge whether Jimmy Carter's presidency will be remembered in history as one of the most unsuccessful of the postwar period. Carter, an outsider from the South, came to Washington promising to bring fear into the "bureaucratic establishment" of the capital on the Potomac. The result was that practically no other president achieved so little consensus between the White House and Congress.[208] His foreign policy successes—Camp David and the Panama Canal Treaty—were overshadowed by the invasion of Afghanistan by Soviet troops and the American hostage drama in Iran.

One of Carter's most positive qualities was his desire to purge America of Vietnam and Watergate by attempting to reintroduce the idealistic element into American foreign policy with his "human rights policy." Carter's Secretary of State Cyrus Vance emphasized that American foreign policy traditionally required idealistic as well as realistic components:

I think it's essential that our foreign policy reflects basic principles, and one of those is a strong sense of idealism and adherence to certain fundamental principles such as human rights. At the same time I think foreign policy has to be a realistic foreign policy, so that one has to provide both realism and idealism and that's what we've attempted to do and we didn't do it perfectly. We made mistakes, as I would be one of the first to admit, but I think to suggest that somehow at once the policy has to be either all idealistic or all Realpolitik is unrealistic.[209]

The condemnation of the human rights abuses of totalitarian and authoritarian regimes today is ultimately to be attributed to the Carter administration.[210] Nonetheless, what his fellow Americans hold against Carter most was his skepticism toward the idea of progress: "We have learned that *more* is not necessarily *better,* that even our great nation has its recognized limits, and that we can neither answer all questions nor solve its problems."[211] Evidently impressed by the Club of Rome's visions of the 1970s, Jimmy Carter was the first president of the United States to propagate the idea of material modesty and restraint of technological progress in the country of unlimited possibilities. To Americans, this seems to have been his least forgiveable sin.

Ronald Reagan, as the obliging insider from the West, owes his success to his replacement of Carter's ideology of humility with an ideology of economic strength, military greatness, and technological progress. Reagan's entire philosophy was clearly defined in his first inaugural address:

Well, this Administration's objective will be a healthy, vigorous, growing economy that provides equal opportunities for all Americans with no barriers born of bigotry or discrimination. . . . All must share in the productive work of this "new beginning," and all must share in the bounty of a revived economy. With the idealism and fair play which are the core of our system and our strength, we can have a strong, prosperous America at peace with itself and the world. So as we begin, let us take inventory. . . . It is time for us to realize that we are too great a nation to limit ourselves to small dreams. We're not, as some would have us believe, doomed to an inevitable decline. I do not believe in a fate that will fall on us no matter what we do. I do believe in a fate that will fall on us if we do nothing. So, with all the creative energy at our command, let us begin an era of national renewal. Let us renew our faith and our hope. We have every right to dream heroic dreams. . . . And as we renew ourselves, here in our own land we will be seen as having greater strength throughout the world. We will again be the exemplar of freedom and a beacon of hope for those who do not now have freedom. . . . As for the enemies of freedom, those who are potential adversaries, they will be reminded that peace is the highest aspiration of the American people. We will not negotiate for it, sacrifice for it; we will not surrender for it—now or ever![212]

After an era of national humiliation (Vietnam, Iran) and political decay (Watergate), President Reagan's solution of "national renewal," with his observation that "we are too great a nation to limit ourselves to small dreams," hit home. Reagan, with his spirit of the "nice boy next door and bright sunshine,"[213] actually succeeded in giving back the Americans their courage after the failures of the 1970s and in restoring American virtues such as patriotism, belief in progress, self-confidence, and entrepreneurship.[214]

Not since the days of Franklin Delano Roosevelt or, to some extent, John F. Kennedy, has any president enjoyed such popularity, used his power and freedom as president so cleverly, persuasively influenced Congress and public opinion, or pursued his domestic and foreign strategies with such persistence as Ronald Reagan. In his first one hundred days in office, he established his anti-inflationary, laissez-faire economic program, which was to reduce drastically the role of the state in social and economic matters. "The whole Reagan economic program, enacted just about as he wanted it, in just over six months, was the most formidable domestic initiative any President had driven through since the hundred days of Franklin Roosevelt."[215] This economic program seemingly marked once and for all the end of four decades of the New Deal consensus that Richard Nixon invoked even at the beginning of the 1970s with his statement "we are all Keynesians"—a shocking one for many Republicans.

Reagan's foreign policy program seems to be more difficult to assess. Not least because of Reagan's often crudely ideological rhetoric in respect to the Soviets, many Europeans considered it a resurrection of the Cold War and the containment and rollback policies of the 1950s. But the president's course would ultimately reveal itself to be "mainstream foreign policy."[216] That this was to be was confirmed by Lawrence Eagleburger in 1982:

What I think he's seeking in foreign policy is far less fundamental and, despite the fact that many Europeans would disagree with me, I think what he's seeking in foreign policy terms is much more in the mainstream of American postwar history than what he's doing in the domestic area.[217]

At the moment it would be premature to examine Reagan's domestic and foreign policy concepts in greater detail. And yet, the preliminary conclusions on Ronald Reagan's term of office made by *Time* magazine with its "Yankee Doodle Magic" cover story (July 1986) are worthy of mention:

Perhaps the Reagan era is to be remembered simply as a quietus. Perhaps it is the illusion of a long summer celebration of the past, an illusion necessary before the future can begin. And yet Reagan's significance is larger than that. He has restored the authority of the American presidency. He has given Americans an optimism, a pride in themselves and in their country that they have not possessed since the death of John Kennedy. And he is the first President since F.D.R. to alter the debate over what the role of the government should be. As one keeps score in the art of the possible, that is not bad at all.[218]

Only history can tell how valid this assessment of the Reagan administration will remain.

# 8

# Political Theory and Praxis

The contention that America has no political history of ideas of its own is based merely on recurring European "prejudices." In the following discussion, an attempt will be made to introduce the pragmatic and simultaneously idealistic qualities of American theory. It distinguishes itself from its European counterpart in that it has never contained chiliastic or utopian goals, but only progressivist ideals applicable and realizable in this world. This posture, a typical one for Americans, was once expressed characteristically by Theodore Roosevelt: "No ideal can be right for this world if it is not filtered to be used in this world. . . . words are of use only as they are translated into deeds."[219] A classical philosopher could not have provided a more philosophical and motivating definition of success than that offered by the American philosopher and poet Ralph Waldo Emerson:

To laugh often and to love much, to win respect of intelligent persons and the affection of children; to appreciate beauty; to find the best in others; to give one's self; to leave the world a lot better whether by a healthy child, a garden patch, or a redeemed social condition; to have played and laughed with enthusiasm and sung with exaltation, to know even one life has breathed easier because you have lived—this is to have succeeded.[220]

Since Plato Europeans have engaged primarily in the discussion of the ideal conditions of human thought, progress, and human reason, whereas Americans have limited themselves since the beginning of their independence to consideration of the real conditions of human thought, progress, and human reason.[221] American political theory actually emerged from the revolutionary praxis of the progressivist ideology of the "First New Nation" (Seymour Martin Lipset), which aspired to the realization of the basic values declared important for national survival, such as freedom, liberty, democracy, human rights, and equality. Thus, from the beginning the progressivist quality of American political theory lay in the continuity of revolutionary practice and its constitutional institutionalization, which as a fundamental conservative element of the American political tradition still shapes the historical and political consensus in America today.

It is the American creed, rooted in the English Protestant moralism of the seventeenth century and in the liberal rationalism of the eighteenth, which brought Louis Hartz and Daniel Boorstin to the convincing claim that the political, social, and economic tradition in America was a liberal one from the outset. As a result, feudalism and monarchy were unknown, and significant strains of communism, socialism, or fascism never took hold.[222] According to Samuel Huntington, these circumstances explain why the conflict of ideas did not figure as prominently in political theory in the United States as it did in Europe. Rather, it was conflict between the plurality of groups, all of which recognize liberalism as the American progressivist ideology:

Cleavage in the United States thus does not take the form of idea versus idea, as in Europe, but rather of idea versus fact. The conflict is between two groups who believe in the same political principles. . . . Conflict is the child of consensus, and the most passionate and traumatic controversies among Americans derive from the liberal-democratic values on which they so overwhelmingly agree.[223]

Moreover, Americans do not avoid or repress conflicts; their flexible consensus of liberal values presents them with possibilities for compromise. Thus, they have been spared the bitter dogmatic struggles common to their European counterparts. As Robert McClosky observed, liberal American ideology is "not a consistent body of dogmas tending in the same direction, but a conglomerate of ideas which may be and often are logically inconsistent. It is characteristic of the American mind . . . to hold contradictory ideas simultaneously without bothering to resolve the potential conflict between them."[224] The persistence and acceptance of ambivalent and perhaps even contradictory ideas above all characterize the pragmatic spirit of open, liberal, and pluralistic American society. Through the entire course of its history, American democracy has distinguished itself on the basis of its willing recourse to the method of voluntary consensus and compromise in the interest of overcoming mutual conflicts and crises.

Certain historical and political factors have been crucial for the uniquely homogeneous development of American political theory. A significant indicator of American antipathy toward power and domination is the fact that American thought has no theory of state. The Americans consciously avoided adopting the modern European ideas of a Machiavelli, Hobbes, or Bodin, for the concentration and centralization of state power and authority was suspect from the beginning.

As early as 1891, James Bryce saw fit to explain that "Americans had no theory of the State and felt no need for one. . . . The nation is nothing but so many individuals. The government is nothing but certain representatives and officials."[225]

Historically, powerful leadership regimes generally arise either out of the need to destroy a traditional system or to combat foreign enemies. In comparison to its European counterparts, the American social system has always been weak because the absence of feudal or monarchical regimes to be deposed obviated the need for concentrations of power or the establishment of a strong government. James Madison once remarked laconically that "in Europe power granted charters to liberty, [whereas] in America, liberty granted charters to power."[226] In the same context, Tocqueville remarked that the Americans "arrived at a state of democracy without having to endure a democratic revolution, and . . . are born equal instead of becoming so."[227] As Huntington points out, this mode of thought originated in the political theory of the Founding Fathers, who contended that "men in power would be tempted to do evil and would infringe the rights and liberties of others unless they were restrained by countervailing power. Hence government must be weak because men are evil."[228] Their more optimistic successors, though convinced of an opposing view of human nature, came to the same conclusion concerning the form of government: "Because men are inherently well intentioned and reasonable, strong government is not necessary to control or direct them: government should be weak because men are good."[229]

Similarly, the United States is the most modern society with the most antiquated institutions and the most antiauthoritarian consciousness. As Richard Neustadt wrote, "The constitutional convention of 1787 is supposed to have created a government of 'separated powers.' It did nothing of the sort. Rather, it created a government of separated institutions *sharing* powers."[230] With the system of government of separate, power-sharing institutions, with the system of checks and balances and the separation of church and state ("no bishop, no king"), the United States created a decentralized, weak, democratic, and antiauthoritarian government, reflected in its political thought as tolerance, the capacity for consensus and compromise, and sometimes uniformity. In terms of organization it was diametrically opposed to European systems of government. In Europe opposition to internal social modernization ultimately forced modernization of the political system, whereas in America the acceptance of internal social modernization ruled out modernization of the political system. "The United States," writes Huntington, "thus combines the world's most modern society with one of the world's more antique polities."[231]

A European variant of conservatism could never establish itself in America, for the United States has only liberal traditions and institutions to offer for conservation. The ambivalence of the American idea of progress lies in the "idea versus institution gap" (Samuel P. Huntington), in the realization of ideal institutions.

The following discussion will attempt to present a politicophilosophical mor-
phology of the American idea of progress rooted in five theoretical and practical
concepts: idealism and realism, republicanism and federalism, and liberalism.


## IDEALISM AND REALISM

The American Dream is nothing more than the realization of unrealized European
ideals on the North American continent. As the American poet Archibald
McLeish put it in 1960, some would say that the liberation of humanity, the
freedom of the individual and the mind, is only a dream. In that they were right,
he said, that is the American Dream. The dream of being able to erect a better
world on the other side of the Atlantic, "a Citty upon a Hill," drove the Puritan
pilgrims West at the beginning of the seventeenth century, just as the ideologies
of Yankeeism and the self-made individual drew swarms of European settlers
to the land of unlimited possibilities in the nineteenth century. The American
Dream, the striving toward a better, more reasonable order, toward the greatest
possible individual freedom with the highest possible degree of equal rights, has
become the dominant spiritual element in the New World, one providing it with
structure and progressivist promise. "America is a land of wonders," wrote
Alexis de Tocqueville,


in which everything is in constant motion and every change seems an improvement. The
idea of novelty is there indissolubly connected with the idea of amelioration. No national
boundary seems to be set to the efforts of man; and in his eyes what is not yet done is
only what he has not yet attempted to do.[232]


Thomas Jefferson never tired of proclaiming to his countrymen and the world
his belief in the American Dream ("life, liberty, and the pursuit of happiness"),
the mission of the New World as the leader of humankind, and the rich soil of
North America, on which people could pursue their individual interests and
inclinations freely and equally. The way Americans see themselves, their national
identity, does not rely as much as that of other peoples on a common ancestry,
culture, history, language, or religion. Rather, it is primarily motivated by the
idealist fundamental values of freedom, equality, popular sovereignty, and human
rights on which the nation was constituted. Together these basic convictions
comprise a political creed, a secular religion with a progressive goal: "The
American mission for the future is to realize the values of the past." From the
beginning there was an essential connection between this American idealism and
the real conditions of existence on the North American continent. For it was the
incredible natural wealth of this open, almost unsettled continent that made
possible the realization of the American concept of freedom and the pursuit of
happiness. The close link between the idealist political creed and the actual
conditions of the New World was clear from the very beginning. The "land of

the free'' was simultaneously the ''land of opportunity.'' American idealism and patriotism has always related to both.[233]

The German philosopher Hugo Münsterberg, who came to Harvard University around the turn of the century, characterized the ideals of the American Dream in four basic categories:[234] ''In America's public life it is the spirit of self-determination, in economic life the spirit of self-occupation, in social life the spirit of self-assertion, and in intellectual life the spirit of self-perfection.''[235] Münsterberg thus described the political, social, and economic American culture, which had remained essentially unchanged for centuries.

When attempting to portray the idealism of the political culture, that is, the political attitudes, socioeconomic modes of behavior, and common assumptions prevailing in the United States, one must first of all refer to the basic contrasts within this culture.[236] Particularly noteworthy is that a modern America marked by constant change coexists with elements of a conservative political culture formed by a fundamentalist religious tradition; the social and ethnic heterogeneity of American society contrasts with the homogeneity of a way of life so characteristic for the political, social, and economic culture of the ''middle class'' and ''mainstream politics.'' The American middle class is the foundation of political idealism and realism in American culture and its political establishment. The political attitudes of middle-class Americans are an effortless blend of contradictions between increased mobility and cultural continuity, progressivist optimism and old-fashioned, vaguely religious, moralistic, patriotic virtues. Although the homogeneity of the middle class does not transcend the pluralism of the society and the regional specifics of ethnic groupings, upwardly mobile individuals from almost all social groups conform to middle-class standards. Thus, the social and ideological dominance of the middle class by no means excludes the diversity of ''ethnic politics'' and regionally conditioned differences. At the same time, however, the middle class is the guarantor of ideological continuity in the midst of constant economic and social change.[237]

The middle class takes the idealistic American values for granted. ''Liberty'' and ''freedom,'' that is, the indisputable right to lead one's private life as one will without interference and to express political and religious opinions freely, are ranked first among the values held. In addition, middle-class individuals remain convinced that a good education and some effort will ensure them a chance at personal success and social and economic mobility. Thus, the middle class sees itself as the guardian of the optimistic, uninterrupted American tradition of idealism and individualism. Middle-class thinking also recognizes no essential contradiction between isolated state intervention in the national economy as long as individual opportunities and spheres of action are expanded in the process and as long as the reproduction of conditions guaranteeing individual success in American society, the ''American way of life,'' remain the central task and duty of the government. Here, however, the sense of reality and pragmatic thinking of the middle class fuse into skeptical acceptance.[238] Since the end of the 1960s, the middle-class ethos, with its emphasis on success and performance and its traditional conception of family, religion, and patriotism, has been influenced by the "new morality" of a radically individualist philosophy of self-development and self-realization.[239] The mid-1970s subsequently witnessed a reaction by traditional middle-class and ethnic groups to this rigorous interpretation of "post-materialist and post-bourgeois individualism," which had become particularly widespread among the younger members of the educated upper middle class.[240] Under the Reagan administration traditional middle-class values seem to have reasserted themselves, although today there exists greater diversity and substantially more tolerance for the unusual than there had been in, say, the 1950s.

One should not assume that the idealistic political values of the American middle class, and more or less those of the East Coast establishment, are smoothly integrated into political practice. Although the gulf between political ideal and political reality may be prominent in all social systems, Americans appear to feel it especially keenly because of their "unique commitment to liberal, democratic, and egalitarian values." In his recent work, Samuel P. Huntington refers to this problem, which he identifies as the "promise versus performance gap" and the "idea versus institution gap":

The history of American politics is the repetition of new beginnings and flawed outcomes, promise and disillusion, reform and reaction. American history is the history of the efforts of groups to promote their interests by realizing American ideals. What is important, however, is not that they succeed but that they fail, not that the dream is realized but that it is not and never can be realized completely or satisfactorily. In the American context there will always be those who say that the institutional glass is half-empty and who will spill much passion attempting to fill it to the brim from the spring of idealism. But in the nature of things, particularly in America, it can never be more than half-full. This gap between promise and performance creates an inherent disharmony, at times latent, at times manifest, in American society.[241]

This ambivalence between political ideal and practical realization became particularly manifest in American society during the moralist Creedal Passion periods,[242] and most recently during the student unrest at the end of the 1960s and the beginning of the 1970s. In this period the attempt was made once more, this time by the youth of America, to eliminate or at least reduce the "idea versus institution gap." This most recent Creedal Passion period in the twentieth century

witnessed a dramatic renewal of the democratic spirit in America. . . . The spirit of protest, the spirit of equality, the impulse to expose and correct inequalities were abroad in the land. The themes of the 1960s were those of Jacksonian Democracy and the muckraking Progressives; they embodied ideas and beliefs which were deep in the American tradition but which usually do not command the passionate intensity of commitment that they did in the 1960s. That decade bore testimony to the validity of the democratic idea. It was a decade of democratic surge, of the reassertion of democratic egalitarianism.[243]

The profound difference between the New Left in America and the New Left in Europe is especially important in this context (whereby the German student revolt, again, occupies a special role).[244] The protesting European students aspired to the realization of Marxist ideals, while the vast majority of protesting American students were seeking reform of institutions and the actual realization of American ideals and the American creed. The aims and aspirations of the rebelling American students were clearly articulated in the idealistic speech by the law student Meldon E. Levine at Harvard's graduation ceremonies in 1969. "What is the protest all about?" Levine began his speech:

Our protest is not an attempt to subvert institutions or an attempt to challenge values which have been affirmed for centuries. We are NOT . . . conspiring to destroy America. We are attempting to do precisely the reverse: we are affirming the values which YOU have instilled in us and which you have taught us to respect. You have told us repeatedly that trust and courage were standards to emulate. You have convinced us that equality and justice were inviolable concepts. You have taught us that authority should be guided by reason and tempered by fairness. AND WE HAVE TAKEN YOU SERIOUSLY. . . . You have made us idealists and then told us to go slowly. All we ask is that you allow us to realize the very values which you have held forth.[245]

Young European Marxists would probably have used such a speech to attack the reactionary and traditional values of the older generation in order to proclaim their own radical and revolutionary principles. By contrast, the American students demanded only the realization of the American ideology of progress and idealism, holding on to values shared by the older generation and their own.

Comparing the Western European gap between ideas and institutions with its American counterpart, for example, one notes that the gap is smaller in America than in Western Europe or elsewhere in the world because American political institutions are ultimately more open, more liberal, and more democratic than other social systems were or are. The only danger that could threaten American society would be a new Creedal Passion awakening that would so surpass previous ones in moral vehemence that it would destroy these institutions in the name of its own liberal democratic ideals. "Inoculated against the appeal of foreign ideas, America has only to fear her own."[246]

Another historical factor is of particular importance for the development of American idealism. Whereas progress in Europe generally had to be furthered against history, in America "in the earlier periods, history and progress (in the sense of realizing American ideals) . . . went hand in hand." In later phases, however, "the achievement of American ideals involved more the restoration of the past than the realization of the future, and progress and history worked increasingly at cross purposes."[247] In the future Americans will also have to learn to cope with this specifically American ambivalence in the belief of idealism and progress.

## REPUBLICANISM AND FEDERALISM

If idealism and pragmatism are the moral core of American progressivist optimism, then republicanism and federalism represent the finest achievement of the American Revolution and American Constitution. These two political conceptions were invoked eloquently as Thomas Jefferson took office as the third president of the United States in 1801 saying, "We are all Republicans, we are all Federalists." On these two constitutional pillars, the republican and the federal, the Founding Fathers built the free, democratic, and pluralistically federalist entity of the United States of America, which seems to have lost none of its vitality and willingness to experiment even today.[248] Nelson A. Rockefeller, who in the 1960s advocated the idea of a new and creative federalism, wrote:

The federal system, conceived by the Founding Fathers and embodied in the Constitution, is a crucial stone of our arch of liberty. For us, it has provided unity without the sacrifice of desirable diversity, strength to achieve national goals while simultaneously enhancing human dignity, and an energized environment of law and custom wherein economic and social progress is achieved through equal opportunity for free individuals rather than the totalitarian dictates of a ruling hierarchy.[249]

One of the most significant advantages of the American representative republic over classical democracy was that it had been possible to realize the principle of popular sovereignty within an enormous territorial expanse and a large population. At the same time, the republic was equipped with a society characterized by great social, cultural, and economic diversity and major differences of interest, which, however, had an extremely stabilizing effect on American society at large and its republican system. Clearly, its plurality of interests enables American political life to avoid the old evil of classical democracy, the tyranny of a popular majority.

But the fathers of the Constitution were aware not only of that evil, but also of the independence or even tyranny of democratic governmental organs themselves. It was this latter concern that the anti-Federalists immediately expressed in their main criticism of the new constitutional order of 1787.[250] They considered the idea of rule by a small number of educated and politically experienced aristocrats irreconcilable with the spirit of American democratic values. The anti-Federalists further defended their concept of a small republic with a small, homogeneous population, and opposed the balance created between the individual states and the nation, which, according to them, favored a strong central government. Their explicit rejection of the "Union" contained the implicit proviso that the new situation would endanger republican freedom of the individual states. It was precisely this freedom that they believed the federal government was obliged to protect above all else.[251]

The Federalists themselves were aware of the eventuality that power could become concentrated in the federal government and that such power could be used against the interests of the people. They also understood the ambivalent quality of the federalist model of popular sovereignty: on the one hand, that a large, free republic requires a large degree of governmental power for survival, and, on the other hand, that a lopsided concentration of power poses the greatest danger to the maintenance of freedom. The Federalists expected that these differing conceptions of popular sovereignty would peacefully coexist within the framework of the new republican-federal system. They expected that the people would always identify more closely with individual state governments and that the federal government would be active in federal and foreign policy. Contrary to these expectations of the Founding Fathers, however, the question about the core of republican federal democracy and, above all, about the value of the majority government at the federal level relative to interest group politics and participatory democracy remained unresolved. American political culture has been marked for two centuries by mistrust of all forms of institutionalized state power and anxiety about the centralized abuse of power. Expressed in positive terms, that culture has been determined by the commitment to plural federalist and local grass-roots democracy, to politics formed by the direct involvement of citizens, and to communal self-administration and neighborly assistance.[252]

The continuing political debate about the substance and essence of American federalism can be traced back to the inconclusive definition of the federalist idea in the original constitution of 1787.[253] The Founding Fathers made only cursory note of the fact that their understanding of federalism contained specific dangers and inherent conflicts between the federal government and the individual states (which were granted limited sovereignty). Until the secession of the Southern states in 1860–61, constitutional reality in the United States was formed by the competition between two entities ("dual federalism," "dual sovereignty"), each of which regarded itself as sovereign in the same area. This "dualistic federalism" claimed competence from the Tenth Amendment, which reserves for the states those powers not entrusted to the federal government. It stressed the concept of dual sovereignty of nation and state in disputed spheres, derived the notion of "exclusive" competencies therefrom, and ultimately assured rivalry in the allocation of the contentious spheres.[254] The smouldering conflict broke out in the Civil War, when the Southern states, with the famed theoretician of federalism John C. Calhoun, referred to the federal character of the Union in order to justify their secession. The Union had by no means eliminated the sovereignty of the individual states, which because of customs disputes and the problem of slavery now wanted to obtain their independence by leaving the Union. The doctrine of dual sovereignty was not clarified until 1868, with the passage of the Fourteenth Amendment, which unambiguously gave precedence to membership in the Union. These federal combinations, which were left open when the United States was founded, created the potential for many future conflicts; how and if the problems could be overcome was still uncertain at the end of the eighteenth century.

Nationalization, or the transfer of political equilibrium from the states to the federal level, and a parallel shift of power from Congress to the president and the president's ever increasing bureaucratic apparatus ("big government") characterized twentieth-century development in the American federalist system. This tendency toward centralization, supported and actively promoted by liberal Democrats, was reflected as "cooperative federalism" particularly in the administration of Franklin Delano Roosevelt. The beginnings of contractual cooperation between the federal government and the individual states can be detected quite early. It already appeared in the institutionalization of horizontal self-coordination by the Governor's Conference, first called in 1908, and the Council for State Governments, created in 1933. The New Deal programs made explicit use of the theory of cooperative federalism in their use of "grants in aid" to the states.[255] Cooperative federalism, practiced in the 1960s, was doomed in that it encouraged economic dependence and reduced the independence of the individual states. According to Daniel J. Elazar, the director of the Center for the Study of Federalism,

once the idea that the federal government could act in any area as it willed became accepted as the norm under the theory of cooperative federalism, no further justification was needed, and the programs could be designed to place the thrust of the action on federal shoulders, thereby reducing the state and local roles in the programs that emerged.[256]

The first Republican president after the Second World War, Dwight D. Eisenhower, attempted to hinder this process and revive the old theory of dual federalism in modified and modern form.[257] Eisenhower's efforts to decentralize federal affairs and to return areas of jurisdiction to the individual states ultimately failed, for "in order to achieve this reversal it would first be necessary for the national government to acquire sufficient control over the determination of how functions were to be shared by the several governmental arenas."[258]

In other words, Eisenhower's plans for decentralization would have initially required a centralization of power impossible in a "noncentralized political system." "It is impossible to centralize power in the sense referred to here without changing the essential constitution of the system."[259] This example reflects the ambivalence of contemporary American governmental practice, an ambivalence with which Eisenhower's Republican successors Nixon, Ford, and Reagan also had to struggle. For although the Federalists, Alexander Hamilton and John Adams, had once been the supporters of a strong federal government, with Thomas Jefferson and James Madison wanting to grant more rights and freedom to the individual states, in the twentieth century the progressivist interpretation of federalism was completely reversed. Since the 1930s, the Democrats have been the ones centralizing and expanding the power of the federal government in Washington, while the Republicans became the proponents of decentralization and the dissolution of "big government" in Washington. One can see what a sisyphian task this has become by studying the New Federalism plans of Richard Nixon and Ronald Reagan.

The Republican governor of New York, Nelson A. Rockefeller, first revived the discussion of federalism in the early 1960s in a series of lectures at Harvard University through which he pleaded for a new, creative, innovative, and pluralist federalism.[260] President Johnson borrowed this idea, and the phrase "creative federalism," although he eliminated the concept of cooperative federalism for reducing the growth of federal jurisdiction and intervention. However, during the Johnson administration the subsidies grew larger than ever before, although it should be noted that the large part of these "grants" can be traced back to the initiative of the liberal Democratic federal government and its bureaucracy, and not to demands on the part of the individual states themselves. The programs brought into life by the federal subsidies and administered at the state level extended to almost all of the problematic areas of modern American industrial society: city planning and renovation programs, public housing, education, training and educational programs for the unemployed, measures for the creation of jobs for the young and minorities, unemployment benefits, welfare, "food stamps," assistance for care of children and the poor, health insurance for the poor and elderly, antidrug and anticrime campaigns, public transportation, and so on.

This enormous growth of responsibility and areas of jurisdiction for the federal government necessarily brought with it new modus operandi in federal cooperation. This rapid expansion of the network of federal subsidies led to the creation of new interest groups profiting from the grants-in-aid programs. In addition, the activism of the federal government brought together various officials with direct involvement in subsidized programs, such as administrators and public servants, at the local and state levels. They all organized themselves on the national level as interest groups and, through private lobbies, gained influence over the creation of future governmental programs. In this way cooperative federalism produced a new pluralistic system of organizations and interest groups. The most important "intergovernmental lobbies" to emerge from cooperative federalism included the National Governors' Conference (with fifty-four governors of states and territories), the National Conference of State Legislators (with 7,600 delegates from individual state legislators and their assistants), the National League of Cities (representing 14,700 cities), the U.S. Conference of Mayors (representing 500 big cities), and the National Association of Counties, formed by delegates from 1,500 counties. Today the intergovernmental lobby continues to influence the Federal grants-in-aid programs in its own interest, with the help of its lobbyists and expenditures of several million dollars a year.[261]

Richard Nixon adopted Rockefeller's concept of creative federalism in his State of the Union message in 1969 and presented it as "the New Federalism": "After a third of a century of power flowing from the people and the States to Washington it is time for a New Federalism in which power, funds and responsibility will flow from Washington to the States and to the people."[262] Nixon's suggestions for reform, which were to have halted the process of centralization and aided the independent development of states and communities, were to be implemented through "revenue sharing," an equitable distribution of national tax revenue, and a more flexible management of the grants-in-aid system. The administration also aimed to avoid crippling the initiative, innovativeness, and creativity of the individual state governments with overly restrictive guidelines and controls set in Washington.[263] The creed of the New Federalism was now clothed in appealing phrases in order to make the decentralization measures of the president sound more plausible. Thus, "Publius," alias William Safire, wrote in January 1970:

The purpose of the New Federalism is not to wrap liberal principles in conservative clothing, or vice versa; the purpose is to come to grips with a paradox: a need to protect both individual equality at the national level and individual uniqueness at the local level; and a need to both establish national goals and decentralize government services.[264]

In March 1970 George Shultz, who at that time was secretary of labor, formulated several thoughts on the New Federalism:

We must act as one nation in determining national goals: We must act as a federation of States and localities in meeting those goals providing leeway for local option and individual diversity. . . . Local innovation and voluntary action must be aggressively encouraged, which limits the liability of the failure of worthwhile experiments and raises the chances of finding practical solutions. We must reinstill a new respect for individual responsibility and personal freedom, recognizing that the dignity of work is the counterpart of human dignity. The individual citizen must think and act on two levels: He must contribute to the determination of our national goals and then must involve himself locally in making those goals a reality where he lives. This may not seem like a revolutionary credo, but if it is followed in our time, it could have the same revolutionary impact that followed the acceptance of the ideas of the original Federalists.[265]

The ideas of both texts, which together constituted the heart of the New Federalist philosophy and which are still valid for the "anti–big government" orientation of the Bush administration, were at last incorporated into national policy once and for all when Nixon announced his New Federalism program in 1971:

The time has come for a new partnership between the Federal Government and the States and localities—a partnership in which we entrust the States and localities with a larger share of the Nation's responsibilities, and in which we share our Federal Revenues with them so that they can meet those responsibilities. To achieve this goal, I propose . . . that we enact a plan of revenue sharing historic in scope and bold in concept.[266]

Since 1972, $6 billion, half to individual states and the rest to cities and counties, were to be distributed as general revenue sharing, which (with the exception of education and social programs) could be put to any use by the agencies involved. In reality, however, the degree of independence that the Nixon administration envisioned for individual states was not achieved. At the end of the 1970s, the subsidies of this revenue sharing program amounted to over 12 percent of the federal funds transferred to the individual states and communities. On the other hand, the number of restricted, "categorical" subsidies increased considerably faster than the unrestricted revenue sharing payments from the federal government because the opportunities for interest groups, administrative bodies, and congressional committees to exert influence on the funding depended on the control of specific financial means. Thus, in 1976 restricted subsidies amounted to 79 percent of all federal payments in the revenue-sharing program.[267] Daniel J. Elazar fittingly characterized Nixon's decentralization programs as a genuine attempt at debureaucratization, an experiment that unfortunately coincided with Washington's measures to exert greater control:

Although sincerely presented as an effort to reverse the tide of centralization, . . . Nixon's "New Federalism" actually became a loosely connected series of efforts to concentrate control over programs old and new in Washington. . . . Thus, the Nixon years saw an increase in legislation—in the fields of education, health, welfare, environmental protection, industrial safety—which transferred policy-making authority to Washington from the states, sometimes accompanied by provisions for the devolution of responsibility for implementing the new policies and sometimes not.[268]

In view of these problematic relationships between the individual states and the federal government, it seems doubtful that President Reagan's plan for a New Federalism, as presented in his first inaugural address and then again in his State of the Union Address in January 1982, was actually successful. His "deregulation" plan originally presented a strategy for transferring over 40 (of almost 500) federal subsidy programs to the individual states after an eight-year transitional period financed from a special fund. The proposal also provided for the return of the expensive health care program to the federal government. But the Governors' Conference (1986), with its Democratic majority, rejected the program several times, since the Reagan proposals, while indeed granting greater decisional leeway on an intergovernmental level, linked this increased freedom to drastic cuts in social funding at the federal level. The majority of the individual states would, after transfer of the social expenditures and with no tax increases to offset them, be unable to fund these programs.[269] Peter Korn, the city manager of Rochester, New York, expressed his discontent with Reagan's federalism program in 1981 with the words:

I see the most important part of the Reagan budget as a shifting of the burden. I can see a real bitter struggle on the City Council when various groups clash over reduced money. The problem for local politicians is how to avoid being classified as the S.O.B.'s in all this.[270]

William Safire, an expert on federalism, sharply criticized Reagan's New Federalism philosophy: "Can it be that the Reagan approach is to centralize power, weaken governments and impoverish localities—making him the biggest anti-federalist since FDR?"[271]

That the principle of republican federalism is *the* governmental form of the United States, that the federal idea of "unity amidst diversity" has always been the young republic's motto *e pluribus unum,* and that the federal partnership between the states has steeped the new American society in progress and freedom, today remains undisputed among Democrats as well as Republicans. As Elazar appropriately wrote: "This federal relationship is what has governed the United States of America, what made the American revolution unique in the modern era and kept it from the pitfalls of totalitarianism."[272] It may well be that the policies of the New Federalism have not yet been fully worked out. Nonetheless, the Reagan government proved that it had the will to reduce the monstrous and bloated machinery of "big government" in Washington.

Of course, the "crisis" of American federalism cannot be overcome without taking into account the pluralist phenomenon, which reflects the dilemma and the ambivalence of American federalism: the multitude of interest groups, pressure groups, political action committees (PACs), and so on.[273] These groups may represent the original source of American freedom and progress, but they are anathema to a postmodern federalism.

## LIBERALISM VERSUS CONSERVATISM?

The following account will endeavor to show that neofederalist ideas have had a great deal in common with the development of neoconservatism since the beginning of the 1970s, that neoconservatism in America today is essentially a renaissance of the classic American liberalism dating from the founding of the nation, that there is no genuine American theory of conservatism, and that the modern Republican party is one of Jeffersonian Republicanism, whereas the modern Democratic party supports a Hamiltonian federalism.

Inspired by Thomas Jefferson, Ronald Reagan announced his New Federalism in July 1982 before the convention of the National Association of Counties in Baltimore, as follows:

Together, you and I are involved in an epic struggle to restore the governmental balance intended in our constitution and desired by our people. We are turning America away from yesterday's policies of big brother government. We are determined to restore power and authority to states and localities—returning as much decision-making as possible to the level of government where services are delivered. Thomas Jefferson once said: "I know no safe depository of the ultimate powers of . . . society but the people themselves." I agree with him. . . . The more government we can keep at the local levels in local hands, the better off we are and the more freedom we will have. . . . Let me quote Jefferson again. . . . He said: "Were not this great country already divided into states, that division must be made, that each might do for itself what concerns itself directly, and what it can do so much better than a distant authority. Every state is again divided into counties each to take care of what lies within its local bounds; each county again into townships or wards to manage minute details. . . . Were we directed from Washington when to sow and when to reap, we would soon want for bread."[274]

This is the unambiguous proclamation by a Republican of a revival of the classical liberal axiom of America: "that government governs best that governs least." If Ronald Reagan's landslide victory in November 1980 was celebrated as a conservative revolution, it may well have been because the new president proposed a redistribution of power from the state to society, from institutions to individuals, and from the federal government to the states; in other words, because he promised to restore the liberal tradition of America by means of a conservative revolution. His triumphal reelection in November 1984 conclusively confirmed the trend and general mood of neoconservatism, which appeared to have been irresistibly infiltrating American thought and politics since the Nixon era.[275] For many Europeans, Reagan's "conservative revolution" was an inconceivable phenomenon. Certainly, before making the attempt to explain neoconservatism, it is necessary to analyze American conservatism, or, to put it more precisely, the fact that there is no American conservatism in the European sense.

If one recalls the roots of the American republic, one will note that this country, aided by idealistic principles, evolved from a conservative revolution and that the American nation represents the product of an indestructible belief in progress imported into the United States by immigrants. If, in addition, one pursues the theses of Louis Hartz's classic work *The Liberal Tradition in America,* the liberalism of the founding ideology emerges as the political core of American consensus-oriented thought that has united liberals and conservatives, Democrats and Republicans ever since.[276] In contrast to Europe, in America liberalism was from the outset the only dominant progressivist ideology, and its impacts on American conservatism differed from those on its European conservatism. Because of the lack of feudal, monarchic, and aristocratic social structures, as well as significant class differences, and thanks to the separation of church and state, there remained only liberal traditions, institutions, and social structures for American conservatives to protect since the American Revolution and the institutionalization of their ideals in the Constitution. Clinton Rossiter thus wrote the following about the weak character of American conservatism as doctrine:

The reason that the American Right is not Conservative today is that it has not been Conservative for more than a hundred years. . . . Conservatism first emerged to meet the challenge of democracy. In countries like England it was able to survive the rise of this new way of life by giving way a little at a time under its relentless pounding, but in America the triumph of democracy was too sudden and complete. It came to society as well as to politics; it came early in the history of the Republic and found the opposition only half dug in. . . . The result was a disaster for genuine, old-country Conservatism. Nowhere in the world did the progressive, optimistic, egalitarian . . . thinking invade so completely the mind of an entire people. Nowhere was the Right forced so abruptly into such an untenable position. If there is any single quality that the Right seems always and everywhere to cultivate, it is unquestioning patriotism, and this, in turn, calls for unquestioning devotion to the nation's ideals. The long-standing merger of "American" and "democracy" has meant that to profess Conservatism is to be something less than "one hundred per cent American"; indeed, it is to question the nation's destiny. Worse than that, this merger has doomed outspoken Conservatism to political failure.[277]

Rossiter's remarks make clear that American conservatives would be regarded as "un-American" if they would dare to abandon the liberal American ideology of progress stemming from the time of the country's founding. But as Ralf Dahrendorf has noted, American conservatives are "characterised by the desire to preserve progress rather than to preserve any particular state of affairs."[278] The question that arises then is, whether an American conservatism exists at all, and if so, how it is expressed in a thoroughly liberal country with progressive values, a country thus lacking any significant socialist, communist, and fascist influences, and marked only sporadically by extremism from the Left (Black Panthers, Weathermen)[279] and Right (the KKK since 1867, McCarthyism, the John Birch Society of 1958).[280] In fact, the United States has some elements of conservative thought that must, however, be treated as a specifically American phenomenon. American conservatism has little in common with European conservatism.

The South and the Midwest are considered conservative by American standards. The South's movement to secede in the 1850s and 1860s reflected the conservatism of the separatists, who valued the sovereignty of the individual states more highly than that of the Union, and who interpreted slaveholding as a protected property right and therefore not explicitly forbidden by the Constitution.[281] The fact that their conservative posture conformed neither to the spirit of American federal principles nor to the spirit of the American Constitution can be addressed here only in passing. However paradoxical it might sound, it cannot be disputed that this conservative strain was by no means inherently "un-American," but instead a thoroughly plausible interpretation of the basic and progressivist American ideology that Southerners wanted to preserve. Nonetheless, it was ultimately the Republican Abraham Lincoln whom the Americans had to thank for saving the Union and abolishing the anti-American institution of slavery.

The conservative posture was manifested again in the United States after the Second World War and the rise of communism as a global totalitarian ideology. However, the "conservative intellectual movement" (George H. Nash) imported into America in the 1940s and 1950s principally from Europe never gained a firm foothold.[282] This new conservatism encompassed three separate directions of thought. The first group, whose members called themselves traditionalists, included Richard Weaver, Peter Viereck, Robert Nisbet, Leo Strauss, Eric Voegelin, William F. Buckley, and Russell Kirk. Shocked by totalitarianism and the rise of a secularized, uprooted mass society, the traditionalists pressed for a rejection of moral relativism, which had allegedly eroded the values of Western civilization and created an intolerable vacuum in which polymorphic ideologies were able to spread unchecked. These new conservatives, with their orientation toward Europe, glorified the wisdom of European conservatives such as Edmund Burke and Clemens Metternich, and called for a return to Christian orthodoxy and the classical theory of natural rights.[283] It is hardly surprising that this group, generally regarded as an esoteric circle with "un-American" value concepts, received little attention.[284]

A second group, consisting of ex-communists and ex-Trotskyists such as Whittaker Chambers, James Burnham, and Frank Meyer, all eloquent anticommunists from East and Central Europe who had found a new home in the United States, was characterized by a militant missionary antitotalitarianism marked by the deep conviction that the West was involved in a titanic struggle with the relentless opponent of "communism," which had as its goal the conquest of the world. The influence of these people on contemporary American attitudes was much greater than that of the traditionalists, and their credo may well have unintentionally given McCarthyism key ideas.[285]

The third group represented, and represents, an important and influential, indeed, the genuinely conservative school of thought in the United States: the "libertarians," also known as classical liberals. This group formed in order to resist the threat to freedom, the free market economy, and private initiative posed by a constantly expanding state. Convinced in the 1940s that America was on the brink of an irresistible slide into state planning and "socialism" ("the road to serfdom," as Friedrich Hayek called it), the classical liberals lent their ardent support to laissez-faire politics, which had influence in sections of the academic community and general public in the middle of the 1950s. Beginning with people like Friedrich Hayek and Ludwig von Mises in the 1940s and 1950s and progressing through Milton Friedman and the Chicago School in the 1960s to the neoconservative Arthur Laffer and the representatives of so-called supply-side economic theory of the late 1970s and 1980s, the libertarians—mostly trained economists—developed a subtly differentiated defense of the free market economy, in the process exercising influence on the strategies of Republican presidents.[286]

Elements of all three forms of conservatism made their way into politics on the national level in Senator Barry Goldwater's ideological struggle for the presidency in 1964, a struggle he lost to Lyndon Johnson.[287] After the 1964 election, however, it did not take long for a new conservative strain to manifest itself in the Nixon administration at the beginning of the 1970s. The final breakthrough came with the Reagan administration's compact domestic and foreign policy concept known as neoconservatism.

If representatives of classical liberalism appear in American history time and again as conservatives and are accepted as such, then one reason is their desire to defend and preserve the original progressivist ideology of the liberal American creed from the presumed or actual danger of paramorphosis. It could be said that conservatism as a phenomenon always makes its appearance in American history when its self-awareness is required as a corrective for American liberalism, thereby assuming the task of preserving national and traditional American values. As early as the 1950s, the liberal Samuel P. Huntington formulated in this sense his own neoconservative self-awareness, one he has retained to the present day:

In preserving the achievements of American liberalism, American liberals have no recourse but to turn to conservatism. . . . Conservatism is not, as the aristocratic interpretation argues, the monopoly of one particular class in history. Nor is it, as the autonomous school contends, appropriate in every age and place. It is, instead, relevant in a particular type of historical situation. That is the situation in which American liberalism finds itself today. Until the challenge of communism and the Soviet Union is eliminated or neutralized, a major aim of American liberals must be to preserve what they have created.[288]

From an economic point of view, the classical liberals, alias "new conservatives" of the 1940s and 1950s, made this position their own following Franklin Roosevelt's New Deal programs, which they regarded as the social democratization of laissez-faire liberalism. In their opinion it was precisely this trend that had to be stopped. At the end of the 1960s, after Lyndon Johnson's Great Society programs, the libertarians raised their voices once more, this time as neoconservatives who had set themselves the goal of ending the growth of the American welfare state. When asked in 1982 how American conservatism should be defined in lieu of the various trends since World War II, Norman Podhoretz, the editor of *Commentary* and one of today's best-known conservatives and ex-liberals, replied:

I would say . . . it is impossible to define American conservatism in the abstract or general because the definition of conservatism in this country varies depending on the particular historical context. Once upon a time, as recently as twenty years ago, what was called conservatism in this country was very similar to what was called liberalism in England and various other European countries, and what is called conservatism today in this country bears a greater resemblance to what was called liberalism in this country twenty years ago than it does to conservatism in certain other countries, so it's extremely difficult to define the term in any consistent way. . . . Neoconservatism today is very similar to the point of view of American liberalism at the time of John Kennedy.[289]

The formation of a neoconservative movement at the beginning of the 1970s, and the political achievement of their goals in the 1980s, should be understood as the reaction of conservative liberals to the social, political, and economic culture of the 1960s, as a reaction to the Johnson administration's democratic liberalism based on state intervention, antifederalism, and egalitarianism.[290] It is the protest of former liberals and present members of the Democratic party—academics and publishers like Daniel Bell, Nathan Glazer, Irving Kristol, Seymour Martin Lipset, Daniel P. Moynihan, Aaron Wildavsky, Robert Nisbet, and Jeane Kirkpatrick—against the burgeoning welfare state, especially its Great Society version, that led to a bureaucratization and growth of federal power that is still felt in Washington today. With their publications, such as *Commentary, The Public Interest,* and the editorial page of *The Wall Street Journal,* and their think-tanks, including the American Enterprise Institute, Hoover Institution, and Hudson Institute, the neoconservatives ensure the intellectual cohesion and public status of the group.

The neoconservatives minimize bureaucratic state intervention into individual affairs, have the market recognized as the only respectable instrument for the constant exploitation of resources, healthy growth, and protection of individual business freedom. They attribute responsibility for the decay of American political and social culture to the radical counterculture of the 1960s, a phenomenon which, in their opinion, asserted itself as egalitarianism as opposed to equal opportunity, as racial equality through bureaucratic measures (busing, affirmative action) as opposed to deeper political processes actually bringing about changes of awareness.[291] In foreign policy, now that the Vietnam syndrome and isolationist tendencies have been mostly overcome, the neoconservatives plead for a global offensive military strategy and abandonment of the policy of rapprochement ("appeasement") of the last two decades, which, they argue, has offered Moscow new spheres of influence.[292] The neoconservative progressivist credo of these former liberals, a credo that helped Ronald Reagan to victory, is summarized precisely by Norman Podhoretz:

I think most people who are called conservative today, including neo-conservatives, think that progress means a much greater rate of economic growth and much higher productivity, and a greater emphasis both on the market and on the individual as the source of both political action and economic energy. In terms of foreign policy, progress would mean rearmament as the modernization of the American defense posture, reestablishment of the balance of power, which most conservatives think has tilted toward the Soviet Union, and a stronger American role in international affairs in defense of liberty and democracy and in resistance to the spread of Soviet imperialism and of communist totalitarianism generally.[293]

Another contemporary movement should be mentioned in addition to the neoconservative influences supporting Ronald Reagan's policies: the New Right, which actually has little in common with the more elite East and West Coast brand of conservatism. The New Right, embodied by an anti-elitist, populist, and fundamentalist middle-class rebellion, has also contributed to Reagan's electoral victories. Various religious groupings, most of them organized into private churches by prominent television preachers like Jerry Falwell (head of the aggressive and religiously fanatic Moral Majority), support the goal of transforming the United States into a Christian nation. They proclaim their fundamentalist and moral aims through national organizations such as the National Conservative Political Action Committee and the Conservative Caucus, as well as in the magazines *Policy Review, Conservative Digest,* and *Moral Majority Report.* Among their goals are the elimination of the separation of church and state on a communal level, no emancipation for women, no homosexuality, no pornography, no abortions, censorship of books and television, introduction of prayer in public schools, and increased use of the death penalty. These aims blatantly contrast not only present mainstream liberal morality, the liberal democratic progressivist values of the nation, but also the basic attitude of the secular American constitutional system. Nonetheless, the New Right is represented in the Senate above all by Jesse Helms and Orrin Hatch, and by Phil Crane and Newt Gingrich in the House of Representatives.[294] Their absolutely "un-American" goals and values restrict the fundamentalist New Right to a clear minority in the country's political culture. The Reagan administration's disregard for its demands has also robbed this ultrareactionary movement of some of its militant zeal. At the same time, the New Right, as a symptom of today's anonymous mass democracy that can turn into a dangerous religious fundamentalism, self-righteous moralism, and vigilante justice, has to be taken seriously.[295]

At this point it may be asked whether the conservative Reagan Revolution[296] brought with it a crisis of American liberalism, or whether an already existing "crisis" of liberalism brought about neoconservatism. From the neoconservative point of view, the analysis of the crisis of American liberalism delivered in 1980 by Irving Kristol in the Forum of the Kennedy School of Government at Harvard University may be considered fundamental. Basing his argument on the thesis that "probably the most decisive intellectual political event of the twentieth century is the death of socialism, by which I mean . . . the death of socialism as a viable ideal," Kristol divided the history and tradition of American liberalism into three categories. *Liberalism I,* he says, is the old-fashioned individualistic, laissez-faire liberalism that dominated this country and others for the nineteenth century and a good part thereafter. *Liberalism II* is the welfare state liberalism, a liberalism that sought to place some restrictions on individual liberties, particularly individual rights such as the right of property, in order to achieve a collective good, namely, designating a level beneath which people must not fall into poverty, the provision of medical services, the provision of services and sustenance in old age, and so on. But interestingly, welfare state liberalism did not challenge the values of laissez-faire liberalism. That is, says Kristol, it wanted to make those values more widely shared. Or, to put it very bluntly, it wanted everyone to enjoy the American way of life and so decided to create a welfare state for that purpose. That was the impetus behind the New Deal, behind postwar reforms, and, originally, behind the Great Society.

*Liberalism III,* Kristol believes, born early in the 1960s, is something else again, and the distinctive aspect of contemporary liberalism, radical liberalism, is that it's no longer liberalism. Radical liberalism does not celebrate the American way of life and try to share it with everyone; rather, it holds the American way of life and American traditions in contempt. Kristol emphasizes that radical liberalism gave birth to neoconservatism. That is, suddenly a great many people who had thought of themselves as liberals, found themselves faced with some problems at odds with a liberalism that seemed to have no roots in American society and traditional American values, and certainly no respect for traditional American values.

Kristol defines the differences in liberalism very clearly by an example. He thinks it extraordinary that Jane Fonda, whom he considers a marvelous actress should be regarded by the media as a representative of the extreme left wing of the Democratic party and of American liberalism today. In his view, Jane Fonda is a nice, old-fashioned Maoist.[297]

Here Kristol graphically portrays the transformations of American liberalism that finally compelled the classical liberals to disassociate themselves definitively from radical liberalism and partially from welfare state liberalism. That is, they disavowed the bureaucratization of numerous social welfare programs and the attendant increase of centralized power as well as egalitarian utopias. Just as the liberal mainstream society and politics of the United States offers the New Right's ultra-rightist ideas only a small chance of survival, the same liberal environment makes it equally hard for the ultra-leftist ideas of the New Left to gain a foothold. "It would be a path inconsistent with any sense of identity that we as Americans have with our nation and with our historical past" (Irving Kristol). "Neoconservatism," Kristol stressed in conclusion, "is a heresy within liberalism, . . . an effort to establish a reformation within liberalism by returning to the sources."[298]

Three additional trends can be discerned within liberalism, apart from the neoconservative point of view that are not quite identical to Kristol's portrayal. The first group consists of what Lawrence J. R. Herson calls social space liberals, whose ranks include former, frustrated members of the New Left. Their main leftist thesis of the end of liberalism derives from the insight that pluralistic fractionalism of liberalism into interest-group liberalism brought about its consequent degeneration. Thus, they concentrate on such themes as the quality of life, no growth, and questions of ecology and nuclear weapons (the freeze movement). A well-known spokesman of this group is Tom Hayden, former co-founder of the SDS (Students for a Democratic Society), one of the architects of the counterculture on the Berkeley University campus in the 1960s, and husband of Jane Fonda.[299] These leftist liberals receive important support from their think-tank, the Institute for Policy Studies, founded in 1961 by Richard J. Barnet and Marcus G. Raskin as "Washington's progressive research institute," as well as from the publications *Harper's* and *The Nation*.[300]

The second group consists of supporters of a life space liberalism who occupy themselves with civil liberties, that is, they continue to hold to an equality of outcome and distance themselves from the neoconservative credo of equality of opportunity, while continuing the discussion of welfare state liberalism.[301] Meanwhile, for the intelligentsia John Rawls's *A Theory of Justice* (1971) has become a classic of liberal equality. Rawls's book discards the Anglo-Saxon tradition of individualism for the tradition of Rousseau and Kant and only conditionally accepts the political credo of Hobbes and Locke that the state exists for the individual and not the individual for the state. It criticizes the utilitarian standard of justice of the maximum social happiness, which can come about either as the result of the great happiness of a few or the slight happiness or even misery of a great many. It replaces this standard with the principle that a society is just only if the improvement of the life of any of its classes simultaneously improves the fate of the underprivileged. Rawls's use of a utilitarian criterion of justice oriented to the needs of the commonweal abandons the classical and primary principle of individual well-being in favor of the good of a group, the underprivileged. For good reason, it is interpreted as an attempt to formulate social democratic ideas using the concepts and mental strategies of non-Hegelian Anglo-Saxon political theory.[302] At the same time, other texts representative of this liberal engagement should also be mentioned, such as Ronald Dworkin's *Taking Rights Seriously* (1977) and *A Matter of Principle* (1985), Bruce A. Ackerman's *Social Justice in the Liberal State* (1980), Amy Gutmann's *Liberal Equality* (1980), and Sidney Verba and Gary R. Orren's *Equality in America* (1985).[303]

If one were to trace this intellectual ethos and pathos in favor of welfare state liberalism and "just" liberal egalitarian and civil rights concerns in the platforms of the political parties, one would locate them within the Democratic party in the direct vicinity of Walter Mondale, the loser of the 1984 presidential election. They are also to be found among the think-tanks: in the Brookings Institution and the Center for Democratic Policy founded in 1981 (also in Washington), whose members include the Center's president Ted Van Dyk, former adviser to Hubert Humphrey and George McGovern, and other former presidential advisers such as Nicholas B. Katzenbach and Adam Yarmolinsky (under Johnson) or Stuart Eizenstat and Hodding Carter III (under Carter). These views may also be found in the quarterly publication *democracy,* which also appeared for the first time in 1981.[304] Mondale's close coalition with the unions and his seemingly outmoded ideals of welfare state liberalism were not only unappealing to the voters in 1984, but are still controversial within the Democratic party today. Probably the only part of the 1984 and 1988 campaigns that will remain of historical interest was the dynamic presence of Geraldine Ferraro and Jesse Jackson.

While life space liberalism seems to be "out," the neoliberalism of the neoliberals, and thus the third and most important liberal trend, is all the more "in vogue." The neoliberals were initially characterized by their own claims of opposition to Mondale: "Mondale represents the special interest politics that means the death of the Democratic Party. We're trying to free ourselves from the old liberal prejudices such as being pro-labor or anti-business, while retaining the liberal tradition of compassion or caring."[305] These are the words of Charles Peters, editor of the *Washington Monthly,* one of the press organs of the neoliberals. In their search for a neoliberal credo ("a middle ground between kooky conservatism and affirmative action for gays"[306]) and a neoliberal presidential candidate for 1988, the neoliberals already met with some success. Among their aspirants for the 1988 presidential campaign were Richard Gephardt (representative from Missouri), Joseph R. Biden (senator from Delaware), Dale Bumpers (senator from Arkansas), and Mike Dukakis (governor of Massachussetts). The neoliberal program unites Democratic senators (Paul Tsongas, Ernest Hollings,

Bill Bradley, Albert Gore), members of the House of Representatives (Timothy Wirth, Gephardt), former and incumbent governors (Jerry Brown, Bruce Babbit, Richard Lamm, James Hunt), academics (Lester Thurow, Amitai Etzioni, Robert Reich, David Birch), and journalists (Charles Peters, James Fallows, editor of the *The Atlantic,* Morton Kondracke, editor of *The New Republic*). The program consists of three central themes: investment, appropriate technology, and co-operation between nations, sectors, and in the workplace.[307]

Convinced that the central commitments of New Deal liberalism, such as economic centralization, macroeconomic political strategies, and interest group liberalism have become obsolete, the neoliberals emphasize the importance of steady economic growth as a necessary precondition for social justice, with a policy of investment clearly favored over policies of redistribution. Since in the future growth will be taking place in small economic units, the Keynesian macroeconomic strategies must be replaced by concepts such as entrepreneurial innovation of smaller firms. Since the 1980s, new technologies have been steadily multinationalizing the worldwide economic market and thereby creating additional impetus for growth, so the neoliberals advocate cooperation between business and educational institutions, and defend free-trade policies in the face of protectionist demands. The neoliberal strategy can already be said to include the programs of Governor Hunt of North Carolina and Governor Babbit of Arizona, who have called for a partnership between government, business, and educational institutions in their states. The goal of these partnerships is "the establishment of information archipelagos, that is, junctions of information—and service-based industries with rural or small-town amenities."[308]

Finally, the question may arise as to whether the positions of the neoliberals, though modified to accomodate the demands of a postmodern age, do not in fact coincide with the positions of the old or classical liberals. As Walter Goodman observed accurately in *The New York Times,* "The neoliberals stand today in somewhat the position neoconservatives occupied a decade ago. Their ambition is to attain the influence in liberal politics that the neoconservatives have attained in conservative politics."[309]

If today's neoliberalism is almost identical to the prevailing neoconservatism, then neoconservatism has successfully fulfilled its task. As long as Democratic and Republican politicians are changing camps (Henry Kissinger worked for John F. Kennedy, Richard Nixon, and Gerald Ford; Daniel P. Moynihan, for Lyndon B. Johnson and Gerald Ford; Max Kampelman, for Jimmy Carter and Ronald Reagan), as long as broad consensus on the values of the formative and progressivist American ideology continues to reign, and as long as American conservatism continues to function as a corrective to American liberalism and liberalism as a corrective for conservatism, American liberal tradition and politics, as Louis Hartz remarked three decades ago, will remain unshakeable.

# Notes to Part III

1. See Samuel P. Huntington, *American Politics: The Promise of Disharmony* (Cambridge, Mass., 1981), 4, 86 ff; 160 ff. William G. McLoughlin, *Revivals, Awakenings, and Reform: An Essay on Religion and Social Change in America, 1607–1977* (Chicago, 1978), 2, 10 f; 23.

2. On this issue, see S. P. Huntington, *American Politics,* 10, 94 (quote). See also B. Bailyn, Political Experience and Enlightenment Ideas in Eighteenth-Century America, *American Historical Review* 67 (January 1962); 348.

3. See A. de Tocqueville, *Democracy in America* ed. P. Bradley (New York, 1954), 1:311.

4. Ibid., 1:314; S. M. Lipset, *The First New Nation, The United States in Historical and Comparative Perspective* (New York, 1979) 140–150.

5. See G. K. Chesterton, *What I Saw in America* (New York, 1923), 11–12. Sidney E. Mead, The "Nation with the Soul of a Church", *Church History* 36 (September 1967); 262–83.

6. See Charles H. Hendel, An Exploration of the Nature of Authority, in C. J. Friedrich ed., *Authority* (Cambridge, Mass., 1958), 4–5. S. P. Huntington, *American Politics* (chapter: The Gap: The American Creed versus Political Authority), 33 ff. (quote p. 33).

7. S. P. Huntington, *American Politics,* 33. S. M. Lipset, *The First New Nation,* 277 ff.

8. Hans Kohn, *American Nationalism: An Interpretive Essay* (New York, 1957), 8.

9. See R. E. Neustadt, *Presidential Power, The Politics of Leadership from FDR to Carter* (New York, 1980). Robert S. Hirschfield, ed., *The Power of the Presidency, Concepts and Controversy* (New York, 1982). Edward S. Corwin, *The President: Office and Powers, 1787–1957—History and Analysis of Practice and Opinion* (New York: 1957).

## CHAPTER 6

10. See Denis W. Brogan, *The American Character* (New York, 1944); S. M. Lipset, *The First New Nation* (chapter: The Unchanging American Values and Their Connection with American Character), 110 ff. Alex Inkeles, Continuity and Change in the American National Character, in S. M. Lipset, ed., *The Third Century, America as a Post-Industrial Society* (Chicago, 1980), 390–416.

11. Clinton Rossiter, *Conservatism in America* (New York, 1962), 72.

12. Perry Miller quoted according to K. Krakau, *Missionsbewußtsein und Völkerrechtsdoktrin in den Vereinigten Staaten von Amerika*, 23.

13. See Charles W. Dunn, The Theological Dimensions of Presidential Leadership: A Classification Model, *Presidential Studies Quarterly* 14, no. 1 (Winter 1984); 61–72. Charles W. Dunn, ed., *American Political Theology: Historical Perspectives and Theoretical Analysis* (New York, 1984).

14. D. W. Brogan, *The American Character*, 164.

15. See also Alan Heimert, *Religion and the American Mind: From the Great Awakening to the Revolution* (Cambridge, Mass., 1966). Patricia Caldwell, *The Puritan Conversion Narrative: The Beginnings of American Expression* (New York, 1983).

16. See A. de Tocqueville, *Democracy in America*, 1, 409. For additional background on the role of religion in American life, see Nelson R. Burr, *A Critical Bibliography of Religion in America* (Princeton, N.J., 1961).

17. P. Schaff, *America: A Sketch of Its Political, Social, and Religious Character* (Cambridge, Mass., 1961), 72.

18. See Ann Kibbey, *Rhetoric, Prejudice, and Violence: The Interpretation of Material Shapes in Puritanism* (New York, 1985); Andrew Delbanco, The Puritan Errand Re-Viewed, *Journal of American Studies* 18 (December 1984). Perry Miller and Thomas H. Johnson, *The Puritans* (New York, 1938), 146–49, 160–62.

19. J. Edwards, quoted in A. Heimert and A. Delbanco, *The Puritans in America* (Cambridge, Mass., 1985), 12. See Herbert Wallace Schneider, *The Puritan Mind* (Ann Arbor, Mich., 1958), 96.

20. J. Wise, quoted in P. Miller and T. H. Johnson, *The Puritans*, 268 ff.

21. See Erich Voegelin, *Über die Form des Amerikanischen Geistes* (Tübingen, 1928), 109. K. Krakau, *Missionsbewußtsein*, 39.

22. See Max Weber, *The Protestant Ethic and Spirit of Capitalism*, ed. Talcott Parsons (New York, 1958). Ernst Troeltsch, *Protestantism and Progress: A Historical Study of the Relation of Protestantism to the Modern World* (Boston, 1958).

23. See R. B. Perry, *Amerikanische Ideale* (Nürnberg, 1947), 1, 349–77, especially 364–77.

24. R. B. Perry, *Characteristically American* (New York, 1949), 39. See Paul Seaver, The Puritan Work Ethic Revisted, *Journal of British Studies* 19–20 (1979–81); 35–53.

25. See H. W. Schneider, *The Puritan Mind*, 237 ff. A. Carnegie, *Autobiography*, ed. J. C. Van Dyke (Boston, 1920). Horatio Alger, Jr., Struggling Upward; or Luke Larkin's Luck, in *The American Gospel of Success: Individualism and Beyond*, ed. Moses Rischin (Chicago, 1965). A. de Tocqueville, *Democracy in America*, 2:42–44. G. Gorer, *Die Amerikaner* (Hamburg, 1958). R. Niebuhr, *The Irony of American History* (New York, 1952), 52. R. Niebuhr, The Protestant Movement and Democracy in the United

States, in *The Shaping of American Religion*, ed. J. W. Smith and A. L. Jamison (Princeton, N.J., 1961), 24, 31 f.

26. H. McClosky and J. Zaller, *The American Ethos, Public Attitudes toward Capitalism and Democracy* (Cambridge, Mass., 1984), 1.

27. L. Samson, Americanism as Surrogate Socialism, in *Failure of a Dream?*, ed. John H. M. Laslett and S. M. Lipset (Garden City, N.Y., 1974), 426.

28. D. Sobel, Desire to Be Unique—a Universal Goal, *The New York Times*, December 1, 1980.

29. See also, William R. Brock, Americanism, in *The United States*, ed. D. Welland (London, 1974).

30. John Quincy Adams's speech of July 4, 1821, quoted in Ernest R. May, ed., *The American Foreign Policy* (New York, 1963), 64 and 65.

31. Herbert Hoover, quoted in K. Krakau, *Missionsbewußtsein*, 111. See H. Hoover, *American Individualism*, ed. Frank Freidel (New York, 1979).

32. See Louis Hartz, *The Liberal Tradition in America*, 285, 307.

33. Richard Hofstadter, quoted in Hans Kohn, *American Nationalism: An Interpretive Essay* (New York, 1957), 13.

34. See J. O. Robertson, *American Myth, American Reality*, 92 and 93.

35. Carl J. Friedrich et al., *Problems of the American Public Service* (New York, 1935), 12.

36. Seymour Martin Lipset speaks of the "unchanging American character" due to "unchanging American values"; see S. M. Lipset, *The First New Nation*, 101–39.

37. See also Charles L. Sanford, *The Quest for Paradise. Europe and the American Moral Imagination* (Urbana, Ill., 1961), 93.

38. See also C. R. Snyder and H. L. Fromkin, *Uniqueness: The Human Pursuit of Difference* (New York, 1980).

39. Geraldine Ferraro's speech of July 7, 1984, quoted in *Wireless Bulletin from Washington*, Embassy of the United States of America, U.S. Information Service, July 13 (Bonn, 1984), 7.

40. Don K. Price, *The Scientific Estate* (Cambridge, Mass., 1965), 1.

41. See Adrienne Koch, *Power, Morals, and the Founding Fathers*, 5.

42. On Franklin's scientific works, see Ronald W. Clark, *Benjamin Franklin: A Biography* (New York, 1983). I. Bernard Cohen, *Benjamin Franklin: Scientist and Statesman* (New York, 1972). See also B. Franklin, *Collected Works* (Autobiography; Public Papers and Essays; Scientific Papers), (New York, 1985), The Library of America Series. On Jefferson, see I. B. Cohen, ed., *Thomas Jefferson and the Sciences* (New York, 1980). Henry Steele Commager, *Jefferson, Nationalism and the Enlightenment* (New York, 1975). On Madison, see A. Koch, *Jefferson and Madison: The Great Collaboration* (New York, 1950).

43. G. Washington quoted in A. Koch, *Power, Morals, and the Founding Fathers*, 5 and 6. See Gary Wills, *Cincinnatus: George Washington and the Enlightenment* (Garden City, N.Y., 1984).

44. See Rutherford E. Delmage, The American Idea of Progress, 1750–1800, *Proceedings of the American Philosophical Society* 91 (1947); 307–14. Bernard Cohen, *Science and American Society in the First Century of the Republic* (Columbus, Ohio, 1961). I. Bernard Cohen, *Revolution in Science* (Cambridge, Mass., 1985), 208 ff.

45. B. Franklin quoted in Frank Donovan, *The Benjamin Franklin Papers* (New York, 1962), 199–200.

46. John Adams quoted in A. Koch, *Power, Morals, and the Founding Fathers,* 101. See Zoltan Haraszti, *John Adams and the Prophets of Progress* (Cambridge, Mass., 1952). Eli Ginzberg, James K. Anderson, and John L. Herma, *The Optimistic Tradition and American Youth* (New York, 1962).

47. See Michael Foster, *The Growth of Science in the Nineteenth Century,* Annual Reports of the Smithsonian Institution for 1899 (Washington, D.C., 1901), 163–183. Arthur A. Ekirch, *The Idea of Progress in America, 1815–1860* (New York, 1944). Rush Welter, The Idea of Progress in America, *Journal of the History of Ideas* 16 (1955); 401–15. David Noble, The Religion of Progress in America, 1890–1914, *Social Research* 22 (1955); 417–40. Clarke A. Chambers, The Belief in Progress in Twentieth-Century America, *Journal of the History of Ideas* 19 (1958); 197–224.

48. See Henry Adams, *The Degradation of the Democratic Dogma* (New York, 1919). Brooks Adams, *The Law of Civilization and Decay* (London, 1895). Lewis Mumford, *The Transformation of Man* (New York, 1962).

49. See Vannevar Bush, *Science—The Endless Frontier* (New York, 1980); viii, passim.

50. See Norman Cousins, *Modern Man Is Obsolete* (New York, 1945). Albert Einstein, Peace in the Atomic Era, in *Representative American Speeches,* ed. A. C. Baird, 1949, vol. 22, no. 3 (New York, 1950). A. Whitney Griswold, Balancing Moral Responsibility and Scientific Progress, in *Representative American Speeches,* ed. A. C. Baird), 1951–52, vol. 24, no. 3 (New York, 1952). J. Robert Oppenheimer, Speech of December 26, 1954, on modern man and the changing image of man, in *A Treasury of Great American Speeches,* ed. A. Bauer (New York, 1957). David E. Lilienthal, *Change, Hope, and the Bomb* (Princeton, N.J., 1963). Barton J. Bernstein, Shatterer of Worlds, Hiroshima and Nagasaki, *Bulletin of the Atomic Scientists* 31, no. 10, (1975); 12–22. H. F. York, *The Advisors: Oppenheimer, Teller, and the Superbomb* (San Francisco, 1976). The extent to which opinions about the dropping of the atomic bomb remain divided today is shown by the following articles from *The New York Times* under the heading: The Bomb: Was Truman Justified?; John Connor, Yes, It Was a Necessary Evil, *International Herald Tribune* (August 5, 1985): 4. Gar Alperovitz: No, He Had Other Options, *International Herald Tribune* (August 5, 1985); 4.

51. See D. D. Eisenhower's farewell speech, quoted in *The New York Times* (January 22, 1961); 4E. See Charles J. Hitch and Roland N. McKean, *The Economics of Defense in the Nuclear Age* (Cambridge, Mass., 1960). Leonard Silk, *The Research Revolution* (New York, 1960). Charles P. Snow, *Science and Government* (Cambridge, Mass., 1961).

52. See Don K. Price, *The Scientific Estate* (Cambridge, Mass., 1975). On theses issues, see Norman Kaplan, ed., *Science and Society* (Chicago, 1965). Joseph Ben-David, *The Scientist's Role in Society* (Englewood Cliffs, N.J., 1971). Samuel T. Cohen, Krieg liegt in der Natur des Menschen, "Spiegel-Interview" with the inventor of the neutron bomb, conducted by Frank Wiering, September 14, 1981; Interview with Edward Teller, the inventor of the hydrogen bomb, in *The Playboy Interview,* ed. G. Barry Golson, conducted by Gila Berkowitz (New York, 1981).

53. D. K. Price, *The Scientific Estate,* 162. See Hans J. Morgenthau, *Truth and Power* (chapter: Modern Science and Political Power), (London, 1970).

54. D. K. Price, *The Scientific Estate,* 278.

55. See Lewis Mumford, *Values for Survival* (New York, 1946). George J. Seidel, *The Crisis of Creativity* (Notre Dame, Ind., 1966). Romano Guardini, *The End of the Modern World* (Chicago, 1967). Reinhold Niebuhr, *Faith and Politics, A Commentary*

*on Religious, Social and Political Thought in a Technological Age,* ed. Ronald H. Stone, (New York, 1968). Gunther S. Stent, *The Coming of the Golden Age, A View of the End of Progress* (Garden City, N.Y., 1962). Frank J. Yartz, David J. Hassel, and Allan L. Larson, *Progress and the Crisis of Man* (Chicago, 1976). Robert Nisbet, *History of the Idea of Progress* (chapter: Progress at Bay), (New York, 1980). Hans Jonas, Reflections on Technology, Progress, and Utopia, *Social Research* 48, no. 3 (1981), 411–55. Gabriel A. Almond, Marvin Chodorow, and Roy Harvey Pearce, eds., *Progress and Its Discontents* (Berkeley, Calif., 1982). Robert L. Holmes, The Sleep of Reason Brings Forth Monsters, *Harvard Magazine* 85, no. 4, (March–April 1983): 56a–56h. Hans Jonas, *The Imperative of Responsibility, In Search of an Ethics for the Technological Age* (Chicago, 1984). Roger Sperry, *Naturwissenschaft und Wertentscheidung* (Munich, 1985).

56. For a critical view of scientific research focused primarily on high technology, see Thomas Kuhn, *The Structure of Scientific Revolutions,* (Chicago, 1962). R. Harré, ed., *Problems of Scientific Revolution* (Oxford, 1975). Nicholas Valery, The Declining Power of American Technology, *New Scientist* 71 (1976): 72–73. Robert W. Kates, Christoph Hohenemser, and Jeanne X. Kasperson, eds., *Perilous Progress, Managing the Hazards of Technology* (Boulder, Colo., 1985). On the problems of gene technology, see Elof A. Carlson, *Genes, Radiation, and Society: The Life and Work of H. J. Muller* (Ithaca, N.Y., 1981). Ernst Mayr, *The Growth of Biological Thought. Diversity, Evolution and Inheritance* (Cambridge, Mass., 1985). Edward D. Garber, ed., *Genetic Perspectives in Biology and Medicine* (Chicago, 1985). Under President Carter a research body was founded for investigation and discussion of these issues in 1978. The report of the President's Commission for the Study of Ethical Problems in Medicine and Biomedical and Behavioral Research on Screening and Counseling for Genetic Conditions of 1983, Washington, D.C., is especially informative on this subject.

As a few examples from the critical literature on nuclear technology, see Michael Mandelbaum, *The Nuclear Revolution: International Politics before and after Hiroshima* (New York, 1981). Jonathan Schell, *The Fate of the Earth* (New York, 1982); James E. Dougherty, *The Bishops and Nuclear Weapons: The Catholic Pastoral Letter on War and Peace* (Hamden, Conn., 1984). Robert Dahl, *Controlling Nuclear Weapons: Democracy Versus Guardianship* (Syracuse, N.Y., 1985).

57. See Zbigniew Brzezinski, *Between Two Ages, America's Role in the Technetronic Era* (New York, 1970). Peter Medawar, *The Hope of Progress* (New York, 1973). Peter M. Quay, Progress as a Demarcation Criterion for the Sciences, *Philosophy of Science* 41 (1974); 154–70. Thomas J. Kuehn and Alan L. Porter, eds., *Science, Technology, and National Policy* (Ithaca, N.Y., 1981). Julian L. Simon and Hermann Kahn, *The Resourceful Earth* (New York, 1984). Norman Macrae, *The 2025 Report: A Concise History of the Future, 1975–2025* (New York, 1985).

58. See D. and D. Meadows, E. Zahn, and P. Milling, *The Limits to Growth* (New York, 1972). Richard Sennett, *The Fall of Public Man* (New York, 1978). Lester C. Thurow, *The Zero Sum Society Distribution and the Possibilities for Economic Change* (New York, 1980). J. David Bolter, *Turning's Man, Western Culture in the Computer Age* (Chapel Hill, N.C., 1984). Neil Postman, *Amusing Ourselves to Death: Public Discourse in the Age of Show Business* (New York, 1985).

59. See Jimmy Carter's Inaugural Address of January 20, 1977, in *Representative American Speeches, 1976–77,* ed. W. W. Braden (New York, 1977), p. 21. It was also President Carter who commissioned the Global 2000 report. See The Global 2000 Report to the President, ed. Council on Environmental Quality (Washington, D.C., 1980).

60. See Harriet Zuckerman, *Scientific Elite: Nobel Laureates in the United States* (New York, 1977). "Amerika und Seine Nobelpreisträger," in *Amerika-Dienst*, United Information Service, Embassy of the United States of America, Bonn, December 21, 1983, No. 51.

61. See Horst Rademacher, Desolate Forschungsfinanzierung in Amerika, *Blick durch die Wirtschaft* (April 11, 1986): 4.

62. On SDI, see Ronald Reagan's televised speech of March 23, 1983, printed in *Wireless Bulletin from Washington*, no. 57, 1983, United States Information Service, Embassy of the United States of America, Bonn, 1983. See also George A. Keyworth, *President Reagan's New Defense Initiative: A Road to Stability* (Stanford, Calif., 1984). (Until December 1985, Keyworth was the science adviser of the president.) Robert Jastrow, *How to Make Nuclear Weapons Obsolete* (Boston, 1985). Critical on SDI are John Tirman, Richard L. Garwin, Kurt Gottfried, and Henry W. Kendall, *The Fallacy of Star Wars* (New York, 1984) (A report of the Union of Concerned Scientists). Jonathan B. Stein, *From H-Bomb to Star Wars: The Politics of Strategic Decision Making* (Lexington, Mass., 1984): Gregory Treverton, The Year(s) of SDI, *German Studies Newsletter* (Center for European Studies, Harvard University), no. 6 (November 1985): 1–7.

63. D. K. Price, *The Scientific Estate*, 278.

## CHAPTER 7

64. S. P. Huntington, *American Politics*, 127. On the American Constitution now, see Forrest McDonald, *Novus Ordo Seclorum—The Intellectual Origins of the Constitution* (Lawrence, Kan., 1985).

65. See also D. K. Price, *America's Unwritten Constitution: Science, Religion, and Political Responsibility* (Baton Rouge, La., 1983). Sandra Day O'Connor, Shield of Freedom: The Constitution and the Courts, printed in *U.S. Policy Information and Texts*, United States Information Service, Embassy of the United States of America, no. 50, April 3, 1986, (Bonn, 1986), 7–13.

66. See Ernst Fraenkel, *Das amerikanische Regierungssystem* (chapter: Die Verfassung als traditionsbildender Faktor), (Cologne, 1962), 19 ff. Edward S. Corwin, *The Constitution and What It Means Today* (Princeton, N.J., 1978).

67. Warren E. Burger, The Constitution: A Beacon for Those Seeking Liberty, in *U.S. Policy Information and Texts*, United States Information Service, Embassy of the United States of America, March 5, 1986, no. 32 (Bonn, 1986).

68. See A. Koch, *Power, Morals, and the Founding Fathers*, 140. Klaus Stern, *Grundideen europäisch-amerikanischer Verfassungsstaatlichkeit* (Berlin, 1984), 9.

69. See K. Stern, *Grundideen*, 9. *The Federalist Papers*, ed. Clinton Rossiter, No. 51, 322.

70. K. Stern, *Grundideen*, 9

71. See Bernard Bailyn, *The Origins of American Politics* (New York, 1971). Richard Hofstadter et al., *The United States: The History of a Republic* (Princeton, N.J., 1967). Caroline Robbins, *The Eighteenth Century Commonwealth* (New York, 1968).

72. The Declaration of Independence (July 4, 1776), in Harold C. Syrett, ed., *American Historical Documents* (New York, 1965), 82.

73. John Locke, *Two Treatises of Government* (Cambridge, 1960), 430–31.

74. See Louis Hartz, *The Liberal Tradition in America*, passim. A. Koch, *Power*,

*Morals, and the Founding Fathers,* 27 ff. S. P. Huntington, *American Politics,* 6, 15, 19, 21. For a revisionist view on John Locke, see Richard K. Matthews, *The Radical Politics of Thomas Jefferson: A Revisionist View* (Lawrence, Kan., 1984). Garry Wills, *Inventing America. Jefferson's Declaration of Independence* (New York, 1978).

75. A. de Tocqueville, *Democracy in America,* 2: 108.

76. James Bryce, *The American Commonwealth* (London, 1891), 2, 417–18.

77. S. P. Huntington, *American Politics,* 34.

78. See A. Koch, *Power, Morals, and the Founding Fathers,* 50 ff., 103 ff.

79. See *The Federalist Papers,* ed. Clinton Rossiter, (New York, 1961), No. 10 (Madison, 77 ff.); No. 1 (Hamilton, 33 ff.); No. 9 (Hamilton, 71 ff.); No. 14 (Madison, 99 ff.); No. 15 (Hamilton, 105 ff.); No. 17 (Hamilton, 118 ff.); No. 27 (Hamilton, 174 ff.); No. 37 (Madison, 224 ff.); No. 39 (Madison, 240 ff.); No. 45–49 (Madison and Hamilton, 288–317); No. 51 (Madison and Hamilton, 320 ff.); No. 70–71 (Hamilton, 423–35); No. 78 (Hamilton, 464 ff.). See also S. P. Huntington, The Founding Fathers and the Division of Powers, in *Area and Power,* ed. Arthur Maass, (Glencoe, Ill., 1959).

80. See S. P. Huntington, *American Politics,* 21.

81. See James Bryce, *The American Commonwealth,* vol. 2.

82. See G. Jellinek, Die Erklärung der Menschen- und Bürgerrechte (1895), and E. Boutmy, Die Erklärung der Menschen- und Bürgerrechte und Georg Jellinek (1902), in *Zur Geschichte der Erklärung der Menschenrechte,* ed. R. Schnur (Darmstadt, 1964).

83. See K. Stern, *Grundideen europäisch-amerikanischer Verfassungsstaatlichkeit,* 17.

84. See J. Sandweg, Rationales Naturrecht als revolutionäre Praxis, Untersuchungen zur "Erklärung der Menschen- und Bürgerrechte" von 1789, (Cologne, 1972).

85. See K. Stern, *Grundideen,* 18, 20. E. Angermann, *Der deutsche Frühkonstitutionalismus und das amerikanische Vorbild,* 1 ff. B. Bailyn, *The Ideological Origins of the American Revolution,* 19 ff.

86. See K. Stern, *Grundideen,* 21 (includes additional references). See also A. S. Rosenbaum, *The Philosophy of Human Rights—International Perspectives* (London, 1980).

87. See H. M. Christman, ed., *The Public Papers of Chief Justice Earl Warren* (New York, 1959), 7.

88. Madison, No. 51, in *The Federalist Papers,* 322.

89. Madison quoted in A. Koch, *Power, Morals, and the Founding Fathers,* 115.

90. See A. Koch, *Power, Morals, and the Founding Fathers,* 145.

91. Herbert McClosky, Consensus and Ideology in American Politics *The American Political Science Review,* no. 2 (June 1964): 362 and 363. On the thesis that the values of the American ideology of progress have remained unchanged until the present day, see also Clyde Kluckholm, Have There Been Discernible Shifts in American Values During the Past Generation?, in *The American Style,* ed. Elting E. Morison (New York, 1958), 152. S. M. Lipset, *The First New Nation,* 99 ff. Lloyd A. Free and Hadley Cantril, *The Political Beliefs of Americans, A Study of Public Opinion* (New York, 1968). E. C. Ladd, *Ideology in America* (Ithaca, N.Y., 1969), 174 ff. Donald J. Devine, *The Political Culture of the United States* (Boston, 1972), 65. H. McClosky and J. Zaller, *The American Ethos,* 189 ff.

92. See also C. Carstens, *Grundgedanken der amerikanischen Verfassung und ihre Verwirklichung* (Berlin, 1954).

93. Robert A. Dahl, Decision-Making in a Democracy: The Role of the Supreme

Court as a National Policy-Maker, in: *Readings in American Political Behavior*, ed. Raymond E. Wolfinger (Englewood Cliffs, N.J., 1966), 166. See also Edward S. Corwin, *The Constitution and What It Means Today* (Princeton, N.J., 1978).

94. See Sam C. Sarkesian and Krish Nanda, *Politics and Power in American Government* (chapter: The Supreme Court and Society), (New York, 1976), 292 f.

95. The Constitution of the United States, (Signed and submitted to Congress, September 17, 1787; final ratification, May 29, 1790), Art. III, Sec. 1, in Harold C. Syrett, *American Historical Documents* (New York, 1965), 112.

96. Alexander Hamilton, No. 78, in *The Federalist Papers*, 467.

97. See C. G. Haines, *The American Doctrine of Judicial Supremacy* (Berkeley, Calif., 1932).

98. On Coke, see Catherine Dinker-Bowen, *The Lion and the Throne. The Life and Times of Sir Edward Coke, 1552–1634* (London, 1957). J. Beauté, *Un grand juriste anglais: Sir Edward Coke, 1552–1634. Ses idées politiques et constitutionnelles* (Paris, 1975).

99. Klaus Stern draws attention to Haines's judgment on Coke in *Grundideen*, 26 ff.

100. C. G. Haines, *The American Doctrine of Judicial Supremacy*, 66. Also, B. Bailyn ascribes an important role to Otis in his work *The Origins of the American Revolution*, 176 ff.

101. C. G. Haines, *The American Doctrine of Judicial Supremacy*, 66.

102. See Horst Mewes, *Einführung in das politische System der USA* (chapter: Judikative und Verfassungskontinuität), (Heidelberg, 1986), 39. S. C. Sarkesian and K. Nanda, *Politics and Power*, 294 ff.

103. See Marbury v. Madison, in H. C. Syrett, *American Historical Documents*, 153–57 (1 Cranch 137, 176–80). K. Stern, *Grundideen*, 31 ff.

104. See Gibbons v. Ogden, in H. C. Syrett, *American Historical Documents*, 181–84 (9 Wheaton 1). S. C. Sarkesian and K. Nanda, *Politics and Power*, 304.

105. See Karl Loewenstein, *Verfassungsrecht und Verfassungspraxis der Vereinigten Staaten* (Berlin, 1959). Alexander M. Bickel, *The Least Dangerous Branch: The Supreme Court at the Bar of Politics* (Indianapolis, Ind., 1962). Loren P. Beth, The Supreme Court Reconsidered: Opposition and Judicial Review in the United States, *Political Studies* 16, no. 2 (June 1968); 243–49. Robert A. Goldwin, ed., *How Democratic Is the Constitution* (Washington, D.C., 1982).

106. F. D. Roosevelt quoted in S. C. Sarkesian and K. Nanda, *Politics and Power*, 292.

107. C. A. Beard, *The Supreme Court and the Constitution* (Englewood Cliffs, N.J., 1938) (Introduction).

108. See H. Wechsler, Toward Neutral Principles of Constitutional Law, *Harvard Law Review* 73 (1959–60), 1 ff.

109. See Dred Scott v. Sandford, in H. C. Syrett, *American Historical Documents*, 249–54. See also under p. 396.

110. See H. Mewes, *Einführung in das politische System der USA*, 47, 40. S. C. Sarkesian and K. Nanda, *Politics and Power*, 304–305. Horst Ehmke, *Wirtschaft und Verfassung, Die Verfassungsrechtsprechung des Supreme Court zur Wirtschaftsregulierung* (Karlsruhe, 1961). On the decision-making behavior of the judges of the Supreme Court in the past and present, see D. W. Rohde and H. J. Spaeth, *Supreme Court Decision Making* (New York, 1975).

111. On Roosevelt's conflict with the Supreme Court, see William E. Leuchtenburg, *Franklin D. Roosevelt and the New Deal, 1932–1940* (New York, 1963), 57, 143–45, 161–62, 170–71, 231–38, 259–60. Robert Jackson, *The Struggle for Judicial Supremacy* (New York, 1941). See also Archibald Cox, *The Role of the Supreme Court in American Government* (New York, 1976). On the anticonstitutionality of American federal laws since 1803, see Edward S. Corwin, *The Constitution of the United States, Analysis and Interpretation* (Washington, D.C., 1953).

112. S. C. Sarkesian and K. Nanda, *Politics and Power*, 306–307, 299.

113. See Martin Shapiro, The Supreme Court from Warren to Burger, in Anthony King, ed., *The New American Political System* (Washington, D.C., 1979). Stephan L. Wasby, *Continuity and Change. From the Warren Court to Burger Court* (Pacific Palisades, Calif., 1976).

114. See Richard Kluger, *Simple Justice* (New York, 1977). Henry Abraham, *Freedom and the Courts* (New York, 1977). Gary Orfield, *Congressional Power: Congress and Social Change* (New York, 1975). John Hope Franklin, *From Slavery to Freedom* (New York, 1974).

115. See Barron v. Baltimore, in H. C. Syrett, *American Historical Documents*, 212–13. H. Mewes, *Einführung in das politische System der USA*, 41

116. See H. Mewes, *Einführung in das politische System der USA*, 41f.

117. Article XIV (1868), in H. C. Syrett, *American Political Documents*, 118.

118. See Plessy v. Ferguson, in H. C. Syrett, *American Political Documents*, 311. J. H. Franklin, *From Slavery to Freedom*. H. Mewes, *Einführung in das politische System der USA*, 42–43.

119. See Brown v. Board of Education of Topeka, in H. C. Syrett, *American Political Documents*, 409–12. S. C. Sarkesian and K. Nanda, *Power and Politics*, 306 f. For an evaluation thirty years after, see Curtis J. Sitomer, The Landmark Desegregation Ruling and Its 30-Year Legacy, *The Christian Science Monitor* (May 11, 1984): 21–23.

120. See Frank Freidel, *F.D.R. and the South* (chapter: Roosevelt's Civil Rights Dilemma), (Baton Rouge, La., 1965), 71 ff.

121. See Oscar Handlin, *Fire-Bell in the Night, The Crisis in Civil Rights* (Boston, 1964), 36 ff. H. Mewes, *Einführung in das politische System der USA*, 43.

122. See James C. Duram, *A Moderate Among Extremists: Dwight D. Eisenhower and the School Desegregation Crisis* (Chicago, 1981), 144, 171. See also Robert F. Burk *The Eisenhower Administration and Black Civil Rights* (Knoxville, Tenn., 1984).

123. See James C. Harvey, *Civil Rights During the Kennedy Administration* (Jackson, Miss., 1971), 40 f.

124. See H. Mewes, *Einführung in das politische System der USA*, 44. Donald L. Horowitz, *The Court and Social Policy* (Washington, D.C., 1977). Norman Dorsen, Paul Bender, and Burt Neuborne, *Political and Civil Rights in the United States* (Boston, 1976).

125. See Lino A. Graglia, *Disaster by Decree. The Supreme Court Decisions on Race and the Schools—A Sharply Critical View of the Court Rulings That Led to Forced Busing* (Ithaca, N.Y., 1976).

126. See H. Mewes, *Einführung in das politische System der USA*, 43.

127. Ibid., 45. D. L. Horowitz, *The Court and Social Policy;* J. C. Harvey, *Black Civil Rights During the Johnson Administration* (Jackson, Miss., 1973).

128. See Allan P. Sindler, *Bakke, De Fumis and Minority Admissions* (New York, 1978). Allan Bakke had taken the Medical School of the University of California to court because the school had refused him admission in 1973 and 1974 on the basis of a reservation of sixteen places for members of minority groups that, according to the

charges, were less qualified than Bakke. The California Court decided in Bakke's favor; the University, however, referred the case on appeal to the Supreme Court. The result was a test of the constitutionality of the policies of the Department of Health, Education, and Welfare. Five of the nine judges agreed that explicit "racial quotas" violated the equality principle of the Fourteenth Amendment, thus enabling Bakke to be admitted to the University and forbidding the "quota policy." At the same time, a majority of five judges decided that affirmative action programs for minorities are constitutional as long as they comprise only one factor among many others in the admission process without entailing explicit quotas (H. Mewes, *Einführung in das politische System der USA*, 45ff.)

129. See Sheila K. Johnson, The Future of Woman in America's Third Century, in *The Third Century*, ed. S. M. Lipset (Chicago, 1980), 286–301. Gilbert Y. Steiner, *Constitutional Inequality: The Political Fortunes of the Equal Rights Amendment* (Washington, D.C., 1985).

130. See Sabina Lietzmann, Amerika nach dem Sündenfall, "Frankfurter Allegemeine Zeitung" (Supplement), March 29, 1986, No. 74. Orlando Patterson, The Black Community: Is There a Future?, in *The Third Century*, ed. S. M. Lipset, 244–84.

131. See Hugo Müller-Vogg, Amerikas Frauen verändern den Arbeitsmarkt, *Frankfurter Allgemeine Zeitung* (July 17, 1985); 12.

132. A. M. Bickel, Close of the Warren Era, *The New Republic* (July 12, 1969).

133. A. J. Goldberg, On the Supreme Court, *The New York Times* (April 12, 1971). See Alexander Bickel, *The Supreme Court and the Idea of Progress* (New York, 1970).

134. See, for example, Louis B. Boudin, *Government by Judiciary* (New York, 1932), 2 vols. James T. Brennan, *The Cost of the American Judicial System* (West Haven, Conn., 1966). M. Judd Harmon, ed., *Essays on the Constitution of the United States* (Port Washington, N.Y., 1978).

135. See Martin Shapiro, Judicial Activism, in *The Third Century*, ed. S. M. Lipset, 109–31. Jonathan D. Casper, The Supreme Court and National Policy Making, *The American Political Science Review* 70, no. 1 (1976): 50 ff. Robert McClosky, *The Modern Supreme Court* (Cambridge, Mass., 1973).

136. See also Edward S. Corwin, *The Presidency, Office and Power 1787–1957* (New York, 1957). Michael Nelson, ed., *The Presidency and the Political System* (Washington, D.C., 1984).

137. See Clinton Rossiter, *The Federalist Papers* (Hamilton, No. 1, No. 9, No. 15, No. 17, No. 27, Nos. 70–71, No. 78). Adrienne Koch, *Power, Morals, and the Founding Fathers* (chapter: Adams and the Taming of Power). Lance Banning, *The Jeffersonian Persuasion: Evolution of a Party Ideology* (Ithaca, N.Y., 1978). Robert M. Johnstone, *Jefferson and the Presidency: Leadership in the Young Republic* (Ithaca, N.Y., 1978).

138. See Edward N. Kearny, ed., *Dimensions of the Modern Presidency* (St. Louis, 1981). Rexford G. Tugwell and Thomas E. Cronin, eds., *The Presidency Reappraised* (New York, 1978), 39. Edward S. Corwin, The Aggrandizement of Presidential Power (1941), in *The Power of the Presidency, Concepts and Controversy*, ed. Robert S. Hirschfield (New York, 1968), 282 ff.

139. Adlai E. Stevenson, The Presidency—1984, *Presidential Studies Quarterly*, no. 1 (Winter 1984): 18.

140. See Don K. Price and Harold J. Laski, The Parliamentary and the Presidential Systems, *Public Administration Review* (PAR) 3, no. 4 (Autumn 1943), and PAR 4, no. 4 (Autumn 1944).

141. Author's conversation with Professor Samuel Huntington on May 20, 1982, at the Center for International Affairs, Harvard University.

142. Direct quotation of Professor Richard E. Neustadt from a conversation with the author on May 20, 1982, at the Kennedy School of Government, Harvard University.

143. John McDiarmid, Presidential Inaugural Addresses—A Study in Verbal Symbols, *Public Opinion Quarterly* 1 (July 1937); 79–82.

144. Rhetoric played a vital role as early as the American Revolution, as Gordon S. Wood showed in Rhetoric and Reality in the American Revolution, *William and Mary Quarterly* 23, (1966): 31. "For the ideas, the rhetoric, of the Americans was never obscuring but remarkably revealing of their deepest interests and passions. What they expressed may not have been for the most part factually true, but it was always psychologically true. In this sense their rhetoric was never detached from the social and political reality; and indeed it becomes the best entry into an understanding of that reality." On presidential terminology, see also Theodore Otto Windt, Presidential Rhetoric: Definition of a Field of Study, *Presidential Studies Quarterly* 16, no. 1 (Winter 1986): 102 ff. Roderick P. Hart, The Language of the Modern Presidency, *Presidential Studies Quarterly* 14, no. 2 (Spring 1984): 249 ff. Dante Germino, *The Inaugural Addresses of American Presidents, The Public Philosophy and Rhetoric* (Lanham, Md., 1984), with an introduction by Kenneth W. Thompson. Waldemar Besson, *Die politische Terminologie des Präsidenten Franklin D. Roosevelt, Eine Studie über den Zusammenhang von Sprache und Politik* (Tübingen, 1955).

145. Thomas E. Cronin, The Presidency and Its Paradoxes, in *The Power of the Presidency*, ed., R. S. Hirschfield, 422.

146. See Joseph M. Bessette and Jeffrey Tulis, eds., *The Presidency in the Constitutional Order* (Baton Rouge, La., 1981). Louis W. Koenig, *The Chief Executive* (New York, 1981). Harry A. Bailey, ed., *Classics of the American Presidency* (Oak Park, Ill., 1980). Harold Laski, *The American Presidency: An Interpretation* (New Brunswick, N.J., 1980).

147. Hamilton, No. 70, *The Federalist Papers*, 423.

148. See Richard Loss, Alexander Hamilton and the Modern Presidency: Continuity or Discontinuity?, *Presidential Studies Quarterly* 12, no. 1 (Winter 1982): 20.

149. Ibid., 6 ff.

150. See Donald L. Robinson: The Inventors of the Presidency, *Presidential Studies Quarterly* 12, no. 1 (Winter 1983): 8 ff.

151. R. Gordon Hoxie, The Presidency in the Constitutional Convention, *Presidential Studies Quarterly* 15, no. 1, (Winter 1985): 31.

152. On the rich source material on the American presidency, see the following works: Robert U. Goehlert and Fenton S. Martin, *The Presidency: A Research Guide* (Santa Barbara, Calif., 1985). Jeffrey M. Elliot and Sheikh R. Ali, *The Presidential-Congressional Political Dictionary* (Santa Barbara, Calif., 1984). Henry F. Graff, ed., *The Presidents: A Reference History* (New York, 1984). *The American Presidency: A Historical Bibliography* (Santa Barbara, Calif., 1984). Kenneth E. Davison, *The American Presidency: A Guide to Information Sources* (Detroit, 1983).

153. Richard E. Neustadt, *Presidential Power, The Politics of Leadership from FDR to Carter* (New York, 1980), v.

154. Ibid., 147. See Karlyn Kohrs Campbell and Kathleen Hall Jamieson, Inaugurating the Presidency, *Presidential Studies Quarterly* 15, no. 2 (Spring 1985): 394–411.

155. Emmet John Hughes, *The Living Presidency* (Baltimore, 1973), 74–75.

156. Theodore Roosevelt, quoted in *The Autobiography of Theodore Roosevelt*, ed. Wayne Andrews (New York, 1958), 197.

157. Woodrow Wilson, quoted in *The Power of the Presidency*, ed. R. S. Hirschfield, 96.

158. F. D. Roosevelt, quoted in Anne O'Hare McCormick, Roosevelt's View of the Big Job, *The New York Times Magazine* (September 11, 1932). See Thomas E. Cronin and William R. Hochman, Franklin D. Roosevelt and the American Presidency, *Presidential Studies Quarterly* 15, no. 2 (Spring 1985): 277–86.

159. Hedley Donovan, *Roosevelt to Reagan, A Reporter's Encounters with Nine Presidents* (New York, 1985), 25.

160. R. E. Neustadt, *Presidential Power*, 119.

161. Harry S Truman, Inaugural Address (January 20, 1949), in *Inaugural Addresses of the Presidents of the United States, From George Washington 1789 to Richard M. Nixon 1973* (Washington, D.C., 1974), 256.

162. Harry S Truman, quoted in *The Power of the Presidency*, ed. R. S. Hirschfield, 118–19.

163. Dwight D. Eisenhower, Some Thoughts on the Presidency, *Reader's Digest* (1968), and D. D. Eisenhower, quoted in E. J. Hughes, *The Ordeal of Power, A Political Memoir of the Eisenhower Years* (New York, 1963), 348.

164. John F. Kennedy, The Role of the President (Campaign Speech from January 14, 1960), in *Representative American Speeches*, ed. L. Thonssen, 32, no. 4 (New York, 1960), 126.

165. Lyndon B. Johnson, quoted in *The Power of the Presidency*, ed. R. S. Hirschfield, 152.

166. See Arthur M. Schlesinger, *The Imperial Presidency* (New York, 1974).

167. Richard M. Nixon, quoted in *The Power of the Presidency*, ed. R. S. Hirschfield, 163.

168. See Vincent Davis, ed., *The Post-Imperial Presidency* (New York, 1980).

169. Gerald R. Ford, Congress, the Presidency and National Security Policy, *Presidential Studies Quarterly* 16, no. 2 (Spring 1986): 201.

170. See R. Gordon Hoxie, *The Presidency of the 1970's* (New York, 1973). Thomas E. Cronin, *The State of the Presidency* (Boston, 1975). James MacGregor Burns, *The Power to Lead, The Crisis of the American Presidency* (New York, 1984).

171. Jimmy Carter's "Crisis of Confidence," Speech of July 15, 1979, is quoted in *The Power of the Presidency*, ed. R. S. Hirschfield, 202.

172. Jimmy Carter, quoted in H. Donovan, *Roosevelt to Reagan*, 246.

173. H. Donovan, *Roosevelt to Reagan*, 251.

174. Ronald Reagan's Inaugural Speech is quoted in *Weekly Compilation of Presidential Documents, Administration of Ronald Reagan* 17, no. 4 (Washington, D.C., 1981): 2.

175. See Godfrey Hodgson, *All Things to All Men, The False Promise of the Modern American Presidency from Franklin D. Roosevelt to Ronald Reagan* (New York, 1980). James W. Caeser, Glen E. Thurow, Jeffrey Tulis, and Joseph M. Bessette, The Rise of the Rhetorical Presidency, *Presidential Studies Quarterly* 11, no. 2 (Spring 1981): 158–71. Kenneth W. Thompson, ed., *The American Presidency, Principles and Problems* (Washington, D.C., 1983). Martin Linsky, ed., *Television and the Presidential Elections* (Lexington, Mass., 1983). Jeff Fishel, *Presidents and Promises. From Campaign Pledge to Presidential Performance* (Washington, D.C., 1984). Theodore J. Lowi, *The Personal*

*Presidency: Power Invested, Promise Unfulfilled* (Ithaca, N.Y., 1985). C. Don Livingston, The Televised Presidency, *Presidential Studies Quarterly* 16, no. 1 (Winter 1986): 22–30. Herbert Schmertz, The Media and the Presidency, *Presidential Studies Quarterly* 16, no. 1 (Winter 1986), 11–21.

176. James Bryce, *The American Commonwealth* (London, 1891), 1.

177. The following is quoted in Clinton Rossiter, *The American Presidency* (New York, 1960), 16–39.

178. Thomas E. Cronin, Thinking and Learning about Leadership, *Presidential Studies Quarterly* 14, no. 1 (Winter 1984): 28. On the topic of "leadership qualities," see also C. Rossiter, The Presidency: Focus of Leadership, *The New York Times Magazine* (November 11, 1956). Stephen R. Graubard and Gerald Holton, eds., *Excellence and Leadership in a Democracy* (New York, 1962). James MacGregor Burns, *Presidential Government, The Crucible of Leadership* (Boston, 1965). Frank Kessler, *The Dilemmas of Presidential Leadership: Of Caretakers and Kings* (Englewood Cliffs, N.J., 1982). Bert A. Rockman, *The Leadership Question: The Presidency and the American System* (New York, 1984). Leslie L. Gahl, Moral Courage: The Essence of Leadership, *Presidential Studies Quarterly* 14, no. 1 (Winter 1984): 43–60.

179. See James David Barber, *The Presidential Character, Predicting Performance in the White House* (Englewood Cliffs, N.J., 1972). Kenneth W. Thompson, *The President and the Public Philosophy* (Baton Rouge, La., 1981). Charles Funderburk, *Presidents and Politics: The Limits of Power* (Monterey, Calif., 1982). John A. Gueguen, Reflections on Statesmanship and the Presidency, *Presidential Studies Quarterly* 12, no. 4 (Fall 1982): 470–84.

180. F. D. Roosevelt, quoted in Samuel I. Rosenmann, *Working with Roosevelt* (New York, 1952): 260, 264.

181. Author's conversation with Senator William Fulbright in Washington, D.C., on April 27, 1982.

182. Harry S Truman, Inaugural address, 251, 252, 253.

183. Author's conversation with Professor Richard E. Neustadt, Kennedy School of Government, Harvard University, on April 26, 1985.

184. Author's conversation with Clark Clifford in Washington, D.C., on April 27, 1982.

185. D. D. Eisenhower, Second Inaugural Address, in *Inaugural Addresses of the Presidents of the United States,* 265.

186. Author's conversation with Senator William Fulbright, April 27, 1982.

187. A summary is provided in Herbert von Borch, Der General im Weißen Haus, Dwight D. Eisenhower—ein unterschätzter Präsident, *Süddeutsche Zeitung* (February 15–16, 1986), no. 38. Anthony James Joes, Eisenhower Revisionism: The Tide Comes in, *Presidential Studies Quarterly,* 15, no. 3 (Summer 1985): 561–71.

188. Author's conversation with Governor Sherman Adams in Lincoln, New Hampshire, on April 13, 1982.

189. R. Gordon Hoxie, *Command Decision and the Presidency, A Study of National Security Policy and Organization* (New York, 1977), 252, Foreword by President Gerald R. Ford.

190. Herbert von Borch, *John F. Kennedy, Amerikas Unerfüllte Hoffnung* (Munich, 1986), 32 ff.

191. David Halberstam, *The Best and the Brightest* (New York, 1969).

192. John F. Kennedy, The New Frontier (Democratic National Convention, Speech

in Los Angeles on July 15, 1960), in *Representative American Speeches, 1960–1961*, ed. Lester Thonssen, 33, no. 3 (New York, 1961), 12.

193. John F. Kennedy, Inaugural Address, in *A Treasury of Great American Speeches*, ed. C. Hurd and A. Bauer (New York, 1970), 361–62.

194. Author's conversation with Dean Rusk, University of Georgia, Dean Rusk Center, Athens, Georgia, on April 19, 1982.

195. Author's conversation with Walt W. Rostow in Bonn on June 8, 1984.

196. Jack Valenti, *A Very Human President* (New York, 1975).

197. See Eric F. Goldman, *The Tragedy of Lyndon Johnson* (New York, 1974).

198. Lyndon B. Johnson, Inaugural Address, in *Inaugural Addresses of the Presidents of the United States*, 273.

199. Walt W. Rostow, *Lyndon Johnson, 1908–1973*, unpublished manuscript of 1982, 5.

200. Robert A. Caro, *The Years of Lyndon Johnson, the Path to Power* (New York, 1982), vol. 1. For a critical view, see Vaughn Davis Bornet, *The Presidency of Lyndon B. Johnson* (Lawrence, Kan., 1983).

201. The Road Back, *Newsweek* (May 19, 1986).

202. Richard M. Nixon, Second Inaugural Address, in *Inaugural Addresses of the Presidents of the United States*, 280.

203. R. M. Nixon, Inaugural Address, 278.

204. Ibid., 276; Second Inaugural Address, 283.

205. See Fawn M. Brodie, *Richard Nixon, The Shaping of His Character* (Cambridge, Mass., 1983).

206. Gerald R. Ford, The Pardon of Richard Nixon (September 8, 1974), in Theodore Windt, *Presidential Rhetoric (1961–1980)*, (Dubuque, Iowa, 1980), 225.

207. Gerald R. Ford, *A Time to Heal* (New York, 1979).

208. See Haynes Johnson, *In the Absence of Power, Governing America* (New York, 1980).

209. Author's conversation with Cyrus Vance in New York on April 21, 1982.

210. For a summary, see Friedbert Pflüger, *Die Menschenrechtspolitik der USA, Amerikanische Außenpolitik zwischen Idealismus und Realismus 1972–1982* (Munich, 1983).

211. Jimmy Carter, Inaugural Address, in *Representative American Speeches, 1976–77*, ed. W. W. Braden (New York, 1977), 21.

212. Ronald Reagan, Inaugural Address, 2, 3, 4.

213. See H. Donovan, *Roosevelt to Reagan*, 250.

214. For a critical view of these "old Republican" values, see Robert Dallek, *Ronald Reagan, The Politics of Symbolism* (Cambridge, Mass., 1984).

215. H. Donovan, *Roosevelt to Reagan*, 252. For a critical view of Reagan's economic policies, see John F. Palmer and Isabel V. Sawhill, eds., *The Reagan Record, An Assessment of America's Changing Domestic Priorities* (Cambridge, Mass., 1984).

216. See Dennis L. Bark, ed., *To Promote Peace, U.S. Foreign Policy in the Mid-1980s* (Stanford, Calif., 1984). Ryan J. Barrilleaux, *The President and Foreign Affairs: Evaluation, Performance, and Power* (New York, 1985).

217. Author's conversation with Lawrence Eagleburger in Washington, D.C., on April 30, 1982.

218. Yankee Doodle Magic, What Makes Reagan So Remarkably Popular a President?, *Time* (July 7, 1986): 10.

## CHAPTER 8

219. Theodore Roosevelt, *Realizable Ideals* (San Francisco, 1911), 36, 127.

220. Ralph Waldo Emerson, quoted in Thomas E. Cronin, *Thinking and Learning about Leadership,* 31.

221. See Richard Hofstadter, *The American Political Tradition and the Men Who Made It* (chapter: The Founding Fathers: An Age of Realism), 3–21.

222. See Louis Hartz, *The Liberal Tradition in America, An Interpretation of American Political Thought since the Revolution* (New York, 1955). Daniel J. Boorstin, *The Genius of American Politics* (Chicago, 1953). See Werner Sombart, *Why Is There No Socialism in the United States?* (New York, 1976). Daniel Bell, Socialism: The Dream and the Reality, *Antioch Review* 12 (March 1952): 3–17. D. Bell, *The End of Ideology* (chapter: The Failure of American Socialism), (Glencoe, Ill., 1960). S. M. Lipset, Why No Socialism in the United States?, in Seweryn Bialer and Sophia Sluzar, eds., *Sources of Contemporary Radicalism* (Boulder, Colo., 1977), 31–149.

223. Samuel P. Huntington, *American Politics,* 32 and 33.

224. Robert McClosky, The American Ideology, in *Continuing Crisis in American Politics,* ed. Marian D. Irish (Englewood Cliffs, N.J., 1963), 14.

225. James Bryce, *The American Commonwealth,* 2, 417–18.

226. See S. P. Huntington, *American Politics,* 36–40.

227. Alexis de Tocqueville, *Democracy in America,* ed. Phillips Bradley), (New York, 1945), 2:108.

228. S. P. Huntington, *American Politics,* 37.

229. Ibid.

230. R. E. Neustadt, *Presidential Power,* 26.

231. S. P. Huntington, *Political Order in Changing Societies* (chapter: Political Modernization: America vs. Europe), (New Haven, Conn., 1968), 129.

232. Alexis de Tocqueville, *Democracy in America,* vol. 1.

233. See S. P. Huntington, *American Politics,* 13 ff.

234. See also John J. Herz, *Political Realism and Political Idealism* (Chicago, 1951).

235. Hugo Münsterberg, *Die Amerikaner* (Berlin, 1912), 1, 59.

236. See Lloyd A. Free and Hadley Cantril, *The Political Beliefs of Americans, A Study of Public Opinion* (New York, 1968). Donald J. Devine, *The Political Culture of the United States* (Boston, 1972).

237. See H. Mewes, *Einführung in das politische System der USA,* 77. Richard Suzman, Social Changes in America and the Modernization of Personality, in *We the People,* ed. Gordon DiRenzo (Westport, Conn., 1977): Alex Inkeles, Continuity and Change in the American National Character, in *The Third Century, America as a Post-Industrial Society,* ed. S. M. Lipset (Chicago, 1979), 389–416. S. P. Huntington, *American Politics,* 6, 20, 26–27, 230.

238. See H. Mewes, *Einführung in das politische System der USA* (Heidelberg, 1986), 78, 81.

239. Ibid. See Daniel Yankelovich, *New Rules* (New York, 1981). M. D. Hancock and G. Sjoberg, eds., *Politics in the Post-Welfare-State, Responses to the New Individualism* (New York, 1972).

240. See George C. Lodge, *The New American Ideology* (New York, 1975). S. P. Huntington, Postindustrial Politics: How Benign Will It Be?, *Comparative Politics* 6 (January 1974).

241. S. P. Huntington, *American Politics*, 11 and 12. See also S. M. Lipset and W. Schneider, *The Confidence Gap: Business, Labor and Government in the Public Mind* (Boston, 1972).

242. See also Part III, p. 215.

243. S. P. Huntington, The United States, in *The Crisis of Democracy*, ed. M. Crozier, S. P. Huntington, and J. Watanuki (New York, 1975), 59–60.

244. On the German student revolt, see Part I, pp. 26 ff.

245. Meldon E. Levine, quoted in S. P. Huntington, *American Politics*, 2. On the American Left, see also E. C. Ladd and S. M. Lipset, Public Opinion and Public Policy, in The United States in the 1980s, ed. Peter Duignan and Alvin Rabushka (Stanford, Calif., 1980), 72–74. Lawrence Lader, *Power on the Left, American Radical Movements Since 1946* (New York, 1979), 167 ff. Norman H. Nie, Sidney Verba, and John R. Petrocik, *The Changing American Voter* (Cambridge, Mass., 1976), 365–69. Edward J. Bacciocco, *The New Left in America* (Stanford, Calif., 1974), 228–29.

246. S. P. Huntington, *American Politics*, 235.

247. Ibid., 222.

248. See A. W. McMahon, ed., *Federalism* (New York, 1955): Martin Diamond, Democracy and the Federalist. A Reconsideration of the Framer's Intent, *American Political Science Review* 53 (March 1959): 52–68. M. J. C. Vile, *The Structure of American Federalism* (Oxford, 1961). Aaron Wildavsky, *American Federalism in Perspective* (Boston, 1967).

249. Nelson A. Rockefeller, *The Future of Federalism* (New York, 1963), v.

250. See Vincent Ostrom, *The Political Theory of a Compound Republic: A Reconstitution of the Logical Foundations of an American Democracy as Presented in the Federalist* (Blacksburg, Va., 1971). Martin Diamond, *Notes on the Political Theory of the Founding Fathers* (Philadelphia, 1971).

251. See Herbert J. Storing, ed., *The Anti-Federalist: Writings by the Opponents of the Constitution* (Chicago, 1985), abridgement by Murray Dry. H. J. Storing, *What the Anti-Federalists Were For* (Chicago, 1981). Alpheus T. Mason, *The States Rights Debate: The Anti-Federalists and the Constitution* (Englewood Cliffs, N.J., 1964).

252. See Robert Dahl, *Pluralist Democracy in the US: Conflict and Consensus* (Chicago, 1967): Gabriel Almond and Sidney Verba, *The Civic Culture, Political Attitudes and Democracy in Five Nations* (Boston, 1965).

253. See William Anderson, *The Nation and the States, Rivals or Partners* (Minneapolis, Minn., 1953). Carl J. Friedrich, Federal Constitutional Theory and Emergent Proposals, in *Federalism*, ed. A. W. McMahon, 510 ff. Robert T. Golembiewski and Aaron Wildavsky, eds., *The Cost of Federalism* (New Brunswick, N.J., 1984).

254. See E. S. Corwin, *The Passing of Dual Federalism*, in *Essays in Constitutional Law*, ed. R. McCloskey (New York, 1957), 185 ff.

255. See V. O. Key, *The Administration of Federal Grants to States* (Chicago, 1937). Jane Perry Clark, *The Rise of a New Federalism* (New York, 1938). Henner Ehringhaus, *Der kooperative Föderalismus in den Vereinigten Staaten von Amerika* (Frankfurt am Main, 1972).

256. Daniel J. Elazar, Constitutionalism, Federalism, and the Post-Industrial American Policy, in S. M. Lipset, *The Third Century*, 87.

257. See Morton Grodzins, *The American System* (Chicago, 1974), 277.

258. Daniel J. Elazar, Constitutionalism, in S. M. Lipset, *The Third Century*, 84.

259. Ibid. See in addition the report of the Kerstenbaum Commission, charged by

Eisenhower to check state and community charges of Washington's excessive bureau-cratism, *Commission on Intergovernmental Relations: A Report to the President for Transmittal to the Congress* (Washington, D.C., 1955).

260. See Nelson A. Rockefeller, *The Future of Federalism*, 6–10, passim.

261. See James Sundquist, *Making Federalism Work* (Washington, D.C., 1969). D. J. Elazar, *American Federalism, A View from the States* (New York, 1972). Donald M. Haider, *When Governments Come to Washington* (New York, 1974). Leon Epstein, The Old States in a New System, in *The New American Political System*, ed. Anthony King (Washington, D.C., 1979), 342 ff. Horst Mewes, *Einführung in das politische System der USA*, 245 f.

262. Richard Nixon, Address to the Nation on August 8, 1969, in *Public Papers of the Presidents of the United States* (Washington, D.C., 1970).

263. See Michael Reagan, *The New Federalism* (New York, 1972).

264. William Safire's article appeared in January 1970 in New Federalist Paper, No. 1, quoted here from W. Safire, *Safire's Political Dictionary* (New York, 1978), 454.

265. George Shultz's speech of March 19, 1970, quoted here from W. Safire, *Safire's Political Dictionary*, 454–55.

266. Richard Nixon, State of the Union Address of January 22, 1971, in *Public Papers of the Presidents of the United States* (Washington, D.C., 1972), 53–54. On Nixon's positions on federalism, see also New Federalist Papers, in *The Publius Symposium on the Future of American Federalism, Publius* 2, no. 1 (Spring 1972).

267. See W. E. Oates, ed., *Financing the New Federalism. Revenue Sharing, Conditional Grants, and Taxation* (Baltimore, 1975). Richard P. Nathan and Charles P. Adams,. *Revenue Sharing: The Second Round* (Washington, D.C., 1977). H. Mewes, *Einführung in das politische System der USA*, 246.

268. D. J. Elazar, Constitutionalism, Federalism, and the Post-Industrial American Policy, in S. M. Lipset, *The Third Century*, 85. See Howard Ball, *Controlling Regulatory Sprawl. Presidential Strategies from Nixon to Reagan* (Westport, Conn., 1984).

269. On Reagan's New Federalism programs, see chapter 3 of Walter E. Volkomer's book *American Government* (Englewood Cliffs, N.J., 1983). See also C. Boyden Gray, Regulation and Federalism, *Yale Journal of Regulation* 1, no. 1 (1983): 93–110. George E. Peterson, Federalism and the States: An Experiment in Decentralization, in *The Reagan Record, An Assessment of America's Changing Domestic Priorities*, ed. John Z. Palmer and Isabel V. Sawhill (Cambridge, Mass., 1984), Urban Institute Study, 222 ff. David R. Beam, New Federalism, Old Realities: The Reagan Administration and Intergovernmental Reform, in *The Reagan Presidency and the Governing of America*, ed. Lester M. Salomon and Michael S. Lund (Washington, D.C., 1984), Urban Institute Study.

270. Peter Korn, quoted in John Herbers, What Shape for the New Federalism?, *The New York Times* (March 29, 1981).

271. William Safire, Yes, Reagan Has a Philosophy, But It Won't Work, *International Herald Tribune* (August 27, 1985): 4.

272. D. J. Elazar, Constitutionalism, in S. M. Lipset, *The Third Century*, 81.

273. See also Vincent Ostrom, *The Intellectual Crisis in American Public Administration* (University, Ala., 1974). Norman J. Ornstein, *Interest Groups, Lobbying and Policy Making* (Washington, D.C., 1978). Thomas Dye and L. Harmon Ziegler, *The Irony of Democracy* (Monterey, Calif., 1981). Robert Dahl, *Dilemmas of Pluralist Democracy* (New Haven, Conn., 1982). A. Cigler and P. Loomis, *Interest Group Politics* (Washington, D.C., 1983). Larry J. Sabato, *Pac Power* (New York, 1984). R. T. Go-

lembiewski and Aaron Wildavsky, eds., *The Cost of Federalism* (New Brunswick, N.J., 1984)—see in particular the essays of Nelson Polsby, Theodore Lowi, Fred Greenstein, David Caputo, and Donald Kettl.

274. Ronald Reagan on New Federalism, in *Wireless Bulletin from Washington*, United States Information Service, No. 131, July 14, 1982, Embassy of the United States of America, (Bonn, 1982), 9, 10.

275. See Norman Podhoretz, The New American Majority, *Commentary* 71, no. 1 (January 1981): 19–28.

276. See Louis Hartz, *The Liberal Tradition in America*, passim.

277. Clinton Rossiter, *Conservatism in America* (New York, 1962), 201–202.

278. Ralf Dahrendorf, European Sociology and the American Self-Image, *European Journal of Sociology* 2 (1961): 364.

279. See Lawrence Lader, *Power on the Left, American Radical Movements Since 1946* (New York, 1979) passim.

280. See Ben Haas, *KKK* (Evanston, Ill., 1963). Benjamin R. Epstein and Arnold Forster, *The Radical Right, Report on the John Birch Society and Its Allies* (New York, 1967). Seymour Martin Lipset and Earl Raab, *The Politics of Unreason, Right-Wing Extremism in America 1790/1970* (New York, 1970). Daniel Bell, ed., *The Radical Right* (New York, 1979).

281. See Donald Davidson, The New South and the Conservative Tradition, *National Review* 9 (September 10, 1960). Allen Guttmann, *The Conservative Tradition in America* (New York, 1967).

282. See George H. Nash, *The Conservative Intellectual Movement in America Since 1945* (New York, 1976), passim. Irving Louis Horowitz, *Ideology and Utopia in the United States 1956–1976* (chapter: New Conservatism in America), (London, 1977), 133–61.

283. See Richard M. Weaver, *Ideas Have Consequences* (Chicago, 1948). P. Viereck, *The Unadjusted Man, A New Hero for Americans, Reflections on the Distinction between Conforming and Conserving* (New York, 1956). Robert Nisbet, *The Quest for Community* (New York, 1953). Leo Strauss, *Natural Right and History* (Chicago, 1953). Eric Voegelin, *The New Science of Politics* (Chicago, 1952). William F. Buckley, *Up from Liberalism* (New York, 1959) (Introduction by Barry Goldwater; Foreword by John Dos Passos). W. F. Buckley, *American Conservative Thought in the Twentieth Century* (Indianapolis, 1970). Russel Kirk, *The Conservative Mind* (Chicago, 1953). See also Walter Lippmann, *The Public Philosophy, On the Decline and Revival of the Western Society* (Boston, 1955). Ludwig Freund, The New American Conservatism and European Conservatism, *Ethics* 66 (October, 1955). Ralph L. Ketcham, The Revival of Tradition and Conservatism in America, *Bulletin of the American Association of University Professors* 41 (Autumn 1955).

284. See Arthur M. Schlesinger, Jr., The New Conservatism: Politics of Nostalgia, *Reporter* 12 (June 16, 1955). George H. Nash, Historische, philosophische und soziologische Wurzeln des Konservativismus, in *Der Neo-Konservativismus in den Vereinigten Staaten und seine Auswirkungen auf die Atlantische Allianz*, ed. Hans Rühle, Hans-Joachim Veen, and Walter F. Hahn (Melle, 1982), 42 ff.

285. See Whittaker Chambers, *Witness* (New York, 1952). J. Burnham, *The Coming Defeat of Communism* (New York, 1950). Frank S. Meyer, Communism Remains Communism, *National Review* 2 (October 13, 1956). F. S. Meyer, The Meaning of McCarthyism, *National Review* 5 (June 14, 1958). For a retrospective and succinct account,

see the study by Richard H. Pells, *The Liberal Mind in a Conservative Age: American Intellectuals in the 1940s and 1950s* (New York, 1985).

286. See Friedrich A. Hayek, *The Road to Serfdom* (Chicago, 1944). Ludwig von Mises, *Omnipotent Government* (New Haven, Conn., 1944). Milton Friedman, *Capitalism and Freedom* (Chicago, 1962). George Gilder, *Wealth and Poverty* (New York, 1981). Tod Loofbourrow, Erik Brynjolfsson, and Menzie Chinn, Supply Side for the World: An Interview with Arthur Laffer, *Harvard International Review* 4, no. 6 (March–April 1982): 20–23.

287. See Barry Goldwater, *The Conscience of a Conservative* (Shepherdsville, Ky., 1960). B. Goldwater, *Why Not Victory?* (New York, 1962).

288. S. P. Huntington, Conservatism as an Ideology, in *American Political Science Review* 5 (June 1957): 455.

289. Author's conversation with Norman Podhoretz on May 12, 1982, in New York.

290. See Harvey C. Mansfield, *The Spirit of Liberalism* (Cambridge, Mass., 1978). Edward H. Crane, Libertarianism, in *Emerging Coalitions in American Politics*, ed. S. M. Lipset (San Francisco, 1978). Robert A. Nisbet, The Dilemma of Conservatives in a Populist Society, in *Emerging Coalitions in American Politics*, ed. S. M. Lipset. R. A. Nisbet, The Quintessential Liberal, *Commentary* 72, no. 3 (September 1981).

291. On the neoconservative positions, see Nathan Glazer, The Limits of Social Policy, *Commentary* 52 (September 1971). Daniel P. Moynihan, America's Crisis of Confidence, *Current* (December 1975). Irving Kristol, What Is a Neo-Conservative? *Newsweek* (January 19, 1976). "Is There a Crisis of Spirit in the West"? A Conversation with Dr. Henry A. Kissinger and Senator Daniel P. Moynihan, *Public Opinion* (May/June 1978). Peter Steinfels, *The Neoconservatives, The Men Who Are Changing America's Politics* (New York, 1979–80). Theodore H. White, Summing Up, A Chronicle of two decades of social experiment . . . and the disillusionment that swept Ronald Reagan into the White House, *The New York Times Magazine* (April 25, 1982).

292. See Norman Podhoretz, Making the World Safe for Communism, *Commentary* (April 1976). N. Podhoretz, *The Present Danger, Do We Have the Will to Reverse the Decline of American Power?* (New York, 1980). Robert W. Tucker, The Purposes of American Power, *Foreign Affairs* 52, no. 2 (Winter 1980–81).

293. Author's conversation with Norman Podhoretz on May 12, 1982, in New York.

294. On the ideology of the New Right, see Michael Johnston, The "New Christian Right" in American Politics, *Political Quarterly* 53, no. 2 (April/June 1982). Robert W. Whitaker ed., *The New Right Papers* (New York, 1982) (with articles by the most exposed representatives of the New Right: William A. Rusher, Richard Viguerie, Paul M. Weyrich, et al.). Paul M. Weyrich, Reagan Crowd Out of Touch with Middle America, *Conservative Digest* 8, no. 9, (August 1982). R. A. Viguerie, *The New Right: We're Ready to Lead* (Falls Church, Va., 1980). Lee Edwards, *You Can Make the Difference* (chapter: The New Right and the Conservative Movement), (Westport, Conn., 1980). For a critical view of the New Right, see Democrats for the 80's, *The New Right: A Threat to America's Future* (Chairman of the Board of Directors, Pamela C. Harriman), (Washington, D.C., 1981). Peter Ross Range, Thunder from the Right, *The New York Times Magazine* (February 8, 1981): 23 ff. Friedbert Pflüger, Reagan, die Konservativen und die Gefahr der Neuen Rechten, *Sonde*, no. 1 (1981): 40–61. Alan Crawford, *Thunder on the Right, The "New Right" and the Politics of Resentment* (New York, 1980). William A. Hunter, *The "New Right": A Growing Force in State Politics*, ed. Thomas W. Bonnett, (Washington, D.C., 1980).

295. See Margaret Canovan, *Populism* (New York, 1981). Kevin P. Phillips, *Post-Conservative America. People, Politics, and Ideology in Time of Crisis* (New York, 1982).

296. Rowland Evans and Robert D. Novak, *The Reagan Revolution* (New York, 1981).

297. Irving Kristol on Neoconservatism, Lecture at the Kennedy School of Government, Harvard University, February 5, 1980, unpublished manuscript.

298. Quotations from I. Kristol, ibid.

299. See Lawrence J. R. Herson, *The Politics of Ideas: Political Theory and American Public Policy* (Homewood, Ill., 1984). Tom Hayden, *American Future: New Frontiers Beyond Old Frontiers* (Boston, 1980). Henry S. Kariel, *Beyond Liberalism, Where Relations Grow* (New York, 1977). Irving Louis Horowitz, *Ideology and Utopia in the United States 1956–1976* (chapter: The Pluralistic Bases of Modern American Liberalism), 162–79. Theodore J. Lowi, *The End of Liberalism: Ideology, Policy and the Crisis of Public Authority* (New York, 1969).

300. See Joshua Muravchik, The Think Tank of the Left, *The New York Times Magazine* (March 29, 1981): 36 ff.

301. See L. J. R. Herson, *The Politics of Ideas.*

302. John Rawls, *A Theory of Justice* (Cambridge, Mass., 1971).

303. See Robert Paul Wolff, *The Poverty of Liberalism* (Boston, 1969). Ronald Dworkin, *Taking Rights Seriously* (Cambridge, Mass., 1977–80). R. Dworkin, Liberalism, in *Public and Private Morality*, ed. Stuart Hampshire (Cambridge, Mass., 1978). R. Dworkin, *A Matter of Principle* (Cambridge, Mass., 1985). Bruce A. Ackerman, *Social Justice in the Liberal State* (New Haven, Conn., 1980). Amy Gutmann, *Liberal Equality* (Cambridge, Mass., 1980). Sidney Verba and Gary R. Orren, *Equality in America, The View from the Top* (Cambridge, Mass., 1985). For opposing theoretical positions on this subject, see Robert Nozick, *Anarchy, State and Utopia* (New York, 1974). R. Nozick, *Philosophical Explanations* (Cambridge, Mass., 1982).

304. See Walter F. Mondale, The Re-Education of Walter Mondale, *The New York Times Magazine* (November 8, 1981), 67 ff. Wanted: A Liberal Agenda, *Newsweek* (March 30, 1981): 46–48. Liberalism in America, *The Center Magazine* 14, no. 2 (March/April 1981) (the entire issue is dedicated to the theme of liberalism, articles by Barton J. Bernstein, Al Stern, Otis L. Graham, and others).

305. Charles Peters, quoted in Walter Goodman, As Neoliberals Search for Closest Fit, Hart Is Often Mentioned, *The New York Times* (May 15, 1984): A 24.

306. Morton Kondracke quoted in Wanted: A Liberal Agenda, *Newsweek,* 47.

307. See Randall Rothenberg, *The Neoliberals: Creating the New American Politics* (New York, 1984), passim.

308. See ibid. Morton Kondracke and Michael A. Scully, Liberalism's Brave Neo World?, Two Views, *Public Opinion* (April/May 1982): 3–5. The Agenda After Reagan, *The New Republic* (March 31, 1982) (the entire issue is dedicated to the above-mentioned theme, articles by Daniel Yergin, Walter Laqueur, Lester Thurow, Robert Reich, and others). Paul Tsongas, *The Road from Here, Liberalism and Realities in the 1980s* (New York, 1982). E. J. Kahn, Paul Tsongas Interview, *The Boston Magazine* 73, no. 2 (February 1981): 59 ff.

309. Walter Goodman, As Neoliberals Search, *New York Times,* A24.

# Part IV

## DOMESTIC POLITICAL MANIFESTATIONS OF THE AMERICAN IDEA OF PROGRESS

*Any understanding of the essence and orientation of the American ideology of progress would be incomplete without an examination of its key domestic manifestations. The persistent recurrence of frontier and manifest destiny thinking, which is a typical variant of America's domestic and foreign policy belief in progress, is especially meaningful. During the Puritan age in New England, the idea of a New Jerusalem and the "City upon a Hill" fused into the progressivist ideology of the East; in the age of the Founding Fathers the archaic myth (Atlantis, Arcadia) of the continuous westward course of American civilization was infused with new energy. Thomas Jefferson gave the guiding visions and motifs of the American Revolution ("independence, expansion, and nationalism") a new, westwardly oriented framework in the ideology of the frontier:*

*[He] tied the nation and its nationalism to an expanding western dream, and to the independence of isolation. American independence and expansion (America as fortress and as crusader) became in the mythology of manifest destiny logically inseparable ideals and concepts, connected intimately with the creation of the American nation.[1]*

*The nineteenth-century image of the Western hero was personified in its archetype, Andrew Jackson:*

*the outstanding Western hero of the early nineteenth century, and the symbol of . . . the West and its mythology by the entire nation was Andrew Jackson. . . . The West, as symbolized by Jackson, was not merely an acceptable adjunct of the United States but a permanent and essential part of the nation, of its society, and its politics. . . . The democratic West represented the lasting hopes of the American nation, and with Andrew Jackson as President, those hopes were permanently part of the nation. The integration of the West proved, in the logic of mythology, that expansion was necessary to the health of the nation and its ideals, and that it was morally good—beneficial to the liberty, equality, and pursuit of happiness (as well as the democracy) of all humanity.[2]*

*After the East and then the West of the country had been settled, all that remained for America was the mission in the rest of the world: "The mission of the East—to send 'missionaries' to civilize the West—was the same as the mission of America to the world."[3]*

*At this point it is necessary to portray the motivation and problems of this initially innercontinental missionary zeal, which continues to manifest itself in the policies of American presidents. The American historian Frederick Jackson Turner, in his path-breaking lecture entitled "The Significance of the Frontier in American History" in 1893, drew attention to the importance of the frontier, the incessant push westward into the land of unlimited opportunity, as an ideological factor and one of the most critical elements of the American sense of progress.[4] At the same time, before becoming president, Theodore Roosevelt wrote a four-volume work on the frontier:* The Winning of the West *(1906). In the 1960s, this motif would return in John F. Kennedy's "New Frontier," this time, symbolically rather than as a geographic reference since the country had been settled for a number of decades. Today only this symbolic character of frontier ideology has been retained. Ronald Reagan's attempt to dare a new frontier in space with his SDI project seems, however, to remain controversial also in the Bush administration.*

*This section is dedicated to understanding the middle period of American history and politics and the motivations and problems associated with its frontier ideology (such as the expulsion of the Indians). This period heralded the coming of a new Creedal Passion phase during the Jacksonian democracy. As idol of the common man, Andrew Jackson propagated the democratization and popularization of progressivist thought in his model of agrarian democracy, envisioned as an anti-elitist foil to the more aristocratic Jeffersonian idea of democracy. At the same time, the reawakening of American nationalism in the first half of the nineteenth century and the emergence of doubts about American progressivism in the romantic movement, whose radical and critical spokesman was Henry David Thoreau, will also be discussed here.*

*The following investigation will attempt to treat and explain the most important domestic political crises of American progressivism. The discussion begins with the biggest crisis in American history, the Civil War, which was resolved through the policies of Abraham Lincoln. At the same time, Lincoln succeeded in abolishing the sorest point in American progressivism—slavery. Thus, he was able to take his place of honor in American history not only as the most exceptional American president of the nineteenth century, but also as one of the most significant personalities of American politics.*

*The period following the Civil War brought with it a new phase of American history and politics, the age of industrialization and urbanization. This period, with its new wave of immigration and the establishment of large monopolies, or trusts, was variously interpreted as the Gilded Age or reconstruction phase, the era of Spoilsmen and robber barons, a period of rugged individualism or plutocratic reaction. In response to this rise of a socially unregulated American industrial age, an agrarian fundamentalist populist movement was founded toward the end of the century. This movement perceived itself as David against the Goliath trusts and felt itself isolated from the* Promise of American Life *(Herbert Croly, 1909). The movement could be labeled as the most vigorous, active critical reaction to American civilization. The eventual stemming of this new tide of creedal passion and its integration into the Progressive movement may be credited to the progressive presidents Theodore Roosevelt ("New Nationalism") and Woodrow Wilson ("New Freedom") and their reform policies.*

*The Progressive era (lasting from 1890 to 1920) constitutes one of the most interesting periods in domestic American history and politics. It was the prototype for the first open conflict between* Progress and Poverty *(Henry George, 1880), the first antagonisms between government and big business, and the first crisis of the laissez-faire principle in the United States. With the aid of neo-Jeffersonian ideals (Woodrow Wilson) and neo-Hamiltonian strategies (Theodore Roosevelt), the Progressive movement created a true masterpiece of American consensus and progressivist politics by managing to convince both the Democratic and Republican parties to embrace progressivist politics. Capitalism and democracy were preserved and reconciled with each other through reform of the American government, economy, and society, rather than revolution, as extreme leftists and rightists had propounded. This occasioned revisionist historians to dismiss this era as* The Triumph of Conservatism *(Gabriel Kolko, 1963).[5] But it was this age of Progressivism, mugwump intelligentsia, muckraking spirit, and the emancipation of women that heralded the modern American presidency and thereby a strong government with centralized power, as well as the beginnings of the American welfare state. Theodore Roosevelt's unsuccessful candidacy for the presidency in 1912 in the Progressive party (Bull Moose party), which he himself had founded, ultimately proved that the modern Republican party could no longer afford to inure itself to questions of social justice and social welfare.[6]*

*Finally, this discussion will try to shed light on the American economic depression of the 1930s, a depression overcome by FDR's continuation of progressivist politics with his New Deal program. In addition, the question must be discussed of whether or not the New Deal consensus, which survived for three decades after the Second World War and had a major influence on American economic policy, has been rendered obsolete today by a postmodernist economic and ecologic culture and by a neolibertarian renaissance.*

# 9

## Frontier and Manifest Destiny

If one attempts to follow the traces of American frontier ideology and the image of the American West, one will inevitably encounter two plausible interpretations, as the American historian Ray A. Billington has indicated. The modern concept of the American West blends two different images that emerged during the eighteenth and nineteenth centuries. The one pictured the frontier as lawless, brutal, and repelling, molded by a savage environment that reduced the frontiersman to semibarbarism. The other painted the West as a transplanted Eden, overflowing with the bounties of nature, and beckoning the dispossessed to a new life of abundance and freedom.[7]

It is a well-known fact that environmental conditions almost always influence the psychological and intellectual development of the individual, as well as the people and the politics of a country. The continental expanse of the United States, with its immense natural resources and riches and its seemingly unlimited opportunities, has made America seem like the promised land to Americans and foreigners alike. The presence of these exceptional circumstances produced a progressivist belief in the special destiny of this people, in their electness, and their charge to demonstrate to themselves and to the rest of the less privileged world the liberal and democratic ways of life by means of "conduct" and "example." These beliefs were simultaneously to be actively communicated to the world, that is, Americans were to be missionaries.[8] The ideology of the frontier and manifest destiny can only be interpreted against the background of this combination of unusual natural conditions, the progressivist belief in freedom and democracy, and a missionary sense of providence.

The experience of the frontier and the pioneers ultimately affected American self-understanding and missionary zeal in two ways. On the one hand, the actual frontier experience directly influenced the character of Americans, particularly those who were geographically and chronologically closest to the frontier and its legacy in the nineteenth century. On the other hand, this historical experience and the frontier tradition resulting from it fused into an independent politico-historical factor that helped shape the American view of the past and image of the world.[9] In this way there emerged a myth of the frontier that became a solid component of the American progressivist credo and continues to the present in both these conceptual images. This experience of the Western frontier, as instrumentalized into a variant of progressivist American ideology, was described by Frederick Jackson Turner, one of the Progressive historians, in the following way: "American democracy is fundamentally the outcome of the experiences of the American people in dealing with the West."[10] Walt W. Rostow explains the persistence of American values on the basis of the myth of success and the American sense of adventure and pioneering enterprise:

[The] classic American style . . . emerged distinctively toward the end of the seventeenth century as the imperatives and opportunities of a wild but ample land began to assert themselves over various transplanted autocratic attitudes and institutions which proved inappropriate to the colonial scene . . . [and] came fully to life . . . after the War of 1812. . . . The cast of American values and institutions and the tendency to adapt them by cumulative experiment rather than to change them radically has been progressively strengthened by the image of the gathering success of the American adventure.[11]

According to Turner's "single factor" interpretation (Louis Hartz)[12] of American history, the frontier strengthened Puritan and democratic convictions and experiences such as idealism, individualism, the idea of uniqueness and electness, produced and deepened the idea of manifest destiny, and thus had a lasting effect on the American character and American politics. In addition, it influenced America's relationship to its surroundings. Thus, the frontier hypothesis can be understood as a secular counterpart to the Puritan founding of American progressivist ideology.[13] It promoted the intracontinental tendencies and ideals of the American idea of mission, and it diverted these same factors into a foreign policy mission once the West and the rest of the country had been settled.

Above all, the frontier was a historical experience, and as such it was a dynamic, flowing process; it was the settlement of the North American continent from the East, the pushing back of the frontier toward the West, that compelled Turner to use the concept of "the West" synonymously with the frontier.[14] The pioneer existence of the Americans on the frontier, in their constant struggle with nature and the Indians, dependent only on themselves and a few neighbors, favored qualities still considered typically American today: self-confidence, thirst for independence, mistrust of authority, activism, optimism, individualism, and aspiration for success. Whether interpreted in the sense of Puritanism, democracy, or the frontier, success has time and again been regarded as proof of the fundamental correctness of American ideology and its institutions.[15] The frontier was the actual "melting pot" of America; under its influence immigrants of any origin became "Americans." At the same time it produced a nationalizing motivation.

Andrew Jackson, the incarnation of this democracy constructed on individualistic pioneer virtues, pointed to the progressive aspects of the frontier or the West: "free land," the surplus of natural resources, open spaces, freedom, and "opportunity" for all. Equality and personal freedom became the catchwords of President Jackson, for whom the internal continental expansion of the United States "extended the area of freedom."[16] Thus, the frontier experience, the migrations of the pioneers, the dynamic expansion of civilization into the West— all gave a new impulse to the already extant American missionary zeal, that combination of the Puritan concept of salvation and its secularized form of enlightened democratic belief in progress. This third element of American frontier and missionary consciousness consists of the task of promoting democracy; that is, ensuring the progress of humankind. With the help of this ideology, the belief that the rise and expansion of democracy is the task and triumph of the American frontier could be renewed.[17]

Long after the frontier itself had disappeared, this missionary impulse was transformed into the lasting power of the frontier as progressivist ideology and myth. In the twentieth century, the spirit of discovery and "opportunity" awakened by the frontier experience shifted to intellectual and political areas, such as science, technology, politics, and economics. The frontier of "opportunities" was now expanded within established geographical boundaries by enhancement of technological and economic conditions. Here, however, lie the problems inherent in a missionary belief in the frontier: the United States has often tended to transfer to the international level the frontier ideas of the expansion of economic opportunities and democratic compromise. This tendency has often contributed to a moralistic ethos and idealistic overambition in American foreign policy.

Presidents Theodore Roosevelt, Franklin Delano Roosevelt, John F. Kennedy, and Ronald Reagan are all representatives of this modern frontier ideology. As mentioned previously, Theodore Roosevelt explored the phenomenon of the "frontier" quite thoroughly in his work *The Winning of the West*.[18] In office the application of frontier ideology thus meant for him the pursuit of an expansionist and proselytizing foreign policy toward the United States' neighbor, the Philippines.

Under Franklin Delano Roosevelt, American science and technology once again set out for new frontiers. The postwar bases of U.S. scientific and technological progress were laid down in the report "Science—The Endless Frontier," submitted in July 1944 to President Roosevelt by Vannevar Bush, the director of the Office of Scientific Research and Development.[19] In the letter commissioning Bush to write the study, Roosevelt wrote: "New frontiers of the mind are before us, and if they are pioneered with the same vision, boldness, and drive with which we have waged this war we can create a fuller and more fruitful employment and a fuller and more fruitful life."[20] Frontier ideology experienced a veritable renaissance during the presidency of John F. Kennedy. Here the democratic credo of the frontier, the inseparable bond between *democracy, progress,* and *liberty,* was redefined in new missionary-like terms. On July 15, 1960, the new presidential candidate John F. Kennedy proclaimed to the Democratic National Convention in Los Angeles:

For I stand tonight facing West on what was once the last frontier. From the lands that stretch three thousand miles behind me, the pioneers of old gave up their safety, their comfort and sometimes their lives to build a new world here in the West. . . . They were determined to make that new world strong and free, to overcome its hazards and its hardships, to conquer the enemies that threatened from without and within. Today some would say . . . that there is no longer an American frontier. But I trust that . . . we stand today on the edge of a New Frontier—the frontier of the 1960s—a frontier of unknown opportunities and perils—a frontier of unfulfilled hopes and threats. . . . I am asking each of you to be new pioneers on that New Frontier.[21]

Kennedy cultivated this resurrection of frontier ideology as a motto of progress ("getting America moving") throughout his term of office. In the second year of his presidency, he once again invoked the frontier in his State of the Union Address of 1962, in connection with American research in space: "our objective in making this effort, which we hope will place one of our citizens on the moon, is to develop in a new frontier of science, commerce and cooperation, the position of the United States and the Free World."[22]

The attempt to establish a new frontier in space in the 1980s is the latest manifestation of expansion of the American frontier in science and technology, as well as military areas. In his famous speech of March 23, 1983, on national security, President Ronald Reagan introduced a new long-term military strategy to be called the Strategic Defense Initiative (SDI):

Let me share with you a vision of the future which offers hope. It is that we embark on a program to counter the awesome Soviet missile threat with measures that are defensive. Let us turn to the very strengths in technology that spawned our great industrial base and that have given us the quality of life we enjoy today. What if free people could live secure in the knowledge that their security did not rest upon the threat of instant U.S. retaliation and destroy strategic ballistic missiles before they reached our soil or that of our allies? I know this is a formidable technical task, one that may not be accomplished before the end of this century. . . . It will take years, probably decades, of effort on many fronts. . . . Our only purpose—one all people share—is to search for ways to reduce the danger of nuclear war. My fellow Americans, tonight we are launching an effort which holds the promise of changing the course of human history. There will be risks, and results take time. But . . . I believe we can do it.[23]

As far as the development of frontier ideology is concerned, this was certainly a new, challenging technological way of overcoming the "frontier of the frontier." However, the uncertainty about the success of this plan, and the risks mentioned by Reagan himself, have brought critics of the SDI project on both sides of the Atlantic into the arena. Whether the SDI program actually means progress will become clear only over the course of the next decades.

In this context, one more aspect of frontier ideology needs to be mentioned: the idea of manifest destiny. Manifest destiny can be understood as the activation of the original American missionary idea, originally as the intracontinental justification for the expansion and settlement of the United States during the nineteenth century.[24] Julius Pratt credits the classic and politically momentous definition of the idea of manifest destiny to the journalist John O'Sullivan, the editor of *United States Magazine and Democratic Review*. In articles from July and November 1839, O'Sullivan wrote that the destiny of the United States was to fulfill "manifest destiny to overspread the continent allotted by Providence for the development of our . . . millions." Then he went on to speak of the "mission of American democracy,"

the nation of many nations [which] is destined to manifest to mankind the excellence of divine principles: to establish on earth the noblest temple. . . . Its floor shall be a hemisphere, its congregation of a Union of many Republics . . . governed by God's national law of equality, the law of brotherhood.[25]

The idea of electness and of fulfilling a particular mission, first on the American continent, then for all humankind, has occupied the American mind since the Puritan age. This idea of mission was, however, only passively conceived in the symbol of "a New Israel" and the idea of "conduct and example." With the rise of the ideology of manifest destiny, this previously abstract idea of mission changed for the first time into an active, dynamic, and practical political principle in which all of the previously discussed missionary elements of American thought (Puritan and democratic moralism, idealistic universalism, providential sanction of the American existence and chosenness, the moral conviction of a new progressivist beginning and of America's superiority over the Old World) came to fruition first within the continent, then outside of it. The new moment that gave the imminent sense of political mission the opportunity to unfold was the concrete example of the frontier experience: "A free, confederated, self-governed republic on a continental scale."[26] The rationale and justification of this continental expansion, the active propagation of American ideals in the name of manifest destiny, initially remained restricted to the American continent. The rest of the world was involved only to the degree that the New World had been elected "to manifest to all mankind the excellence of divine principles" (O'Sullivan), that is, to serve as a model through "conduct and example."[27]

Continental manifest destiny and its ideology of expansion and frontier brought with it the problem of expelling "savages," the Indians, a policy seemingly sanctioned by providence. The problem had already come to light in 1823, in the words of the Massachusetts Congressman Francis Baylies:

The swelling tide of our population must and will roll on until that mighty ocean interposes its waters, and limits our territorial empire. . . . To diffuse the arts of life, the light of science, and the blessings of the Gospel over a wilderness, is no violation of the laws of God; it is no invasion of the rights of man to occupy a territory over which the savage roams, but which he never cultivates. . . . The stream of bounty which perpetually flows from the throne of the Almighty ought not to be obstructed in its course.[28]

The spreading of the mission, in this case the expulsion of the Indians, from their own land, was interpreted as "no violation of the laws of God." Indeed, it was regarded as the duty "to spread the blessings of the Gospel over a wilderness . . . over which the savage roams, but which he never cultivates."

A counterpart to the ideology of manifest destiny is presented by the speech made in 1855 by the chief of the Duwamish, Chief Seattle, a speech that gives eloquent testimony to the thinking and character of the Indians. What is now the state of Washington in the American Northwest was the home of the Duwamish Indians, who like all Indians considered themselves a part of nature, to which they paid tribute and respect, and with which they had lived in complete harmony for generations. When, in 1855, the Democratic President Franklin Pierce proposed to the Duwamish that they sell their land to white settlers and move to a reservation, Chief Seattle responded to the "Great Chief of the white men" as follows:

The White Chief says that Big Chief at Washington sends us greetings of friendship and good will. This is kind of him for we know he has little need of our friendship in return. His people are many. They are like the grass that covers vast prairies. My people are few. They resemble the scattering trees of a storm-swept plain. The Great—and I presume—good White Chief sends us word that he wishes to buy our lands but is willing to allow us enough to live comfortably. This indeed appears just, even generous, for the Red Man no longer has rights that he need respect, and the offer may be wise also, as we are no longer in need of an extensive country.

There was a time when our people covered the land as the waves of a wind-ruffled sea cover its shell-paved floor, but that time long since passed away with the greatness of tribes that are now but a mournful memory. I will not dwell on, nor mourn over, our untimely decay, nor reproach my pale face brothers with hastening it as we too may have been somewhat to blame.

Youth is impulsive. When our young men grow angry at some real or imaginary wrong, and disfigure their faces with black paint, it denotes that their hearts are black—and then they are often cruel and relentless, and our old men and old women are unable to restrain them. Thus it has ever been. Thus it was when the white man first began to push our forefathers westward. But let us hope that the hostilities between us may never return. We would have everything to lose and nothing to gain. Revenge by young braves is considered gain, even at the cost of their own lives, but old men who stay at home in times of war, and mothers who have sons to lose, know better.

Our good father at Washington—for I presume he is now our father as well as yours, since King George has moved his boundaries further north—our great and good father, I say, sends us word that if we do as he desires he will protect us. His brave warriors will be to us a bristling wall of strength, and his wonderful ships of war will fill our harbors so that our ancient enemies far to the northward—the Hidas and Timpsions, will cease to frighten our women, children and old men. Then in reality will he be our father and we his children. But can that ever be? Your God is not our God! Your God loves your people and hates mine. He folds his strong protecting arms lovingly about the pale face and leads him by the hand as a father leads his infant son—but He has forsaken His red children—if they are really His. Our God, the Great Spirit, seems also to have forsaken us. Your God makes your people wax strong every day. Soon they will fill all the land. Our people are ebbing away like a rapidly receding tide that will never return. The white man's God can not love our people or He would protect them. They seem to be orphans who can look nowhere for help. How then can we be brothers? How can your God become our God and renew our prosperity and awaken in us dreams of returning greatness. If we have a common Heavenly Father He must be partial—for He came to His pale-face children. We never saw Him. He gave you laws but had no word for His red children whose teeming multitudes once filled this vast continent as stars fill the firmament. No. We are two distinct races with separate origins and separate destinies. There is little in common between us.

To us the ashes of our ancestors are sacred and their resting place is hallowed ground. You wander far from the graves of your ancestors and seemingly without regret. Your religion was written on tables of stone by the iron finger of your God so that you could not forget. The Red Man could never comprehend nor remember it. Our religion is the traditions of our ancestors—the dreams of our old men, given them in the solemn hours of night by the Great Spirit; and the visions of our sachems, and is written in the hearts of our people.

Your dead cease to love you and the land of their nativity as soon as they pass the portals of the tomb and wander away beyond the stars. They are soon forgotten and never return. Our dead never forget the beautiful world that gave them being. They still love its verdant valleys, its murmuring rivers, its magnificent mountains, sequestered vales and verdant-lined lakes and bays, and ever yearn in tender, fond affection over the lonely hearted living, and often return from the Happy Hunting Ground to visit, guide, console and comfort them.

Day and night can not dwell together. The Red Man has ever fled the approach of the White Man as the morning mist flees before the rising sun.

However, your proposition seems fair, and I think that my folks will accept it and will retire to the reservation you offer them. Then we will dwell apart in peace for the words of the Great White Chief seem to be the voice of Nature speaking to my people out of dense darkness.

It matters little where we pass the remnant of our days. They will not be many. The Indian's night promises to be dark. Not a single star of hope hovers above his horizon. Sad-voiced winds moan in the distance. Grim Nemesis seems to be on the Red Man's trail, and wherever he goes he will hear the approaching footsteps of his fell destroyer and prepare to stolidly meet his doom, as does the wounded doe that hears the approaching footsteps of the hunter.

A few more moons. A few more winters—and not one of the descendants of the mighty hosts that once moved over this broad land or lived in happy homes, protected by the Great Spirit, will remain to mourn over the graves of a people—once more powerful and hopeful than yours. But why should I mourn at the untimely fate of my people? Tribe follows tribe, and nation follows nation, like the waves of the sea. It is the order of nature, and regret is useless. Your time of decay may be distant—but it will surely come, for even the White Man whose God walked and talked with him as friend with friend, can not be exempt from the common destiny. We may be brothers after all. We will see.[29]

## JACKSONIAN DEMOCRACY

The first populist manifestation of progress in American domestic politics took place during the middle period (1820–60) of American history, which spanned the age of the frontier and manifest destiny, the Indian and slavery questions, and the presidency of Andrew Jackson (1829–37).[30] A democratic-populist trend began in the 1820s (the Creedal Passion period), and was directed against the "aristocratic character of the elitist politics of the patrician generation of the country's founders." It was borne along in the wake of the stormy expansion into the West and eventually penetrated the entire American middle class and its spiritual, social, and economic ways of life, finally culminating in the "Jacksonian Revolution."[31] With Jackson's inauguration as the first Westerner to move into the White House, the era of the presidents from New England and Virginia drew to a close. This change of systems struck the Easterners almost apocalyptically. This impression was intensified by the scenes of Jackson's wild boisterousness and raw, unbridled, short-tempered eruptions ("dangerous egomania") that took place after his inauguration in Washington and even in the White House itself ("cleansing the Augean stables").[32]

Andrew Jackson assumed office with a plan to "democratize" the American republic, its institutions, and the organizational structures of the American political parties. As the first president to regard himself as a representative of the middle class, as the archetype of the "self-made man and man of the frontier" from Tennessee, as a "man of the people," as a champion of independence of local government and the individual states, as an advocate of laissez-faire economic policies, and as an opponent of firmly entrenched and hierarchically structured bureaucracies instilled with their own professional class consciousness, Jackson wanted to popularize American democracy and progressivist ideology and establish a government of the people within the bureaucracies themselves.[33] Henceforth, the functionaries of governmental power were to be elected directly and freely at the local and individual state level, and all political officeholders in official nonelective positions were to be appointed by the president of the United States, the governors, and mayors along party lines.[34] In the area of economics, this populist president advocated a strictly laissez-faire policy, called for absolute legal equality (blacks and Indians excluded), and sought to abolish all economic privileges.

Richard Hofstadter outlined the Jacksonian Revolution in the following terms:

The Jacksonian movement grew out of expanding opportunities and a common desire to enlarge these opportunities still further by removing restrictions and privileges that had their origin in acts of government; thus, with some qualifications, it was essentially a movement of laissez-faire, an attempt to divorce government and business.[35]

The fact that Jackson's open hostility had negative, even catastrophic, effects on the national economy was demonstrated by the president's struggle against the national bank, which was popularly regarded as a threat because of the monopoly it had. The national bank was made the scapegoat for a whole variety of problems. In 1832 Jackson used his veto to block the application of the Second Bank of the United States for a renewal of its charter, which was due to expire in 1836 and which Congress was entirely willing to approve. Feeling sufficiently strong after his reelection in the fall of 1832, Jackson destroyed the Bank by withdrawing the deposits of the federal government. This action was hailed by his populist supporters and adherents of ''grass-roots democracy'' but precipitated a severe financial and economic crisis from which the country would not recover until the 1840s.[36]

The rise of Jacksonian democracy was accompanied by the consolidation of the American two-party system, first in the establishment of the Democratic party in 1828, to which Jackson himself belonged; and second, in reaction to this, in the establishment of the Whig party under the leadership of John Quincy Adams, Henry Clay, and Daniel Webster. On both sides a party machine now began to entrench itself, amateur politicians were replaced with professionals, and appointment to office came to be viewed as the reward or incentive for outstanding service to the party. Jackson clearly recognized the opportunities ensuing from this development by building up a ''spoils system'' within the government and the Democratic party, a system more extensive than that of any of his predecessors.[37] Hofstadter wrote fittingly of Jackson that ''He was a simple, emotional, and unreflective man with a strong sense of loyalty to personal friends and political supporters; he swung to the democratic camp when the democratic camp swung to him.''[38] By drastically reducing the periods of office and encouraging swift turnover in the higher reaches of the bureaucracy (''rotation in office''), the populist president was able to reward many of his loyal adherents and friends, to bring a number of ''middle-class'' citizens into active political life, and to put a stop to the seemingly corrupt process of bureaucratization. He thus created the impression that the entire governmental and administrative apparatus was undergoing democratization and was likewise being purged of incompetents.

Jackson himself formulated his populist social philosophy in these words:

It is to be regretted that the rich and powerful too often bend the acts of government to their selfish purposes. Distinctions in society will always exist under every just government. Equality of talents, of education, or of wealth cannot be produced by human institutions. In the full enjoyment of the gifts of Heaven and the fruits of superior industry, economy, and virtue, every man is equally entitled to protection by law; but when the laws undertake to add to these natural and just advantages artificial distinctions, to grant titles, gratuities, and exclusive privileges, to make the rich richer and the potent more powerful, the humble members of society—the farmers, mechanics, and laborers—who have neither the time nor the means of securing like favors to themselves, have a right to complain of the injustice of their Government. There are no necessary evils in government. Its evils exist only in its abuses. If it would confine itself to equal protection, and, as Heaven does its rains, shower its favors alike on the high and the low, the rich and the poor, it would be an unqualified blessing.[39]

This was an unambiguous definition of the progressivist philosophy of the rising middle class, of the movement of the common man. This philosophy was adopted and supported by the Jacksonian Revolution, and articulated an agrarian-populist protest against the emerging economic society with its tendencies toward the concentration of power and the attendant formation of classes.[40] Jackson had promised a democratization of American institutions and organizations as a response to aristocratic wealth, prestige, and relations.[41] In some quarters his electoral victory was celebrated as "a demand for the restoration of morality and virtue in civic life, and a reform of those practices that had corrupted officials, expanded government, and endangered freedom. It represented a reaffirmation of the republican doctrines of the Revolution."[42] Yet, his term of office also resulted in the formation of a "party machinery," which tended to serve Jackson's populistic party functionaries and friends more as an instrument of manipulation than as a vehicle for emancipation of the masses.

Ernst Fraenkel has graphically characterized the consequences of Jackson's "debureaucratization, progressivist popularization, and democratization" for the country's party culture. According to him, the Jacksonian Revolution brought about

—the development of political parties whose primary goals were to provide their active members with official offices and government contracts (patronage parties);

—rule of these parties by "bosses," who distributed "spoils" in return for fees to the candidates for public office and government contracts designated by local party machines;

—the corruption of public administration (especially at the community level), which was frequently forced to finance, directly or indirectly, the "bosses," party machines, campaigns, and party followers;

—the fostering of an "underworld" whose immunity from prosecution by the equally "beholden" police and justice officials was guaranteed by the party machine (and not only in isolated instances) in return for a "license fee" paid to the "boss." This practice allowed for the maintenance of illegal enterprises (casinos, bookmaking parlors, brothels) and the pursuit of prohibited professions (by bookies, pimps, and bootleggers). Candidates of both parties for election to parliamentary, administrative, or judicial positions were nominated by bodies stacked with functionaries appointed by the "bosses" primarily from the ranks of former or incumbent officials or candidates for public office, depending on whether the party in question was "in" or "out";

—care of the needy segments of the population (especially new immigrants) by the party machine, which created reliable election "fixers" and a pliable electorate with the help of its charitable and social welfare activity, the whole apparatus made possible in the first place by the lack of labor, welfare, and social security authorities.[43]

The most recent trilogy about the Jackson era ignores such negative qualities of progress. On the contrary, in his three-volume work, the historian Robert V. Remini praises Jackson as a "great hero," "the first grand champion of American democracy," and "the key figure in transforming America from a republic into a democracy." According to Remini, Jackson's two principles were "the right of the majority to govern is absolute," and "the will of the majority, once it is expressed, must be obeyed absolutely." Furthermore, writes Remini, "the president and the president alone" must represent the people as the spokesperson of the majority. Finally, "all branches of the government, including the Congress and the courts," must "obey the popular will."[44] Remini's idealization of these "un-American," "authoritarian," and "absolute" principles, as well as his admiration of Jackson's personality, are unmistakable.

In fact, Jackson's populist ideological concept of democracy ("the popular will") entails a *reversal* of the constitutional ideology originally conceived by the Founding Fathers. The minority, once protected from the tyranny of the majority, was now supposed to obey the will of the majority "absolutely." If Jackson's predecessors still regarded themselves merely as the "heads of the *executive branch* of the government," Jackson now offered a new definition of this role: "the President, not Congress, (is) . . . the instrument of popular will."[45] In line with this view, he even gave himself the rank of "head of the government," something that had been done by no other president before him. The question then quite naturally arises as to who makes the final determination of "the popular will." Jackson himself never once doubted what the "popular will" was: he was its very embodiment. One is tempted to identify in Jackson's doctrine of the "popular will" an American version of Rousseau's *volonté générale*. Another question that begs irresistibly to be answered is, what was *democratic* about the Jacksonian democracy when "all branches of the government, including Congress and the courts, must obey the popular will," which in this case meant nothing other than "obey the President."

## NATIONALISM AND ROMANTICISM

The intellectual and social life, as well as the politics and economy of the Jackson era and the years immediately following it were marked by the prevalence of individualistic-democratic and nationalistic-romantic currents. The mixture of the frontier experience, manifest destiny, and nagging questions of imperfection spurred intellectual efforts to improve social conditions:

The spread of political democracy through extension of the franchise and the accompanying spate of social reform movements changed significantly the lives and expectations of ordinary folk, and progress accordingly took on a variety of democratic connotations. The expansion of the frontier provided a psychological, as well as an economic, safety valve for the growing tensions of urban life in the East. The rise of an acute sense of American nationalism linked intimately developments in the nation at large with each individual's perception of himself and his destiny. Advances in public education and communications technology put detailed news of the day's events in everyone's hands, thus raising the general level of awareness of historical change.[46]

All of these changes, which emerged not least as the result of the radical democracy of the West (Jacksonian democracy), were expressed in a romantic and individualistic interpretation of the idea of progress. The fact that the American progressivist idea received new energy during the middle period was confirmed by the historian Arthur Ekirch, who maintained that "the idea of progress" around 1860 "was the most popular American philosophy, thoroughly congenial to the ideas and interests of the age."[47]

The main figure of American Romanticism and the philosophical school of the transcendentalists was Ralph Waldo Emerson (1803–82), whose essays, which were also familiar to many Europeans, propagated an idealized moral individualism.[48] His image of the individual as a part of the divine totality of nature was rooted in Puritanism and the rationalist ideas of the Enlightenment but at the same time remained indebted to the world-view of Romanticism. At any rate, he regarded the idea of progress with ambivalence:

Emerson, though he subscribed generally to the notion of individual improvement, was also skeptical that technological or scientific advance signified progress in either knowledge or society. The measure of a civilization's progress was the moral quality of men it produced, and Emerson to the last was uncertain that the modern age had in this regard made progress over the past.[49]

Henry David Thoreau (1817–62) was genuinely skeptical of progress; indeed, he was antiprogressivist and scornful of the "American way of life." He can be characterized as the cultural pessimist of American Romanticism. When he repeatedly refused to pay taxes in protest against the Mexican War and slavery, he spent a brief period in jail. His essay on civil disobedience (1849), which would later have a strong influence on Mahatma Gandhi, was a manifesto of passive resistance against a state power that was, for him, morally suspect ("I find that we should first be men, then subjects"):[50]

I meet this American government, or its representative, the state government, directly, and face to face, once a year—no more—in the person of its tax-gatherer; this is the only mode in which a man situated as I am necessarily meets it; and it then says distinctly, Recognize me; and the simplest, most effectual, and, in the present posture of affairs, the indispensablest mode of treating with it on this head, of expressing your little satisfaction with and love for it, is to deny it then.[51]

In "Civil Disobedience," which clearly originated from his Romantic and pantheistic feelings (today one would speak of an "alternative ethos"), Thoreau made out citizens of the world to be superior to citizens serving a firmly established order: "It is not many moments that I live under a government, even in this world. If a man is thought-free, fancy-free, imagination-free, that which *is not* never for a long time appearing *to be* to him, unwise rulers or reformers cannot fatally interrupt him."[52] From the outset Thoreau's critics reproached him for having failed to say how the border between justified resistance and limitless anarchy could be defined in the conscience of the individual. Thoreau, who had his own ideas about the "ideal state," was apparently unwilling to subordinate himself to the democratic state as long as it did not meet his ideal:

There will never be a really free and enlightened State until the State comes to recognize the individual as a higher and independent power, from which all its own power and authority are derived, and treats him accordingly. I please myself with imagining a State at last which can afford to be just to all men, and to treat the individual with respect as a neighbor; which even would not think it inconsistent with its own repose if a few were to live aloof from it, not meddling with it, nor embraced by it, who fulfilled all the duties of neighbors and fellow-men. A State which bore this kind of fruit, and suffered it to drop off as fast as it ripened, would prepare the way for a still more perfect and glorious State, which also I have imagined, but not yet anywhere seen.[53]

Before publishing his masterpiece *Walden* (1854), the self-sufficient philosopher wrote translations from Greek (Aeschylus and Pindar), poems, studies of neo-Platonic philosophers, and articles on oriental philosophy (on Buddha and Confucius, among others) for *The Dial*. All of these preliminary exercises flowed into his "back to nature" critique of culture, with its Rousseauean tenor. For two years he secluded himself at Walden Pond in the woods of Massachusetts, attempting to make a practical demonstration that the individual, as a creation of God and nature, could live a life of worldly holiness and natural dignity dependent only on himself and in direct intercourse with nature. The human qualities of wildness, rawness, and instinct were, according to Thoreau, just as natural as fitness, civility, morality, and nobility. Together nature and mind comprised the absolute center of all things and creatures, of all heights and depths. Thus, the synthesis of nature and mind required constant refinement, spiritualization, and aesthetic cleansing of natural qualities to the point of their absolute perfection. *Walden* documents one of the first manifestations of American cultural pessimism in the form of a Romantic worship of nature and flight from civilization,[54] which would also prove to be a critique of technological progress. "Modern improvements," such as the railroad, meant for Thoreau simply "improved means to an unimproved end." "While they accelerated the pace of life, it was doubtful whether they enhanced its quality." And so he came to the conclusion that "we do not ride on the railroad, it rides upon us." Equally suspect to him was the newly installed telegraph connection between Massachusetts and Texas: "Thoreau suspected the two states had little of enduring value to say to one another."[55] Once the father of the modern American critique of civilization, Thoreau has today become the guru of American "counterculture."

Along with these Romantic manifestations, a host of other social and national ideas for reform were making themselves felt, above all in New England and the Midwestern states. The first initiatives in the struggle for equal rights for women became apparent (Margaret Fuller), and the first American peace movement, which was seized by the idea of pacifism in the age of democracy, proclaimed the following through its intellectual spokesman William Ellery Channing:

The tendencies of civilization are decidedly towards peace. The influence of progressive knowledge, refinement, arts, and national wealth, are pacific. The old motives for war are losing power. . . . It is now thoroughly understood, that the development of a nation's resources in peace is the only road to prosperity; . . . We have another pacific influence at the present moment, in the increasing intelligence of the middle and poorer classes of society, who in proportion as they learn their interests and rights, are unwilling to be used as materials of war, to suffer and bleed in serving the passions and glory of a privileged few. Again, science, commerce, religion, foreign travel, new facilities of intercourse, new exchanges of literature, new friendships, new interests, are overcoming the antipathies of nations, and are silently spreading the sentiment of human brotherhood.[56]

However, Channing's pious Romantic vision of the progress of humankind would remain unfulfilled.

Other experiments of social reform were made under the influence of English and French efforts to found "Progressive-Romantic" settlements and communities. One of the earliest among these, "New Harmony" in Indiana (1825), became famous as a place not only where equal rights and the absolute freedom of opinion and speech were practiced but where even private property was abolished. This undertaking, whose improbable leader was an industrialist (Robert Owen), soon proved to be an economic failure. Even so, the experiment had many imitators, such as the legendary "Brook Farm" (1841) in Massachusetts. This socialist community was founded

in order more effectually to promote the great purpose of human culture; to establish the external relations of life on a basis of wisdom and purity; to apply the principles of justice and love to our social organization in accordance with the laws of Divine Providence; to substitute a system of brotherly cooperation for one of selfish competition . . . ; to prevent the exercise of worldly anxiety by the competent supply of our necessary wants; to diminish the desire of excessive accumulation by making the acquisition of individual property subservient to upright and disinterested uses; to guarantee to each other the means of physical support and of spiritual progress.[57]

A large number of New England intellectuals from the circle of the transcendentalists, among them Albert Brisbane, Orestes A. Brownson, and William

Henry Channing, supported this utopian project, which was abandoned in 1847 after the farm was destroyed by fire.[58]

Another movement from this era of romantic-national and individualist-democratic spirit was the abolitionist movement, which became active at the beginning of the nineteenth century and whose goal was the unconditional abolition of slavery. Abolitionism would come to play an important role in the worsening conflict between the North and the South.

Though all the currents of thought described above—romantic, alternative, esoteric, or socialist—were significant, they exerted little influence because they clearly deviated from the American mainstream ideology of progress. Nonetheless, they illustrate the colorful diversity of American society.

# 10

## Between Crisis, Protest, and Reform

In the mid–nineteenth century, the United States experienced its worst political crisis. It was triggered by the economic and ideological estrangement between the slave-holding South and the slave-free North and ultimately led to the Civil War. The promising nation would have been divided with a single stroke if Abraham Lincoln had not succeeded in radically defending the Union and abolishing slavery. The American Civil War can be interpreted not least as a struggle for the establishment of human rights, in this case specifically those of black Americans, rights that were rooted in American constitutional and progressivist ideology.

The years following the Civil War were also marked by turbulence and social tensions. Protest movements began to form, directed against the increasing institutionalization of all economic and social areas since the breakthrough of large-scale industrialization and the end of Reconstruction after the Civil War. These groups consisted primarily of farmers from the Midwest and South and became known as the Populist movement, which in 1891–92 appeared as the People's or Populist party. This phenomenon of populist industrialization was taken up at the beginning of the twentieth century in the progressive reforms (primarily concerning economic areas) of presidents Woodrow Wilson and Theodore Roosevelt.

It remains now to sketch the topic of welfare state versus laissez-faire, a subject of controversy in the United States since the Progressive era.

## CIVIL WAR AND EMANCIPATION

"A house divided against itself cannot stand." With these words, a still relatively unknown Republican politician, Abraham Lincoln, addressed the Illinois Republican convention in June 1858.

We are now far into the fifth year since a policy was initiated with the avowed object and confident promise of putting an end to slavery agitation. Under the operation of that policy, that agitation has not only not ceased, but has constantly augmented. In my opinion, it will not cease until a crisis shall have been reached and passed. A house divided against itself cannot stand. I believe this government cannot endure permanently half slave and half free. I do not expect the Union to be dissolved; I do not expect the house to fall; but I do expect that it will cease to be divided. It will become all one thing, or all the other.[59]

In the seven debates on slavery held during the congressional elections of 1858 with the Democratic Senator Stephen A. Douglas, whose Senate seat the young frontier lawyer was challenging, Lincoln condemned slavery as a moral, social, and political injustice. He characterized it as a problem that could only be resolved on the national level.[60] Thus, in July 1858 he appealed to his audience in Chicago:

Let us discard all this quibbling about this man and the other man, this race and that race and the other race being inferior, and therefore they must be placed in an inferior position. Let us discard these things, and unite as one people throughout this land, until we shall once more stand up declaring that all men are created equal.[61]

When in May 1860 Lincoln's party nominated him as its presidential candidate, the South regarded this action as a provocation and made an undisguised threat to secede. In the eyes of the Southerners, the unceasing growth of the economic, demographic, and political superiority of the North could no longer be countered with any other means than the long-planned withdrawal from the Union. They felt that such a move had to be made then or never. James Oliver Robertson characterized the escalation of this conflict into crisis with the following words: "the conflict which brought on the Civil War was basic to the very existence of the nation. The nation . . . was between freedom and slavery, between the national ideals and a perversion of those ideals, between the agrarianism of the past and the industrialism of the future."[62]

The first state to leave the Union was South Carolina in December 1860; within the next few months Mississippi, Florida, Alabama, Georgia, Louisiana, and Texas followed. In February 1861 the new Confederate States of America was founded in Montgomery, Alabama, led by Jefferson Davis as provisional president. As late as March 1861, in his inaugural address, Lincoln promised that he would not begin a war, but he also stated unequivocally that he was prepared to preserve the Union and to defend its legal authority:

The Union is much older than the Constitution. It was formed, in fact, by the Articles of Association in 1774. It was matured and continued by the Declaration of Independence in 1776. It was further matured, and the faith of all the then thirteen States expressly plighted and engaged that it should be perpetual, by the Articles of Confederation in 1778. And, finally, in 1787 one of the declared objects for ordaining and establishing the Constitution was "to form a more perfect Union." . . . It follows from these views that no State upon its own mere motion can lawfully get out of the Union. I therefore consider that, in view of the Constitution and the laws the Union is unbroken and to the extent of my ability I shall take care, as the Constitution itself expressly enjoins upon me, that the laws of the Union be faithfully executed in all the States. . . . In doing this there needs to be no bloodshed or violence, and there shall be none unless it be forced upon the national authority. . . . Plainly the central idea of secession is the essence of anarchy. . . . In *your* hands, my dissatisfied fellow-country-men, and not in *mine,* is the momentous issue of civil war. . . . *You* have no oath registered in heaven to destroy the government, while I shall have the most solemn one to "preserve, protect, and defend it."[63]

The actual outbreak of the Civil War in April 1861 was primarily a result of unresolved conflict over the slavery question.

The Union's narrow victory after the Battle of Antietam in September 1862, which halted the Confederate Army's advance on Washington, gave Lincoln his long-awaited opportunity to deliver the Emancipation Proclamation, which was first announced in the form of a preliminary proclamation and finally became effective permanently on January 1, 1863. As Lincoln said,

That on the first day of January in the year of our Lord, one thousand eight hundred and sixty-three, all persons held as slaves within any State, or designated part of a State, the people whereof shall then be in rebellion against the United States shall be then, thenceforward, and forever free; and the executive government of the United States, including the military and naval authorities thereof, will recognize and maintain the freedom of such persons and will do no act or acts to repress such persons, or any of them, in any efforts they may make for their actual freedom.[64]

The liberation of the slaves in all rebellious areas was proclaimed, and in the process an important step was taken toward reestablishing the American national identity and the liberal political self-understanding of Americans. The Emancipation Proclamation also benefited the Northern states in terms of foreign policy; it was welcomed in many European countries and accordingly put the Confederacy on the defensive. However, it was not until the decisive Union victory at Gettysburg in 1863 that the path seemed clear for a national reconsolidation of the United States.

Lincoln, the "emancipator, war leader, frontier hero and spokesman of charity, freedom and democracy," once more demonstrated his greatness when, in his Gettysburg Address, he called on his fellow countrymen to remember that

Fourscore and seven years ago our fathers brought forth on this continent, a new nation, conceived in Liberty, and dedicated to the proposition that all men are created equal. . . . that this nation, under God, shall have a new birth of freedom—and that government of the people, by the people, for the people, shall not perish from the earth.[65]

Had the South sought an armistice after their defeat at Gettysburg, then it might have been spared total catastrophe. Lincoln had often demonstrated a willingness to cease hostilities, but only under the condition that the Southern states return to the Union and acknowledge the emancipation of the slaves. The Confederacy's ultimate capitulation and thereby the renaissance of the Union, took place on April 9, 1865, at the Appomattox Court House.

Lincoln's statesmanship and farsightedness, sense of national justice, and convincing leadership would exhibit themselves once more—before he fell victim to an assassin's bullet on April 14, 1865—in his Reconstruction speech of April 12. In this speech he pleaded for moderation and compassion in the treatment of the South.[66] Lincoln felt

that the seceded States, so called, are out of their proper practical relation with the Union, and that the sole object of the Government, civil and military, is to again get them into their practical relation. I believe that it is not only possible, but in fact easier, to do this without deciding, whether those States have ever been out of the Union than with it. Finding themselves safely at home, it would be utterly immaterial whether they had ever been abroad. Let us all join in doing the acts necessary to restoring the . . . Union; and each forever after, innocently indulge his own opinion whether, in doing the acts, he brought the States from without, into the Union, or only gave them proper assistance, they never having been out of it.[67]

In the attempt to analyze Lincoln's historical significance for the American political and national (progressivist) ideology, one comes to the conclusion, as LaWanda Cox writes in her most recent study, that his "radical" human rights policy was of primary importance.[68] The republican Union and democracy that had originated in the Revolution and had been conceived by the Founding Fathers had faced a serious crisis in the form of the Civil War: "The nation and its destiny, its independence and its expansion, its mission to the world were challenged and tested in the Civil War."[69] The nation would probably have met its downfall without Lincoln's awareness of tradition and political commitment to the ideas of freedom, unity, democracy, and human rights. America, as a progressivist experiment and democratic example for all humankind, would have failed. It is understandable that Americans still honor Abraham Lincoln as one of their great national heroes, the savior and preserver of their ideology of progress.[70]

## POPULISM AND PROGRESSIVISM

After the war, Lincoln's progressivist policies were reflected in efforts toward a social renewal and political democratization of the South; above all in three constitutional amendments. The Thirteenth Amendment (1865) declared slavery illegal in the entire country and thus confirmed the Emancipation Proclamation; the Fourteenth Amendment (1868) guaranteed the freed slaves ("freedmen") citizenship and human rights; and the Fifteenth Amendment (1870) secured for blacks the right to vote and participate in elections. It must be acknowledged that it was only after long and bitter conflict that these principles were finally realized, a century later, in the 1960s.

At the same time, the postwar period from 1865 to the end of the 1870s, the Reconstruction, was characterized by numerous attempts to normalize the social and economic life of the Southern states and to reintegrate the former Confederacy into the Union. However, the question of how this goal was to be achieved was dominated by such deep-seated differences between North and South that a comprehensive Reconstruction of the nation could not be considered. At the end of the war, the government in Washington was unable to produce an effective program for restoring the Union. Lincoln's generous Reconstruction plan of December 1863, which provided for swift reestablishment of the Southern state governments and which Lincoln had tried to implement until his assassination, was rejected by the radical Republicans in his own ranks, who hated the earlier leaders of the South and wanted to punish them for the secession. Lincoln's weak successor, Andrew Johnson, was unable to get Reconstruction onto the right track.

While the former Confederacy lay paralyzed in defeat, uninhibited greed, speculation, and general unscrupulousness spread through the North. In almost all sectors of the economy, a new class of rapacious profit seekers, speculators, and "robber barons" grew and took advantage of the defeated South. This moral degeneration ("spoilsmen age") also worked its way into politics and administration, inflicting severe damage on the credibility of many institutions and influential personalities. This Gilded Age (Mark Twain), or the Age of Cynicism, as Hofstadter called it, coincided, especially in the North, with a rapidly accelerating process of industrialization, a new influx of immigrants from Western and Northern European countries, an increasing concentration of the urban population, and the limitless laissez-faire approach of the Carnegies (*The Gospel of Wealth*, 1889) and Rockefellers.[71] The enormous economic discrepancy that arose between the industrial magnates and the metropolitan slum dwellers (Henry George, *Progress and Poverty*, 1880) and that steadily expanded as the pressure of new immigration increased should be seen against this background of technological and industrial progress and the ideology of the "survival of the fittest." This situation in turn led to the articulation of a sharply accusatory critique of society, civilization (Edward Bellamy, *Looking Backward*, 1888), and the economic system (Thorstein Veblen, *The Theory of the Leisure Class*, 1899).[72]

The call for extensive economic and social reforms was first heard from the Populists, who, in 1867, had organized themselves into an agrarian protest movement. After 1867, the populist movements increasingly campaigned against the political predominance of the big cities, the monopolies and railroad companies, banks and trusts, middleman profiteering, and the government's deflationary currency policies as the result of the gold standard declared in 1873. They articulated the interests of the farmers of the Midwest and South in particular, but also of the West and Southwest, demanding cheap credits and railroad cargo rates, as well as higher prices for their most important products. They also promoted the reestablishment of the old and presumably tested ideals of Jeffersonian and Jacksonian "agrarian democracy."

By agrarian democracy the Populists meant grass-roots democracy, the direct, participatory democracy that emerged from the comprehensible unity of a relatively homogeneous society of farming families and self-reliant settlers. Because of their lack of class tradition, these farmers were not peasants in the traditional European sense, but rather individual capitalistic private property owners.[73]

The idea and the realization of direct democracy in North America can be traced back to colonial times and had already become noticeable during the fights for independence and the constitutional deliberations (anti-Federalists). Toward the end of the eighteenth century, it emerged as a broad radical countertrend. Since then, direct democracy, along with the representative components in the American constitutional and governmental system, has been a recurrent theme in the political culture of the United States, a tradition that has been closely connected, since the age of Jacksonian Democracy, with egalitarian rhetoric stressing the common man or little man and directed against special interests.

All populist movements were similarly committed to the ideal of agrarian democracy, despite their large differences from state to state. These differences were especially marked between the Midwest and the South, where each had its own interests, rhetoric, and colorful folklore. The most important general demands of these movements included the direct election of senators, initiation of primaries, women's suffrage, the right of recall, the introduction of initiatives and referendums, and a progressive income tax. The Farmer's Alliance, a populist group that dominated the 1880s, also demanded the expansion of cooperative markets and credit organizations, the establishment of postal savings banks, tax relief measures, government subsidies for agriculture, the nationalization of the railroads, and the introduction of the eight-hour work day. These various movements provided the basis for the formation of the Populist party in 1891–92, the first influential third party alongside the Republicans and Democrats. At times, the Populist party was even able to win a string of states in the Midwest and South. At their first convention in Omaha, Nebraska, on July 4, 1892, they proclaimed their radically progressive program, the product of a variety of populist ideas:[74]

We believe that the powers of government—in other words, of the people—should be expanded . . . to the end that oppression, injustice, and poverty shall eventually cease in the land. We declare . . .

First, that the union of the labor forces of the United States this day consummated shall be permanent and perpetual; may its spirit enter into all hearts for the salvation of the Republic and the uplifting of mankind.

Second, wealth belongs to him who creates it, and every dollar taken from industry without an equivalent is robbery. "If any will not work, neither shall he eat." The interests of rural and civil labor are the same; their enemies are identical.

Third, we believe that the time has come when the railroad corporations will either own the people or the people must own the railroads; and should the government enter upon the work of owning and managing all railroads, we should favor an amendment to the constitution by which all persons engaged in the government service shall be placed under a civil-service regulation of the most rigid character, so as to prevent the increase of the power of the national administration by the use of such additional government employees.[75]

The Populist party platform also included the following planks:

We demand a graduated income tax.

We believe that the money of the country should be kept as much as possible in the hands of the people, and hence we demand that all State and national revenues shall be limited to the necessary expenses of the government, economically and honestly administered.

We demand that postal savings banks be established by the government for the safe deposit of the earnings of the people and to facilitate exchange.[76]

Three of the Platform Committee's closing ten resolutions should be mentioned here:

Resolved, that we condemn the fallacy of protecting American labor under the present system, which opens our ports to the pauper and criminal classes of the world and crowds out our wage-earners; and we denounce the present ineffective laws against contract labor, and demand the further restriction of undesirable immigration.

Resolved, that we favor a constitutional provision limiting the office of President and Vice-President to one term, and providing for the election of Senators of the United States by a direct vote of the people.

Resolved, that we oppose any subsidy or national aid to any private corporation for any purpose.[77]

The presidential campaign of 1892 brought the Populist party huge successes in the West and South, but their candidate, James B. Weaver, was defeated. In the campaign of 1896, which was fought on all sides with great passion, the Populists decided to support William Jennings Bryan,[78] the popular Democratic candidate whose campaign revolved around social justice.[79] After its titanic rise, the Populist movement found itself already exhausted in 1896 as a result of having backed Bryan's unsuccessful candidacy. However, its demands for the expansion of direct democracy and for control of the monopolies were historical examples for later politicians, for instance, in the Progressive movement immediately following the Populist Age, then in the interventionist agricultural policies of FDR's New Deal, and even later in Lyndon Johnson's social reforms and building programs.

Measured against the realization of concrete individual demands and the preservation of certain interests, Populism comprised one of the most successful political fringe movements in American history. Of course, the realization of Populist demands promoted and accelerated tendencies toward a "strong government" and expansion of the central bureaucracy.[80] Franklin Delano Roosevelt and Lyndon Johnson, proponents of drastic expansion in state intervention mechanisms, referred to the populist tradition as did, in part, their ideological opponents Jimmy Carter (who brings to mind William Jennings Bryan) and Ronald Reagan. George McGovern, the unsuccessful Left liberal Democratic presidential candidate of 1972, was also a populist in the basic democratic tradition of the Midwestern corn belt. George Wallace, the former governor of Alabama, stood firmly in the tradition of turn-of-the-century Southern Populism with his rhetoric and program, his appeal to the "little people," and his segregationist, but social-welfare-oriented, paternalism toward poor farmers. By contrast, the aggressive, fundamentalist populism of today's New Right is based on a populistic conglomeration of ideas from the Jacksonian era, the agrarian revolts of the late nineteenth century, and cultivation of the baser instincts of modern mass democracy.

Populist ideology turned out to be two-faced. On the one hand, the Populists were rural, authoritarian, fundamentalist, xenophobic, and anti-Semitic; on the other, they were progressive social reformers and promoters of grass-roots democracy. They were not, however, social revolutionaries or social democrats, and they did not agitate against American capitalism. Rather, they merely opposed the onesidedness of a few private capitalistic forms of organization that favored industry and big business. The American farmers were themselves capitalistic businessmen, but compared to industry they were insignificant. American Populism was ultimately the revolt of small and middle-sized businessmen against the giants. Although the movement was a failure as a revolt, it managed to register some successes in the form of a consistent long-term impetus for reform. But even the most radically fundamental democratic, egalitarian, and participatory claims of the Populists were revolutionary only in the specifically Populist sense of the word, in which "revolution" meant the reestablishment of original values and conditions they considered to have been perverted. Thus, the Populists demanded neither more democracy nor more social justice, but simply the reestablishment of the old, idealized, less institutionalized, and less technological form of democracy as represented by the agrarian democracy of the late eighteenth century.[81]

Populist ideology, therefore, was primarily regressive. According to Populist credo, economic freedom, equal status, and the chance to return a profit, all of which had been eroded by the increasing concentration, organization, and complexity of the economy, should be returned to the farmer and small businessman, regardless of the size, structure, and solvency of the business involved. However, contrary to the Populists' original intentions, the means regarded as appropriate for such reform cleared the way for "big government" and at the same time, due to market mechanisms, actually strengthened the larger and more progressive organizations.

American historiography of the early twentieth century willingly interpreted Populism as the direct predecessor of the Progressive movement.[82] Since the 1950s, however, Populism's nationalist tendencies have been recognized with greater clarity, its hostile posture toward the immigrants in general and its anti-Semitism in particular.[83] The fact that the Populist movement also had its share of pessimistic, even reactionary, elements, in spite of the progressiveness of its social and economic programs and demands, cannot be denied: "Yet, Populism denied not the idea of progress but its realization in existing society. Optimistic in reforming zeal, Populism was still essentially pessimistic in its awareness of the ensuing obstacles. Not surprisingly, the result was an ambivalence with pessimism the overriding factor."[84]

The political legacy of the Populist protest movements against the social and economic effects of industrialization and technological progress in the period from around 1900 to 1920 was the Progressive movement. A creedal passion that had returned in the Populist era continued in the progressive age of reform and sought to redefine the political tradition and its progressivist ideology in view of the social and economic transformation of modern America.[85] The Progressive platform centered on the Hamiltonian and Jeffersonian models of government and was thus able to guarantee further application of their political concepts modified to apply to the twentieth century, to preserve the "American creed" of liberalism and individualism.

The protagonists of the Progressives were, as is well known, the Republican Theodore Roosevelt ("the Conservative as Progressive") and the Democrat Woodrow Wilson ("the Conservative as Liberal").[86] With their goals of (1) public regulation and control of big business, (2) amelioration of social distress, and (3) democratization of government, they pursued a reformation (not revolution) of America's economy, society, and politics. These reforms were intended to bring the country into line with the new requirements of the technological and industrial twentieth century, and ultimately represented a middle road between the demands of the radical Left and the radical Right. The skillful integration of Progressive reforms in Republican and Democratic policies enabled both presidents to create a new consensus on modern capitalism and modern democracy, thus reestablishing the liberal American ideology of progress.[87]

In many respects the political, social, and economic orientation of the Progressives proved to be a watershed for the progressive development of America. As was the case for many of their radical populist predecessors, the progressivists' central premise lay in the promotion of an active interventionist political leadership, rather than a federal government passive in the face of the unfair competition engaged in by the modern American trusts. The experience that private initiative and local experiments in reform could contribute to the permanent solution of social and political inadequacies only if backed by government legislation also contributed to the progressivists' main motives.[88] Of course, the call for more state responsibility eventually brought with it, as Samuel Huntington remarked, an increase in presidential power and the buildup of "big government": "The efforts to make government more responsible increased the growth of presidential power."

A particularly clear example of Progressive ideology is provided in the influential book *The Promise of American Life* (1909), by Herbert Croly, an intellectual who had served as an adviser to Roosevelt.[89] In Croly's view, American society stood at a turning point in its history, for the earlier preconditions for the fulfillment of the American way of life had undergone extensive change. From the outset the American progressivist system had promised not only democracy and individual freedom, but also material reward in the pursuit of happiness. "America" thus stood, above all, for a better life.[90] Arthur Schlesinger summarized Croly's assumptions as follows:

that American life is committed to the fulfillment of a national promise; that the American assumption had been that the Promise would fulfill itself automatically; that new social and economic conditions meant that, if this was ever true, it was true no longer; and that to preserve the Promise it would be necessary to abandon the traditional American patriotic fatalism and transform the national Promise into a closer equivalent of a national purpose, the fulfillment of which is a matter of conscious work.[91]

According to Croly, this belief in an "automatic" connection between individual desires and a better life had been shown to be unjustified. On the contrary, the pursuit of private property had created, at the turn of the century, a massive concentration of economic power, political corruption, and unwarranted privilege. On the basis of these facts, Croly drew the conclusion that the future fulfillment of the American "promise" of a better life could be achieved only through conscious and focused national planning and construction by a strong federal government. At the same time he emphasized that, henceforth, "technical efficiency, moral conversion, structural reorganization and individual emancipation had to make progress together."[92]

Supported by the progressivist ideals of the American political tradition, the Progressives tried by means of democratic reforms to impede plutocracy and socialism at the same time. A progressivist "Mugwump" intelligentsia, which had formed in the meantime, criticized political, economic, and social problems, particularly those of big cities, in a series of newly established Progressive mass-circulation magazines ("muckraking" journalism). Their approval of a strong national government was linked with the insight that overarching reforms of society could be realized only with active cooperation of the citizenry at local and state levels.[93]

The Progressive wave of reform set in around 1900 in the Midwest, particularly in Wisconsin, where the Republican governor and radical Progressive Robert M. La Follette streamlined the administration of his state into a model of efficiency and organization. He cleared away the corrupt rule of the party bosses, established close cooperation between the government and the renowned state university in Madison, appointed numerous expert commissions that supplied him with recommendations and advice for the solution of economic and social problems, introduced legislation for direct primaries, initiatives, and referendums, cut back the influence of banking and railroad lobbies, and created the first state income tax. Wisconsin became, in the words of Theodore Roosevelt, a "laboratory of democracy" that impressed the entire country.

Similar governmental programs were also carried out in other agricultural states such as Iowa, Minnesota, Oregon, Mississippi, Arkansas, and South Carolina. But the Progressive movement scored important successes even in the industrial states. In New Jersey, for example, the struggle against the power of large private corporations and their influence on public administration and politics was led with dedication by the reform politician and New Jersey Governor Woodrow Wilson (1911–12).[94]

The Progressives also succeeded in introducing a series of welfare laws at the state level. In 1914 all the states—with one exception—forbade employment of children under the age of fourteen. By 1920 almost all of the states had accident insurance. In the 1920s thirteen states improved conditions in clinics and hospitals and introduced social security. After 1914, when eleven states had recognized women's voting rights, Congress passed in 1919 a constitutional amendment securing national women's suffrage. In 1913 the direct election of senators was recognized at the national level with the Seventeenth Amendment.[95]

That the objectives of the Progressive movement in the first decade of the twentieth century were elevated to a concern of the federal government must be credited to Theodore Roosevelt. This multifaceted, inquisitive, and talented statesman and Nobel Prize winner had published a number of historical and political works before his inauguration.[96] He fulfilled the duties of his office with a moral dynamism ("bully pulpit") that had not been seen since the days of Lincoln. Many of the conservative "Old Guard" Republicans were suspicious of his energetic personality and willingness to reform, while Progressive politicians of both parties pinned great hopes on him. In his first year in office, Roosevelt demonstrated that he had recognized the problems brought about by the republic's economic upturn and was ready to work toward a solution.[97] He certainly did not want to submit the existing economic system to revolutionary change, but to liberate it from corruption and the abuse of power: "we Republicans hold the just balance and set our faces resolutely against the improper corporate influence on the one hand as against demagogy and mob rule on the other."[98] Roosevelt, the neo-Hamiltonian, was convinced that the federal government was obligated to control private business, to support the regulation of capital, to put an end to the monopolies, and to provide more security for salaried employees. He formulated his progressivist philosophy quite pragmatically before Congress on December 2, 1902:

Our aim is not to do away with corporations; on the contrary, these big aggregations are an inevitable development of modern industrialism, and the effort to destroy them would be futile unless accomplished in ways that would work the utmost mischief to the entire body politic. . . . We draw the line against misconduct, not wealth.[99]

Despite his willingness for reform, Roosevelt was not interested in undercutting the American economy: "somehow or other we shall have to work out methods of controlling the big corporations *without* paralyzing the energies of the business community."[100] In his own words (1901), his concern was to make possible a "square deal" for all of the interest groups involved in the economic process: "We demand that big business give the people a square deal. . . . We do not wish to destroy corporations, but we do wish to make them subserve the public good."[101] In 1910, when Roosevelt was no longer president, he spoke again of a square deal in his New Nationalism speech in Kansas:

I stand for the square deal. But when I say that I am for the square deal, I mean not merely that I stand for fair play under the present rules of the game, but that I stand for having those rules changed so as to work for a more substantial equality of opportunity and of reward for equally good service. . . . When I say I want a square deal for the poor man, I do not mean that I want a square deal for the man who remains poor because he has not got the energy to work for himself. If a man who has had a chance will not make good, then he has got to quit.[102]

During his two terms as president, Roosevelt put through railroad legislation (the Elkins Act, 1903, and the Hepburn Act, 1906) for central regulation of the railroad industry, which dissolved the railroads' control over the coal mines and which enabled the federal government to intervene in interstate rate issues. Roosevelt further compelled Congress to create a Department of Commerce and Labor, whose leader was given cabinet status. A Bureau of Corporations, a central control authority, was in turn subordinated to this department. This bureau illuminated the business practices of the big companies, drew up reports of these practices, and published them in the press. Roosevelt's fight against the trusts strengthened his popularity, especially among people in the middle and lower income brackets, yet his successes were in general more propagandistic than practical. The legal bases of the antimonopoly movement were not significantly expanded. Nonetheless, he created a general awareness of the "socialization of democracy" (Arthur M. Schlesinger) and the necessity of having entrepreneurs exercise more social responsibility ("social stewardship," Richard Striner), attitudes that actually compelled some trusts to proceed with greater caution and moderation. At the same time, Roosevelt advocated the first legislation for food and drug protection (the Pure Food and Drug Act, 1906).[103]

Some of the most remarkable achievements of Roosevelt's Progressive domestic policy resulted from his commitment to environmental protection, to the conservation of the forests and the other natural resources of the country. As the first American president to show ecological awareness, he promoted the creation of national land and wildlife preserves and the protection of natural waterways. In a message to Congress on December 3, 1907, he said:

The conservation of our national resources and their proper use constitute the fundamental problem which underlies almost every other problem of our national life.... We are prone to speak of the resources of this country as inexhaustible; this is not so. The mineral wealth of the country, the coal, iron, oil, gas, and the like, does not reproduce itself, and therefore is certain to be exhausted ultimately; and wastefulness in dealing with it today means that our descendants will feel the exhaustion a generation or two before they otherwise would. But there are certain other forms of waste which could be entirely stopped—the waste of soil by washing, for instance, which is among the most dangerous of all wastes now in progress in the United States, is easily preventable, so that this enormous loss of fertility is entirely unnecessary. The preservation or replacement of the forests is one of the most important means of preventing this loss.[104]

In May 1908, Roosevelt convened the National Conservation Conference in Washington, in which forty-four governors and numerous experts participated. The environmental congress laid the ground for regular governors' conferences and led to the emergence of individual state environmental protection commissions. Six decades later another Republican president, Richard Nixon, would deal intensively with the topic of environmental protection and create the Environmental Protection Agency (1970).

Theodore Roosevelt, in a certain sense the father of the modern Republican party, had seen very clearly that a highly technologized society with concentrated private property required Hamiltonian methods to realize Jeffersonian goals.[105] During his attempted political comeback he was to use his New Nationalism, the ideas of which had been preformulated by Croly,[106] to present himself not only as the new Progressive personality, but also as the initiator of the concept of the welfare state and strong government. In his New Nationalism speech, Roosevelt emphasized that

Our country—this great Republic—means nothing unless it means the triumph of a real democracy.... The absence of effective State, and especially, national, restraint upon unfair money-getting has tended to create a small class of enormously wealthy and economically powerful men, whose chief object is to hold and increase their power. The prime need is to change the conditions which enable these men to accumulate power which it is not for the general welfare.... This, I know, implies a policy of a far more active governmental interference with social and economic conditions in this country than we have yet had, but I think we have got to face that such an increase in governmental control is now necessary.... I do not ask for overcentralization; but I do ask that we work in a spirit of broad and far-reaching nationalism when we work for what concerns our people as a whole.... The betterment which we seek must be accomplished ... mainly through the National Government. The American people are right in demanding that New Nationalism, without which we cannot hope to deal with new problems.... The New Nationalism regards the executive powers as the steward of the public welfare. It demands of the judiciary that it shall be interested primarily in human welfare rather than in property, just as it demands that the representative body shall represent all the people rather than any one class or section of the people.... The material progress and prosperity of a nation are desirable chiefly so far as they lead to the moral and material welfare of all good citizens. . . . The prime problem of our nation is to get the right type of good citizenship, and to get it, we must have progress, and our public men must be genuinely progressive.[107]

In this way Theodore Roosevelt became the first modern statesman of the United States to lay the groundwork for an activist and interventionist presidency and the gradual buildup of the welfare state.[108] He proudly defended his socialization of democracy before his Republican critics, claiming: "What I have advocated . . . is not wild radicalism; it is the highest and wisest kind of conservatism."[109] He wanted to save American liberalism and pluralism from socialism and plutocracy with his national Progressive concept.[110] His 1912 attempt, supported by Herbert Croly and Walter Lippmann, to play a role in the future of America once again as the presidential candidate of the Progressive ("Bull Moose") party he had founded himself was destined to fail, however.

The election was won by the Democratic candidate Woodrow Wilson, also a Progressive and a former president of Princeton University, who confronted Roosevelt's New Nationalism vision with his own New Freedom concept. As a neo-Jeffersonian, Wilson was convinced that the changed economic situation had made government intervention unavoidable. He, too, believed it necessary to block the increasing formation of trusts, which were preventing fair opportunities for small and even big business, but his demands for state interventionist policies were by no means as radical as Roosevelt's.[111] As Wilson emphasized during his campaign of 1912:

The big trusts, the big combinations, are the most wasteful, the most uneconomical, and, after they pass a certain size, the most inefficient, way of conducting the industries of this country. . . . A trust is an arrangement to get rid of competition, and a big business is a business that has survived competition by conquering in the field of intelligence and economy. A trust does not bring efficiency to the aid of business; it *buys efficiency out of business*. I am for big business, and I am against the trusts.[112]

Wilson believed from the outset that he should steer his domestic policies on a middle course between "plutocracy and the masses" in order to give his government, as an "impartial agency," the chance to assume the role of arbitrator between the extreme forces ("socialism represents a danger of the very sort we seek to escape, a danger of centralized and corruptible control") and the "common interest."[113] He defined the role of the government in the convincing formula: "The business of government is to organize the common interest against the special interest."[114] His Progressive conservative philosophy was reflected paradigmatically in the following sentences: "America will insist upon recovering in practice those ideals which she has always professed. . . . If I did not believe that to be progressive was to preserve the essentials of our institutions, I for one could not be a Progressive."[115] As Hofstadter interpreted this position, for Wilson it was important "that the force of the State be used to restore pristine American ideals, not to strike out sharply in a new direction."[116]

Wilson's political thought was characterized by intellectual discipline as well as a high degree of idealism. His personal integrity invariably induced him to fight for his moral convictions with an unwavering missionary fervor.[117] Like Roosevelt, Wilson also possessed a keen sense of contemporary social injustice. Unlike Roosevelt, however, he was convinced that the interventional function of the government was merely a corrective, a means to restore "opportunities" for the free and fair play of economic forces. In his inaugural address of March 4, 1913, he announced his progressive reform program:

At last a vision has been vouchsafed us of our life as a whole. We see the bad with the good, the debased and decadent with the sound and vital. With this vision we approach new affairs. Our duty is to cleanse, to reconsider, to restore, to correct the evil without impairing the good, to purify and humanize every process of common life without weakening or sentimentalizing it. There has been something crude and heartless and unfeeling in our haste to succeed and be great. Our thought has been "let every man look out for himself, let every generation look out for itself," while we reared giant machinery which made it impossible that any but those who stood at the levers of control should have a chance to look out for themselves. . . . Our work is a work of restoration. We have itemized with some degree of particularity the things that ought to be altered and here are some of the chief items: a tariff which cuts off from our proper part in the commerce of the world, violates the just principles of taxation, and makes the Government a facile instrument in the hands of private interest; a banking and currency system based upon the necessity of the Government to sell its bonds fifty years ago and perfectly adapted to concentrating cash and restricting credits; an industrial system, which takes it on all its sides, financial as well as administrative, holds capital in leading strings, restricts the liberties and limits the opportunities of labor, and exploits without renewing or conserving the national resources of the country; a body of agricultural activities never yet given the efficiency of great business undertakings or served as it should be through the instrumentality of science taken directly to the form, or afforded the facilities of credit best suited to its practical needs; . . . We have studied as perhaps no other nation has the most effective means of production, but we have not studied cost or economy as we should either as organizers of industry, as statesmen, or as individuals. Nor have we studied and perfected the means by which government may be put at the service of humanity, in safeguarding the health of the Nation, the health of its men and women and its children, as well as their rights in the struggle for existence. This is no sentimental duty. The firm basis of government is justice, not pity. . . . There can be no equality or opportunity, the first essential of justice in the body politic, if men and women and children be not shielded in their lives, their very vitality, from the consequences of great industrial and social processes, which they cannot alter, control, or singly cope with. Society must see to it that it does not itself crush or weaken or damage its own constituent parts.[118]

Woodrow Wilson's New Freedom program meant freeing the economy from monopolies, the government from corruption, and the individual from social injustice. Wilson also largely succeeded in realizing his three main goals: (1) trust legislation, (2) tariff reduction, and (3) banking reform. "The first Wilson administration, in fact, produced more positive legislative achievements," wrote

Hofstadter, "than any administration since the days of Alexander Hamilton."[119] Wilson was the first president since Jefferson to personally present to the Congress his legislative proposals for new tariff policies in a special session that he convened. To eliminate the weaknesses of the more than thirty thousand more or less independent banking institutes, which were notoriously prone to crises, the Federal Reserve Act (1913) established a new national central and reserve banking system that proved an effective instrument for the control of the economy. In 1916 the Federal Farm Loan Board with twelve regional lending banks for the support of agriculture was formed. This was followed in 1914 by the Federal Trade Commission, which took the place of the Bureau of Corporations as the agency for the control of large businesses in interstate commerce, and, in the same year, the Clayton Act, with its new antitrust regulations. Federal control over child labor began in 1916, and in the same year the eight-hour day for railroad workers was introduced at the president's initiative.[120]

With his Progressive liberal New Freedom strategy, Wilson pursued his aim "to restore for capitalism the condition of economic opportunity within a competitive framework," and "to provide the individuals the means of obtaining social and economic justice for themselves," at which point he added that "government should assist individuals in their efforts to organize for collective action in the pursuit of social justice."[121] Whereas Theodore Roosevelt's concept of progressivism was the neo-Hamiltonian restoration and conservation of the national progressivist ideology in an age of rapid economic and technological change, Woodrow Wilson's idea of progressivism was manifested in the neo-Jeffersonian restoration and conservation of liberal ideals of progress. In this way, the Progressives were successful in reformulating the consensus of American political tradition and accommodating modern circumstances. At the end of his presidency (1919), Wilson wrote a letter in which he described for one last time the spirit of the Progressive era:

The world is going to change radically, and I am satisfied that governments will have to do many things which are now left to individuals and corporations. I am satisfied for instance that the government will have to take over all the great natural resources . . . all the water power, all the coal mines, all the oil fields, etc. They will have to be government-owned. If I should say that outside, people will call me a socialist, but I am not a socialist. And it is because I am not a socialist that I believe these things. I think the only way we can prevent communism is by some such action as that.[122]

The era of American progressivism ended with the outbreak of the First World War. However, the initiatives for practical economic and social reform would awaken in the Franklin D. Roosevelt administration, and their results would surpass the Progressive movement's achievements.

## SOCIAL WELFARE VERSUS LAISSEZ-FAIRE?

Discussion of the proper extent of welfare-state and free-market politics has been underway in America at least since the Progressive era. Theodore Roosevelt was the last Republican president to see the realization of the American progressivist ideology in an active interventionist federal government. With Franklin Delano Roosevelt's presidency and its breakthrough to a centralist and actively interventionist federal government, it would henceforth be the Democrats who revived the Hamiltonian principle of a strong state for the welfare of society and declared it to be their principle for progress in the twentieth century. The Republicans, by contrast, increasingly tied themselves to the Jeffersonian motto that "that government is best which governs least."

Franklin Delano Roosevelt, who had served as a high official under President Wilson and was one of his greatest admirers, came to office during the most serious economic crisis America had ever known. This economic emergency, and later the Second World War, made possible an enormous increase of presidential power and with it the tendency toward an almost (for American standards) social-democratic planned economy, manifested in Roosevelt's New Deal programs. In 1936 liberalism in America meant the promotion of new government agencies, such as the NRA (National Recovery Administration), the AAA (Agricultural Adjustment Administration), the PWA (Public Works Administration), the CCC (Civilian Conservation Corps), and the TVA (Tennessee Valley Authority). All were tools of the modern liberal bureaucratic invasion of a new economic and social order envisioned by the Democratic party.[123] The New Deal received theoretical support from the macroeconomic strategies of John Maynard Keynes (*The General Theory of Employment, Interest and Money,* 1936), which was to exercise an enormous influence on the economic policies of the United States until the end of the 1960s.[124]

The legacy of the Roosevelt era, especially the experience of the Great Depression and the Second World War, was a strong and powerful presidency as the embodiment of liberal Democratic nationalism. The fact that this legacy was to remain neither undisputed nor unchallenged was already clear during the Truman administration (Friedrich A. Hayek, *Individualism and the Economic Order,* 1948) and the Eisenhower years that followed. Harry Truman's effort to continue the liberal Democratic economic attitudes of the Roosevelt era after the end of the war, under the name of the Fair Deal, was partly rejected by a Republican Congress.[125] But even during the Eisenhower era, when the liberal Democratic concept of a strong presidential office lost ground, the government was unable and unwilling to dismantle the structures of the welfare state that had already been built. This reluctance was particularly noticeable during the phase of unprecedented economic growth that characterized the 1950s. Of course, even this epoch had its critics who sounded warnings from the Left (John Kenneth Galbraith, *The Affluent Society,* 1958) and the Right (Milton Friedman, *Capitalism and Freedom,* 1962).

Roosevelt's New Deal legacy had its final triumph in the Johnson administration, during which the influence of liberal presidential democracy on the country's social and economic policies once more reached its prior zenith. In the elections of 1964, the Democrats were able to form a progressive congressional majority for the first time since 1938. As a result, Johnson succeeded in passing a series of social laws that went far beyond Roosevelt's laws. Lyndon Johnson's Great Society vision and his will to realize the American Dream for all, to redeem Croly's *Promise of American Life,* transformed liberal Democratic interest politics from a mainly defensive strategy toward poverty and unemployment effective since FDR, into a practical, offensive, government initiated strategy of a prosperous society for all.[126] The 1960s witnessed one last performance of the Keynesian Revolution and its American ideal of the "pursuit of happiness" made possible by a modern progressive economy and technology, before the decades-old New Deal consensus, or as Theodore Lowi prophesied in 1968, "the end of the welfare state," succumbed to apparently inexorable decay.

The New Deal consensus finally collapsed completely with the monetarist revolution of Ronald Reagan, which Walt W. Rostow characterized as *The Barbaric Counter-Revolution* (1984). A new school of supply-side economists such as Arthur Laffer, George Gilder, Charles Murray, and Martin Feldstein saw the progressive income tax for the financing of the welfare state as America's main source of economic misery over the preceding fifteen years. In their view, the tax system of recent decades had hindered the country's efficiency and productivity. President Reagan's proposed tax deductions favoring those income groups ready and able to invest were simultaneously connected with radical cutbacks in social programs and were intended to initiate a new epoch of continuing economic growth.[127] The renaissance of the laissez-faire principle (Jack Kemp, *An American Renaissance,* 1980), of tried-and-tested liberal economic individualism, aspired to growth without inflation and the reduction of unemployment by means of tax relief. However, the economic policies of the Reagan administration have been marred by high budget deficits.

Reagan's daring attempt to dismantle the American welfare state seemed just as revolutionary as the statist New Deal program undertaken by Roosevelt back in the 1930s. The neoconservative mood is clearly more receptive to the traditional values of an individualistic self-help principle and laissez-faire capitalism, as shown in the study by Herbert McClosky and John Zaller, *The American Ethos, Public Attitudes Toward Capitalism and Democracy* (1984). Yet, total elimination of the welfare state in the land of idealism and realism seems unlikely. A long-term consensus based on an exclusively laissez-faire oriented coalition of business and technology seems just as unlikely as the restoration of the New Deal coalition of blue collar workers, blacks, minorities, and unions. The new global technological and economic challenges of the future will require a new consensus on progress between neoconservatism and neoliberalism, between social welfare and laissez-faire concepts, as well as new forms of cooperation between the state, business, science, and society.

# Notes to Part IV

1. James Oliver Robertson, *American Myth, American Reality* (New York, 1982), 74.

2. Ibid., 80, 81.

3. Ibid., 83.

4. F. J. Turner, *The Frontier in American History* (New York, 1920). See also the analysis of K. D. Bracher, Der "Frontier-Gedanke": Motiv des amerikanischen Fortschrittsbewußtseins, Ein ideologienkritischer Versuch, *Zeitschrift für Politik* 2 (1955): 228 ff.

5. Gabriel Kolko, *The Triumph of Conservatism: A Reinterpretation of American History* (New York, 1963). Critical here is Arthur M. Schlesinger, *The Crisis of the Old Order, 1919–1933* (Boston, 1957), 11–36.

6. On Theodore Roosevelt, See John Morton Blum, *The Republican Roosevelt* (Cambridge, Mass., 1977). On the development of the Republican party, see Milton Viorst, *Fall from Grace, The Republican Party and the Puritan Ethic* (New York, 1971).

## CHAPTER 9

7. See Ray A. Billington, Cowboys, Indians, and the Land of Promise: The World Image of the American Frontier, in *Representative American Speeches, 1975/76*, ed. W. W. Braden (New York, 1976), 176–92, 179 (Keynote Address at the XIV International Congress of Historical Science in San Francisco, August 2, 1975.)

8. See Knut Krakau, *Missionsbewußtsein und Völkerrechtsdoktrin in den Vereinigten Staaten*, 127.

9. See ibid., 156; Frederic L. Paxon, *History of the American Frontier, 1763–1893* (Boston, 1924), passim.

10. F. J. Turner, *The Frontier in American History*, 266.

11. W. W. Rostow, The National Style, in *The American Style: Essays in Value and Performance*, ed. Elting E. Morison (New York, 1958), 247, 259.

12. Louis Hartz, *The Liberal Tradition in America*, 22.

13. See K. D. Bracher, Demokratie als Sendung: Das amerikanische Beispiel, in *Deutschland zwischen Demokratie und Diktatur*, 313 ff.

14. See Henry Nash Smith, *Virgin Land: The American West as Symbol and Myth* (Cambridge, Mass., 1970).

15. See George W. Pierson, The Frontier and American Institutions, *New England Quarterly* 15 (1942): 253. K. Krakau, *Missionsbewußtsein*, 158f.

16. See Rush Welter, *The Mind of America, 1820–1860* (New York, 1975). Ray A. Billington, *America's Frontier Heritage* (New York 1966). K. Krakau, *Missionsbewußtsein*, 159.

17. See K. D. Bracher, Der "Frontier-Gedanke," 229 ff.

18. See Theodore Roosevelt, *The Winning of the West* (New York, 1906), 4 vols.

19. See Vannevar Bush, *Science—The Endless Frontier*, A Report to the President on a Program for Postwar Scientific Research (Washington, D.C. 1980).

20. Franklin Delano Roosevelt's letter to Bush of November 17, 1944, is printed in V. Bush, *Science*, 4.

21. John F. Kennedy's speech is printed in C. Hurd and A. Bauer, eds., *A Treasury of Great American Speeches* (New York, 1970), 355, 356.

22. J. F. Kennedy, State of the Union Address of January 11, 1962, in *Public Papers of the Presidents of the United States 1962* (Washington, D.C., 1963), 11.

23. Ronald Reagan's national security address is printed in *Wireless Bulletin from Washington*, No. 57, March 24, 1983, United States Information Service, Embassy of the United States of America (Bonn, 1983), 9, 10.

24. See John Carl Parish, *The Emergence of the Idea of Manifest Destiny* (Los Angeles, 1932). Frederick Merk, *Manifest Destiny and Mission in American History* (New York, 1963). Albert K. Weinberg, *Manifest Destiny. A Study in Nationalist Expansionism in American History* (New York, 1963).

25. John O'Sullivan, in Julius W. Pratt, The Origin of "Manifest Destiny," *American Historical Review* 32 (1927): 795–98, here p. 797. J. W. Pratt, John O'Sullivan and Manifest Destiny, *New York State Historical Association* 14 (1933): 213 ff. K. Krakau, *Missionsbewußtsein* 128 f.

26. F. Merk, *Manifest Destiny and Mission in American History*, 29. See also K. Krakau, *Missionsbewußtsein*, 129.

27. O'Sullivan, in K. Krakau, *Missionsbewußtsein*, 130.

28. Francis Baylies, in J. O. Robertson, *American Myth*, 72.

29. The speech of Seattle is printed in Clarence B. Bagley, Chief Seattle and Angeline, *Washington Historical Quarterly* 22, no. 4 (October 1931):252–55.

30. See Rush Welter, *The Mind of America: 1820–1860* (New York, 1975). Arthur A. Ekirch, *The American Democratic Tradition: A History* (New York, 1963). Frank Otto Gatell, ed., *Essays on Jacksonian America* (New York, 1970).

31. See Arthur M. Schlesinger, *The Age of Jackson* (Boston, 1945), passim. H. R. Guggisberg, *Geschichte der USA, Entstehung und nationale Konsolidierung* (Stuttgart, 1979), 94 ff.

32. See Robert V. Remini, *Andrew Jackson and the Course of American Freedom, 1822–1832* (New York, 1981), 2, 148. Marquis James, *The Life of Andrew Jackson* (Indianapolis, 1938), 2 vols.

33. See Carl R. Fish, *The Rise of the Common Man, 1830–1850* (New York, 1927). Thomas Perkins Abernethy, *From Frontier to Plantation in Tennessee* (Chapel Hill, N.C., 1932). John William Ward, *Andrew Jackson, Symbol for an Age* (New York, 1955). Edward Pessen, *Jacksonian America: Society, Personality, and Politics* (Homewood, Ill., 1969). Harold D. Moser, Sharon McPherson, and Charles F. Bryan, Jr., eds., *The Papers of Andrew Jackson, 1804–1813,* vol. 2 (Knoxville, Tenn., 1984).

34. See A. M. Schlesinger, *The Age of Jackson.*

35. Richard Hofstadter, *The American Political Tradition* (chapter: Andrew Jackson and the Rise of Liberal Capitalism), 70.

36. See Ralph C.H. Catterall, The Second Bank of the United States (Chicago, 1903). Bray Hammond, Jackson, Biddle, and the Bank of the United States, *Journal of Economic History* 7 (May 1947): 1–23. R. V. Remini, *Andrew Jackson,* 2, 369; R. V. Remini, *Andrew Jackson and the Course of American Democracy, 1833–1845* (New York, 1984), vol. 3, 108, 222. Remini describes Jackson's ignorance of American financial and economic policy, as well as the role of the Bank of the United States. He states that Jackson had "a terribly naive view of the public debt."

37. See H. R. Guggisberg, *Geschichte der USA,* 96. Glyndon G. Van Deusen, *The Jacksonian Era, 1828–1848* (New York, 1959).

38. R. Hofstadter, *The American Political Tradition,* 69.

39. Andrew Jackson, quoted in R. Hofstadter, *The American Political Tradition,* 77, 78. See Joseph L. Blau, ed., *Social Theories of Jacksonian Democracy* (New York, 1954).

40. See Marvin Meyers, *The Jacksonian Persuasion* (Stanford, Calif., 1957), 6, 16 ff, 158.

41. R. Hofstadter, *The American Political Tradition.*

42. R. V. Remini, *Andrew Jackson,* 2, 148.

43. Ernst Fraenkel, *Das amerikanische Regierungssystem* (Cologne, 1962), 47.

44. R. V. Remini, *Andrew Jackson,* 3, preface.

45. Ibid., 159.

46. David W. Marcell, *Progress and Pragmatism,* 70.

47. Arthur A. Ekirch, *The Idea of Progress in America, 1815–1860* (New York, 1944), 267. See also W. O. Clough, ed., *Intellectual Origins of American National Thought* (New York, 1955).

48. On Emerson's works, see the recent edition by Joel Porte, ed., *Ralph Waldo Emerson, Essays and Lectures* (Cambridge, Mass., 1984), The Library of America Series.

49. D. W. Marcell, *Progress and Pragmatism,* 85. See also Mildred Silverman, Emerson and the Idea of Progress, *American Literature* 12 (March 1940): 1–19.

50. See G. E. Müller, *Amerikanische Philosophie* (chapter: Der "Transzendentalismus": Die romantische Bewegung), (Stuttgart, 1950), 76 ff.

51. H. D. Thoreau, Civil Disobedience, in *Thoreau: Walden and Other Writings,* ed. Joseph Wood Krutch (New York, 1980), 93.

52. Ibid., 101, 102.

53. Ibid., 103, 104.

54. See P. Laver, Contradiction, Eclecticism and Integration, Social and Political Ideas in the Writings of Henry David Thoreau, with Particular Reference to Walden, Ph.D. diss., Newcastle upon Tyne University, 1977, passim.

55. Quote in D. W. Marcell, *Progress and Pragmatism,* 85.

56. W. E. Channing, *Works* (Boston, 1846), 4, 240, 241.

57. Quote in John T. Codman, *Brook Farm, Historic and Personal Memoirs* (Boston, 1894), 11–12. See Yehoshua Arieli, Individualism and Nationalism in American Ideology (chapter: Social Criticism in America), (Baltimore, 1966), 233 f. A. M. Schlesinger, *The Age of Jackson*, 361–68.

58. See Y. Arieli, Individualism and Nationalism, 231–72.


## CHAPTER 10

59. Abraham Lincoln's "House Divided" speech of June 16, 1868, is printed in H. C. Syrett, *American Historical Documents*, 254, 255.

60. H. R. Guggisberg, *Geschichte der USA*, 111 f. Ronald D. Rietveld, Lincoln and the Politics of Morality, *Illinois State Historical Society Journal* 68 (1975): 27–43. Stephen B. Oates, *Our Fiery Trial: Abraham Lincoln, John Brown and the Civil War Era* (Amherst, Mass., 1979). David Brion Davis, Slavery and the Idea of Progress, in *Oceans Apart? Comparing Germany and the United States*, ed. Erich Angermann and Marie Louise Frings (Stuttgart, 1981).

61. A. Lincoln, quoted in R. Hofstadter, *The American Political Tradition and the Men Who Made It*, 148.

62. J. O. Robertson, *American Myth*, 89.

63. A. Lincoln's Inaugural Address is published in H. C. Syrett, *American Historical Documents*, 271, 272, 273, 275. See also David Donald, *Lincoln Reconsidered: Essays on the Civil War Era* (New York, 1959).

64. A. Lincoln quoted in H. C. Syrett, *American Historical Documents*, 280.

65. A. Lincoln's Gettysburg Address, in H. C. Syrett, *American Historical Documents*, 281. See also Philip B. Kunhardt, *A New Birth of Freedom: Lincoln at Gettysburg* (Boston, 1983).

66. See Hans J. Morgenthau and David Hein, *Essays on Lincoln's Faith and Politics* (Washington, D.C., 1983).

67. A. Lincoln, quoted in R. Hofstadter, *Great Issues in American History, 1864–1957*, 2, 14.

68. See LaWanda Cox, *Lincoln and Black Reform: A Study in Presidential Leadership* (Columbia, S.C., 1981), passim.

69. J. O. Robertson, *American Myth*, 86.

70. See also Richard Nelson Current, *Speaking of Abraham Lincoln: The Man and His Meaning for Our Times* (Urbana, Ill., 1983).

71. See R. Hofstadter, *The American Political Tradition* (chapter: The Spoilsmen: An Age of Cynicism), 211–239. Richard Jensen, *The Winning of the Midwest: Social and Political Conflict, 1888–1896* (Chicago, 1971). H. R. Guggisberg, *Geschichte der USA*, 121ff.

72. See John L. Thomas, *Alternative America, Henry George, Edward Bellamy, Henry Demarest Lloyd and the Adversary Tradition* (Cambridge, Mass., 1983).

73. See Eric F. Goldman, *Rendezvous with Destiny, A History of Modern American Reform* (New York, 1956), 24 ff. Richard Hofstadter, *The Age of Reform, From Bryan to F.D.R.* (New York, 1955), 46 ff.

74. See E. F. Goldman, *Rendezvous with Destiny*. R. Hofstadter, *The Age of Reform*. Helen Campbell, *Prisoners of Poverty: Woman Wage-Workers, Their Trades and Their Lives* (Boston, 1887).

75. Populist Party Platform (July 4, 1892), printed in R. Hofstadter, *Great Issues in American History, A Documentary Record: 1864–1957* (New York, 1958), vol. 2, 150, 151.

76. Populist Party Platform, 151.

77. Ibid., 152, 153.

78. On Bryan, see R. Hofstadter, *The American Political Tradition* (chapter: William Jennings Bryan: The Democrat as Revivalist), 240–65. H. R. Guggisberg, *Geschichte der USA*, 148.

79. See W. J. Bryan, *The First Battle* (Chicago, 1896). Bryan's "Cross of Gold" Speech (July 8, 1896), printed in H. C. Syrett, *American Historical Documents*, 308–11. W. J. Bryan, Individualism Versus Socialism, *Century Magazine* 71 (1906): 856–57. H. R. Guggisberg, *Geschichte der USA*, 148.

80. See Hans-Jürgen Puhle, Was Ist Populismus?, *Politik und Kultur*, no. 1 (1983), 26–30. H. R. Guggisberg, *Geschichte der USA*, 148.

81. See D. Noble, The Religion of Progress, 1890–1914, *Social Research* (1955), 417–40. Gerald W. McFarland, *Mugwumps, Morals and Politics, 1884–1920* (Amherst, Mass., 1975). H.-J. Puhle, Was Ist Populismus?,'' 29 f.

82. See John D. Hicks, *The Populist Revolt: A History of the Farmer's Alliance and the People's Party* (Minneapolis, 1931).

83. This train of thought is supported especially by the historians Eric F. Goldman, *Rendezvous with Destiny,* and Richard Hofstadter, *The Age of Reform.*

84. Norman Pollack, *The Populist Response to Industrial America, Midwestern Populist Thought* (Cambridge, Mass., 1976), 23.

85. See Samuel P. Hays, *The Response to Industrialism, 1885–1914* (Chicago, 1957). Franklin D. Mitchell and Richard O. Davies, *America's Recent Past* (chapter: The Progressive Movement) (New York, 1969), 1–8. Stanley P. Caine, The Origins of Progressivism, in Lewis L. Gould, ed., *The Progressive Era* (New York, 1974), 11–34. A. A. Ekirch, *Progressivism in America* (New York, 1974).

86. See R. Hofstadter, *The American Political Tradition* (chapter: Theodore Roosevelt: The Conservative As Progressive, 266–307, and chapter: Woodrow Wilson: The Conservative As Liberal, 308–67).

87. See Louis L. Gould, *Reform and Regulation: American Politics, 1900–1916* (New York, 1978). Henry F. May, *The End of American Innocence, A Study of the First Years of Our Own Time, 1912–1917* (Chicago, 1959), 20–29, 30 ff. David W. Noble, *The Paradox of Progressive Thought* (Minneapolis, 1958). For a critical view of the achievements of the Progressive Movement, see Gabriel Kolko, *The Triumph of Conservatism: A Reinterpretation of American History* (New York, 1963). Kenneth McNaught, American Progressivism and the Great Society, *Journal of American History* 53 (December 1966): 504–20.

88. See John D. Buenker, *Urban Liberalism and Progressive Reform* (New York, 1978).

89. Herbert Croly, *The Promise of American Life,* ed. A. M. Schlesinger, (Cambridge, Mass., 1965).

90. See Charles Forcey, *The Crossroads of Liberalism, Croly, Weyl, Lippmann and the Progressive Era, 1900–1925* (New York, 1967), 3–51. Eric F. Goldman, *Rendezvous with Destiny* (chapter: Mr. Croly Writes a Book), 146 ff.

91. A. M. Schlesinger, ed., *The Promise of American Life by Herbert Croly* (Introduction), xiv–xv.

92. H. Croly, *The Promise of American Life,* ed. A. M. Schlesinger, (Introduction), xxii.

93. See Louis Filler, *Appointment at Armageddon: Muckraking and Progressivism in the American Tradition* (Westport, Conn., 1976). Walter Lippmann, *Drift and Mastery (1914)*, (chapter: The Themes of Muckraking), (Englewood Cliffs, N.J., 1961). R. Hofstadter, *The Age of Reform* (chapter: Muckraking: The Revolution in Journalism), 186 ff.

94. See R. Hofstadter, *The Age of Reform*, 131 ff. John D. Buenker, *Urban Liberalism and Progressive Reform*, 163–239.

95. See J. D. Buenker, *Urban Liberalism*. Lois W. Banner, *Woman in Modern America: A Brief History* (New York, 1974). David J. Rothman, *Conscience and Convenience, The Asylum and Its Alternatives in Progressive America* (Boston, 1980).

96. On Theodore Roosevelt's works, see Aloysius A. Norton, *Theodore Roosevelt* (Boston, 1980). Hermann Hagedorn, ed., *The Works of Theodore Roosevelt*, Memorial Edition (New York, 1923–25), 24 vols.

97. See John Morton Blum, *The Republican Roosevelt* (Cambridge, Mass., 1978). J. M. Blum, *The Progressive Presidents. Theodore Roosevelt, Woodrow Wilson, Franklin D. Roosevelt, Lyndon B. Johnson* (New York, 1980), 23–60.

98. T. Roosevelt, quoted in R. Hofstadter, *The Age of Reform*, 285, 286.

99. Ibid., 292.

100. Ibid., 298.

101. T. Roosevelt, quoted in William Safire, *Safire's Political Dictionary*, 683.

102. T. Roosevelt, The New Nationalism, in *Contemporary Forum, American Speeches on Twentieth-Century Issues*, ed. Ernest J. Wrage and Barnet Baskerville, (New York, 1962), 31.

103. See George E. Mowry, *The Era of Theodore Roosevelt and the Birth of Modern America, 1900–1912* (New York, 1958). J. M. Blum, *The Republican Roosevelt*, 73 ff. J. M. Blum, *The Progressive Presidents*.

104. T. Roosevelt's Seventh Annual Message to Congress, printed in H. C. Syrett, *American Historical Documents*, 321, 323.

105. See Arthur M. Schlesinger, *The Vital Center* (Boston, 1962), 176 ff.

106. See H. Croly, *The Promise of American Life*.

107. T. Roosevelt, *The New Nationalism*, 27, 33, 37, 38, 39.

108. See A. M. Schlesinger, *The Crisis of the Old Order, 1919–1933* (chapter: The New Nationalism), (Boston, 1957), 17–26.

109. T. Roosevelt, quoted in R. Hofstadter, *The Age of Reform*, 301.

110. See Y. Arieli, *Individualism and Nationalism in American Ideology* (Epilogue), 337.

111. See William Diamond, *The Economic Thought of Woodrow Wilson* (Baltimore, 1943). A. M. Schlesinger, *The Vital Center*, 179 f.

112. Woodrow Wilson, The New Freedom, in R. Hofstadter, *Great Issues in American History*, 296.

113. See R. Hofstadter, *The American Political Tradition* (chapter: Woodrow Wilson: The Conservative as Liberal), 323.

114. W. Wilson, quoted in R. Hofstadter, *The American Political Tradition*, 330.

115. Ibid., 332.

116. R. Hofstadter, *The American Political Tradition*, 336.

117. See David Mervin, Woodrow Wilson and Presidential Myths, *Presidential Studies Quarterly* 11, no. 4 (Fall 1981): 559–64.

118. W. Wilson, Inaugural Address (March 4, 1913), in *Inaugural Addresses of the*

*Presidents of the United States, from George Washington 1789 to Richard M. Nixon 1973* (Washington, D.C., 1974), 200, 201.

119. R. Hofstadter, *The American Political Tradition*, 334.

120. See A. S. Link, *Woodrow Wilson and the Progressive Era* (New York, 1953). J. M. Blum, *The Progressive Presidents* (chapter: Woodrow Wilson), 61 ff. H. R. Guggisberg, *Geschichte der USA*, 156 ff.

121. See A. M. Schlesinger, *The Crisis of the Old Order* (chapter: The New Freedom), 27 ff. A. M. Schlesinger, *The Vital Center*, 178 f.

122. W. Wilson, quoted in R. Hofstadter, *The American Political Tradition*, 361.

123. See William E. Leuchtenburg, *Franklin D. Roosevelt and the New Deal, 1932–1940* (New York, 1963). A. M. Schlesinger, *The Age of Roosevelt, The Crisis of the Old Order, 1919–1933*.

124. See Lawrence B. Klein, *The Keynesian Revolution* (New York, 1963). W. W. Rostow, *Politics and the Stages of Economic Growth* (London, 1971). Herbert Stein, *Presidential Economics, The Making of Economic Policy from Roosevelt to Reagan and Beyond* (New York, 1984).

125. See Alonzo L. Hamby, *Beyond the New Deal, Harry S. Truman and American Liberalism* (New York, 1973).

126. See J. M. Blum, *The Progressive Presidents* (chapter: Lyndon Johnson and the Uncertain Legacy), 163–203. James E. Anderson and Jared E. Hazleton, *Managing Macroeconomic Policy, The Johnson Presidency* (Austin, Tex., 1985).

127. See G. Gilder, *Wealth and Poverty* (New York, 1981); H. Stein, *Presidential Economics*.

# Part V

---

## FOREIGN POLICY AND THE AMERICAN IDEA OF PROGRESS

*This final section will analyze the realization of the progressivist idea beyond America's own borders. First, the international impacts of the American Revolution, including its function as an example for the rest of the world, will be evaluated. Its effects extend from the French Revolution to the most recent past, in the decolonization processes and independence movements of the Third World. Second, the idea of progress is outlined in light of a foreign policy dualism between the expansionist ideological sense of mission and continental isolationism, from the Washington Doctrine to the Reagan Doctrine.*

# 11

## The International Impact of the American Revolution

This chapter deals with (1) the effects of the American Revolution's progressivist ideals on other countries of the period, particularly France, Germany, Latin America, Scandinavia, Italy, Greece, and Russia ("the American Revolution's child, though an unwanted and unacknowledged one"[1]); and (2) the reflection of these ideals in the decolonization processes and liberation movements of many countries in the early and mid–twentieth century. As Charles William Eliot, the president of Harvard, emphasized in a speech in 1896, it was above all "five American contributions to civilization—freedom, democracy, justice, progress, and welcoming of newcomers—by which the American nation had set a glorious example to the whole world."[2]

### FROM THE FRENCH REVOLUTION TO THE DISSOLUTION OF THE COLONIAL EMPIRES

In Europe the American Revolution was welcomed by the philosophers (Voltaire, Lessing, and others) mainly as the practical confirmation and realization of Enlightenment thought. The constitutions of the individual states met with particular interest; in France they were quickly translated and reprinted several times, and in 1781 they appeared in Dutch translation in the Netherlands. Joseph Garat wrote in 1783 that "the philosophers of all Europe see in the new constitutions . . . the noblest and perhaps the last hope of mankind."[3] After a four-month stay in Paris in May 1777, Benjamin Franklin wrote emphatically:

All Europe is on our side of the Question, as far as Applause and good Wish can carry them. Those who live under arbitrary Power do nevertheless approve Liberty, and wish for it; they almost despair of recovering it in Europe; they read the Translations of our separate Colony Constitutions with Rapture. . . . Hence 'tis a Common Observation here, that our Cause is the *Cause of all Mankind,* and that we are fighting for their liberty in defending our own.[4]

Even if Franklin's claim about "all Europe" may be exaggerated, European public opinion of the Revolution was positive. In 1782 Mirabeau expressed himself in terms similar to Franklin's: "All Europe has applauded the sublime manifesto of the United States of America."[5]

The general European enthusiasm was also manifested in the fact that volunteers from Europe crossed the Atlantic to fight with the Americans for their revolutionary ideals: Lafayette from France, Kosciusko and Pulaski from Poland, von Steuben from Prussia. Inspired by the American revolutionary spirit, Kosciusko returned to Poland and fought for Polish independence; in the same way Lafayette returned to France to fight for the French Revolution.[6]

Without question, the American Revolution found the most sympathy in France. France had not only been allied with the rebellious colonies since 1778 and sent troops to America, but also had an enlightened official opinion whose progressivist ideas stood in sharp opposition to the existing absolutist system. Even if Brissot's famous remark to the effect that "the American Revolution was the mother of the French"[7] may sound overstated (although a modern French historian characterized the revolt of the English colonies as "the most important direct cause of the French Revolution"[8]), the American Revolution definitely contributed to the preparation and outbreak of revolution in France in various ways. Above all it had a demonstrative effect, a positive counterimage to the Ancien Régime. At the same time it proved that a successful revolution was possible and that a new political order initiated by the people could be realized. Through the American Revolution the notion of revolution in France took on a positive character (*heureuse révolution*), thereby removing reservations toward a revolution at home. Tocqueville, who conceded the great influence of the American Revolution on the French Revolution, emphasized the French philosophers' receptivitity to this event: "The Americans simply seemed to be carrying out what our writers had envisioned; they made into reality that of which we could only dream."[9]

Probably one of the most important connections between the two revolutions was indirect, however. It was the French government's decision to support the North American colonies in their struggle for independence from England, to compensate for France's defeat in the Seven Years' War. This led to an insoluble financial crisis within the Ancien Régime, which in turn triggered the Revolution.[10]

During the French Revolution, the human rights proclaimed in America exercised some influence on the French declarations of human and civil rights. It is difficult, however, to determine how much of an effect the American Revolution had outside of America and what particular contribution it made to liberal democratic movements after 1789. As Robert R. Palmer has noted, the more time that passes, the harder the attempt to analyze the specific effects of the American Revolution.[11]

There has been no shortage of efforts, on the part of both liberals and conservatives, to isolate the American Revolution from other revolutions precisely because of its moderate objectives and its relatively moderate course of events. As early as the 1790s, conservative federalists in the Netherlands had used the American example to counter the French one.[12] In France itself, Victor Hugo, who wanted to break out of the pattern of violence and terroristic ritual (Jacobins) created in his country by the "mother revolution" of 1789, issued the motto, "let us speak less of Robespierre and somewhat more of Washington."[13] In Germany, "the reception of the American Revolution remained confined largely to the area of theory and contemplation." A form of abstract enthusiasm developed that could be put to little practical use in Germany.[14]

In 1793, and emphatically again in 1800, Friedrich von Gentz, a conservative poet, juxtaposed the American and the French revolutions. The former he justified as a "defensive revolution" oriented according to the law, and the latter he dismissed as the embodiment of "absolute lawlessness."[15] In his preface to David Ramsay's *History of the American Revolution,* which appeared in 1794–95 in German translation, the Berlin gymnasium instructor G.F.K. Seidel wrote:

The philanthropist who unwillingly lays aside the sad story of the spoiled French Revolution should then be advised to take to the study of the origins of the free American state, in order to hearten himself with the conviction that even the huge uneducated mass of men can contribute to noble goals if it is only led by honest men.[16]

Later, in the nineteenth century, "revolution-shy German liberals" considered the American Revolution, against the background of the negatively regarded French counterpart, as an ideal revolution, whose moderation, continuity, and maintenance of the principle of freedom appeared exemplary.[17] It was precisely the conservative, "nonrevolutionary" traits that appealed to the conservative German historians. Johann Gustav Droysen wrote in 1846 that

If one wants to name what happened here a revolution, then it was of the sort that disturbed none of the important internal conditions, which did not interrupt the continuity of the domestic legal order in any matter, and did not change the condition of people and property any more than the ongoing war did.[18]

Progressivist elements of the American Revolution were taken over by many other countries as well. In the Western Hemisphere, it served as a model for Latin American movements of liberation from Spanish colonialism.[19] The liberal Russian poet Radistschev, in a section of his book *Journey from Petersburg to*

*Moscow* (ca. 1780–84) directed against Czarist censorship, cited American constitutions and their bills of rights that guaranteed freedom of the press.[20] The founders of the Russian revolutionary tradition, the Decembrists, were equally influenced by American examples and adopted many details from the Federal Constitution of 1787 when making their own constitutional plans for Russia.[21] In Italy, the great prophet of the Italian Risorgimento, the poet Vittorio Alfieri, published a volume of odes in 1784 that he called *America liberata*. A year later he dedicated his revolutionary drama *Bruto* to George Washington, the first president of the United States.[22] At the other end of Europe, in Sweden, the American Constitution was immediately translated and distributed:

Members of the nobility, infected by the American ideas, began whispering about a *coup* against the absolute monarch, and when finally, in 1809, the revolution was achieved, some of them wanted to establish a congress after the American pattern. Class interests, however, proved superior, and the old Riksdag of four estates was reconstituted.[23]

A freedom fighter of the Norwegian Revolution of 1814, Judge C. M. Falsen, also known as the father of the Norwegian Constitution, named his son George Benjamin in honor of Washington and Franklin.[24] The American Revolution also served as an example for the revolution in Belgium, which led to the country's independence in 1830. Belgium was the first European country to realize the radical principle of the absolute separation of church and state. Two decades after the adoption of the Belgian Constitution in 1830, Désiré de Haerne, a priest and a member of the Belgian Parliament, accounted for the American influence before the House of Representatives:

We are the only nation that has remained faithful in spirit to traditional rights and has followed America from the foundation of her political establishment and her liberal institutions. Yes, we looked upon England, on the one hand, as worthy of imitation in the march of progress in the path of true and practical liberty; but, at the same time, we were conscious that there were certain customs in the institutions of that country we could not adopt, and we cast our eyes beyond the Atlantic, where we found a great people worthy of entire imitation, and it is the institutions of that people we have chiefly inscribed upon our organic charter. We have followed their example in all that regards public liberty, the distribution of power, the election of representatives, and decentralization of rule.[25]

America also played a role in the Greek struggle for independence (1821–29) from the domination of the Ottoman Empire. President James Monroe was the first statesman to recognize the Greek people as an independent nation in his message to Congress on January 7, 1822. At the same time he asked Congress to approve the sending of an American minister to Greece to support the country's independence. "The United States was the only country in the world to officially declare itself in favor of Greek independence and to publicly express its encouragement for the new government, sentiments pronounced by President Monroe himself.''[26] Additional steps to promote Greek independence, such as the provision of three fleets and a loan of $2 million, were announced in Monroe's speech of December 2, 1823 (Monroe Doctrine). John Quincy Adams was finally able, however, to dissuade the president from his ''sentimental references to the revolutionary movement in Greece,'' as he noted in his memoirs (VI, pp. 194–99).[27] The president mentioned the Greek struggle for independence in his speech noting that

A strong hope has been long entertained, founded on the heroic struggle of the Greeks, that they would succeed in their contest and resume their equal station among the nations of the earth. It is believed that the whole civilized world take a deep interest in their welfare. . . . That she may obtain that rank is the object of our most ardent wishes.[28]

Edward Everett, then a famous publicist, was also fired with enthusiasm for the Greek cause. In his article ''Affairs of Greece'' (1823), he called for individual contributions to be passed on to the Greek freedom fighters.[29] Everett's article was motivated by the Greek appeal for aid addressed to the American people on May 25, 1821, the same plea that had impressed Monroe so greatly:

Having formed the resolution to live or die for freedom, we are drawn toward you by a just sympathy; since it is in your land that Liberty has fixed her abode, and by you that she is prized as by our fathers. Hence, in invoking her name, we invoke yours at the same time, trusting that in imitating you, we shall imitate our ancestor, and be thought worthy of them if we succeed in resembling you. Though separated from you by mighty oceans, your character brings you near us. We esteem you nearer than the nations on our own frontiers; and we possess, in you, friends, fellow-citizens, and brethren, because you are just, humane and generous;—just because free, generous and liberal because Christian. . . . You are desirous that all men should share the same blessings. . . . This glory, Americans, is yours alone, and raises you above all the nations which have gained a name of liberty and laws. . . . what friendship and zeal will [Greece] not manifest to you, when through your aid [Greece] will have broken [her] chains. . . . the bands of gratitude and fraternity will forever unite the Greeks and the Americans.[30]

Daniel Webster, then representative from Massachusetts, proposed the following resolution to Congress for the support of Greece on January 19, 1824: ''That provision ought to be made by law, for defraying the expense incident to the appointment of an Agent or Commissioner to Greece, whenever the President shall deem it expedient to make such appointment.''[31]

These announcements of American sympathy found resonance in Greece. The aura of the American Revolution is immortalized in the twenty-second verse of the Greek freedom hymn composed by the poet Dionysos Solomos. With all its heart, so the song goes, the country of Washington had rejoiced at the news of Greece's independence, and in so doing had recalled the iron bars that once held it prisoner as well.[32]

The Bolshevik Revolution (1917) did not arouse the sympathy of the United States. Communism was seen as a "powerful and malevolent force" during Wilson's administration, and there was a belief that this revolutionary ideology was doomed to failure because of its fundamentally incorrect assumptions.[33] In November 1920 Woodrow Wilson wrote: "As to Russia, I cannot but feel that Bolshevism would have burned out long ago if let alone."[34] The Anglo-Americans' attempt to influence the course of the Russian Revolution with their own troops, an effort attributable in particular to Wilson's "crusade idealism," failed.[35] Interestingly, Senator William Fulbright sees the Wilson administration as responsible for the beginning of the end of U.S.-Soviet relations:

The West, we and the British, particularly sought to abort that Revolution (1917) by force . . . , very mildly we sent forces over there and it started, right from the beginning, an antagonism between the newfound communist country and the West. That was our fault, I think. It was a very stupid thing to do, especially since we couldn't . . . and didn't pursue it to success. . . . Ever since then there has been this antagonism which still exists.[36]

However, the diametrically opposed objectives of the American and Russian Revolutions make the antagonism of the two countries understandable.

The thesis that, in succeeding decades, the decolonization process in Third World countries was similar to the American revolutionary experience has been strengthened by Seymour Martin Lipset's "first new nation" theory. According to him, the United States was "the first nation of any consequence to emerge from the colonial dominance of Western Europe as a sovereign state in its own right, and to that extent it shares something in common with the 'emerging nations' of today, no matter how different they may be in other respects."[37] In fact, during Franklin D. Roosevelt's era a wave of sympathy, indeed, a veritable American anticolonial tide set in against European interests and for the emancipation of the developing countries. The maturation of entire continents and peoples, and particularly in conjunction with the universal values and standards of the American and other European revolutions, was to be promoted by the Americans. The Atlantic Charter (1941) initiated by Roosevelt included the phrase "respect the right of all peoples to choose the form of government," an important precondition for the decolonization process.[38] His son Elliott Roosevelt recalled that his father made the following remarks about decolonization:

When we've won the war, I will work with all my might and main to see to it that the United States is not wheedled into the position of accepting any plea that will further France's imperialistic ambitions or that will aid and abet the British empire in its imperial ambitions.[39]

Especially in the 1960s, during John F. Kennedy's administration, independence movements in Latin America and the liberation struggles in the Third World obtained assistance, especially from Kennedy's Peace Corps strategy. It was during these years that a Ghanian student in the United States commented: "We have two home countries, our own and America."[40] Jefferson had once said the same thing about his own country and France.

The many Marxist or newly arisen Islamic movements obviously have little chance of American support, for their guiding ideals and visions are not even remotely similar to the freedom-oriented, revolutionary American creed.[41] Nonetheless, for some of its critics the United States is a reactionary country that only supports the liberation movements in nations close to it ideologically.[42] In the 1960s Arnold Toynbee even invoked parallels to Rome:

Today America is no longer the inspirer and leader of the World Revolution, and I have an impression that she is embarassed and annoyed when she is reminded that this was her original mission. . . . By contrast, America is today the leader of a world-wide anti-revolutionary movement in defence of vested interests. She now stands for what Rome stood for. Rome consistently supported the rich against the poor in all foreign countries that fell under her sway; and, since the poor, so far, have always and everywhere been far more numerous than the rich, Rome's policy made for inequality, for injustice, and for the least happiness of the greatest number.[43]

The fact that progressive ideals of the American Revolution have lost none of their power was ultimately proven by Carter's human rights policies.

# 12

## Between Continental Isolationism and Expansionist Mission

"A country's foreign policy is inevitably influenced by its history and the specifics of its political development," wrote Gordon A. Craig.[44] This statement is especially relevant to the United States. From the outset, Americans strongly doubted whether foreign policy was a legitimate sphere of activity for their country. The first pioneers had, of course, come to America with the intention of founding a *novum ordo saeculorum* and would have been happiest to have broken off every connection to the commerce, intrigue, diplomatic entanglements, and conflicts of the Old World. At the beginning of the twentieth century, Colonel George Harvey articulated a deeply rooted bias when he announced that "the foreign policy of the United States consists of not having any foreign policy at all." Two decades later, Demaree Bess analyzed "Why the Americans Hate the State Department." In her article of the same name, she came to the conclusion that they felt it to be a superfluous, and thus annoying, establishment.

Whenever Americans directed their gaze to the outside world, writes Gordon Craig, they were usually unable to spot any clear differences there between the various negotiations, alliances, systems, and wars. It appeared to them that the first three involuntarily led to the last. In particular, the Americans perceived balance-of-power or balance-of-forces systems to be threatening. American statesmen from John Adams to Woodrow Wilson and Cordell Hull despised European power politics. This conception was so deeply rooted in general that Henry Kissinger declared in the 1970s that the most important and most difficult task of the Nixon government consisted of "making the American people familiar with the requirements of the balance of power."[45]

American foreign policy was basically designed to express not only the political will of the American people, but their moral superiority as well. Since the founding of their nation, Americans have felt that their foreign policy was both effective and expedient. They also believed that because they were morally sound, their foreign policy could be based on idealistic rather than purely pragmatic motives. Strategies betraying a pragmatic political form in European style have remained suspect to Americans to the present.[46]

The history of American foreign policy begins with the American Revolution. According to the American Dream, the progressivist ideals of the New World were to become the starting point and model of an international order in which the freedom of individuals would be respected everywhere. America's conviction of its own historical mission in the world has been preserved for over two hundred years. Naturally, the best method for bringing the values of free America to the rest of the world always remained controversial.[47] Should the young republic actively bring its progressivist ideals out into the world, directly proselytizing other peoples? Or would it perhaps be better for America to remain aloof from entanglement in world politics and simply trust that the example of its freedom, its democracy, and a realization of its human rights would also be able to effect progress in other countries?

The Puritan age was dominated by the idea that the New World, as "a Citty upon a Hill," the New Jerusalem, could attract the attention of people in the entire world and serve as an example for them.[48] Interference in the affairs of foreign countries in order to effect changes was strictly ruled out in the decades that followed. This isolationist concept in American foreign policy continued from the end of the eighteenth century until the First World War, when Woodrow Wilson involved himself in the European war.[49] After Wilson the United States fell back into an isolationist foreign policy, only to abandon its continental isolationism once and for all during and after the Second World War in response to the threat of totalitarianism from the Right and Left.[50] The historical turmoil of the Second World War convinced the United States of the necessity of abandoning its isolationist stance and intervening militarily in the war so that Europe and the Free World could be rescued and their politics restructured. Since then American foreign policy has been defined in world political categories of responsibility. Considering the constant oscillations between power and morality in American foreign policy, it is clear that an acceptable balance between the two has been very difficult to strike since the emergence of the dialectic of national interest and idealism after 1945.[51]

These problems have left their mark in scholarly discussion of the question of when and why the United States found itself torn between a historical and political cycle of continental isolationism and an expansionist ideological mission.[52] The definitions of the idealistic school, the realistic school, and the interventionist school vary. Where one sees the realization of moral progressivist strategies in mission and crusading idealism, others are convinced that realistic progressivist strategies can only flourish in a climate of isolationism and equilibrium of power.[53] America can renounce neither idealism nor realism in foreign policy owing to its own self-understanding rooted in the Revolution. This fact is reflected in all the political change in the progressivist policies pursued from George Washington to Ronald Reagan.

## FROM WASHINGTON'S FAREWELL ADDRESS TO REAGAN'S UNILATERALISM DOCTRINE

The renunciation of active intervention in the name of freedom and progress dominated American foreign policy during the first half of the nineteenth century. It was based primarily on the warning of the first American president, George Washington. In his Farewell Address of 1796, which was to become the main isolationist doctrine of the United States, Washington rationally advised against an interventionist foreign policy. Why should the United States, he asked, entangle itself in the web of European ambition, rivalry, interest, humor, or caprice? The separate geographic situation of America was especially suited to enable America to disassociate itself from the intrigues of European politics:

Europe has a set of primary interests which to us have none or a very remote relation. Hence she must be engaged in frequent controversies, the cause of which are essentially foreign to our concerns. Hence, therefore, it must be unwise in us to implicate ourselves by artificial ties in the ordinary vicissitudes of her politics or the ordinary combinations and collisions of her friendships or enmities. Our detached and distant situation invites and enables us to pursue a different course. If we remain one people, under an efficient government, the period is not far off when we may defy material injury from external annoyance; when we may take such an attitude as will cause the neutrality we may at any time resolve upon to be scrupulously respected; when belligerent nations, under the impossibility of making acquisitions upon us, will not lightly hazard the risk giving us provocation; when we may choose peace or war, as our interest, guided by injustice, shall counsel. Why forego the advantages of so peculiar a situation? Why quit our own to stand upon foreign ground? Why, by interweaving our destiny with that of any part of Europe, entangle our peace and prosperity in the toils of European ambition, rivalship, interest, humor, or caprice? It is our true policy to steer clear of permanent alliances with any portion of the foreign world, so far, I mean, as we are now at liberty to do it; for let me not be understood as capable of patronizing infidelity to existing engagements. I hold the maxim no less applicable to public than to private affairs that honesty is always the best policy. I repeat, therefore, let those engagements be observed in their genuine sense. But in my opinion it is unnecessary and would be unwise to extend them.[54]

James Monroe, influenced by John Quincy Adams, supported a similar isolationist view (Monroe Doctrine) that the United States should avoid interfering in European politics. As Monroe said, "the citizens of the United States [would continue to] cherish sentiments the most friendly in favor of the liberty and happiness of their fellow-men on that side of the Atlantic." Yet the Americans could not and did not want to interfere in European affairs. They also expected that the Europeans, for their part, would renounce expansion of their system "to any portion" of the Western Hemisphere.

In the wars of the European powers in matters relating to themselves we have never taken any part, nor does it comport with our policy so to do. It is only when our rights are invaded or seriously menaced that we resent injuries or make preparation for our defense. With the movements in this hemisphere we are of necessity more immediately connected, and by causes which must be obvious to all enlightened and impartial observers. The political system of the allied powers is essentially different in this respect from that of America. This difference proceeds from that of our own, which has been achieved by the loss of so much blood and treasure, and matured by the wisdom of their most enlightened citizens, and under which we have enjoyed unexampled felicity, this whole nation is devoted. We owe it, therefore, to candor, and to the amicable relations existing between the United States and those powers to declare that we should consider any attempt on their part to extend their system to any portion of this hemisphere as dangerous to our peace and safety.[55]

Albert Gallatin, one of the leading American politicians of his time, was also one of the supporters of an isolationist foreign policy. He stated that the mission of the United States was to be a "model for all other governments," abide by the highest principles of political morality, and improve its own institutions so as to use the American example to "exert a blessed moral influence on mankind."[56]

This same principle of American restraint would soon be challenged. In December 1849 Lewis Cass of Michigan proposed to the Senate that it consider breaking off diplomatic relations with Austria as a protest against the repression of the Hungarian Revolution by Austrian and Russian troops in 1848–49. The proposal turned out to be significant, because a short time later Ludwig Kossuth, the leader of the Hungarian uprising, visited the United States and, in a number of speeches, called on the Americans to more active support of their cause. Kossuth criticized the United States on its policy, noting that the country was always debating about its mission for liberty, whereas in practice it was unready to take on an active role in the control of affairs beyond its borders. America could not, his argument continued, count on the radiant power of its "example" and hope that its moral appeals would simply succeed on their own. He, Kossuth, had never heard of a dictator practicing restraint merely because of "moral influence." Even though the Cass proposal was finally rejected in the Senate, it did effect a debate on the passive ambivalence of America's missionary and progressivist convictions. Many of the arguments for and against foreign interventions would resurface in coming years, retaining their relevance to the present day.[57]

The moral and idealistic missionary ethos typical of Americans, which had expressed itself at the beginning of the nineteenth century in the ideology of the frontier and manifest destiny, next served the United States as a motivation and justification to conquer the continent and push the frontier westward. Americans regarded the settlement and proselytization of North America as their natural right, through which divine providence fulfilled its task of bringing Christianity, freedom, democracy, and progress to the world. In the 1840s and 1850s, America was seized by a wave of intracontinental expansion, resulting in the annexation of Oregon and the Southwest, including California and Texas. This territorial expansion required a war against Mexico (1846–48), which was considered justified on the basis of the Monroe Doctrine. Besides economic issues and consideration of national security, the belief that expansion would fulfill a preordained task for the good of humankind remained a potent impulse.[58]

This urge to expand did not encompass only North America, however. In the middle of the nineteenth century, the United States extended its influence to Central America and to Pacific regions such as China and Japan, where conflicts with European powers were reckoned with for the first time.[59] The doctrine of manifest destiny soon expanded as well. Henceforth, it was regarded not only as a formula for justifying expansion on the North American continent, but increasingly as legitimation for extending interests beyond the United States.

The great turning point in American foreign policy, from its purely commercial orientation to an "imperial" aspiration for power, is generally acknowledged to have taken place in 1898. Cuba's independence from Spain and America's takeover of the Philippines, Guam, and Puerto Rico were both consequences of the Spanish-American War. In the same year the Americans annexed Hawaii and split Samoa with the German Reich.[60] Was the United States, born in the struggle for independence from the colonial power of England, now setting up its own "imperial" colonies?[61]

William H. Seward, for example, who had served as secretary of state under Abraham Lincoln and Andrew Johnson, had repeatedly proposed the expansion of an "informal empire." According to Seward, the United States, as a world power, had to expand toward the North, South, and West, to make the Pacific into a *mare americanum*, and turn Asia into the commercial domain of the United States.[62] Similar demands were also made by the historian and head of the United States Naval Academy, Alfred Thayer Mahan, who had dreamed of building up a strong navy for the conquest of new markets and bases.[63]

Along with the United States' indisputable economic and commercial motives, idealistic elements also played a role in American expansionist desires around the turn of the century. Even the revisionist school has characterized the great power politics of the United States since the McKinley administration (1897–1901) as "idealistic and moral imperialism." Under McKinley, the American creed, the belief in the superiority of American values and America's traditional missionary and progressivist optimism, flourished once more.[64] Along the same lines, the Protestant preacher Josiah Strong, in his book *Our Country* (1885), called on the American people to remake the world in America's sense: "It seems to me that God . . . prepared the Anglo-Saxon race for a moment which will come irresistibly in the future of the world." According to Strong, "the last struggle of the races" was nearing. The struggle would lead to the "rep-

resentative of the greatest freedom, the purest Christianity, the highest civilization
. . . spreading itself over the entire world."[65] In the same way, President
McKinley declared before the Congress on April 11, 1898, that intervention in
Cuba was a "question of humanity," "to secure in the island the establishment
of a stable government, capable of maintaining order and observing its international obligations, insuring peace and tranquility and the security of its citizens
as well as our own."[66] McKinley justified the annexation of the Philippines in
similar terms in a speech given in Boston in 1899: "The Philippines, like Cuba
and Puerto Rico, were entrusted to our hands by war, and to that great trust,
under the providence of God and in the name of human progress and civilization
we are committed."[67] The idealistic belief in progress was indeed an essential
reason for American expansionist policy toward the end of the nineteenth century.

McKinley's successor, Theodore Roosevelt, took up where this foreign policy
had left off. Toward China, he initially pursued the Open Door Policy that had
been adopted by McKinley's Secretary of State, John Hay. Roosevelt mediated
successfully in the Russo-Japanese War of 1904–1905, pushed back the British
with his Latin American policies, and made possible the beginning of construction
on the Panama Canal in 1904.[68] However, the core of his foreign policy was
the extension of the Monroe Doctrine by the so-called Roosevelt Corollary, by
which the United States obligated itself to prevent the economic ruin and strategic
instability of Latin American states and to impede any intervention by European
governments as a result of such instability. As Roosevelt said:

If a nation shows that it knows how to act with reasonable efficiency and decency in
social and political matters, if it keeps order and pays its obligations, it need fear no
interference from the United States. Chronic wrongdoing, or an impotence which results
in a general loosening of the ties of civilized society, may in America, as elsewhere,
ultimately require intervention by some civilized nation, and in the Western hemisphere
the adherence of the United States to the Monroe Doctrine may force the United States,
however reluctantly, in flagrant cases of such wrongdoing or impotence, to the exercise
of an international police power. . . . Our interests and those of our Southern neighbors
are in reality identical. They have great natural riches, and if within their borders the
reign of law and justice obtains, prosperity is sure to come to them. . . . We would interfere
with them only in the last resort, and then only if it became evident that their inability
or unwillingness to do justice at home and abroad had violated the rights of the United
States or had invited foreign aggression to the detriment of the entire body of American
nations.[69]

For Roosevelt, American foreign policy was a matter of being able "to speak
softly and carry a big stick."[70]

Even more emphatically than Roosevelt, Woodrow Wilson grounded his foreign policy in idealistic visions.[71] Although he was initially at pains to preserve
America's neutrality during the First World War, German policies and the impending defeat of the Allies finally compelled him to intervene.[72] Wilson's
argument for America's entry into the war was not, however, national security,

but rather the fundamental moral excellence of the American nation, which committed the government, as the "single champion" of democracy, to combat the "natural enemy of freedom":

It is a fearful thing to lead this great peaceful people into war, into the most terrible and disastrous of all wars, civilization itself seeming to be in the balance. But the right is more precious than peace, and we shall fight for the things which we have always carried nearest to our hearts,—for democracy, for the right of those who submit to authority to have a voice in their own governments, for the rights and liberties of small nations, for a universal dominion of right by such a concert of free peoples as shall bring peace and safety to all nations and make the world itself at last free. To such a task we can dedicate our lives and our fortunes, everything that we are and everything that we have, with the pride of those who know that the day has come when America is privileged to spend her blood and her might for the principles that gave her birth and happiness and the peace which she has treasured.[73]

In effect, Wilson described his "crusading idealism" as democratic America's last struggle against the forces of evil. In a speech given in Boston in February 1919, he explained that, in the name of the American people, he declared the goal of this great war to be ideals and nothing but ideals, and it was in this spirit that the war was won.[74]

Wilson's idea of an order of world peace, guaranteed by a League of Nations that would abolish foreign policy and replace it with a *world domestic policy*, soon proved to be utopian. These ideas were not only rejected by the Europeans, but in particular by the Americans themselves. No one in America wanted to take on responsibility for the European postwar order.[75] A new phase of isolationism abruptly broke out in Washington at precisely the moment when the American ideals of progress could have served more urgently than ever as an example.[76]

Only twenty-four years after Wilson's Declaration of War, the provisional isolationist policy of the United States was abandoned once and for all with its entry into the Second World War. Even though the rise of national socialism had at first changed nothing in America's policies of neutrality, Franklin D. Roosevelt decided in favor of American intervention in the face of the increasing totalitarian threat toward Europe and the rest of the Free World. In his Four Freedoms speech of January 6, 1941, he elaborated to the American people the necessity of American intervention, even though he was still unable to make any concrete statements as to the extent of American commitment:

Let us say to the democracies, "We Americans are vitally concerned in your defense of freedom. We are putting forth our energies, our resources and our organizing powers to give you the strength to regain and maintain a free world. We shall send you, in ever-increasing numbers, ships, planes, tanks, guns. This is our purpose and our pledge."[77]

Franklin Roosevelt saw the threat to freedom and democracy as the main danger presented by national socialism. In this same speech he proclaimed his famous four freedoms as a bulwark, so to speak, against German dictatorship:

In the future days, which we seek to make secure, we look forward to a world founded upon four essential human freedoms. The first is freedom of speech and expression—everywhere in the world. The second is freedom of every person to worship God in his own way—everywhere in the world. The third is freedom from want, which, translated into world terms, means economic understanding which will secure to every nation a healthy peace-time life for its inhabitants—everywhere in the world. The fourth is freedom from fear—which, translated into world terms, means a world-wide reduction of armaments to such a point and in such a thorough fashion that no nation will be in a position to commit an act of physical aggression against any neighbor—anywhere in the world.[78]

For Roosevelt it was important to formulate idealistic, but realistic, goals for a postwar order that would serve American interests as much as the interests of liberal and democratic states.

Soon after the war ended, it became clear once more that the establishment of a harmonious world order was not possible. As a victorious power, the Soviet Union pursued an aggressive foreign policy in Eastern and Southern Europe, erected an Iron Curtain as Winston Churchill termed it, and introduced the era of the Cold War.[79]

The United States' reaction was the so-called Truman Doctrine, in which the Americans pledged assistance to free and independent nations against the expansionist intentions of totalitarian regimes. This doctrine also contained an appeal to Americans to promote freedom, democracy, and human rights in the world. In his speech, Harry Truman emphasized that, in the present bipolar world, every country on the globe had to make a choice between two forms of government: either democracy or dictatorship, either the rule of the majority, free institutions, individual freedom, and freedom of speech and religion, or terror, oppression, press and broadcast censorship, and the suppression of personal freedoms. According to Truman, it was now the task of the United States to ensure freedom of decision for these countries and to support the free nations: "The free peoples of the world look to us for support in maintaining their freedoms. If we falter in our leadership we may endanger the peace of the world."[80] For the first time in its history the United States became a member of an alliance founded in and for peacetime, an alliance whose aim was mutual military security for its members. The troika of President Truman, George Marshall, and George Kennan, assisted by Ernest Bevin, Robert Schuman, Jean Monnet, and other allies, laid the foundations of the postwar order—the strategy of containment, the Marshall Plan with its philosophy of economic and military support for allies, and the NATO alliance. The speed with which this task was accomplished, and the fact that the United States has to this day remained true to the principles embodied in those agreements, imbued American foreign policy vis-à-vis the Soviet great-power dictatorship with a new pragmatism, consistency, and continuity that is virtually as credible today as it was immediately after the Second World War.[81]

The strategy formulated by George Kennan during the Truman administration for stemming Soviet imperialism and preserving the Free World[82] would determine American foreign policy until the end of the 1960s, although the Kennedy presidency reintroduced idealistic elements in 1961. The Eisenhower administration had occupied itself with reacting to Soviet initiatives and defining its foreign policy primarily in terms of military action ("rollback") and power politics ("liberation"). Secretary of State John Foster Dulles sought to encircle the Soviet Union and China with a global ring of multilateral and bilateral alliances united by anticommunist commitments. The main result of this undertaking, as Townsend Hoopes wrote, was "the institutionalization and multiplication in American life of the structures and attitudes of the Cold War."[83] By contrast, Kennedy put far greater emphasis on the basic idealistic motivation that had provided the basis for containment. In addition, Kennedy dedicated himself increasingly to the problems of the Third World and attempted to fight poverty and human rights violations in Latin America with his Alliance for Progress strategy.[84]

In his inaugural address in 1961, Kennedy referred to the progressivist ideals and values of the American Revolution. He promised "a grand and global alliance . . . against the common enemies of man: tyranny, poverty, disease, and war itself." To the Soviet Union he sent the message that Americans would not be willing to tolerate the undercutting of democracy, freedom, and human rights. Indeed, every nation should know, "that we shall pay any price, bear any burden, meet any hardship, support any friend, oppose any foe to assure the survival and the success of liberty."[85] After the policy of containment and the global involvement accompanying it had reached their pinnacle in the Vietnam War, and after the failure of this policy had become clear,[86] the desire for a change of American foreign policy began to grow. In the Johnson administration's bloody jungle war in Vietnam, the United States widely appeared to have repudiated the very values it was attempting to defend against communist aggression.[87] The broad foreign policy consensus once forged by Truman was suddenly endangered.

After Richard Nixon took office as president in 1969 and named the experienced Henry Kissinger as his security adviser, new accents in American foreign policy soon emerged. In Guam on July 25, 1969, Richard Nixon proclaimed the so-called Nixon Doctrine, which provided for a reduction of the military "overcommitment" of past decades in conjunction with a simultaneous stabilization and strengthening of regional structures.[88] The new Asia Doctrine, announced by Secretary of State William Rogers, implied the protection of national interests without an automatic military reaction on the part of the United States in response to threats. The Nixon Doctrine was not an isolationist retreat, as many critics claimed, but rather a substitute, although primarily in Asia and the Pacific, for military strength, for a unilateral *pax americana*.[89] The corollary to the Nixon

Doctrine, the policy of the balance of forces—a strategy attributable to the virtuousity of "Metternissinger" in foreign policy (Gordon A. Craig)—sought a restructuring of the international system, a codification of principles that would lead to a peaceful management and remodeling of East-West competition. The intent behind this neorealistic foreign policy was to reshape a previously "esoteric military strategy" that had confused power with diplomacy, as Kissinger contended, into a deideologized, political strategy of containment known as détente. Just as Roosevelt in the 1940s had contained national socialism with the help of Stalin and the totalitarian policies of the Soviets with the help of Churchill, Nixon and Kissinger aspired to check the Russians with the help of the Chinese, a strategy to be reached via relaxed relations with both of the other great powers. The containment of the geopolitical expansion of the Soviet Union was possible only with a change in Moscow's international behavior, and this, in turn, could only take place by means of a policy of détente that would be useful to both. Kissinger's realpolitik approach ultimately represented a policy of containment by other means (containment as détente).

After the Cold War era of bipolar confrontation had been relegated to the past, an age of dialogue, negotiation, coexistence between the superpowers, détente, and peace dawned. It was important to connect the *reality of competition to the imperative of coexistence* (Kissinger) in order to achieve a balance of power, to set into motion a "dialectic of rapprochement and delimitation" between East and West, and to neutralize the sources of conflict between the two great powers.

The historical opportunity of a "change through rapprochement," however, could not be successfully exploited, for a genuine deepening of détente by the East would have meant an erosion of the Soviet system. The consequence of an inexorable slackening of tensions would have been the Europeanization of Russia.[90]

Under Nixon, Ford, and Kissinger, the United States returned to a foreign policy aimed primarily at stability, maintenance of the world political status quo, consolidation of spheres of influence, and the securing of freedom. The prime aim of foreign policy was realism, not idealism. The missionary idea ebbed, and America once again limited itself to serving other countries as an example, as the "Citty upon a Hill," without actively carrying its own values out into the rest of the world. Henry Kissinger succinctly described this posture:

As the greatest democracy the world has ever known, we are a living reminder that there is an alternative to tyranny and oppression. The revolution that we began two hundred years ago goes on, for most of the world still lives without the freedom that has for so long been ours. To them we remain a beacon of hope and an example to be emulated.[91]

Kissinger also professed the U.S. commitment to the idea of freedom and self-determination. Whereas presidents Wilson, Roosevelt, and Kennedy had made these idealistic objectives the cornerstone of their foreign policy, the pragmatic Kissinger was more interested in other tasks, to which, however, he also applied moral grounds. "As far as the ancient antagonism between freedom and tyranny is concerned, we are not neutral," said Kissinger before the Senate Committee on Foreign Relations on September 19, 1974. But there were, he contended, other compelling necessities that imposed limits on the ability of the United States to bring about change in other countries. It was no longer "the principal goal of American foreign policy to transform the domestic structures of societies with which we deal." "The awareness of our limits corresponds to the recognition of the necessity of peace—and not to a lack of moral feeling." Kissinger then concluded his speech by noting that the maintenance of human life and of human society was also a moral value.[92]

Under Nixon, Ford, and Kissinger, after numerous manifestations of American missionary zeal in questions of basic freedoms and human rights, American foreign policy seemed to hark back to the maxims of George Washington and John Quincy Adams. Deideologization and pragmatization of international relations now went hand in hand with the concepts of stability, equilibrium, interest, power, security, détente, and peace.

The equilibrium that Kissinger had achieved between his pragmatic policies of the balance of power and his strategy of enlightened interest began to collapse in the United States in the mid-1970s. All sides of the political spectrum bemoaned a "moral vacuum" in American foreign policy. It was Gerald Ford's successor, Jimmy Carter, who was destined to plunge into this vacuum. In his inaugural address on January 20, 1977, Carter declared:

Because we are free, we can never be indifferent to the fate of freedom elsewhere. Our moral sense dictates a clearcut preference for those societies which share with us an abiding respect for individual human rights. We do not seek to intimidate, but it is clear that a world which others can dominate with impunity would be inhospitable to decency and a threat to the well-being of all people.[93]

Although Kissinger's key foreign-policy concepts had included such words as equilibrium and status quo, Carter's rhetoric was dominated by expressions such as freedom, human rights, morality, principles, belief, the "spiritual strength of our nation," and the "nobility of ideas."[94] Carter attempted to restore optimism and idealism to an America tortured by moralistic self-criticism after Vietnam and Watergate. The president saw a global trend directed toward the realization of human rights. He felt that the United States had to be identified with this trend:[95]

The world itself is now dominated by a new spirit. Peoples more numerous and politically aware are craving, and now demanding, their place in the sun—not just for the benefit of their own physical condition, but for basic human rights. The passion for freedom is on the rise. Tapping this new spirit, there can be no nobler nor more ambitious task for

America to undertake on this day of a new beginning than to help shape a just and peaceful world that is truly humane.[96]

The rebirth of American idealism, shown clearly in these words, characterized Carter's entire presidency. He continued his public expressions of sympathy for Eastern European dissidents, and unlike his predecessors, he supported the efforts of the Congress to make foreign aid for the Third World dependent on the human rights record of the recipient country in each case.

In the eyes of the world, this position did indeed distance Washington from totalitarian and authoritarian dictatorships all across the globe, but these campaigns exposed the president to charges of inconsistency. Time and time again the Carter administration found itself faced with the problem of linking lofty human rights standards to the vast number of the United States' concrete foreign policy goals. Relations with Moscow were not merely a matter of human rights; there was also détente to consider, specifically SALT II, which was finally signed in the summer of 1979. In respect to the Third World, the ideal of human rights was accompanied by the goal of national security and the task of ensuring economic markets. How strongly, for example, could the Marcos regime in the Philippines be affected by the refusal of foreign aid, if it was simultaneously necessary to keep the two U.S. military bases there for the security of the entire region?

Thus, Carter's human rights policy remained a high moral standard—"crusading idealism," as Stanley Hoffmann called it—but it was realized only occasionally. Good motives, bad craftsmanship, was a frequent charge raised in his own country against Carter's policy.[97] Abroad, his human rights policies were often called "containment as idealism."

Apart from his human rights policy, Carter achieved three foreign policy successes during his time in office: the signing of the Panama Canal treaty, the establishment of diplomatic relations with the People's Republic of China, and the Camp David agreement between Israel and Egypt. The elimination of American paternalism toward Latin America, equilibrium, nonproliferation policies, and disarmament were the main points of Carter's foreign policy program. The president did not change his policy until December 1979, after the Soviet invasion of Afghanistan. Afghanistan and the taking of American citizens as hostages in Iran compelled him in his last year in office to pursue a "harder line."[98] The president announced the so-called Carter Doctrine, the objective of which was to secure the Near East's oil pipelines for the Western world.[99] Suddenly, power politics and Western security interests were back at the center of Washington's foreign policy. Jimmy Carter tried to take the new mood in the country into account: "We don't want to be kicked around anymore." But Carter had taken too long to make the change. He lost the presidential campaign against his Republican challenger, Ronald Reagan.

As did his predecessor, Reagan had fluent command of "freedom rhetoric" from the outset. It reached one of its high points in his address before the British

Parliament on June 8, 1982, when the president called for a "crusade for freedom" to liberate all oppressed people in the world.[100] Even in respect to Latin America the idea of human rights played a certain role in the Reagan administration, and not just rhetorically.[101] But while Carter's human rights policy had been supported primarily by idealism and a bad conscience after Vietnam and Watergate, Reagan used the topic exclusively as a means of restraining the Soviet Union.[102]

It was Reagan's goal to make America great and strong, politically, economically, and militarily. This included the successful execution of an armaments program unique in American history, which was culminated with the vision of the Strategic Defense Initiative (SDI), or Star Wars, as its opponents soon called it.[103] An enormous economic upsurge came about in conjunction with the massive program of rearmament and an ideological confrontation reminiscent of the 1950s. "America is back again" was the slogan with which Reagan assured his reelection in 1984, thus achieving a popularity enjoyed by only a few presidents before him.

America had finally left the trauma of Vietnam behind, had won back its sense of optimism, and was looking with new optimism into the future. In Spring 1985 Secretary of State George Shultz declared:

as we head toward the 21st century, it is time for the democracies to celebrate their system, their beliefs and their success. We face challenges, but we are well poised to master them. . . . The free nations, if they maintain their unity and their faith in themselves, have the advantage—economically, technologically, morally. History is on freedom's side.[104]

This credo had also been affirmed by Jimmy Carter, but now—under Reagan—it seemed to achieve credibility. Idealism was given support from power politics, and the administration did not shy away from giving the traditional American mission of freedom and progress military support. On February 6, 1986, in his State of the Union Address, Reagan clarified this approach, which would later be regarded as the core of the Reagan Doctrine:

Freedom is not the sole prerogative of a chosen few, it is the universal right of all God's children. Look to where peace and prosperity flourish today. It is in homes that freedom built. Victories against poverty are the greatest and most secure where people live by laws that ensure free press, free speech and freedom to worship, vote and create wealth. Our mission is to nourish and defend freedom and democracy and to communicate these ideals everywhere we can. We must stand by all our democratic allies. And we must not break faith with those who are risking their lives on every continent, from Afghanistan to Nicaragua, to defy Soviet-supported aggression and secure rights which have been ours from birth.[105]

This frequently invoked solidarity with the freedom fighters of the world had already become quite clear in the fall of 1983, when the Reagan administration toppled the Marxist-Leninist regime in Grenada with American troops. Reagan also decided to support the Contras in Nicaragua, the resistance of Afghan partisans, the anticommunist liberation movement in Cambodia, and the underground fighters of Western-oriented UNITA in Angola. Against the background of the traditional strategy of containment, which had shaped American foreign policy in various forms since the end of the Second World War and which was primarily characterized by its defensive character, the policy of the Reagan Doctrine appeared to have an unambiguously offensive orientation: the "rollback" was successful in Grenada, why wouldn't it also be successful one day in Nicaragua, for example?

It came as no surprise that Reagan's policy met with strong condemnation among his opponents in the communist camp. But criticism was also to be heard time and again in the countries of the Third World and especially from European allies. The Reagan administration was accused of defining its policies exclusively according to American interests without taking the interests of friends and allies into account. In 1982, on the basis of this criticism, Joseph Nye charged Reagan with pursuing a policy of "global unilateralism."[106] The most recent incident in which the United States showed that it would act without the consent if necessary and even despite the express refusal, of its closest partners, was the attack on Libya in the spring of 1986. Was moral self-righteousness once again the result of America's missionary urge?[107]

In its final days, the Reagan administration seemed prepared to reach an understanding with the Kremlin on questions of global disarmament. The May 1987 INF agreement to eliminate medium-range nuclear missiles from Eastern and Western Europe was considered a historic step toward disarmament. For the time being, one would be well advised to wait out future developments and to be wary of conclusive judgments about the Reagan administration. Nonetheless, it has already been established that Ronald Reagan will go down in American history as the president who met the global challenge of totalitarianism ideologically, economically, and militarily with more decisiveness and more emphasis on the offensive than any of his predecessors. Whether this policy will prove successful in the long term, and whether it will really help spread freedom in the world, remains to be seen.

# Notes to Part V

## CHAPTER 11

1. Arnold J. Toynbee: If We Are to Be the Wave of the Future, *The New York Times Magazine* (November 13, 1960): 123.

2. Charles William Eliot, quoted in Halvdan Koht, *The American Spirit in Europe, A Survey of Transatlantic Influences* (Philadelphia, 1949), 79.

3. J. Garat, quoted in Durand Echeverria, *Mirage in the West, A History of the French Image of American Society to 1815* (Princeton, N.J., 1968), 109.

4. B. Franklin, quoted in H. Koht, *The American Spirit in Europe,* 14.

5. Mirabeau, quoted in H. Koht, *The American Spirit in Europe,* 14.

6. See H. Koht, *The American Spirit in Europe,* 14 ff.

7. See Claude Fohlen, The Impact of the American Revolution on France, in *The Impact of the American Revolution Abroad,* Library of Congress Symposia on the American Revolution (Washington, D.C., 1976), 23.

8. See George Lefèbvre, *The Coming of the French Revolution* (Princeton, N.J., 1967), 21.

9. Alexis de Tocqueville, *The Old Regime and the French Revolution,* (New York, 1955).

10. See H.-C. Schröder, *Die Amerikanische Revolution,* 165.

11. See R. R. Palmer, The Impact of the American Revolution Abroad, in *The Impact of the American Revolution Abroad,* 6.

12. See J. W. Schulte Nordholt, The Impact of the American Revolution on the Dutch Republic, in *The Impact of the American Revolution Abroad,* 44 f.

13. V. Hugo, quoted in *Thomas v. Vegesack: Die Macht und die Phantasie, Schriftsteller in den Revolutionen* (Hamburg, 1979), 101.

14. See Horst Dippel, Die Wirkung der amerikanischen Revolution auf Deutschland und Frankreich, in *200 Jahre Amerikanische Revolution und moderne Revolutionsfor-*

*schung, Geschichte und Gesellschaft*, ed. H.-U. Wehler (Göttingen, 1976), special issue 2, 120.

15. See H. Dippel, Deutschland und die Amerikanische Revolution, Ph.D. diss., Cologne, 1972, 257–61. H. Dippel, *Germany and the American Revolution, 1770–1880. A Sociohistorical Investigation of Late Eighteenth-Century Political Thinking* (Chapel Hill, N.C., 1977).

16. G.F.K. Seidel, quoted in *Die Amerikanische Revolution in Augenzeugenberichten*, ed. W. P. Adams and A. M. Adams (Munich, 1976), 357 f.

17. See Michael Neumüller, *Liberalismus und Revolution, Das Problem der Revolution in der deutschen liberalen Geschichtsschreibung des 19. Jahrhunderts* (Düsseldorf, 1973), 75 f.

18. J. G. Droysen, quoted in ibid., 233.

19. See Mario Rodriguez, The Impact of the American Revolution on the Spanish- and Portuguese-Speaking World, in *The Impact of the American Revolution Abroad*, 115.

20. A. N. Radistschev, *Reise von Petersburg nach Moskau*, (East Berlin, 1961), 166, 183 f. H.-C. Schröder, *Die Amerikanische Revolution*, 161.

21. See N. N. Bolkhovitinov, The American Revolution and the Russian Empire, in *The Impact of the American Revolution Abroad*, 91 ff.

22. See the article by Gabrieli, in A.N.J. Den Hollander, ed., Contagious Conflict. See also Paul R. Baker, *The Fortunate Pilgrims: Americans in Italy, 1800–1860* (Cambridge, Mass., 1964).

23. H. Koht, *The American Spirit in Europe*, 21.

24. Ibid., 22.

25. D. de Haerne, quoted in H. Koht, *The American Spirit in Europe*, 24.

26. Jean Dimakis, La Guerre de l'indépendance Grecque vue par la presse Française (Période de 1821 à 1824), (Thessaloniki, 1969, Institute for Balkan Studies), 109.

27. See Norman Graebner, ed., *Ideas and Diplomacy* (New York, 1964), 139 ff.

28. J. Monroe, quoted in ibid., 142.

29. See E. Everett, Affairs of Greece, *North American Review* 17 (October 1823): 417–24.

30. The appeal is quoted in N. Graebner, ed., *Ideas and Diplomacy*, 144 and 145.

31. Daniel Webster, quoted in *Ideas and Diplomacy*, 148, ed. N. Graebner. See Harris Y. Vouras, *Hellenic Independence and America's Contribution to the Cause* (Putland, Vt., 1934).

32. See Dionysos Solomos, *Apanta* (Athens, 1965), 5.

33. See: Lloyd C. Gardner, *Safe for Democracy: The Anglo-American Response to Revolution, 1913–1923* (New York, 1984).

34. W. Wilson, quoted in Linda Killen, *The Russian Bureau: A Case Study in Wilsonian Diplomacy* (Lexington, Ky., 1983), 130.

35. See L. C. Gardner, *Safe for Democracy*, 326.

36. Author's conversation with Senator William Fulbright on April 27, 1982, in Washington, D.C.

37. S. M. Lipset, quoted in S. P. Huntington, *Political Order in Changing Societies*, 134.

38. See D. C. Watt, American Anti-Colonialist Policies and the End of the European Colonial Empires 1941–1962, in *Contagious Conflict*, ed. A.N.J. Den Hollander, 95.

39. F.D.R., in Elliott Roosevelt, *As He Saw It* (New York, 1946), 114.

40. See Waldemar Besson, Struktur und Entwicklung der gegenwärtigen Weltpolitik,

in *Perspektiven für das letzte Drittel des 20. Jahrhunderts* (Stuttgart, 1968), 173 ff. F. Ansprenger, *Die Auflösung der Kolonialreiche* (Munich, 1968).

41. See N. L. Hoepli, ed., *Aftermath of Colonialism* (New York, 1973).

42. See Hans-Jürgen Schröder, *Amerika als Modell? Das Dilemma der Washingtoner Außenpolitik gegenüber revolutionären Bewegungen im 20. Jahrhundert*, ed. E. Angermann, (Munich, 1979).

43. Arnold Toynbee, *America and the World Revolution* (New York, 1962), 16 and 17.

## CHAPTER 12

44. Gordon A. Craig, Die Supermacht und das Gute, Amerikanische Außenpolitik von 1919–1983, *Frankfurter Allgemeine Zeitung* (Supplement), (January 7, 1984).

45. See ibid. Knud Krakau, American Foreign Relations—An American Style?, in *Oceans Apart?*, ed. E. Angermann and M.-L. Frings, 121–45.

46. See G. A. Craig, Die Supermacht. Knud Krakau, American Foreign Relations. Hans J. Morgenthau, *The Purpose of American Politics* (New York, 1960).

47. See G. A. Craig, The Democratic Roots of American Diplomatic Style, in *Vom Staat des Ancien Régime zum modernen Parteinstaat*, H. Berdin et al. ed. (Festschrift for Theodor Schieder), (Munich, 1978), 117–31.

48. See Larzer Ziff, *Puritanism in America, New Culture in a New World* (New York, 1974). S. Bercovitch, *The Puritan Origins of the American Self* (New Haven, Conn., 1977).

49. See Arnold Wolfers and Lawrence Martin, eds., *The Anglo-American Tradition in Foreign Affairs* (New Haven, Conn., 1976), 263–79. Alexander Conde, *A History of American Foreign Policy, Growth to World Power (1700–1914)*, vol. 1 (New York, 1978).

50. See Klaus Schwabe, *Der amerikanische Isolationismus im 20. Jahrhundert, Legende und Wirklichkeit* (Wiesbaden, 1975). Alexander Conde, *A History of American Foreign Policy, Global Power (1900 to the Present)*, vol. 2 (New York, 1978).

51. See Hans J. Morgenthau, *In Defense of the National Interest* (New York, 1951). W. W. Rostow, *The United States in the World Arena* (New York, 1960), 17–38. Werner J. Feld, *American Foreign Policy: Aspirations and Reality* (New York, 1984).

52. See Michael Wolffsohn, 200 Jahre Außenpolitik der Vereinigten Staaten, *Aus Politik und Zeitgeschichte*, B 6/81 (February 7, 1981): 15–24. Frank L. Klingenberg, Cyclical Trends in American Foreign Policy Moods and Their Policy Implications, in *Challenges to America: U.S. Foreign Policy in the 1980s, Sage International Yearbook of Foreign Studies*, 4, ed. Charles W. Kegley and Patrick J. McGowan (1979). Norman Graebner, ed., *Traditions and Values: Studies in American Diplomacy, 1865–1945* (Lanham, N.Y., 1985).

53. See H. J. Morgenthau, *American Foreign Policy* (London, 1952). Robert Endicott Osgood, *Ideals and Self-Interest in America's Foreign Relations, The Great Transformations of the Twentieth Century* (Chicago, 1953). George F. Kennan, *Realities of American Foreign Policy* (Princeton, N.J., 1954). Kenneth W. Thompson, *Political Realism and the Crisis of World Politics, An American Approach to Foreign Policy* (Princeton, N.J., 1960). Stanley Hoffmann, *The State of War, Essays on the Theory and Practice of International Politics* (London, 1965). Stanley Hoffmann, *Primacy or World Order, American Foreign Policy Since the Cold War* (New York, 1980). John G. Stoes-

singer, *Crusaders and Pragmatists, Movers of Modern American Foreign Policy* (New York, 1979).

54. G. Washington's Farewell Address (September 17, 1796), printed in H. C. Syrett, *American Historical Documents*, 146. See Felix Gilbert, *To the Farewell Address, Ideas of Early American Foreign Policy* (Princeton, N.J., 1961).

55. Monroe Doctrine, printed in H. C. Syrett, *American Historical Documents*, 180.

56. A. Gallatin, quoted in F. Pflüger, *Die Menschenrechtspolitik der USA*, 33.

57. See *Congressional Globe*, 31st Congress, 2nd Session from January 7, 1850, 113–16. F. Pflüger, *Die Menschenrechtspolitik der USA*, 34 f.

58. See Albert K. Weinberg, *Manifest Destiny, A Study in Nationalist Expansionism in American History* (New York, 1963).

59. See Dan E. Clark, Manifest Destiny and the Pacific, *Pacific Historical Review* 1 (March 1932): 1–17.

60. See E. May, *Imperial Democracy, The Emergence of America as a Great Power* (New York, 1973), 243 ff., Hans Ulrich Wehler, *Grundzüge der amerikanischen Außenpolitik 1750–1900* (Frankfurt am Main, 1984), 1 (1750–1900), 193 ff.

61. See H.-U. Wehler, Der amerikanische Imperialismus vor 1914, in *Der moderne Imperialismus*, ed. W. J. Mommsen (Stuttgart, 1971), 172 ff. H.-U. Wehler, *Der Aufstieg des amerikanischen Imperialismus, Studien zur Entwicklung des Imperium Americanum 1865–1900* (Göttingen, 1974).

62. See E. May, *Imperial Democracy*. H.-U. Wehler, *Der amerikanische Imperialismus vor 1914*.

63. See A. Wolfers and L. Martin, eds., *The Anglo-American Tradition in Foreign Affairs*, 234 ff.

64. See William A. Williams, *The Tragedy of American Diplomacy* (New York, 1978). Yves-Henri Nouailhat, *Histoire des doctrines politiques aux Etats-Unis* (Paris, 1977) (chapter: Progressisme et impérialisme), 75 ff. See also T. A. Shannon, Manifest Destiny and Anti-Imperialists of 1898: An American Dissent, Ph.D. diss., Oxford University, 1983.

65. J. Strong, quoted in F. Pflüger, *Die Menschenrechtspolitik der USA*, 37.

66. McKinley's War Message, quoted in H. C. Syrett, *American Historical Documents*, 312, 313. See also Whitney T. Perkins, *Constraints of Empire: The United States and Caribbean Interventions* (Oxford, 1982).

67. McKinley, quoted in *Boston Herald* (February 17, 1899).

68. See John Milton Cooper, *The Warrior and the Priest: Theodore Roosevelt and Woodrow Wilson* (Cambridge, Mass., 1983). K. Krakau, Die Lateinamerika-Politik der USA, *Aus Politik und Zeitgeschichte*, B 9/86 (March 1, 1986), 31 f.

69. Roosevelt Corollary to the Monroe Doctrine (December 6, 1904), printed in H. C. Syrett, *American Historical Documents*, 319, 320.

70. See Frederick W. Marks, Theodore Roosevelt and the Conservative Revival, in *Traditions and Values: Studies in American Diplomacy, 1865–1945*, ed. Norman Graebner (Lanham, N.Y., 1985).

71. See J. M. Blum, *Woodrow Wilson and the Politics of Morality* (Boston, 1956).

72. See A. Lentin, *Lloyd George, Woodrow Wilson and the Guilt of Germany* (Baton Rouge, La., 1985).

73. W. Wilson's Speech for a Declaration of War Against Germany (April 2, 1917), printed in H. C. Syrett, *American Historical Documents*, 342.

74. W. Wilson, quoted in G. A. Craig, *Die Supermacht und das Gute*. See Daniel

P. Moynihan, Was Woodrow Wilson Right? Morality and American Foreign Policy, *Commentary* 57, no. 4 (May 1974): 25–31.

75. See Lloyd Abrosius, Woodrow Wilson and the Quest for Orderly Progress, in *Traditions and Values: Studies in American Diplomacy, 1865–1945*, ed. Norman Graebner (Lanham, N.Y., 1985).

76. See David A. Shannon, ed., *Progressivism and Postwar Desillusionment 1898–1928* (New York, 1965).

77. F. D. Roosevelt's "Four Freedoms" Speech (January 6, 1941), printed in H. C. Syrett, *American Historical Documents*, 385.

78. Ibid., 386.

79. See Michael Wolffsohn, *Die Debatte über den Kalten Krieg* (Opladen, 1982). A. Conde, *A History of American Foreign Policy, Global Power (1900 to the Present).*

80. Truman Doctrine (March 12, 1947), printed in H. C. Syrett, *American Historical Documents*, 396.

81. See G. Kennan, *American Diplomacy* (Chicago, 1951), 89 ff. Raymond Aron, *The Imperial Republic: The United States and the World, 1945–1973* (Englewood Cliffs, N.J., 1974).

82. See G. Kennan, The Sources of Soviet Conduct, *Foreign Affairs* 25 (1946–47), 566–82.

83. T. Hoopes, quoted in G. A. Craig, *Die Supermacht und das Gute.* K. Krakau, *Missionsbewußtsein und Völkerrechtsdoktrin, in den Vereinigten Staaten von Amerika*, 206 ff.

84. See K. Krakau, *Die Lateinamerika-Politik der USA*, 32 f. A. Schlesinger, *A Thousand Days: John F. Kennedy in the White House* (New York, 1965), 176 ff.

85. J. F. Kennedy's Inaugural Address, printed in Richard Hofstadter, *Great Issues in American History, From Reconstruction to the Present Day, 1864–1969* (New York, 1969), 453.

86. See J. William Fulbright, *The Arrogance of Power* (New York, 1966). Henry Kissinger, *White House Years* (Boston, 1979), 63 ff. S. Hoffmann, *Primacy or World Order*, 20 ff.

87. See R. Aron, *The Imperial Republic.*

88. On the Nixon-Doctrine, see H. Kissinger, *White House Years*, 233 f., 460, 519. Christian Hacke, *Die Ära Nixon-Kissinger 1969–1974, Konservative Reform der Weltpolitik* (Stuttgart, 1983), 30 ff.

89. See Peter Weilemann, *Weltmacht in der Krise, Isolationistische Impulse in der amerikanischen Außenpolitik der siebziger Jahre* (Stuttgart, 1982).

90. See M. Mathiopoulos, Zur Containment-Politik der USA: Strategien von Roosevelt bis Reagan, *Politik und Kultur*, no. 3 (1983): 72 ff.

91. Henry Kissinger, The Moral Foundations of Foreign Policy, in H. Kissinger, *American Foreign Policy* (New York, 1977), 211, 213.

92. H. Kissinger, *Détente with the Soviet Union: The Reality of Competition and the Imperative of Cooperation, Speech before the Senate Committee on Foreign Relations*, September 19, 1974.

93. Jimmy Carter's Inaugural Address, in *Representative American Speeches, 1976–77*, ed. W. W. Braden (New York, 1977), 21, 22.

94. See F. Pflüger, *Die Menschenrechtspolitik der USA*, 130 f.

95. See Arthur Schlesinger, Human Rights and the American Tradition, *Foreign Affairs* 57 (1978–79): 503–526. Kurt R. Spillmann, "Die Stadt auf dem Berge," Carter's

Menschenrechtspolitik und die amerikanische Tradition, *Schweizer Monatshefte* 58 (1978), 179–82.

96. Jimmy Carter's Inaugural Address, 21.

97. See F. Pflüger, *Die Menschenrechtspolitik der USA*, 248 ff. Jeane Kirkpatrick, Dictatorship and Double Standards, *Commentary* (November 1979): 34 ff. S. Hoffmann, A View from at Home: The Perils of Incoherence, *Foreign Affairs* 57 (1978–79): 463–91. S. Hoffmann, *Duties Beyond Borders, On the Limits and Possibilities of Ethical Politics* (Syracuse, N.Y., 1981).

98. See J. Carter, *Keeping Faith, Memoirs of a President* (New York, 1982), 431 ff.

99. See Zbigniew Brzezinski, *Power and Principle, Memoirs of the National Security Advisor 1977–1981* (New York, 1983), 426 ff.

100. See R. Reagan, Speech before the British Parliament, June 8, 1982, in *Wireless Bulletin*, Embassy of the United States, Bonn, June 9, 1982.

101. See F. Pflüger, US-Menschenrechtspolitik-Von Carter zu Reagan, in *Außenpolitik*, No. 4/84, 345 ff.

102. See, for example, Charles Maechling, Human Rights Dehumanized, *Foreign Policy* (Fall 1983): 118 ff.

103. See Caspar W. Weinberger, U.S. Defense Strategy, *Foreign Affairs* 64, no. 4 (Spring 1986): 675–97. See also Lee H. Hamilton, National Security and National Defense, *Political Studies Quarterly* 15, no. 2 (Spring 1985): 261–70.

104. George P. Shultz, Shaping American Foreign Policy, New Realities and New Ways of Thinking, *Foreign Affairs* 63, no. 4 (Spring 1985): 721.

105. R. Reagan, quoted in Stephen S. Rosenfeld, The Reagan Doctrine: The Guns of July, *Foreign Affairs* 64, no. 4 (Spring 1986): 701, 702. On the Reagan Doctrine see J. J. Kirkpatrick, *The Reagan Doctrine and U.S. Foreign Policy* (Washington, D.C., 1985). J. J. Kirkpatrick, *Implementing the Reagan Doctrine* (Washington, D.C., 1985) (The Heritage Foundation, National Security Record No. 82). Robert Tucker, Intervention and the Reagan Doctrine, New " 'Rollback' Revisited: A Reagan Doctrine for Insurgent Wars?'' (Washington, D.C., 1986).

106. See Joseph Nye, Maintaining the Western Alliance, *Harvard International Review* 4, no. 6 (March–April 1982): 6 f.

107. On the dilemma of morality and politics, see George F. Kennan: Morality and Foreign Policy, *Foreign Affairs* 64, no. 2 (Winter 1985–86): 205–18.

# Concluding Remarks

Instead of concluding this volume with an extensive summary or repetition of the results of the study, this final section presents a few ideas important for contemporary inquiries about America and Europe.

1. Europe and America are inseparably bound to one another. The idea of progress, so important for America, as well as the spirit of freedom, the idea of democracy, and aspirations toward justice all have their roots in Europe. Greek philosophy, Roman law, Christian faith, and ideas of the Enlightenment are definitive influences on the New World and Old World alike. The basic ideas of modernism spread outward from Europe and affected the American Revolution and Constitution. If Europe were to separate itself from America, or America to separate itself from Europe, both would not only be surrendering their own security but would simultaneously be revolting against history and endangering their common values of liberty, democracy, and human rights.

2. History and progress have developed in America and Europe in directions that display significant diversity as well as common characteristics. The American idea of progress—freedom, democracy, equality, human rights—was born in the American Revolution and has since, as the American creed, continuously shaped the national identity and political reality of the United States down to the present day.

By contrast, the European sense of history and concept of progress have been disrupted, often dramatically. The negative ideologization of progressivist thought began in the French Revolution, where the ideals of revolt were dogmatized, absolutized, and totalitarianized in the terrorist regime of Robespierre. This development provided the basis for the great ideological movements of the nineteenth century—Marxism and nationalism—the destructive potential of which was experienced in the twentieth century as progress became synonymous with totalitarian rule under national socialism and communism.

Against this background the question emerges as to whether Europe after the Second World War will ever be in a position to overcome its historical crisis and division and to think of progress again. Europe's lack of vision, loss of intellectual radiance, inability to maintain a sense of history because of past discontinuities, self-torturing pessimism toward the future, and lack of élan and innovativeness—where will all of this lead? Certainly, contemporary Europe, East and West, is searching for itself, searching for historical awareness and identity. The central question is whether these efforts will be powerful enough to secure Europe's future.

3.    Utopia and reality produce a tension that is dealt with differently in America and Europe. Since classical antiquity the seduction of humankind by utopian thought has exercised a virulent influence. The goal of the realization of a state of paradisiac happiness free of all power relationships has always ultimately brought unhappiness to humanity. The grand design often justifies the worst means. In the thinking of a Europe shaken by war, and in the disruptions of the Old World's idea of progress, utopian seductions had an ambivalent appeal and were thus able to bring about conditions favorable to totalitarian thought.

In America it is different. The idea of the American Revolution is indeed decisively progress-oriented and aspires to a freer and more just world. In this sense it also possesses visionary characteristics. On the other hand, from the very beginning American thought accepted the individual as such, with all of his or her weaknesses and imperfections. In this sense the American Revolution was also pragmatic.

It is this that distinguishes the American idea of progress from most of the intellectual visions of the past. The American Revolution set idealistic goals while keeping its feet on realistic ground. It aspired to unconditional progress for humankind while knowing that the chiliastic endpoint of history would never be reached.

This view is not only attributable to the realistic view of humankind prevalent during the revolutionary period. Nor is it merely the result of anthropological modesty. Rather, it is related to the fact that eschatology has never been perceived to be desirable. "What shall become of us without any barbarians? These people were a kind of solution" (Cavafy). What would the empire of good be without the empire of evil?

4.    Will Europe and America, working in concert, be able to meet the ethical, political, and economic challenges of the technological age? To do so, both must be aware of their common intellectual foundations. Perhaps it will require the dissolution of the differentiation between the scientific disciplines—the humanities and natural sciences—in short, the revival of Aristotelian unity. Finally, does not human survival require a new concept of progress, one that can overcome the gap between science and philosophy, technology and ethics? Europe and America depend upon each other.

# Select Bibliography

## INTERVIEWS

Governor Sherman Adams, chief of staff under President Eisenhower, April 13, 1982, Lincoln, N.H.

Former Secretary of Defense Clark Clifford, adviser to Presidents Truman, Johnson, and Carter, April 27, 1982, Washington, D.C.

Deputy Secretary of State Lawrence Eagleburger, Reagan administration, April 30, 1982, Washington, D.C.

Senator William Fulbright, April 27, 1982, Washington, D.C.

Editor of *Commentary* Norman Podhoretz, May 12, 1984, New York.

Former National Security Adviser Walt W. Rostow under President Johnson, June 8, 1984, Bonn.

Former Secretary of State Dean Rusk, Kennedy and Johnson administrations, April 19, 1982, Athens, Georgia.

Former Secretary of State Cyrus Vance, Carter administration, April 21, 1982, New York.

## NEWSPAPERS

*Boston Globe*

*Frankfurter Allgemeine Zeitung*

*International Herald Tribune*

*Los Angeles Times*
*New York Times*
*Der Spiegel*
*Süddeutsche Zeitung*
*Washington Post*
*Die Zeit*

## BOOKS

Abraham, D. *The Collapse of the Weimar Republic: Political Economy and Crisis.* Princeton, N.J., 1983.

Abrosius, L. Woodrow Wilson and the Quest for Orderly Progress. In *Traditions and Values: Studies in American Diplomacy, 1865–1945,* ed. N. Graebner. New York, 1985.

Acheson, D. *Present at the Creation: My Years in the State Department.* New York, 1969.

Ackerman, B. A. *Social Justice in the Liberal State.* New Haven, Conn., 1980.

Adams, B. *The Law of Civilization and Decay.* London, 1895 (with an Essay as Foreword from Theodore Roosevelt).

Adams, H. *Mont-Saint-Michel and Chartres.* Boston, 1904.

Adams, H. *The Education of Henry Adams.* Boston, 1918.

Adams, H. *The Tendency of History.* New York, 1919.

Adams, H. B. *Life and Writings of Jared Sparks.* 2 vols. Boston, 1883.

Adams, W. P., and Krakau, K., eds. *Deutschland und Amerika: Perzeption und historische Realität.* Berlin, 1985.

Adenauer, K. *Erinnerungen,* vols. 1–4. Stuttgart, 1965–68.

Adorno, T. W. *Negative Dialektik.* Frankfurt am Main, 1967.

Alden, J. R. *George Washington.* Baton Rouge, La. 1984.

Allen, H. C. *Great Britain and the United States: A History of Anglo-American Relations.* London, 1954.

Almond, G. A. and Verba, S. *The Civic Culture, Political Attitudes and Democracy in Five Nations.* Princeton, N.J., 1963.

Almond, G. A., and Verba, S., eds. *The Civic Culture Revisited.* Boston, 1980.

Almond, G. A., Chodorow, M., and Pearce, R. H., eds. *Progress and Its Discontents.* Berkeley, Calif., 1982.

Alt, F. *Frieden ist möglich.* Munich, 1983.

*America and the Mind of Europe.* (Collection, introduction by Lewis Galantiere.) London, 1951.

"America," or a General Survey of the Political Situation of the Several Powers of the Western Continent, with Conjectures on Their Future Prospects: By a Citizen of the United States. Philadelphia, 1827.

Ames, S., ed. *The Works of Fisher Ames.* Boston, 1854.

Anderson, J. E., and Hazleton, J. E. *Managing Macroeconomic Policy, The Johnson Presidency.* Austin, Tex., 1985.

Anderson, T. *Brooks Adams, Constructive Conservative.* Ithaca, N.Y., 1951.

Andrews, W., ed. *The Autobiography of Theodore Roosevelt.* New York, 1958.

Angermann, E. *Die Amerikanische Revolution im Spiegel der Geschichte*. Ed. E. Angermann. Munich, 1979.

Angermann, E., and Frings, M.-L., eds. *Oceans Apart? Comparing Germany and the United States*. Stuttgart, 1981.

Angermann, E., et al., eds. *New Wine in Old Skins. A Comparative View of Socio-Political Structures and Values Affecting the American Revolution*. Stuttgart, 1976.

Arendt, H. *The Origins of Totalitarianism*. New York, 1951.

Arieli, Y. *Individualism and Nationalism in American Ideology*. Cambridge, Mass., 1964.

Aristotle. *The Politics* (translated and with an Introduction, Notes, and Glossary by Carnes Lord). Chicago, 1984.

Aron, R. *Introduction to the Philosophy of History*. Boston, 1962.

Aron, R. *The Elusive Revolution*. London, 1968.

Aron, R. *Progress and Disillusion, The Dialectics of Modern Society*. London, 1968.

Aron, R. *The Imperial Republic: The United States and the World, 1945–1973*. Englewood Cliffs, N.J., 1974.

Assaum, P.-L. *Freud et Nietzsche*. Paris, 1980.

Avineri, S. *Hegel's Theory of the Modern State*. Cambridge, 1972.

Bacciocco, E. J. *The New Left in America*. Stanford, Calif., 1974.

Badian, E. *Roman Imperialism in the Late Roman Republic*. Oxford, 1968.

Badian, E. "Crisis Theories" and the Beginning of the Principate. In *Romanitas-Christianitas, Untersuchungen zur Geschichte und Literatur der römischen Kaiserzeit*, Festschrift for Johannes Straub, ed. G. Wirth. Berlin, 1982.

Bagley, C. B. Chief Seattle and Angeline. *Washington Historical Quarterly* 22, no. 4 (October 1931):243–75.

Bahr, E., et al., ed. *Mut zur Einheit* (Festschrift for Johann Baptist Gradl). Cologne, 1984.

Bahro, R. *Die Alternative*. Cologne, 1977.

Bailey, T. A. *Probing America's Past: A Critical Examination of Major Myths and Misconceptions*. Lexington, Mass., 1973.

Baillie, J. *The Belief in Progress*. New York, 1950.

Bailyn, B. *The Ideological Origins of the American Revolution*. Cambridge, Mass., 1967.

Bailyn, B. *The Origins of American Politics*. New York, 1971.

Bailyn, B. The Central Themes of the American Revolution. An Interpretation. In *Essays on the American Revolution*, ed. Stephen G. Kurtz and James H. Hutson. New York, 1973.

Baird, A. C., ed. *Representative American Speeches, 1937–1959*. New York, 1937–59.

Baker, K. L., Dalton, R. J., and Hildebrandt, K. *Germany Transformed: Political Culture and the New Politics*. Cambridge, Mass., 1981.

Baker, P. R. *The Fortunate Pilgrims: Americans in Italy, 1800–1860*. Cambridge, Mass., 1965.

Baldry, H. C. *The Unity of Mankind in Greek Thought*. Cambridge, 1965.

Ball, H. *Controlling Regulatory Sprawl. Presidential Strategies from Nixon to Reagan*. Westport, Conn. 1984.

Bancroft, G. *The History of the United States of America from the Discovery of the Continent*. Boston, 1934–74. 10 vols.

Bancroft, G. *Literary and Historical Miscellanies*. New York, 1985.

Banner, L. W. *Woman in Modern America: A Brief History*. New York, 1974.

Banning, L. *The Jeffersonian Persuasion: Evolution of a Party Ideology.* Ithaca, N.Y., 1978.

Barber, J. D. *The Presidential Character, Predicting Performance in the White House.* Englewood Cliffs, N.J., 1972–77.

Baring, A. *Außenpolitik in Adenauers Kanzlerdemokratie, Bonns Beitrag zur Europäischen Verteidigungsgemeinschaft.* Munich, 1969.

Bark, D. L., ed. *To Promote Peace, U.S. Foreign Policy in the mid-1980s.* Stanford, Calif., 1984.

Barnes, S. H., Kaase, M., et al. *Political Action, Mass Participation in Five Western Democracies.* London, 1979.

Barrilleaux, R. J. *The President and Foreign Affairs: Evaluation, Performance, and Power.* New York, 1985.

Barth, H. *Masse und Mythos, Die ideologische Krise an der Wende zum 20. Jahrhundert und die Theorie der Gewalt: Georges Sorel.* Hamburg, 1959.

Bauer, A., ed. *A Treasury of Great American Speeches.* New York, 1957.

Beam, D. R. New Federalism, Old Realities: The Reagan Administration and Intergovernmental Reform. In *The Reagan Presidency and the Governing of America,* ed. Lester M. Salomon and Michael S. Lund. Washington, D.C., 1984. Urban Institute Study.

Beard, C. *An Economic Interpretation of the Constitution of the United States.* New York, 1913.

Beard, C. Grounds for a Reconsideration of Historiography. In *Theory and Practice in Historical Study: A Report of the Committee on Historiography.* New York, 1946.

Beard, C. and Beard, M. *The American Spirit: A Study of the Idea of Civilization in the United States.* New York, 1962.

Beard, C. and Beard, W. *The American Leviathan.* New York, 1930.

Beard, M. *The Making of Charles A. Beard.* New York, 1955.

Beard, M., and Crawford, M. *Rome in the Late Republic.* Ithaca, N.Y., 1985.

Beauté, J. *Un grand juriste anglais: Sir Edward Coke, 1552–1634. Ses idées politiques et constitutionnelles.* Paris, 1975.

Beauvoir, S. de. *L'Amérique au jour le jour.* Paris, 1955.

Becker, C. *Progress and Power.* New York, 1936.

Becker, C. *The Declaration of Independence: A Study in the History of Political Ideas.* New York, 1956.

Beetham, D. *Max Weber and the Theory of Modern Politics.* London, 1974.

Bell, D. *The End of Ideology: On the Exhaustion of Political Ideas in the Fifties.* Glencoe, Ill., 1960.

Bell, D. Technology, Nature, and Society. In *The Frontiers of Knowledge.* The Frank Nelson Doubleday Lectures, 1st Series. Garden City, N.Y., 1975.

Bell, D. *The Cultural Contradictions of Capitalism.* London, 1976.

Bell, D., ed. *The Radical Right.* New York, 1979.

Beloff, M. *The United States and the Unity of Europe.* Washington, D.C., 1963.

Ben-David, J. *The Scientist's Role in Society.* Englewood Cliffs, N.J., 1971.

Bender, P. *Das Ende des ideologischen Zeitalters, Die Europäisierung Europas.* Berlin, 1981.

Bercovitch, S. *The Puritan Origins of the American Self.* New Haven, Conn., 1975.

Berg, P. *Deutschland und Amerika 1918–1929, Über das deutsche Amerikabild der zwangiger Jahre.* Hamburg, 1963.

Berger, M. *The British Traveller in America, 1836–1860*. New York, 1943.

Berghan, U. R., and Kitchen, M., eds. *Germany in the Age of Total War* (Festschrift for F. L. Carsten). London, 1981.

Bergstraesser, A. *Europa als Idee und Wirklichkeit*. Freiburg, 1955.

Berkin, C., ed. *Woman of America*. Boston, 1979.

Berlin, I. *Four Essays on Liberty*. New York, 1970.

Berlin, I. *Against the Current*. Ed. Henry Hardy, with an introduction by Roger Hausheer. London, 1980.

Berman, M. *John Fiske: The Evolution of a Popularizer*. Cambridge, Mass., 1961.

Bernier, O. *Lafayette: Hero of Two Worlds*. New York, 1983.

Bernstein, B. J., ed. *Towards a New Past. Dissenting Essays in American History*. New York, 1968.

Besson, W. *Die politische Terminologie des Präsidenten Franklin D. Roosevelt, Eine Studie über den Zusammenhang von Sprache und Politik*. Tübingen, 1955.

Bestuschew-Lada, I. *Die Welt im Jahr 2000. Eine sowjetische Prognose für unsere Zukunft*. Freiburg, 1984.

Beuys, B. C. Das Thema der Einheit und Einigkeit in den Antrittsreden der Amerikanischen Präsidenten von 1789–1945. Ph.D. thesis. Cologne, 1969.

Bialer, S., and Sluzar, S., eds. *Sources of Contemporary Radicalism*. Boulder, Colo., 1977.

Bickel, A. M. *The Supreme Court and the Idea of Progress*. New York, 1970.

Biddiss, M. *The Age of the Masses. Ideas and Society in Europe since 1870*. New York, 1978.

Biedenkopf, K. *Die neue Sicht der Dinge, Plädoyer für eine freiheitliche Wirtschafts- und Sozialordnung*. Munich, 1985.

Billington, J. H. *Fire in the Minds of Men, Origins of the Revolutionary Faith*. New York, 1980.

Billington, R. A. *America's Frontier Heritage*. New York, 1966.

Billington, R. A., ed. *The Reinterpretation of Early American History*. San Marino, Calif., 1966.

Bismarck, P. von, Rovan, J., Weidenfeld, W., and Windelen, H. *Die Teilung Deutschlands und Europas*. Bonn, 1984 (with a foreword by Walter Scheel).

Blackbourn, D. and Eley, G. *Mythen deutscher Geschichtsschreibung*. Berlin, 1980.

Blackmer, D. L. M., and Kriegel, A. *The International Role of the Communist Parties of Italy and France*. Cambridge, Mass., 1975.

Blau, J. L., ed. *Social Theories of Jacksonian Democracy*. New York, 1954.

Bleicken, J. *Die athenische Demokratie*. Paderborn, 1984.

Bloch, E. *Differenzierungen im Begriff Fortschritt, Tübinger Einleitung in die Philosophie I*. Frankfurt am Main, 1963.

Bloch, M. *Die Feudalgesellschaft*. Frankfurt, 1982.

Bloom, A. *The Closing of the American Mind*. New York, 1987.

Blum, J. M. *The Progressive Presidents: Roosevelt, Wilson, Roosevelt, Johnson*. New York, 1980.

Bolkhovitinov, N. N. The American Revolution and the Russian Empire. In *The Impact of the American Revolution Abroad*. Library of Congress Symposia on the American Revolution. Washington, D.C., 1976.

Boller, P. F. *American Thought in Transition: The Impact of Evolutionary Naturalism, 1865–1900*. Chicago, 1969.

Bolter, J. D. *Turning's Man, Western Culture in the Computer Age.* Chapel Hill, N.C., 1984.

Boorstin, D. J. *The Genius of American Politics.* Chicago, 1953.

Boorstin, D. J. *The Americans.* Vol. 1: *The Colonial Experience;* Vol. 2: *The National Experience.* New York, 1958, 1965.

Boorstin, D. J. *America and the Image of Europe.* New York, 1960.

Borch, H. von. *Amerika—Dekadenz und Größe.* Munich, 1981.

Borch, H. von. *John F. Kennedy, Amerikas Unerfüllte Hoffnung.* Munich, 1986.

Bornet, V. D. *The Presidency of Lyndon B. Johnson.* Lawrence, Kan., 1983.

Boyers, R., ed. *The Legacy of the German Refugee Intellectuals.* New York, 1972.

Bracher, K. D. Demokratie als Sendung: das amerikanische Beispiel. In *Deutschland zwischen Demokratie und Diktatur.* Bern, 1964.

Bracher, K. D. *The German Dictatorship: The Origins, Structure, and Effects of National Socialism.* Translated by Jean Steinberg. New York, 1970. Originally published as *Die deutsche Diktatur, Entstehung, Struktur, Folgen des Nationalsozialismus* (Cologne, 1969).

Bracher, K. D. *The German Dilemma: The Throes of Political Emancipation.* London, 1974. Originally published as *Das deutsche Dilemma, Leidenswege der politischen Emanzipation.* Munich, 1971.

Bracher, K. D. Totalitarianism. In *Dictionary of the History of Ideas.* Vol. 4. New York, 1973.

Bracher, K. D. *Die Krise Europas, 1917–1975 (Propyläen Geschichte Europas,* vol. 6). Frankfurt am Main, 1976.

Bracher, K. D. *Die Auflösung der Weimarer Republik, Eine Studie zum Problem des Machtverfalls in der Demokratie.* Villingen, 1978.

Bracher, K. D. *Geschichte und Gewalt, Zur Politik im 20. Jahrhundert.* Berlin, 1981.

Bracher, K. D. *The Age of Ideologies: A History of Political Thought in the Twentieth Century.* Translated by Ewald Osers. New York, 1984. Originally published as *Zeit der Ideologien: Eine Geschichte politischen Denkens im 20. Jahrhundert* (Stuttgart, 1982).

Bracher, K. D., ed. *Geschichte der Bundesrepublik Deutschland.* 5 vols. *Deutsche Verlagsanstalt.* Stuttgart, 1983–86.

Bracher, K. D. *Totalitarian Democracy and After.* Jerusalem, 1984. (Israel Academy of Sciences and Humanities.)

Bracher, K. D. *Zeitgeschichtliche Kontroversen. Um Faschismus, Totalitarismus, Demokratie.* Munich, 1984.

Braden, W. W., ed. *Representative American Speeches, 1975–76.* New York, 1976.

Brand, K. W., Brüsser, D., and Rucht, D. *Aufbruch in eine andere Gesellschaft, Neue soziale Bewegungen in der Bundesrepublik.* Frankfurt am Main, 1983.

Brandt, P., and Ammon, H. Patriotismus von Links. In W. Venohr, *Die deutsche Einheit kommt bestimmt,* ed. W. Venohr. Bergisch-Gladbach, 1982.

Brandt Commission. *Common Crisis, North-South: Cooperation for World Recovery.* London, 1983 (with a foreword by Willy Brandt).

Brandt, W., Kreisky, B., and Palme, O. *Briefe und Gespräche 1972–1975.* Eds. G. Grass, E. Jäckel, and D. Lattmann. Frankfurt am Main, 1975.

Brissot, J. P. *New Travels in the United States of America Performed in 1788.* London, 1792.

Bristed, J. *The Resources of the United States of America;* or a *View of the Agricultural,*

*Commercial, Manufacturing, Financial, Political, Literary, Moral, and Religious Capacity and Character of the American People.* New York, 1818.

Brock, W. R. Americanism. In The United States, ed. D. Welland. London, 1974.

Brodie, F. M. *Richard Nixon, The Shaping of His Character.* Cambridge, Mass., 1983.

Brogan, D. W. *The American Character.* New York, 1959.

Broszat, M. *Der Nationalsozialismus, Weltanschauung, Programm und Wirklichkeit.* Stuttgart, 1960.

Broszat, M., et al., eds. *Deutschlands Weg in die Diktatur.* Berlin, 1983.

Brown, K. C., ed. *Hobbes Studies.* Oxford, 1965.

Brown, U. *Bury My Heart at Wounded Knee: An Indian History of the American West.* New York, 1971.

Brugmans, H. *L'idée européenne 1920 à 1970.* Brugge, 1970.

Bruhn, J. and Bavendamm, D. *Roosevelts Weg zum Krieg.* Munich, 1983.

Brunowsky, R.-D., and Wicke, L. *"Der Öko-Plan"—Durch Umweltschutz zum neuen Wirtschaftswunder.* Munich, 1984.

Bryan, W. J. *The First Battle.* Chicago, 1896.

Bryce, J. *The American Commonwealth.* London, 1891. vols. 1 and 2.

Brzezinski, Z. K. *Totalitarian Dictatorship and Autocracy.* Cambridge, Mass., 1956.

Brzezinski, Z. K. *Between Two Ages, America's Role in the Technetronic Era.* New York, 1970.

Brzezinski, Z. K. *Power and Principle, Memoirs of the National Security Advisor, 1977–1981.* New York, 1983.

Buckley, W. F. *American Conservative Thought in the Twentieth Century.* Indianapolis, Ind., 1970.

Buel, R. *Securing the Revolution. Ideology in American Politics 1789–1815.* Ithaca, N.Y., 1972.

Buenker, J. D. *Urban Liberalism and Progressive Reform.* New York, 1978.

Bullock, A. *Hitler: A Study in Tyranny.* New York, 1962.

Burgess, J. W. *Political Science and Comparative Constitutional Law.* Vol. 1: *Sovereignty and Liberty.* Boston, 1896.

Burk, R. F. *The Eisenhower Administration and Black Civil Rights.* Knoxville, Tenn., 1984.

Burnet, M. F. *Genes, Dreams, Realities.* New York, 1970.

Burnham, J. *The Coming Defeat of Communism.* New York, 1950.

Burns, E.M.N. *The American Idea of Mission.* New Brunswick, N.J., 1957.

Burns, J.M.G. *The Power to Lead, The Crisis of the American Presidency.* New York, 1984.

Burr, N. R. *A Critical Bibliography of Religion in America.* Princeton, N.J., 1961.

Burus, R. D., ed. *Guide to American Foreign Policy Relations Since 1700.* 1982 (ABC-Clio).

Bury, J. B. *The Idea of Progress: An Inquiry into Its Growth and Origin.* New York, 1955.

Bush, V. *Science—The Endless Frontier, A Report to the President on a Program for Postwar Scientific Research.* Washington, D.C., 1980.

Butterfield, H. *The Whig Interpretation of History.* London, 1931.

Caine, St. P. The Origins of Progressivism. In: *The Progressive Era,* ed. Lewis L. Gould. Syracuse, N.Y., 1974.

Caldwell, P. *The Puritan Conversion Narrative: The Beginnings of American Expression.* New York, 1983.

Calleo, D. P. *The German Problem Reconsidered, Germany and the World Order 1870 to the Present.* Cambridge, 1978.

Calleo, D. P. *Beyond American Hegemony: The Future of the Western Alliance.* New York, 1987.

Camus, A. *The Rebel: An Essay on Man in Revolt.* Translated by Anthony Bower. New York, 1956. Originally published as *L'Homme révolté* (Paris, 1951).

Canovan, M. *Populism.* New York, 1981.

Capra, F. *The Turning Point: Science, Society, and the Rising Culture.* New York, 1982.

Carlson, E. A. *Genes, Radiation, and Society: The Life and Work of H. J. Muller.* Ithaca, N.Y., 1981.

Carnegie, A. *Autobiography,* Ed. J. C. Van Dyke. Boston, 1920.

Caro, R. A. *The Years of Lyndon Johnson, the Path to Power.* New York, 1982. Vol. 1.

Carr, E. H. *What Is History?* New York, 1962.

Carstens, K. *Grundgedanken der amerikanischen Verfassung und ihre Verwirklichung.* Berlin, 1954.

Carter, J. *Keeping Faith, Memoirs of a President.* New York, 1982.

Cartwright, W. H. and Watson, R. L., eds. *The Reinterpretation of American History and Culture.* Washington, D.C., 1973.

Cavill, W. H., and Randle, T. W. *Cooperation in Europe since 1945 as Presented in Resources for the Teaching of History, Geography and Civics in Secondary Schools.* Strasbourg, 1979 Doc. DELS/EGT 79/61 (case-study on the United Kingdom, which was prepared for the Committee of Cultural Cooperation of the European Council.)

Chambers, W. *Witness.* New York, 1952.

Channing, W. E. *Works.* Boston, 1846. Vol. 4.

Chastellux, F. J. Marquis de. *Travels in North America in the Years 1780–1781, and 1782.* London, 1787.

Chénu, M.-D. *L'Eveil de la conscience dans la civilisation médiévale.* Paris, 1969.

Chesterton, G. K. *What I Saw in America.* New York, 1923.

Churchill, W. S. *The Second World War.* Boston, 1948–53.

Cigler, A., and Loomis, P. *Interest Group Politics.* Washington, D.C., 1983.

Clark, R. W. *Benjamin Franklin: A Biography.* New York, 1983.

Clough, W. O., ed. *Intellectual Origins of American National Thought.* New York, 1961.

Cobb, R. *Reactions to the French Revolution.* London, 1972.

Codman, J. T. *Brook Farm, Historic and Personal Memoirs.* Boston, 1894.

Cohen, I. B. *Science and American Society in the First Century of the Republic.* Columbus, Ohio, 1961.

Cohen, I. B. *Benjamin Franklin: Scientist and Statesman.* New York, 1972.

Cohen, I. B., ed. *Thomas Jefferson and the Sciences.* New York, 1980.

Cohen, I. B. *Revolution in Science.* Cambridge, Mass., 1985.

Cohen, L. H. *The Revolutionary Histories: Contemporary Narratives of the American Revolution.* Ithaca, N.Y., 1980.

Cohen, W. J. *The American Revisionists: The Lessons of Intervention in World War I.* Chicago, 1967.

Cohn, N. *The Pursuit of the Millenium, Revolutionary Messianism in Medieval and*

*Reformation Europe and Its Bearing on Modern Totalitarian Movements.* New York, 1961.

Collingwood, R. G. *The Idea of History.* New York, 1956.

Commager, H. S. *The Growth of the American Republic.* New York, 1942–69. 2 vols.

Commager, H. S. *The American Mind: An Interpretation of American Thought and Character since the 1880's.* New Haven, Conn., 1950.

Commager, H. S. *Jefferson, Nationalism, and the Enlightenment.* New York, 1975.

Commager, H. S. *The Empire of Reason, How Europe Imagined and America Realized the Enlightenment.* London, 1978.

Commager, H. S., and Giodanetti, E., eds. *Was America a Mistake? The Eighteenth-Century Controversy.* New York, 1967.

Committee of the EEC, ed. *Eine Industriestrategie für Europa.* 11/84 (June/July 1984), ''Europe.'' Luxembourg, 1984.

Committee of the EEC, ed. *Die Stärkung der technologischen Grundlagen und der Wettbewerbsfähigkeit der Gemeinschaftsindustrie.* Communique by the European Commission to the European Council, March 29–30, 1985, KOM (85).

Conde, A. *A History of American Foreign Policy, Growth to World Power (1700–1914).* Vol. 1. New York, 1978.

Conde, A. *A History of American Foreign Policy, Global Power (1900 to the Present).* Vol. 2. New York, 1978.

Connor, W. R. *The New Politicians of Fifth-Century Athens.* Princeton, N.J., 1971.

Conradt, D. P. Changing German Political Culture. In *The Civic Culture Revisited,* ed. Gabriel A. Almond and Sidney Verba. Boston, 1980.

Cooney, J. A., Craig, G. A., Schwarz, H.-P., and Stern, F., eds. *The Federal Republic of Germany and the United States.* Boulder, Colo., 1984.

Cooper, J. M. *The Warrior and the Priest: Theodore Roosevelt and Woodrow Wilson.* Cambridge, Mass., 1983.

Corwin, E. S. The Passing of Dual Federalism. In *Essays in Constitutional Law,* ed. R. McCloskey. New York, 1957.

Corwin, E. S. *The President: Office and Powers, 1787–1957. History and Analysis of Practice and Opinion.* New York, 1957.

Corwin, E. S. *The Constitution and What It Means Today.* Princeton, N.J., 1978.

Cowling, M. *The Impact of Hitler, British Politics and British Policy 1933–1940.* Cambridge, 1975.

Cox, A. *The Role of the Supreme Court in American Government.* New York, 1976.

Cox, L. *Lincoln and Black Freedom: A Study in Presidential Leadership.* Columbia, S.C., 1981.

Craig, G. A. *Germany, 1866–1945.* New York, 1978.

Craig, G. A. *The Germans.* New York, 1982.

Craig, G. A. Germany and the US: Some Historical Parallels and Differences and Their Reflection in Attitudes toward Foreign Policy. In: *The Federal Republic of Germany and the United States,* ed. J. A. Cooney, G. A. Craig, H. P. Schwarz, and F. Stern. Boulder, Colo., 1984.

Craig, G. A. Roosevelt and Hitler: The Problem of Perception. In *Deutsche Frage und europäisches Gleichgewicht,* ed. K. Hildebrand, and R. Pommern. (Festschrift for Andreas Hillgruber). Cologne, 1985.

Craig, G. A., and George, A. L. *Force and Statecraft: Diplomatic Problems of Our Time.* New York, 1983.

Crawford, A. *Thunder on the Right, The "New Right" and the Politics of Resentment.* New York, 1980.

Crèvecoeur, H. St. J. What Is an American?. Reprinted from *Letters from an American Farmer (1782).* In *The Character of Americans,* ed. Michael McGiffert. Homewood, Ill., 1964.

Croly, H. *The Promise of American Life, New York 1909.* Ed. A. M. Schlesinger. Cambridge, Mass., 1965.

Cronin, T. E. *The State of the Presidency.* Boston, 1975.

Cronin, T. E. The Presidency and Its Paradoxes. In *The Power of the Presidency,* ed. R. S. Hirschfield. New York, 1982.

Crouzet, M. *The European Renaissance since 1945.* New York, 1971.

Crozier, M. France's Cultural Anxieties under Gaullism: The Cultural Revolution Revisited. In *Culture and Society in Contemporary Europe,* ed. S. Hoffmann and P. Kitromilides. Cambridge, Mass., 1981.

Crozier, M. *Le mal américain.* Paris, 1981.

Cunliffe, M., and Winks, R. W., eds. *Pastmasters. Some Essays on American Historians.* New York, 1969.

Current, R. N. *Speaking of Abraham Lincoln: The Man and His Meaning for Our Times.* Urbana, Ill., 1983.

Dahl, R. *Dilemmas of Pluralist Democracy.* New Haven, Conn., 1982.

Dahl, R. *Controlling Nuclear Weapons: Democracy Versus Guardianship.* Syracuse, N.Y., 1985.

Dahrendorf, R. *Die angewandte Aufklärung, Gesellschaft und Soziologie in Amerika.* Frankfurt am Main, 1968.

Dahrendorf, R. *Plädoyer für die Europäische Union.* Munich, 1973.

Dahrendorf, R. ed. *Trendwende, Europas Wirtschaft in der Krise* (with a foreword by Gaston Thorn). Zurich, 1981.

Dahrendorf, R. *Die Chancen der Krise, Über die Zukunft des Liberalismus.* Stuttgart, 1983.

Dallek, R. *Ronald Reagan, The Politics of Symbolism.* Cambridge, Mass., 1984.

Daniels, G., ed. *Darwinism Comes to America.* Waltham, Mass., 1968.

Daniels, J. *Ordeal of Ambition: Jefferson, Hamilton, Burr.* Garden City, N.Y., 1970.

Danto, A. C. *Nietzsche as Philosopher.* New York, 1965.

Danto, A. C. *Jean-Paul Sartre.* New York, 1975.

Danzin, A. *Wissenschaft und Wiedergeburt Europas.* Frankfurt am Main, 1980.

Darwin, C. *The Descent of Man, and Selection in Relation to Sex.* New York, 1871.

Davis, D. B. *The Problem of Slavery in the Age of Revolution, 1770–1823.* Ithaca, N.Y., 1975.

Davis, V., ed. *The Post-Imperial Presidency.* New York, 1980.

Davison, K. E. *The American Presidency: A Guide to Information Sources.* Detroit, 1983.

Dean, V. M. *Europe and the United States.* New York, 1950.

Debo, A. *A History of the Indians of the United States.* Norman, Okla., 1970.

Debouzy, M. Influence of American Political Dissent on the French New Left. In *Contagious Conflict, The Impact of American Dissent on European Life,* ed. A.N.J. Den Hollander. Leiden, 1973.

Dell'Omodarme, M. *Europa-Mito e Realtà del Processo d'Integrazione.* Milan, 1981.

Democrats for the 80's. *The New Right: A Threat to America's Future*. Washington, D.C., 1981.

Den Hollander, A.N.J., ed. *Diverging Parallels, A Comparison of American and European Thought and Action*. Leiden, 1971.

Den Hollander, A.N.J. On "Dissent" and "Influence" as Agents of Change. An introduction. In *Contagious Conflict, The Impact of American Dissent on European Life*, ed. A.N.J. Den Hollander. Leiden, 1973.

*Der Traum der Vernunft, Vom Elend der Aufklärung*. Darmstadt, 1985. (A Series of lectures of the Academy of Arts in Berlin.)

Dettling, W., ed. *Deutsche Parteien im Wandel*. Munich, 1983.

Deutsch, K. W. Soziale und politische Aspekte der Informationsgesellschaft. In *Die Zukunft der Informationsgesellschaft*, ed. P. Sonntag. Frankfurt am Main, 1983.

Devine, D. J. *The Political Culture of the United States*. Boston, 1972.

Dewey, J. *The Influence of Darwin on Philosophy*. New York, 1910.

Diamond, M. *Notes on the Political Theory of the Founding Fathers*. Philadelphia, 1971.

Dickens, C. *American Notes (1842)*. London, 1893.

*Die Bundesrepublik Deutschland 1985/1990/2000. Die Entwicklung von Wirtschaft und Gesellschaft in der Bundesrepublik und den Bundesländern bis 2000*. Reworked by Peter Hofer, Stefan Rommerskirchen, Detlef Franzen and Heinfrid Wolf. Stuttgart, 1983.

Dimakis, J. *La Guerre de l'indépendance Grecque vue par la presse Française*. Thessaloniki, 1968.

Dippel, H. *Germany and the American Revolution, 1770–1880. A Sociohistorical Investigation of late Eighteenth-Century Political Thinking*. Chapel Hill, N.C., 1977.

Dippel, H. *Die Amerikanische Revolution 1763–1787*. Frankfurt am Main, 1985.

Dodds, E. R. *Der Fortschrittsgedanke in der Antike*. Munich, 1977.

Donovan, H. *Roosevelt to Reagan, A Reporter's Encounters with Nine Presidents*. New York, 1985.

Donovan, T. P. *Henry Adams and Brooks Adams: The Education of Two American Historians*. Norman, Okla., 1961.

Dorsen, N., Bender, P., and Neuborne, B. *Political and Civil Rights in the United States*. Boston, 1976.

Dougherty, J. E. *The Bishops and Nuclear Weapons: The Catholic Pastoral Letter on War and Peace*. Hamden, Conn., 1984.

Doughty, H. *Francis Parkman*. New York, 1962.

Drachmann, A. G. *The Mechanical Technology of Greek and Roman Antiquity*. Copenhagen, 1963.

Droz, J. *Le Romantisme politique en Allemagne*. Paris, 1963.

Drummond, G. D. *The German Social Democrats in Opposition, 1949–1960: The Case Against Rearmament*. Norman, Okla., 1982.

Dudley, D. R. *A History of Cynicism from Diogenes to the Sixth Century AD*. London, 1937.

Duignan, P., and Rabushka, A., eds. *The United States in the 1980s*. Stanford, Calif., 1980.

Dunn, C. W., ed. *American Political Theology: Historical Perspectives and Theoretical Analysis*. New York, 1984.

Dunn, J. *Western Political Theory in the Face of the Future*. Cambridge, 1980.

Duverger, M. *Demokratie im technischen Zeitalter*. Munich, 1973.

Duverger, M. *Janus les Deux. Faces de l'Occident.* Paris, 1985.

Dworkin, R. *Taking Rights Seriously.* Cambridge, Mass., 1977.

Dworkin, R. Liberalism. In *Public and Private Morality,* ed. Stuart Hampshire. New York, 1978.

Dworkin, R. *A Matter of Principle.* Cambridge, Mass., 1985.

Dye, T., and Ziegler, L. H. *The Irony of Democracy.* Monterey, Calif., 1981.

East, R. A. *John Adams.* Boston, 1979.

Echeverria, D. *Mirage in the West: A History of the French Image of American Society to 1815.* Princeton, N.J., 1968.

Edelstein, L. *The Idea of Progress in Classical Antiquity.* Baltimore, 1967.

Ehmke, H. *Wirtschaft und Verfassung, Die Verfassungsrechtsprechung des Supreme Court zur Wirtschaftsregulierung.* Karlsruhe, 1961.

Ehmke, H. *Demokratischer Sozialismus und demokratischer Staat.* Bonn-Bad Godesberg, 1973.

Einstein, A. Peace in the Atomic Era. In *Representative American Speeches, 1949–50,* ed. A. C. Baird, Vol. 22, no. 3. New York, 1950.

Eisenstadt, G. M., and Oberndörfer, D., eds. *200 Jahre deutsch-amerikanische Beziehungen.* Bonn, 1976.

Ekirch, A. A. *The Idea of Progress in America, 1815–1860.* New York, 1944–51.

Ekirch, A. A. *The Decline of American Liberalism.* New York, 1955.

Ekirch, A. A. *The American Democratic Tradition: A History.* New York, 1963.

Ekirch, A. A. *Progressivism in America.* New York, 1974.

Elazar, D. J. *American Federalism, A View from the States.* New York, 1972.

Elazar, D. J. Constitutionalism, Federalism, and the Post-Industrial American Policy. In *The Third Century, America as a Post-Industrial Society,* ed. S. M. Lipset. Chicago, 1980.

Elias, N. *Über den Progress der Zivilisation.* Vols. 1 and 2. Frankfurt am Main, 1978.

Elkins, S., and McKitrick, E., eds. *The Hofstadter Aegis. A Memorial.* New York, 1974.

Ellett, E. F. *The Woman of the American Revolution.* New York, 1853–54. 3 vols.

Elliot, J., and Ali, S. R. *The Presidential-Congressional Political Dictionary.* Santa Barbara, Calif., 1984.

Ellul, J. *The Technological Society.* New York, 1967.

Elvin, L. *The Education Systems in the European Community. A Guide.* Windsor, 1981.

Emerson, D. E. *Richard Hildreth.* Baltimore, 1946.

Engle, P. *Woman in the American Revolution.* Chicago, 1976.

Eppler, E. *Ende oder Wende, Von der Machbarkeit des Notwendigen.* Stuttgart, 1975.

Epstein, K. *The Genesis of German Conservatism.* Princeton, N.J., 1975.

Erdmann, K. D. *Die Weimarer Republik.* Munich, 1980.

Eschenburg, T., ed. *Geschichte der Bundesrepublik Deutschland.* (5 vols.). *Deutsche Verlagsanstalt.* Stuttgart, 1983–86.

Essinger, H., and Ucar, A., eds. *Erziehung in der multikulturellen Gesellschaft. Versuche und Modelle zur Theorie und Praxis einer Interkulturellen Erziehung.* Baltmannsweiler, 1984.

Europa im Unterricht. *Bibliographie.* Collected by Cornelia Hagemann, ed. Bonn, 1981.

*Europäische Defizite, europäische. Perspektiven—eine Bestandaufrahme für morgen.* Ed. Werner Weidenfeld, Forschungsgruppe Europa. Gütersloh, 1988.

*"Europe," or, a General Survey of the Present Situation of the Principal Powers, with*

*Conjectures on Their Future Prospects: By a Citizen of the United States.* London, 1822.

European Parliament, ed. *Entwurf eines Vertrags zur Gründung der Europäischen Union.* Luxembourg, 1984.

European Parliament, ed. *Plan für den wirtschaftlichen Wiederaufschwung in Europa.* Luxembourg, 1984.

European Parliament. ed. *Stellung der Frau in Europa.* Luxembourg, 1984.

Evans, R., and Novak, R. D. *The Reagan Revolution.* New York, 1981.

Evans, R. J., ed. *Society and Politics in Wilhelmine Germany.* New York, 1978.

Faulenbach, B. *Deutscher Sonderweg, Zur Geschichte und Problematik einer zentralen Kategorie des deutschen Weges.* Munich, 1980.

Fay, B. *The Revolutionary Spirit in France and America: A Study of Moral and Intellectual Relations between France and the United States at the End of the Eighteenth Century.* New York, 1929.

*Federalist Papers, The.* Alexander Hamilton, James Madison, John Jay. Introduction by Clinton Rossiter. New York, 1961.

Feigenbaum, E., and McCorduck, P. *Die Fünfte Computer-Generation—Künstliche Intelligenz und die Herausforderung Japans.* Basel, 1984.

Feld, W. J. *American Foreign Policy: Aspirations and Reality.* New York, 1984.

Ferguson, M. *Die sanfte Verschwörung—Persönliche und gesellschaftliche Transformation im Zeichnen des Wassermannes.* Munich, 1984.

Ferguson, W. K. *The Renaissance in Historical Thought: Five Centuries of Interpretation.* Boston, 1948.

Ferro, M. *De Gaulle et l'Amérique.* Paris, 1973.

Fess, G. M. *The American Revolution in Creative French Literature (1775–1932).* Columbia, Mo., 1941.

Fest, J. C. *Hitler, Eine Biographie.* Berlin, 1973.

Fest, J. C., ed. *Geschichte der Bundesrepublik Deutschland.* 5 vols. *Deutsche Verlagsanstalt.* Stuttgart, 1983–86.

Festinger, L. *The Human Legacy.* New York, 1983.

Fetscher, I. *Überlebensbedingungen der Menschheit, Ist der Fortschritt noch zu retten?* (updated edition of 1976). Munich, 1985.

Feyerabend, P. K. *Ausgewählte Schriften.* Vol. 1: *Der Wissenschaftliche Realismus und die Autorität der Wissenschaften;* vol. 2: *Irrwege der Vernunft.* Wiesbaden, 1979.

Field, G. G. *Evangelist of Race, The Germanic Vision of Houston Steward Chamberlain.* New York, 1981.

Filler, L. *Appointment at Armageddon: Muckraking and Progressivism in the American Tradition.* Westport, Conn., 1976.

Fine, J.V.A. *The Ancient Greeks, A Critical History.* Cambridge, Mass., 1985.

Finley, M. I. *The World of Odysseus.* New York, 1965.

Fischer, F. *Griff nach der Weltmacht. Die Kriegszielpolitik des kaiserlichen Deutschland 1914/18.* Düsseldorf, 1961.

Fischer, J. *Von Grüner Kraft und Herrlichkeit.* Reinbeck bei Hamburg, 1984.

Fischer, M.M.J. *Iran from Religious Dispute to Revolution.* Cambridge, Mass., 1980.

Fishel, J. *Presidents and Promises. From Campaign Pledge to Presidential Performance.* Washington, D.C., 1984.

Fiske, J. *Outlines of Cosmic Philosophy.* Boston, 1875. Vol. 1.

Fiske, J. *Manifest Destiny: American Political Ideas Viewed from the Standpoint of Universal History*. New York, 1885.

Fiske, J. *The Critical Period of American History, 1783–1789*. Boston, 1888.

Fleming, D., Bailyn, B., ed. *The Intellectual Migration, Europe and America, 1930–1960*. Cambridge, Mass., 1969.

Flexner, J. T. *Washington, The Indispensable Man*. Boston, 1974.

Fohlen, C. The Impact of the American Revolution on France. In *The Impact of the American Revolution Abroad*. Library of Congress Symposia on the American Revolution. Washington, D.C., 1976.

Forcey, C. *The Crossroads of Liberalism, Croly, Weyl, Lippermann, and the Progressive Era, 1900–1925*. London, 1961.

Ford, G. R. *A Time to Heal*. New York, 1979.

Forman, J. D. *Communism: From Marx's Manifesto to 20th Century Reality*. New York, 1972.

Foster, M. *The Growth of Science in the Nineteenth Century*. Annual Reports of the Smithsonian Institution for 1899. Washington, D.C., 1901.

Foucault, M. *The Archaeology of Knowledge*. New York, 1972.

Fraenkel, E. *Amerika im Spiegel des deutschen politischen Denkens*. Cologne, 1959.

Fraenkel, E. *Das amerikanische Regierungssystem*. Cologne, 1962.

Frankel, C. *The Faith of Reason: The Idea of Progress in the French Enlightenment*. New York, 1948.

Franklin, B. *Collected Works*. The Library of America Series. New York, 1985.

Franklin, J. H. *From Slavery to Freedom*. New York, 1974.

Franklin, J. H. *John Locke and the Theory of Sovereignty*. Cambridge, 1978.

Franz, E. G. *Das Amerikabild der deutschen Revolution von 1848/49*. Heidelberg, 1958.

Free, L. A., and Cantril, H. *The Political Beliefs of Americans, A Study of Public Opinion*. New York, 1968.

Freidel, F., ed. *Harvard Guide to American History*. Cambridge, Mass., 1974. 2 vols.

Freud, S. *Civilization and Its Discontents*. London, 1951.

Frey, P. Spanien und Portugal. In *Jahrbuch der Europäischen Integration*, ed. W. Weidenfeld and W. Wessels. Bonn, 1984.

Friedan, B. *The Feminine Mystique*. New York, 1963.

Friedländer, S. *Kitsch und Tod. Der Widerschein des Nazismus*. Munich, 1984.

Friedman, J. E. and Shade, W. G. *Our American Sisters, Woman in American Life and Thought*. Boston, 1976.

Friedman, L. *Inventors of the Promised Land*. New York, 1975.

Friedman, M. *Capitalism and Freedom*. Chicago, 1962.

Friedmann, G. *La Crise du progrès: esquisse d'histoire des idées, 1895–1935*. Paris, 1936.

Friedrich, C. J. *Totalitarian Dictatorship and Autocracy*. Cambridge, Mass., 1956.

Friedrich, C. J., ed. *Authority*. Cambridge, Mass., 1958.

Fritz, K. von. *The Theory of the Mixed Constitution in Antiquity. A Critical Analysis of Polybios' Political Ideas*. New York, 1955.

Fritz, K. von. *Grundprobleme der Geschichte der antiken Wissenschaft*. Berlin, 1971.

Fritz, K. von. *The Relevance of Ancient Social and Political Philosophy for Our Times*. Berlin, 1974.

Fromm, E. *To Have or to Be?* New York, 1976.

Fulbright, J. W. *The Arrogance of Power*. New York, 1966.

*Fundamental Testaments of the American Revolution*. Library of Congress Symposia on the American Revolution. Washington, D.C., 1973.

Funderburk, C. *Presidents und Politics: The Limits of Power*. Monterey, Calif., 1982.

Funke, M., ed. *Terrorismus*. Düsseldorf, 1977.

Furet, F. *1789—Vom Ereignis zum Gegenstand der Geschichtswissenschaft*. Frankfurt am Main, 1980.

Galbraith, J. K. *The Affluent Society*. Boston, 1958.

Galtung, J. *Strukturelle Gewalt*. Reinbek bei Hamburg, 1977.

Garber, E. D., ed. *Genetic Perspectives in Biology and Medicine*. Chicago, 1985.

Gardner, L. C. *Safe for Democracy: The Anglo-American Response to Revolution, 1913–1923*. New York, 1984.

Gatell, F. O., ed. *Essays on Jacksonian America*. New York, 1970.

Gaus, G. *Wo Deutschland Liegt, Eine Ortsbestimmung*. Hamburg, 1983.

Gay, P. *Voltaire's Politics: The Poet as Realist*. Princeton, N.J., 1959.

Gay, P. *Weimar Culture, The Outsider As Insider*. New York, 1968. (With an introduction by K. D. Bracher.)

Gay, P. *The Enlightenment*. Vol. 2: *The Science of Freedom*. New York, 1969.

Gay, P. *Style in History*. New York, 1974.

Gentz, F. von. *The American and French Revolutions Compared*. Chicago, 1955. Originally published as *Der Ursprung und die Grundsätze der amerikanischen Revolution verglichen mit dem Ursprunge und den Grundsätzen der Französischen*. Berlin, 1800.

George, A. L. *Force and Statecraft: Diplomatic Problems of Our Time*. New York, 1983.

George, H. *Progress and Poverty*. New York, 1880.

Gerbet, P. *La Construction de l'Europe*. Paris, 1982.

Gerbi, A. *The Dispute of the New World. The History of a Polemic, 1750–1900*. Pittsburgh, 1973.

Germino, D. *The Inaugural Addresses of American Presidents, The Public Philosophy and Rhetoric*. Lanham, Md., 1984. (With an introduction by Kenneth W. Thompson.)

Gibbon, E. *Decline and Fall of the Roman Empire*. Vols. 1 and 2. (Chicago, 1952).

Gigon, O. *Der Begriff der Freiheit in der Antike*. Munich, 1977.

Gilbert, F. *To the Farewell Address, Ideas of Early American Foreign Policy*. Princeton, N.J., 1961.

Gilbert, F. *The End of the European Era, 1890 to the Present*. New York, 1970.

Gilder, G. *Wealth and Poverty*. New York, 1981.

Ginsberg, M. *The Idea of Progress: A Revaluation*. London, 1953.

Ginzberg, E., Anderson, J. K., and Herman, J. L. *The Optimistic Tradition and American Youth*. New York, 1962.

*Global Future; Time to Act*. Second Report to the President on Global Resources, Environment and Population. Ed.: Council on Environmental Quality and U.S.-State Department. Washington, D.C., 1981.

*The Global 2000 Report to the President*. Ed. Council on Environmental Quality. Washington, D.C., 1980.

Glotz, P. *Die Arbeit der Zuspitzung, Über die Organisation einer regierungsfähigen Linken*. Berlin, 1984.

Glotz, P. *Manifest für eine Neue Europäische Linke*. Berlin, 1985.

Glucksmann, A. *Philosophie der Abschreckung*. Stuttgart, 1984.

Godechot, J. *The Counter-Revolution*. London, 1972.

Goehlert, R. V., and Martin, F. S. *The Presidency: A Research Guide*. Santa Barbara, 1985.

Goldman, E. F. *Rendez-Vous with Destiny, A History of Modern American Reform*. New York, 1952.

Goldman, E. F. *The Tragedy of Lyndon Johnson*. New York, 1974.

Goldsmith, M. M. *Hobbes' Science of Politics*. New York, 1966.

Goldwater, B. *The Conscience of a Conservative*. Shepherdsville, Ky., 1960.

Goldwin, R. A., ed. *How Democratic Is the Constitution*. Washington, D.C., 1982.

Golembiewski, R. T., and Wildavsky, A., eds. *The Cost of Federalism*. New Brunswick, N.J., 1984.

Gombrich, E. H. *Ideals and Idols: Essays on Values in History and Art*. New York, 1979.

Gorer, G. *Die Amerikaner*. Hamburg, 1958.

Gottschalk, L. *Lafayette between the American and the French Revolution, 1783–1789*. Chicago, 1950.

Gould, L. L., ed. *The Progressive Era*. Syracuse, N.Y., 1974.

Gould, L. L., ed. *Reform and Regulation, American Politics, 1900–1916*. New York, 1978.

Graebner, N., ed. *Ideas and Diplomacy*. New York, 1964.

Graebner, N., ed. *Traditions and Values: Studies in American Diplomacy, 1865–1945*. Lanham, N.Y., 1985.

Graff, H. F., ed. *The Presidents: A Reference History*. New York, 1984.

Graml, H. *Europa zwischen den Kriegen*. Munich, 1964.

Grant De Pauw, L. *Conover Hunt, Miriam Schneir: Remember the Ladies. Woman in America, 1750–1815*. New York, 1976.

Grass, G., Jäckel, E., and Lattmann, D., eds. *Willy Brandt, Bruno Kreisky, Olof Palme: Briefe und Gespräche 1972–1975*. Frankfurt am Main, 1975.

Graubard, S. G. *A New Europe?* Boston, 1964.

Graubard, S. R., and Holton, G., eds. *Excellence and Leadership in a Democracy*. New York, 1962.

Greene, J. P., ed. *The Encyclopedia of American Political History: Studies of the Principal Movements and Ideas*. New York, 1985. 3 vols.

Gregor, A. J. *Young Mussolini and the Intellectual Origins of Fascism*. Berkeley, Calif., 1979.

Greiffenhagen, M. *Das Dilemma des Konservatismus*. Munich, 1977.

Griffith, W. E., ed. *The European Left, Italy, France and Spain*. Lexington, Mass., 1979.

Groeben, H. von der. *Aufbaujahre der Europäischen Gemeinschaft, Das Ringen um den Gemeinsamen Markt und die Politische Union (1958–66)*. Baden-Baden, 1982.

Grosjean, M., and Renner, G. *Die europäische Integration in den Rahmenplänen für Unterricht der Länder der Bundesrepublik Deutschland*. Berlin, 1981.

Grosser, A. *Das Bündnis, Die westeuropäischen Länder und die USA seit dem Krieg*. Munich, 1978.

Grosser, A. *Affaires Extérieures, La Politique de la France 1944/84*. Paris, 1984.

Grossner, C. *Der Verfall der Philosophie*. Hamburg, 1971.

Gruen, E. S. *The Last Generation of the Roman Republic*. Berkeley, Calif., 1974.

Grundmann, H. *Geschichtsschreibung im Mittelalter*. Göttingen, 1978.

Guardini, R. *The End of the Modern World*. Chicago, 1967.

Guggisberg, H. R. *Das europäische Mittelalter im amerikanischen Geschichtsdenken des 19. und 20. Jahrhunderts*. Basel, 1964.

Guggisberg, H. R. William Hickling Prescott und das Geschichtsbewußtsein der amerikanischen Romantik. In *Jahrbuch für Amerikastudien*, vol. 11, 1966.

Guggisberg, H. R. Jacob Burckhardt und Amerika. In *Jahrbuch für Amerikastudien*, vol. 13, 1968.

Guggisberg, H. R. The Uses of the European Past in American Historiography. In *Diverging Parallels, A Comparison of American and European Thought and Action*, ed. A.N.J. Den Hollander. Leiden, 1971.

Guggisberg, H. R. Sozialpolitisches Engagement in der amerikanischen Historiographie des 20. Jahrhunderts. In *Alte und Neue Welt in historischer Perspektive, Sieben Studien zum amerikanischen Geschichts- und Selbstverständnis*, ed. H.R. Guggisberg. Bern, 1973.

Gummere, R. M. *The American Colonial Mind and the Classical Traditions—Essays in Comparative Culture*. Cambridge, Mass., 1963.

Guthrie, W.K.C. *A History of Greek Philosophy*. Vol. 3. Cambridge, 1969.

Gutman, A. *Liberal Equality*. Cambridge, 1980.

Guttmann, A. *The Conservative Tradition in America*. New York, 1967.

Haack, F. W. *"Jugendsekten" und die neue Religiosität*. Gelsenkirchen-Buer, 1982.

Haas, E. B. *Uniting of Europe, Political, Social and Economic Forces 1950–1957*. Stanford, Calif., 1968.

Habermas, J. *Technik und Wissenschaft als Ideologie*. Frankfurt am Main, 1968.

Habermas, J., ed. *Stichworte zur geistigen Situation der Zeit*. vols. 1 and 2. Frankfurt am Main, 1980.

Habermas, J. *Die Neue Unübersichtlichkeit*. Frankfurt am Main, 1985.

Habermas, J. *Der philosophische Diskurs der Moderne*. Frankfurt am Main, 1985.

Hacke, C. *Die Ära Nixon-Kissinger 1969–1974, Konservative Reform der Weltpolitik*. Stuttgart, 1983.

Haefner, K. *Mensch und Computer im Jahre 2000. Ökonomie und Politik für eine human computerisierte Gesellschaft*. Basel, 1984.

Haines, C. G. *The American Doctrine of Judicial Supremacy*. Berkeley, Calif., 1932.

Halberstam, D. *The Best and the Brightest*. New York, 1973.

Hale, O. *The Great Illusion 1900–1914*. New York, 1971.

Hall, B. *Travels in North America in the Years 1827 and 1828*. Edinburgh, 1829. 3 vols.

Hamby, A. L. *Beyond the New Deal: Harry S. Truman and American Liberalism*. New York, 1973.

Hancock, M. D., and Sjoberg, G. *Politics in the Post-Welfare State*. New York, 1972.

Handler, E. *America and Europe in the Political Thought of John Adams*. Cambridge, Mass., 1964.

Handlin, L. *George Bancroft: The Intellectual as Democrat*. New York, 1984.

Handlin, O. *This Was America: True Accounts of People and Places, Manners and Customs, as Recorded by European Travelers at the Western Shore in the Eighteenth, Nineteenth, and Twentieth Centuries*. Cambridge, Mass., 1949.

Haraszti, Z. *John Adams and the Prophets of Progress*. Cambridge, Mass., 1952.

Harich, W. *Kommunismus ohne Wachstum? Babeuf und der "Club of Rome."* Reinbek bei Hamburg, 1975.

Harmon, M. J., ed. *Essays on the Constitution of the United States*. Port Washington, N.Y., 1978.

Harpprecht, K. *Der fremde Freund Amerika—eine innere Geschichte*. Stuttgart, 1982.

Harré, R., ed. *Problems of Scientific Revolution*. Oxford, 1975.

Hartmann, J. *Politische Profile der westeuropäischen Industriegesellschaft. Ein vergleichendes Handbuch*. Frankfurt am Main, 1984.

Hartz, L. *The Liberal Tradition in America. An Interpretation of American Political Thought since the Revolution*. New York, 1955.

Harvey, J. C. *Civil Rights During the Kennedy Administration*. Jackson, Miss., 1971.

Harvey, J. C. *Black Civil Rights During the Johnson Administration*. Jackson, Miss., 1973.

Hasselblatt, D., ed. *1984—Orwells Jahr*. Berlin, 1984.

Hatch, N. O. *The Sacred Cause of Liberty, Republican Thought and the Millenium in Revolutionary New England*. New Haven, Conn., 1977.

Hättich, M. Geschichtsbild und Demokratieverständnis. In *Die Zweite Republik, 25 Jahre Bundesrepublik Deutschland—eine Bilanz*, ed. R. Löwenthal and h.-P. Schwarz. Stuttgart, 1974.

Hawke, D. F. *Paine*. New York, 1974.

Hax, H., Kraus, W., and Kryoshi, T., eds. *Structural Change: The Challenge to Industrial Societies*. Eighth German-Japanese Economics and Social Sciences Seminar. Cologne, September 25–27, 1984. Berlin, 1985.

Hayden, T. *American Future: New Frontiers Beyond Old Frontiers*. Boston, 1980.

Hayek, F. A. *Individualism and Economic Order*. Chicago, 1948.

Hays, S. P. *The Response to Individualism, 1885–1914*. Chicago, 1957.

Hazard, P. *La crise de la conscience européenne 1680–1715*. Paris, 1961.

Heilbroner, R. *The Future as History, The Historic Currents of Our Time and the Direction in Which They Are Taking America*. New York, 1960.

Heimert, A. *Religion and the American Mind: From the Great Awakening to the Revolution*. Cambridge, Mass., 1966.

Heimert, A., and Delbanco, A., eds. *The Puritans in America*. Cambridge, Mass., 1985.

Heinemann, U. *Die verdrängte Niederlage—Politische Öffentlichkeit und Kriegsschuldfrage in der Weimarer Republik*. Göttingen, 1983.

Helbich, W. ''Amerika ist ein freies Land...,'' Auswanderer schreiben nach Deutschland. Darmstadt, 1985.

Hellwig, R., ed. *Die Christdemokratinnen, Unterwegs zur Partnerschaft*. Stuttgart, 1984. (With a foreword by Helmut Kohl.)

Henningsen, M. *Der Fall Amerika, Zur Sozial- und Bewußtseinsgeschichte einer Verdrängung, Das Amerika der Europäer*. Munich, 1974.

Hennis, W. *Politik und praktische Philosophie*. Stuttgart, 1977.

Hentig, H. von, *Das allmähliche Verschwinden der Wirklichkeit. Ein Pädagoge ermutigt zum Nachdenken über die Neuen Medien*. Munich, 1984.

Herbst, J. *The German Historical School in American Scholarship*. Ithaca, N.Y., 1965.

Herder-Dornreich, Ph., Klages, H., and Schlotter, H.-G., eds. *Überwindung der Sozialstaatskrise*. Baden-Baden, 1984.

Herf, J. *Reactionary Modernism: Technology, Culture, and Politics in Weimar and the Third Reich*. Cambridge, 1984.

Hermet, G., Hassner, P., and Rupnik, J. *Totalitarismes*. Paris, 1984.

Herson, L.J.R. *The Politics of Ideas: Political Theory and American Public Policy.*
  Homewood, Ill., 1984.

Herz, J. J. *Political Realism and Political Idealism.* Chicago, 1951.

Heuß, A. *Versagen und Verhängnis. Vom Ruin deutscher Geschichte und ihres Verständnisses.* Berlin, 1984.

Hicks, J. D. *The Populist Revolt: A History of the Farmer's Alliance and the People's
  Party.* Minneapolis, 1931.

Higham, J. *Strangers in the Land. Patterns of American Nativism, 1860–1925.* New
  York, 1963.

Higham, J., and Conkin, P. K. *New Directions in American Intellectual History.* Baltimore, 1980.

Higham, J., Krieger, L., and Gilbert, F. *History, Humanistic Scholarship in America.*
  Englewood Cliffs, N.J., 1965.

Hildebrand, K., and Pommern, R., eds. *Deutsche Frage und europäisches Gleichgewicht*
  (Festschrift for Andreas Hillgruber). Cologne, 1985.

Hildreth, R. *The History of the United States of America, New York 1849–52.* 6 vols.

Hillgruber, A. *Die Last der Nation. Fünf Beiträge über Deutschland und die Deutschen.*
  Düsseldorf, 1984.

Himmelfarb, G. *Darwin and the Darwinian Revolution.* New York, 1968.

Himmelfarb, G. *On Liberty and Liberalism: The Case of John Stuart Mill.* New York,
  1974.

Hingley, R. *Joseph Stalin, Man and Legend.* New York, 1974.

Hirschfield, R. S., ed. *The Power of the Presidency, Concepts and Controversy.* New
  York, 1982.

Hitch, Ch. J., and McKean, R. N. *The Economics of Defense in the Nuclear Age.*
  Cambridge, Mass., 1960.

Hodgson, G. *America in Our Time: From World War II to Nixon, What Happened and
  Why.* New York, 1976.

Hodgson, G. *All Things to All Men, The False Promise of the Modern American Presidency from Franklin D. Roosevelt to Ronald Reagan.* New York, 1980.

Hoepli, N. L., ed. *Aftermath of Colonialism.* New York, 1973.

Hofer, W. *Mächte und Kräfte im 20. Jahrhundert.* Düsseldorf, 1985.

Hoffmann, S. *Decline or Renewal? France since the 1930s.* New York, 1977.

Hoffmann, S. *Primary or World Order? American Foreign Policy since the Cold War.*
  New York, 1980.

Hoffmann, S. *Duties Beyond Borders, On the Limits and Possibilities of Ethical Politics.*
  Syracuse, N.Y., 1981.

Hoffmann, S. Fragments Floating in the Here and Now: Is There a Europe, Was There
  a Past, and Will There Be a Future? or, The Lament of a Transplanted European.
  In *Culture and Society in Contemporary Europe,* ed. S. Hoffmann and P. Kitromilides. Winchester, Mass., 1981.

Hoffmann, S., ed. *The Rise of the Nazi Regime, Historical Reassessment.* Boulder, Colo.,
  1985.

Hoffmann, S., and Kitromilides, P., eds. *Culture and Society in Contemporary Europe.*
  Cambridge, Mass., 1981.

Hofstadter, R. *The American Political Tradition and the Men Who Made It.* New York,
  1948. (With a foreword by Christopher Lasch.)

Hofstadter, R. *The Age of Reform, From Bryan to F.D.R.* New York, 1955.

Hofstadter, R. *Social Darwinism in American Thought*. Boston, 1955.

Hofstadter, R. *Great Issues in American History*. Vol. 2: 1864–1957. New York, 1958.

Hofstadter, R. *The Progressive Historians*. *Turner, Beard, Parrington*. New York, 1970.

Hofstadter, R., et al. *The United States: The History of a Republic*. Princeton, N.J., 1967.

Holmes, C., and Pollard, S. *The End of the Old Europe, 1914–1939*. New York, 1973.

Holmes, K. The Origins, Development, and Composition of the Green Movement. In *The Greens of West Germany*, ed. R. L. Pfaltzgraff et al. Cambridge, Mass., 1983.

Holmes, K. *The West Germany Peace Movement and the National Question*. Cambridge, Mass., 1984.

Holst, H. V. *Verfassung und Demokratie der Vereinigten Staaten von Amerika*. Vol. 1: *Düsseldorf, 1873*; vols. 2–5: *Berlin 1878–92* [The Constitutional and Political Theory of the United States, 8 vols., Chicago, 1889–92.]

Hook, S. *Academic Freedom and Academic Anarchy*. Boston, 1971.

Hoover, H. *American Individualism*. Ed. Frank Friedel. New York, 1979.

Horkheimer, M., and Adorno, T. W. *Dialektik der Aufklärung*. Frankfurt am Main, 1969.

Horowitz, I. L. *Ideology and Utopia in the United States 1956–1976*. London, 1977.

Horx, M. *Das Ende der Alternativen oder Die Verlorene Unschuld der Radikalität*. Munich, 1985.

Hotze, H. *Skandal Europa*. *Die Europäische Gemeinschaft oder: Wie sich eine Idee zu Tode subventioniert*. Frankfurt, 1985.

Hoxie, R. G. *The Presidency of the 1970's*. New York, 1973.

Hoxie, R. G. *Command Decision and the Presidency*. A Study of National Security Policy and Organization. New York, 1977. (Foreword by President Gerald R. Ford.)

Hübener, T. *The Germans in America*. Philadelphia, 1962.

Huber, A., ed. *Die Sozialdemokratinnen, Verdient die Nachtigall Lob, wenn sie singt?* Stuttgart, 1984. (With a foreword by Herbert Wehner.)

Hübner, K. *Kritik der wissenschaftlichen Vernunft*. Freiburg, 1978.

Hübner, K. *Die Wahrheit des Mythos*. Munich, 1985.

Hughes, D. A., ed. *Perspectives on Pornography*. New York, 1970.

Hughes, E. J. *The Ordeal of Power, A Political Memoir of the Eisenhower Years*. New York, 1963.

Hughes, E. J. *The Living Presidency*. Baltimore, 1973.

Hughes, H. S. *Consciousness and Society: The Reorientation of European Social Thought 1890–1930*. New York, 1958.

Hughes, H. S. *Oswald Spengler—A Critical Estimate*. London, 1962.

Hughes, H. S. *Contemporary Europe: A History*. Englewood Cliffs, N.J., 1966.

Huhle, C. *Vom Nahziel Kommunismus zu den Grenzen des Wachstums? Sowjetische Kommunismus-Konzeptionen seit 1961*. Frankfurt am Main, 1980.

Hull, D. *Darwin and His Critics*. Cambridge, Mass., 1973.

Hunt, R. N. *The Political Ideas of Marx and Engels* Vol. 1: *Marxism and Totalitarian Democracy 1818–1850*. London, 1975.

Hunter, W. A. *The "New Right": A Growing Force in State Politics*. Ed. Thomas W. Bonnett. Washington, D.C., 1980.

Huntington, S. P. The Founding Fathers and the Division of Powers. In *Area and Power*, ed. Arthur Maass. Glencoe, Ill., 1959.

Huntington, S. P. *Political Order in Changing Societies*. New Haven, Conn., 1968.

Huntington, S. P. The United States. In *The Crisis of Democracy*, ed. M. Crozier, S. P. Huntington, and J. Watanuki. New York, 1975.

Huntington, S. P. *American Politics: The Promise of Disharmony*. Cambridge, Mass., 1981.

Huntington, S. P., and Moore, C. H., eds. *Authoritarian Politics in Modern Society*, New York, 1970.

Hurd, C., and Bauer, A., eds. *A Treasury of Great American Speeches*. New York, 1970.

Huxley, A. *Brave New World*. New York, 1932 (Revised 1958).

*Impact of the American Revolution Abroad, The*. Washington, D.C., 1976.

*Inaugural Addresses of the Presidents of the United States, from George Washington 1789 to Richard Milhous Nixon 1973*. Washington, D.C., 1974.

Inge, W. R. *The Idea of Progress*. Oxford, 1920.

Ingersoll, D. E. *Communism, Fascism and Democracy, The Origins and Development of Three Ideologies*. Columbus, Ohio, 1971.

Inglehart, R. *The Silent Revolution: Changing Values and Political Styles among Western Publics*. Princeton, N.J., 1977.

Inkeles, A. Continuity and Change in the American National Character. In *The Third Century, America as a Post-Industrial Society*, ed. S. M. Lipset, Chicago, 1980.

Inkeles, A., and Levinson, D. National Character: The Study of Modal Personality and Sociocultural Systems. In *Handbook of Social Psychology*, ed. Gardner Lindzey. Cambridge, Mass., 1954.

Institut für Zeitgeschichte, ed. "Deutscher Sonderweg—Mythos oder Realität?" with contributions by H. Möller, Th. Nipperdey, K. Sontheimer, E. Nolte, M. Stürmer, and K. D. Bracher. Munich, 1982.

Jäckel, E. *Hitlers Weltanschauung, Entwurf einer Herrschaft*. Stuttgart, 1981.

Jäckel, E., ed. *Geschichte der Bundesrepublik Deutschland*. 5 vols. *Deutsche Verlagsanstalt*. Stuttgart, 1983–86.

Jackson, R. *The Struggle for Judicial Supremacy*. New York, 1941.

Jacobsen, H.-A. *Nationalsozialistische Außenpolitik 1933–1938*. Frankfurt am Main, 1968.

Jacoby, H. *Die Bürokratisierung der Welt*. Frankfurt am Main, 1984.

Jaher, F. C. *Doubters and Dissenters: Cataclysmic Thought in America, 1885–1918*. New York, 1964.

James, W. *Pragmatism and the Meaning of Truth*. (Introduction by A. J. Ayer). Cambridge, Mass., 1978.

Jansen, T., and Mahnke, D., eds. *Persönlichkeiten der Europäischen Integration, Vierzehn biographische Essays*. Bonn, 1981.

Jaspers, K. *Über Bedingungen und Möglichkeiten eines neuen Humanismus*. Munich, 1951.

Jaspers, K. *Vom Ursprung und Ziel der Geschichte*. Frankfurt am Main, 1955.

Jaspers, K. *Die geistige Situation der Zeit*. Berlin, 1979 (Reprint).

Jastrow, R. *How to Make Nuclear Weapons Obsolete*. Boston, 1985.

Jennings, F. *The Invasion of America: Indians, Colonialism, and the Cant of Conquest*. Chapel Hill, N.C., 1975.

Jennrich, P. *Die Okkupation des Willens, Macht und Methoden der neuen Kultbewegungen*. Hamburg, 1985.

Jensen, L., ed. *Machiavelli: Cynic, Patriot, or Political Scientist?* Boston, 1960.

Johnson, H. *In the Absence of Power, Governing America*. New York, 1980.

Johnson, S. K. The Future of Woman in America's Third Century. In *The Third Century*, ed. S. M. Lipset. Chicago, 1980.

Johnstone, R. M. *Jefferson and the Presidency: Leadership in the Young Republic*. Ithaca, N.Y., 1978.

Joll, J. *Intellectuals in Politics*. London, 1960.

Joll, J. *Europe since 1870*. New York, 1973.

Joll, J. *The Origins of the First World War. Origins of the Modern Wars*. Ed. H. Hearder. London, 1984.

Jonas, H. *The Imperative of Responsibility, In Search of an Ethics for the Technological Age*. Chicago, 1984.

Jonas, M. *The United States and Germany, A Diplomatic History*. Ithaca, N.Y., 1985.

Jones, H. M. *America and French Culture, 1750–1848*. Chapel Hill, N.C., 1927.

Jones, H. M. *The Pursuit of Happiness*. Cambridge, Mass., 1953.

Jones, H. M. *O Strange New World*. New York, 1964.

Jordan, W. D. *White over Black. American Attitudes toward the Negro, 1550–1812*. Chapel Hill, N.C., 1968.

Jordy, W. H. *Henry Adams: Scientific Historian*. New Haven, Conn., 1952.

July, R. W. *The Origins of Modern African Thought*. London, 1968.

Kaiser, K., and Schwarz, H. P., eds. *Amerika und Westeuropa*. Stuttgart, 1977.

Kaiser, K., Merlini, C., Montbrial, T. de, Wallace, W., and Wellenstein, E. *Die EG vor der Entscheidung, Fortschritt oder Verfall*. Bonn, 1983.

Kaltefleiter, W. Changes in Social Values in Industrial Societies: The Example of the Federal Republic of Germany. In *Structural Change: The Challenge to Industrial Societies*. Eighth German-Japanese Economics and Social Sciences Seminar, Cologne, September 24–27, 1984, ed. H. Hax, W. Kraus, and T. Kiyoshi. Berlin, 1985.

Kaltenbrunner, G. K., ed. *Rekonstruktion des Konservatismus*. Freiburg, 1972.

Kamenka, E., ed. *Nationalism, the Nature and Evolution of an Idea*. London, 1976.

Kammen, M. *People of Paradox: An Inquiry Concerning the Origins of American Civilization*. New York, 1972.

Kammen, M. *A Season of Youth. The American Revolution and the Historical Imagination*. New York, 1978.

Kammen, M., ed. *The Past Before US: Contemporary Historical Writing in the United States*. Foreword by John Hope Franklin. Ithaca, N.Y., 1980.

Kaplan, N., ed. *Science and Society*. Chicago, 1965.

Karasek, F. *Zusammenarbeit in Europa und Erziehung in Europa*. Wien, 1981.

Kariel, H. S. *Beyond Liberalism, Where Relations Grow*. New York, 1977.

Kates, R. W., Hohenemser, C., and Kasperson, J. X., eds. *Perilous Progress, Managing the Hazards of Technology*. Boulder, Colo., 1985.

Keller, M. *Affairs of State. Public Life in Late Nineteenth Century America*. Cambridge, Mass., 1977.

Kelley, D. R. *The Beginning of Ideology, Consciousness and Society in the French Reformation*. Cambridge, Mass., 1981.

Kelly, G. A. *Idealism, Politics and History: Sources of Hegelian Thought.* Cambridge, Mass., 1969.

Kennan, G. *Realities of American Foreign Policy.* Princeton, N.J., 1954.

Kennan, G. *Democracy and the Student Left.* Boston, 1968.

Kennedy, E. M. and Hatfield, M. O. *FREEZE! How You Can Help Prevent Nuclear War.* Washington, D.C., 1982.

Kennedy, G. *The Art of Persuasion in Greece.* Princeton, N.J., 1963.

Kennedy, G. *The Art of Rhetoric in the Roman World.* Princeton, N.J., 1972.

Kennedy, J. F. The Role of the President. In *Representative American Speeches,* ed. L. Thonssen. Vol. 32, no. 4. New York, 1960.

Kennedy, P. *The Rise and Fall of the Great Powers: Economic Change and Military Conflict from 1500 to 2000.* New York, 1988.

Kessler, F. *The Dilemmas of Presidential Leadership: Of Caretakers and Kings.* Englewood Cliffs, N.J., 1982.

Keynes, J. M. *The Economic Consequences of the Peace.* London, 1950.

Keyworth, G. A. *President Reagan's New Defense Initiative: A Road to Stability.* Stanford, Calif., 1984.

Kibbey, A. *Rhetoric, Prejudice, and Violence: The Interpretation of Material Shapes in Puritanism.* New York, 1985.

Kielmansegg, P. G. *Deutschland und der Erste Weltkrieg.* Stuttgart, 1980.

Killen, L. *The Russian Bureau: A Case Study in Wilsonian Diplomacy.* Lexington, Ky., 1983.

King, A., ed. *The New American Political System.* Washington, D.C., 1979.

Kirk, R. *The Conservative Mind.* Chicago, 1953.

Kirkpatrick, J. *The Reagan Doctrine and US Foreign Policy.* Washington, D.C., 1985.

Kissinger, H. A. *The Meaning of History, Reflections on Spengler, Toynbee and Kant.* Unpublished Honors Thesis, Harvard University, 1951.

Kissinger, H. A. *A World Restored. Castlereagh, Metternich and the Restoration of Peace, 1812–1822.* Boston, 1957.

Kissinger, H. A. The Moral Foundations of Foreign Policy. In *American Foreign Policy,* ed. H. A. Kissinger. New York, 1977.

Klages, H. *Überlastete Staatverdrossene Bürger? Zu den Dissonanzen der Wohlfahrtsgesellschaft.* Frankfurt am Main, 1981.

Klayes, H., and Kmieciak, P., eds. *Wertewandel und gesellschaftlicher Wandel.* Frankfurt am Main, 1979.

Klee, E. *"Euthanasie" im NS-Staat.* Frankfurt am Main, 1983.

Klein, L. B. *The Keynesian Revolution.* New York, 1963.

Kleinewefers, H. *Reformen für Wirtschaft und Gesellschaft, Utopien, Konzepte, Realitäten.* Frankfurt am Main, 1985.

Klingenberg, F. L. Cyclical Trends in American Foreign Policy Moods and Their Policy Implications. In *Challenges to America: U.S. Foreign Policy in the 1980's,* ed. Charles W. Kegley and Patrick J. McGowan. Sage International Yearbook of Foreign Policy Studies, vol. 4, 1979.

Klotzbach, K. *Der Weg zur Staatspartei, Programmatik, praktische Politik und Organisation der deutschen Sozialdemokratie 1945 bis 1965.* Berlin, 1982.

Kluckhol, C. Have There Been Discernible Shifts in American Values during the Past Generation? In *The American Style,* ed. Elting E. Morison. New York, 1958.

Klussmann, P. G., and Mohr, H., eds. *Probleme deutscher Identität—Zeitgenössische Autobiographien, Identitätssuche und Zivilisationskritik.* Bonn, 1983.

Koch, A. *Jefferson and Madison: The Great Collaboration.* New York, 1950.

Koch, A. *Power, Morals, and the Founding Fathers. Essays on the Interpretation of the American Enlightenment.* Ithaca, N.Y., 1966.

Koch, A., and Peden, W., eds. *The Selected Writings of John and John Quincy Adams.* New York, 1946.

Koenig, L. W. *The Chief Executive.* New York, 1981.

Kohn, H. *American Nationalism: An Interpretative Essay.* New York, 1957.

Koht, H. *The American Spirit in Europe, A Survey of Transatlantic Influences.* Philadelphia, 1949.

Kolakowski, L., and Hampshire, S., eds. *The Socialist Idea: A Reappraisal.* London, 1974.

Kolko, G. *The Triumph of Conservatism: A Reinterpretation of American History.* New York, 1963.

König, F., and Rahner, K., eds. *Europa, Horizonte der Hoffnung.* Cologne, 1983.

Koselleck, R. Fortschritt und Beschleunigung, Zur Utopie der Aufklärung. In *Der Traum der Vernunft.* Darmstadt, 1985.

Koselleck, R. *Vergangene Zukunft, Zur Semantik geschichtlicher Zeiten.* Frankfurt am Main, 1979.

Koyré, A. *From the Closed World to the Infinite Universe.* New York, 1958.

Krakau, K. *Missionsbewußtsein und Völkerrechtsdoktrin in den Vereinigten Staaten von Amerika.* Frankfurt am Main, Berlin, 1967.

Krakau, K. American Foreign Relations—An American Style? In *Oceans Apart? Comparing Germany and the United States,* ed. E. Angermann and M.-L. Frings. Stuttgart, 1981.

Kraus, W. *Nihilismus heute oder die Geduld der Weltgeschichte.* Vienna, 1983.

Kremendahl, H. *Pluralismustheorie in Deutschland.* Leverkusen, 1977.

Krieger, L. *European History in America.* In *History, Humanistic Scholarship in America,* ed. J. Higham, L. Krieger, and F. Gilbert. Englewood Cliffs, N.J., 1965.

Krieger, L., and Stern, F. *"Editors' Introduction." The Responsibility of Power, Historical Essays in Honor of Hajo Holborn,* Garden City, N.Y., 1967.

Kucharsky, D. *The Mind and Spirit of Jimmy Carter.* New York, 1977.

Kuehn, T. J., and Porter, A. L., eds. *Science, Technology, and National Policy.* Ithaca, N.Y., 1981.

Kuhn, H. *Krisenbewußtsein in Amerika, Jahrbuch für Amerikastudien.* Ed. W. Fischer. Heidelberg, 1956.

Kuhn, T. S. *The Structure of Scientific Revolutions.* Chicago, 1970.

Kunhardt, P. B. *A New Birth of Freedom: Lincoln at Gettysburg.* Boston, 1983.

LaCapra, D. *History and Criticism.* Ithaca, N.Y., 1985.

Ladd, E. C. *Ideology in America.* New York, 1969.

Ladd, E. C., and Lipset, S. M. Public Opinion and Public Policy. In *The United States in the 1980s,* ed. Peter Duignan and Alvin Rabushka. Stanford, Calif., 1980.

Lader, L. *Power on the Left, American Radical Movements since 1946.* New York, 1979.

Lafontaine, O. *Der andere Fortschritt, Verantwortung statt Verweigerung.* Hamburg, 1985.

Lakatos, I., and Musgrave, A., eds. *Criticism and the Growth of Knowledge.* Cambridge, Mass., 1970.

Landes, D. *The Unbound Prometheus: Technological Change and Industrial Development in Western Europe from 1750 to the Present*. Cambridge, 1969.

Langguth, G. *Protestbewegung—Entwicklung, Niedergang, Renaissance, Die neue Linke seit 1968*. Cologne, 1983.

Langguth, G. *Der grüne Faktor, Von der Bewegung zur Partei*. Zürich, 1984.

Laqueur, W. Z. *Weimar: A Cultural History*. New York, 1975.

Laqueur, W. Z., ed. *Literature and Politics in the Twentieth Century*. New York, 1967.

Lasch, C. *The Culture of Narcissism: American Life in an Age of Diminishing Expectations*. New York, 1979.

Laski, H. *The American Democracy*. New York, 1948.

Laski, H. *The American Presidency: An Interpretation*. New Brunswick, N.J., 1980.

Laslett, J. H. M., and Lipset, S. M., eds. *Failure of a Dream?* Garden City, N.Y., 1974.

Laudam, L. *Progress and Its Problems, Toward a Theory of Scientific Growth*. Berkeley, Calif., 1977.

Leavis, F. R. *Two Cultures? The Significance of C. P. Snow*. London, 1963.

Lefèbvre, G. *The Coming of the French Revolution*. Princeton, N.J., 1967.

Le Goff, J. *Kultur des europäischen Mittelalters*. Zürich, 1970.

Leisler Kiep, W. *Good Bye Amerika—was dann?* Stuttgart, 1972.

Leisner, W. *Der Gleichheitsstaat, Macht durch Nivellierung*. Berlin, 1980.

Leiss, W. *The Domination of Nature*. New York, 1972.

Lekachman, R. *Creed Is Not Enough: Reaganomics*. New York, 1982.

Lemisch, J. *On Active Service in War and Peace. Politics and Ideology in the American Historical Profession*. Toronto, 1975.

Lentin, A. *Lloyd George, Woodrow Wilson and the Guilt of Germany*. Baton Rouge, La., 1985.

Leonhard, W. *The Three Faces of Marxism: The Political Concepts of Soviet Ideology, Maoism, and Humanist Marxism*. Translated by Ewald Osers. New York, 1970. Originally published as *Die Dreispaltung des Marxismus, Ursprung und Entwicklung des Sowjet-Marxismus, Maoismus und Reformkommunismus* (Düsseldorf, 1970).

Leonhard, W. *Eurokommunismus—eine Herausforderung an Ost und West*. Gütersloh, 1978.

Lerner, M. *America as a Civilization*. New York, 1957.

Levin, D. *History as Romantic Art: Bancroft, Prescott, Motley, and Parkman*. Stanford, Calif., 1959.

Levine, P. The Writer as Independent Witness: An Interview with E. L. Doctorow. In *E. L. Doctorow: Essays and Conversations*, ed. R. Trenner. Princeton, N.J., 1983.

Lévi-Strauss, C. *Structural Anthropology*. London, 1968.

Lewis, R. W. B. *The American Adam*. Chicago, 1959.

Libiszowska, Z. *Tomasz Jefferson*. Warsaw (Ossolineum), 1984.

Library of Congress, European Affairs Division. *The United States and Postwar Europe. A Bibliographical Examination of Thought Expressed in American Publications During 1948–1952*.

Lichtheim, G. *Europe in the Twentieth Century*. New York, 1972.

Lilienthal, D. E. *Change, Hope, and the Bomb*. Princeton, N.J., 1963.

Link, A. S. *Woodrow Wilson and the Progressive Era*. New York, 1953.

Link, W. *Die amerikanische Stabilisierungspolitik in Deutschland 1921–1932*. Düsseldorf, 1970.

Linsky, M., ed. *Television and the Presidency Elections*. Lexington, Mass., 1983.

Lipgens, W. *Sources for the History of European Integration, 1945–1955*. Stuttgart, 1980.

Lipgens, W. *A History of European Integration, 1945–1947*. New York, 1982.

Lippmann, W. *The Public Philosophy, On the Decline and Revival of the Western Society*. Boston, 1955.

Lipset, S. M. Why No Socialism in the United States? In *Sources of Contemporary Radicalism*, ed. Seweryn Bialer and Sophia Slazar. Boulder, Colo., 1977.

Lipset, S. M., ed. *Emerging Coalitions in American Politics*. San Francisco, 1978.

Lipset, S. M. *The First New Nation, The United States in Historical and Comparative Perspective*. New York, 1979.

Lipset, S. M. *The Third Century, America as a Post-Industrial Society*. Chicago, 1980.

Lipset, S. M., and Raab, E. *The Politics of Unreason, Right-Wing Extremism in America 1790–1970*. New York, 1970.

Lipset, S. M., and Schneider, W. *The Confidence Gap: Business, Labor and Government in the Public Mind*. Boston, 1972.

Lodge, G. C. *The New American Ideology*. New York, 1975.

Lovejoy, A. O. *Essays in the History of Ideas*. New York, 1960.

Löwenthal, R. *Der romantische Rückfall*. Stuttgart, 1970.

Löwenthal, R., ed. *Demokratischer Sozialismus in den 80er Jahren*. Cologne, 1979.

Löwenthal, R. *Gesellschaftswandel und Kulturkrise, Zukunftsprobleme der westlichen Demokratien*. Frankfurt am Main, 1979.

Löwenthal, R., and Schwarz, H.-P., eds. *Die Zweite Republik, 25 Jahre Bundesrepublik Deutschland—eine Bilanz*. Stuttgart, 1974–79.

Lowi, T. J. *The End of Liberalism. Ideology, Policy and the Crisis of Public Authority*. New York, 1969.

Lowi, T. J. *The Personal President: Powers Invested, Promise Unfulfilled*. Ithaca, N.Y., 1985.

Löwith, K. *From Hegel to Nietzsche: The Revolution in Nineteenth Century Thought*. London, 1964.

Lübbe, H. *Geschichtsbegriff und Geschichtsinteresse—Analytik und Pragmatik der Historie*. Basel, 1977.

Lübbe, H. *Zeit-Verhältnisse. Zur Kulturphilosophie des Fortschritts*. Graz, 1983.

Lührs, G., et al., eds. *Kritischer Rationalismus und Sozialdemokratie*. Berlin, 1975. (With a foreword by Helmut Schmidt.)

Lundberg, E. Aufstieg und Fall des schwedischen Modells. In *Trendwende, Europas Wirtschaft in der Krise*, ed. R. Dahrendorf (with a foreword by Gaston Thorn). Zurich, 1981.

Lutz, P. C., ed. *Spengler heute*. Munich, 1980.

Lynd, S. *Intellectual Origins of American Radicalism*. New York, 1968.

Mably, G. B. de. *Observations on the Government and Laws of the United States of America*. London, 1784.

MacIntyre, A. *A Short History of Ethics*. New York, 1966.

Macrae, N. *The 2025 Report: A Concise History of the Future, 1975–2025*. New York, 1985.

Macridis, R. C. *Greek Politics at a Crossroads, What Kind of Socialism?* Stanford, Calif., 1984.

Mahan, A. T. *The Influence of Sea Power upon History, 1660–1783.* Boston, 1890.

Mahan, A. T. *The Interest of America in Sea Power, Present and Future.* London, 1890.

Maier, C. S., ed. *The Rise of the Nazi Regime, Historical Reassessments.* Boulder, Colo., 1985.

Maier, P. The Beginnings of American Republicanism. In *The Development of a Revolutionary Mentality.* Library of Congress Symposia on the American Revolution. Washington, D.C., 1972.

Malin, J. C. *Confounded Rot about Napoleon. Reflections upon Science and Technology, Nationalism, World Depression of the Eighteen-Nineties, and Afterwards.* Lawrence, Kan., 1961.

Mandelbaum, M. *The Nuclear Revolution: International Politics before and after Hiroshima.* London, 1981.

Mann, G. *Vom Geist Amerikas, Eine Einführung in amerikanisches Denken und Handeln im zwanzigsten Jahrhundert.* Stuttgart, 1954.

Mannheim, K. *Ideology and Utopia.* London, 1954.

Mansfield, H. C. *The Spirit of Liberalism.* Cambridge, Mass., 1978.

Manuel, F. E. *Utopias and Utopian Thought.* Boston, 1966.

Marcell, D. W. *Progress and Pragmatism. James, Dewey, Beard, and the American Idea of Progress.* Westport, Conn., 1974.

Marcuse, H. *One-Dimensional Man.* Boston, 1964.

Marcuse, L. Kultur-Pessimismus. In *Club Voltaire I,* ed. G. Szczesny. Munich, 1964.

Marks, F. W. Theodore Roosevelt and the Conservative Revival. In *Traditions and Values: Studies in American Diplomacy, 1865–1945,* ed. Norman Graebner. Lanham, Md., 1985.

Martin, E. T. Thomas Jefferson and the Idea of Progress. Ph.D. diss., University of Wisconsin, 1941.

Martin, L., ed. *The Anglo-American Tradition in Foreign Affairs,* New Haven, Conn., 1956.

Martineau, H. *Society in America.* New York, 1837. Vols. 1 and 2.

Marwick, A. *War and Social Change in the Twentieth Century, A Comparative Study of Britain, France, Germany, Russia, and the United States.* London, 1974.

Masur, G. *Prophets of Yesterday, Studies in European Culture 1890–1914.* New York, 1965.

Mathias, P., ed. *Science and Society: 1600–1900.* Cambridge, 1972.

Mathiopoulos, M. The American Presidency: A German Perspective. In *The American Presidency, Perspectives from Abroad,* ed. K. W. Thompson. Lanham, Md., 1986.

Matthews, R. K. *The Radical Politics of Thomas Jefferson: A Revisionist View.* Lawrence, Kan., 1984.

May, E. *Imperial Democracy, The Emergence of America as a Great Power.* New York, 1973.

May, H. F. *The End of American Innocence, A Study of the First Years of Our Own Time, 1912–1917.* Chicago, 1959.

May, H. F. *The Enlightenment in America.* Oxford, 1978.

Mayer, A. J. *The Persistence of the Old Regime, Europe to Great War.* New York, 1981.

Mayne, R., ed. *Europe Tomorrow, 16 Europeans Look Ahead,* London, 1972.

Mayr, E. *The Growth of Biological Thought. Diversity, Evolution and Inheritance.* Cambridge, Mass., 1985.

McClelland, C. E., and Scher, S. P., eds. *Postwar German Culture: An Anthology.* New York, 1974.

McClosky, H., and Brill, A. *Dimensions of Tolerance.* New York, 1983.

McClosky, H., and Zaller, J. *The American Ethos, Public Attitudes toward Capitalism and Democracy.* Cambridge, Mass., 1984.

McClosky, R., ed. *Essays in Constitutional Law.* New York, 1957.

McClosky, R. The American Ideology. In *Continuing Crisis in American Politics,* ed. Marian D. Irish. Englewood Cliffs, N.J., 1963.

McClosky, R. *The Modern Supreme Court.* Cambridge, Mass., 1973.

McCreary, E. A. *The Americanisation of Europe. Americans and American Companies in the Uncommon Market.* New York, 1964.

McDonald, F. *Novus Ordo Seclorum. The Intellectual Origins of the Constitution.* Lawrence, Kan., 1985.

McFarland, G. S. *Mugwumps, Morals and Politics, 1884–1920.* Amherst, Mass., 1975.

McGiffert, M., ed. *The Character of Americans.* Homewood, Ill., 1964.

McLoughlin, W. G. *Revivals, Awakening, and Reform: An Essay on Religion and Social Change in America, 1607–1977.* Chicago, 1978.

McMahon, A. W., ed. *Federalism.* New York, 1955.

McNeill, W. H. *The Pursuit of Power, Technology, Armed Force and Society Since A.D. 1000.* Chicago, 1983.

Meadows, D. V. D., Zahn, E., and Milling, P. *The Limits of Growth.* New York, 1972.

Meier, C. *Res publica Amissa, Eine Studie zu Verfassung und Geschichte der späten römischen Republik.* Frankfurt, 1980.

Meinecke, F. *Die Idee der Staatsräson in der neueren Geschichte.* Munich, 1927.

Melandri, P. *La politique extérieure des Etats-Unis de 1945 à nos jours.* Paris, 1982.

Merk, F. *Manifest Destiny and Mission in American History.* New York, 1963.

Mesick, J. L. *The English Traveler in America, 1785–1835.* New York, 1922.

Mewes, H. *Einführung in das politische System der USA.* Heidelberg, 1986.

Meyer-Abich, K. M. *Wege zum Frieden mit der Natur, Praktische Naturphilosophie für die Umweltpolitik.* Munich, 1984.

Meyers, M. *The Jacksonian Persuasion.* Stanford, Calif., 1957.

Michalka, W., ed. *Die nationalsozialistische Machtergreifung.* Paderborn, 1984.

Miller, J. C. *Hamilton: Portrait in Paradox.* New York, 1969.

Miller, P. *Jonathan Edwards.* New York, 1949.

Miller, P. *Roger Williams, His Contribution to the American Tradition,* Indianapolis, Ind., 1953.

Miller, P. *Errand into the Wilderness.* Cambridge, Mass., 1956.

Miller, P., and Johnson, T. H. *The Puritans.* New York, 1938.

Mises, L. von. *Omnipotent Government.* New Haven, Conn., 1944.

Mitscherlich, M. *Die friedfertige Frau.* Frankfurt am Main, 1985.

Mohler, A. *Die Konservative Revolution in Deutschland 1918–1932.* Darmstadt, 1972.

Moltmann, G. *Revisionist Historiography in the United States and Its Importance for German-American Relations in the Weimar Period, Germany and the USA 1918–1933.* Braunschweig, 1968.

Moltmann, G. Deutscher Anti-Amerikanismus heute und früher. In *Vom Sinn der Geschichte*, ed. F. Otmar. Stuttgart, 1976.

Moltmann, G., ed. *Germans to America. 300 Years of Immigration, 1683–1983*. Stuttgart, 1982.

Momigliano, A. *Alien Wisdom: The Limits of Hellenization*. Cambridge, 1975.

Monnet, J. *Memoirs*. Garden City, N.Y., 1978.

Moore, B. *Social Origins of Dictatorship and Democracy*. Boston, 1967.

Morgan, E. S., ed. *The American Revolution: Two Centuries of Interpretation*. Englewood Cliffs, N.J., 1965.

Morgan, E. S. *The Puritan Family*. New York, 1966.

Morgan, E. S. *The Birth of the Republic, 1763–89*. Chicago, 1977.

Morgan, H. W., ed. *The Gilded Age*. Syracuse, N.Y., 1970.

Morgenthau, H. J. *In Defense of the National Interest*. New York, 1951.

Morgenthau, H. J. *The Purpose of American Politics*. New York, 1960.

Morgenthau, H. J. *Truth and Power*. London, 1970.

Morgenthau, H. J., and Hein, D. *Essays on Lincoln's Faith and Politics*. Washington, D.C., 1983.

Morris, G. S. *Hegel's Philosophy of the State and of History*. Chicago, 1887.

Morris, R. B. *The American Revolution Reconsidered*. New York, 1967.

Moser, H. D., McPherson, S., and Bryan, C. F., Jr., eds. *The Papers of Andrew Jackson, 1804–1813*, vol. 2. Knoxville, Tenn., 1984.

Mosse, G. L. *Nazi Culture: Intellectual, Cultural, and Social Life of the Third Reich*. New York, 1966.

Mosse, G. L., ed. *Literature and Politics in the Twentieth Century*. New York, 1967.

Mosse, G. L. *Towards the Final Solution*. New York, 1978.

Mosse, G. L. *Masses and Man, Nationalist and Fascist Perceptions of Reality*. New York, 1980.

Motley, J. L. *Democracy, the Climax of Political Progress and the Destiny of Advanced Races: An Historical Essay*. London, 1869.

Motley, J. L. *History of the United Netherlands from the Death of William the Silent to the Twelve Year's Truce*. London, 1901, vol. 1.

Motley, J. L. Historic Progress and American Democracy. In *Representative Selections, with Introduction, Bibliography, and Notes*, ed. Chester P. Higby and B. T. Schantz. New York, 1939.

Mowry, G. E. *The Era of Theodore Roosevelt and the Birth of Modern America, 1900–1912*. New York, 1958.

Muchembled, R. *Kultur des Volkes. Kultur der Eliten. Die Geschichte einer erfolgreichen Verdrängung*. Stuttgart, 1982.

Müller, H. J. *Out of Night. A Biologist's View of the Future*. New York, 1935.

Müller, R. *Die Konzeption des Fortschritts im antiken Geschichtsdenken*. Berlin, 1983.

Mullin, G. W. *Flight and Rebellion, Slave Resistance in Eighteenth Century Virginia*. New York, 1972.

Multhoff, R. *Das Bild der Deutschen Geschichte im Spiegel amerikanischer Geschichtslehrbücher*. The Alumni Funnel: US Educational Commission in the Federal Republic of Germany, vol. 2, no. 1, 1960.

Mumford, L. *Values for Survival*. New York, 1946.

Münsterberg, H. *Die Amerikaner*. Berlin, 1912. 2 vols.

Myrdal, G. *An American Dilemma, The Negro Problem and American Democracy.* New York, 1944.

Nagel, P. C. *One Nation Indivisible. The Union in American Thought, 1776–1861.* New York, 1964.

Nagel, P. C. *This Sacred Trust. American Nationality, 1789–1898.* New York, 1971.

Nash, G. H. *The Conservative Intellectual Movement in America since 1945.* New York, 1976.

Nash Smith, H. *Virgin Land: The American West as Symbol and Myth.* Cambridge, Mass., 1970.

National Institute of Mental Health. *Television and Behaviour. Ten Years of Scientific Progress and Implications for the Eighties.* Washington, D.C., 1982.

Nef, J. U. *War and Human Progress, An Essay on the Rise of Industrial Civilization.* Cambridge, Mass., 1950.

Nef, J. U. *Western Civilization since the Renaissance. Peace, War, Industry, and the Arts.* New York, 1963.

Negley, G., and Patrick, J. M. *The Quest for Utopia: An Anthology of Imaginary Societies.* New York, 1952.

Negt, O. *Lebendige Arbeit, enteignete Zeit. Politische und Kulturelle Dimensionen des Kampfes um die Arbeitszeit.* Frankfurt am Main, 1984.

Neill, A. S. *Summerhill: A Radical Approach to Child Rearing.* New York, 1960.

Nell, O. *Acting on Principle: An Essay on Kantian Ethics.* New York, 1975.

Nelson, M., ed. *The Presidency and the Political System.* Washington, D.C., 1984.

Neumann, F. L. The Social Sciences. In F. L. Neumann et al., *The Cultural Migration: The European Scholar in America.* Philadelphia, 1953.

Neumüller, M. *Liberalismus und Revolution, Das Problem der Revolution in der deutschen liberalen Geschichtsschreibung des 19. Jahrhunderts.* Düsseldorf, 1973.

Neustadt, R. E. *Presidential Power: The Politics of Leadership from FDR to Carter.* New York, 1980.

Neustadt, R. E., and May, E. R. *Thinking in Time: The Uses of History for Decision Makers.* New York, 1986.

Nevins, A. *America through British Eyes.* New York, 1948.

Newhouse, J. *De Gaulle and the Anglo-Saxons.* London, 1970.

Newman, K. J. *Zerstörung und Selbstzerstörung der Demokratie. Europa 1918–1938.* Cologne, 1972.

Nie, H. H., Verba, S., and Petrocik, J. R. *The Changing American Voter.* Cambridge, Mass., 1976.

Niebuhr, R. *The Irony of American History.* New York, 1952.

Niebuhr, R. *Moral Man and Immoral Society, A Study in Ethics and Politics.* New York, 1960.

Niebuhr, R. The Protestant Movement and Democracy in the United States. In *The Shaping of American Religion,* ed. J. W. Smith and A. L. Jamison. Princeton, N.J., 1961.

Nipperdey, T. *Im Zwielicht der Geschichte. Vom Nutzen und Nachteil der Geschichte für das Leben.* Münster, 1985.

Nisbet, R. *Tradition and Revolt.* New York, 1968.

Nisbet, R. *History of the Idea of Progress.* New York, 1980.

Noble, D. W. *The Paradox of Progressive Thought.* Minneapolis, 1958.

Noelle-Neumann, E., and Strümpel, B. *Macht Arbeit krank, macht Arbeit glücklich*, Munich, 1984.

Nolte, E. *Marxismus und Industrielle Revolution*. Stuttgart, 1983.

Nordholt, J. W. S. The Impact of the American Revolution on the Dutch Republic. In *The Impact of the American Revolution Abroad*. Washington, D.C., 1976.

Nore, E. *Charles A. Beard: An Intellectual Biography*. Carbondale, Ill., 1983.

Norton, A. A. *Theodore Roosevelt*. Boston, 1980.

Nouailhat, Y.-H. *Histoire des doctrines politiques aux Etats-Unis*. Paris, 1977.

Nozick, R. *Anarchy, State and Utopia*. New York, 1974.

Nozick, R. *Philosophical Explanations*. Cambridge, Mass., 1982.

Nussbaum, B. *Das Ende unserer Zukunft*. Munich, 1983.

Oakeshott, M. *Rationalism in Politics*. London, 1962.

Oates, S. B. *Our Fiery Trial: Abraham Lincoln, John Brown, and the Civil War Era*. Amherst, Mass., 1979.

Oates, W. E., ed. *Financing the New Federalism. Revenue Sharing, Conditional Grants, and Taxation*. Baltimore, 1975.

Offe, C. *"Arbeitsgesellschaft." Strukturprobleme und Zukunftsperspektiven*. Frankfurt am Main, 1984.

Ogburn, W. F. *Social Change*. New York, 1922.

Öko-Institut, Projektgruppe ökologische Wirtschaft, ed. *Arbeiten im Einklang mit der Natur*. Freiburg, 1985.

Orfield, G. *Congressional Power: Congress and Social Change*. New York, 1975.

Ornstein, N. J. *Interest Groups, Lobbying and Policy Making*. Washington, D.C., 1978.

Ortega y Gasset, J. *The Revolt of the Masses*. Notre Dame, Ind., 1985.

Osgood, R. E. *Ideals and Self-Interest in America's Foreign Relations, The Great Transformation of the Twentieth Century*. Chicago, 1953.

Ostrom, V. *The Political Theory of a Compound Republic: A Reconstruction of the Logical Foundations of an American Democracy as Presented in The Federalist*. Blacksburg, Va., 1971.

Palme, O. Demokratischer Sozialismus und der Kampf der Vollbeschäftigung. In *Demokratischer Sozialismus in den 80er Jahren*, ed. R. Löwenthal. Cologne, 1979.

Palmer, J. L., and Sawhill, I. V., eds. *The Reagan Record, An Assessment of America's Changing Domestic Priorities*. Cambridge, Mass., 1984.

Palmer, R. R. *The Age of Democratic Revolution*. Princeton, N.J., 1959, vols. 1 and 2.

Papadakis, E. *The Green Movement in West Germany*. New York, 1984.

Parish, J. C. *The Emergence of the Idea of Manifest Destiny*. Los Angeles, 1932.

Parrington, V. L. *Main Currents in American Thought*. Vol. 1: *The Colonial Mind, 1620–1800;* vol. 2: *The Romantic Revolution in America, 1800–1860;* vol. 3: *The Beginnings of Critical Realism in America, 1860–1920*. New York, 1927, 1930, 1954.

Pasquier, Y. *La coopération en Europe depuis 1945 présentée comme ressources pour l'enseignement de l'histoire, géographie et sciences civiques dans les écoles secondaires*. Strasbourg 1979. Doc. DECS, EGT, 79, 56 (Case-study on France, which was prepared for the Committee of Cultural Cooperation of the European Council.)

Passmore, J. *Man's Responsibility for Nature: Ecological Problems and Western Traditions*. London, 1974.

Paxton, R. O. *Europe in the Twentieth Century*. New York, 1975.

Pearce, R. H. *The Savages of America: A Study of the Indian and the Idea of Civilization.* Baltimore, 1965.

Pells, R. H. *The Liberal Mind in a Conservative Age: American Intellectuals in the 1940s and 1950s.* New York, 1985.

Perry, R. B. *Puritanism and Democracy.* Vols. 1 and 2. New York, 1944.

Perry, R. B. *Characteristically American.* New York, 1949.

Peterson, G. E. Federalism and the States: An Experiment in Decentralization. In *The Reagan Record, An Assessment of America's Changing Domestic Priorities,* ed. John Z. Palmer and Isabel V. Sawhill. Cambridge, Mass., 1984.

Pfaltzgraff, R. L., et al., ed. *The Greens of West Germany.* Cambridge, Mass., 1983.

Pflüger, F. *Die Menschenrechtspolitik der USA, Amerikanische Außenpolitik zwischen Idealismus und Realismus 1972–1982.* Munich, 1983.

Philbrick, F. S. *The Rise of the West, 1754–1830.* New York, 1965.

Phillips, J. A. *Machine Dreams.* New York, 1984.

Phillips, K. P. *Post-Conservative America, People, Politics, and Ideology in Time of Crisis.* New York, 1982.

Picht, G. *Mut zur Utopie.* Munich, 1969.

Pierce, Ch. *Principles of Philosophy.* Cambridge, Mass., 1931.

Pierson, G. W. *Tocqueville and Beaumont in America.* New York, 1938.

Piltz, T., ed. *Die Deutschen und die Amerikaner.* Munich, 1977.

Platon. Laws 923b. Manchester University Press, 1921, vol. 2.

Plessner, H. *Die verspätete Nation, Über die Verführbarkeit des bürgerlichen Geistes.* Stuttgart, 1959.

Pocock, J. G. A. *The Machiavellian Moment. Florentine Political Thought and the Atlantic Republican Tradition.* Princeton, N.J., 1975.

Podewills, C. Graf von, ed. *Tendenzwende, Zur geistigen Situation der Bundesrepublik.* Stuttgart, 1975.

Podhoretz, N. *The Present Danger, Do We Have the Will to Reverse the Decline of American Power?* New York, 1980.

Pohrdt, W. *Endstation.* Berlin, 1982.

Pole, J. R. *The Pursuit of Equality in American History.* Berkeley, Calif., 1978.

Pole, J. R. *The Gift of Government: Political Responsibility from the English Restoration to American Independence.* Athens, Ga., 1983.

Pollack, N. *The Populist Response to Industrial America.* Cambridge, Mass., 1962.

Pollard, S. *The Idea of Progress, History and Society.* New York, 1968.

Pollard, S., and Holmes, C. *The End of the Old Europe. 1914–1939,* New York, 1973.

Popper, K. *The Open Society and Its Enemies.* London, 1957.

Popper, K. *Objective Knowledge.* Oxford, 1972.

Popper, K. *Auf der Suche nach einer besseren Welt. Vorträge und Aufsätze aus dreißig Jahren.* Munich, 1984.

Porte, J., ed. *Ralph Waldo Emerson, Essays and Lectures.* Cambridge, 1984.

Postman, N. *Amusing Ourselves to Death.* New York, 1985.

Potter, D. M. *People of Plenty.* Chicago, 1954.

Pöttering, H.-G., ed. *Sicherheit in Freiheit für Europa, Plädoyer für eine europaische Sicherheitspolitik.* Bonn, 1988.

Pradt, D.-G.-F., Dufour de. *Des colonies et de la révolution actuelle de l'Amérique.* Paris, 1817. (English edition, London, 1817).

Pradt, D.-G.-F., Dufour de. *L'Europe et l'Amérique en 1821*. Paris, 1822. (2 parts.). (English edition, 1822).

President's Commission for the Study of Ethical Problems in Medicine and Biomedical and Behavioral Research. *On Screening and Counseling for Genetic Conditions*. Washington, D.C., 1983.

Presse und Informationsamt der Bundesregierung, ed. *Geschichte mahnt, 30. Jan. 1933– 30. Jan. 1983* (especially the speeches of R. von Weizsäcker, W. Brandt, and K. D. Bracher). Bonn, 1983.

Price, D. *Observations on the Importance of the American Revolution and the Means of Rendering it a Benefit to the World*. London, 1784.

Price, D. K. *The Scientific Estate*. Cambridge, Mass., 1965.

Price, D. K. *America's Unwritten Constitution: Science, Religion, and Political Responsibility*. Baton Rouge, La., 1983.

Pritchett, H. *The American Constitution*. New York, 1977.

Pross, H. *Die deutsche akademische Emigration nach den Vereinigten Staaten 1933– 1941*. Berlin, 1955.

Pye, L. W., and Verba, S., eds. *Political Culture and Political Development*. Princeton, N.J., 1966.

Quandt, S., ed. *Geschichtswissenschaft und Massenmedien*. Gießen, 1981.

Radistschew, A. N. *Reise von Petersburg nach Moskau*. Berlin, 1961.

Radkau, J. *Die deutsche Emigration in den USA. Ihr Einfluß auf die amerikanische Europapolitik 1933–1945*. Düsseldorf, 1971.

Rawls, J. *A Theory of Justice*. Cambridge, Mass., 1971.

Reagan, M. *The New Federalism*. New York, 1972.

Reeves, R. *American Journey: Travelling With Tocqueville in Search of America*. New York, 1982.

Reichel, P., ed. *Politische Kultur in Westeuropa. Bürger und Staaten in der Europäischen Gemeinschaft*. Frankfurt am Main, 1984.

Reill, P. H. *The German Enlightenment and the Rise of Historicism*. Berkeley, Calif., 1975.

Reinhold, M., ed. *The Classic Pages: Classical Reading of Eighteenth-Century Americans*. University Park, Pa. 1975.

Remini, R. V. *Andrew Jackson and the Course of American Freedom, 1822–1832*. New York, 1981. Vol. 2.

Remini, R. V. *Andrew Jackson and the Course of American Democracy 1833–1845*. New York, 1984. Vol. 3.

Rémond, P. *Les Etats-Unis devant l'opinion française 1815–1852*. Paris, 1962.

Rescher, N. *Wissenschaftlicher Fortschritt, Eine Studie über die Ökonomie der Forschung*. Ed. Roland Posner. Berlin, 1982.

Revel, J.-F. *Without Marx or Jesus*. New York, 1971.

Revel, J.-F. *The Totalitarian Temptation*. New York, 1977.

Revel, J.-F. *How Democracies Perish*. New York, 1984.

Rhodes, J. M. *The Hitler Movement, A Modern Millenarian Revolution*. Stanford, Calif., 1980.

Ribeiro, D. *Der Zivilisatorische Prozeß*. Ed. H. R. Sonntag. Frankfurt am Main, 1971.

Richonnier, M. *Les Métamorphoses de l'Europe de 1764 à 2001*. Paris, 1985.

Richter, E. *Die erste Direktwahl des Europäischen Parlaments, Motive, Wahlkampf, Resultate und Perspektiven*. Bonn, 1981.

Riedl, R. *Die Strategie der Genesis*. Munich, 1984.

Riesman, D. *The Lonely Crowd, A Study of the Changing American Character*. New Haven, Conn., 1950.

Riesman, D. *Abundance for What?* New York, 1964.

Rischin, M., ed. *The American Gospel of Success: Individualism and Beyond*. Chicago, 1965.

Ritter, A., ed. *Deutschlands literarisches Amerikabild*. Hildesheim, 1977.

Roazen, P. *Freud, Political and Social Thought*. New York, 1968.

Robbins, C. *The Eighteenth Century Commonwealth Man*. New York, 1968.

Robertson, J. O. *American Myth, American Reality*. New York, 1982.

Robinson, J. H. *The New History, Essays Illustrating the Modern Historical Outlook*. New York, 1912.

Rockefeller, N. A. *The Future of Federalism*. New York, 1963.

Rockman, B. A. *The Leadership Question: The Presidency and the American System*. New York, 1984.

Rodriguez, M. The Impact of the American Revolution on the Spanish- and Portuguese-Speaking World. In *The Impact of the American Revolution Abroad*. Washington, D.C., 1976.

Röhrich, W. *Die verspätete Demokratie. Zur politischen Kultur der Bundesrepublik Deutschland*. Cologne, 1983.

Romilly, J. de. Thucidide et l'Idée de Progrès. In *Annali della Scuola Normale Superiore di Pisa*, Ser. 2, 1966.

Romilly, J. de. Der Optimismus des Thukydides und das Urteil des Historikers über Perikles (Thuk. II 65). In *Perikles und seine Zeit*, ed. G. Wirth, Darmstadt, 1979.

Romoser, G. K., and Wallach, P., eds. *West German Politics in the Mid-Eighties—Crisis and Continuity*. New York, 1985.

Roosevelt, T. *The Winning of the West*. New York, 1906. 4 vols.

Roosevelt, T. The New Nationalism (1910). In *An American Primer*, ed. Daniel J. Boorstin. New York, 1966.

Roosevelt, T. *Realizable Ideals*. San Francisco, 1911.

Rorvik, D. *In This Image: The Cloning of a Man*. New York, 1978.

Rossiter, C. *Seedtime of the Republic, The Origins of the American Tradition of Political Liberty*. New York, 1953.

Rossiter, C. *Conservatism in America*. New York, 1955.

Rossiter, C. *The American Presidency*. New York, 1960.

Rossiter, C. *The American quest, 1790–1860. An Emerging Nation in Search of Identity, Unity, and Modernity*. New York, 1971.

Rostand, J. *L'homme*. Paris, 1961.

Rostock, M. *Die antike Theorie der Organisation staatlicher Macht*. Meisenheim, 1975.

Rostow, W. W. The National Style. In *The American Style: Essays in Value and Performance*, ed. Elting E. Morison. New York, 1958.

Rostow, W. W. *The United States in the World Arena: An Essay in Recent History*. New York, 1960.

Rostow, W. W. *Politics and the Stages of Economic Growth*. London, 1971.

Rostow, W. W. Lyndon Johnson, 1908–1973. Unpublished Manuscript, 1982.

Rostow, W. W. *The Barbaric Counter-Revolution, Cause and Cure*. London, 1984.

Roszack, T. *The Making of a Counterculture: Reflections on the Technocratic Society and Its Youthful Opposition*. London, 1969.

Roth, J. J. *The Cult of Violence: Sorel and the Sorelians.* Berkeley, Calif., 1980.

Roth, W. *Der Weg aus der Krise, Umrisse einer sozialökologischen Marktwirtschaft.* Munich, 1985.

Rothenberg, R. *The Neoliberals: Creating the New American Politics.* New York, 1984.

Rothschild, J., and Wolf, S. B. *The Children of the Counterculture.* New York, 1976.

Rush, B. *Three Lectures upon Animal Life.* Philadelphia, 1799.

Ruth, S. *Issues in Feminism: A First Course in Woman's Studies.* Boston, 1980.

Rüther, G., and Weigelt, K., eds. *Die Grünen und der Parlamentarismus.* Melle, 1985.

Rutkoff, P. M., and Scott, W. B. *New School, A History of the New School for Social Research.* New York, 1986.

Sabato, L. J. *Pac Power,* New York, 1984.

Sabine, G. H. *A History of Political Theory.* London, 1966.

Salomon, L. M., and Lund, M. S., eds. *The Reagan Presidency and the Governing of America.* Washington, D.C., 1984.

Salvadori, M., ed. *European Liberalism.* New York, 1972.

Samson, L. *Americanism as Surrogate Socialism.* In *Failure of a Dream?,* ed. John H. M. Laslett and S. M. Lipset. Garden City, N.Y., 1974.

Sanford, C. L. *The Quest for Paradise. Europe and the American Moral Imagination.* Urbana, Ill., 1961.

Santayana, G. *Winds of Doctrine.* New York, 1913.

Sauer, W., ed. *Der dressierte Arbeiter, Geschichte und Gegenwart der industriellen Arbeitswelt.* Munich, 1984.

Sauzay, B. *Le Vertige Allemand.* Paris, 1985.

Saveth, E. *American Historians and European Immigrants, 1875–1925.* New York, 1948.

Schaff, P. *America: A Sketch of Its Political, Social, and Religious Character.* Cambridge, Mass., 1961.

Schapiro, L. *Totalitarianism.* London, 1972.

Schell, J. *The Fate of the Earth,* New York, 1982.

Schelsky, H. *Die skeptische Generation, Eine Soziologie der deutschen Jugend.* Düsseldorf, 1957.

Schlesinger, A. *The Age of Jackson.* Boston, 1945.

Schlesinger, A. *The Imperial Presidency.* New York, 1974.

Schlesinger, A. *The Birth of a Nation: A Portrait of the American People on the Eve of Independence.* Boston, 1982.

Schlesinger, A. M. *The Vital Center, The Politics of Freedom.* Boston, 1949.

Schlesinger, A. M. *The Crisis of the Old Order, 1919–1933.* Boston, 1957.

Schlesinger, A. M. Richard Hofstadter. In *Pastmasters. Some Essays on American Historians,* ed. Marcus Cunliffe and Robin W. Winks. New York, 1969.

Schlesinger, A. M. *The Cycles of American History.* Boston, 1986.

Schmid, C. *Europa und die Macht des Geistes.* Bern, 1973.

Schmidt-Phiseldeck, L. von. *Europa und Amerika, oder die künftigen Verhältnisse der zivilisierten Welt.* Copenhagen, 1820.

Schmitt, C. *Die Diktatur.* Munich, 1921.

Schonfeld, W. R. *Obedience and Revolt: French Behaviour toward Authority.* Beverley Hills, Calif., 1976.

Schröder, H.-C. *Die Amerikanische Revolution.* Munich, 1982.

Schröder, H.-J. *Amerika als Modell? Das Dilemma der Washingtoner Außenpolitik ge-*

*genüber revolutionären Bewegungen im 20. Jahrhundert,* Ed. E. Angermann. Munich, 1979.

Schulz, E. *Die deutsche Nation in Europa, Internationale und historische Dimensionen.* Bonn, 1982.

Schulz, E., and Danylow, P. *Bewegung in der Deutschen Frage? Die ausländischen Besorgnisse über die Entwicklung in den beiden deutschen Staaten.* Bonn, 1985.

Schulze, H. *Weimar, Deutschland 1917–1933.* Berlin, 1983. (Vol. 4 of the 6-vol. series *Die Deutschen und ihre Nation.*)

Schumpeter, J. A. *Capitalism, Socialism and Democracy.* New York, 1942.

Schwabe, K. 200 Jahre amerikanische Unabhängigkeit: Jüngste Tendenzen der amerikanischen Historiographie in Erforschung und Deutung der amerikanischen Revolution. In *Geschichte in Wissenschaft und Unterricht* 28, 1977.

Schwan, A. *Weimar, Selbstpreisgabe einer Demokratie.* Düsseldorf, 1980.

Schwan, G. *Sozialismus in der Demokratie?* Stuttgart, 1982.

Schwartze, J., and Bieber, R., eds. *Eine Verfassung für Europa. Von der Europäischen Gemeinschaft zur Europäischen Union.* Baden-Baden, 1984.

Schweitzer, A. *Kultur und Ethik.* Munich, 1960.

Scott, W. B. *In Pursuit of Happiness: American Conceptions of Property from the Seventeenth to the Twentieth Century.* Bloomington, 1977.

Seidel, G. J. *The Crisis of Creativity.* Notre Dame, Ind., 1966.

Seidenberg, R. *Post-historic Man: An Inquiry.* Boston, 1957.

Seligman, E.R.A. *The Economic Interpretation of History.* New York, 1902.

Sennett, R. *The Fall of Public Man.* New York, 1978.

Servan-Schreiber, J. J. *The American Challenge.* New York, 1968.

Severini, E. *Vom Wesen des Nihilismus.* Stuttgart, 1983.

Shaffer, A. H. *The Politics of History, Writing the History of the American Revolution, 1783–1815.* Chicago, 1975.

Shannon, D. A., ed. *Progressivism and Postwar Dissillusionment 1898–1928.* New York, 1965.

Shannon, T. A. Manifest Destiny and Anti-Imperialists of 1898: An American Dissent. Ph.D. diss., Oxford University, 1983.

Shapiro, M. The Supreme Court from Warren to Burger. In *The New American Political System,* ed. Anthony King, Washington, D.C., 1979.

Shapiro, M. Judicial Activism. In *The Third Century, America as a Post-Industrial Society,* ed. S. M. Lipset. Chicago, 1980.

Shell, K. L. The American Impact on the German New Left. In *Contagious Conflict.* Leiden, 1973.

Shklar, J. N. *After Utopia: The Decline of Political Faith.* Princeton, N.J., 1957.

Silk, L. *The Research Revolution.* New York, 1960.

Simon, J. L. and Kahn, H. *The Resourceful Earth.* London, 1984.

Simpson, L. P., ed. *The Federalist Literary Mind.* Baton Rouge, La., 1962.

Sinowjew, A. *Kommunismus als Realität.* Zurich, 1981.

Skinner, B. F. *About Behaviorism.* New York, 1974.

Skinner, Q. *The Foundation of Modern Political Thought.* Vol. 1. Cambridge, 1978.

Sklair, L. *Sociology of Progress.* London, 1970.

Skotheim, R. *American Intellectual Histories and Historians,* Princeton, N.J., 1966.

Sloterdijk, P. *Kritik der zynischen Vernunft.* 2 vols. Frankfurt am Main, 1983.

Smith, D. M. *Mussolini: A Biography.* London, 1981.

Snow, C. P. *The Two Cultures and the Scientific Revolution.* Cambridge, 1959.

Snow, C. P. *Science and Government.* Cambridge, Mass., 1981.

Snyder, C. R., and Fromkin, H. L. *Uniqueness: The Human Pursuit of Difference,* New York, 1980.

Sola Pool, I. de. *Technologies of Freedom.* Cambridge, Mass., 1983.

Solomos, D. *Apanta.* Athens, 1965.

Sombart, W. *Why Is There no Socialism in the United States?* Foreword by Michael Harrington. New York, 1976. Originally published as *Warum gibt es in den Vereinigten Staaten keinen Sozialismus?* (Tübingen, 1906).

Sontag, R. J. *A Broken World 1919–1939.* New York, 1971.

Sontheimer, K. *Zeitenwende? Die Bundesrepublik Deutschland zwischen alter und alternativer Politik.* Hamburg, 1983.

Sorel, G. *Les Illusions du progrès.* Paris, 1908.

Sorman, G. *Der neue Liberalismus. Die Macht des Individuums in der verwalteten Gesellschaft.* Düsseldorf, 1986.

Sparks, J., ed. *Diplomatic Correspondence of the American Revolution.* Boston, 1829–30. 12 vols.

Späth, L. *Wende in die Zukunft, Die Bundesrepublik auf dem Weg in die Informationsgesellschaft.* Hamburg, 1985.

Spencer, H. *Social Statics,* New York 1865.

Spengler, O. *The Decline of the West.* New York, 1932. Originally published as *Der Untergang des Abendlandes.* (Munich 1922–23).

Sperry, R. *Naturwissenschaft und Wertenscheidung.* Munich, 1985.

Spink, J. S. *French Free Thought from Gassendi to Voltaire.* London, 1960.

Stark, W. *America, Ideal and Reality, The United States of 1776 in Contemporary European Philosophy.* Ed. Karl Mannheim. London, 1947.

Stein, H. *Presidential Economics, The Making of Economic Policy from Roosevelt to Reagan and Beyond.* New York, 1984.

Stein, J. B. *From H-Bomb to Star Wars: The Politics of Strategic Decision Making.* Lexington, Mass., 1984.

Steiner, G. Y. *Constitutional Inequality: The Political Fortunes of the Equal Rights Amendment.* Washington, D.C., 1985.

Steinfels, P. *The Neoconservatives, The Men Who Are Changing America's Politics.* New York, 1980.

Stent, G. S. *The Coming of the Golden Age, A View of the End of Progress.* Garden City, N.Y., 1962.

Stern, F., ed. *The Varieties of History, From Voltaire to Present.* Cleveland, 1956.

Stern, F. *The Politics of Cultural Despair, A Study in the Rise of the Germanic Ideology.* Berkeley, Calif., 1961.

Stern, F. *The Failure of Illiberalism, Essays on the Political Culture of Modern Germany.* New York, 1972.

Stern, K. *Grundideen europäisch-amerikanischer Verfassungsstaatlichkeit.* Berlin, 1984.

Sternsher, B. *Consensus, Conflict, and American Historians.* Bloomington, Ind., 1975.

Stoessinger, J. G. *Crusaders and Pragmatists, Movers of Modern American Foreign Policy.* New York, 1979.

Stojanovic, S. *Kritik und Zukunft des Sozialismus.* Munich, 1970.

Stone, N. *Europe Transformed 1878–1919.* Glasgow, 1983.

Storing, H. J. *What the Anti-Federalists Were For.* Chicago, 1981.

Storing, H. J., ed. *The Anti-Federalist: Writings by the Opponents of the Constitution.* Chicago, 1985.

Stourzh, G. Die deutschsprachige Emigration in den Vereinigten Staaten: Geschichtswissenschaft und politische Wissenschaft. In *Jahrbuch für Amerikastudien,* vols. 10 and 11, 1965.

Stourzh, G. *Alexander Hamilton and the Idea of Republican Government.* Stanford, Calif., 1970.

Strauss, L. *Natural Right and History.* Chicago, 1953.

Strauss, L. *Thoughts on Machiavelli.* Glencoe, Ill., 1958.

Stromberg, R. N. *After Everything: Western Intellectual History since 1945.* New York, 1975.

Stromberg, R. N. *An Intellectual History of Europe.* Englewood Cliffs, N.J., 1975.

Strout, C. *The Pragmatic Revolt in American History: Carl Becker and Charles Beard.* New Haven, Conn. 1958.

Struve, W. *Elites against Democracy, Leadership Ideals in Bourgeois Political Thought in Germany, 1890–1933.* Princeton, N.J., 1973.

Strzelewicz, W., and Wiebecke, F. Bildungspolitik. In *Die Zweite Republik, 25 Jahre Bundesrepublik Deutschland—eine Bilanz.* Ed. R. Löwenthal and H.-P. Schwarz. Stuttgart, 1974–79.

Stürmer, M. *Dissonanzen des Fortschritts, Essays über Geschichte und Politik in Deutschland.* Munich, 1986.

Suzman, R. Social Changes in America and the Modernization of Personality. In *We the People,* ed. Gordon DiRenzo. Westport, Conn., 1977.

Syme, R. *The Roman Revolution.* Oxford, 1952.

Szczesny, G. *Vom Unheil der totalen Demokratie, Erfahrungen mit dem Fortschritt.* Munich, 1983.

Talmon, J. L. *The Myth of the Nation and the Vision of Ideological Polarization in the Twentieth Century.* London, 1981.

Taylor, C. *Hegel.* Cambridge, 1975.

Taylor, P. *The Limits of European Integration.* New York, 1983.

Teggart, F. J. *Theory and Processes of History* (summarized edition with a foreword by Kenneth Bock). Berkeley, Calif., 1941. (The Idea of Progress and the Foundations of the Comparative Method.)

Teilhard de Chardin, P. *The Phenomenon of Man.* New York, 1959.

Thelin, B. *Cooperation in Europe since 1945 as Presented in Resources for the Teaching of History, Geography and Civics in Secondary Schools.* Strasbourg, 1979. Doc. DECS/EGT/79/60. (Case-study on Sweden, which was prepared for the Committee of Cultural Cooperation of the European Council.)

Thomas, J. L. *Alternative America, Henry George, Edward Bellamy, Henry Demarest Lloyd and the Adversary Tradition.* Cambridge, Mass., 1983.

Thomas, M. The Idea of Progress in the Writings of Franklin, Freneau, Barlow, and Rush. Ph.D. diss., University of Wisconsin, 1938.

Thompson, K. W. *Political Realism and the Crisis of World Politics, An American Approach to Foreign Policy.* Princeton, N.J., 1960.

Thompson, K. W. *The President and the Public Philosophy.* Baton Rouge, La., 1981.

Thompson, K. W., ed. *The American Presidency, Principles and Problems.* Washington, D.C., 1984.

Thompson, K. W. *Moralism and Morality in Politics and Diplomacy*. Lanham, Md., 1985. (The Credibility of Institutions, Policies and Leadership Series, vol. 1.)

Thompson, K. W. *The American Presidency, Perspectives from Abroad*. Lanham, Md., 1986.

Thonssen, L., ed. *Representative American Speeches*. Vol. 32, no. 4. New York, 1960.

Thoreau, H. D. Civil Disobedience. In *Thoreau: Walden and Other Writings*, ed. Joseph Wood Krutch. New York, 1980.

Thorndike, L. *A History of Magic and Experimental Science*. New York, 1923–58. 8 vols.

Thurow, C. *The Zero-Sum-Society, Distribution and the Possibilities for Economic Change*. New York, 1980.

Tillich, P. *Politische Bedeutung der Utopie im Leben der Völker*. Berlin, 1951.

Tirman, J., Garwin, R. L., Gottfried, K., and Kendall, H. W. *The Fallacy of Star Wars*. New York, 1984. (A report from the Union of Concerned Scientists.)

Tocqueville, A. de. *Democracy in America*. Ed. P. Bradley. New York, 1945. Vols. 1 and 2.

Tolstoy, L. *What Is Art? and Essays on Art*. Oxford, 1959.

Topitsch, E., and Salamun, K. *Ideologie*. Munich, 1972.

Touraine, A. *Die postindustrielle Gesellschaft*. Frankfurt am Main, 1982.

Toynbee, A. J. *A Study of History*. 2 vols. New York, 1947.

Toynbee, A. J. *Civilization on Trial*. New York, 1958.

Toynbee, A. J. *America and the World Revolution*. London, 1962.

Trenner, R., ed. *E. L. Doctorow: Essays and Conversations*. Princeton, N.J., 1983.

Tresolini, R. J., and Shapiro, M. *American Constitutional Law*. London, 1970.

Troeltsch, E. *Protestantism and Progress, A Historical Study of the Relation of Protestantism to the Modern World*. Boston, 1958.

Troge, A. *Technik und Umwelt*. Cologne, 1985.

Trollope, F. M. *Domestic Manners of the Americans*. New York, 1949.

Trommler, F., ed. *Amerika und die Deutschen, Bestandsaufnahme einer 300 jährigen Geschichte*. Opladen, 1986.

Trueblood, E. J. *The Dawn of the Post-Modern Era*. New York, 1954.

Tsongas, P. *The Road from Here, Liberalism and Realities in the 1980s*. New York, 1982.

Tucker, R. *Intervention and the Reagan Doctrine, New " 'Rollback' Revisited: A Reagan Doctrine for Insurgent Wars?"* Washington, D.C., 1986.

Tucker, R. C. *The Marxian Revolutionary Idea*. London, 1970.

Tugwell, R. G., and Cronin, T. E., eds. *The Presidency Reappraised*. New York, 1978.

Turner, F. J. *The Frontier in American History*. New York, 1920.

Turner, J. *Without God, Without Creed. Origins of Unbelief in America*. Baltimore, 1985.

Tuveson, E. L. *Redeemer Nation: The Idea of America's Millenial Role*. Chicago, 1968.

Ulam, A. B. *Stalin, The Man and His Era*. New York, 1973.

Unger, I. *The Movement. A History of the American New Left, 1959–1972*. New York, 1974.

Utter, W. T. Vernon Louis Parrington. In *The Marcus W. Jernegan Essays in American Historiography*, ed. W. T. Hutchinson. Chicago, 1937.

Valenti, J. *A Very Human President*. New York, 1975.

Valjavec, F. *Die Entstehung des europäischen Konservatismus*. Ed. G. G. Schumann. Cologne, 1974.

Van Doren, C. *The Idea of Progress.* Ed. M. J. Adler. New York, 1967.

Vecoli, R. J. European Americans: From Immigrants to Ethnics. In *The Reinterpretation of American History and Culture,* ed. William H. Cartwright and Richard L. Watson. Washington, D.C., 1973.

Vegesack, T. von. *Die Macht und die Phantasie, Schriftsteller in den Revolutionen.* Hamburg, 1979.

Venohr, W., ed. *Die deutsche Einheit kommt bestimmt.* Bergisch-Gladbach, 1982.

Venturi, F. *Utopia and Reform in the Enlightenment.* Cambridge, 1971.

Verba, S. *The Civic Culture, Political Attitudes and Democracy in Five Nations.* Princeton, N.J., 1963.

Verba, S. Germany: The Remaking of Political Culture. In *Political Culture and Political Development,* ed. Lucian W. Pye and S. Verba. Princeton, N.J., 1966.

Verba, S., and Orren, G. R. *Equality in America, The View from the Top.* Cambridge, Mass., 1985.

Vernant, J.-P. *Die Entstehung des griechischen Denkens.* Frankfurt am Main, 1983.

Viereck, P. *Conservatism Revisited: The Revolt against Revolt.* New York, 1949.

Viereck, P. *The Unadjusted Man, A New Hero for Americans, Reflections on the Distinction Between Conforming and Conserving.* New York, 1956.

Vignes, G. T. *Six Months in America.* London, 1832. Vol. 2.

Viguerie, R. A. *The New Right: We're Ready to Lead.* Falls Church, Va., 1980.

Voegelin, E. *Über die Form des Amerikanischen Geistes.* Tübingen, 1928.

Volkommer, W. E. *American Government.* Englewood Cliffs, N.J., 1983.

Vollmer, A. "*. . . und wehrt Euch täglich! Bonn—ein Grünes Tagebuch.*" Gütersloh, 1984.

Vossler, O. *Die amerikanischen Revolutionsideale in ihrem Verhältnis zu den europäischen.* Munich, 1929.

Vouras, H. Y. *Hellenic Independence and America's Contribution to the Cause.* Putland, Vt., 1934.

Vovelle, M. *Die Französische Revolution—Soziale Bewegung und Umbruch der Mentalitäten (Ancien Régime, Aufklärung und Revolution,* vol. 7). Munich, 1982.

Wansey, H. *An Excursion to the United States of America, in the Summer 1794.* Salisbury, 1798.

Ward, J. W. *Andrew Jackson, Symbol for an Age.* New York, 1955.

Wasser, H. *Die Vereinigten Staaten von Amerika, Porträt einer Weltmacht.* Stuttgart, 1980.

Watkins, F. M. *The Political Tradition of the West: A Study in the Development of Modern Liberalism.* Cambridge, 1948.

Watt, D. C. American Anti-Colonialist Policies and the End of the European Colonial Empires 1941–1962. In *Contagious Conflict, The Impact of American Dissent on European Life,* ed. A.N.J. Den Hollander. Leiden, 1973.

Weaver, R. M. *Ideas Have Consequences.* Chicago, 1948.

Weber, A. *Farewell to European History.* New Haven, Conn., 1949.

Weber, E. J. *Varieties of Fascism, Doctrines of Revolution in the Twentieth Century.* London, 1964.

Weber, G. *Die europapolitische Rolle der Bundesrepublik Deutschland aus der Sicht ihrer EG Partner. Deutscher Sonderweg oder europäische Musterrolle?* Bonn, 1984.

Weber, M. *The Protestant Ethic and Spirit of Capitalism*. Ed. Talcott Parsons. New York, 1958.

Webster, C. *The Great Instauration: Science, Medicine and Reform 1626–1669*. London, 1975.

Wecter, D. *The Hero in America. A Chronicle of Hero-Worship*. New York, 1941.

Weems, M. L. *The Life of George Washington*. With various anecdotes equally honourable to himself and exemplary to his young countrymen. Philadelphia, 1808.

Wehler, H.-U. *Der Aufstieg des amerikanischen Imperialismus, Studien zur Entwicklung des Imperium Americanum 1865–1900*. Göttingen, 1974.

Wehler, H.-U. *200 Jahre amerikanische Revolution und moderne Revolutionsforschung*. Göttingen, 1976.

Wehler, H.-U. *Grundzüge der amerikanischen Außenpolitik 1750–1900*. Frankfurt am Main, 1984.

Weidenfeld, W. *Europa 2000, Zukunftsfragen der europäischen Einigung*. Munich, 1980.

Weidenfeld, W., ed. *Die Vermittlung der europäischen Einigung in Schule und Massenmedien*. Bonn, 1981.

Weidenfeld, W. *Ratlose Normalität. Die Deutschen auf der Suche nach sich selbst*. Zurich, 1984.

Weil, F. D. Post-Fascist Liberalism: The Development of Political Tolerance in West Germany Since World War II. Ph.D. diss., Harvard University, 1981.

Weinberg, A. K. *Manifest Destiny, A Study in Nationalist Expansionism in American History*. New York, 1963.

Weismer, S. *The Social Impact of Revenue Sharing*. New York, 1976.

Weizsäcker, C. F. von. Aufzeichnungen zur Begründung eines Max-Planck-Instituts zur Erforschung der Lebensbedingungen der wissenschaftlich-technischen Welt. In *Verfall der Philosophie*, ed. L. Grossner. Hamburg, 1971.

Weizsäcker, C. F. von. *Der bedrohte Friede, Politische Aufsätze 1945–1981*. Munich, 1981.

Weizsäcker, C. F. von.*Wahrnehmung der Neuzeit*. Munich, 1983. (Articles from 1945–83.)

Weizsäcker, R. von. *Die deutsche Geschichte geht weiter*. Berlin, 1983.

Weizsäcker, R. von. *Von Deutschland aus*. Berlin, 1985.

Welland, D., ed. *The United States*. London, 1974.

Wellek, R. *Confrontations: Studies in the Intellectual and Literary Relations Between Germany, England and the United States During the Nineteenth Century*. Princeton, N.J., 1965.

Wellmer, A. *Zur Dialektik von Moderne und Postmoderne, Vernunftkritik nach Adorno*. Frankfurt am Main, 1985.

Welter, R. *The Mind of America, 1820–1860*. New York, 1975.

Wendorf, R. *Zeit und Kultur*. Opladen, 1980.

Whitaker, R. W., ed. *The New Right Papers*. New York, 1982.

White, J. The Americans on Herbert Spencer: Some Reaction to His Social and Evolutionary Thought 1860–1940. Ph.D. diss., Hull University, 1975.

White, K. D. *Greek and Roman Technology*. Ithaca, N.Y., 1983.

White, L. The Historical Roots of Our Ecology Crisis. In *Dynamo and Virgin Reconsidered, Essays in the Dynamism of Western Culture*. Cambridge, Mass., 1968.

White, M. *The Philosophy of the American Revolution*. New York, 1978.

Whitney, L. *Primitivism and the Idea of Progress*. Baltimore, 1934.

Wildavsky, A. *American Federalism in Perspective*. Boston, 1967.

Williams, R. *Culture and Society 1780–1950*. New York, 1958.

Williams, W. A. *The Tragedy of American Diplomacy*. New York, 1962.

Williams, W. A. *America Confronts a Revolutionary World, 1776–1976*. New York, 1976.

Wills, G. *Inventing America. Jefferson's Declaration of Independence*. New York, 1978.

Wills, G. *Cincinnatus: George Washington and the Enlightenment*. Garden City, N.Y., 1984.

Wilson, R. J., ed. *Darwinism and the American Intellectual*. Homewood, Ill., 1967.

Wilson, W. *Constitutional Government in the United States (1908)*. New York, 1961.

Wilson, W. *The New Freedom*. New York, 1913.

Windt, T. *Presidential Rhetoric (1961–1980)*. Dubuque, Iowa, 1980.

Winter, K. *Das europäische Bildungswesen im Prozeß seiner Internationalisierung*. Weinheim, 1980.

Wirsing, G. *Der maßlose Kontinent*. Jena, 1942.

Wirth, G., ed. *Perikles und seine Zeit*. Darmstadt, 1979.

Wirth, G., ed. *Romanitas-Christianitas, Untersuchungen zur Geschichte und Literatur der römischen Kaiserzeit* (Festschrift for Johannes Straub). Berlin, 1982.

Wolfers, A., and Martin, L., eds. *The Anglo-American Tradition in Foreign Affairs*. New Haven, Conn., 1956.

Wolff, R. P. *The Poverty of Liberalism*. Boston, 1968.

Wolfinger, R. E., ed. *Readings in American Political Behavior*. Englewood Cliffs, N.J., 1966.

Wood, G. S. *The Creation of the American Republic, 1776–1787*. Chapel Hill, N.C., 1969.

Wrage, E. J., and Baskerville, B., eds. *Contemporary Forum, American Speeches on Twentieth-Century Issues*. New York, 1962.

Wust, K., and Moos, H., eds. *300 Jahre deutsche Einwanderer in Nordamerika*. Munich, 1983.

Yankelovich, D. *New Rules*. New York, 1981.

Yartz, F. J., Hassel, D. J., and Larson, A. L. *Progress and the Crisis of Man*. Chicago, 1976.

York, H. F. *The Advisors: Oppenheimer, Teller, and the Superbomb*. San Francisco, 1976.

Young, A. F., ed. *Dissent-Explorations in the History of American Radicalism*. De Kalb, Ill., 1968.

Ziff, L. *Puritanism in America, New Culture in a New World*. New York, 1974.

Zinn, H. *Politics of History*. Boston, 1970.

Zinn, H. *A People's History of the United States*. New York, 1980.

Zuckerman, H. *Scientific Elite: Nobel Laureates in the United States*. New York, 1977.

## PERIODICALS

Adams, F. B. The New Industrial Revolution. *Atlantic Monthly* 87 (February 1901).

Adams, F. B. The American Democratic Ideal. *Yale Review* 5 (January 1916).

Adams, H. B. Jared Sparks and Alexis de Tocqueville. *John Hopkins University Studies in Historical and Political Science* 16, no. 12 (1898).

Almeder, R. F. Science and Idealism. *Philosophy of Science* 40 (1973).

Alter, P. Nationalbewußtsein und Nationalstaat der Deutschen. *Aus Politik und Zeitgeschichte,* B 1/86 (January 4, 1986).

Angermann, E. Der deutsche Frükonstitutionalismus und das amerikanische Vorbild. *Historische Zeitschrift* 219 (1974).

Appleby, J. America as a Model for the Radical French Reformers of 1789. *William and Mary Quarterly,* Series 3, no. 28 (1971).

Aron, R. Nations and Ideologies. *Encounter* 4 (1955).

Ashcraft, R. Ideology and Class in Hobbes' Political Theory *Political Theory,* 6, no. 1 (February 1978).

Bailey, T. A. The Mythmakers of American History. *Journal of American History* 55 (June 1968).

Bailyn, B. Political Experience and Enlightenment Ideas in Eighteenth-Century America. *American Historical Review* 67 (January 1962).

Beard, C. Written History as an Act of Faith. *American Review* 39 (January 1934).

Beard, C., and Vogts, A. Currents of Thought in Historiography. *American Historical Review* 42 (April 1937).

Behrmann, G. C. Geschichte und aktuelle Struktur des Antiamerikanismus. Aus Politik und Zeitgeschichte, B 29–30 (1984).

Bell, D. Socialism: The Dream and the Reality. *Antioch Review* 12 (March 1952).

Benda, E. Erprobung der Menschenwürde am Beispiel der Humangenetik. *Aus Politik und Zeitgeschichte,* B 3/85 (January 19, 1985).

Bercovitch, S. The Typology of America's Mission. *American Quarterly* 25 (1978).

Bernstein, B. J. Shatterer of Worlds, Hiroshima and Nagasaki. *Bulletin of the Atomic Scientists* 31, no. 10 (1975).

Bickel, A. M. Close of the Warren Era. *The New Republic* (July 12, 1969).

Bracher, K. D. Der "Frontier-Gedanke": Motiv des amerikanischen Fortschrittsbewußtseins, Ein ideologienkritischer Versuch. *Zeitschrift für Politik* 2 (1955).

Bracher, K. D. Europa zwischen National- und Weltpolitik: Historische Wandlungen und politische Entscheidungen. *Integration* (March 1980).

Bracher, K. D. Zeitgeschichtliche Erfahrungen als aktuelles Problem. *Aus Politik und Zeitgeschichte,* (March 14, 1987).

Brasche, V. Strukturwandel am Arbeitsmarkt. *Aus Politik und Zeitgeschichte,* B 45/84 (November 10, 1984).

Bredow, W. von. Friedensbewegung und Deutschlandpolitik. *Aus Politik und Zeitgeschichte,* B 46/83, (November 19, 1983).

Bryan, W. J. Individualism Versus Socialism. *Century Magazine* 71 (1906).

Bullinger, D. Die Neuen Technologien. *Aus Politik und Zeitgeschichte,* B 4/85 (January 26, 1985).

Casper, J. D. The Supreme Court and National Policy Making. *American Political Science Review* 70, no. 1, (1976).

Ceaser, J. W., Thurow, G. E., Tulis, J., and Bessette, J. M. The Rise of the Rhetorical Presidency. *Presidential Studies Quarterly* 11, no. 2 (Spring 1981).

Chambers, C. A. The Belief in Progress in Twentieth-Century America. *Journal of the History of Ideas* 19 (1958).

Craig, G. A. The War of the German Historians. *The New York Review* (January 15, 1987).

Cronin, T. E. Thinking and Learning about Leadership. *Presidential Studies Quarterly* 14, no. 1 (Winter 1984).

Cronin, T. E., and Hochman, W. R. Franklin D. Roosevelt and the American Presidency. *Presidential Studies Quarterly* 15, no. 2 (Spring 1985).

Crowe, C. The Emergence of Progressive History. *Journal of the History of Ideas* 27 (1966).

Dahrendorf, R. European Sociology and the American Self-Image. *European Journal of Sociology* 2 (1961).

Dana, J. D. Science and the Scientific Schools. *American Journal of Education* 2 (September 1956).

Delbanco, A. The Puritan Errand Re-Viewed. *Journal of American Studies* 18 (December 1984).

Delmage, R. E. The American Idea of Progress, 1750–1800. *Proceedings of the American Philosophical Society* 91 (1947).

Diamond, M. Democracy and the Federalist. A Reconsideration of the Framer's Intent. *American Political Science Review* 53 (March 1959).

Eisenhower, D. D. Some Thoughts on the Presidency. *Reader's Digest*, 1968.

Ekirch, A. A. Parrington and the Decline of American Liberalism. *American Quarterly* 3 (1951).

Ellis, J. Habits of Mind and an American Enlightenment. *American Quarterly* 28 (1976).

Everett, E. Affairs of Greece. *North American Review* 17 (October 1823).

Fay, S. B. The Idea of Progress. *American Historical Review* 52 (January 1947).

Finley, M. I. The Freedom of the Citizen in the Greek World. *Talanta* 7 (1975–76).

Fiske, J. A Century's Progress in Science. *Atlantic Monthly* 78 (July 1986).

Fläming, C. Die genetische Manipulation des Menschen. *Aus Politik und Zeitgeschichte*, B 3/85 (January 19, 1985).

Fontaine, A. The Real Divisions of Europe. *Foreign Affairs* no. 2 (January 1971).

Ford, G. R. Congress, The Presidency and National Security Policy. *Presidential Studies Quarterly* 16, no. 2 (Spring 1986).

Freund, L. The New American Conservatism and European Conservatism. *Ethics* 66 (October 1955).

Gahl, L. L. Moral Courage: The Essence of Leadership. *Presidential Studies Quarterly* 14, no. 1 (Winter 1984).

Gibbens, V. E. Tom Paine and the Idea of Progress. *Pennsylvania Magazine of History and Biography* 66 (April 1942).

Glazer, N. The Limits of Social Policy. *Commentary* 52 (September 1971).

Goldmann, E. F. Hermann E. von Holst. Plumed Knight of American Historiography. *Mississippi Valley Historical Review* 23 (1936–37).

Goodson, I. European Cooperation in Education: Historical Background and Contemporary Experience. *European Journal of Teacher Education* no. 5 (1982).

Gray, C. B. Regulation and Federalism. *Yale Journal of Regulation* 1, no. 1 (1983).

Gueguen, J. A. Reflections on Statesmanship and the Presidency. *Presidential Studies Quarterly* 12, no. 4 (Fall 1982).

Gutman, H. G. Whatever Happened to History? *The Nation* (November 21, 1981).

Hamilton, L. H. National Security and National Defense. *Presidential Studies Quarterly* 15, no. 2 (Spring 1985).

Hartz, L. The Coming of Age of America. *American Political Science Review* 51 (June 1957).

Haskins, C. H. European History and American Scholarship. *American Historical Review* 2 (January 1923).

Henningsen, M. Das Amerika von Hegel, Marx und Engels. *Zeitschrift für Politik* 3 (1973).

Higby, C. P. The Present Status of Modern European History in the United States. *Journal of Modern History* 1 (March 1929).

Higham, J. The Cult of the "American Consensus." Homogenizing Our History. *Commentary* 27 (1959).

Higham, J. Beyond Consensus: The Historian as Moral Critic. *American Review* 67 (1962).

Himmelfarb, G. American Democracy and European Critics. *The Twentieth Century* 151 (1952).

Hirschfield, C. Brooks Adams and American Nationalism. *American Historical Review* 69, no. 2 (January 1964).

Hoffman-Lange, U. Eliteforschung in der Bundesrepublik Deutschland. *Aus Politik und Zeitgeschichte*, B 47/83 (November 26, 1983).

Hoffmann, S. Europe's Identity Crisis: Between the Past and America. *Daedalus* 93 (Fall 1964).

Hofstadter, R. Parrington and the Jeffersonian Tradition. *Journal of the History of Ideas* 2 (1941).

Holmes, R. L. The Sleep of Reason Brings Forth Monsters. *Harvard Magazine* 85, no. 4 (March–April 1983).

Hommes, U. Brauchen Wir die Utopie? *Aus Politik und Zeitgeschichte*, B 20 (1977).

Hoxie, R. G. The Presidency in the Constitutional Convention. *Presidential Studies Quarterly* 15, no. 1 (Winter 1985).

Hrbek, R. 30 Jahre Römische Verträge, Eine Bilanz der EG-Integration. *Aus Politik und Zeitgeschichte*, B 18/87 (May 2, 1987).

Huntington, S. P. Conservatism as an Ideology. *American Political Science Review* 5 (June 1957).

Huntington, S. P. Postindustrial Politics: How Benign Will It Be? *Comparative Politics* 6 (January 1974).

Iggers, G. G. The Image of Ranke in American and German Historical Thought. *History and Theory* 2, 1962.

Iggers, G. G. The Idea of Progress: A Critical Reassessment. *American Historical Review* 71 (October 1965).

Ingersoll, D. E. Machiavelli and Madison: Perspectives on Political Stability. *Political Science Quarterly* 85, no. 2 (June 1970).

*Integration.* January 1984. Special issue on the draft of the treaty of the European Parliament.

Is There a Crisis of Spirit in the West? A Conversation with Dr. Henry A. Kissinger and Senator Daniel P. Moynihan. *Public Opinion* (May/June 1978).

Joes, A. J. Eisenhower Revisionism: The Tide Comes in. *Presidential Studies Quarterly* 15, no. 3 (Summer 1985).

Johnston, M. The "New Christian Right" in American Politics. *The Political Quarterly* 53, no. 2 (April/June 1982).

Jonas, H. Reflections on Technology, Progress, and Utopia. *Social Research* 48, no. 3 (1981).

Jones, H. M. The Influence of European Ideas in Nineteenth-Century America. *American Literature* 7 (March 1935–January 1936).

Kahn, E. J. Paul Tsongas/Interview. *The Boston Magazine* 73, no. 2 (February 1981).

Kelley, R. Ideology and Political Culture from Jefferson to Nixon. *American Historical Review* 82, no. 3 (June 1977).

Kennan, G. F. The Sources of Soviet Conduct. *Foreign Affairs* 25 (1946–47).

Kennan, G. F. Morality and Foreign Policy. *Foreign Affairs* 64, no. 2 (Winter 1985–86).

Kern, H., and Schumann, M. Industriearbeit im Umbruch. *Aus Politik und Zeitgeschichte*, B 45/84 (November 10, 1984).

Ketchman, R. L. The Revival of Traditions and Conservatism in America. *Bulletin of the American Association of University Professors* 41 (Autumn 1955).

Kirkpatrick, J. Dictatorship and Double Standards. *Commentary* (November 1979).

Klein, J. Zur französischen Debatte über die europäische Verteidigung. *Integration* (February 1985).

Klindleberger, C. P. U.S. Foreign Economic Policy, 1776–1976. *Foreign Affairs* 55, no. 2 (January 1972).

Kohrs Campbell, K., and Jamieson, K. H. Inaugurating the Presidency. *Presidential Studies Quarterly* 15, no. 2 (Spring 1985).

Kondracke, M., and Scully, M. A. Liberalism's Brave Neo World?, Two Views. *Public Opinion* (April/May 1982).

Krakau, K. Die Lateinamerika-Politik der USA. *Aus Politik und Zeitgeschichte*, B 9/86 (March 1, 1986).

Laski, H. J. The Parliamentary and the Presidential Systems. *Public Administration Review* 3, no. 4 (Autumn 1943), and 4, no. 4 (Autumn 1944).

Libby, O. G. Some Pseudohistorians of the American Revolution. *Proceedings of the Wisconsin Academy of Sciences and Arts* 13 (1900).

Liberalism in America. *The Center-Magazine* 14, no. 2 (March/April 1981).

Livingston, C. D. The Televised Presidency. *Presidential Studies Quarterly* 16, no. 1 (Winter 1986).

Livingston, R. G. Once Again, The German Question. *German Studies Newsletter* no. 2 (April 1984).

Loss, R. Alexander Hamilton and the Modern Presidency: Continuity or Discontinuity? *Presidential Studies Quarterly* 12, no. 1 (Winter 1982).

Löwenthal, R. Reflections on the "Greens," Roots, Character, and Prospects. *German Studies Newsletter* no. 4 (February 1985).

Maechling, C. Human Rights Dehumanized. *Foreign Policy* (Fall 1983).

Mann, G. Der Fortschrittsglaube Amerikas. *Universitas* no. 10 (1950).

Markovits, A. S. On Anti-Americanism in West Germany. *New German Critique* no. 34 (Summer 1985).

Mathiopoulos, M. Fortschritt und Ideologie. *Liberal* no. 3, (March 1982). (Festschrift for Karl Dietrich Bracher.)

Mathiopoulos, M. Containment-Politik der USA: Strategien von Roosevelt bis Reagan. *Politik und Kultur* no. 3 (1983).

Mathiopoulos, M. The American President Seen Through German Eyes; Continuity and Change from the Adenauer to the Kohl Era. *Presidential Studies Quarterly* no. 4 (Fall 1985).

Mayer-Tasch, P. C. Die internationale Umweltpolitik als Herausforderung für die Nationalstaatlichkeit. *Aus Politik und Zeitgeschichte*, B 20/85 (May 18, 1985).

McClosky, H. Consensus and Ideology in American Politics. *American Political Science Review* no. 2 (June 1964).

McDiamid, J. Presidential Inaugural Addresses—A Study in Verbal Symbols. *Public Opinion Quarterly* 1 (July 1937).

Mead, S. E. "The Nation with the Soul of a Church." *Church History* 36 (September 1967).

Meier, Chr. Ein antikes Äquivalent des Fortschrittsgedankens. *Historische Zeitschrift* 226, (Munich 1978).

Mervin, D. Woodrow Wilson and Presidential Myths. *Presidential Studies Quarterly* 11, no. 4 (Fall 1981).

Meyer, F. S. Communism Remains Communism. *National Review* 2 (October 13, 1956).

Mickel, W. W. Der Begriff der "europäischen Dimension" im Unterricht. *Aus Politik und Zeitgeschichte,* B 41/84 (October 13, 1984).

Morison, S. E. Faith of a Historian. *American Historical Review* 56 (1950–51).

Morris, R. B. "We the People of the United States": The Bicentennial of a People's Revolution. *American Historical Review* 2, no. 1 (February 1977).

Moynihan, D. P. Was Woodrow Wilson Right? Morality and American Foreign Policy. *Commentary* 57, no. 4 (May 1974).

Moynihan, D. P. America's Crisis of Confidence. *Current* (December 1975).

Müller, H. J. Should We Strengthen or Weaken Our Genetic Heritage? *Daedalus* (Summer 1961).

Mumford, H. M. Henry Adams and the Tendency of History. *New England Quarterly* 32 (March 1959).

Muravchik, J. The Think Tank of the Left. *New York Times Magazine* (March 29, 1981).

*New Federalist Papers*. In the Publius Symposium on the Future of American Federalism. *Publius* 2, no. 1 (Spring 1972).

Nisbet, R. The Quintessential Liberal. *Commentary* 72, no. 3 (September 1981).

Noble, D. The New Republic and the Idea of Progress. *Mississippi Valley Historical Review* 38 (December 1951).

Noble, D. The Religion of Progress in America, 1890–1914. *Social Forces* 22 (Winter 1955).

Noelle-Neumann, E., and Herdegen, G. Die europäische Gemeinschaft in der öffentlichen Meinung: Informationsdefizite und enttäuschte Entwartungen. *Integration* (March 1983).

Nye, J. Maintaining the Western Alliance. *Harvard International Review* 4, no. 6 (March–April 1982).

O'Hare McCornick, A. Roosevelt's View of the Big Job. *The New York Times Magazine* (September 11, 1932).

O'Sullivan, J. Julius W. Pratt: The Origin of "Manifest Destiny." *American Historical Review* 32 (1927).

Paetzold, K. E. Kyklos und Telos im Geschichtsdenken des Polybios. *Saeculum* 28 (1977).

Parkman, F. The Failure of Universal Suffrage. *North American Review* 127 (1878).

Pflüger, F. US Human Rights Policy—From Carter to Reagan. *Aussenpolitik* (Engl. edition) 35, no. 4 (1984).

Pierson, G. W. The Frontier and American Institutions. *New England Quarterly* 15 (1942).

Podhoretz, N. Making the World Safe for Communism. *Commentary* April 1976.

Podhoretz, N. The New American Majority. *Commentary* 71, no. 1 (January 1981).

Pogodda, H. Technik und Natur, Technik und Kunst. *Deutsche Zeitschrift für Philosophie, Ost-Berlin*, no. 1 (1970).

Pole, J. R. The American Past: Is It Still Usable? *Journal of American Studies* 1 (1967).

Pratt, J. W. John O'Sullivan and Manifest Destiny. *New York State Historical Association* 14 (1933).

Price, D. K., and Laski, H. J. The Parliamentary and the Presidential Systems. *Public Administration Review* 3, no. 4 (Autumn 1943) and *Public Adminstration Review* 4, no. 4 (Autumn 1944).

Quay, P. M. Progress as a Demarcation Criterion for the Sciences. *Philosophy of Science* 41, 1974.

Range, P. R. Thunder from the Right. *The New York Times Magazine* (February 8, 1981).

Recum, H. von. Dimensionen des Wertewandels. *Aus Politik und Zeigeschichte*, B 25/84 (June 23, 1984).

Reid, H. G., and Yanarella, E. J. Political Science and the Post-Modern Critique of Scientism and Domination. *Review of Politics* 3 (July 1975).

Rietveld, D. R. Lincoln and the Politics of Morality. *Illinois State Historical Society Journal* 68 (1975).

Rifkind, M. Für ein stärker geeintes Europa—ein praktisches Programm. *Integration* (February 1985).

Robinson, D. L. The Inventors of the Presidency. *Presidential Studies Quarterly* 12, no. 1 (Winter 1983).

Rosenfeld, St. S. The Guns of July. *Foreign Affairs* 64, no. 4 (Spring 1986).

Rossiter, C. The American Mission. *The American Scholar* 20 (1950–51).

Rossiter, C. The Presidency: Focus on Leadership. *The New York Times Magazine* (November 11, 1956).

Rüsen, J. Geschichtsbewußtsein und menschliche Identität. *Aus Politik und Zeitgeschichte*, B 41/84 (October 13, 1984).

Salomon, A. The Religion of Progress. *Social Research* 13 (December 1946).

Schlesinger, A. M. The New Conservatism: Politics of Nostalgia. *Reporter* 12 (June 16, 1955).

Schlesinger, A. M. America: Experiment or Destiny? *American Historical Review* 82, no. 3 (1977).

Schlesinger, A. M. Human Rights and the American Tradition. *Foreign Affairs* 57, 1978–79.

Schmertz, H. The Media and the Presidency. *Presidential Studies Quarterly* 16, no. 1 (Winter 1986).

Schorske, C. Weimar and the Intellectuals. *The New York Review of Books* 11, nos. 9, 10 (May 7/May 21, 1970).

Schulze, H. Die Versuchung des Absoluten, Zur deutschen politischen Kultur im 19. und 20. Jahrhundert. *Aus Politik und Zeitgeschichte*, B 7/84 (February 18, 1985).

Seaver, P. The Puritan Work Ethic Revisited. *Journal of British Studies* 19–20 (1979–81).

Shultz, G. P. Shaping American Foreign Policy, New Realities and New Ways of Thinking. *Foreign Affairs* 63, no. 4 (Spring 1985).

Silverman, M. Emerson and the Idea of Progress. *American Literature* 12 (March 1940).

Skotheim, R. A., and Vanderbilt, K. Vernon Louis Parrington: The Mind and Art of a Historian of Ideas. *Pacific Northwest Quarterly* 53 (1962).

Sorenson, L. R. Charles A. Beard and German Historical Thought. *Mississippi Valley Historical Review* 42 (September 1955).

Sternberger, D. Komponenten der geistigen Gestalt Europas. *Merkur* 34 (1980).

Susman, W. I. The Useless Past: American Intellectuals and the Frontier Thesis: 1910–1930. *Bucknell Review* 11 (1963).

Susman, W. I. History and the American Intellectual: Uses of a Usable Past. *American Quarterly* 16 (Summer 1964).

Thomas, J. L. Romantic Reform in America, 1815–1865. *American Quarterly* 17 (Winter 1965).

Toynbee, A. J. If We Are to Be the Wave of the Future. *The New York Times Magazine* (November 13, 1960).

Treverton, G. The Year(s) of SDI. *German Studies Newsletter,* no. 6 (November 1985).

Tsanoff, R. A. Ancient Classical Alternatives and Approaches to the Idea of Progress. *Greek and Byzantine Studies* 1, no. 2 (1958).

Tucker, R. W. The Purposes of American Power. *Foreign Affairs* 52, no. 2 (Winter 1980–81).

Ulrich, O. Computer, Wertewandel und Demokratie. *Aus Politik und Zeitgeschichte,* (June 23, 1984).

Ulrich, O. Informationstechnik und gesellschaftliche Zukünfte. *Aus Politik und Zeitgeschichte,* (March 2, 1985).

Unger, I. The "New Left" and American History. Some Recent Trends in United States Historiography. *American Historical Review* 72 (1966–67).

Uterwiedde, H. Mitterrands Wirtschaftspolitik—Was bleibt vom Sozialismus? *Aus Politik und Zeitgeschichte,* B 19/85 (May 11, 1985).

Valery, N. The Declining Power of American Technology. *New-Scientist* 71 (1976).

Veen, H. J. Wer wählt Grün?, *Aus Politik und Zeitgeschichte,* B 35/36/1984 (September 1, 1984).

Vogt, J. Die Sklaverei im antiken Griechenland und Die Sklaverei im antiken Rom. *Antike Welt* 9, nos. 2, 3 (1978).

Warnat, B. Gleichberechtigung von Männern und Frauen—Ist der Staat am Zuge? *Aus Politik und Zeitgeschichte,* B 45/81 (November 7, 1981).

Weidenfeld, W.: Was ist die Idee Europas? *Aus Politik und Zeitgeschichte,* B 23-24/74 (June 9, 1984).

Weinberger, C. W. U.S. Defense Strategy. *Foreign Affairs* 64, no. 4 (Spring 1986).

Welter, P. The Idea of Progress in America. *Journal of the History of Ideas* 16 (June 1955).

Weyrich, P. M. Reagan Crowd Out of Touch with Middle America. *Conservative Digest* 8, no. 9 (August 1982).

Wheeler, R. H. The Effect of Climate on Human Behaviour in History. *Cycles* (1963).

White, T. H. Summing Up, A Chronicle of Two Decades of Social-Experiment . . . and the Disillusionment That Swept Ronald Reagan into the White House. *The New York Times Magazine* (April 25, 1982).

Windt, T. O. Presidential Rhetoric: Definition of a Field of Study. *Presidential Studies Quarterly* 16, no. 1 (Winter 1986).

Winegarten, R. The Idea of Decadence. *Commentary* 58, no. 3 (September 1974).

Wood, G. S. Rhetoric and Reality in the American Revolution. *William and Mary Quarterly* 23 (1966).

Woodward, C. V. The Aging of America. *American Historical Review* 82, no. 3 (June 1977).
Zilsel, E. The Genesis of the Concept of Scientific Progress. *The Journal of the History of Ideas* 6 (1945).

# Index

## About the Author

MARGARITA MATHIOPOULOS was born in Bonn, West Germany, in 1956. She studied Political Science, History, Italian Philology, and Psychology at the University of Bonn, where she received M.A. and Ph.D. degrees in Political Science. From 1980 to 1982 she conducted research for her doctoral dissertation at the Government Department of Harvard University on a scholarship of the Friedrich-Neumann Foundation.

Since 1976 Dr. Mathiopoulos has also been active as a journalist for German and Greek press and television. She is currently Assistant Director of the international Aspen Institute in Berlin and Assistant Professor at the History and Political Science Department of the Free University of Berlin.

She is the author of the book *Amerika—Das Experiment des Fortschritts: Ein Vergleich des politischen Denkens in den USA und Europa*. Her previous publications include articles on the American presidency, European-American security relations, and the German-American partnership in *Presidential Studies Quarterly*, *Harvard International Review*, *Außenpolitik*, and *Cosmopolitiques*.